Pro Android Web Game Apps

Using HTML5, CSS3, and JavaScript

Juriy Bura

Apress®

Pro Android Web Game Apps: Using HTML5, CSS3, and JavaScript

ISBN 978-1-4302-3819-5

ISBN 978-1-4302-3820-1 (eBook)

President and Publisher: Paul Manning
Lead Editor: Chris Nelson
Technical Reviewer: Charles Cruz
Editorial Board: Steve Anglin, Mark Beckner, Ewan Buckingham, Gary Cornell, Jonathan Gennick, Jonathan Hassell, Michelle Lowman, James Markham, Matthew Moodie, Jeff Olson, Jeffrey Pepper, Douglas Pundick, Ben Renow-Clarke, Dominic Shakeshaft, Matt Wade, Tom Welsh
Coordinating Editor: Brigid Duffy
Copy Editor: Kimberly Burton
Compositor: Bytheway Publishing Services
Indexer: SPi Global
Artist: SPi Global
Cover Art By: Sergey Lesiuk
Cover Designer: Anna Ishchenko

To Elena and Alysa

Contents at a Glance

Contents

About the Authors

■ **Juriy Bura** is an independent consultant living between Kiev, Ukraine, and Zurich, Switzerland. His main area of expertise is games and real-time web applications for both desktop and mobile platforms. He is a co-owner of Deadline Solutions (`http://deadline-solutions.com/about.html`). Juriy is also a leader of the JavaScript User Group in Ukraine, a frequent conference speaker, and a passionate web developer seeking how to push the browser to its limits. Having more than seven years of experience in Java and JavaScript, he is sure that game development is the area with the most fun concentrated within a line of code.

Juriy spends his spare time with his family and playing board games in a small "geek" club. Juriy blogs at `http://juriy.com` and tweets as `@juriy`.

■ **Paul Coates** is a freelance copy editor and EFL teacher, based in Burton Upon Trent, UK, and Kyiv, Ukraine. He made sure that Juriy's ingredients had the right touch of English flavor for publication. When not teaching students of all ages how to speak his native tongue, Paul provides copy editing and proofreading for foreign works in English, as well as Russian and Ukrainian translations. Paul enjoys video gaming, cinema, and traveling.

Paul occasionally blogs at http://psykspopcornjungle.blogspot.com and occasionally tweets at @Psyklax.

Acknowledgments

This book would be impossible without the help and support from many great people. I'm most grateful to my wife, Elena, whose love gave me inspiration when I needed it most, and my parents, Alexander and Vera Bura.

I'm grateful to my good friends: Vadim Voituk for his brilliant ideas and technical expertise; Alexey Kondratov, who was the first to explain to me how a book is different from a 600-page blog; and Artyom Volkhonskiy. I'm so glad that you guys have always been there when I needed your support and opinion. Your help has improved this book tremendously.

A very special thanks to a brilliant artist—Sergey Lesiuk (`http://nitro-killer.deviantart.com`), who created the cover art and graphical assets for the isometric engine, and the guys at Marcus Studio (`www.marcusstudio.com.ua/`) for the fabulous animated knight character. With their help, we now have more free high-quality art to use in our game projects.

Thanks to the Apress team, who did a great job bringing this book to life: Steve Anglin, Brigid Duffy, Charlie Cruz, Kimberly Burton, Anna Ishchenko, Stephen Moles, Jonathan Gennick, Jean Blackburn, and many others working behind the scenes to publish this book.

Personal thanks to Chris Nelson for his review, advice, and for dealing with never-ending changes to the chapters' structure. With your help, this book shaped up. Working with you is a great pleasure.

Thanks to Paul Coates for his invaluable contribution to this book and his readiness to review all those "last minute edits" in the middle of the weekend.

And, of course, thank you, my little angel Alysa. No more "Daddy is working again tonight." I promise.

—Juriy Bura

I want to thank Juriy for a great job, Stephen and Chris at Apress for making our first book a pleasure to write, and most of all Sasha, without whom none of this would be possible.

—Paul Coates

Introduction

This book is about making web games with JavaScript for today's most promising mobile platform—Android. Game development is a challenging subject. Games aim to simulate life in some form or another, and the more realistic you want a simulation to be, the more knowledge and skill you have to apply to make it believable. Video games is the place where mathematics—which is quite typical in programming—meets kinematics, optics, acoustics, artificial intelligence, art, music, and storytelling. Where else can you find a mix like that?

Why JavaScript and HTML5? If you are holding this book in your hands, then you probably already have your answer to that question. If you are curious about *my* reasoning, it's because JavaScript is the most popular cross-platform client-side solution that developers have at their disposal. Every device that has Internet access also has a browser—from desktop computers and smartphones to tablets and set-top boxes. And without a doubt, every browser has JavaScript. An application built with a standard HTML5 stack will run on most devices. You want your game to be fast? You want it on desktops, mobiles, and tablets on Windows, iOS, Linux, and Android? You don't want to rewrite the code for a set of heterogeneous platforms in different programming languages? HTML5 comes to rescue!

The goal of this book is to give you a deep understanding of the algorithms and approaches that stand behind the most common types of games. I prefer this approach to that of streamlined how-to guides that often sacrifice important details in favor of immediate results. While the "how-to" approach might look like a quicker way to get to the goal, it usually leaves readers with knowledge gaps to fill on their own. Of course, this book has plenty of how-to examples in addition to thorough coverage of the underlying concepts.

That's why I couldn't avoid putting some math in the book. Yeah, there are few formulas on the pages. Real gamedev is impossible without fair amount of math. You don't need to have any special knowledge of mathematics beyond what you already know from school to master every subject in this book. If you are already proficient with math, you might find some explanations too obvious—feel free to skip them.

In this book, I deliberately avoided using any existing "Swiss Army knife"–style libraries like jQuery, prototype.js, or Underscore.js because I didn't want the examples to be hard-wired with any of them. While there are many great libraries, every developer has his own preferences. I find library-agnostic code to be the friendliest.

What This Book Is About

This book is about making games for the Android platform with HTML5 and JavaScript. It will guide you from an empty HTML page to a full-blown HTML5 game with animations, sound, endless worlds, and multiplayer support.

The following are among the many things you learn in this book:

- How to draw game elements with the Canvas element; how to use sprites and sprite sheets; and how to capture user input.

- How the exciting world of 3D programming works—including WebGL, one of the most promising APIs for web game development.

- How to create multiplayer games with the help of Node.js—the tool that brings the power of JavaScript to the server.

- How to establish real-time communication between users and let them play against each other in online matches. All of this is possible with JavaScript. You don't need to know any other server-side language to write efficient server-side code!

- How to make computer-controlled characters behave intelligently—have them find their way through the world and make decisions with the help of AI algorithms.

- How to add some neat sound effects.

- How to publish our masterpiece in the Android Market.

This book covers many gamedev algorithms and optimizations, most of which are not limited to JavaScript. Once you learn them, you will be able to quickly master game development on other platforms. Understanding how 3D rendering or pathfinding works will help you to build games for any platform, not just the web.

This book is about making games and writing the most exciting applications in the world—and having real fun while doing so.

What This Book Is Not About

This book is not about web programming in general. I will not cover what HTML is or how HTTP works. I assume that you already know how to write basic JavaScript and embed it into an HTML page. You don't need to be a web development guru, but at the very least, you need understand the language core. Operators, functions, objects, and variables should be familiar to you. If you don't feel comfortable with these concepts, you might want to start with Terry McNavage's *JavaScript for Absolute Beginners* (Apress, 2010).

This book is not about game design—creating levels, building character personalities, or designing economics for the online world. Everything related to the gameplay, story, plot, characters, and game mechanics is out of scope. While these topics are extremely interesting, there are special books devoted to them. One such book that I would recommend is *Game Design: Theory and Practice*, Second Edition, by Richard Rouse III (Jones & Bartlett, 2004).

Who Is This Book For?

This book is for programmers. It will guide you through the technical aspects of creating a game—rendering 2D and 3D graphics, user input, networking, sound, artificial intelligence, and publishing the game on the application market. Every concept explained here is illustrated with code examples that you can run on your Android smartphone or tablet. I tried to make the book as practical as possible—working code is a very important way to provide a kick-start.

If you are a web developer and you want to learn how to make games for Android devices, this book is for you. You don't need experience with any specific JavaScript library—or even experience making sites for mobile platforms—to get the most out of this book. If you know how to make a personal web page from the scratch with some JavaScript in it, that's about enough to get started.

If you are a game developer who created games for other platforms, and you want to leverage your experience to HTML5 and Android, this book is also for you. If this is the case, some sections might look familiar or even obvious to you. For example, if you have worked with OpenGL from within a Java application, you probably know what a shader is or how to map texture to polygons. Feel free to skip such sections and focus on practical aspects—JavaScript listings and examples that come with the book.

About the Art Files

This book comes with some great art created especially for it by Sergey Lesiuk (isometric tiles and buildings) and the guys at Marcus Studio (an animated knight character). You may use this art in your own projects—free or commercial—without tricky restrictions. The complete license text is distributed with the files.

Free and unrestricted art is very important in the early stages of development. It feels so much better to work on a game that looks like a game rather than a mess of stub graphics. The initiative to share commercial-looking sprites for free was inspired by Daniel Cook on his wonderful web site at www.lostgarden.com. I encourage you to join and share your gamedev assets for free—the developer community will be most grateful.

How This Book Is Structured

The book is divided into four parts that we jokingly call "worlds."

2D Worlds

This part of the book is devoted to 2D graphics and the Canvas element. It also gets you started in Chapter 1, "Preparing the Environment," by setting up required tools: the IDE, the web server, Java SDK, and the Android emulator. Once all of these are set, you are ready for action.

Chapter 2, "Graphics in the Browser: The Canvas Element," is where the magic starts. You will learn how to render shapes on HTML5 Canvas, how to use paths and curves, gradients and fills, transformations, and states of the 2D context.

In Chapter 3, "Creating the First Game," you create your first project—the Four Balls game. This small project uses elements you created in Chapter 2 and illustrates important, basic game development concepts, such as game state, mechanics, turn validation, and win/lose conditions.

Modern games are impossible without colorful animations. Chapter 4, "Animation and Sprites," guides you through the process of loading the images and drawing a running character frame by frame. You will also learn more advanced animation effects, such as interpolation, acceleration, deceleration, and easing functions.

Chapter 5, "Event Handling and User Input," will introduce you to the methods of working with input in your game. You'll learn how to capture browser events and build a high-level API for complex input models. We'll explore drag-and-drop and pixel-perfect picking with color masks.

At this point, you will be able to create your own simple games, as you will have all the "starter tools" under your belt. So it is time to move to the more advanced topics—rendering game worlds.

In Chapter 6, "Rendering Virtual Worlds," you'll learn how to render Really Big Worlds. We start with the simplest tile-map technique and gradually optimize it. You learn how to cache the fragments of the map, how to use the offscreen buffer, and render the world objects such as trees and rocks.

Chapter 7, "Making an Isometric Game," is the longest chapter of the book. It is devoted to isometric 2D game engines. The isometric view is the most popular way to represent the game world in strategy games, RPGs, tactics, and many other popular genres. You will learn about isometric projection, the shape of tiles, and the ways to render them. In addition to techniques described in Chapter 6, we'll introduce more rendering optimizations—the dirty rectangles algorithm and clustering of world objects. The result of this chapter is our second big project—an isometric engine ready to be used in the next strategy game or RPG.

3D Worlds

The "3D Worlds" part introduces 3D graphics—from the basic rendering concepts to WebGL.

In Chapter 8, "3D in a Browser," we learn what 3D is, how it works, and the math behind it.

Chapter 9, "Using WebGL," is devoted to WebGL—a very promising web standard that is making its way into the mobile world. You'll learn how to initialize WebGL, write shaders, work with geometry data, load textures, and work with 3D models.

Connecting Worlds

"Connecting Worlds" is all about communication and talking to the server. We start with learning Node.js and the Express framework in Chapter 10, "Going Server-Side." This chapter ranges from Node installation to a simple game server with proper templates, session handling, logging, error handling, and notifications.

In Chapter 11, "Talking to the Server," we move back to the client-side and learn how to connect to a server from a web page and exchange data with other players. We will look at different ways of communication, often called transports, and learn their pros and cons.

In Chapter 12, "Making Multiplayer Games," you make your third big project—the multiplayer version of Four Balls—with Node.js, Express, and Socket.IO.

Improving Worlds

The final part is devoted to various small aspects of game development.

Chapter 13, "AI in Games," is about artificial intelligence—breathing life into computer-controlled opponents. You will learn basic approaches to pathfinding and decision making—a good start to making bots look intelligent.

Chapter 14, "JavaScript Game Engines," discusses game engines and introduces Crafty.js—a small yet quite powerful game engine written in JavaScript. Here's where you complete a fourth project—an Escaping Knight game.

Chapter 15, "Building Native Applications," explains what it takes to publish an HTML5 game as the native application to the Android Market. We will go through all steps of the process—packaging the game, signing it with the key, preparing it for market, and publishing—and then update the game to the next version.

Chapter 16, "Adding Sound," adds the final touch to the game—sound. In this chapter, you'll use SoundManager2 to load and play sounds in the Escaping Knight game. You will learn how to loop background MP3s, play "click sounds," and notify the user about game events.

Appendix

Appendix A, "Debugging Web Applications," explains how to debug JavaScript games. We try hard to write good code, but we're all human—mistakes are unavoidable. This appendix will give you a good understanding of how to find bugs and quickly eliminate them, saving more time for development.

Contacting the Author

If you have any questions, suggestions, comments, or ideas regarding this book or HTML5 game development in general, I'd be happy to receive your feedback via e-mail at juriy.bura@gmail.com, my web site at http://juriy.com, or on Twitter at @juriy.

Getting Started

The goal of this chapter is to prepare a comfortable workspace for development. The environment and tools for mobile development are always a little more complicated than regular desktop projects. When it comes to Android *and* JavaScript in a single application, the right tools in the right place can make a huge difference. But a workspace is not only about tools. It is also very important to set up coding standards and best practices to follow during the development process. Coding conventions and basic architectural decisions are also discussed in this chapter.

Being a seasoned developer, you already have certain preferences in tools and coding approaches. For example, every web programmer has his favorite integrated development environment (IDE) and browser for basic testing. You probably also have your own vision on writing good and maintainable JavaScript code. If you are comfortable with your preferences, use them. At the very least, I encourage you to try the tools and techniques that are described in this chapter. You might find some of them more convenient.

This chapter is divided into two parts—tools and techniques—each describing its own important aspect of development. In this chapter, we will do the following:

- Tools:
    - Install Java Development Kit
    - Compare IDEs with good support of JavaScript
    - Install web server (nginx in the first part of the book)
    - Install Android SDK and configure the emulator

      ▨   Create a basic web page and make sure that it loads in a desktop browser, a real device, and the emulator

    ▨   Techniques:

      ▨   Review the JavaScript best coding practices

      ▨   Implement a simple inheritance mechanism that will be used for OOP code throughout the book

Tools

In this section, we review and set up tools that are required to build JavaScript applications. JavaScript is a mature platform that is used to create complex state-of-the-art software. Naturally, there are a lot of software components that help to create, test, and debug rich JavaScript pages.

JavaScript is a dynamic language, unlike Java or C++. The major difference between static and dynamic languages is that a static language must define the data structures *before* runtime. In a static language, for example, a programmer who wants to create a class called Van has to explicitly describe all the properties and methods that it has: `color`, `maxSpeed`, `drive()`, and so forth. Every object of the Van type has the same strictly defined interface. No surprises here.

Dynamic languages like JavaScript allow adding, removing, or changing the structure of any class or object *at* runtime. So, tricks like the following are possible and valid:

```
var van = getTheRandomVan();
van.drive = racingCar.makeUTurn; // valid assignment of the new property
```

Just like that, you can take the method from the object of a different class and use it instead of the existing method. In this case, only one instance of van is affected, the rest of the objects stay intact!

As you can see, a lot of things can happen with the JavaScript data structures at runtime: the variables can change their types, and existing objects can be extended with the new methods using the local code or the code that was downloaded from the remote server via Ajax call.

The dynamic behavior gives extreme power to the language, but makes it way harder for tools like IDEs to predict the structure of the objects and their types. The dynamic nature of JavaScript prevents code analyzers from helping you in the same way they help with the "classic" static-typed languages.

What We'll Need

Since we are going to make games for the web, we need to set up a small web-like infrastructure that mimics a real environment. As a bare minimum, we need the following three components:

- An integrated development environment (IDE)
- A web server to serve static files: HTML pages, JavaScript files, images, and others
- A device emulator or a real device to test the product

This list is far from complete, of course, but it's a good start.

The goal of this section is to create a plain "Hello World" HTML page that can be viewed with an emulator, a real device, and a desktop browser. Once you see that this setup works, you can forget about the environment and focus on writing applications.

Almost every tool, except for the emulator, gives you some options. For example, there's no "best" IDE for JavaScript and there are around a dozen popular web servers that are good at serving static files. Once you get a basic setup going, feel free to experiment with individual components, and fine-tune them.

> **NOTE:** When I write about software products, I often mention prices and versions. I think this information is useful. It is nice to know upfront how much you are expected to invest in a tool. This kind of information is, of course, subject to change and should be read as the "price at the time of writing." For the most up-to-date information, please refer to the respective companies' web sites.

> **NOTE:** Everybody who writes code makes mistakes. No matter how experienced you are, if you are human, you will eventually introduce bugs in your program. Debugging is part of the process, just like development, and not the easiest part I must admit. Debugging tools are also very important to set and use. But this topic is outside the scope of this chapter. A more in-depth discussion about hunting bugs in mobile-oriented code is found in Appendix A.

Environment Variables

Most tools that we use in this book follow the same installation pattern:

- Install the tool or extract archive

- Set environment variable TOOL_HOME, for example, JAVA_HOME or ANT_HOME

- Add the folder with executables, usually TOOL_HOME/bin to the PATH so that you can call the tool straight from the console or terminal without typing the whole path

Setting and changing environment variables depends on your OS.

Windows 7

In Windows 7, right-click My Computer and select Properties from the drop-down menu. In the opened window, click Advanced System Settings ➤ Environment Variables. Under System Variables, click New. Enter a variable name (for example, JAVA_HOME), the variable value, and then click OK. Note that you have to reopen any opened console windows to make them "see" the changes.

Adding certain folders to PATH works the same way. Find the variable called PATH in the environment variable list and click Edit. Put the cursor at the end of the line, add a semicolon (;), and type the path to the folder. Usually when you add the new tool to the path, you refer the existing variable, as follows:

```
;%JAVA_HOME%\bin
```

To check that the variable is set correctly, open a new console window and execute:

```
> echo %JAVA_HOME%
```

Use the name of your variable instead of JAVA_HOME, of course. You should see the path immediately printed in the console window.

Mac OS X Lion

In Mac OS X Lion, first create the file called .bash_profile in your home folder. Open the terminal window and execute:

```
$touch ~/.bash_profile
$ open -e ~/.bash_profile
```

The file should now be opened in the text editor. Add the following line for every environment variable that you want to create:

```
export TOOL_HOME=/path/to/tool
```

For example:

```
export NODE_PATH=~/node
export ANDROID_HOME=~/android
```

The last line of this script should be the line that updates the PATH variable:

```
export PATH=$PATH:$ANDROID_HOME/tools:$NODE_PATH
```

PATH is a colon-separated list of paths where Mac OS looks for programs when you call them from the terminal without providing the exact location of the executable file. Save the .bash_profile, go back to the terminal window, and execute the following to reload the newly defined variables:

```
$ . .bash_profile
```

Now check that the variables are available. Type the following:

```
$ echo $VARIABLE_NAME
```

Use your own variable instead of VARIABLE_NAME, of course. You should immediately see the path defined for this variable. If you ever need to edit one of the variables, edit the file and change the value appropriately.

Paths

When you work with tools, you are often asked to enter different kinds of paths. In this book, I usually refer to them explicitly, like "IDE installation path" or "the project path" (meaning the path to your project folder). It is easy to understand what it means most of the time. There are cases, however, when I can't use that kind of explanation; for example, the screenshots usually show a certain state of the program, and if I take the screenshot from my system, it shows my paths, of course. Code listings and config files sometimes refer to paths too; in this case, I also use the real paths that I use for development.

The paths are different for Windows users and Mac users, but since the software that we use is mostly cross-platform, any path format can be used. Most tools accept the forwardslash(/) in Windows paths for distinguishing between the path separator and escape characters. If you try to use code like var path = "c:\nginx", for example, it will not work correctly. The \n will be treated as the escape sequence and transformed to the "new line" character. This issue is not JavaScript specific; most programming languages use the backslash(\ ) to denote that the character standing after it will be processed in a special way. You must use either "c:\\nginx" or "c:/nginx" to specify the valid path, and both strings will work fine. I recommend using the second approach (it is easier to read at least). The cases when you need to specify the absolute paths in JavaScript are quite rare and usually relate to server-side development.

Personally, I like to use the c:\apps folder for the development-related tools like IDEs, development kits, emulators, and everything else that can be executed. I keep my projects in c:\apps\projects. You are free to use your own conventions, of course. Just keep in mind that when you see a path like c:\apps\projects\myproject in this book, you have to use your own value instead.

The other good reason to use the real paths in listings is that you know the expected format straightaway. There are many ways to specify the location of a file or folder in a file system: absolute, relative, or in the form of URI (with file:// protocol). The relative paths may be calculated either from the current working folder or from the folder where the currently executing file is located, and so forth. It is often good to see a real example rather than a placeholder like %YOUR_PROJECT_PATH%.

Java Development Kit

Java Development Kit, or simply JDK, is an essential part of Android development, even if you don't plan to write a single line of Java code. The Android emulator requires Java to run and some JavaScript IDEs require it too. JDK is a set of tools used to compile and run programs written in Java. We will not use JDK directly in this book, but several components that we will need require it.

For windows users, JDK can be downloaded from the official site at www.oracle.com/technetwork/java/javase/downloads/index.html (click Java on this page), select the version according to your OS, and install it. Once this is done, you will have to set the environment variable called JAVA_HOME to let other programs know where they can find Java. Also, add JAVA_HOME/bin to PATH.

For Mac users, open the terminal and type:

```
$ java -version
```

If you see the version number, then JDK is already installed. Otherwise, you will be prompted to install the best available package. Type the same command once again after the installation to make sure that JDK is ready. The installation path on Mac OS X 10.7.x is:

```
/System/Library/Java/JavaVirtualMachines/1.6.0.jdk/Contents/Home
```

It might be slightly different, depending on the particular Java version. Create the new variable called JAVA_HOME and point to this folder.

That's it. You have just installed Java and you're ready for more exciting things.

Integrated Development Environment

Sometimes JavaScript projects are as simple as a couple of scripts that can hide fields from an HTML form or load some content with Ajax. In this case, you can get by with a text editor—it loads faster than an IDE, has a simple interface, and saves a lot of memory (IDEs are really memory-hungry these days). For tiny projects all you need is a syntax highlighter to make your code look pretty and to save you from trivial typos.

For anything bigger than that, an IDE is essential. You will need a set of advanced features that a typical text editor doesn't have: good code analysis, inspections, checking for potential errors, autocompletion, refactoring tools, integration with version control systems, bug trackers, and many others.

As I mentioned already, there's no perfect IDE in the market. Some are good for JavaScript while others are not. They differ in price, system requirements, supported platforms, and featuresets. When choosing an IDE, it is most important that you feel comfortable with it. The first steps with a new IDE might seem hard, but if you feel like you're struggling with each line of code even after a couple of weeks, you should try other products. The increase in productivity will most likely make up for the lack of a feature or two.

If you've worked with JavaScript before, you might have picked a favorite IDE already. If not, then the following are a couple of options:

- **IntelliJ Idea** (www.jetbrains.com/idea/) has good support for the whole web stack: HTML, CSS, JavaScript, and server-side languages like PHP and Java. If your project is open-sourced, IntelliJ Idea is free—otherwise you will have to pay around $200 for it. IntelliJ has several lightweight IDEs derived from Idea. WebStorm is the one for HTML and JavaScript, and it is only $69.

- **Aptana Studio** (http://aptana.com) is based on the glorious and powerful Eclipse project (www.eclipse.org). It is extremely feature-rich, and has a plug-in for virtually anything from exploring databases and building enterprise reports to reminding you that your tea is ready. Aptana is free and open source.

The choice between the two usually comes down to one's own preference. There is an army of Eclipse fans and a similar army of IntelliJ fans, which tend to start a holy war each time one side releases a new version. If you're in doubt, try both and choose the IDE you like best. Next, I give you a brief look at these IDEs and demonstrate how they work by making a Hello World project in each of them.

IntelliJ Idea

Download the installer from the official site (`www.jetbrains.com/idea/download/index.html`) and launch it. Follow the regular installation process (there are no odd questions here; IntelliJ Idea only wants to know an installation folder location).

After the installation has completed and you launch IntelliJ Idea for the first time, you will need to choose which plug-ins to enable. If you plan to use IntelliJ as your IDE, it is better to review the lists and select only the plug-ins that you will really use. A smaller number of enabled plug-ins improves the startup time. Otherwise, just leave all the checkmarks with default values. Finally, you see the Welcome screen shown in Figure 1-1; it has several rows of buttons. Click Create New Project to see the New Project window, and choose Create Project from Scratch.

Figure 1-1. *IntelliJ Idea welcome screen*

IntelliJ Idea treats a "project" as a set of one or more modules. For example, if you write a chat application, the "chat application" as a whole is the project. The modules of this project could be Server, Android Client, Desktop Client, and so forth. The idea behind the modules is to separate the different components of the projects since they might have different dependencies or build steps, or they may use different programming languages. The project doesn't have to use many modules, of course. For a simple application, one module is enough.

Each module has a type: Java, J2ME, Android, Grails, and the most important type of module for this book—a Web Module. Select it from the list on the left, as shown in Figure 1-2. If you decide to use IntelliJ Idea as your main IDE, use these steps for every new project that you make.

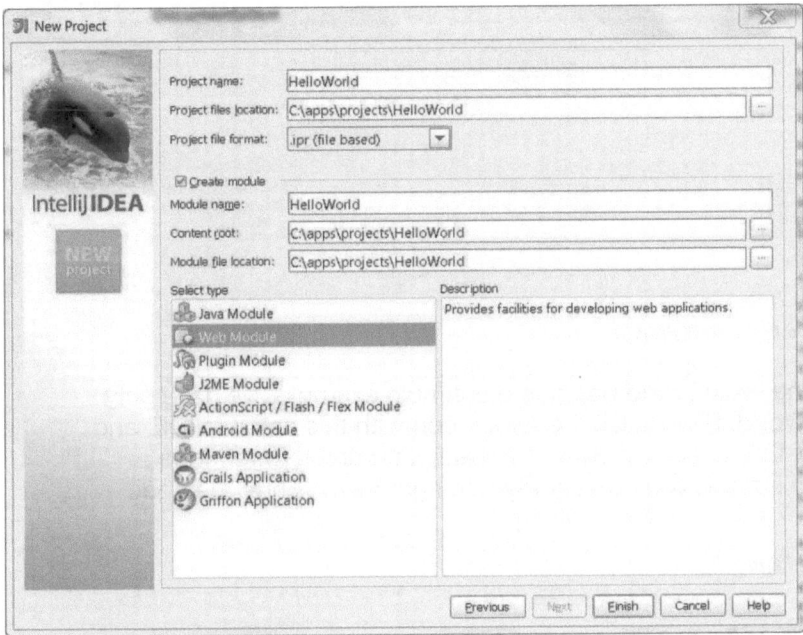

Figure 1-2. *Creating a new project*

Enter the project name and the location you wish to use for project files, and then click Finish. Your project is created and you are presented with a blank workspace, as shown in Figure 1-3.

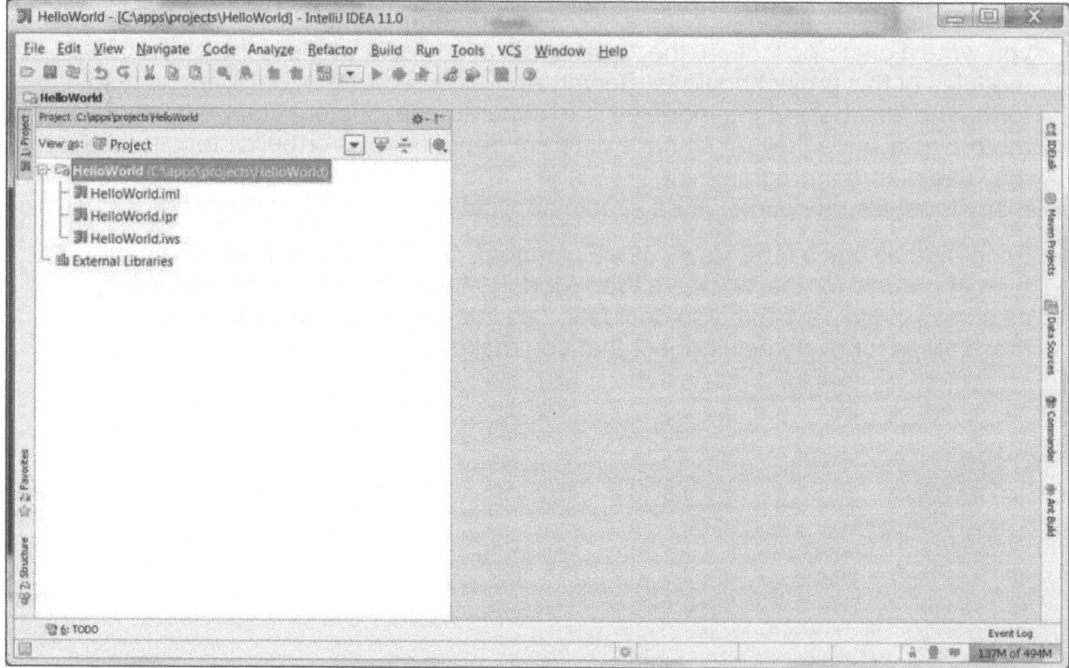

Figure 1-3. *The look of the blank new project*

Now you can write the Hello World page. In our simple example, we have only one module—HelloWorld. Right-click the folder icon with this name in IDE, and then select New File. Enter `index.html` in the dialog and press Enter. Idea creates a new empty file and you can start typing right away. Enter the code from Listing 1-1.

Listing 1-1. *Basic HTML5 Page*

```
<!DOCTYPE html>
<html lang="en">
<head>
<title>Hello World</title>
</head>
<body>
        It Works!
</body>
</html>
```

Open the newly created file in your favorite desktop browser and make sure that it renders the page. We still cannot open this file with a mobile device or in an emulator since both of them need the file to be accessible via HTTP. Neither a device nor an emulator has direct access to the filesystem on your PC, which is why we will need a web server. I explain how to launch the page in a mobile device later in this chapter.

IntelliJ Idea is a very powerful tool, yet it takes some time to get used to it and start utilizing its full potential. Make sure to check the default hotkeys reference: Help ➤ Default Keymap Reference. It is a single PDF page of the most frequently used hotkeys grouped by category.

If you plan to work only with the standard web stack (CSS, HTML, JavaScript, etc.) then you can use the lighter (and cheaper) version of Idea, which is WebStorm. The steps required to create and run a new project in WebStorm are simpler. Go to File ➤ New Project, and enter the name and the path. When the project is created, you work with it in exactly the same way as you would work with Idea.

Now let's compare Idea to Aptana Studio.

Aptana Studio

Start by downloading the latest release of Aptana from `www.aptana.com`. Select the standalone version, wait until the download is complete, and install the IDE to the folder of your choice. When the installation is completed and you launch the IDE, you will see the Start page, which has a summary of new features and fixed bugs, as well as links to the forums, documentation, and bugs database (see Figure 1-4).

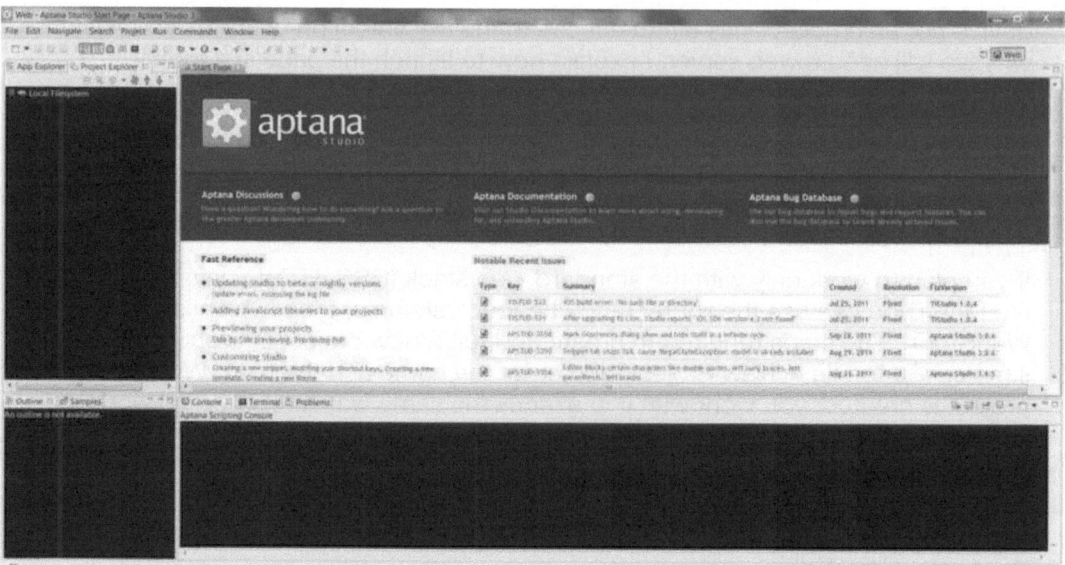

Figure 1-4. *The Start page in Aptana Studio*

Aptana utilizes a slightly different approach to naming. The *project* in Aptana is similar to *module* in IntelliJ, and a set of projects is called a *workspace*. Using the example from the previous section, if you make a chat application in Aptana, you will have a separate workspace that contains several projects: Server, Android Client, and Desktop Client. Aptana uses the same concept, but different words to describe it. Like IntelliJ, it allows you to clearly separate the components of the application and treat them in a different way when required.

Let's create the same Hello World page as in the previous section. To create a new project, select File ➤ New ➤ Web Project. On the first screen, enter the name and the path to the project folder (uncheck Use Default Location if you want to enter the custom path). The next screen presents you with several templates (see Figure 1-5). Project templates work like prebuilt Hello World skeletons for different cases. Uncheck the Create Project with One of the Templates if it is checked, and then click Finish.

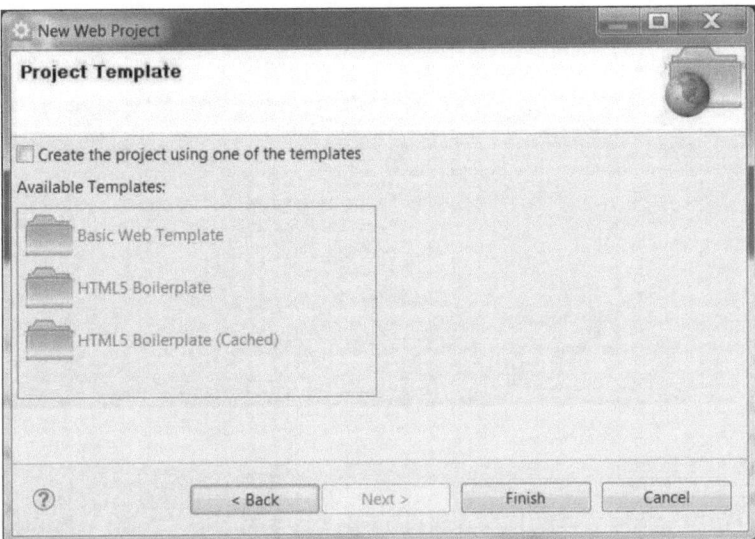

Figure 1-5. *The new web project wizard in Aptana Studio*

The dialog is now closed and the new folder called Hello World appears in the Project Explorer (the area in the top-left section of the screen). Right-click the folder and select New... ➤ File from the context menu. Enter index.html in the opened window. Paste the code from Listing 1-1 in the file. The result should look like Figure 1-6. Save the file and open it in the desktop browser. The page should say It Works!

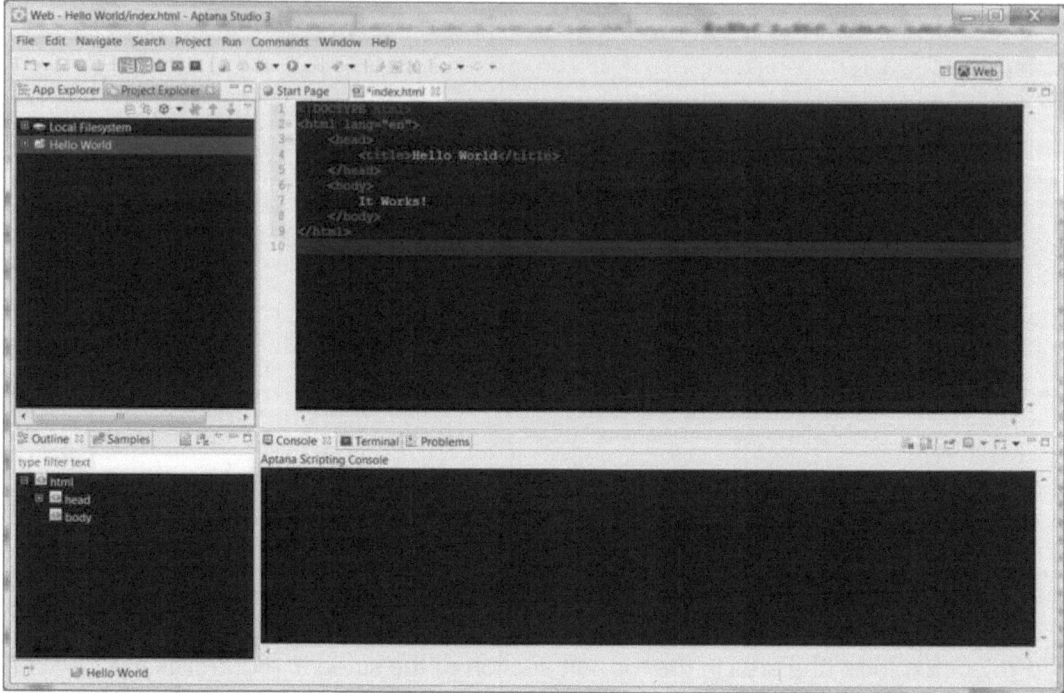

Figure 1-6. *The code is pasted into the newly created filein Aptana Studio*

Choosing the IDE that fits you is the first step to writing good code. Once the page is ready, it should be tested in an environment that is as close to production as possible. In our case, this is either a real device or an emulator. To do this, we will need to install a web server.

Web Server

Your device cannot access the filesystem on your PC and load the web page directly from a folder. That's why we will need a web server, a tool that can serve web pages via HTTP. After you install a web server and configure it, you access the project files the same way as you access regular web sites on the Internet: type the address in the browser to see the rendered HTML pages.

There are at least a dozen popular commercial-grade products that can do the job. We'll use the smallest one, nginx (http://nginx.com). At only 800 KB when compressed, it proudly holds third-place on the list of the most popular web servers in the world, ranking after Apache (http://httpd.apache.org) and IIS (www.iis.net). 12 percent of the world's top-million web sites use nginx, and this

number is increasing according to W3Techs
(`http://w3techs.com/technologies/cross/web_server/ranking`).

Why don't *we* use Apache, "the world's most popular web server"? You can if
you want, but it is a little too complex for the simple task of serving static pages.

> **NOTE:** Web servers usually work on port 80. Sometimes programs like Skype may
> use the same port for its own needs. If you're having problems starting nginx while
> Skype is in operation, open Skype, go to Tools ➤ Options ➤ Advanced ➤ Connection
> and remove the checkmark from Use Ports 80 and 443 as Alternatives for Incoming
> Connections.
>
> Alternatively, you can configure nginx to use a different port, for example port 8080.
> If you choose to do so, you should remember to add the port number to the address
> to view your pages. If nginx is configured to use port 80, for example, you can type
> `http://localhost` in the browser to load the page; otherwise, you should set the
> port correctly in the address bar as `http://localhost:8080`.

Setting Up nginx

Download the latest version of nginx from `http://nginx.org/en/download.html`.
The installation process of nginx is very easy—you just unzip it. This is enough
to get it up and running, but it will only serve files from a predefined internal
folder, and you will have to copy all of the project's contents over and over
again to test even the smallest edit. We will reconfigure nginx to point web root
as the project directory instead.

Go to the `conf` folder inside the nginx installation and open `nginx.conf` in a text
editor. Find the following lines:

```
location / {
root    html;
index  index.html index.htm;
}
```

and change the `html` to the path to your project as follows (I used
`c:\apps\projects\myproject`):

```
location / {
root    c:/apps/projects/myproject;
index  index.html index.htm;
}
```

> **NOTE:** nginx uses the hash symbol (#) for commenting-out lines in config files. If you see a line starting with #, you can safely ignore it or even delete it to keep the config clean. The original purpose of the commented blocks is to show how to work with a certain aspect of configuration—a kind of inline help.

The bolded code is the path to your project folder. If you decide to change the default port, find the following lines:

```
server {
    listen      80;
    server_name  localhost;
```

and change 80 (bolded in the code) to whatever port you like.

Save the changes and launch nginx. You will not see any UI or window with settings; this is OK. nginx is working in the background and doesn't have a UI; you control it via commands, not buttons and menus.

Open your favorite desktop browser once more and type `http://localhost`. You should see your Hello World web page up and running. If you see something like "Welcome to nginx!" it means that the web server is using the wrong folder to read the HTML files. Make sure that you completed the instructions and set the root parameter in the `nginx.conf` appropriately.

Opening the Page on a Mobile Device

Now, if you have a mobile device handy, you can open the same web page and see how it looks on your Android!

The easiest way to do this is to connect your Android and PC to the same network via Wi-Fi. You'll need to find the IP address of your computer and point the mobile browser to it. For example, if the IP address of your PC on the local network is 192.168.0.15, you should open the browser and enter `http://192.168.0.15` in the address bar. You will see the page that you have just created.

What if you don't have a mobile device or you don't have a Wi-Fi access point and you can't connect your PC and Android to the same network? Well, the best choice is to buy the missing hardware. What can be easier? But seriously, you can install the Android emulator and test your web applications with it.

The Android SDK and Emulator

The good news is that you don't have to choose between a dozen products or download a separate tool for every device on the market. You download and install the Android SDK, configure the profile of the device, and run the emulator with the given profile. Then you work with the emulator the same way that you would with a mobile device: open browser, enter address, load page, and so on.

Even though Android emulators are really good, you should perform testing on real devices as soon as possible. A real device might have its own vendor-specific and hardware-specific peculiarities that will affect the way the application behaves. You also can't evaluate the usability of your product on the emulator since the real device feels different. Clicking inside the virtual copy of a smartphone is not the same as holding the real phone or tablet in your hands.

Emulators are useful when it comes to checking if an application runs fine on all supported Android versions and screen resolutions. Usually, you don't have a few dozen spare Android devices for testing—emulators are way cheaper (actually, they are free).

> **TIP:** Even if everything is working as expected on the emulator, the real device might still behave oddly. In the later phases of testing, it is useful to actually test your product on lots of devices. A service like Perfecto Mobile (`www.perfectomobile.com`) helps you to do that without having to buy or borrow every device that you want to try. It allows you to remotely control almost any model of mobile device; you pay for the time that you've spent testing on them.

Installing the SDK

The Android emulator is a part of the Android SDK—a set of tools for Android development, just as the Java SDK is a set of tools for Java.

Download the Android SDK from `http://developer.android.com/sdk/index.html` and install it. On the last step of the install wizard, leave the checkmark checked to launch the SDK Manager.

The SDK itself comes with a couple of essential tools (hence, the size of the installer is only 40 MB). The rest of the components are to be downloaded separately. The SDK Manager checks the list of available components and allows you to choose what to download (see Figure 1-7).

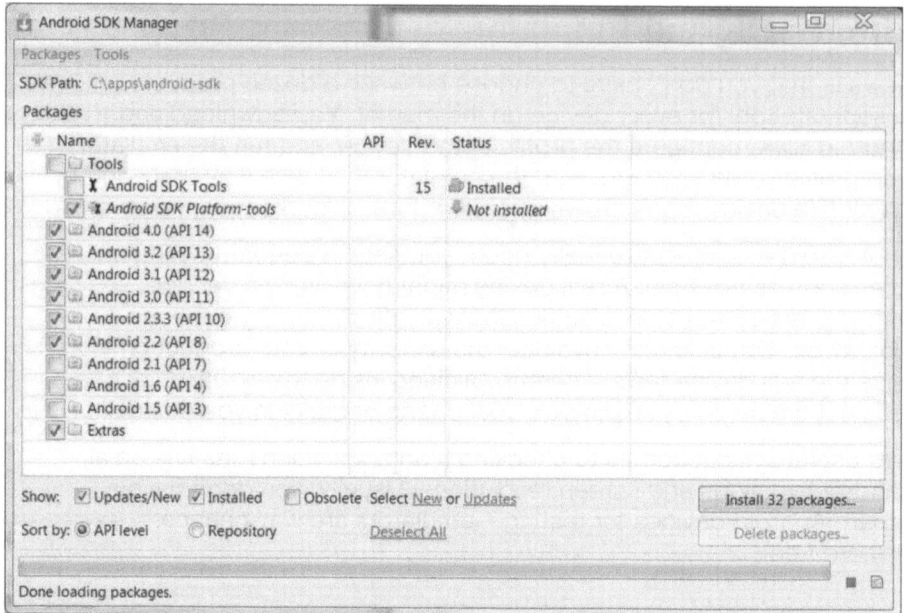

Figure 1-7. *Installing optional packageson the SDK Manager*

Choose the components that you are planning to work with and then click Install. If you use emulators for testing, you should put checkmarks against all platforms that you are going to support. Also, mark the Tools ➤ Android SDK Platform-Tools and Extras. Take a look at Figure 1-7 for reference. Now is a good time to brew some coffee since the process is not that fast and the files are not that small.

Setting Up AVDs

Once the download is finished, you are ready to configure and launch the emulator. Launch AVD Manager; it is located in the folder where you installed the SDK. AVD stands for Android Virtual Device; it is the profile of the platform that will be emulated. When you first open the application, it doesn't have any preconfigured AVDs. The list of devices will be empty and the window will look like that shown in Figure 1-8.

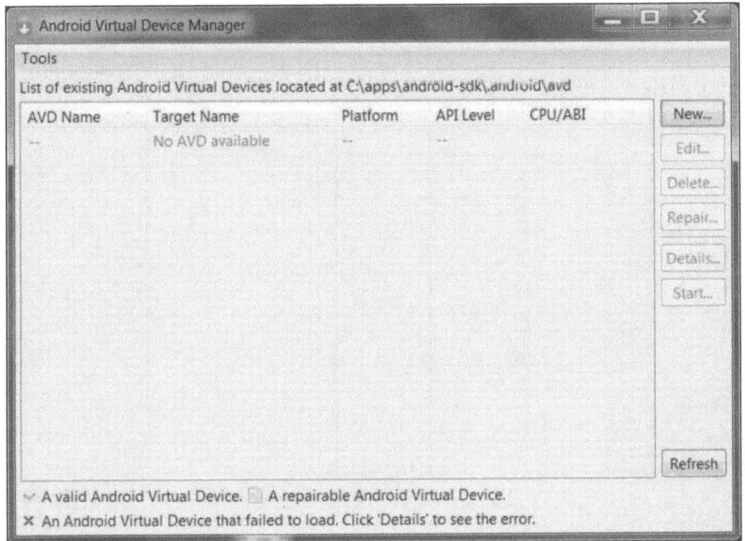

Figure 1-8. *The Android Virtual Device Manager window, which has no configured AVDs yet*

Click the New button to create the first AVD. In the dialog box, set the emulator parameters (see Figure 1-9). Device Name is a label that identifies this configuration; enter whatever sounds good to you. Target is the version of the Android API that the emulator will use. In this book, we will work with Android 2.2 and above, so select Android 2.2–API Level 8 for the first device. You may leave the size of the SD card blank or set it to some value. The last option allows you to set the skin. The *skin* determines the resolution of the emulator; pick any, but make sure that the skin fits your PC screen size, otherwise it will be hard to use. When you press the Create AVD button, the device profile appears in the list. Repeat the process for every configuration that you plan to work with.

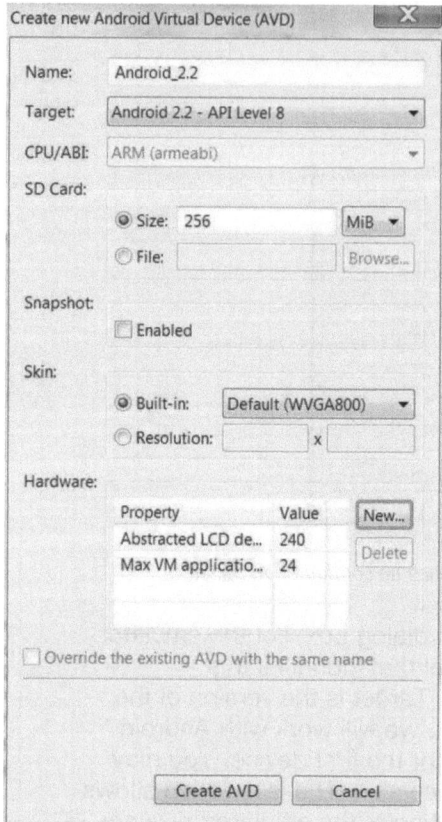

Figure 1-9. *Creating a new AVD*

To launch the emulator, select the AVD from the list and click Start…. You will be presented with several startup options, and you can safely leave the default values. The emulator takes a pretty long time to load so be patient; give it at least a couple of minutes. Once you see the Android home screen, you can navigate to the HTML page, shown in Figure 1-10, that we created earlier in this chapter.

> **NOTE:** Emulator takes a significant amount of time to start, so it makes sense to leave it open during the whole development session and simply update the page in the browser once you need to check the changes.

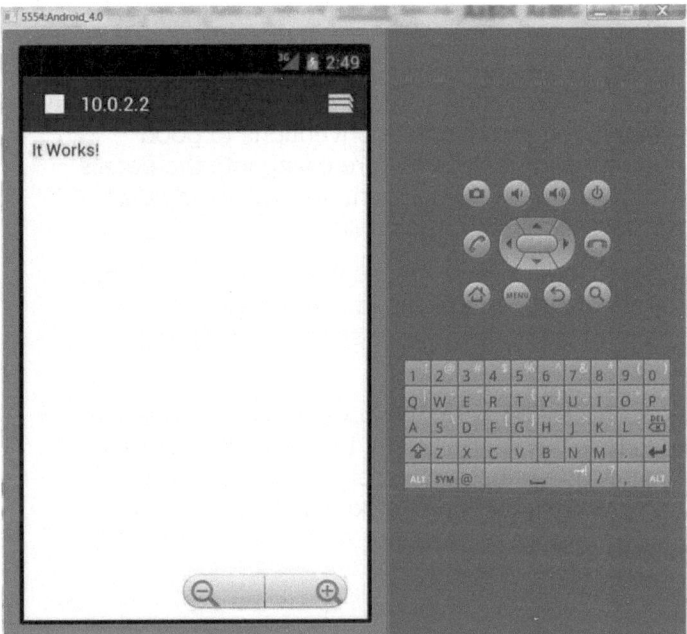

Figure 1-10. *Creating a new device profile for the Android emulator*

NOTE: Usually when you want to refer your own machine, you type
`http://127.0.0.1` or `http://localhost`. But when you are in the emulator's
browser, these addresses access the emulator itself, not the host machine. The
address that you should use is `http://10.0.2.2`. Type this address in the
emulator; you should see the test page. Don't forget to add the port number if you're
using a port other than 80.

Create the environment variable called `ANDROID_HOME` and point it to the SDK
installation path. Then update the `PATH` variable with `ANDROID_HOME/tools` and
`ANDROID_HOME/platform-tools`. Android SDK has two folders with executable
scripts. Make sure to add both of them to `PATH`.

At this point, we have all the basic tools required to start writing code and
testing the results. However, there is one other aspect of development:
debugging. When you write the code, bugs are unavoidable, and finding them is
often harder than writing the code itself. Debugging is a broad topic that is
covered in Appendix A of this book. It is best to read the techniques described
there as soon as possible.

Techniques

This section is devoted to the next very important aspect of creating an application: techniques of development—from code conventions to good practices and important architectural approaches. Before diving into the details of this section, I want to give a simple, yet very important tip: *write code that you can be proud of.* This is the best metric of code quality.

You must have heard a lot of "good coding" advice: use meaningful names for variables, write comments, format your code nicely, and avoid huge, unmanageable functions. Let me add some JavaScript-specific tips in this section.

We will look into the two aspects of development: the code and OOP. The first subsection is devoted to writing clean JavaScript code; the second is working with OOP. JavaScript has the somewhat unusual "prototype-based" model of inheritance that causes a lot of misunderstanding and confusion, so it is worth devoting a separate section to clarifying it.

The Code

How do you write good JavaScript code? Let's forget about the program structure for a moment—classes, inheritance, coupling, and cohesion—and instead look at the plain JavaScript code. How do you make it look good? How do you make it predictable and maintainable? This section is devoted to some basic advice on the subject.

Style

Style is the way your code looks. There is plenty of generic advice on how to write beautiful code. Let's look at those specific to JavaScript.

Naming "Private" Parameters and Functions

JavaScript doesn't have a `private` keyword to restrict the access to certain variables. So a good way to secure the access to the private state of the object is the use of the underscore symbol and a little discipline. Put the underscore before the name of the method that should not be accessed outside of the object, and never call these "private" methods from an external API. The following is a simple example:

```
function Person() {
    this._age = 20;

    this.setAge = function(age) {
        if (age < 0)
            throw "Age can not be negative";

        // Ok, since the private member is accessed from within the object
        this._age = age;
    };

    this.getAge = function() {
        return this._age;
    }
}

var person = new Person();

// Illegal, you're accessing the private property from outside of the object
person._age = 25;

// The right way to do it.
person.setAge(25);
```

> **NOTE:** There is another way to hide the variable from the outer world using scopes.
> The JavaScript-specific pattern, called *module*, describes this idea. The main
> purpose of this technique is different—we look into the details of modules in the
> Chapter 11, where we share components between client- and server-side JavaScript.

Avoid the "Cool but Scary" Look

When you get the black belt in JavaScript and understand some advanced
features, you might be tempted to write pieces of code that look extremely
"hardcore" and "advanced." For instance, the function that writes the
arguments of the method into the console can be written with a line like the
following:

```
console.log([tag, "(", Array.prototype.join.call(arguments, "|"),
")"].join(""));
```

If I were you, I wouldn't do that. You're better off spending another line or two,
breaking the code into smaller pieces, and making it readable and obvious even
for a js-novice. Writing code that is easy to read and understand is harder than
writing messy, unreadable code.

The Structure

The code might look clean, but it's still far from perfect. JavaScript is a single-threaded, dynamic, and weakly-typed language. These three features are very powerful when they are used in the right way, but they can cause all kinds of problems when misused.

Avoid Setting "Magic" Parameters to Objects

JavaScript allows you to add any property to any object at runtime—it is a dynamic language. When you create simple data structures like point coordinates on the fly or use an object as a hash map, this feature is very nice. The following code shows how it can be used correctly.

```
function getCurrentCoordinates() {
    {
        x: getCurrentX(),
        y: getCurrentY();
    }
}
```

```
var userStatus = {}
userStatus["John"] = IDLE;
userStatus["Mary"] = ONLINE;
userStatus["Peter"] = AWAY;
```

There are cases, however, when you should avoid such structural changes. If there is a predefined data structure, for example, you should not extend it in that way.

Why is it a bad habit? Imagine that you're on a team working on the same code. You start adding the custom fields to the objects since you need them in your functions. The other developers see that there are new useful properties, so they start to rely on them in their own code.

Here is a simple example: a programmer is making a function that should print the date in a certain format. He can write the following kind of code:

```
function printNiceDate(date) {
    date.niceFormat = "";
    date.niceFormat += date.getFullYear() + " ";
    date.niceFormat += date.getMonth() + " ";
    date.niceFormat += date.getDate() + " ";
    console.log(date.niceFormat);
}
```

Even though this code is 100 percent correct, it creates an unexpected field on the object. The same "enriched" Date object can then be passed to the different layers of the application and another programmer might think that the extra field is the standard functionality that he can rely on. He will write code that uses the new field, as follows:

```
// Cool, I love this extra field, probably it is a new standard
console.log ("Date is " + date.niceFormat.substr(4))
```

At some point, the author decides to change the format of the custom field: remove it or rename it. He thinks that the new field is his property—it is not standard, probably not even mentioned in the documentation, and it was introduced by him: that means that he can do whatever he likes with his custom field.

If he decides to delete the field, the project breaks. The code that utilized the `niceFormat` will not work anymore. Both programmers will waste their time on debugging and restoring the original flow. Summary: if you really, really need custom fields, make sure they don't leak.

Even if you're a "lone wolf" working in your garage, you still have other team members: yourself in a month or two. Trust me, you'll forget most of your undocumented conventions after a while, even if they look perfectly logical right now.

> **NOTE:** Recent versions of JavaScript introduce the way to formally protect the state of the object with `Object.freeze`, `Object.seal`, and `Object.preventExtensions`. If you need stronger guarantees of object immutability, you can use one of these methods.
>
> The opposite case is also important. You should not delete any properties from the object unless you know what you are doing. The structure of the object must remain predictable at all times.

There is an exception to this rule. If the dynamically added methods and properties are part of the framework design, it is perfectly fine to use them. For example, the Crafty.js framework that we will try in Chapter 14 implements the Entity Component System, an approach that works best by customizing particular objects at runtime.

Use It As If It Is (Almost) Static-Typed

No need to explain this rule. It is always good to know that if the variable is boolean at the start of the script, it will stay boolean until the end.

Whenever Possible, Use Asynchronous Calls

JavaScript is single-threaded, meaning the application is "frozen" when it executes the code. Avoid using blocking long-running operations inside this single thread because they can grind your application to a halt. The UI becomes unresponsive, which leads to a terrible user experience.

This is especially important for the XHR requests; synchronous calls might look really fast when you work with a local server, but almost certainly become a problem in the wild. You should never use the synchronous XHR.

Using an asynchronous API is even more important on the server. Writing a dozen bytes to a file on the hard drive might sound like an operation that can't slow anything down; it's just too fast. It might be true if you're testing the server alone. When you have 30,000 visitors, each requiring your server to write a dozen bytes, this code fragment will become a bottleneck if not written properly.

The Environment

Development and production environments differ in many ways. When you have everything on your local PC, your project lives in a small and unrealistic paradise. In the real world, network packets take much more time to deliver: sometimes they are lost, connections are broken, and resources are not available all the time.

Notify the User About Long Operations

So you do everything right: your code is asynchronous and the UI is never unresponsive. But let's say you need to load a large set of sprites for the next level, load level data, generate random terrain, or calculate the optimal strategy for artificial intelligence.Or maybe you have to do it all together. In such cases, users sometimes have to wait a considerable amount of time before something interesting happens.

Don't leave your user sitting in front of an empty screen and wondering, "How long will it actually take—a minute, five minutes, more?!"

Use some sort of progress bar or "liveness" indicator whenever you suspect that an operation will take more than a second.

NOTE: The following is a very good metric of *a long operation* described by Jakob Nielsen, an expert in web usability, at `www.useit.com/papers/responsetime.html`:

0.1 second is about the limit for having the user feel that the system is reacting instantaneously, meaning that no special feedback is necessary except to display the result.

1.0 second is about the limit for the user's flow of thought to stay uninterrupted, even though the user will notice the delay. Normally, no special feedback is necessary during delays of more than 0.1 but less than 1.0 second, yet the user loses the feeling of operating directly on the data.

10 seconds is about the limit for keeping the user's attention focused on the dialog. For longer delays, users will want to perform other tasks while waiting for the computer to finish, so they should be given feedback indicating when the computer expects to be done. Feedback during the delay is especially important if the response time is likely to be highly variable and users won't know what to expect.

Don't Think That Resources Are Always There

Resources—such as images for textures, sounds, or XMLs—are essential parts of the application. Usually, you defer the loading of these types of dependencies. The usual mistake is to assume that the resource will always be where you expected it to be—in your favorite `res` folder, for example. Yet there are at least two reasons why a resource may become unavailable:

1. *Connectivity*. You can simply lose the connection to the server. This'll give you an ugly error instead of a nice picture.

2. *Simple coding errors like typos or different conventions*. You can type `casle.png` instead of `castle`, while the real file is called `castle_big.png`.

Usually, losing the resource in that way means that the user will not see or hear something, or a 3D model will appear solid black. A good solution is to log those kinds of errors and to use the "no-image" images to make it obvious that something is wrong. Sometimes the missing image is not a good reason to show the critical error dialog, since the game might still be playable.

Quick Summary: Writing Good Code

Writing good code in JavaScript is not that hard if you follow simple rules. Good code must be

- *Clear*. The person who reads it should quickly understand what it does.

- *Predictable*. Variables should not change their type and structure when they are not expected to.

- *Freeze-tolerant and fault-tolerant*. Real-world mobile data connections are far from perfect, so make sure that the user knows how long he has to wait to download. Expect that data might not be available all the time and use asynchronous calls whenever possible.

> **TIP:** If you want to learn more about testing connection problems in the real world, read on to Chapter 11, which explains how to simulate the packet loss and network delays in the local environment.

Object-Oriented Programming

Object-oriented programming (OOP) is the most widely-used programming paradigm. It has helped build complex programs for more than half a century. The most popular languages, like Java and C#, work with the concept of classes—the blueprints that define the common structure of the object. JavaScript doesn't have classes; instead, it has functions and prototypes that give similar functionality. This section of the chapter is devoted to implementing the OOP approach in JavaScript.

> **NOTE:** The description of best OOP practices is beyond the scope of this book. This section only shows how to implement a basic OOP system, not how to build the effective architectures based on objects. We will have a lot of practice with objects throughout the remaining chapters, however, and we will try to utilize the best OOP approaches.

Constructing Objects

There are several ways to define the object in JavaScript. The simplest way is to declare it as the usual hash, as shown in Listing 1-2.

Listing 1-2. *Simplest Way to Define the Object*

```
var car = {
    color: "red",
    drive: function() {
        console.log(this.color + " car moved");
    }
};
car.drive();
```

This method is not very useful since you create one individual object that does not relate in any way to any common data structure. To create a second instance of the car, you'll have to describe its structure once again.

In object-oriented languages like Java, we got used to the idea of classes that describe the common structure of the objects and that can be used to construct any number of them.

In JavaScript, there are no classes. But there's a similar mechanism to describe the common blueprint: functions and objects. In fact, any function or object can be used to create a new object. Listing 1-3 shows an example that creates the object with the same structure as before.

Listing 1-3. *Creating a New Object with the Constructor Function*

```
function Car() {
    this.color = "red";
    this.drive = function() {
        console.log(this.color + " car moved");
    };
}

var car = new Car();
car.drive();
```

With this approach, we can create a second instance of the Car without describing the structure again. Obviously, this approach is better, since the object description is now stored in one place. If you ever need to change it, you will not have to search through the whole code base, but instead fix only the Car() function; objects that are created via new Car() will be changed too. The functions like Car that are primarily used to create new objects are commonly called *constructors*. Properties defined with this keyword will be available to every object created with the same constructor.

Prototypes

Prototypes work similar to classes in other languages: they define the common structure for the objects created with the same constructor.Prototypes are a source of constant confusion among JavaScript developers. I will try to describe this topic without making it even more confusing than it already is.

Every object in JavaScript has a prototype, and the prototype itself is an object. It works like a parent: it shares all its properties with the child object, allowing the child to use them as if they were its own. Take a look at Figure 1-11. The car object (the bottom box in the figure) has only one own property, color, but the car's prototype has the drive function. Since all properties of the prototype are available to the object, you can call car.drive() as if it is a regular function of car.

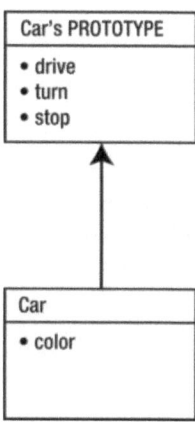

Figure 1-11. *The properties defined on the prototype are available to the object*

> **NOTE:** In JavaScript there's a term, *own property*, which refers to the property that is defined directly on the object. In the following code, the color property is the own property of the car object since it is defined directly by car and not in the car's prototype.
>
> ```
> var car = new Car();
> car.color = "red";
> ```

Since the prototype is a regular object, it can have its own prototype too. The methods of that "super" prototype are available to the object as well. Figure 1-12 illustrates this idea. When JavaScript needs to find a variable or call a method, it first looks through the object's properties. If the property is not found, it then looks at the prototype, then the prototype of the prototype, and so on until it reaches the top level. This idea is known as the *prototype chain.*

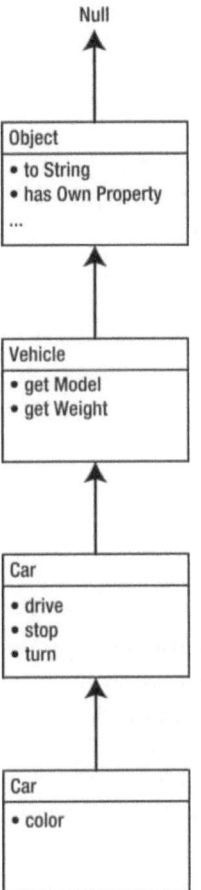

Figure 1-12. *The prototype chain*

At the top of the prototype chain stands the prototype of the Object. It defines the methods and functions common to every created object, like toString, hasOwnProperty, and others.

> **NOTE:** There are two ways to access the prototype of an object. The standard way is by using the `Object.getPrototypeOf` function. The other is by using the call to `__proto__` property. `car.__proto__` is the prototype of the `car` object. The second way is not standard, but it is implemented in most browsers. Even though the `__proto__` property is deprecated, it is still convenient for debugging.

Every function in JavaScript has a property called `prototype`. If the function is used as the constructor, this property is automatically assigned as the prototype of the objects created via the `new` call. Let's look at another example in Listing 1-4.

Listing 1-4. *Simple Use-Case of the Prototype Property*

```
function Car() {
    this._color = "red";
}

Car.prototype.drive = function () {
    console.log(this._color + " car is driving");
};

var car = new Car();
car.drive();
```

All changes that you make to the `prototype` property are instantly available to every object constructed with `new Car()`, no matter if they were created before or after the change. Take a look at Listing 1-5. The first object, car1, is created as usual. Its prototype is `Car.prototype`, as described. Next, we add the new function to `Car.prototype`. This function is instantly available to every object that shares the same prototype, no matter if the object was constructed before or after the change.

Listing 1-5. *Updating the Prototype*

```
function Car(color) {
    this._color = color;
}

Car.prototype.drive = function () {
    console.log(this._color + " car is driving");
};

var car1 = new Car("red");
console.log(Object.getPrototypeOf(car1) === Car.prototype); // true
car1.drive();
```

```
// Adding the new function to the prototype
Car.prototype.stop = function () {
    console.log(this._color + " car has stopped");
};

var car2 = new Car("blue");
// Objects share the same object for prototype
console.log(Object.getPrototypeOf(car1) === Object.getPrototypeOf(car2));
// true

// Both objects can now access the new method
car2.stop();
car1.stop();
```

When you execute this script, you'll see that the new methods are available to both car1 and car2. Figure 1-13 illustrates this idea. Each object that is created with the new Car()call shares the same object as its prototype. Obviously, by sharing the prototype, they share the whole prototype chain.

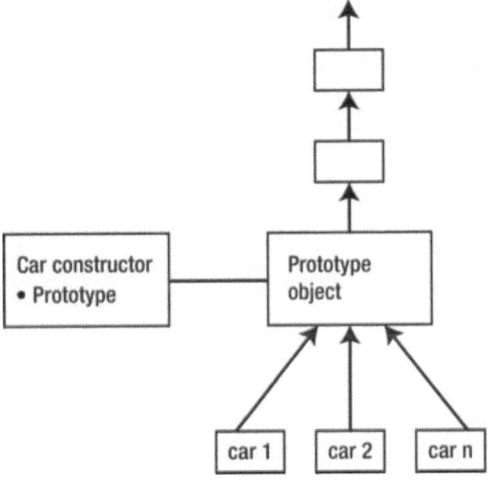

Figure 1-13. *All objects created with new Car() share the same prototype defined in Car.prototype*

Inheritance

Inheritance is one of the core concepts of OOP. It allows reusing the common functionality defined in a "parent" object and extends it with the specifics of "child" objects. Let's look at an example of an application that operates several different types of cars: fire trucks, racing cars, and ice cream vans. All of these cars have common features. They can all move, turn, and stop. But each car has special features that are only available to it: fire trucks can rotate a water cannon, a racing car can drift, and an ice cream van can play melodies. Figure 1-14 illustrates this architecture.

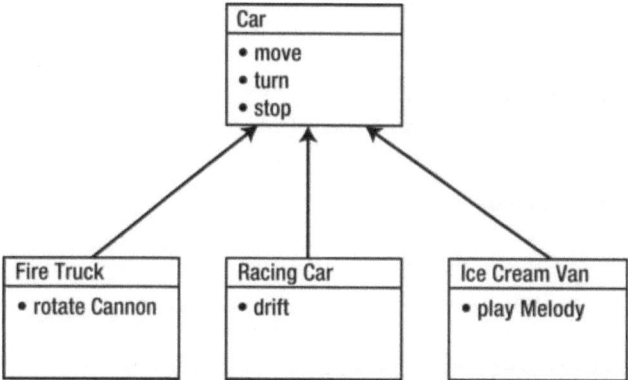

Figure 1-14. *The idea of inheritance. The "parent" (Car) defines the common methods, while "children" (FireTruck, RacingCar, and IceCreamVan) define only the specific extensions.*

As you can see, the prototype chain does exactly the same thing: it allows you to reuse the methods and variables from the prototypes on the upper levels. Let's start with the code for two constructors that define the required methods (see Listing 1-6).

Listing 1-6. *The Basic Setup for Inheritance*

```
function Car(color) {
    this._color = color;
}

Car.prototype.move = function() {
    console.log(this._color + " car moves");
};

Car.prototype.turn = function(direction) {
    console.log(this._color + "car turns " + direction);
};

Car.prototype.stop = function() {
    console.log(this._color + " car stops");
};

function FireTruck() {}

FireTruck.prototype.turnCannon = function(direction) {
    console.log("Cannon moves to the " + direction);
```

```
};
```

```
// Link prototypes of FireTruck and Car into the chain somehow
```

```
var truck = new FireTruck();
// Will not work, because the Car.prototype is not in the prototype chain
// of the truck object yet, so method move() is not available
truck.move();
truck.turnCannon("right");
```

> **NOTE:** As you see, the code uses console.log to trace the execution. To learn how to capture the console output in both mobile and desktop browsers, refer to Appendix A.

The code will not work. The truck.move() call results in an error since the move method is not available to FireTruck. Fixing this code and adding the Car into the chain is surprisingly easy. There is a special method in JavaScript called Object.create(proto, properties). It creates a new blank object and sets its prototype to proto—the first argument of the function. Listing 1-7 shows how to fix the code.

Listing 1-7. *Corrected Inheritance*

```
function FireTruck() {}
```

```
FireTruck.prototype = Object.create(Car.prototype);
// Check just in case
console.log(Object.getPrototypeOf(FireTruck.prototype) === Car.prototype);
// true
// Now the Car.prototype is added to the chain
```

```
FireTruck.prototype.turnCannon = function(direction) {
    console.log("Cannon moves to the " + direction);
};
```

```
var truck = new FireTruck();
// Will now work, because the Car.prototype is in the prototype chain
// of the truck object
truck.move();
truck.turnCannon("right");
```

The example now runs, but the output is still somewhat wrong.

```
true
undefined car moves
Cannon moves to the right
```

The color of the car is set in the Car constructor. The constructor itself was not executed, and the color left undefined. This issue is easy to fix too. Alter the FireTruck constructor and add the call to the Car constructor in it. This way we allow the Car to initialize its own variables of the object.

```
function FireTruck() {
    Car.call(this, "red");
}
```

Run the code again and enjoy the correct output.

Even though the code works, it has a tiny issue that needs solving. When you create the new function, its prototype property is not empty. It has one property called constructor that refers back to the function itself. When we call

```
FireTruck.prototype = Object.create(Car.prototype);
```

this property is lost since the newly created object doesn't have its own properties. We can pass the missing property as the second argument to create.

```
FireTruck.prototype = Object.create(Car.prototype, {
    constructor: {
        value: FireTruck, // the same as FireTruck.prototype.constructor
        enumerable: false,
        writable: true,
        configurable: true
    }
});
```

The constructor is not the usual property. It doesn't appear when you loop through the keys of the object, but it is available if you access it directly by name. We can achieve the same result by passing the property "descriptor" to the second argument of create(). Descriptor has several fields, as follows:

- value: The initial value

- enumerable: If property should appear in the list of object properties; in loops like for... in or Object.keys

- writable: If property can be assigned a different value

- configurable: True if the rules described with the descriptor can be changed or the property can be deleted

This way we mimic the behavior of the real constructor, preserving the structure of the prototype that ECMA (European Computer Manufacturers Association, an organization responsible for the standards behind JavaScript) specification defines. This is the practical implementation of the coding principle described earlier: preserve the structure of the object. Even if you don't know why this property might ever be required, you must keep it.

Let's look at Listing 1-8, the final version of the example. It shows how to implement inheritance and build custom prototype chains. The code for inheritance is moved into the separate function. Doing so has several benefits: at the very least, we eliminate code duplication (in case we have a dozen objects in the application). Besides, if you back-port your game to an older browser, you might need to implement a different strategy of inheritance since older browsers might not support the described features.

Listing 1-8. *The Final Version of the Inheritance Example*

```
function extend(subConstructor, superConstructor) {
    subConstructor.prototype = Object.create(superConstructor.prototype, {
        constructor: {
            value: subConstructor,
            enumerable: false,
            writable: true,
            configurable: true
        }
    });
}


function Car(color) {
    this._color = color;
}

Car.prototype.move = function() {
    console.log(this._color + " car moves");
};

Car.prototype.turn = function(direction) {
    console.log(this._color + "car turns " + direction);
};

Car.prototype.stop = function() {
    console.log(this._color + " car stops");
};

function FireTruck() {
    Car.call(this, "red");
}

extend(FireTruck, Car);

FireTruck.prototype.turnCannon = function(direction) {
    console.log("Cannon moves to the " + direction);
```

```
};

var truck = new FireTruck();
truck.move();
truck.turnCannon("right");
```

The extend function is used in each and every script throughout this book. Create a new file called utils.js and put the code for the function there. In upcoming chapters, we will add other useful functions to this file.

> **NOTE:** The implementation of OOP in JavaScript has evolved several times during the last few years. There are multiple approaches to solving the same task: some are better, while others are a little worse or outdated. The described approach is the cleanest one so far. Also, Node.js (the server-side JavaScript engine that we learn in Chapter 10) uses the same method of extending objects. Using it makes porting objects from client to server a much easier task. In fact, I cheated a little and used the function from the Node core module to keep this sort of consistency.

A final note on naming. In this chapter, I did my best to avoid using the word "class". It turns out, however, that class is a great word to describe the concept of the blueprint that you can use to construct new objects. Using words like "constructor" and the "prototype chain" is very inconvenient. In upcoming chapters, I use the word "class" to refer any constructor function together with the prototype. In other words, the whole set of properties that define the object. Since now we have clarified the mechanics behind JavaScript OOP, it will not cause any misunderstanding.

OOP presents great possibilities for structuring your code. Even though JavaScript doesn't have classes, it is still an object-oriented language. For a long time, JavaScript was used for simple scripts, and OOP approaches seemed like an unnecessary level of complexity. When the code base grew, however, OOP showed its full potential.

A Word About Mobile Browsers

Android is an open and relatively new platform—a sweet target for every company that makes browsers. Major browser-market players are competing to make "the ultimate mobile Android browser." At the time of writing, there are a lot of alternatives available for the user: Firefox, Dolphin HD, Dolphin Mini, Opera Mini, and several other products. It seems that we'll have another browser war really soon.

This enthusiasm is really great since the competition is the force that improves the quality of the product, especially when browsers are free and quality is the only distinction. On the other hand, it makes your life a little harder. As a web application developer, you are responsible to write the code that runs fine on all the chosen platforms. More supported browsers means more happy users, but it also means more sleepless nights, ugly hacks, and longer development time.

Whatever strategy you or your boss picks, the rule about browser families stays the same: if you are optimizing the code for a stock browser, make sure it looks good on Chrome. With mobile Firefox, make sure that the application works fine on the desktop version.

Summary

In this chapter, we reviewed the set of tools needed to start the development of Android web applications. We installed JDK (Java Development Kit) and tried out two IDEs to write the simplest possible Hello World application. We installed the nginx web server to make the page available to the emulator and/or device, and we configured nginx to use the folder of our Hello World application as the root for static files. Now when we change the file in the IDE, we can instantly see the changes in the browser by simply reloading the page.

We installed Android SDK and configured the emulator to test our page with it. We learned how to create new emulators and how to set various options like API version and screen resolution.

In the second part of the chapter, we reviewed the best practices for coding. We learned how to use the strengths of JavaScript while avoiding pitfalls. We determined several development principles that are especially important for JavaScript.

We learned how OOP works in JavaScript. This topic causes a lot of confusion and it was important to understand the basic principles that we will use later. We learned what a prototype is and where it comes from. We also learned what a prototype chain is and how the JavaScript engine resolves the property of the object when it needs to access it.

We built a simple example to test the advantages of OOP and created a simple function to "chain" the prototypes of the constructor functions.

The environment is now prepared and you are ready to start the development of real applications. Read on to the next chapter to make your first game.

Graphics in the Browser: The Canvas Element

In this chapter, we will learn how to "draw" on a web page—or specifically, display arbitrary shapes using the canvas element. We will experiment with the drawing API, trying the most common things, such as drawing a line and filling a rectangle with the gradient fill. The code from this chapter serves as the basis for the complete game that we create in Chapter 3: Four Balls, a web version of a popular logical game where players try to arrange a line of four, same-colored tokens to win. (If you're eager to take a peek at the final result, look at the first page of the next chapter.) We learn how to create the game's visuals—the board and the tokens—in this chapter.

We'll cover the following topics:

- A bird's-eye view of the typical video game structure
- Different approaches to rendering graphics on the web page
- The canvas element and its contexts
- Context2D API
    - Coordinate system, fractional coordinates, and anti-aliasing
    - Drawing basic shapes

- Rendering paths
- Curves
- Fills, types of gradients, and gradient-based effects
- Canvas transformations and states

These topics act like small building blocks that allow you to make a broad range of applications: from simple 2D games (Chapter 3) to the complex isometric engines (Chapters 6 and 7), or even 3D engines (Chapter 8).

The Anatomy of the Game

Have you ever played games? I'm sure you have. Let's start with a simple question: what are video games all about? Mostly about having fun, right? Each game presents the player with a virtual world ruled by its own laws and mechanics. The world may be as simple as *Tetris*—a screen with bricks falling from above—or as sophisticated as modern online games with knights and wizards, clans and politics.

The player is trying to accomplish a goal: score points, connect dots in a line, or conquer a galaxy or two. The game itself is the interaction between the gamer and the game world. The player perceives the state of the game in some way: by reading text, looking at a 3D landscape, or examining a web page. The player takes all of this in and takes action. The world is then updated, and it is the player's turn again. He takes another action, and so on, until the end of the game.

So what are the essential components of a game that make it all happen?

Nowadays, games are strongly focused on graphical content. Actually, game graphics might be the only chance to attract the player and make him try your product. Players want the game to be beautiful, and web application games are no exception. Most games have a graphical engine that draws the world on the screen. Some are complex, others are simple, but there are almost no games that have no graphics at all.

Graphics aren't the whole game; they are just the visuals. Games are all about interaction. Players want to move those starships on a screen and send them into a battle. The second essential part of every game development project is user input processing.

We got used to controllers, mice, and keyboards, but mobile platforms offer completely different ways of interaction: touchscreens, accelerometers, gyroscopes, and other sensors. Users can't perform a "right mouse-click" but they can tap, slide, shake, or rotate their devices. Intuitive controls might sound like an easy task to implement, at least before you start to write the real code.

A gamer can excuse flaws in graphics, but he will never tolerate poorly designed controls. Imagine how unhappy the user who accidentally tapped All In instead of Fold in the middle of a poker round would be.

The last component, but certainly not the least, is the game logic: the rules and laws of the game world. It is responsible for a wide range of tasks: artificial intelligence, physics engines, generation of random game content, and many, many others. The code that handles logic may be distributed between the client and the server, or completely client-side. For simple games, like the one that we are going to make in the next chapter, there will be no server at all; everything that the game needs will be on a web page. We will add some server-side logic to the game in Chapter 12 when we create the multiplayer version of Four Balls.

You might have noticed that I didn't mention networking. Even though network communication plays an extremely important role in game development, I believe that it is not a part of the game itself. It is the function, the tool that helps to bring bytes of data from your shiny Android device to the gray box, far away in the datacenter, and back. The magic is happening elsewhere. Nevertheless, it is an extremely important and typically complex component that we learn in-depth in Chapters 10 through 12.

We start our exploration of web game development with the most basic and essential feature of the games, the graphics. The following sections cover the simple, yet very powerful canvas API: the HTML5 DOM (Document Object Model) element that introduced the biggest change in web gaming since Ajax.

Drawing Inside the Browser

The task of drawing inside the browser is not entirely new or unique to game development. Once browsers started to show their full power, the capability of displaying arbitrary dynamic graphics became essential for a broad range of rich web applications. There are three ways to display graphics in the browser:

- arrange divs with CSS image backgrounds
- use Scalable Vector Graphics (SVG)
- use the canvas element

The first approach, sometimes referred to as "floating divs," is considered outdated. It was used to make games in the browsers that did not support canvas. The idea behind it is to create a div element for every object on the scene. The div is then styled with the background-image CSS property; that's how it renders the image. This approach has an obvious drawback: it doesn't allow you to draw arbitrary graphics; only static images. If a developer wants to draw a line between two points, it is not possible unless there is an image with that line somewhere on the server. This method is just a workaround that web game developers had to use before canvas appeared.

The second approach is to use SVG, an XML-based vector graphics standard. SVG has somewhat limited use for Android game development; this standard is not supported by stock Android 2.x browsers. Even if a browser did support it, SVG is somewhat hard to use due to its XML nature. Any action, even drawing a simple line or filling a rectangle, involves the manipulation of XML nodes, which is not as intuitive as using the canvas API.

The best option for game development is to use the canvas element, which is well-supported by modern devices and also has an intuitive drawing API. The rest of this chapter focuses on it.

The Basic HTML Setup

Before turning to canvas, we first need an HTML page. For this book, we will use the simple setup shown in Listing 2-1.

Listing 2-1. *The HTML Skeleton*

```
<!DOCTYPE html>
<html lang="en">
<head>
    <meta charset="utf-8" />
    <style>
    </style>
    <script>
        function init() {

        }
    </script>
</head>
<body onload="init()">

</body>
</html>
```

As you see, this is a standard HTML5 boilerplate. Android perfectly understands this style. There's no need to follow outdated HTML4 guidelines—long doctypes, explicit declarations of language in script blocks, and so forth—since all modern browsers already support HTML5, at least at its basic level. This HTML page is empty, yet it has the entry point for JavaScript code: the init()

method. This method is executed once the HTML file is loaded, parsed, and the document is fully available to JavaScript. This is the perfect place to put your initialization logic: show the "loading" screen, initialize and assign event listeners, or start loading the external resources. For now, the method is empty, but we will soon add drawing code to it. The code for the basic HTML skeleton is available in the 1.skeleton.html file for this chapter.

Now we are ready to start the exploration of canvas.

What Is Canvas?

Canvas is a relatively new HTML element. The concept of such an element was introduced in 2004 by Apple. It allows you to draw arbitrary graphics such as geometry primitives, shapes and images, gradients, strokes, and fills. It also has a rich API to control the output that supports transformations like scaling, rotation, and per-pixel image processing. With some extra effort, it can be used for image-processing and applying advanced effects.

The canvas works differently than regular HTML rendering. With HTML, you create elements and attach them to the DOM tree. Once they are attached, you can change their look and position with CSS. If you move the div 100 pixels left, the area where it was before is magically empty and the div appears in the new position. Working with HTML nodes is like having a dozen papers with images lying on your table; you can move them around, put one on top of the other, or throw them away, as shown in Figure 2-1.

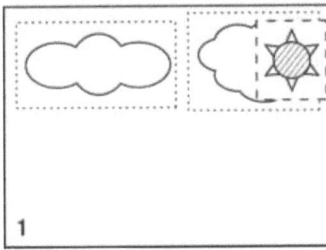 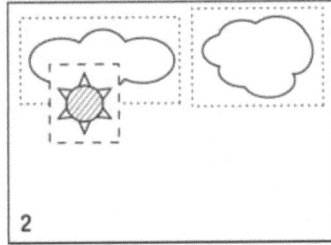

Figure 2-1. *When you move a div on an HTML page, you don't have to worry about clearing the content; you change coordinates, and a div is rendered in a new location. Dotted borders show divs; dashed borders show the div that is moving.*

The canvas is more like painting on a ... canvas. Yes, the real-life one that is made of fabric. Once you paint something, it is there until you erase it or paint something else on top of it. To "move" the image, you first need to erase the old image, restore all the other objects that might have been affected by the move, and then paint the image again in the new place. Look at Figure 2-2, which illustrates this idea.

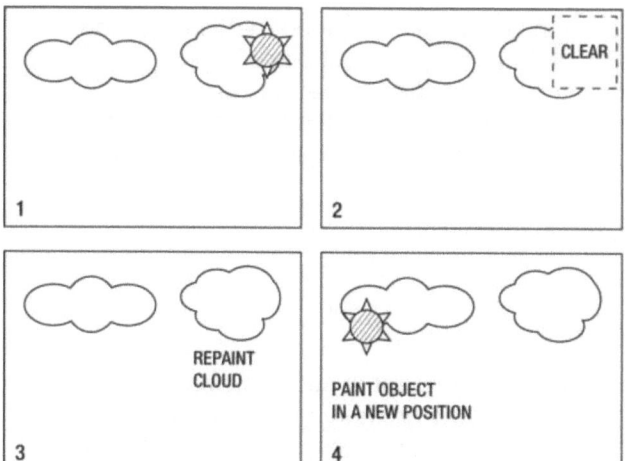

Figure 2-2. *To change the position of an image, you first have to clear its original position, restore other objects that might have been affected, and then paint the image in a new location.*

Listing 2-2 is the example that demonstrates the canvas API. Read through the code to get a feeling of the "canvas style" of web development.

Listing 2-2. *Canvas API Example*

```
<!DOCTYPE html>
<html lang="en">
<head>
    <meta charset="utf-8" />
    <style>
    </style>
    <script>
        function init() {
            var canvas = document.getElementById('mainCanvas');
            var ctx = canvas.getContext('2d');
            ctx.clearRect(0, 0, 300, 300);
            ctx.fillStyle = "lightgray";
            ctx.fillRect(10, 10, 50, 50);
        }
    </script>
</head>
<body onload="init()">
    <canvas id="mainCanvas" width="300px" height="300px"></canvas>
</body>
</html>
```

As you see, canvas is a regular DOM element just like div or table. It behaves exactly the same way as the other nodes: it can be created via document.createElement(), appended to parent, or styled with CSS. It can have margins, paddings, borders, position, and so on. The magic starts to happen after the line var ctx = canvas.getContext('2d').

The Context

The context (the ctx in Listing 2-2) determines the "drawing mode" of the canvas. From a practical point of view, this is the object that acts like the access point to the whole set of drawing methods. Look at the listing once again. Context is the object that is responsible for setting paint colors and for drawing shapes. The type of ctx is CanvasRenderingContext2D, but we'll call it just context for simplicity. If you are still confused about the relationship between canvas and its context, think of canvas as the dull DOM element that looks like the transparent rectangle. The context is the entry point to draw on it; a collection of functions that you use to paint something.

> **NOTE:** At this point, one might ask: Why do I call canvas.getContext('2d')? Why '2d'? Maybe there are other types of context like '3d'? The W3C specification defines that getContext "returns an object that exposes an API for drawing on the canvas. The first argument specifies the desired API. Subsequent arguments are handled by that API."
>
> It basically means that you can get the different context out of the canvas, which exposes the different set of API, like 3D API. What exactly you will get depends on the browser. The result for 2D context is clearly defined by the W3C specification.
>
> In 2007, Opera published the first experimental build that had a support for custom 3D canvas; you had to get the "opera-3d" context to access it. The WebGL specification (https://www.khronos.org/registry/webgl/specs/1.0/), released on March 3, 2011, defines its own context called "webgl" to access the standardized 3D context. (We will take a deeper look into WebGL in Chapter 9.)
>
> So '2d' is not just an arbitrary term that can be omitted.

This explanation should make it obvious why it is not completely correct to say "the canvas can draw a curve." It is not the canvas that can or can't draw, it is the graphical context, the API, that is responsible for drawing. What makes perfect sense in one context (like curves in 2D), can be impossible to accomplish in the other context (like curves in WebGL).

The Coordinate System

Coordinates define where exactly you want a certain figure to be painted or how big it will be. Almost every call to the canvas API involves the coordinates. If you want to draw a rectangle, you have to set the top-left corner, width, and height. For the circle, you need the center point and radius. What exactly are those coordinates and how do they work?

The 2D context defines the rectangular bitmap area. The context uses a classic Cartesian coordinate system to refer to individual points inside it. There are two axes: the horizontal axis is called x and vertical is y. The x axis increases when going to the right; and the y axis increases when going down. The point with both x and y set to 0 is called an *origin;* it is located in the top-left corner of a bitmap. Figure 2-3 shows four points, one of which is the origin. Each point has the coordinates near it written in parentheses.

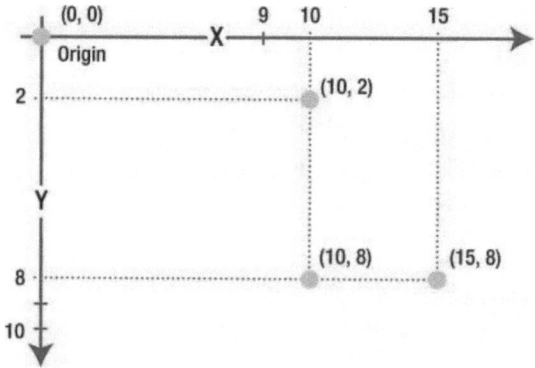

Figure 2-3. *The coordinate system of 2D context*

In 2D space, each point is referred to by the pair of coordinates: x and y. In this book, I use the regular mathematical notation: (x, y); for example, (10, 2) means that the x coordinate of a point is 10 and the y coordinate is 2. The coordinates of origin are (0, 0). In a graphical context the point (10, 8) will be to the left of (15, 8), and to the bottom of (10, 2).

There is one more important rule that is worth mentioning here. Sometimes the graphics APIs and software do not distinguish between the points of the coordinate grid and pixels of the screen, and use these terms interchangeably. The 2D context works in a different and somewhat unintuitive way (at least it is unintuitive for people when they start to write the code for the canvas). Coordinates *are not* pixels. Coordinates are small points *inside* of the pixels or *between* them; for example, the (0, 0) coordinate is a top-left corner of a top-left pixel. The center of the same pixel will have the decimal coordinates (0.5, 0.5).

Imagine that you want to draw a thin vertical line from (1, 0) to (1, 4). You want it to be one pixel wide and have a black color. The context will treat it as a line that lies *between* the first and the second pixel of the screen. Figure 2-4 shows how 2D API treats such a call.

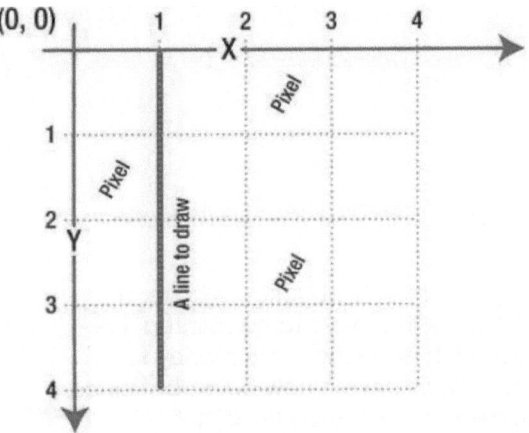

Figure 2-4. *Context treats the line with integer coordinates as if it lies between pixels.*

The width of the line is one pixel, so the context should paint half of the left pixel and half of the right pixel to make a total of one. Obviously, a device display can't handle this task since the pixel is the atomic element—it cannot be painted with two different colors at the same time. So the line will overlap *both left and right* pixels. To compensate for the increased width of the line, the context renders both pixels semitransparent, making the line look lighter in color. Figure 2-5 shows the model of such a one-pixel line that is positioned on the boundary between real, physical pixels.

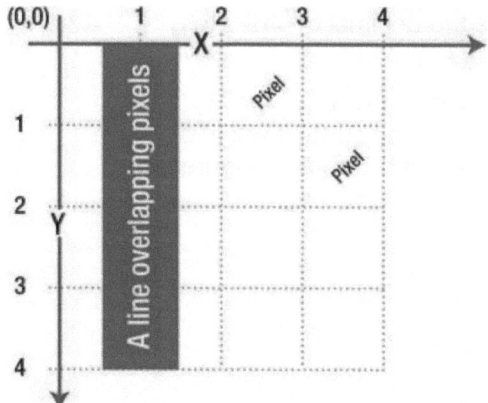

Figure 2-5. *The line is one pixel wide; it overlaps half of two pixels since it is positioned over their boundary.*

A context works like a painter with just enough paint in his bucket to cover a wall. Suddenly, he realizes that there are *two* walls that have to be painted. He decides to dilute his paint with water to get the job done (no extra money for another bucket of paint—that's life). Now both walls have a new color, but since the layer of the paint is so thin, you can see the old wallpaper through it.

That is how the context draws the line: the stroke color is "divided" between the left and the right pixel. The resulting color that the user sees will not be black; it will be light gray. The resulting color also depends on the color of the background since it is visible through a translucent line. Also, the resulting line will be two pixels wide since both the left and right pixels are "covered" by the original line. Figure 2-6 shows the result of such a call on 2D context. The white dashed line is the line that was meant to be drawn. It lies between the pixels. The resulting line is painted with 50 percent transparency; because of that, the background affects the resulting color of the line. It is dark red on the top and dark gray on the bottom.

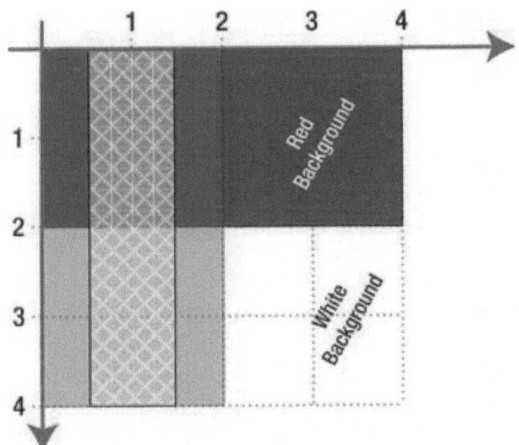

Figure 2-6. *The result of using integer coordinates to draw the vertical one-pixel line*

To draw the one-pixel black line, you have to set the decimal coordinates by adding an extra half of a pixel. If a line from (1.5, 0) to (1.5, 4) goes through the center of every pixel, it is exactly one pixel wide; and since it doesn't overlap any extra space, it has the pure black color.

What if you want a two-pixels-wide line? Correct. You have to switch back to integer coordinates, otherwise it will effectively cover three pixels—one solid pixel at the center and two semitransparent pixels on the sides.

Treating coordinates like that may be a little confusing, but it makes perfect sense once you start to deal with shapes that are more complex. You shouldn't care a lot about the *exact* pixels that make up a figure if the figure is nicely rendered and looks natural to the user. Smooth colors and soft edges look natural; aliased "ladders," where pixels are either black or white, do not. Figure 2-7 shows the practical difference between the two. The top row shows the aliased version of the line and the circle (the normal size and zoomed fragments), while the bottom row shows the same figures drawn with anti-aliasing, as 2D context draws them. As you can see, the bottom images look much nicer.

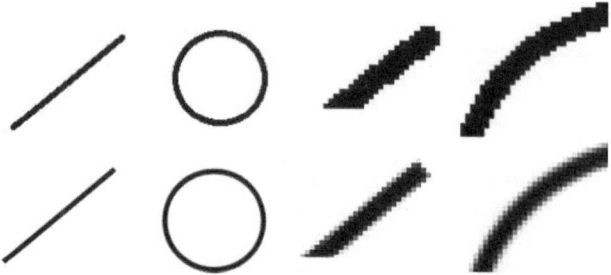

Figure 2-7. *Comparing aliased figures with smoothed figures*

> **NOTE:** The 2D context is anti-aliased by default. That's why those semitransparent pixels appear. What if you want the old, jaggy pixel-art style? Can you turn the anti-aliasing off? The simple answer would be no. If you still want to get full control over the pixels, you'll have go to the lower level and work directly with the bitmap image data. We'll show how to do it in upcoming chapters (Chapter 5 explains the basics of this technique).

Now that we know how coordinate system works, we can start drawing actual graphics.

Drawing Shapes

The 2D context defines two types of shapes: simple shapes and complex shapes. *Simple shapes* is a geeky name for rectangles. Everything that is not a rectangle is a *complex shape*, even a line. We'll start the drawing experiments with the simplest possible figure, a rectangle. Then we'll look into more complex shapes and paths.

As I promised at the start of the chapter, we will prepare some code for our first big project, a Four Balls game. Now that we know the tricky coordinate system of the context, we can handle the first task: drawing a background for the game board. The board is rectangular, so we'll start by learning how to draw a rectangle outline and fill it with some color. The default white background is a little dull, so we'll change it to something better!

Rectangles

Drawing a rectangle is a straightforward task (see Listing 2-3). There are two functions for it: drawRect() and fillRect(). The first function draws only the outline of the rectangle, which we will use for the border. The second draws a filled shape, which is suitable for the background. Both methods take four arguments: x and y of the top-left corner of the rectangle, and its size: width and height.

***Listing 2-3.** Drawing a Rectangle*

```
<!DOCTYPE html>
<html lang="en">
<head>
    <meta charset="utf-8" />
    <style>
    </style>
    <script>
        function init() {
            var canvas = document.getElementById("mainCanvas");
            var ctx = canvas. getContext("2d");
            ctx.fillStyle = "gray";
            ctx.strokeStyle = "blue";

            ctx.lineWidth = 3;
            ctx.fillRect(50, 50, 100, 120);
            ctx.strokeRect(4.5, 30.5, 70, 70);
        }
    </script>
</head>
<body onload="init()">
    <canvas id="mainCanvas" width="300px" height="300px"></canvas>
</body>
</html>
```

The output looks like what is shown in Figure 2-8.

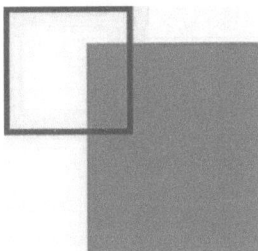

***Figure 2-8.** Drawing rectangles with drawRect and fillRect*

Insert the code from Listing 2-3 into the HTML template from the beginning of the chapter. In the following listings, I omit the HTML wrapper since it usually doesn't change. You have to write your code straight into the init() method and give it a try.

> **NOTE:** This copy/paste approach is only used for short, hands-on examples because now we learn how to draw things. In the next chapter, when we are done with the basics, we will create a good object-oriented architecture for the game.

Don't forget to use the coordinate guidelines from the previous section. The stroke is a line; use the half-pixel coordinates when the stroke width is odd and the integer coordinates when it is even, otherwise the line will be blurry and semitransparent. For the fillRect operation, you can use the integer coordinates all the time since you usually want to fill the whole pixel, not half of it.

> **NOTE:** I didn't mention how to use these strokes and fills. I explain them in detail in the next sections. For now, think of a fill as the "paint bucket" tool in a graphical editor and a stroke as the "border" of a shape.

To fill the whole available space, you can use canvas.width and canvas.height properties. Listing 2-4 shows how to fill the background with a very light-yellow color (like old paper) and how to draw a two-pixel border afterwards.

Listing 2-4. *Drawing the Board Background*

```
var canvas = document.getElementById("mainCanvas");
var ctx = canvas.getContext("2d");
ctx.fillStyle = "#fffbb3";
ctx.strokeStyle = "#989681";

ctx.lineWidth = 2;
ctx.fillRect(0, 0, canvas.width, canvas.height);
ctx.strokeRect(1, 1, canvas.width - 2, canvas.height - 2);
```

The output from this code looks like Figure 2-9.

Figure 2-9. *A filled and stroked rectangle*

Paths

In 2D context, everything that is not a rectangle is a complex shape, which is another geeky name. A complex shape is a "virtual" path that you draw on the context. Why is it virtual? Because it is not visible until you stroke or fill it.

The dotted line on the first image in Figure 2-10 does not show on the display; I put it there for reference. Fill works like the paint bucket; stroke is the border. You can use either one of these, or both together, but the path will stay invisible until you use either to "paint" it. Setting a path is like drawing a sketch with a very thin pencil; to finish the picture, paint should be applied on top of it. Figure 2-10 illustrates this idea.

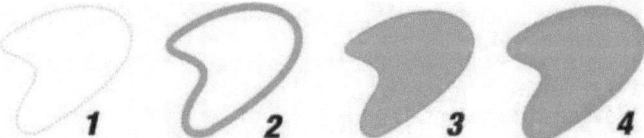

Figure 2-10. *(1) Path without strokes and fills (invisible). (2) Path with stroke only. (3) Path with fill only. (4) Path with both stroke and fill.*

Context2D API has three "instruments" for building paths: lines, arcs, and curves (quadratic and Bézier).

We will start learning how paths work from drawing a grid on the game board. Then we look at arcs and draw tokens for the game. Finally, we will use curves to draw some nice board decorations.

Lines

Line is the simplest of the paths. The code to render a line on the canvas is very straightforward:

```
ctx.beginPath();
ctx.moveTo(50, 50);
ctx.lineTo(120, 100);
ctx.strokeStyle = "#000";
ctx.stroke();
```

First of all, we need to let context know that we are starting a new path: beginPath does exactly that. The moveTo method means "we are going to draw the next path segment from this point." Or, continuing the analogy with the pencil and paper, "take your pencil off the paper and put it to that point without drawing anything." The next line of the code is self-explanatory: draw the line from wherever you are to (120, 100). At this point, the line is not drawn yet; it exists only as a virtual path. The final two lines stroke the path; the line finally becomes visible. The result is not surprising: the line from (50, 50) to (120, 120), as shown in Figure 2-11.

Figure 2-11. *Drawing a line*

Now you know how to draw lines. Let's use this knowledge to draw a grid for the board (see Listing 2-5).

Listing 2-5. *Drawing a Grid*

```
// For now, set cell size explicitly, later
// we will calculate it based on device dimensions
var cellSize = 40;
ctx.beginPath();

// Drawing horizontal lines
for (var i = 0; i < 8; i++) {
    ctx.moveTo(i*cellSize + 0.5, 0);
    ctx.lineTo(i*cellSize + 0.5, cellSize*6)
}

// Drawing vertical lines
for (var j = 0; j < 7; j++) {
    ctx.moveTo(0, j*cellSize + 0.5);
    ctx.lineTo(cellSize*7, j*cellSize + 0.5);
```

```
}

// Stroking to show them on the screen
ctx.lineWidth = 1;
ctx.strokeStyle = "#989681";
ctx.stroke();
```

The board has seven columns and six rows, so we need to draw eight vertical and seven horizontal lines. Note that we don't stroke each line individually. The lines are joined into one big path that is stroked afterwards with a single `ctx.stroke()` call. The individual line is called a *subpath*. More about subpaths later in this chapter.

> **NOTE:** As you see, I'm hard-coding the cell size here. Don't do this in the real application if your game needs to scale to fit screens with different resolutions. We will rewrite the code and make it adapt to the screen size later in the next chapter.

If you add this code after the code from Listing 2-4, the result will look almost like the board. The grid is not yet perfectly centered inside the board, but that's easy to fix as we will see in the final sections of this chapter.

We've used a method called `beginPath`, but we haven't used anything like `closePath`, even though there is a method with such a name. In terms of 2D context, to "close" a path means to put a straight line between the last and the first point of the subpath. If you need to create a triangle, for example, you only need to define two lines out of three. When you close the path, the API will add the third line for you.

Arcs

An arc is painted in a slightly different way than a line. You don't have to "move" your pencil anywhere; you call the arc method straight away, passing six parameters: the x and y coordinates of the center, radius, start angle, end angle, and counterclockwise flag.

> **NOTE:** Why is there no method called "draw circle" in the API? The Context2D API is trying to be as compact as possible. It doesn't have a lot of convenience methods; it is left to developers to make them. An arc is a segment of circle, like a slice of pizza. So the circle is the special case of the arc, the pizza that has only one big slice.

Quick math hint. There are two metrics to describe angles: degrees and radians. Degrees are the usual metric for everyday life: a right angle is 90 degrees, the Earth's axial tilt is around 23.4 degrees, and so on. Radians are mostly used in math and ... the canvas API. A full circle is 360 degrees or 2*pi (2π) radians, so one radian is about 57 degrees. It doesn't make much sense to convert every angle with a calculator to radians if you are used to degrees, or even write a code that does so. It is best to get used to radians.

Radians expressed as plain numbers don't make much sense; they are almost always shown with pi (π) number. A full circle is 2π radians; a right angle is $\pi/2$; 45 degrees is $\pi/8$, and so forth. In JavaScript, there's a handy constant defined in Math class: Math.PI. Use it whenever you need to set the angle in radians. Figure 2-12 illustrates how the arc is drawn and how the angles are expressed in radians.

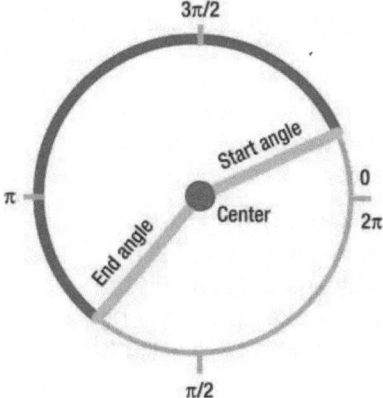

Figure 2-12. *The arc appears between the start angle and end angle, following the direction set by the clockwise flag.*

To draw a token we need a circle. A full circle is 2π radians. The following code illustrates how to draw it:

```
var x = 90;
var y = 70;
var radius = 50
ctx.beginPath();
ctx.arc(x, y, radius, 0, 2*Math.PI, false);

// Setting stroke and fill style
ctx.fillStyle="darkgoldenrod";
ctx.lineWidth=5;
ctx.strokeStyle="black";
```

```
ctx.fill();
ctx.stroke();
```

The last parameter in the `arc` function is the "direction" of the arc: if it is true, then the arc will move between angles in a counterclockwise direction (by default, it will move in a clockwise direction). When we draw a complete circle, the direction doesn't matter, so we leave the default.

Before looking at the output, let's make another step towards the game: create a two-dimensional array and fill it with the board data: 0 for no piece, 1 for a red piece, and 2 for a green piece. Then we will draw pieces on the top of the grid that we created in the previous section. Listing 2-6 shows the code.

Listing 2-6. *Drawing Pieces*

```
var data = [
    [0, 0, 0, 0, 0, 0, 0],
    [0, 0, 0, 0, 0, 0, 0],
    [0, 0, 0, 0, 0, 0, 0],
    [0, 0, 0, 0, 0, 0, 0],
    [0, 0, 0, 2, 1, 0, 0],
    [0, 0, 2, 1, 1, 2, 0]
];

ctx.strokeStyle = "#000";
ctx.lineWidth = 3;

for (var i = 0; i < data.length; i++) {
    for (var j = 0; j < data[i].length; j++) {
        var value = data[i][j];
        if (!value)
            continue;

        switch (value) {
            case 1:
            ctx.fillStyle = "red";
            break;

            case 2:
            ctx.fillStyle = "green";
            break;
        }

        ctx.beginPath();
        ctx.arc((j+0.5)*cellSize, (i+0.5)*cellSize, cellSize/2 - 5, 0,
2*Math.PI, false);
        ctx.fill();
        ctx.stroke();
    }
}
```

Look at Figure 2-13. The result is starting to look like a real game.

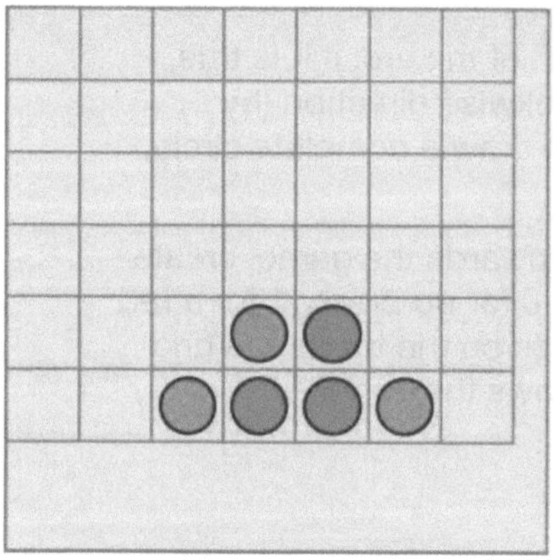

Figure 2-13. *The game field with grid and pieces*

So far, we have the board background, the grid, and the pieces that we will use in the game project in Chapter 3.

Curves

Besides the straight lines and arcs, the 2D context supports two other complex types of paths: quadratic curves and Bézier curves. The math behind them is somewhat more complex than the math for drawing a rectangle or circle, but I'll try to explain it without going too deep into the details.

Both types of curves use the "control points" to set the shape of the curve. The first and the last control points are the *anchors*. They are the start and the end of the curve itself. Other control points don't belong to the curve, they rather act like magnets that can twist and twirl it. Quadratic curves use three control points, whereas Bézier curves use four. Let's start with quadratic curves. Once you get the idea, the mechanics behind the Bézier curve will be obvious. The API to draw a curve is very simple, just one line of the code:

```
ctx.bezierCurveTo(0, 100, 60, 200, 30, 300);
```

To use it wisely, we'll first take a step into the math.

Quadratic Curves

The curve is painted point-by-point. The position of each point of the curve is defined by the position of control points. Let's say we want to draw five points that belong to the curve; the first point is the start of the curve, the last point is the end of the curve, and the other three are points in the middle. Let's use the parameter t to refer to the points of the curve. It will "move" from 0 to 1 as the curve is drawn from the start to the end. t will be 0 for the first point, 0.25 for the second point, 0.50 for the third point, 0.75 for the fourth, and 1 for the last. Now we build a curve.

First, we have the control points: A, B, and C. The initial setup is shown in image 1 of Figure 2-14.

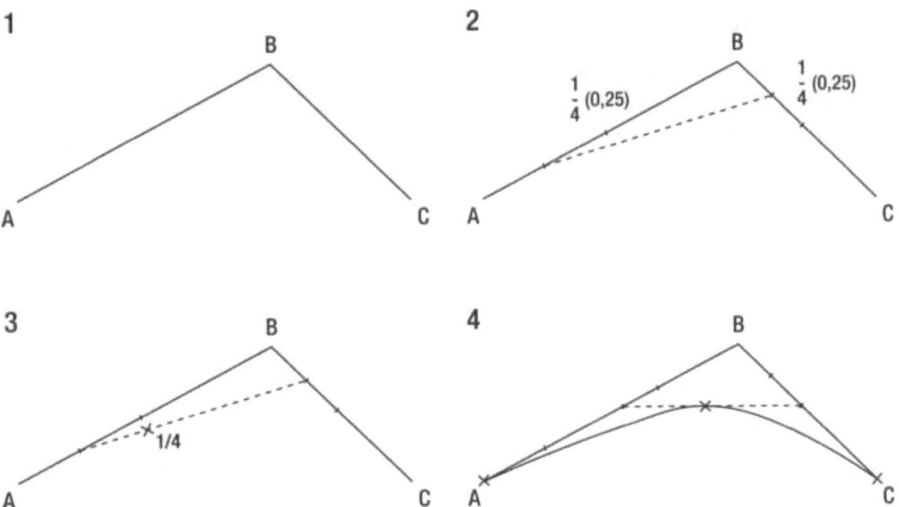

Figure 2-14. *The math behind the curves*

The start of the curve (when t is 0) is the point A. Now let's deal with the second point (t = 0.25). Measure one quarter (0.25) of the AB segment and one quarter of the BC segment, and then draw the line between these two points, as shown on image 2. Now we have a dotted "supporting line." Take one quarter of this new line and you'll have the point of a curve! Image 3 shows this point marked with a small cross.

Repeat these steps for the third point. The value of t is 0.5 (which is ½), so instead of taking the quarters of segments, you have to measure the halves. Draw the supporting dotted line between the middle of AB and the middle of BC. Find the middle of the dotted line; this is the third point. The result is shown in image 4 of Figure 2-14.

One more step for the fourth point, (t = 0.75), and the final point is point C (see Figure 2-15). Now you have five points to build a curve! Join them with the smooth curve, as shown on Figure 2-15, and the quadratic curve is ready.

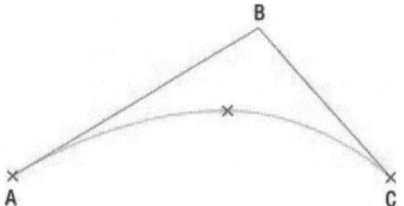

Figure 2-15. *The quadratic curve built point-by-point*

This mechanism is very powerful. With only three control points at your disposal, you can build a curve that best suits your needs! Figure 2-16 shows more examples of quadratic curves.

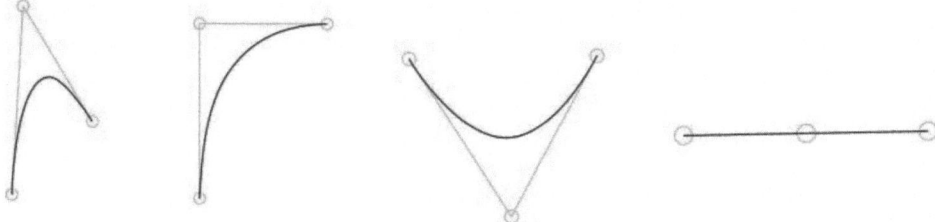

Figure 2-16. *More quadratic curves*

Bézier Curves

Bézier curves work the same way as quadratic curves, except that they use four control points instead of three and they need three supporting lines instead of one.

> **NOTE:** Actually, both quadratic and Bézier curves in Context2D API *are* Bézier curves from a mathematical point of view. It would be more intuitive if they were called "cubic" curves since Bézier curves can be of any order. There are fourth and fifth order Bézier curves too, but they are not supported by the `canvas` API.

Look at the example of a Bézier curve in Figure 2-17. To find the position of the point, you first need to build a helper segment between AB and BC, then between BC and CD. The algorithm of building these segments is absolutely the same as for the quadratic curve. You pick a value from 0 to 1, call it t for convenience, and find the piece of each segment that is proportional to the value. (t = 0) is the start of the segment, (t = 1/3) is one-third of the segment, and so on. After doing these steps on the Bézier curve, you build three supporting points. Deal with them as if they are the control points of the quadratic curve. You have exactly the same setup as in the previous section (three points and a t value) and you know how to find the point of such curve already.

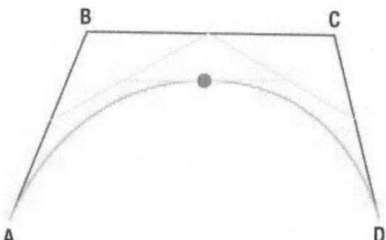

Figure 2-17. *Example of a Bézier curve*

Bézier curves are more flexible than quadratic curves: four points give you more control over the shape. The Bézier curve can cross itself, but the quadratic curve can't. Figure 2-18 illustrates the behavior of different Bézier curves.

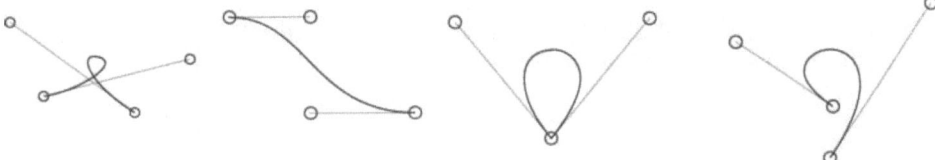

Figure 2-18. *More Bézier curves*

Drawing Curves

Drawing curves on the canvas is way easier than understanding the math behind them. The only thing that you have to do is to pass the coordinates of control points to one of two methods: quadraticCurveTo() or bezierCurveTo(), depending on which type of curve you want. The first control point is implicitly the point where your "virtual pencil" is standing before the call. To illustrate, if you called moveTo(10, 20), then lineTo(40, 50), your "current" coordinates are (40, 50); they will be used as the first control point of the curve. The following is an example of the Bézier curve:

```
ctx.beginPath();
ctx.moveTo(50, 50);
ctx.bezierCurveTo(0, 100, 60, 200, 30, 300);
ctx.stroke();
```

This code draws a Bézier curve that has four control points: (50, 50)—the start of the curve, (0, 100); (60, 200)—the magnets; and (30, 300)—the end of the curve.

Let's use imagination and add some kind of abstract figure on the background of the game board. How about drawing two Bézier curves? Add the code in Listing 2-7 right after you fill the background with the solid color, but before you stroke the border (otherwise the curve will overlap it):

Listing 2-7. *Drawing Curves on Background*

```
// Drawing curves
ctx.strokeStyle = "#6f6e62";
ctx.fillStyle = "#e8b948";

ctx.beginPath();
ctx.moveTo(50, 300);
ctx.bezierCurveTo(450, -50, -150, -50, 250, 300);
ctx.fill();

ctx.beginPath();
ctx.moveTo(50, 0);
ctx.bezierCurveTo(450, 350, -150, 350, 250, 0);
ctx.fill();
```

The result looks … somewhat abstract. A little bit of practice, and I'm sure you can make it better than what is shown in Figure 2-19.

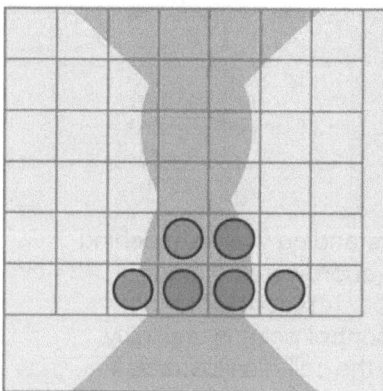

Figure 2-19. *Using curves to decorate a background*

Curves can do much more than drawing waves or hills. In fact, Bézier curves are used very heavily in game development: for defining the movement paths, for advanced easing functions, and for describing rather complex 3D geometry such as B-splines or NURBS surfaces. The power of the Bézier curve lies in the way it represents the shape; only a few points that are easy to transmit over a network or save in a file.

Subpaths

The path in 2D context may consist of several independent figures, called subpaths; for example, you may draw two triangles as the components of the single "path." When you call stroke() or fill(), every subpath is stroked or filled as the separate figure.

There are two ways to start a new subpath: calling moveTo() or closePath(). The difference is that closePath adds the line from the current point to the first point of the subpath to make it closed; whereas moveTo simply starts the new subpath.

> **NOTE:** The name closePath is extremely misleading; the path itself is not closed. All new geometry—lines, curves, and arcs—are added to the same path. The path is closed (in fact, discarded) only when you call beginPath again.

Listing 2-8 shows the example of two triangles rendered with the help of subpaths. The result is the same as rendering them with separate paths.

Listing 2-8. *Two Triangles Rendered As the Subpaths*

```
ctx.beginPath(); // Begin the path

ctx.moveTo(150, 150);   // Start first subpath
ctx.lineTo(200, 200);
ctx.lineTo(100, 200);
// No need to add the line to (150, 150), it will be added by closePath
ctx.closePath();        // End subpath (not the path itself)

ctx.moveTo(250, 200);   // Start second subpath
ctx.lineTo(300, 250);
ctx.lineTo(200, 250);
ctx.closePath();        // End second subpath

ctx.fill();
ctx.stroke();
// Both triangles are filled and stroked at this point,
// since they are the subpaths of the same path

ctx.beginPath(); // The old path is discarded. New paths starts here
… // next subpath code goes here
```

The result of the code is two triangles, filled and stroked as the single path (see Figure 2-20).

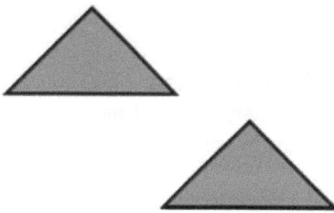

Figure 2-20. *Two triangles drawn as subpaths of a single path*

Most of the time, however, you create a separate path per figure. Subpaths make a difference when you need to draw a lot of figures that have the same stroke and fill style; for example, it is about 1.5 times faster to draw the grid as one big path than stroke each line individually. Such cases are quite rare though.

We've learned how to draw shapes, now it is time to learn how to paint them in attractive colors. We've seen already how to change the color of fills and strokes, but the canvas 2D API has many more options than just dull solid fills.

Strokes and Fills

You have already seen a few examples of strokes and fills in the preceding sections. The following code shows how to set a fill color, a stroke color, and a line width:

```
ctx.fillStyle = "gray";
ctx.strokeStyle = "blue";
ctx.lineWidth = 3;
```

Strokes and fills are really easy to understand. Stroke describes the outline of a shape, while fill describes the internal area. Stroke is the "border" of a path, and fill is its color. Both fillStyle() and strokeStyle() accept the same types of values: solid colors, gradients, and patterns.

Solid Colors

CSS colors are the simplest way to define the style. You can use any format you like: color name, color code, or rgb and rgba functions (see Listing 2-9).

Listing 2-9. *Several Ways to Define a Color for Strokes and Fills*

```
ctx.fillStyle = "#987654"; // Using the code of the color
ctx.strokeStyle = "blue"; // Using predefined CSS color name
ctx.fillStyle = "rgb(255, 0, 0)"; // using the rgb function
ctx.strokeStyle = "rgba(255, 0, 0, 0.5)"; // using the rgba function
```

The context "remembers" the fill and stroke settings. It will use the latest values until you override them explicitly.

Now let's try gradients!

Gradients

Gradient is a smooth transition between two or more colors, or between shades of the same color. The sky at sunset, changing from blue to red or a rainbow, is an example of natural gradients. In computer graphics, gradients are used to simulate light effects like flare, glow, or soft shadows. Figure 2-21 shows several uses of gradients.

Figure 2-21. *Gradients. The image on the left is a screenshot from the game* Commander Keen; *a jaggy gradient is used on the sky background. On the right, multiple radial gradients are used to simulate inner glow and shiny gloss.*

Canvas supports two types of gradients: linear gradients and radial gradients.

Linear Gradients

To make a linear gradient, you first need to create the gradient object:

```
var gradient = ctx.createLinearGradient(10, 10, 50, 50);
```

The parameters that you pass to `createLinearGradient` are x and y coordinates of two points: the start of the gradient and the end of the gradient. In the previous example, I initialized the gradient that starts at (10, 10) and ends in (50, 50). Next, you have to set color stops for the gradient:

```
gradient.addColorStop(0, "blue");
gradient.addColorStop(0.3, "green");
gradient.addColorStop(1, "red");
```

Each call associates a certain color with the point on the gradient line. The first argument is the *offset:* 0 means the start of the line; 1 means the end of the line. In this example, we add three colors. The gradient starts blue. One-third into the line, it changes to pure green, and then ends as red. The areas before the start and after the end of the gradient line is a solid color. In our example, the gradient starts at (10, 10); the point (5, 5) is blue since it lies before the start, and (70, 80) is red because it lies beyond the end of the gradient.

When the gradient is ready, you need to set it as fill or stroke:

```
ctx.fillStyle = gradient; // set gradient as fill
ctx.strokeStyle = gradient; // set gradient as stroke
```

It is much easier to understand if you try this code yourself: color gradients don't look that good on a book page. LED displays render them much better. Still, the result of applying the simple linear gradient to the background of our board is shown in Figure 2-22.

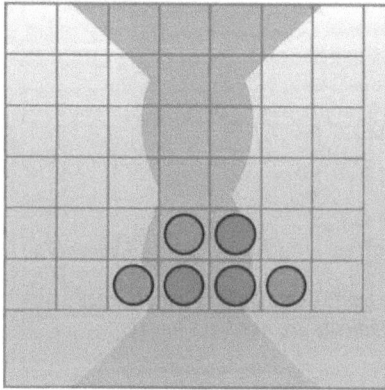

Figure 2-22. *Linear gradient used as the board background*

The code follows:

```
var gradient = ctx.createLinearGradient(0, 0, 0, 300);
gradient.addColorStop(0, "#ffffff");
gradient.addColorStop(1, "#c6c602");
ctx.fillStyle = gradient;
ctx.fillRect(0, 0, canvas.width, canvas.height);
```

> **NOTE:** The colors used in this example are rather bright in order to demonstrate how the curves and gradients look. In the real product, the background should not distract the user from the game. The rest of the code in this chapter use the production version of the colors, which are dimmer and more attractive on the device screen.

Radial Gradients

Radial gradients work exactly the same way, with the only exception that they use circles instead of lines to define the start and the end of the gradient. The start of the gradient is *inner circle*, and the end is the other *outer circle*. To set them both, you specify their center and radius, which are a total of six parameters:

```
c.createRadialGradient(x0, y0, r0, x1, y1, r1);
```

The parameters are as follows:

- y0 and y0: the center of the first circle

- r0: the radius of the first circle

- x1, y1: the center of the second circle

- r1: the radius of the second circle

The radial gradient makes a smooth color transition between the inner and outer circles. Listing 2-10 shows the whole code.

Listing 2-10. *Using Radial Gradients*

```
var gradient = ctx.createRadialGradient(30, 30, 5, 45, 30, 60);
gradient.addColorStop(0, "blue");
gradient.addColorStop(0.3, "green");
gradient.addColorStop(1, "red");
ctx.fillStyle = gradient;
ctx.lineWidth = 10;
ctx.fillRect(0, 0, 80, 80);
```

Now let's apply this new knowledge in practice and draw better pieces for the game. The radial gradients work perfectly when it comes to simulating light and fake volume. We will add the light-like flare and a tiny soft outline to the pieces with the help of a single radial gradient (see Listing 2-11).

Listing 2-11. *Using Radial Gradients to Simulate Light and Shadow Effects*

```
var x = y = 50; //center of the token
var gradient = ctx.createRadialGradient(x + 10, y - 10, 10, x, y, radius);
gradient.addColorStop(0, "yellow");
gradient.addColorStop(0.95, "red");
gradient.addColorStop(1, "black");
ctx.fillStyle = gradient;

ctx.beginPath();
ctx.arc(x, y, radius, 0, 2*Math.PI, true);
ctx.fill();
```

The circle that is rendered here is significantly bigger than the token to show how it will look. It is not a big deal to adjust the sizes after you have a big version working. We are shifting the inner circle 10 pixels to the right and top from the center of the piece. The outer circle has the same radius and position as the piece itself.

The gradient has three color stops. The inner circle will be yellow since the nearest color stop (the one at 0 coordinate) is yellow. The last two lines create a shadow-like effect. Since the area for the last color change is very small (only 5 percent of the gradient), the user will see the thin border that looks more like a shadow. Have a look at the image in Figure 2-23. The regular stroke does not give as nice as an effect since the stroke has the same width on every segment of the path, whereas the gradient is slightly thinner on the "lighted" side and thicker on the "shadowed" side.

Figure 2-23. *Using radial gradients to simulate the light and shadow effects*

We can now modify the code that draws pieces to make the pieces appear glossy. The technique is similar to the one described in Listing 2-11, except that the position of the inner and outer circle of the gradient depends on the position of the token itself. The code looks slightly more complex (see Listing 2-12).

Listing 2-12. *Rendering Tokens with the Gradient Fill*

```
// data variable is the array that holds the board state like in Listing 2-6
for (var i = 0; i < data.length; i++) {
    for (var j = 0; j < data[i].length; j++) {
        var value = data[i][j];
        if (!value)
            continue;
```

```
var color;
switch (value) {
    case 1:
    color = "red";
    break;

    case 2:
    color = "green";
    break;
}

var x = (j + 0.5)*cellSize;
var y = (i + 0.5)*cellSize;

// Token radius
var radius = cellSize*0.4;

// Center of the gradient
var gradientX = x + cellSize*0.1;
var gradientY = y - cellSize*0.1;

var gradient = ctx.createRadialGradient(
    gradientX, gradientY, cellSize*0.1, // inner circle (glare)
    gradientX, gradientY, radius*1.2); // outer circle

gradient.addColorStop(0, "yellow"); // the color of the "light"
gradient.addColorStop(1, color); // the color of the token
ctx.fillStyle = gradient;

ctx.beginPath();
ctx.arc(x, y, cellSize/2 - 5, 0, 2*Math.PI, false);
ctx.fill();
    }
}
```

As you see, the radial gradient uses two colors: yellow for the glare effect and
either red or green for the main piece color. Note again that we do not hard-
code any coordinates; they all are calculated based on the token position and
cell size. This approach allows reusing the same code for the various screen
sizes. We don't care about actual screen dimensions as long as the cellSize
holds the correct value. The result was worth the effort. Take a look at Figure
2-24, which shows how the pieces look with the radial gradient.

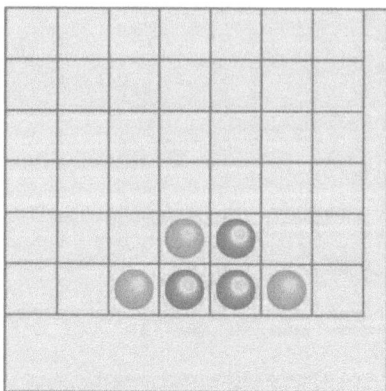

Figure 2-24. *Radial gradient fill applied to the pieces*

Patterns

Patterns are the last type of strokes and fills. Patterns do not work with colors. Patterns take an image and cover a figure's space with it, like the tiles on a kitchen floor. Patterns work as shown in Figure 2-25.

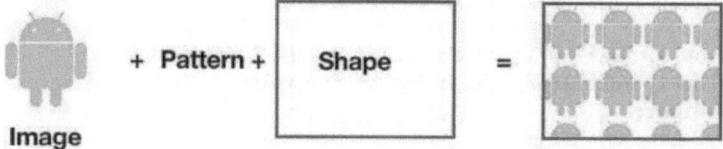

Figure 2-25. *Using patterns as fill*

To create a pattern you will need an image—a JPEG or a PNG or any other web-compatible format—that the browser can handle. Our scene is repainted only once, right after the page is loaded. It means that we need to have a fully loaded image *before* we start to draw anything.

The problem is that browsers load images in an asynchronous manner; you can never be sure that it is already in memory unless you specifically track it. Fortunately, it is not hard at all to implement this logic; we only need to make a couple small adjustments to our initial HTML skeleton. First, we want to download a nice Android logo image from the server (see Listing 2-13).

Listing 2-13. Preloading the Image

```
var logo = new Image();
logo.onload = function() {
    // This function will be called by the browser once the image
    // has loaded
```

```
};
logo.onerror = function() {
    // Always add the error handling code, you never
    // know when it will save you the debugging time
    alert("Could not load the image!");
};
logo.src = "img/logo.png";
```

When you assign the `src` parameter to the image object, the browser starts to load an image from the given path. Our `onload` code will trigger the usual repaint routine, right *after* the loading is completed. This way, we guarantee that the image is available for context's methods when they get executed.

> **NOTE:** In a real-world game, it is often useful to create an `ImageManager`, a separate class that can handle multiple images and hide all the implementation details away from the game logic. Besides, if you have a lot of images to preload, you will need to show some kind of progress bar to the user and let him know that your game isn't stalled. For our purposes, Listing 2-13 is enough to do the job, but we will return to this subject in Chapter 4 and make a better version of the image loading code. Now let's get back to patterns.

Patterns are easier than gradients. You create the pattern with `createPattern()` method. It accepts two parameters: an image and a *repetition strategy* that tells the context what to do if an image is smaller than the area to fill. It works exactly the same way as `background-repeat` CSS property and accepts the following same set of options:

- repeat: repeat image in both directions (default)

- repeat-x: repeat only horizontally

- repeat-y: repeat only vertically, no-repeat—do not repeat the image

Listing 2-14 is the example of patterns. To make the code a little more interesting and clean, I've wrapped the image-loading code into a separate function that executes the callback once the loading is done. The logo variable is global here; in a production environment, it is a rather bad idea to keep these "magic globals." You will find them hard to manage and remember sooner or later. But for this example, it is OK.

Listing 2-14. *Using Patterns*

```
var logo;

function init() {
    loadImage("img/logo.png", function(loadedImg) {
        logo = loadedImg;
        drawScene();
    });
}

function loadImage(imageUrl, callback) {
    var image = new Image();
    image.onload = function() {
        callback(image);
    };
    image.onerror = function() {
        alert("Could not load the image!");
    };
    image.src = imageUrl;
}

function drawScene() {
    var canvas = document.getElementById("mainCanvas");
    var ctx = canvas.getContext('2d');
    var pattern = ctx.createPattern(logo, "repeat");
    ctx.fillStyle = pattern;
    ctx.lineWidth = 10;
    ctx.fillRect(0, 0, 800, 600);
}
```

The bolded lines demonstrate how to create a pattern and use it as a fill. Let's review this code once again, since its structure has changed from the initial HTML5 skeleton. Now we have 3 methods: init(), loadImage(), and drawScene(). The first of these is executed right after the page has finished loading. It is the entry point of the application. It starts the loading of the image that will become a pattern later. When loadImage() is done, it calls the anonymous callback function and passes the loaded Image object as the parameter. Callback executes the drawScene(), the image is used for the pattern and the pattern is used as the default fill. Figure 2-26 shows the result, a nice tiled set of Android logos.

Figure 2-26. *Using patterns*

If you want, you can use a pattern for the board's background (I tried, but I liked gradients better after all). Make sure that the color of the image is not too bright, otherwise you will distract the user from the game itself.

Context State and Transformations

The final part of this chapter is devoted to the *transformations* of the 2D context. Informally, transformation is the rule that is applied to any drawing functions executed on context. If you call ctx.scale(2, 2), for example, everything that you draw afterward will appear twice as big. Context supports the three types of transformations: translate, scale, and rotate.

More formally, transformation changes the coordinate system of the context; for example, after scale(2, 2) each "unit" of coordinate space corresponds to two pixels. So a rectangle with coordinates (10, 10, 5, 5) are drawn as if it is (20, 20, 10, 10).

> **NOTE:** The code that illustrates the use of transformations can be found with the sources for this chapter, the transform-demo.html file. The code is rather large and doesn't have any valuable new material, except for the few lines of transformations, so it is not reprinted in this section. The code uses a slightly different HTML skeleton. Instead of one canvas element, it has several canvas elements. The first element shows the original scene, and the rest show the transformed versions. You can use it as a playground: try different transformations, applying them in different order and to different shapes. The demo uses shapes instead of an image.

The figures in this section show two important things: how coordinate axes are transformed and how the shape changes. The initial scene is schematically presented in Figure 2-27.

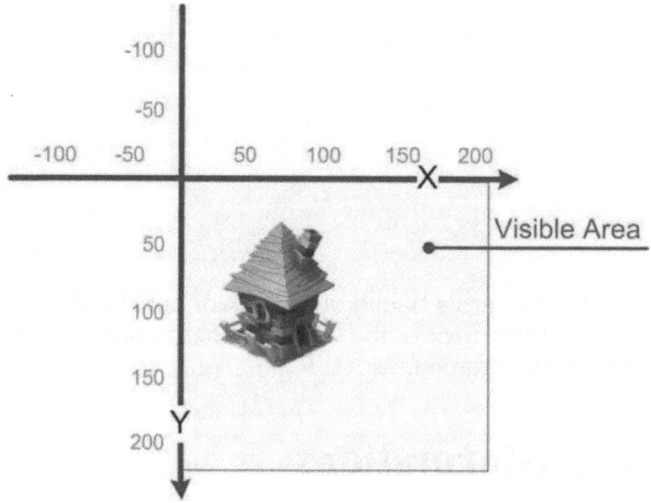

Figure 2-27. *No transformation, the original scene*

By default, when no transformations are applied, the coordinate system looks like what is shown in Figure 2-27: the x axis increasing to the right, and y axis to the bottom, and (0, 0) is in the top-left corner of the canvas. Initially, the only visible part of the coordinate space is where both x and y values are positive.

Translate

Translate is the transformation that shifts every object by a given distance. To apply this transformation call:

```
ctx.translate(50, 100)
```

This code moves the axes, and hence every figure 50 pixels to the right and 100 pixels down (see Figure 2-28). The top-left corner of the canvas is now at point (-50, -100).

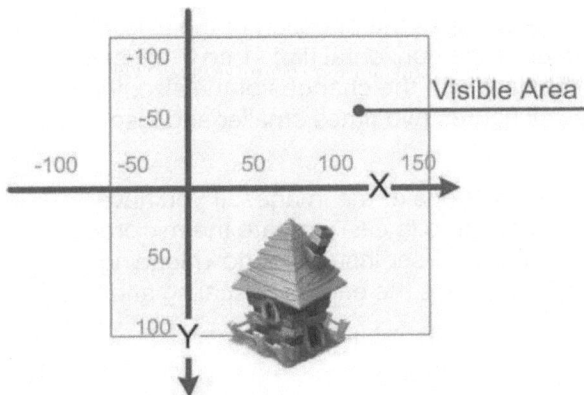

Figure 2-28. *Using the translate function to move the shapes on the scene*

This transformation is often used when you need to change the position of the component without changing its code. Later in this chapter, we see how this transformation might be used to improve the token rendering code by making it more clear and easier to follow.

Scale

Scaling is the transformation that "stretches" or "shrinks" the shapes on the scene. The scale value is set independently for x and y axes. The initial normal scale is 1 for both axes, recorded as (1, 1) for short (in this subsection we use this notion for scale values and not coordinates; the numbers mean the scale value for x and y respectively).

The following are three simple examples to help you understand scaling better:

- *Scaling larger than 1 makes every figure bigger.* (2, 2), for example, makes shapes twice as large.

- *Scaling between 0 and 1 shrinks the shapes.* (0.5, 0.5) makes every shape half of the normal size.

- *Negatively scaling values changes the axis direction and flips shapes.* For example, (-1, 1) flips every shape horizontally.

The following code shows the common use cases of scaling:

```
ctx.scale(2, 2) // Makes all shapes two times larger
ctx.scale(1, 2) // Scales only by the Y axis (the aspect ratio will change)
ctx.scale(1, 1) // Does nothing, and leaves the coordinates intact
ctx.scale(-1, 1) // Flips on X axis
```

When used with the negative values, scale changes the direction of the axis. It looks as if flipping the shape. -1 on X causes the horizontal flip; -1 on Y causes the vertical flip. Of course, you can combine it with the changes of the size; for example, `ctx.scale(0.5, -0.5)` makes all figures two times smaller and also flips the y axis.

Flipping is very useful for creating mirrored versions of the images. If you have an image of a knight facing *left*, for example, you can easily create the mirrored version (the knight facing *right*) straight in the browser instead of downloading the extra image from the server. Figure 2-29 shows the effects of scaling and flipping.

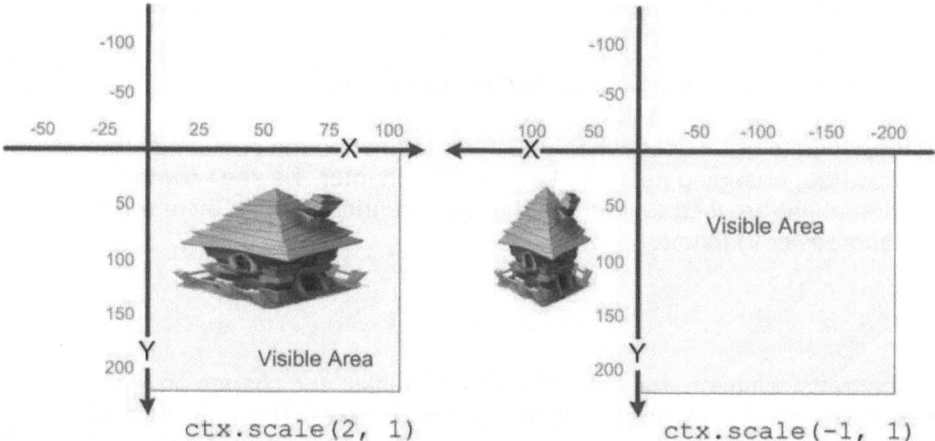

Figure 2-29. *Scaling. The left image is scaled on the x axis; the image on the right shows a flipped scene.*

> **TIP:** You often have to combine "flips" with `translate` calls, since after the flip, the part of the scene can appear out of the visible `canvas` area, like on the right image on Figure 2-29.

The scaling transformation is often used to show the "liveness" of the game objects: the "extra life" icon that shows the beating heart, the deformations of the ball that hits the floor, or the cartoon-style bomb that is anxious to explode. All these effects can be achieved with just a few scale calls.

Rotate

Rotate transformation, as the name implies, rotates the scene around the origin (0, 0). The angle is passed in radians, as in the rest of the API.

```
// rotate around point (0, 0)
ctx.rotate(Math.PI/4);
```

You will often need to rotate the object around an arbitrary point, not just (0, 0); for example, the turret of a tank should turn around its axis, not the origin of the coordinates. In this case, you need to use the simple trick shown in the following code:

```
// Rotate around arbitrary point (150, 150)
ctx.translate(150, 150);
ctx.rotate(Math.PI/4);
ctx.translate(-150, -150);
```

The result looks like the right image in Figure 2-30, compared with rotating around the origin.

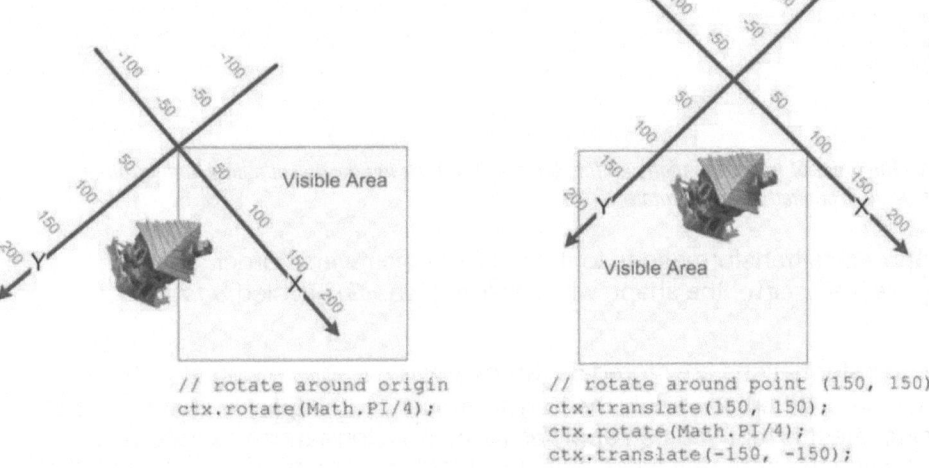

```
// rotate around origin          // rotate around point (150, 150)
ctx.rotate(Math.PI/4);           ctx.translate(150, 150);
                                 ctx.rotate(Math.PI/4);
                                 ctx.translate(-150, -150);
```

Figure 2-30. *Rotating. The left image shows the effect of rotating around the origin; the image on the right shows the effect of rotation around point (150, 150)*

As you can see, we had to use three transformations in order to rotate the scene around (150, 150): translate, rotate, and then translate back. This approach is possible because the modifications of the context stack one on top of another. Let's look how multiple applied transformations affect the scene.

Stacking Transformations

You are not limited to a single transformation per context. In fact, you can apply as many transformations as you want; each one will change the rendering rules. The order of transformations is very important; for example, if we have two transformations (say, rotate by π/2 and scale by 2 on X axis), the result depends on the order of calling corresponding functions.

Look at Figure 2-31. It shows the same scene with two transformations applied in different orders.

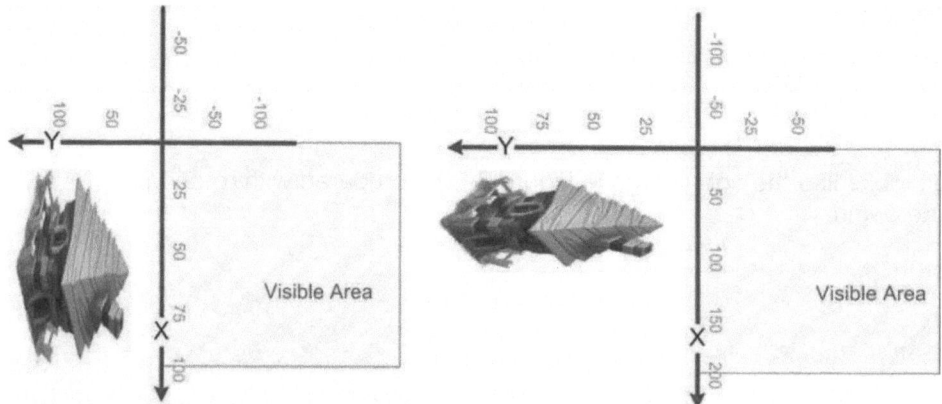

Figure 2-31. *The order of transformations affects the result. On the left, scale is applied before rotate; on the right, scale is applied after the rotate.*

Context applies its transformations to the shape in the reverse order. If you called rotate then scale, the shape will look like it was *first* scaled *and then* rotated.

Internally, transformations are stored as the *matrix*: a two-dimensional 3 × 3 array of numbers. When you apply the transformation, you implicitly change this array. A side effect is that you can apply as many transformations as you want without affecting the performance. Context with 100 applied transformations will not work any slower than the context with two transformations.

If you really know what you are doing, you can pass the transformation matrix to the context manually. There are two methods for this: transform(), which applies the transformation on top of the existing, and setTransform(), which completely resets the matrix.

> **TIP:** Don't worry if you don't understand what the matrix is or how it changes the coordinates of the shapes on the scene. In Chapter 8, we will have an in-depth look into this topic.

Context State

Context state is the collection of different settings that affect the rendering: transformations, fills, strokes, and so forth. Sometimes it is useful to save the state in order to restore it later. Let's look at a simple scenario: a tank game where each of the tanks can change their orientation and can also rotate their cannons.

The code to draw the tank is shown in Listing 2-15.

Listing 2-15. *Transforming a Context State*

```
function drawTank(ctx, x, y, tankRotation, cannonRotation) {
    ctx.translate(x, y);
    ctx.rotate(tankRotation);
    // draw tank body

    ctx.rotate(cannonRotation);
    // draw cannon
}
```

This function transforms the context in order to draw the tank. The problem is that these transformations are not cleared afterward. When you try to draw the second tank, the context is already transformed, and the subsequent transformations are applied on the ones that precede them, as described in the previous section. The result might be incorrect.

To fix the problem, the state of the context must be restored. It is possible, of course, to apply the reverse transformations. If you called translate(x, y), call translate(-x, -y); however, this method is too error-prone and it wastes valuable CPU resources. The better way, shown in Listing 2-16, would be to save() the context state in the first line and then restore() it in the last line.

Listing 2-16. *Saving and Restoring a Context State*

```
function drawTank(ctx, x, y, tankRotation, cannonRotation) {
    ctx.save();
    ctx.translate(x, y);
    ctx.rotate(tankRotation);
    // draw tank body
```

```
    ctx.rotate(cannonRotation);
    // draw cannon
    ctx.restore();
}
```

The state is "saved" in the internal stack. If you call this method multiple times, the states will be pushed to the stack one by one. Then you can pop the states back with restore(). Note that when you call save(), the current state of the context is not reset. It still holds all the transformations and styles that were applied before the call to save().

The rule of thumb: if the function or a block of code changes anything but the fill and stroke styles, it should restore the original state of the context after it is done drawing (see Listing 2-17).

Listing 2-17. *Using save() and restore() with Multiple Transformations*

```
function drawTank(ctx, x, y, tankRotation, cannonRotation) {
    ctx.save();
    ctx.translate(x, y);
    ctx.rotate(tankRotation);
    // draw tank body
    drawBody();

    // draw cannon
    drawCannon(ctx, cannonRotation);

    // draw any other tank features
    ctx.restore();
}

function drawCannon(ctx, cannonRotation) {
    ctx.save();
    ctx.rotate(cannonRotation);
    // actual code here
    ctx.restore();
}
```

Context Transformations in the Sample Project

Now, let's apply a few transformations to our sample project. First of all, we can now implement the correct way of rendering the tokens, as shown in Listing 2-18. (The full version of the code is available in the next section).

Listing 2-18. *Applying save() and restore() to the Sample Project*

```
for (var i = 0; i < data.length; i++) {
    for (var j = 0; j < data[i].length; j++) {
        var value = data[i][j];
```

```
if (!value)
    continue;

// Determine the color of the token
var color;
switch (value) {
    case 1:
    color = "red";
    break;

    case 2:
    color = "green";
    break;
}

// Save the current state of the context,
// to restore it once the token is rendered
ctx.save();

// At this point the context is not yet transformed, we translate the
// coordinates.
ctx.translate((j + 0.5)*cellSize, (i + 0.5)*cellSize);

// After the call, the origin of coordinates (0, 0) is
// on the center of the cell

var radius = cellSize*0.4;

// Gradient offsets are now calculated relatively to the cell center
// such expressions look much cleaner!
var gradientX = cellSize*0.1;
var gradientY = -cellSize*0.1;

// Rest of gradient and fill setup omitted
...

// When fill setup is done, we are ready to draw the token,
// The code is also way easier to read
ctx.arc(0, 0, radius, 0, 2*Math.PI, true);
ctx.fill();

// Finally, restore the state of the context,
// if we don't do that, the transformations will stack and rendering
// code will work with completely wrong positions
ctx.restore();
    }
}
```

As you remember, the grid was not centered in the canvas; it was drawn in the top-left corner of the board. Let's fix this problem with another transformation, shown in Listing 2-19.

Listing 2-19. *Repositioning the Grid*

```
// Apply after the border is drawn
…

var gridOffsetLeft = Math.floor((canvas.width - gridWidth)/2);
var gridOffsetTop = Math.floor((canvas.height - gridHeight)/2);
ctx.save();
ctx.translate(gridOffsetLeft, gridOffsetTop);

// Draw the grid and tokens as in Listing 2-18

ctx.restore(); // always restore the state
```

The result looks much better now.

Context transformation is a very powerful instrument. It allows you to make effects that are impossible to achieve with other means.

The Sample Game Project Result

Now let's review our uses of the canvas 2D API. The game board we've created in this chapter is shown in Figure 2-32. The code that renders the Four Balls game board and some of the pieces is shown in Listing 2-20.

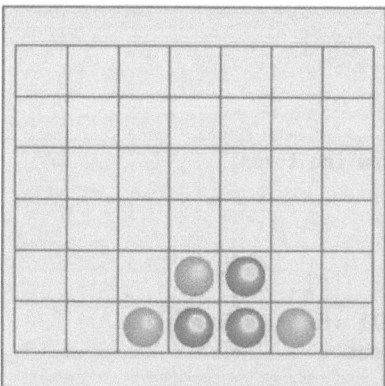

Figure 2-32. *The final version of the game board*

Listing 2-20 shows most of techniques described in this chapter. The fragments of this code, properly divided into the smaller functions, will be used in the game project in Chapter 3. The code is also available in the final.html file with the other materials for this chapter.

Listing 2-20. *The Final Version of the Code That Renders the Game Board and Pieces*

```html
<!DOCTYPE html>
<html lang="en">
<head>
    <meta charset="utf-8" />
    <style>
    </style>
    <script>
        function init() {
            var canvas = document.getElementById("mainCanvas");
            var ctx = canvas.getContext("2d");

            // Background
            var gradient = ctx.createLinearGradient(0, 0, 0, 300);
            gradient.addColorStop(0, "#fffbb3");
            gradient.addColorStop(1, "#f6f6b2");
            ctx.fillStyle = gradient;
            ctx.fillRect(0, 0, canvas.width, canvas.height);

            // Drawing curves
            ctx.strokeStyle = "#dad7ac";
            ctx.fillStyle = "#f6f6b2";

            ctx.beginPath();
            ctx.moveTo(50, 300);
            ctx.bezierCurveTo(450, -50, -150, -50, 250, 300);
            ctx.fill();

            ctx.beginPath();
            ctx.moveTo(50, 0);
            ctx.bezierCurveTo(450, 350, -150, 350, 250, 0);
            ctx.fill();

            // Border
            ctx.strokeStyle = "#989681";
            ctx.lineWidth = 2;
            ctx.strokeRect(1, 1, canvas.width - 2, canvas.height - 2);

            // Grid and pieces (translate to center in on Canvas)
            var cellSize = 40;
            var gridWidth = cellSize*7;
            var gridHeight = cellSize*6;
```

```
var gridOffsetLeft = Math.floor((canvas.width - gridWidth)/2);
var gridOffsetTop = Math.floor((canvas.height - gridHeight)/2);

ctx.save();
ctx.translate(gridOffsetLeft, gridOffsetTop);

// Grid
ctx.beginPath();

// Drawing horizontal lines
for (var i = 0; i < 8; i++) {
    ctx.moveTo(i*cellSize + 0.5, 0);
    ctx.lineTo(i*cellSize + 0.5, cellSize*6)
}

// Drawing vertical lines
for (var j = 0; j < 7; j++) {
    ctx.moveTo(0, j*cellSize + 0.5);
    ctx.lineTo(cellSize*7, j*cellSize + 0.5);
}

// Stroking to show them on the screen
ctx.lineWidth = 1;
ctx.strokeStyle = "#989681";
ctx.stroke();

// Pieces
var data = [
    [0, 0, 0, 0, 0, 0, 0],
    [0, 0, 0, 0, 0, 0, 0],
    [0, 0, 0, 0, 0, 0, 0],
    [0, 0, 0, 0, 0, 0, 0],
    [0, 0, 0, 2, 1, 0, 0],
    [0, 0, 2, 1, 1, 2, 0]
];

ctx.strokeStyle = "#000";
ctx.lineWidth = 3;

for (var i = 0; i < data.length; i++) {
    for (var j = 0; j < data[i].length; j++) {
        var value = data[i][j];
        if (!value)
            continue;

        // Determine the color of the token
        var color;
        switch (value) {
            case 1:
            color = "red";
```

```
                break;

                case 2:
                color = "green";
                break;
            }

            // Center of the token
            var x = (j + 0.5)*cellSize;
            var y = (i + 0.5)*cellSize;

            // Token radius
            var radius = cellSize*0.4;

            // Center of the gradient
            var gradientX = x + cellSize*0.1;
            var gradientY = y - cellSize*0.1;

            var gradient = ctx.createRadialGradient(
                gradientX, gradientY, cellSize*0.1, // inner circle
(glare)
                gradientX, gradientY, radius*1.2); // outer circle

            gradient.addColorStop(0, "yellow"); // the color of the
"light"
            gradient.addColorStop(1, color); // the color of the token
            ctx.fillStyle = gradient;

            ctx.beginPath();
            ctx.arc(x, y, radius, 0, 2*Math.PI, true);
            ctx.fill();
            }
        }
        // Restore the state of the context, since we've changed it
        ctx.restore()
    }

    </script>
</head>
<body onload="init()">
    <canvas id="mainCanvas" width="300px" height="300px"></canvas>
</body>
</html>
```

Summary

In this chapter, we learned the basics of rendering graphics in a browser. To do that, we used the canvas object, a relatively new HTML5 element that pushes the limits of browser graphics and allows us to make browser games that are more advanced.

We had the practical goal of preparing the code for the Four Balls game that we will make in Chapter 3. We created the game board: a grid, tokens, and a background filled with a linear gradient and decorated with Bézier curves. To do all that, we learned the canvas API. Specifically, we learned how to

- draw shapes (simple and complex)
- use fills (colors, patterns, and gradients)
- apply transformations (translate, move, and fill)
- save and restore the state of the context

The code to render the game is almost ready, but it is not a game yet. A game must have certain logic and it must handle user input. The chapters that follow are devoted to covering these topics.

Creating the First Game

The goal of this chapter is to make a simple 2D web game. We have already learned the essentials of the canvas API, the powerful mechanism for rendering arbitrary shapes or images inside the web page. Now it is time to use this knowledge in practice and create a real game project.

We will call our game "Four Balls." This is the web version of the popular logical game that has been known under several names, including "Four in a Row," "Four in a Line," and "Plot Four," and has had several rule variations. According to rumors, the game was played as early as 18th century by Captain James Cook. He loved the game so much, that his crew called it "The Captain's Mistress." A popular commercial version of the game, *Connect Four*, was first sold in 1974 by the Milton Bradley Company. In 1988, *Connect Four* was "mathematically solved." It turned out that the first player can force victory by following a particular optimal strategy. Nevertheless, the game is still very popular in both real-life and electronic versions.

The rules are very simple. The game is played on a vertical seven-column, six-row board. Players drop different colored pieces that fall straight down the board. The player who first makes a line of four pieces of the same color is the winner. The project is quite easy to accomplish, yet it shows several important aspects of game development.

Before getting our hands dirty with the code, we will need a good plan. We'll start from reviewing the HTML5 skeleton. The version that we used in Chapter 2 needs to be adjusted to fit the game development needs.

The game architecture is another issue to address. Adding more and more code to the same file will soon make the project rather hard to improve and maintain. We have to develop a better "logical" structure for it: divide the functionality of the game between several classes so that each one is responsible for its own small task.

Finally, we will have to add user input handling and implement the game logic. User input and browser events are covered in greater detail in Chapter 5; however, we still need to add a little bit of code, without going into the details of how or why it works, because otherwise we can't have a working game.

In this chapter, we will learn how to do the following:

- Update HTML5 skeleton for mobile game development needs

- Create game architecture and separate the code responsible for game logic from the rendering code

- Implement game mechanics: validation of turns, game state, win/lose conditions

- Add the basic input handling to the project

Before we start, take a look at Figure 3-1. It shows what the final version of the game looks like launched in a browser.

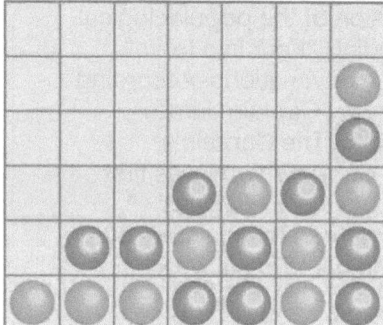

Figure 3-1. *The Four Balls game*

HTML5 Game Skeleton

Games are different from the regular web pages and they require a different HTML skeleton. This section is devoted to making such a skeleton. We start with an overview of the reasons why we should change it, and then we will look at how to implement the new skeleton with HTML, CSS, and JavaScript. In this section, we will first build our skeleton with the basic features we want for our example. One of those features involves enabling graceful screen reorientation. However, sometime you may prefer a specific orientation—either portrait or landscape—so we will look at ways to manage "forced orientation."

The Standard Skeleton

A regular web page can have many elements, and if there is not enough space to display them all, a browser will add scrollbars. Game-oriented mobile web pages often have only one HTML element: the canvas that takes all the available screen space.

The mobile game should do its best to prevent the browser from showing the scrollbars. Scrollbars take precious space and they also "steal" the move event from the game. In a strategy game, for example, the move can be treated as "scroll the *world map*"—which is what the user wants when he swipes the screen. If the page doesn't fit the single screen, however, the same event *must* be treated as "scroll the *browser page*." In this situation, the game engine cannot use the move event for its needs because it is already used for the needs of the browser.

The mobile web game should not allow scaling by the user or the browser. Nowadays, there is a wide variety of mobile devices that have different pixel densities and resolutions. Mobile browsers try to be smart and scale the web page to look best on the given device. This makes perfect sense for regular pages: the fonts will neither be microscopic nor giant, and the page will look roughly the same on old and new devices, smartphones and tablets. Game engines are different. They don't need the browser to be "smart" because they are smart themselves. Games are often made of raster images that do not scale well no matter how hard a browser tries. That's why it is better to turn this feature off from the very beginning.

> **NOTE:** Learn more about the reasons and effects of this browser behavior in the great blog post "A Pixel Is Not a Pixel" at www.quirksmode.org/blog/archives/2010/04/a_pixel_is_not.html.

The skeleton should gracefully handle the change of orientation. Once the user rotates the device, the canvas is resized to fit the new proportions of the screen, and the game rerenders itself, taking the new size into the account.

Let's take the HTML5 skeleton from Chapter 2 and add few more lines of code to it to implement the features described earlier. Listing 3-1 shows the initial skeleton.

Listing 3-1. *The Initial HTML5 Skeleton*

```
<!DOCTYPE html>
<html lang="en">
<head>
    <meta charset="utf-8" />
    <style>
    </style>
    <script>
        function init() {

        }
    </script>
</head>
<body onload="init()">

</body>
</html>
```

First, let's restrict the resize behavior. Add one more meta tag right after the meta charset, like in Listing 3-2.

Listing 3-2. *Viewport Meta Tag: Setting Zooming Options for a Web Page*

```
...
<meta charset="utf-8" />
<meta name="viewport" content="width=device-width, initial-scale=1.0,
maximum-scale=1.0, user-scalable=no, target-densitydpi=device-dpi"/>
<style>
...
```

This code sets the parameters of the *viewport*; in other words, it gives the browser several hints on how to render the page. We instruct the browser to set the initial and maximum scale to 1.0 (which means no scaling), ignore the user's attempts to scale the page (user-scalable=no), and finally, give us the real pixels, so that 1px is exactly what it sounds like—one physical pixel of the device screen (target-densitydpi=device-dpi).

The page, however, might still have scrollbars. To prevent them from appearing, add the style declaration in Listing 3-3.

Listing 3-3. *CSS for the Page: No Scrollbars, Margins, Paddings, or Borders*

```
<style>
    html, body {
        overflow: hidden;
        width: 100%;
        height: 100%;
        margin:0;
        padding:0;
        border: 0;
```

```
    }
</style>
```

The overflow: hidden instruction makes the browser "cut off" everything that goes beyond the visual page bounds, and thus never show the scroll bars. The other lines make sure that the page body uses every available pixel: 100% width and height, no margins, borders, or paddings.

Resizing of the canvas is the trickiest part. Unfortunately, we can't make it with pure CSS, so we'll have to write few lines of JavaScript. The code in Listing 3-4 makes use of browser events that we cover in detail in the Chapter 5. For now, you should just believe that it works.

Listing 3-4. *Listening to Browser Events to Resize the Canvas Once the Page Is Resized*

```
function init() {
    var canvas = initFullScreenCanvas("mainCanvas");
}

/**
 * Resizes the canvas element once the window is resized.
 * @param canvasId - string id of the canvas element
 */
function initFullScreenCanvas(canvasId) {
    var canvas = document.getElementById(canvasId);
    resizeCanvas(canvas);
    window.addEventListener("resize", function() {
        resizeCanvas(canvas);
    });
    return canvas;
}
```

The code in Listing 3-4 has two functions. The first one, init(), is already familiar to you: the browser executes it once the body has finished loading. The second function, initFullScreenCanvas(), makes canvas take all the available screen space, even when the window is resized or a device changes an orientation. It "listens" to the resize event, and every time such event is detected, it calls resizeCanvas(). Next, resizeCanvas() takes care of the resizing: it finds the new size of the page and updates the size of the canvas appropriately. The code for this function, shown in Listing 3-5, is also rather simple.

Listing 3-5. *resizeCanvas, the Function That Finds the New Size of a Page and Updates the Canvas to Fit It*

```
/**
 * Does the actual resize
 */
function resizeCanvas(canvas) {
```

```
        canvas.width  = document.width  || document.body.clientWidth;
        canvas.height = document.height || document.body.clientHeight;
        // Notify the main game class that canva is resized
}
```

When you assign a value to `canvas.width` or `canvas.height`, canvas swipes any content and becomes blank, even if the new value is the same as the previous one and there was no actual resize. In this case, the game must immediately repaint the scene. That's where the last commented line comes from. Once we have the class that knows how to repaint the scene, we notify it about every resize so that it has a chance to redraw the board. For now, we will leave the comment here to remind us that this function is yet to be finished.

> **NOTE:** The size-detection code relies on two properties: `document.width` and `document.body.clientWidth`. Why use both of them? This approach is required for cross-browser compatibility. We will use browsers other than the default Android browser during the course of this book, so it is best to keep the cross-browser version of the code from the very beginning.

The final version of the skeleton looks like Listing 3-6.

Listing 3-6. *HTML5 Skeleton Modified for Game Development Needs*

```
<!DOCTYPE html>
<html lang="en">
<head>
    <meta charset="utf-8" />
    <meta name="viewport"
          content="width=device-width, initial-scale=1.0, maximum-scale=1.0,↵
user-scalable=no, target-densitydpi=device-dpi"/>

    <style>
        html, body {
            overflow: hidden;
            width: 100%;
            height: 100%;
            margin:0;
            padding:0;
            border: 0;
            }

    </style>
    <script>
        function init() {
            var canvas = initFullScreenCanvas("mainCanvas");
        }
```

```
function initFullScreenCanvas(canvasId) {
    var canvas = document.getElementById(canvasId);
    resizeCanvas(canvas);
    window.addEventListener("resize", function() {
        resizeCanvas(canvas);
    });
    return canvas;
}

function resizeCanvas(canvas) {
    canvas.width  = document.width || document.body.clientWidth;
    canvas.height = document.height || document.body.clientHeight;
    // Notify the main game class that Canvas is resized
}

        </script>
    </head>
    <body onload="init()">
        <canvas id="mainCanvas" width="100" height="100"></canvas>
    </body>
</html>
```

Forced Orientation

The skeleton in Listing 3-6 doesn't *force* the screen orientation, but merely rerenders the canvas once it detects that the size of the window has changed. As you know, many native Android games lock the screen in a fixed position—either portrait or landscape—depending on which is best for the game. In a browser environment, forcing orientation is not possible. This practice is considered to be too intrusive and may harm the user's experience. Without doubt, games are very different from the typical web pages that show news or weather forecasts, so what is bad for one type of site might sound like a good idea for others.

The web game is essentially a web page that renders inside the browser, and the user expects certain behaviors from it. If the device is rotated, the browser should reorient. If you change this behavior, you better have a very good reason for it. But wait, I just said that it is impossible to lock the orientation. How we going to change that behavior, then?

The Android browser uses the event called "orientationchange" to notify the page that the device has changed its orientation. The current orientation value is stored in the window.orientation property. Combining the two, you can build a mechanism that gently hints to the user that the game looks better with the other screen orientation. For example, you can create a dialog (preferably not an alert box, but a dialog styled as the game UI element) that outputs some text in the form of advice: "Hint: Four Balls is best played in portrait mode." Make sure to add a "Do not show again" check box or something similar to unsubscribe the user from this notification.

The other possible solution is to mimic the locked orientation. With the help of context transformation, you can rotate the coordinates of the canvas whenever the user is rotating his screen so that game elements always preserve the correct orientation. The code in Listing 3-7 shows how to update the skeleton to lock the game orientation that way.

Listing 3-7. *Locking the Game's Orientation*

```
<script>
    var canvas;
    var ctx;
    function init() {
        canvas = initFullScreenCanvas("mainCanvas");
        ctx = canvas.getContext("2d");
        repaint();
    }

    function initFullScreenCanvas(canvasId) {
        var canvas = document.getElementById(canvasId);
        resizeCanvas(canvas);
        window.addEventListener("resize", function() {
            resizeCanvas(canvas);
        });
        return canvas;
    }

    function resizeCanvas(canvas) {
        canvas.width  = document.width || document.body.clientWidth;
        canvas.height = document.height || document.body.clientHeight;
        // Paint something to see the effect of changed orientation
        repaint();
    }

    function repaint() {
        if (!ctx)
            return;

        // Clear background
        ctx.fillStyle = "white";
        ctx.fillRect(0, 0, canvas.width, canvas.height);

        reorient();
        ctx.fillStyle = "darkgreen";
        ctx.fillRect(10, 10, 250, 30);
```

```
    }

    function reorient() {
        var angle = window.orientation;
        if (angle) {
            var rot = -Math.PI*(angle/180);
            ctx.translate(angle == -90 ? canvas.width : 0,
                    angle == 90 ? canvas.height : 0);
            ctx.rotate(rot);
        }
    }

</script>
```

The new code is in bold. We added a repaint() function, which draws a green figure that looks like the letter T. Before executing the drawing code, it calls reorient(), a function that changes the coordinate system of context once the device changed the orientation. The effect of this is that the screen looks "locked" in a portrait mode, no matter how the user rotates the smartphone. The green "T" is glued to the top of the device. Figure 3-2 shows the normal behavior of the browser vs. the "locked" behavior.

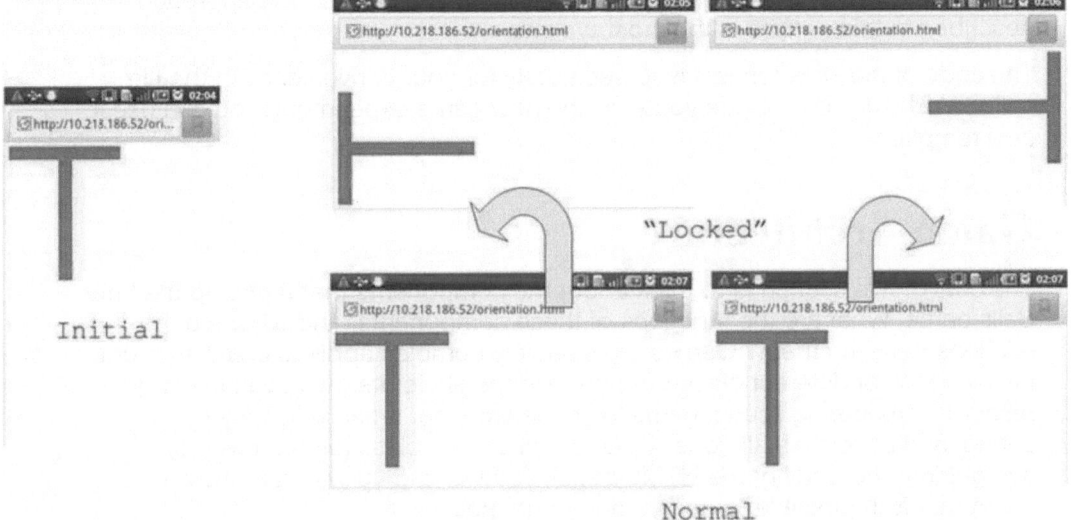

Figure 3-2. *The behavior of the portrait-locked page (top) vs. a normal page (bottom)*

The image at the left of Figure 3-2 shows the initial state of the page, in the portrait screen orientation. The top two images show the rotation behavior of the locked version. As you see, the only element that actually follows the change of orientation is the address bar. The page looks like it doesn't react on change. The bottom two images show the normal behavior of the page.

General advice for the web games: if you can make your game work in both orientations—then do it. This way, you will not violate the standard behavior, and the user will stay happy. If you need to lock the orientation no matter what—use the least intrusive possible way of doing it. The rest of the code in this book relies on a standard browser behavior and does not force any particular orientation.

> **NOTE:** Locking the screen orientation in native Android games is a standard practice, so you should not avoid it if you design your game to be native. More about making native games out of a web application in Chapter 15.

Most of the examples in this book use this basic skeleton, and the project in this chapter is no different. The fullscreen-canvas setup that we just implemented is not the only possible way of laying out a web page, of course. The game may have a smaller canvas and use the rest of the page space for the user interface elements—the in-game chat controls, for example. However, the approach described in this section is the most typical.

The code of the skeleton is saved separately for your convenience in the file called `skeleton.html`. Once you start the new game experiment, you can use it as a template.

Game Architecture

The goal of this section is to think about the components that make up the Four Balls game. What are the functions of these components, and what are the relations between them? Games are relatively complex applications that might have dozens of different classes, each responsible for its own task: loading resources, rendering scene, game logic, networking, artificial intelligence, sound, and so forth. If all code is put into one huge class (or even worse, straight into the body of the HTML page), you will end up with a monstrous script that is impossible to understand or change.

We want our project to be well-written: no global variables to hold states, no "smell" in the code, and a clean, object-oriented API with each class performing a clearly defined set of functions. If you feel uncomfortable with inheritance and prototypes in JavaScript, don't hesitate to peek back to the first chapter of this book. Understanding these principles is very important for this chapter.

Let's start from the game flow and then think about how the game can be broken down into a set of independent components. Here's what happens once the game is loaded:

1. Initially, the user sees the empty board.

2. The user taps the board to place the token. If the turn is invalid, then nothing happens.

3. If the last turn was a "winning" turn, the game reports which player has won: red or green. If there are no more spaces left on the board, the game reports a draw. Otherwise, the next player has a chance to make his move.

4. Once the game is over (ether win or draw), the players should see an alert box with text that says like, "Red player wins."

5. Finally, a new game starts. The board is empty and ready for the game.

Quite simple, right? Now let's take another step, thinking about what exactly the game should be able to do to implement the described flow:

- Draw the board and tokens (rendering)

- Check if the turn is valid and doesn't break the game rules, and check whether the player has won or if the draw state was reached (logic)

- React on user input and determine which column was clicked (event handling)

- Wire components together: pass the events from the browser to the logic-processing, call-rendering routines; update the UI whenever the board changes; manage the game flow; report wins or draws; empty the board for the new game; and so forth (housekeeping).

Now it is very easy to break the whole project into classes. They are as follows:

- Game: The class that is responsible for starting the game, event handling, and housekeeping. Its task is to wire other components together and make them speak to each other. Think of it as the main "orchestration" class for the game.

▧   BoardModel: The meat of the game. The class responsible for the mechanics. It holds the information about the state of the game: which cells are empty, which are occupied by red and green pieces, who is the current player, and what will happen if he drops a piece in a third column. This is where we implement the rules: validation of the turn and checking win conditions.

▧   BoardRenderer: The class responsible for visuals and rendering the game interface on canvas. When BoardRenderer needs to render a cell, it asks the BoardModel about the state of that cell: is it empty, red, or green? BoardModel works like the data source for the renderer. Most of the code for this class was written in Chapter 2.

To make the architecture even more clear, the following is an example of how classes interact with each other once the user taps the screen:

1.   The user taps the screen. The browser fires the event that has the coordinates of the click.

2.   The Game class receives the event and checks which column was under the user's finger. It can translate from browser coordinates to the column coordinates because it knows the position of the board inside the canvas, as well as the width of the columns, so it can tell which column was just tapped.

3.   Having the column index, the Game asks BoardModel if it is OK to make a move. If the column is full, it will ignore the invalid input. A valid move updates the BoardModel: the new token appears in the internal board representation.

4.   Now the turn is made but the user doesn't see any changes on the screen yet. We have updated the model but not the canvas—it still holds the old version of the board. Game uses BoardRenderer to redraw the cell that has the new token in it.

5.   To redraw the cell, BoardRenderer needs to know the color of the token in that cell. It gets the color ID from the BoardModel and renders the cute, gradient-filled ball.

6.   Now the canvas is updated and the player sees the new ball.

7.   Finally, when the match is over, the Game shows the alert box to notify the user about the result.

8.   The Game "resets" the state of BoardModel, uses BoardRenderer
     to redraw the empty board, and starts the new match.

Making the Game

Once we defined the architecture, we are ready to write the code. Start from
creating the empty folder and copying the skeleton from Listing 3-5 to the
index.html file. Create the js folder—we will keep all our scripts there. You can
now point the nginx web server to the project folder, as described in Chapter 1,
to test your game with the real device.

Rendering the Board

We will start from the BoardRenderer—the simplest class in the project. It is
responsible for rendering the interface: a background, a grid, and pieces. Most
of the code in this section is derived from the examples of Chapter 2, so it will
look familiar.

Create the new file called BoardRenderer.js and put in into the js folder. Next,
add the following tag to the index.html file to load the script:

```
<script src="js/BoardRenderer.js"></script>
```

Open the newly created file in your favorite IDE and prepare to write some code.

> **Note:** In this book, every example uses the same naming convention and almost the
> same project structure. When you need to create the new class and add it to the
> project, you start from creating the empty file in <project_folder>/js. The name
> of the file should be <ClassName>.js. For example, the code for BoardModel class
> should go to the file named BoardModel.js. This is a simple and very convenient
> way of organizing your code. It keeps your project folder clean and makes it easy to
> find the class you need. And don't forget to include every script you create into the
> index.html page.

Constructor

Let's start from the constructor. When you write the constructor of the class,
you must think about the type of data that is absolutely essential for this class.
What does it need to function correctly? The BoardRenderer class needs the

context to draw on, otherwise it is useless. It also needs the `BoardModel` to get the color of the pieces. Listing 3-8 shows the first lines of the constructor.

Listing 3-8. *First Version of the BoardRenderer Constructor That Saves the Essential Parameters*

```
function BoardRenderer(context, model) {
    this._ctx = context;
    this._model = model;
}


_p = BoardRenderer.prototype;
```

Now think about the fields that hold the state of the class. Put them in the constructor, even if you can't initialize them with meaningful values straightaway (see Listing 3-9). It is good to have them in one place—once you open the file to read the code, you can navigate to the constructor and see all the variables that hold the state of the class instances.

Listing 3-9. *The BoardRenderer Constructor, All Variables Declared*

```
function BoardRenderer(context, model) {
    this._ctx = context;
    this._model = model;

    // Save for convenience
    this._cols = model.getCols();
    this._rows = model.getRows();

    // top left corner of the board
    this._x = 0;
    this._y = 0;

    // Width and height of the board rectangle
    this._width = 0;
    this._height = 0;

    // the optimal size of the board cell
    this._cellSize = 0;
}
```

Don't worry if you don't understand where those fields come from, I will explain everything in just a minute.

It is convenient to save the reference to the class' prototype in the variable with the short name, as follows:

```
_p = BoardRenderer.prototype;
```

When you start writing functions, the code looks much cleaner. Look at the following snippet that compares two styles. The first line that uses explicit prototype is harder to understand; you have to read the BoardRenderer.prototype part (23 characters!) before you finally reach the name of the function. In the second case, it is only two characters.

```
BoardRenderer.prototype.repaint = function() { … } // Without small variable
_p.repaint = function() { … } // With small variable
```

Working with Different Screen Sizes

One of the most important features of this class is that it should not rely on any hardcoded coordinates or sizes. If you're hard-coding the token size, for example, you're limiting the use of the class to devices with certain resolution and pixel density. The token that looks good on a smartphone might be too small for a Full HD laptop screen. That's why it is important to keep all sizes relative. Listing 3-10 shows how to calculate the radius of the token and offsets of the gradient.

Listing 3-10. *Calculating the Radius of Token and Gradient Offsets*

```
// Token radius
var radius = cellSize*0.4;

// Center of the gradient
var gradientX = cellSize*0.1;
var gradientY = -cellSize*0.1;

var gradient = ctx.createRadialGradient(
    gradientX, gradientY, cellSize*0.1, // inner circle (glare)
    gradientX, gradientY, radius*1.2); // outer circle
```

The cellSize variable is calculated elsewhere (in Game class to be exact) and it represents the optimal size of the board cell in the browser window. The bigger the screen, the bigger the cellSize gets. If we change the value of this variable, the elements simply scale, the token retains its proportions, and the gradients remain correctly positioned. Listing 3-11 is the code for the function that sets the parameters of a game UI: the position and the cellSize.

Listing 3-11. *Setting the Parameters of the Game UI: The Position of the Board Within a Canvas and the Size of a Cell*

```
/**
 * Sets the new position and size for a board. Should call repaint to
 * see the changes
 * @param x the x coordinate of the top-left corner
 * @param y the y coordinate of the top-left corner
 * @param cellSize optimal size of the cell in pixels
 */
_p.setSize = function(x, y, cellSize)  {
```

```
        this._x = x;
        this._y = y;
        this._cellSize = cellSize;
        this._width = this._cellSize*this._cols;
        this._height = this._cellSize*this._rows;
};
```

JSDoc Comments

While the function body is trivial, the style of comments might be new for you. This way of documenting the code is known as JSDoc. It is slightly different from the normal comment: it has special tags that start from the @ character, like @param. These tags denote which aspect of the code is documented: a parameter of the function, the name of the author of the code, or the default value of the variable. These tags are human-readable; they do not make the comments any harder to understand. But the real use of such tags comes when you work with tools that understand them, like IDE. The JSDocs tags are quick to parse and they allow creating better-structured documentation. Figure 3-3 shows how WebStorm renders JSDoc from the function shown in Listing 3-11.

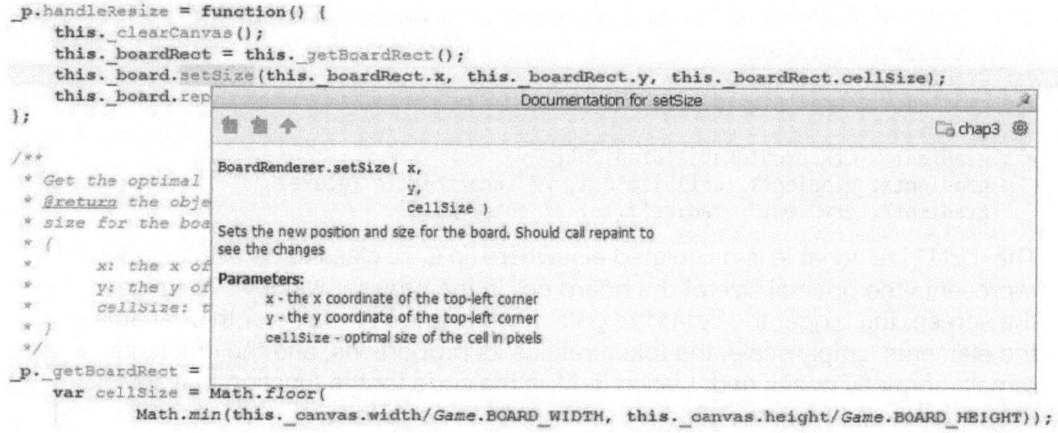

Figure 3-3. *JSDoc rendered in WebStorm*

There are several tools, such as jsdoc-toolkit (http://code.google.com/p/jsdoc-toolkit/), that generate the documentation for the whole project in the form of static HTML files, ready for publishing on a web site. The wiki page of a jsdoc-toolkit project (see http://code.google.com/p/jsdoc-toolkit/w/list) is a good source of inspiration on how to make maximum use of this format.

Of course, it is up to you to decide whether you want to use this format or stick to the old-school, plain-text comments. I advocate using JSDoc at least for documenting parameters and return values of the function.

> **NOTE:** The JSDoc is the JavaScript version of the JavaDoc—the utility for automated docs generation of Java. JavaDoc is the standard way to document Java code. Developers have used it for more than 15 years. In the JavaScript world, it is not yet a de facto standard but rather a convenient way to write the expressive documentation.

We often trim the comments from the code listings in this book because the code is usually discussed straight in the text. The source code for chapters is commented much better.

Rendering Board

Getting back to the BoardRenderer, the following three functions are the polished versions of the code from Chapter 2: _drawBackground(), _drawGrid(), and drawToken() (see Listing 3-12). Each function draws one of the elements of the UI: the gradient background with curves, the grid, or a token.

Listing 3-12. *Functions That Render the UI of the Board: A Background, a Grid, and a Token in a Given Cell*

```
_p._drawBackground = function() {
    var ctx = this._ctx;

    // Background
    var gradient = ctx.createLinearGradient(0, 0, 0, this._height);
    gradient.addColorStop(0, "#fffbb3");
    gradient.addColorStop(1, "#f6f6b2");
    ctx.fillStyle = gradient;
    ctx.fillRect(0, 0, this._width, this._height);

    // Drawing curves
    var co = this._width/6; // curve offset
    ctx.strokeStyle = "#dad7ac";
    ctx.fillStyle = "#f6f6b2";

    // First curve
    ctx.beginPath();
    ctx.moveTo(co, this._height);
    ctx.bezierCurveTo(this._width + co*3, -co,
                -co*3, -co, this._width - co, this._height);
```

```
        ctx.fill();

        // Second curve
        ctx.beginPath();
        ctx.moveTo(co, 0);
        ctx.bezierCurveTo(this._width + co*3, this._height + co,
                          -co*3, this._height + co, this._width - co, 0);
        ctx.fill();

};

_p._drawGrid = function() {
    var ctx = this._ctx;
    ctx.beginPath();
    // Drawing horizontal lines
    for (var i = 0; i <= this._cols; i++) {
        ctx.moveTo(i*this._cellSize + 0.5, 0.5);
        ctx.lineTo(i*this._cellSize + 0.5, this._height + 0.5)
    }

    // Drawing vertical lines
    for (var j = 0; j <= this._rows; j++) {
        ctx.moveTo(0.5, j*this._cellSize + 0.5);
        ctx.lineTo(this._width + 0.5, j*this._cellSize + 0.5);
    }

    // Stroking to show them on the screen
    ctx.strokeStyle = "#CCC";
    ctx.stroke();
};

_p.drawToken = function(cellX, cellY) {
    var ctx = this._ctx;
    var cellSize = this._cellSize;
    var tokenType = this._model.getPiece(cellX, cellY);

    // Cell is empty
    if (!tokenType)
        return;


    var colorCode = "black";
    switch(tokenType) {
        case BoardModel.RED:
            colorCode = "red";
        break;
        case BoardModel.GREEN:
            colorCode = "green";
        break;
    }
```

```
    // Center of the token
    var x = this._x + (cellX + 0.5)*cellSize;
    var y = this._y + (cellY + 0.5)*cellSize;
    ctx.save();
    ctx.translate(x, y);

    // Token radius
    var radius = cellSize*0.4;

    // Center of the gradient
    var gradientX = cellSize*0.1;
    var gradientY = -cellSize*0.1;

    var gradient = ctx.createRadialGradient(
        gradientX, gradientY, cellSize*0.1, // inner circle (glare)
        gradientX, gradientY, radius*1.2); // outer circle

    gradient.addColorStop(0, "yellow"); // the color of the "light"
    gradient.addColorStop(1, colorCode); // the color of the token
    ctx.fillStyle = gradient;

    ctx.beginPath();
    ctx.arc(0, 0, radius, 0, 2*Math.PI, true);
    ctx.fill();
    ctx.restore();
};
```

> **NOTE:** Functions of BoardRenderer rely on BoardModel to get the color of the
> token in a cell. We create this class in the next section, so you can't run the code
> straightaway. If you are still eager to try how it works, you can hard-code the values,
> test the rendering, and then switch back to using BoardModel once it is ready.

The last function that we need to create is repaint (see Listing 3-13). It renders
the whole board step-by-step: first the background, then the grid, and, finally,
the tokens.

Listing 3-13. *The Repaint Function Renders the Whole Board from Scratch*

```
_p.repaint = function() {
    this._ctx.save();
    this._ctx.translate(this._x, this._y);
    this._drawBackground();
    this._drawGrid();
    this._ctx.restore();

    for (var i = 0; i < this._cols; i++) {
```

```
        for (var j = 0; j < this._rows; j++) {
            this.drawToken(i, j);
        }
    }
};
```

The BoardRenderer is now ready. Let's review the class structure once again. There are two public methods for drawing: repaint() and drawToken(). The first method is used to rerender the *whole* board; for example, when the orientation of the screen has changed. The latter is used to draw a *single token* after the user makes a valid move. Of course, we could rerender the whole board every time, but it would be a waste of resources (not really noticeable, but we want things done right).

The BoardRenderer doesn't attempt to determine the optimal size of the board by itself. This job is left to the other classes because BoardRenderer doesn't know anything about the environment it works in: the screen size, the canvas size, or the pixel density. This class is responsible for drawing—and only for drawing.

> **NOTE:** Fine-grained classes that only do the small tasks are a sign of well-designed API. This principle is called "single responsibility." It is one of five fundamental principles of OOP. If you're interested in reading about the other four principles, start with the Wikipedia entry at http://en.wikipedia.org/wiki/SOLID_(object-oriented_design).

The final version the class code is included in the source code for this chapter. The file is called BoardRenderer.js.

Game State and Logic

We have the class that can render the current state of the board, but we don't have a class to hold this state. Let's create one! Start as usual: create the new file called BoardModel.js in the js folder of your project, and add the extra <script> tag to index.html to load it. Now you can write the code for the class. Let's start with the constructor, shown in Listing 3-14.

Listing 3-14. *The BoardModel Constructor*

```
function BoardModel(cols, rows) {
    this._cols = cols || 7;
    this._rows = rows || 6;
    this._data = [];
```

```
    this._currentPlayer = BoardModel.RED;
    this._totalTokens = 0;

    this.reset();
}

_p = BoardModel.prototype;
```

The constructor accepts two *optional* parameters: the number of columns and the number of rows on the board. JavaScript doesn't have the notion of optional parameters at the language level. To make the parameter optional, you check if it is set, and use the default value if it is not.

The line

```
this._cols = cols || 7
```

is equivalent to

```
if (cols) {
    this._cols = cols;
} else {
    this._cols = 7;
}
```

The _data variable holds the current state of the game—a two-dimensional array of numbers: 0 for empty cell, 1 for red token, and 2 for green token. Referring tokens by such IDs is rather error-prone. Consider the code that follows; it checks if the token in the cell is green:

```
if (this._data[i][j] == 2) {
    /* what is 2? what's happening here? */
}
```

This code is hard to understand straightaway. Let's create the variable for each ID and use them instead. Add the code in Listing 3-15 into the BoardModel class.

Listing 3-15. *The Code That Uses "Constants" Instead of Numbers Are Easier to Read*

```
BoardModel.EMPTY = 0;
BoardModel.RED = 1;
BoardModel.GREEN = 2;
```

The same color-checking line becomes much easier now:

```
if (this._data[i][j] == BoardModel.GREEN) {
    /* ok, got it, it is green, let's do something */
}
```

> **NOTE:** The `CAPITAL_CASED` variables is another code convention, just like the `_underlinedPrivateVariables`. It means that variable is a "constant"—you must not change its value once it is initialized.

The initialization code is split into two functions: the constructor and the function called `reset`. The reason to have a separate `reset` function is that we use the same `BoardModel` for many rounds of the game. It returns the object into the initial state, as it was right after the construction: empty board, 0 total tokens, the first player to move is RED. The code for the `reset()` function is shown in Listing 3-16.

Listing 3-16. *Resetting the Game Board to the Initial State*

```
_p.reset = function() {
    this._data = [];
    for (var i = 0; i < this._rows; i++) {
        this._data[i] = [];
        for (var j = 0; j < this._cols; j++) {
            this._data[i][j] = BoardModel.EMPTY;
        }
    }

    this._currentPlayer = BoardModel.RED;
    this._totalTokens = 0;
};
```

The code outside of `BoardModel` needs to access the game state. The `BoardRenderer` needs to read the state of a cell in order to draw a token, for example. Let's add a few public functions to support that (see Listing 3-17).

Listing 3-17. *Functions to Access the State of the Game Board*

```
_p.getPiece = function(col, row) {
    return this._data[row][col];
};

_p.getCols = function() {
    return this._cols;
};

_p.getRows = function() {
    return this._rows;
};
```

The initialization code is now in place, so we can move to the most interesting part: the implementation of the game logic.

Making Moves

What happens when the player taps the screen? According to the flow, once we have the ID of the column, we do the following:

1. Check if the move is valid (if it isn't valid—return straightaway),

2. Update the game state (switch the player, increase the moves counter, put the piece into the cell)

3. Check if we met the win or draw condition

The validity of the move means that the column ID is within the range (placing a token in column 10 when there are only seven columns is not allowed) and that the target column has at least one empty cell. Both conditions are very easy to check. If the move is valid, BoardModel places the token and checks win conditions (we will implement this kind of check in the next section). The code in Listing 3-18 is well-commented, so it is not hard to follow.

Listing 3-18. *Checking the Validity of a New Move and Updating the Board*

```
_p.makeTurn = function(column) {

    // The color of the piece that we're dropping
    var piece = this._currentPlayer;

    // Check if the column is valid
    if (column < 0 || column > this._cols) {
        return {
            status: BoardModel.ILLEGAL_TURN
        }
    }

    // Check if there's the empty row in the
    // given column, if there's no empty row, then the
    // turn is illegal
    var row = this._getEmptyRow(column);
    if (row == -1) {
        return {
            status: BoardModel.ILLEGAL_TURN
        }
    }

    // We found the empty row, so we can drop the piece
    this._totalTokens++;
    this._data[row][column] = piece;

    // Change the next player
    this._toggleCurrentPlayer();
```

```
        // Return the successful turn together with the new
        // state of the game (NONE, WIN or DRAW)
        return {
            status: this._getGameState(column, row),
            x: column,
            y: row,
            piece: piece
        }
};

_p._getEmptyRow = function(column) {
    for (var i = this._rows - 1; i >= 0; i--) {
        if (!this.getPiece(column, i)) {
            return i;
        }
    }
    return -1;
};

_p._toggleCurrentPlayer = function() {
    if (this._currentPlayer == BoardModel.RED)
        this._currentPlayer = BoardModel.GREEN;
    else
        this._currentPlayer = BoardModel.RED;
};
```

The makeTurn function returns the object that describes the result of the turn: Was it successful? What was the color of the piece and the position that the piece fell to? We have to introduce several more constants to identify the different states of the game: NONE (normal state, game in progress), WIN (the last turn was a winning turn), DRAW (no more empty cells left, it is a draw), and ILLEGAL_TURN (the state has not changed because the turn is not permitted). The reason to use constants and not numbers directly is the same as before: code that is written with the use of constants is way easier to read (see Listing 3-19).

Listing 3-19. *Defining More "Constants" to Refer the State of the Game*

```
/**
 * Game state after the turn
 */
BoardModel.NONE = 0; // No win or draw
BoardModel.WIN = 1; // The player who just dropped a piece has won
BoardModel.DRAW = 2; // No more free cells in the board - it is a draw
BoardModel.ILLEGAL_TURN = 3; // The last attempted move was illegal
```

The only function that is left to write is _getGameState(), which checks if the game has reached the win condition.

Win Condition

The goal of the game is obvious from its name—Four Balls. If the last move completed a straight line that consists of four or more same-colored pieces, then the player who dropped the last piece is the winner. The algorithm is implemented in the _getGameState() function. It is much easier than, for example, the algorithm for chess. Still, it deserves a few more words to explain.

It is obvious that the last fallen piece *must* be the part of the winning line; otherwise, the game would have been over before the current turn. We need to check if there's a straight line of four or more same-colored pieces that lies through the given cell—the cell that the last piece dropped to. We calculate the number of pieces in all possible directions that make up the straight line. If there are two pieces of the same color straight to the left, for example, and one piece of the same color straight to the right, then we have a line of four pieces: two at the left, one at the right, and one between them—the piece from the last move. We do this check for a horizontal line, for a vertical line, and then for two diagonal lines.

Figure 3-4 illustrates how these checks work. There is a win condition because there is a horizontal line of four balls. Two balls to the left of the last dropped ball and one to the right give a total of four.

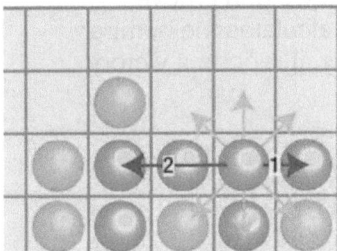

Figure 3-4. *Checking win conditions*

The code that implements this check is quite small. It is split into two functions. One of them, _checkWinDirection(), calculates how many balls of the same color are present in a certain direction starting from the last dropped ball. The other function, _getGameState(), returns the state of the game once every possible direction is checked. The direction is set by two numbers: deltaX and deltaY. On each step of the loop, these values are added to the coordinates of the cell. If deltaX is -1, for example, it means that we will decrease the *column* index at each step (moving to the left); if deltaY is 0, it means that the *row* index stays the same at each step. Combined, it gives the movement in a left direction. If the cell coordinates are (4, 2), then the following cells are checked:

(3, 2), (2, 2), (1, 2). Of course, the check will end earlier if one of the cells is empty or has a piece of a different color. Listing 3-20 shows the code for _checkWinDirection, the function that calculates the number of same-colored balls in a given direction.

Listing 3-20. *Checking the Number of Same-Colored Balls That Fall in a Particular Direction*

```
_p._checkWinDirection = function(column, row, deltaX, deltaY) {
    var pieceColor = this.getPiece(column, row);
    var tokenCounter = 0;
    var c = column + deltaX;
    var r = row + deltaY;
    while(c >= 0 && r >= 0 && c < this._cols && r < this._rows &&
            this.getPiece(c, r) == pieceColor) {
        c += deltaX;
        r += deltaY;
        tokenCounter++;
    }
    return tokenCounter;
};
```

The "line" consists of two opposite directions. The winning line in Figure 3-3, for example, has two directions: left and right. We change the values of deltaX and deltaY in a loop from -1 to 1, trying out every possible direction. We skip this step when both deltaX and deltaY are 0. It is obvious that if we don't move anywhere, we end up in an infinite loop. _getGameState() calculates the number of pieces in every line, and if that number is bigger than four, it reports a victory (see Listing 3-21).

Listing 3-21. *Checking for the Win State*

```
_p._getGameState = function(column, row) {
    if (this._totalTokens == Game.BOARD_WIDTH*Game.BOARD_HEIGHT)
        return BoardModel.DRAW;

    for (var deltaX = -1; deltaX < 2; deltaX++) {
        for (var deltaY = -1; deltaY < 2; deltaY++) {
            if (deltaX == 0 && deltaY == 0)
                continue;
            var count = this._checkWinDirection(column, row, deltaX, deltaY)
                        + this._checkWinDirection(column, row, -deltaX, -deltaY) +
1;
            if (count >= 4) {
                return BoardModel.WIN;
            }
        }
    }
    return BoardModel.NONE;
};
```

Now we have created the BoardModel—the most complex class in the entire project. The complete commented code for this class is found with the sources for this chapter in the BoardModel.js file. We now have the game logic, and we have the class that renders the board on the canvas. If we make them work together, we will have the game!

Wiring Components Together: The Game Class

The main class of the application is the Game class. It is responsible for wiring together the Board and the BoardModel, reacting on user input and orientation changes, and managing the game lifecycle. The lifecycle of the application is pretty simple. The game starts and players tap the screen one by one to take turns. When one player wins or the board is full, the application displays the alert dialog and resets the board for the next round. The Game class also determines the best position and size for the Board.

Start by creating another file called Game.js in the js folder, and add the script tag to the index.html file. I'm sure that you already caught the idea—we do the same steps every time we make a new class. In the following examples, I'll assume that you already know how to do it. Let's start from the constructor, as usual (see Listing 3-22).

Listing 3-22. *The Constructor of the Game*

```
function Game(canvas) {
    this._boardRect = null;
    this._canvas = canvas;
    this._ctx = canvas.getContext("2d");
    this._boardModel = new BoardModel();

    this._boardRenderer = new BoardRenderer(this._ctx, this._boardModel);
    this.handleResize();
}

_p = Game.prototype;
```

The constructor takes one argument—the canvas DOM element. The _boardRect variable is the object that holds the information about the current position of the board inside the canvas, as well as the size of the cell. We need it to handle clicks and translate canvas coordinates into the board coordinates. We create two objects, _boardModel and _boardRenderer, straightaway. They implement the most important parts of the game: graphics and logics.

The constructor calls the handleResize function in the last line. This function repaints the whole UI. It is called in two cases, either in the constructor (to render the initial board) or after the browser window has resized (to rerender the board because the canvas flushed the contents). The code for this function is shown in Listing 3-23.

Listing 3-23. *Handling Resizes*

```
_p.handleResize = function() {
    this._clearCanvas();
    this._boardRect = this._getBoardRect();
    this._boardRenderer.setSize(this._boardRect.x, this._boardRect.y,
        this._boardRect.cellSize);
    this._boardRenderer.repaint();
};
```

After clearing the background of the canvas, the handleResize() updates the parameters of the board (a position and a size) with the help of the _getBoardRect() function. The new parameters are then passed to the _boardRenderer, and then it repaints the new version of the board on the blank canvas. The algorithm behind _getBoardRect() is very straightforward: find the biggest possible area that fits, and then center the board on the screen (see Listing 3-24).

Listing 3-24. *Resizing the Board: Take the Maximum Space for the UI and Put It on the Center of the Screen*

```
_p._getBoardRect = function() {
    var cols = this._boardModel.getCols();
    var rows = this._boardModel.getRows();
    var cellSize = Math.floor(
            Math.min(this._canvas.width/cols, this._canvas.height/rows));

    var boardWidth = cellSize*cols;
    var boardHeight = cellSize*rows;

    return {
        x: Math.floor((this._canvas.width - boardWidth)/2),
        y: Math.floor((this._canvas.height - boardHeight)/2),
        cellSize: cellSize
    }
};
```

Now the most important part: the Game class must handle the clicks and translate them into player moves (see Listing 3-25). Let's call the method responsible for this handleClick() (even though it processes both clicks and taps). Every time the user taps the screen, this method translates the click coordinates into the ID of the column and initiates the whole "new move" flow. Valid moves update the UI: we draw the new piece in the position where it fell. The last thing to do is to check the win condition. If we had a winner or the board is full, we show the alert box and reset the game.

Listing 3-25. *Handling Clicks*

```
_p.handleClick = function(x, y) {
    // get the column index
    var column = Math.floor((x - this._boardRect.x)/this._boardRect.cellSize);

    // Make the turn and check for the result
    var turn = this._boardModel.makeTurn(column);

    // If the turn was legal, update the board, draw
    // the new piece
    if (turn.status != BoardModel.ILLEGAL_TURN) {
        this._boardRenderer.drawToken(turn.x, turn.y);
    }

    // Do we have a winner after the last turn?
    if (turn.status == BoardModel.WIN) {
        // Tell the world about it and reset the board for the next game
        alert((turn.piece == BoardModel.RED ? "red" : "green") + " won the
match!");
        this._reset();
    }

    // If we have the draw, do the same
    if (turn.status == BoardModel.DRAW) {
        alert("It is a draw!");
        this._reset();
    }
};
```

The final two functions to highlight are _reset() and _clearCanvas() (see Listing 3-26). They both are simple. _reset() prepares everything for the new game and _clearCanvas() fills the canvas with a solid white color.

Listing 3-26. *The _reset and _clearCanvas Functions*

```
_p._reset = function() {
    this._clearCanvas();
    this._boardModel.reset();
    this._boardRenderer.repaint();
};

_p._clearCanvas = function() {
    this._ctx.fillStyle = "white";
    this._ctx.fillRect(0, 0, this._canvas.width, this._canvas.height);
};
```

The full and extensively documented version of this class is distributed with the source code for this chapter in the Game.js file.

Adding the Game to the HTML Skeleton

The final task is to add the user-input handling and update the index.html file so that it launches our game when the page is loaded and passes every important browser event to it. Open index.html and modify the code as shown in Listing 3-27.

Listing 3-27. *The Game Is Added to the Skeleton*

```html
<!DOCTYPE html>
<html lang="en">
<head>
    <meta charset="utf-8" />
    <meta name="viewport"
        content="width=device-width, initial-scale=1.0, maximum-scale=1.0,
user-scalable=no, target-densitydpi=device-dpi"/>

    <style>
        html, body {
            overflow: hidden;
            width: 100%;
            height: 100%;
            margin:0;
            padding:0;
            border: 0;
        }
    </style>

    <script src="js/BoardRenderer.js"></script>
    <script src="js/BoardModel.js"></script>
    <script src="js/Game.js"></script>

    <script>
        var game;

        function init() {
            var canvas = initFullScreenCanvas("mainCanvas");
            game = new Game(canvas);

            if (isTouchDevice()) {
                canvas.addEventListener("touchstart", function(e) {
                    var touch = event.targetTouches[0];
                    game.handleClick(touch.pageX, touch.pageY);
                    e.stopPropagation();
                    e.preventDefault();
                }, false);
            } else {
                canvas.addEventListener("mouseup", function(e) {
                    game.handleClick(e.pageX, e.pageY);
```

```
                    e.stopPropagation();
                    e.preventDefault();
            }, false);
        }
    }

    function initFullScreenCanvas(canvasId) {
        var canvas = document.getElementById(canvasId);
        resizeCanvas(canvas);
        window.addEventListener("resize", function() {
            resizeCanvas(canvas);
        });
        return canvas;
    }

    function resizeCanvas(canvas) {
        canvas.width  = document.width || document.body.clientWidth;
        canvas.height = document.height || document.body.clientHeight;
        game && game.handleResize();
    }

    function isTouchDevice() {
        return ('ontouchstart' in document.documentElement);
    }

    </script>
</head>
<body onload="init()">
<canvas id="mainCanvas" width="100" height="100"></canvas>
</body>
</html>
```

Let's briefly review the code. Three <scripts> blocks were added during the course of the chapter, each loading one of the classes: BoardRenderer, BoardModel, and Game. To start the game, we create the new instance of the Game. At this point, the user sees the rendered board, ready to play. We have added the line to the resizeCanvas() function that notifies the game instance about every resize: game && game.handleResize(). This line is equivalent to the following:

```
if (game) {
    game.handleResize();
}
```

We need to check if the game variable exists because the first time we call this function, it is not yet created.

The big part of the bolded code at the end of the init() function is handling the taps and clicks. When the user hits the mouse button or taps the screen, the game is notified about this event. Don't worry if you don't feel comfortable with handling DOM events right now; I explain the details in the next chapter. For now, just believe that the code magically passes the click coordinates to the Game.

> **NOTE:** In the next chapter, we take a deeper look into the processing of user input. For now, you'll have to believe that the code is actually working. We're making this game compatible with both touchscreen-controlled Android devices and desktop browsers from the WebKit family. That's why we have to handle both types of input: touch events and mouse clicks.
>
> It is worth the effort, even if you don't plan to release the game on desktops. The mouse-handling code adds only a few extra lines, but in turn it allows debugging the application on the desktop. To read more about debugging mobile web applications, please refer to Appendix A.

That is it. The game is ready to launch and enjoy. This version is very simple. It has a lot of areas for improvement: it would be nice to put the names of the players somewhere, indicate whose turn is it next, and make a scoreboard. Besides, most of the commercial-grade games have artificial intelligence (AI) since a user doesn't always have a real buddy to play with. (We learn more about AI in Chapter 13.) You could add animations—show the pieces falling down (animations are described in Chapter 4), add sound (covered in Chapter 16), or create a native Android application and distribute your game via the Android Market (Chapter 15 is a good starting point for that). The most important thing, however, is that you now have your first real game!

Summary

In this chapter, we created a simple game called Four Balls. We started by learning about the structure of the HTML page that web games use. We then created a separate HTML skeleton for games and related experiments, which we'll use in upcoming chapters of the book.

We analyzed the game and divided the code into three classes, each having its own set of responsibilities.

We built the BoardRenderer, the class responsible for drawing the board and pieces; the BoardModel, the class responsible for validation of turns and checking the win conditions; and the Game, the class that orchestrates the other two and manages the game lifecycle. The logic of the game is separated from its UI and from user input handling and lifecycle management.

The components of our game are independent of each other. We can change the look of the board without touching the code in BoardModel or Game. We can modify the game rules—for example, we can make the random player take the first move, and this change will not affect the other components. The bigger your project, the more important it is to think about architecture and maintainability.

All the graphics in this game are rendered at runtime. There are no static images at all. We designed the game interface in a way that it supports various screen sizes and densities. The game looks fine on mobile devices, tablets, and PCs. To do this, we had to implement the proper handling of orientation change and resizing of a browser window.

The completed game is the first and most important step. Now we can add new exciting features or explore different types of games that are much more complex, with animated characters, large worlds, and multiplayer capabilities. All of this would be impossible, however, without understanding the material from the first three chapters: the object-oriented approach in JavaScript, the canvas API, and the basics of game architecture.

Chapter

4

Animation and Sprites

In the previous chapter, we created our first web game: a two-player version of *Four Balls*. This game is very simple. We only used graphical primitives to display the board: lines, circles, and gradients. Of course, there are a lot of other games that can be created with exactly the same set of tools, but what if we want to do something more exciting? A 2D platform shooter, perhaps?

Platform shooters usually have much richer graphics than puzzle games (see Figure 4-1). These games have a main character that can run, jump, and, obviously, shoot. Shooters also have "enemies," items, terrain, and a lot of other elements to entertain the player. In other words, you need something more than circles and squares. You need to use custom graphics and animations, usually created by a graphics artist.

Figure 4-1. *A screenshot from* Contra, *a platform shooter (or run-and-gun game) released by Konami in the late '80s. As you see, it is pretty hard to draw complex elements like these with lines and circles.*

Let's say that you already have an experienced artist: someone who will bring some life into the heap of pixels, and make outstanding graphics for your game.

You explain to your artist an idea for a game—you need a character that can run, jump, and shoot. You also need a couple of backgrounds, world elements, and several "bad guys." After a week or two, the artist gives you several PNG files that look like those in Figure 4-2. Now your job is to make a game out of it.

Figure 4-2. *Graphical resources that you might receive from your artist*

In this chapter, we will learn three crucial game development concepts: working with bitmap graphics, making an animation out of set of frames, and implementing user input.

> **NOTE:** The fabulous animated knight that is used throughout this chapter was kindly provided by MarcusFilm (`www.marcusstudio.com.ua`). You may use the knight for free in your own projects—hobby or commercial. Visit the MarcusFilm home page for more art.

Sprites

In game development, a raster image is often called a *sprite*. It might be a static image or a frame of an animation sequence, like in Figure 4-2. When a lot of sprites are placed in a single file, it is called a *sprite sheet*. Figure 4-2 is a fragment of the sprite sheet that has 18 images. Each one is a single frame of a character animation jumping, running, or walking.

NOTE: There are two opposite concepts in 2D graphics: vector and raster graphics. Vector graphics are stored as formulas and coordinates. For example, the circle can be stored as the coordinates of its center and the value of the radius. If you want to scale circle and make it 30 percent bigger, you just multiply the radius by 1.3 and rerender the figure. The same concept applies to any other graphical primitive— lines, curves, and rectangles. That's why vector graphics are easily scaled up or down. Try to run our Four Balls on different devices with different screens, and you will see that it looks fairly good everywhere.

Sprites are an example of a *bitmap* or *raster* graphics. Raster graphics don't have any brain-killing math underneath. You can think of it as a two-dimensional array of pixels. Raster graphics look perfect only in their original size. Once you start scaling them up or down, they don't look very good anymore. Besides the poor look, scaling images hits performance. There is more about that later on in this chapter.

The main difference between the graphical primitives that we used in the previous chapter and the raster images that we'll try out soon is the way they are represented. Primitives are represented by the parameters that define the shape, while a raster image is a two-dimensional array of pixel colors. Images require much more memory, but grant a certain performance boost, especially when it comes to complex graphics. Rendering sprites is a matter of copying pixels from the image to the screen—no math means fewer calculations and faster rendering. The main advantage of sprites is that you can make significantly more complex and attractive graphics. But a sprite is essentially a set of pixels, which means they don't scale well.

The Four Balls game that we made in the previous chapter will look fine at any resolution since every element is described by one or many "formulae." The circle is defined by its center and radius, for example. If you make a circle twice as big, it will still look nice—just bigger. The graphics API does its best to draw a smooth figure. Sprites are images; if you increase the size of a sprite, the graphics API tries to increase every pixel. So when the sprite is twice as big, it looks choppy or blurry, depending on your scaling approach. Take a look at Figure 4-3 to see what happens with a sprite once you start scaling it.

Figure 4-3. *Scaling works badly with sprites. The more you scale it, the more it looks like a big mess of pixels.*

This means that you have to put in some extra effort if you want to make your game look nice on each and every screen resolution and density. The good news is that canvas does a reasonably good job with scaling sprites. So if you don't scale them too much, they still look fairly good. The rule of thumb is "avoid scaling raster images if you can."

You have a PNG on your server, now we have to load it and draw it!

Loading Images

The first step that you need to take before rendering images is to load them: transfer the image bytes from the server or provide them straight in the JavaScript code; let the browser parse data; store the image in the internal format; and make sure that the result was successful. The description of this process is much longer than the actual code that performs all these steps. In this section, we learn how to load an image and how to organize the loading process for multiple images. We will look at two approaches: loading an image from the file and loading image from the data URL—the string that encodes the pixel data.

Loading Images from Files

Loading an image in JavaScript is a very simple task. You don't have to care about parsing the image format, networking, or caching: the browser does the hard part for you. All you have to do is create an `Image` object and assign the `src` property to it. Once you've done that, the browser starts to load the image from the server or from its cache. Once the image is loaded, the browser notifies the registered callback function that the operation is done.

Let's have a look at the code, shown in Listing 4-1.

Listing 4-1. *Loading an Image, the Simplest Example*

```
var img = new Image(); // Create the new Image object. Loading hasn't started yet.
img.onload - function() { // This function is called when loading is done
    alert ("Image is loaded"); // At this point you know that image is ready
};

img.src = "img/knight.png"; // When you assign the src property the browser starts
                            // to download the file.
```

The image loading is an asynchronous operation: once you assign the src property, the browser starts loading the bytes, but the script continues to run. When loading is done, the browser uses one of the registered callbacks to notify your script about the result of the operation.

You can load several images simultaneously, but the browser will not guarantee any particular order of loading. For example, a small image that started to load last might finish loading first. In practice, it means that you always have to check the state of every image that you queued for loading, and assumptions like "if b.png is loaded then a.png is probably loaded too" are not reliable.

> **NOTE:** Another important rule of working with all resources (not only images): you should never rely on good networking or assume that the resource that you're waiting for is available 100 percent of the time. When you create a game, you're usually working with a local environment that works like clockwork. In the real world, internet connections can be interrupted when you least expect it. You should be prepared for it and either retry to download the resource, notify the user about the problem, and quit or continue without it. Continuing without the resource doesn't mean that you have to ignore the accident. With images, you might use a placeholder image instead of the proper one if the image wasn't important (OK, we failed to load the texture for the wizard's hat, but the rest of the game loaded, so why should we end the world?).

Listing 4-2 shows how you handle problems with the image. Notice the bold lines.

Listing 4-2. *Using Error Callbacks*

```
var img = new Image();
img.onload = function() {
    alert("Image loaded");
};
```

```
img.onerror = function() { // This callback is invoked when something went wrong.
    alert("Failed to load the image");
};
img.src = "img/knight.png";
```

The bolded lines show the second callback that you should register on the Image object —onerror. This function is called when the image could not be loaded, and gives you the chance to run the fallback mechanisms.

> **NOTE:** Why do we use PNG images? The PNG has become the de facto standard for game development. It is a *lossless* format, meaning that even after compression it stays pixel-perfect (unlike JPEG). It is open and free to use. Besides, it supports transparency and translucency. What else might one want for his sprites?

Loading Multiple Images

Usually you need more than one image for your game. You've got to track the loading of each sprite, react to problems, and do other small housekeeping tasks. It is a good idea to create a utility class that is responsible for tasks like these. We want to simplify the image loading even more!

We need to manage the loading of multiple images, firing a single callback when the loading is done. We need some sort of progress indication since image loading is a relatively slow operation. Given that we're making a user-friendly interface, we want to show a progress bar. The final task that we want to achieve is to give each image an alias: a string to identify the image in the project. Using an alias is way more convenient than using file names. File names change often, while aliases stay the same.

Let's start from the end. Listing 4-3 shows how we use the ImageManager to preload the image that we will need for the game.

Listing 4-3. *The ImageManager API, a Slightly Better Way to Load an Image*

```
function init() {
    var canvas = initFullScreenCanvas("mainCanvas");

    var imageManager = new ImageManager();
    imageManager.load({
        "arch-left": "img/arch-left.png",
        "arch-right": "img/arch-right.png",
        "knight": "img/knight.png"
    }, onDone, onProgress);
}
```

```
function onProgress(loaded, total, key, path, success) {
    if (success) {
        // Progress bar
        console.log("loaded " + loaded + " of " + total);
    } else {
        // Error handling
        console.log("ERROR: could not load " + path);
    }
}

function onDone() {
    console.log("All images are loaded");
}
```

First, we add three images (their aliases and paths) to the queue. The loading starts immediately. We pass two callback functions: onLoaded and onProgress. onLoaded is called when the whole set of images is loaded and ready. onProgress is called per image whenever the loading result is known—failed or successful. We can use this callback to update the progress bar or to notify the user about the error. The callback accepts the following five parameters:

- loaded: The number of the images loaded so far; useful to move the progress bar.

- total: The total number of the images in the queue.

- key: The alias of the image.

- path: The actual path of the image file; useful for debugging loading problems.

- success: The flag that indicates if the loading ended up well. It is true if everything's fine and the image is ready to be rendered, and false if something went wrong.

Now let's get our hands dirty with the code and write the manager.

> **NOTE:** I assume that you already got used to creating new classes and that you know you should create the new file called ImageManager.js, put it into the js folder, and add the extra script tag to the HTML page to load it.

Let's start with the constructor. Listing 4-4 shows the code.

Listing 4-4. *The Constructor of the ImageManager*

```
function ImageManager(placeholderDataUri) {
    this._images = {};
}
```

`this._images` is the object that holds every loaded image; the key of `this._images` is the image alias; and the value is the actual image object. After images are loaded, the object will be something like the following:

```
this._images = {
    "knight": [loaded image],
    "arch-left": [loaded image],
    "arch-right": [loaded image]
}
```

Once images are loaded it is very easy to get them, as shown in Listing 4-5.

Listing 4-5. *The get Function Returns the Loaded Image by Its Alias*

```
_p.get = function(key) {
    return this._images[key];
};
```

The most interesting part of the `ImageManager` class is, of course, the `load` function that queues the loading of the images. Listing 4-6 shows the complete code for this function. I'll explain it next.

Listing 4-6. *The Core of the ImageManager Class: The Load Function That Initiates the Loading of Images*

```
_p.load = function(images, onDone, onProgress) {
    // The images queue
    var queue = [];
    for (var im in images) {
        queue.push({
            key: im,
            path: images[im]
        });
    }

    if (queue.length == 0) {
        onProgress && onProgress(0, 0, null, null, true);
        onDone && onDone();
        return;
    }

    var itemCounter = {
        loaded: 0,
        total: queue.length
    };

    for (var i = 0; i < queue.length; i++) {
        this._loadItem(queue[i], itemCounter, onDone, onProgress);
    }
};
```

We create a queue of images that the user wants to load. For each image, we store the key (alias) and the path. If it turns out that the queue is empty, we immediately notify both listeners that the loading is complete (indeed, if there is nothing to load, then the loading is done straightaway without any errors). Notice the expression:

```
onProgress && onProgress(0, 0, null, null, true);
```

It reads as "if onProgress exists (not null or undefined) then call it, otherwise do nothing." The expression is a simple logical AND operation. The trick is: when the first part of the expression is false (null and undefined are converted to false), the result is guaranteed to be false and the JavaScript interpreter will not bother calling the second part at all. In other words, the expression says, "call the function if it is defined." This is equivalent to

```
if (onProgress)
    onProgress(0, 0, null, null, true)
```

but is written as a one-liner. It is up to you to decide which notion you like better.

Next, we create the itemCounter—the object that tracks the execution progress for this particular queue: the number of items that are in the queue and the number of that are loaded. Note that the itemCounter is a local variable and it is "associated" with the single queue, not with the whole object. If you decide to call load() twice,

```
imageManager.load({
    "arch-left": "img/arch-left.png",
    "arch-right": "img/arch-right.png"
}, onArchLoaded, onArchProgress);

imageManager.load({
    "knight": "img/knight.png",
}, onKnightLoaded, onKnightProgress);
```

then you have two different queues, two different counters, and a set of different callback functions. The counters will not clash and the simultaneous calls will work absolutely fine. If we were to use a single shared object to hold the items, we would have all kinds of errors. Even though this feature might not be widely used, it is good to have your code as bulletproof as possible.

In the final lines, we call the _loadItem()—the function that creates the Image objects for every item and assigns src property to make the browser load the image. The code is for this function is in Listing 4-7.

Listing 4-7. *The _loadItem Function That Initiates the Loading and Sets onload and onerror Callbacks for Every Image in the Queue*

```
_p._loadItem = function(queueItem, itemCounter, onDone, onProgress) {
    var self = this;
    var img = new Image();
    img.onload = function() {
        self._images[queueItem.key] = img;
        self._onItemLoaded(queueItem, itemCounter, onDone, onProgress, true);
    };

    img.onerror = function() {
        self._onItemLoaded(queueItem, itemCounter, onDone, onProgress, false);
    };
    img.src = queueItem.path;
};
```

The line

```
var self = this;
```

is the typical pattern that you use when you need to work with callbacks. Inside the callback body, the `this` keyword refers to the image that changed the state, not the `ImageManager` object. To save the reference to the instance of `ImageManager`, we introduced the extra variable called `self`. Without the `self` variable, it would be impossible to refer the `ImageManager` functions from within the callback code. Another way to address this issue is by using the `bind()` function, which we'll explore later in this book.

The rest of the code in `_loadItem()` function is quite easy to understand. For every image in the queue, it registers the `onload` and `onerror` listeners. If the image was loaded fine, it is added to internal store with the appropriate key.

The `_onItemLoaded()` function simply calls the listeners passed to the original load function. Take a look at the code in Listing 4-8.

Listing 4-8. *_onItemLoaded function handles the result of loading the image, both success and failure.*

```
_p._onItemLoaded = function(queueItem, itemCounter, onDone, onProgress, success)
{
    itemCounter.loaded++;
    onProgress && onProgress(itemCounter.loaded, itemCounter.total,
queueItem.key, queueItem.path, success);
    if (itemCounter.loaded == itemCounter.total) {
        onDone && onDone();
    }
};
```

Since the image has finished loading (successfully or not), this function increases the counter and calls `onProgress` with the appropriate parameters. If the counter has reached the total number of images, the `onItemLoaded()` also calls `onDone()`.

That's it. The small (only around 50 lines) class makes the loading of the images even easier! Moreover, it has a few very nice features. First, you can load images in the parallel queues without the risk of clashing the counters. Second, both callbacks are optional. So if you only need to know when images are loaded and you don't care about the progress, your code becomes even simpler, as shown in the following:

```
imageManager.load({
    "arch-left": "img/arch-left.png",
    "arch-right": "img/arch-right.png"
}, function() {
    alert("both arch parts are loaded");
});
```

The complete example that shows how to load images with the help of ImageManager is available in 01.basic_image_manager.html file together with the source code for this chapter.

Using a Data URL As an Image

Remember that I mentioned it might be a good idea to create a placeholder image that will be used when one of the noncritical images is not loaded. In 3D applications, for example, the loss of a single texture is not reason enough to stop the game with an error.

Now let's consider a couple of questions. What should we do if we can't load the placeholder image? Is there a way to make sure that the image is loaded, no matter what? It turns out that there is a way. An image is a set of bytes after all, so what if we store these bytes right in the JavaScript code and transfer them straight into the image object?

There's a way to do it. The `src` property of the `Image` object supports so-called data URLs. A data URL looks like the following:

```
data:image/png;base64,iVBORw0KGgoAAAANSUhEUgAAADIAAAAyCAYAAAAeP4ixAAAAmOlEQVRoQ+
3YMRWAMBQEwcRT/Cv4nuAhYYtQDQDQaAyXIFe2aedfk65+zLt1jbiwRiJxKwpBWwlrSClrQClrQKlrSKlt
UKWtIKWFarYEmraFmtoCWtgGW1CpaOipbVClrXf5x9z/LHvzMvVEk7diRQsaRUtH3vQklbAsloFS1pFy2
oFLWkFLKtVsKRVtKxW0JJJWWLJaBUtaRctqBaOX1+W43qGn25cAAAAASUVORK5CYII=
```

> **NOTE:** There's no magic behind the data URL. The format is very simple: `data:[<MIME-type>][;charset=<encoding>][;base64],<data>`. In our case, `MIME-type` is image/png and the charset/encoding part is skipped. There's no binary image encoding, and the charset/encoding part makes sense only for textual information. Then, after `base64` comes the Base64-encoded PNG data.
>
> Base64 is the format for encoding binary data in the form of a text string. Base64 is used to store binary data in systems that work with text. There's no way to put an image in an XML node, for example, since the image file has a binary format; while an XML node may contain only text. Since Base64 is a text format, you can encode the image in Base64 and store in an XML node. Data URI is another example. URI is a text and it can't have any attached binary data in its original form, but Base64 encoding solves this issue and allows storing image data within the valid URI.

Essentially, the data URL is a string representation of some binary data with metadata in front of it. This URL, for instance, represents a small 50 × 50 pixel image with two gray rectangles on a white background—the one that I use as a "no image" placeholder (see Figure 4-4).

Figure 4-4. *A no-image placeholder*

The code to build an image from this string is fairly simple, as shown in Listing 4-9.

Listing 4-9. *Creating an Image from the Data URL*

```
var image = new Image();
image.src = "data:image/png;base64,iVBORw0KGgoAAAAN … 5CYII=";
```

This is a guaranteed way to create a valid image in JavaScript. There's no networking involved and image data is transferred straight into the Image object. Even though it looks like the image is created instantly, this is not the case with data URL. The image is loaded in exactly same way as with the network-downloaded one—before the onload listener is fired, you can't use it. On the other hand, the loading process is very fast and you can safely assume that the image will be created faster than any other image downloaded from a server.

The full example of using data URLs as the source of image data can be found in the 02.data_url.html file with the source code for this chapter.

Let's update our manager so that it uses the data URL for the no-image placeholder (see Listing 4-10).

Listing 4-10. *Updating ImageManager to Use a Data URL for a Placeholder*

```
function ImageManager(placeholderDataUri) {
    this._imageQueue = [];
    this._images = {};
    if (placeholderDataUri) {
        this._placeholder = new Image();
        this._placeholder.src = placeholderDataUri;
    }
}
_p._loadItem = function(queueItem, itemCounter, progressListener) {
    ...

    img.onerror = function() {
        self._images[queueItem.key] = self._placeholder ? self._placeholder :
null;
        self._onItemLoaded(queueItem, itemCounter, progressListener, false);
    };
    img.src = queueItem.path;
};
```

Now, if the ImageManager is supplied with the placeholder, it creates an image and uses it in the _images array for images that failed to download.

The last question to discuss is how to get the data URL for the image. The simplest way is to give this job to canvas. Listing 4-11 shows how I created my placeholder image.

Listing 4-11. *Generating a Data URL with Canvas*

```
ctx.fillStyle = "#CCC";
ctx.fillRect(0, 0, 25, 25);
ctx.fillRect(25, 25, 25, 25);

alert(canvas.toDataURL("image/png"));
```

The toDataURL method creates a "screenshot" of canvas content and encodes it in a given format. After you have the string with a URL, you can use it any way you want – as a placeholder, for example, or to send it to the server to store as the user's screenshot. It is all up to your imagination.

Listing 4-12 is the complete source code for our ImageManager class, with the support for the placeholder image.

Listing 4-12. *The Full Source Code for ImageManager with the Support of Placeholder Image*

```
function ImageManager(placeholderDataUri) {
    this._images = {};
    if (placeholderDataUri) {
        this._placeholder = new Image();
        this._placeholder.src = placeholderDataUri;
    }
}

_p = ImageManager.prototype;


_p.load = function(images, onDone, onProgress) {
    // The images queue
    var queue = [];
    for (var im in images) {
        queue.push({
            key: im,
            path: images[im]
        });
    }

    if (queue.length == 0) {
        onProgress && onProgress(0, 0, null, null, true);
        onDone && onDone();
        return;
    }

    var itemCounter = {
        loaded: 0,
        total: queue.length
    };

    for (var i = 0; i < queue.length; i++) {
        this._loadItem(queue[i], itemCounter, onDone, onProgress);
    }
};

_p._loadItem = function(queueItem, itemCounter, onDone, onProgress) {
    var self = this;
    var img = new Image();
    img.onload = function() {
        self._images[queueItem.key] = img;
        self._onItemLoaded(queueItem, itemCounter, onDone, onProgress, true);
    };

    img.onerror = function() {
        self._images[queueItem.key] = self._placeholder ? self._placeholder :
null;
```

```
        self._onItemLoaded(queueItem, itemCounter, onDone, onProgress, false);
    };
    img.src = queueItem.path;
};

_p._onItemLoaded = function(queueItem, itemCounter, onDone, onProgress, success)
{
    itemCounter.loaded++;
    onProgress && onProgress(itemCounter.loaded, itemCounter.total,
queueItem.key, queueItem.path, success);
    if (itemCounter.loaded == itemCounter.total) {
        onDone && onDone();
    }
};

_p.get = function(key) {
    return this._images[key];
};
```

Tips on Loading Images

You now know how to load an image from a server and how to embed image data straight in the JavaScript code with data URL. But which is better: to download a hundred small images or one huge image that contains all the graphics? Or maybe it makes a lot of sense to embed all the images as a single, huge data URL and guarantee that it will be loaded.

Size vs. Quantity

Supporting dozens of small images is a headache. The process of downloading an image involves sending a separate request to a server that takes time to complete. More images means more requests, more traffic, and more time to wait.

On the other hand, one big image means that the user interface won't show any sensible progress while it is being downloaded. Although you could implement a retry strategy to redownload a broken image, it is better to have small pieces of data instead of one big piece.

When you decide on your image-loading strategy, you should take into the account that images are the perfect candidates for caching. Browsers cache image files very aggressively since it is highly unlikely that an image will change. In game development, images are often updated. You might make new editions to the game, or add new items or levels. You might want to put a Santa hat on the main character during Christmas or add a palm tree in the background. If you have a single huge image, you'll force the client to redownload all the game content, even after a small update. In other words, it's really annoying.

The general recommended way is to break sprites into categories; for example, one image for the main character, one image for the bad guys, an image for the level items, and so forth. If you decide to update an item, there'll be only one image to redownload.

You should also take into account that it is highly unlikely that you will need all the game's graphics in the first minute of the game. Platform shooters usually have levels, for example. Each level might have unique graphics—such as unique backgrounds or unique enemies—that are not required for other levels. Obviously, you should not download these graphics before the user reaches a level. It'd be a waste of time and bandwidth.

Files vs. Data URLs

Data URLs are not a common way to work with images. Even though data URLs have a lot of advantages, they have disadvantages too.

The first and most obvious disadvantage is that data URLs are not manageable. You can loop through the images in the viewer application and easily find the image you need. A data URL is a heap of letters; you cannot distinguish between a car image encoded as the data URL and a hamster image encoded the same way (unless you're a robot or you have special super powers that let you decode Base64 on the fly).

Images take up less space when they are stored as binary files. The size of a data URL is around 30 percent bigger than the size of the same image as a file. If the web server that you're using is zipping the content, this ratio is slightly better, but binary files still win.

By using data URLs, you "couple" the script with the resources, which is a bad thing to do. Once you change either of them, you have to redownload the whole file on the client. After editing an image, you have to regenerate the data URL. Each time the designer changes a single pixel, you must update your code.

The good thing about data URLs is that they are text. They can be transferred via systems that accept only text. They *can* be embedded into the code, but that doesn't mean that they *should* be embedded in the code. The example in the previous section—the placeholder image—is the correct usage of data URL. We want to guarantee that the image is always available to the script, and that's why we're using the data URL.

So What's the Strategy?

Check that your game needs all the graphics on startup, or some of the files might wait until the player reaches some point in the game. If that's the case, you should separate the graphics that can be loaded later, and load them only when they are needed.

A good size for an image is something between 50 KB and 250 KB. Anything less is going to generate a lot of requests, so you should combine several files into a bigger one (the big image that holds multiple small sprites is known as the sprite sheet, which we discuss later in this chapter). If your files are considerably bigger, they will lock up the progress indicator. Besides, if you change even a single pixel in it, you'll have to download it from the server again.

Use data URLs when there's a good reason to use them; otherwise, use good old image files.

Drawing an Image

Loading an image is not very fun by itself, but once you know how to load it, you can draw it on canvas. Let's proceed with our drawing experiments.

How to Draw an Image

There's a single function in Context2D API responsible for drawing an image; it's called drawImage(). The idea behind it is to take a rectangular area of pixels from the image (the source) and fit it into the rectangular area in the canvas (the destination), as shown in Figure 4-5.

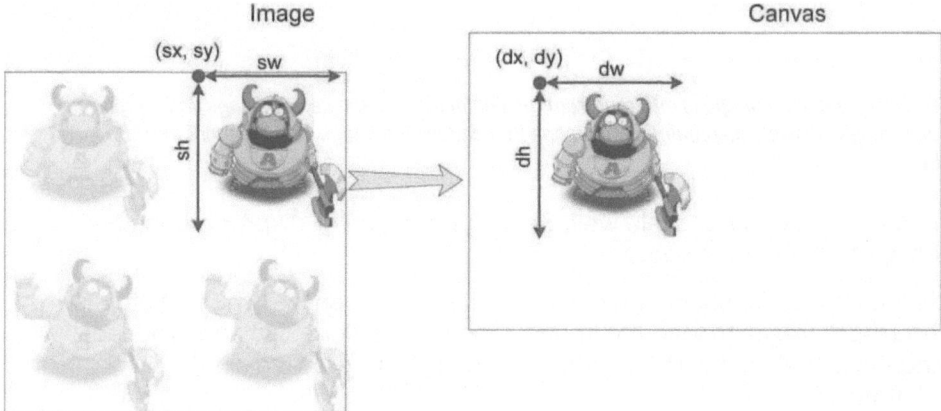

Figure 4-5. Drawing an image on the canvas

The function takes eight parameters:

```
drawImage(image, sx, sy, sWidth, sHeight, dx, dy, dWidth, dHeight)
```

The first parameter is the `Image` object that we loaded. The next four parameters: `sx`, `sy`, `sWidth`, and `sHeight` define the part of the image to draw; everything outside of this rectangle is ignored. The small "s" in the parameter name stands for "source." The last four parameters define the rectangle on a canvas to draw the part of the image into. The lowercase "d" in the name of parameters stands for "destination."

If the destination rectangle is different from the source rectangle (it's bigger, smaller, or has a different proportion of the sides), the image is resized to fit the destination area (see Figure 4-6). Raster graphics look best when they are not resized, so you should attempt to keep the size of the source and destination rectangles the same. This effect can be used for nice-looking animations, however.

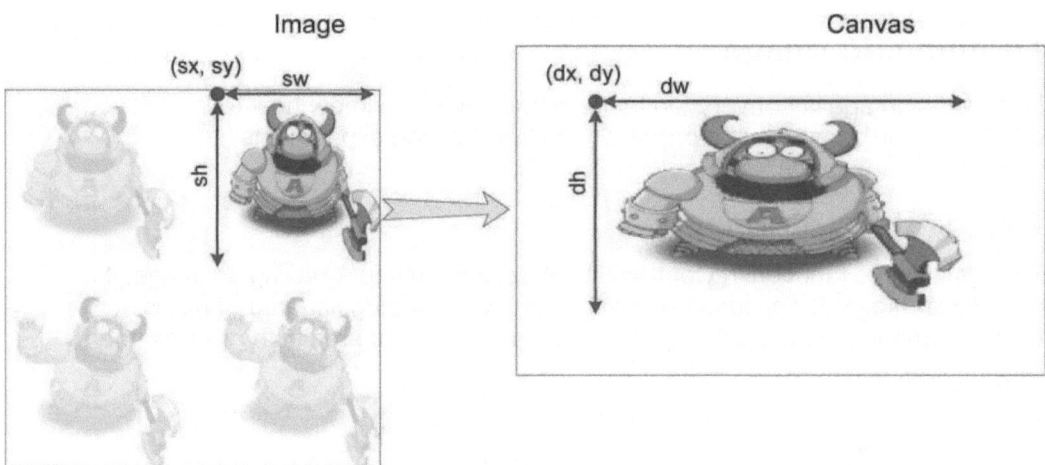

Figure 4-6. *If the source rectangle is different from the destination rectangle, the image will be resized to fit it. This example shows a disproportional change that causes the image to scale more in width than height.*

As you recall, sprites do not scale well. Scaling too much or disproportionately can make sprites look quite bad.

Now let's load the sprite sheet and draw a sprite on the canvas. The first step is to use the `ImageManager` to load the image. Once this is done, we can proceed to drawing the actual sprite. The function in Listing 4-13 draws a single animation frame.

Listing 4-13. *The Function That Draws a Single Sprite from the Sprite Sheet*

```
function drawPlayer() {
    var canvas = document.getElementById("mainCanvas");
    var ctx = canvas.getContext("2d");

    var playerImage = imageManager.getImage("player");
    ctx.drawImage(playerImage, 8, 8, 40, 40, 50, 50, 40, 40);
}
```

As you see, we limit the area of the image—the first rectangle (8, 8, 40, 40) covers one animation frame. The size of the source rectangle is the same as the size of the destination rectangle, so the image is not resized. This is the usual way to draw sprites from a sprite sheet. The complete example of how to draw an image on the canvas is available in the 03.drawing_image.html file with the source code for this chapter.

There are two other ways to draw an image, as shown in Listing 4-14.

Listing 4-14. *Shorthand Versions of the drawImage*

```
// Draws the whole image without scaling at (dx, dy) point of the canvas.
ctx.drawImage(image, dx, dy);
// This is a shorthand version of
ctx.drawImage(im, 0, 0, im.width, im.height, dx, dy, im.width, im.height);

// Scales the image to fit the rectangle (dw, dh) and draws at (dx, dy)
drawImage(image, dx, dy, dw, dh)
// This is a shorthand version of
ctx.drawImage(im, 0, 0, im.width, im.height, dx, dy, dw, dh);
```

These versions of the drawing function have a smaller numbers of parameters. But they both work with the whole source image and do not allow picking the exact frame from the sprite sheet. That's why they are less useful for game development.

Drawing Performance

When it comes to a sprite-based game, everybody asks the same questions: how many sprites can I actually draw per frame? Is it better to draw four small 32 × 32 images or use one big 64 × 64 instead? The answer very much depends on three parameters: hardware, software, and the image that you are using. I've written several tests on http://jsperf.com/draw-image to see how it really works on different browsers and hardware. I checked how PNG transparency, image size, image content, and scaling affect drawing performance.

When I first executed these tests, I was surprised by the results. It looks like different browsers are optimized for the rendering of different types of images.

Google Chrome, for example, rendered every type of image with almost the same speed: big or small, transparent or not, cut from the sprite sheet or painted as is. Other browsers performed in a totally different manner. Opera preferred the image with an opaque background to the same image with a solid background. Safari preferred the transparent image.

It is virtually impossible to give optimization advice in a way that suits every browser: some browsers render graphics faster, some work slightly slower. There are a few relatively constant behaviors that should be used for the optimizations, however.

> **NOTE:** The result of the `jsperf.com` test is the number of iterations per second. In other words, it tells you how many times you can run a certain task during one second—more is better. These numbers should not be treated as some absolute values to determine how fast a certain operation is. The results of the tests are used to compare how much faster one operation is than another. Which operation is faster: multiplying the number by 0.5 or dividing it by 2? This is exactly the type of question that `jsperf.com` aims to answer.
>
> If you ever have any doubt about the effectiveness of a certain approach versus another one, don't hesitate to use this small and very useful tool.

Smaller images are usually painted faster than bigger ones. This sounds like an obvious observation, but the interesting point is that it is "cheaper" to paint one large image rather than cover the same area with several small pictures. I tested sets of 25 sprites. A set of 64 × 64 sprites did 306 repaints per second while a 32 × 32 set managed 506 (bigger is better, remember). I'd need to paint 100 small sprites to cover the same area that I covered with the big ones because the 64 × 64 sprite covers an area four times larger than that of the 32 × 32 sprite. The relative numbers that take the area into account would be 306 (big sprites covering the area) versus 127 (506 ÷ 4 = 127) small sprites covering the area. Big sprites do the job almost three times faster!

Scaling is evil. Almost every browser showed an extreme drop in performance when I tested how the scaling of the image behaves. Drawing a 32 × 32 image scaled to the size of 64 × 64 takes twice the time as drawing the big (64 × 64) unscaled image in a standard Android 2.2 browser. Firefox Mobile draws it nine times slower (at the time of writing). Conclusion: if you want to support the different sizes of sprites, it is best to create different sets of resources—one for Low Res, one for High Res. If you try to scale at runtime, the CPU will not thank you.

Sprite sheets work a little slower than the individual images. Wait! But you just said that sprite sheets are good! Yes, they are—especially when it comes to transferring the image vla 3G networks; but when you need to draw it, an individual image wins the race. How bad is the loss of performance? Not *that* bad: 306 operations per second for the individual image versus 267 operations for the same image cut out from the sprite. In a sprite-intensive game, it is still important to squeeze every CPU cycle you can, but loading images frame by frame is not an option. You've seen already how to build an image out of the canvas object using the data URL. You can use the same approach here: transfer the image as a sprite sheet, but transform it to a set of individual images right in the browser. A couple of extra seconds in loading time is usually a good price for the boost of the performance.

Decimal pixels kill performance. On most browsers, drawing the sprite in decimal coordinates like (1.5, 1.5) is significantly slower than drawing the same image in either (1, 1) or (2, 2). The loss of performance is the same order as with the scaled image. Remember the blurry lines described in Chapter 1? Sprites work the same way: the browser uses anti-aliasing to draw the sprite in a decimal coordinate, bringing up image preprocessing and semitransparent pixels on the border, both of which tend to like eating the CPU (see Figure 4-7). The solution is simple: do `Math.round()` on the coordinates before drawing. No decimal part, no problem.

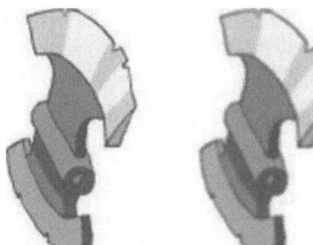

Figure 4-7. *Drawing with integer (left) and decimal coordinates (right). The right image takes nine times longer to output, and doesn't look all that good anyway.*

At the time of writing, the standard browser in Android 2.2 ignored the subpixel values, drawing the image exactly the same way. That's why it works equally well on both integer and decimal coordinates. You should not ignore this issue, however, even if you're developing only for Android—you never know which browser will be the default on your player's system. It could be Firefox Mobile, which doesn't trim coordinates for you.

Still, the question is not answered. How many sprites can I draw per second? The exact answer, of course, is "it depends on this and that…" but I think you've had enough of answers like that from political TV shows. I have written a simple test case to check how much you can expect from both mobile and desktop browsers. I assumed that the game needs around 30 FPS to feel smooth, and tested the number of 32 × 32 sprites I could draw without falling below the FPS cap. In my opinion, there's no sense to use smaller sprites—on modern screen densities, 32 × 32 pixels look tiny already.

My Galaxy S proudly held around 370 sprites on Dolphin HD, and the stock browser Fennec stuck at around 100.

Desktop PCs are way better at handling simple sprites. Safari can render around 2200 sprites; Google Chrome 15 and Opera 11 easily hit 3200 sprites; IE9 got 4500; and Firefox 7 managed 5500. You need around 2000 sprites to fully cover the Full HD screen.

> **NOTE:** For every test case, I'm checking whether or not the browser is capable of covering the area that is supposed to be a game screen. If you can rerender the whole screen each frame, covering it with a completely new set of sprites, then your game should run just fine. This is a very rough metric since it assumes the worst case scenario. Ninety-nine percent of the time, you will not need to update the whole screen. There are a lot of techniques on how to optimize this process and render only the parts of the canvas that actually need to be rendered.
>
> Also, I'm not taking into account the game logic that might be pretty involved. In games like *Angry Birds*, far more CPU time is spent calculating realistic physics than rendering those few boxes. The techniques to optimize rendering speed are covered in detail in Chapter 7.
>
> If you don't have enough processing power to cover the screen with tiles, it doesn't mean that your game won't run, but that you need to do a more accurate benchmark, and probably build a prototype and run it on the target device. It is good practice to do that for every new game that you create. You never know what kind of issues you may uncover with this small experiment.

Sprite Sheets

Let's have a closer look at the character image. It has a set of animation frames for a dozen animations. Each frame has its own position on the sheet and doesn't overlap with the other frames. Frames are of different sizes: a frame with the character standing still is smaller than the frame with the character waving hand since the raised hand takes up some space.

The position of the character inside the frame also differs from one frame to another. It changes depending on the character's pose or action. When he is standing still, he is roughly in the middle of the frame; when he is crouching, he might be shifted a little bit to the right; when he's swinging his weapon, he might be shifted to the left, and so on.

When we render a smooth animation, we need to know this position, or anchor point. When the character is bowing, his feet must stay in a fixed location of the game world, and does not depend on the dimensions of the frame. The "center of the character" is the anchor of the frame.

> **NOTE:** In this chapter, I show how to draw sprites straight from the sprite sheet. Even though this technique is a little slower than rendering individual images, it is fairly easy to adjust the code to prerender each frame once you know how to draw it.

The anchor point is used to position the frame on the screen. When we need to draw a frame in point (x, y), it means that the anchor point should go there, not the top-left corner or any other point on the image (see Figure 4-8).

Figure 4-8. *The anchor points of animation frames. In each frame, the anchor point may have different coordinates.*

We just figured out what we need to know about the frame before drawing an animated character in a given set of coordinates: the size of the frame and the coordinates of the anchor point within that frame. A dozen sprite sheets—each having up to a hundred frames—soon becomes unmanageable without the proper API. So it's time to make a new class! SpriteSheet sounds good enough.

So far, SpriteSheet is one of the simplest classes in the book. I'm showing the code in Listing 4-15.

Listing 4-15. *The SpriteSheet Class Responsible for Drawing Individual Frames*

```
/**
 *
 * @param image the image object to use for drawing
 * @param frames the array describing the frames of the sprite sheet in a
format:
 * [
 *      [x, y, width, height, anchorX, anchorY] // - frame 1
 *      [x, y, width, height, anchorX, anchorY] // - frame 2
 *      ...
 * ]
 */
function SpriteSheet(image, frames) {
    this._image = image;
    this._frames = frames;
}

SpriteSheet.FRAME_X = 0;
SpriteSheet.FRAME_Y = 1;
SpriteSheet.FRAME_WIDTH = 2;
SpriteSheet.FRAME_HEIGHT = 3;
SpriteSheet.FRAME_ANCHOR_X = 4;
SpriteSheet.FRAME_ANCHOR_Y = 5;

/**
 * Draws the frame of the sprite sheet in the given coordinates of the
 * Context.
 * @param ctx the context to draw at
 * @param index the index of the frame
 * @param x x coordinate where the anchor will appear
 * @param y y coordinate where the anchor will appear
 */
_p.drawFrame = function(ctx, index, x, y) {
    var frame = this._frames[index];

    if (!frame)
        return;

    ctx.drawImage(this._image,
        frame[SpriteSheet.FRAME_X], frame[SpriteSheet.FRAME_Y],
        frame[SpriteSheet.FRAME_WIDTH], frame[SpriteSheet.FRAME_HEIGHT],
        x - frame[SpriteSheet.FRAME_ANCHOR_X],
        y - frame[SpriteSheet.FRAME_ANCHOR_Y],
        frame[SpriteSheet.FRAME_WIDTH], frame[SpriteSheet.FRAME_HEIGHT]);
};
```

The constructor accepts two parameters: an image and the description of the frames. Each frame is described by an array that has six elements: four to describe the frame size and position within the sheet, and two for the coordinates of the anchor point. The drawing function is very simple too: it calculates the offset for the given frame so that the anchor point appears in the (x, y) position.

> **NOTE:** You might have noticed that I created several constants to refer to the indices of the frame array. Their only purpose is to make code more readable. Compare the code in the listing with the same code rewritten without constants:
>
> ```
> ctx.drawImage(this._image, frame[0], frame[1], frame[2],
>         frame[3], x - frame[5], y - frame[6], frame[2],
> frame[3]);
> ```
>
> This code looks a little more compact, but if you read it later, I bet you won't remember the meaning behind the indices.

Now we can separate the sprite sheet description from the drawing code, as shown in Listing 4-16.

Listing 4-16. *Using SpriteSheet to Draw Sprites*

```
var frames = [
        [9, 8, 38, 37, 10, 36],
        [57, 8, 39, 37, 10, 36],
        [107, 8, 45, 37, 10, 36],
        [163, 8, 45, 37, 10, 36]
];
var spriteSheet = new SpriteSheet(imageManager.getImage("player"), frames);
spriteSheet.drawFrame(ctx, current, 10, 40);
```

> **TIP:** Where do these frame-description numbers come from? Usually your artist gives them to you, but make sure to explain to him that you need the description of the frames before he starts working. Otherwise, you will spend an evening with your favorite graphical editor measuring pixels—just like I did while writing this chapter.

Raster Fonts

There's another interesting use for the sprite sheet—rendering in-game raster fonts. Games might use very fancy fonts presented as bitmaps, with each sprite representing a letter or character.

The task of building a class that can render strings using bitmap fonts can be trivial or rather complex, depending on the set of features that you need. If you need a one-line bitmap representation of the string, it'll take five minutes to build a class that can do it. On the other hand, the advanced solution that takes into the account line breaks, alignment, and intervals can be very complex. Typography is a broad and interesting topic that is beyond the scope of this book.

Basics of Animation

We're getting closer to the one of the most exciting parts of game development: animation. When pictures start to move, your game becomes "alive." It is a truly incredible feeling to see your first animated sprite moving on the screen.

The Simplest Animation

Nowadays everybody knows how animation works. There's no mystery behind it. When you change frames fast enough and update the picture on the screen (change its shape, position, step to the next frame in the animation sequence, or all of the above), the user experiences the illusion of movement. The picture becomes alive—spaceships fly and shoot, Pac-Man runs away from the chase, and tanks turn their turrets.

To create the animation, we have to implement three steps.

1. Update the state of the picture with time (move it, change frames, etc).

2. Draw the picture on the screen.

3. Wait some time and repeat the previous two steps, drawing the new frame (do not forget to clear the contents of the previous frame).

The faster frames change, the smoother the animation looks to the user. The speed of frame change is called the *frame rate* and it is measured in frames per second, or FPS.

Implementing the plan that we just outlined, we should create a function that renders the frame and call it every 30 to 50 milliseconds. Listing 4-17 shows the code that does the trick.

Listing 4-17. *The Simplest Possible Canvas Animation*

```
var currentFrame = -1;
function animate(timestamp) {
    ctx.fillStyle = "white";
    ctx.fillRect(0, 0, canvas.width, canvas.height);
    currentFrame = ++currentFrame%5;
    spriteSheet.drawFrame(ctx, current, 10, 40);
    requestAnimationFrame(arguments.callee);
}
animate();
```

Let's look closer at this code since it is the basis for the whole animation framework that we're going to make during this chapter. The first two lines of the function are well known from Chapter 2: we're clearing the whole canvas with a solid white color. We have to clear the old frame before drawing the new one since canvas doesn't clear itself automatically and will draw the new content on top of the old. The full example of this approach is available in a file called 05.sprite_sheet_anlimation.html together with the source code for this chapter.

The variable called `current` holds the index of the current frame in the animation sequence. The sequence has a total of five frames. The next line, `currentFrame = ++currentFrame%5`, increases the counter by one and performs a modulo operation (returns the remainder from the division by five) to make sure that the number is never greater than four. This line could be rewritten in the following, more verbose way:

```
current++;
if (current > 4)
    current = 0;
```

It does exactly the same as the line in Listing 4-17: after the counter reaches 4, it drops back to 0 and continues from there. The next line draws the frame, and the last line schedules the execution of the same function after 50 milliseconds.

The last line of the `animate()` function is a new and important concept. JavaScript *timers* are a simple yet very powerful mechanism for scheduling fragments of code for later execution. Redrawing the frame every few milliseconds is one of the core tasks that we need to implement in order to create animation. That's what we will do now.

> **NOTE:** `arguments.callee` is the reference to the function itself. For example, when I'm inside the function called `animate`, then `arguments.callee` refers to this function—`animate()`. When you need to refer the function from within itself, it is the best way to do it. Referencing by name has its drawbacks. If you refactor your code, for example, you should remember to update another reference. In JavaScript it is common for a function not to have a name at all. In this case, `arguments.callee` is the only way to access it after it was created. The last line can be read as "call the same function again in 50 milliseconds".

For the sake of an example, let's consider another approach to pausing the script. Let's tell JavaScript to "wait five milliseconds, and then continue the execution." The ugliest and usually unacceptable way to do it is to throw a useless task to the CPU, and ask to repeat it in a loop. After each cycle, you check how much time has passed and decide if you need to move on (see Listing 4-18). Don't try this at home.

Listing 4-18. *The Naïve Way to Make Browser Wait for 5 Seconds Before Moving On*

```
var delay = 5000; // Five seconds
var start = new Date().getTime();
while (true) {
    // Find something to occupy CPU with, how about some math?
    Math.sin(Math.random()*2*Math.PI) + Math.cos(Math.random()*2*Math.PI);
    var passed = new Date().getTime() - start;
    if (passed > delay)
        break;
}
```

To understand how to organize the animation in the best way, look deep into JavaScript's internals to see why the code in the Listing 4-18 is one of the worst things that you can do, how to avoid the pitfalls of long-running tasks, and schedule the animation loops correctly.

JavaScript Threading Model

JavaScript is a *single-threaded language*. That means that at any given time there's at most one piece of the code that is executing. For example, if an image has finished loading at the moment that another function was executing, the callback will not run immediately in parallel. JavaScript schedules the execution of that code after the end of the current function. If there are several listeners, they will be queued and executed one by one.

Image loading is not the only part of JavaScript that uses callbacks. The user input handling code (which we'll examine in detail in the next chapter) relies on a similar mechanism to react to touches and mouse clicks. This means that while a long task is executed by your script, the rest of the world is frozen until it is finished. Figure 4-9 illustrates this.

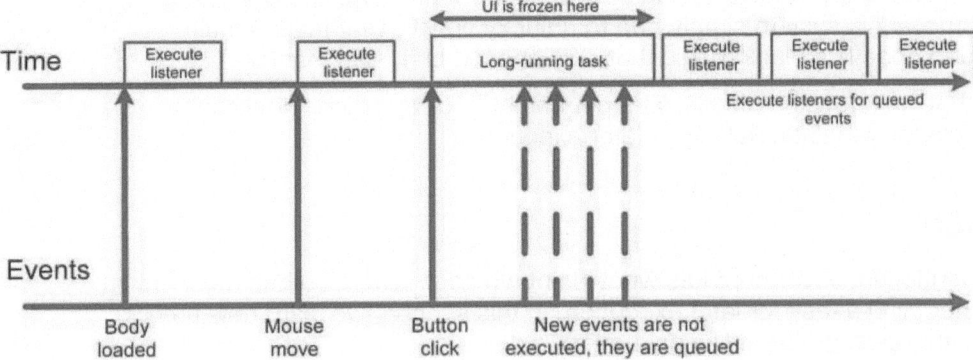

Figure 4-9. *The threading model of JavaScript. Since JavaScript is single-threaded, only one piece of the code can be executed simultaneously. Long running tasks block UI and make the application unresponsive.*

Let's say that you're in the middle of a heavyweight function that runs for a long time. The user moves the mouse cursor over the UI component. This action generates several dozen events, but neither of those are processed until the long-running function has completed.

What is the practical conclusion from all of the preceding? There are two.

- You can be sure that the currently executed code is the only fragment of code that is running. If you are inside a listener, you should not worry about what will happen if the animate() is repainting the scene at this exact moment; it just can't happen.

- Any long-running functions blocks the input. If your chess AI calculates the best strategy in 5 seconds, it means the user will not see the feedback for at least 5 seconds. The long-running tasks can be broken down into smaller ones that do not stop the rest of the world.

The second point might sound like a headache. In practice, it is not a headache at all. You need to put just a little bit more effort into the design of an application with long-running tasks.

The main advantage of the described approach is that designing a single-threaded application (and every JavaScript application is single-threaded) is way simpler than writing multi-threaded code. Languages like Java utilize the full power of threading for the price of complex and very complex APIs that coordinate the execution of multiple threads. To make matters worse, bugs in multi-threaded environments can stay unnoticed for months and eventually crash the whole system simply due to unlucky timing. Unit testing multi-threaded code is a black magic that only chosen ones can master.

Now that we know the pitfalls, let's get back to our question. How can we schedule the repaint function for later execution?

Timers

As I mentioned, JavaScript has what is known as *timers*, a built-in mechanism for scheduling a task for later execution. In this section, we learn how timers help with repeating tasks like animation.

Setting Timers

JavaScript has three functions for scheduling the code for later execution: `setInterval()`, `setTimeout()`, and `requestAnimationFrame()`. All three functions do similar things—they tell the browser: "Hey, please schedule the execution of the code that I'm giving to you. Call in around N milliseconds when you have some free cycles."

After N milliseconds, the browser queues the execution of the function as if it is a simple event listener. If the queue is empty, then you're lucky and your function is executed immediately. If the queue is full of other tasks—well, your function will have to wait, no matter how important is it.

> **NOTE:** This is an important concept about the timers: they are not guaranteed to fire exactly at the time when they are scheduled to fire. One of the reasons was shown earlier; if another piece of code is executing, the timer waits for its turn. Even when timers work in a perfectly dull page without any events and user activities, they are not guaranteed to run in time. The delay might happen because of the resolution of the OS timer, for example (but this is far outside the scope of this book).

There are only two things that you can rely on.

- The timer will never fire before its scheduled time.

⬛ The browser will do its best to fire it on time.

> **TIP:** Don't worry that the timer fires a millisecond later. Usually, the user won't notice the glitch. Don't be a perfectionist and don't try to make the timer perfect. When I was working as a Java game developer, I spent a huge amount of time trying to make the animation loop in Java a little better. Java, being an enterprise platform, had the same timer issues—you couldn't rely on timer accuracy. It was making me crazy and I wrote dozens of tests, native modules, and workarounds. The effect was hardly noticeable. It is way better to spend this time writing real gaming code.

Now let's get back to the scheduling functions and see how they differ.

setInterval() schedules the execution of the function every N milliseconds (see Listing 4-19).

Listing 4-19. *An Example of setInterval*

```
setInterval(
    function() {
        console.log("Hello")
    }, 500);
```

The code in Listing 4-19 outputs the word "Hello" into the console twice a second.

setTimeout() schedules the *single* execution of the function. Of course, you can call setTimeout() at the end of your function once again, thus imitating the work of setInterval(). You have two different ways to call setTimeout; both are shown in Listing 4-20. The first call schedules a single execution, whereas the second call schedules the execution again after each loop.

Listing 4-20. *Two Ways of Calling setTimeout*

```
// Will fire once
setTimeout(function() {
        console.log("Hello")
    }, 500);

// Will work almost like setInterval, will fire forever
setTimeout(function() {
        setTimeout(arguments.callee, 500);
        console.log("Hello")
    }, 500);
```

requestAnimationFrame() is the last timer function, and the most recently added one. It is supported by the vast majority of desktop browsers, but unfortunately not by the stock Android browser (it is supported by mobile Firefox). As the name suggests, it was created specifically for handling animations. You can't pass the timeout value into the requestAnimationFrame; it is up to the browser to decide the best time for the next animation loop. The browser synchronizes the requestAnimationCallback with the other animations on the page—CSS transitions, DOM animations, SVG SMIL, and so forth—improving overall performance of the page. Besides, requestAnimationFrame() will not fire if the browser tab is invisible. If nobody is looking at the animation, why waste precious cycles and battery power on it? This is the supposed method to schedule animations in JavaScript games. Listing 4-21 shows the way to use this function to schedule animation in JavaScript games (for browsers that support it).

Listing 4-21. *An Example of the Usage of requestAnimationFrame*

```
function animate(timestamp){
    console.log("Hello");
    requestAnimationFrame(animate);
}
```

At the time of writing, this function is still implemented with vendor-specific prefixes. In WebKit browsers, it is called webkitRequestAnimationFrame(); in Opera, it is oRequestAnimationFrame(), an so forth. When the function is standardized, browser vendors will eventually remove the prefix; but for now, it is convenient to use the following shim layer in Listing 4-22, which was implemented by Paul Irish.

Listing 4-22. *Shim Layer for requestAnimationFrame*

```
window.requestAnimationFrame = (function(){
    //Check for each browser
    //@paul_irish function
    //Globalises this function to work on any browser as each browser has a
different namespace for this
    return  window.requestAnimationFrame          || //Chromium
            window.webkitRequestAnimationFrame || //Webkit
            window.mozRequestAnimationFrame    || //Mozilla Geko
            window.oRequestAnimationFrame      || //Opera Presto
            window.msRequestAnimationFrame     || //IE Trident
            function(callback, element){           //Fallback function
                return window.setTimeout(callback, 1000/60);
            }
})();
```

Note how this code gracefully degrades to setTimeout(). Even if the browser doesn't support requestAnimationFrame(), your code will not break! Moreover, once the browser adds support to this magical little feature, you do not need to change anything to use it.

> **NOTE:** The construction that Paul used may look confusing at first glance. Let's take a minute to explain it. Paul created an anonymous function that returns the function (remember, in JavaScript, the function acts just like any other object and it can be returned from methods) and called it straightaway. The function checks for the available implementation of `requestAnimationFrame` and assigns it to the `window.requestAnimationFrame` property:
>
> ```
> window.requestAnimationFrame = (function(){
>     // actual shim code here
> })();
> ```

Add this code to `utils.js`, as we will need it in most of the chapters throughout the book.

Stopping Timers

Sometimes you want to cancel the timer—for example, when the game has ended and there's no more need to animate anything, you might want to stop `requestAnimationFrame()` or the other timer. Each function that we described earlier has a counter-function that stops the timer and prevents the next call from happening.

To stop the timer set with `setTimeout()`, you call `clearTimeout()` like this:

```
var handler = setTimeout(function() {alert ("Boom");}, 1000);
clearTimeout(handler);
```

Each timer function returns the "handler" that identifies the timer. The handler is used to distinguish between different timers in case you have many of them in your script. Intervals follow exactly the same pattern, with the only difference being that the function that stops the execution is called `clearInterval()`:

```
var handler = setInterval(function() {alert ("Tick");}, 1000);
clearInterval(handler);
```

Finally, clearing the `animationFrame` is a little bit more involved because of different naming conventions. We will need another shim layer to use `cancelRequestAnimationFrame()` in a browser-agnostic way and, of course, provide the fallback to the standard `clearTimeout()` implementation (see Listing 4-23).

Listing 4-23. *Cancelling requestAnimationFrame*

```
window.cancelRequestAnimFrame = ( function() {
    return window.cancelAnimationFrame              ||
        window.webkitCancelRequestAnimationFrame    ||
        window.mozCancelRequestAnimationFrame       ||
        window.oCancelRequestAnimationFrame         ||
        window.msCancelRequestAnimationFrame        ||
        clearTimeout
} )();
```

Improving Animation

Now that we know how to organize the animation sequence, it is time to think about ways to improve the simple solution. Take into account that the current frame rate can be far below the desired 60 FPS and deal with the possible glitches, for example. The end of this section introduces the Animator class—the class for handling the more complex animation strategies.

Frame Rate and the Time Between Frames

Let's review the animation example from the start of the section once again. This version of the code (see Listing 4-24) doesn't take the frame rate into the account. The animation renders faster on faster devices.

Listing 4-24. *Basic Implementation of Animation*

```
var currentFrame = -1;
function animate(timestamp) {
    ctx.fillStyle = "white";
    ctx.fillRect(0, 0, canvas.width, canvas.height);
    currentFrame = ++currentFrame%5;
    spriteSheet.drawFrame(ctx, current, 10, 40);
    requestAnimationFrame(arguments.callee);
}
animate();
```

If you add more sprites and try it out on different devices, you will notice that the speed of the animation heavily depends on CPU and frame rate (just make sure to add enough sprites). The animation doesn't take time into account, and it will look inconsistent over different browsers and hardware.

If you build the graphics-intensive game with the animation approach shown in Listing 4-24, you soon notice that the speed of animation depends on the device hardware: it runs slower on less powerful devices that can't hold a steady 60 FPS or faster rate on newer multicode smartphones. This is not the behavior that a user expects from a game. The speed of the animation should stay constant and should not depend on the frame rate. Let's fix this.

We need to keep the frame on the screen for a certain fixed amount of time, like 50 milliseconds, before switching to the next one. This way, we make the game slightly more consistent. The second version of the code, shown in Listing 4-25, implements this idea.

Listing 4-25. *The Improved Version of the Code That Checks the Time Elapsed Between the Frames*

```
function animate(t) {
    var now = t || new Date().getTime();
    ctx.fillStyle = "white";
    ctx.fillRect(0, 0, canvas.width, canvas.height);

    var timeSinceFrameStart = now - currentFrameStart;
    if (timeSinceFrameStart > timePerFrame) {
        currentFrame = ++currentFrame%5;
        console.log(currentFrame);
        currentFrameStart = now;
    }

    spriteSheet.drawFrame(ctx, currentFrame, 10, 40);
    requestAnimationFrame(arguments.callee);
}
animate(0);
```

If you try to run the script, you'll notice the result is roughly the same for both the desktop browser and the Android browser.

> **NOTE:** The requestAnimationFrame() should pass the timestamp parameter to the listener function, but since we are using a trick described in a previous section, any browser that doesn't support the new timer will fall back to setTimeout(). In this case, we need to determine the current time ourselves (luckily, this is not a heavyweight operation). That's where that extra line comes from:
> ```
> var now = t || new Date().getTime();
> ```

This approach has its drawbacks, however. Look at Figures 4-10 and 4-11, which show the animation flow. We'll start with Figure 4-10, which shows the perfect case. In a perfect world, the timer hits exactly when we need it to hit—every 50 milliseconds—giving a very predictable interval between the frames.

Perfect case

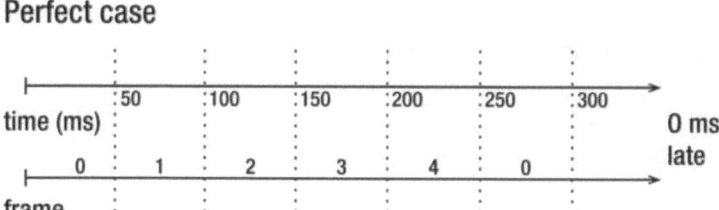

Figure 4-10. *In a perfect world, timers are never late and all animations finish in time.*

In the real world, it looks somewhat different. We planned to keep the frame on the screen for 50 milliseconds. A timer running at 60 FPS hits our function approximately every 16 milliseconds (60 frames per second = 1000 ÷ 60 milliseconds per frame). It means that timer will *not* hit at exactly 50 milliseconds after the start of the animation sequence. The first time the function is executed at 16 milliseconds, then at 32, 48, and 64. When will the frame change? Right after 64 milliseconds (instead of 50, as planned). Figure 4-11 illustrates this idea. Following the same logic, the next frame is rendered at the next hit, after 64 + 50 (the current frame time plus the time between frames), which is 128 milliseconds from the start. And so on, until the end of the animation.

Real World

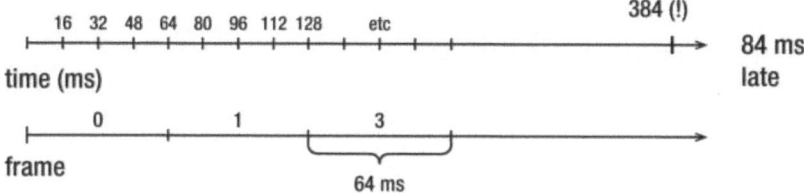

Figure 4-11. *In the real world, timers are inaccurate and animations are running late.*

If the animation has six frames, one may think that it will end in 300 milliseconds (50 milliseconds per frame), but since we are 14 milliseconds late each frame (spending 64 instead of 50), the animation will instead last 384 milliseconds.

The problem with this approach is that we calculate the time from the start of the last frame to decide if we need to render a new one. Since the timer is inaccurate, each frame introduces inaccuracy into the calculation. The more frames we have, the bigger the difference between what we expect and what we get.

Let's try a different model. Instead of using the time from the start of the frame, we will use the time from the start of the animation. Since we know the amount of time the animation lasts, we can determine what fraction of the time has passed. When 100 milliseconds have passed since the start of an animation that takes 300 milliseconds to complete, the completed fraction is 100 ÷ 300 = 1/3, or one-third. At this point, we should be drawing frame 2—no matter how much time has passed since the last frame.

This way we eliminate the increase of inaccuracy and keep the animation as close to the timing as probably possible. To understand the idea better, let's look at Figure 4-12, which illustrates our final approach. The middle axis is the fraction of time passed since the start of the animation. The first frame renders exactly the same way: it stays on the screen for as long as 64 milliseconds. The first frame must be changed when we reach one-sixth of the total time. One-sixth is approximately 0.167; it takes four iterations to reach this threshold. The third iteration starts at 0.16—very close to the next frame, but still not enough. The fourth iteration is at 64 milliseconds or 0.21; that's when the frame actually changes. The second frame should finish at 0.333, so it takes only three more iterations to reach it (from fractions 0.21 to 0.37). The second frame stays on the screen for 48 milliseconds—2 milliseconds less than it should. However, this number is much closer to the desired 50 milliseconds than it was in the first frame.

Better case

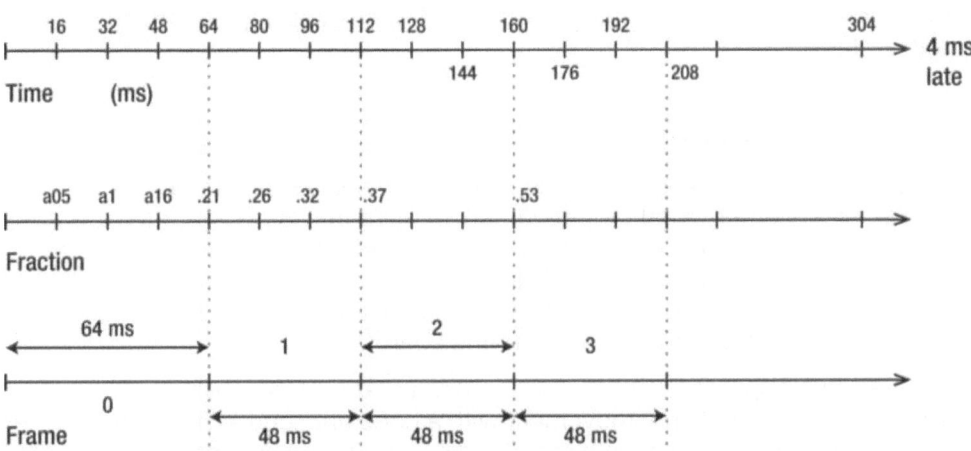

Figure 4-12. *A better approach. We are not relying on the time since the last frame, but rather on the time fraction passed since the start of the animation sequence.*

In this case, the overall animation finishes only 4 milliseconds late—much better than 84. Let's implement this approach and finally make a good version of the animation function. The code is shown in Listing 4-26.

Listing 4-26. *The Final Version of the Animation Function*

```
var numFrames = 6;
var duration = numFrames*50;
var animationStartTime = new Date().getTime();
function animate(t) {
    var now = t || new Date().getTime();

    // Make sure that we don't run out of bounds
    var timePassed = (now - animationStartTime)%duration;
    var fraction = timePassed/duration;
    var currentFrame = Math.floor(fraction*numFrames);

    ctx.fillStyle = "white";
    ctx.fillRect(0, 0, canvas.width, canvas.height);

    spriteSheet.drawFrame(ctx, currentFrame, 10, 40);
    requestAnimationFrame(arguments.callee);
}
animate(0);
```

What if we have multiple sprites on the screen, each with its own animation parameters—time per frame, number of frames, and so forth? Storing this data as we did in the example will soon become messy. Sounds like a good time to make another class.

Implementing Animator

Animation is not limited to changing frames. In fact, any change of shape, position, color, or any other visual property of an element that is performed in a smooth and progressive way is an animation. We just looked at the simplest case: each frame stays on the screen for the same fixed amount of time, changed by the next frame, and so on, until the animation reaches its end. Once it is there, the next loop starts from the first frame again.

If we apply the same approach to changing the *coordinates* of the object, we get a different type of animation—movement with a constant speed. There are a lot of examples of such movement in a real life: a car driving on an empty highway is one. Nevertheless, there are many more examples of movement happening with either acceleration or deceleration (an apple falling from a tree), changing its direction (a swinging pendulum), or following even more complex laws.

These more complex animation cases are often required in casual and arcade games. For example, when a character is swinging on a rope, his speed is not constant; it accelerates while going down and decelerates while going back up. There are many other examples of movement that involve acceleration and deceleration, so it is worth implementing these mechanics in the `Animator` class that we cover in this section.

`Animator` has two main use cases. The first is playing the animation with constant speed, as we just did in the previous section. In this case, `Animator` acts solely as a wrapper around the code that calculates the fraction of the animation loop. The second case is updating animation with acceleration and deceleration.

We will start with looking at the code that uses `Animator`, and then we'll discuss the implementation. Listing 4-27 shows an example that uses `Animator` for simple switching of frames. We create the `Animator` instance and set the parameters for the animation—for now, only the duration of the sequence. After that, `Animator` returns a fraction for the animation passed from the beginning.

Listing 4-27. *The Basic Usage of the Animator*

```
// Total number of frame in the animation
var numFrames = 5;

// Time per frame
var TIME_PER_FRAME = 50;

var animator = new Animator(numFrames*TIME_PER_FRAME);
// Start the animation sequence
animator.start();

function animate(t) {
    var deltaTime = getTimePassedFromLastFrame();
    var fraction = animator.update(deltaTime);

    // Given the fraction and the total number of frames, get the current frame
    var currentFrame = Math.floor(fraction*numFrames);

    // Draw the actual frame
    drawFrame(currentFrame);

    // Loop again
    requestAnimationFrame(arguments.callee);
}
animate(0);
```

`drawFrame()` and `getTimePassedSinceLastFrame()` are placeholder functions that are quite easy to implement. The main idea behind the `Animator` class is to decouple the code that calculates the current fraction of the animation from the code that updates the screen. If you need to animate the *position* of the object, rather than the frame, the changes to the code are minimal, as shown in the Listing 4-28.

Listing 4-28. *Updating the Position of the Object. The Object Moves from (0, 0) to (300, 300) in 500 Milliseconds.*

```
// Total time of the animation - half of a second
var animator = new Animator(500);

// Start the sequence
animator.start();

function animate(t) {
    var deltaTime = getTimePassedFromLastFrame();
    var fraction = animator.update(deltaTime);

    var pos = fraction*500;
    drawToken(pos);

    // Loop again
    requestAnimationFrame(arguments.callee);
}
animate(0);
```

The changed code is in bold. Simply a few lines changed, and we moved from the frame animation to the position animation! What if we want to add the acceleration and deceleration? This change should not affect the way we rerender our screen; the only thing that changes is the algorithm that calculates the new fraction. The actual code is hidden within the animator, so the client code has only two extra lines, as shown in Listing 4-29.

Listing 4-29. *Setting Acceleration and Deceleration*

```
var animator = new Animator(500);
animator.setAcceleration(0.5);
animator.setDeceleration(0.3);
//…
```

The rest of the code stays unchanged!

> **NOTE:** The overall solution is inspired by the Timing Framework
> (http://java.net/projects/timingframework), which was created to
> simplify the animation of user interface elements in Java desktop programs. You may
> want to check it out for inspiration.

Besides acceleration and deceleration, `Animator` should allow setting the number of loops, and toggling the direction of the animation. It should also have a way to notify the user about interesting animation events, and provide simple controls like pause, stop, reset, and so forth. It doesn't make much sense to write this class step by step, since the code doesn't really have anything to do with gamedev-specific algorithms. Let's just look through it to understand how it works.

The full code can be found with the other source code for this chapter in the js/Animator.js file. In this chapter, we just review the most interesting parts of it. At first, I wanted to put the whole thing here, but when I was finally happy with the set of nice small features, fool-proof checks, and workarounds for corner-cases, I realized that I needed six pages just to print the listing. So you better grab the source code and try it out. You've already seen several basic usages of Animator. Besides, the source code for this chapter contains a few completed examples.

Animator has several properties, each with a getter and setter. Debugging code that doesn't work well on an Android device might be a very tough experience (read Appendix A to learn how to deal with it) with hours and hours spent in console.log output. That's why it makes a lot of sense to write a foolproof code that checks that restrictions on the parameters are met. Animator checks every parameter before assigning it to the field (see Listing 4-30).

Listing 4-30. *An Example of Setting the Parameter of Animator—It Checks the Range*

```
_p.setDuration = function(duration) {
    // Do not allow to change the parameters
    //if animation is running
    this._throwIfStarted();

    if (duration < 1) {
        throw "Duration can't be < 1";
    }
    this._duration = duration;
};
```

No one will likely try to launch the Animator with an explicit duration of 0, but if the value for the duration is somehow generated, or received via network, it is technically possible to get to such a condition. The question is: what happens next? Possibly the best way to deal with it in the code is to throw an exception and notify the programmer about the problem. Allowing an unacceptable parameter to pass might do no harm, but more often than not, it will cause unpredictable bugs that are hard to track. This approach is called *fail fast*.

Notice the first line of the function. We don't want the Animator to be reconfigured on the go since it may cause errors as well. If the user is trying to set a property while the animator is running, he will get an exception.

Following the same approach, we define setter and getter for other properties too.

- `duration`: The duration of one loop of animation.

- `repeatCount`: The number of loops; can be an integer or -1 for infinite looping.

- `repeatBehavior`: Either `Animator.RepeatBehavior.LOOP` (default) or `Animator.RepeatBehavior.REVERSE`. Default behavior means that after reaching the end of the animation, Animator starts the next loop from 0 again and moves to 1; it is "playing forward" each time. REVERSE means that animator switches the direction on every loop. For example, even loops go from 0 to 1, while odd loops go from 1 to 0. This model is often referred to as "play forward, then backward."

- `acceleration`: The fraction of time to accelerate.

- `deceleration`: The fraction of time to decelerate.

The acceleration and deceleration values deserve a better explanation. When we use the approach that we've discussed, the fraction value moves from 0 to 1 with a constant rate. The rate is determined by the overall time of animation and it doesn't change during the loop. This approach is good for animating the frames of a sprite, but it has its limitations when it comes to physical processes.

Car movement that is animated in that manner looks unrealistic: the vehicle that was standing still a moment ago now moves 80 miles per hour! In the real world, it will first accelerate, then move with constant speed, and then decelerate. Or accelerate, continue to accelerate, accelerate a little more, and then hit a wall if it's a crash test.

To simulate events from the real world, we need to operate with acceleration and deceleration. The values that are used in `Animator` are fractions of the animating time— from 0 to 1. If we have an animation that runs for 1000 milliseconds, for example, and we set acceleration to 0.5 and deceleration to 0.3, we see the following behavior: the car starts at a speed of 0 (standing still); the speed increases during the first 500 milliseconds (acceleration of 0.5 means half of the time, or 500 milliseconds); then it runs at a constant speed from 500 to 700 milliseconds; and then it decelerates back to 0.

The heart of the animator is a function called `update()`. We keep track of the time spent between the scene repaints and pass that value to the update function. This function returns a fraction, and we know how to use it already. Let's peek into the code for this function. It is the most important part of Animator, shown in Listing 4-31.

Listing 4-31. *The Update Function: the Heart of the Animator*

```
/**
 * This function should be called by the external timer to update the state
 * of the animator.
 * @param deltaTime - time passed since the last update. 0 is valid value.
 */
_p.update = function(deltaTime) {

    // Will return undefined
    if (!this._started) {
        return;
    }

    // If the animator is paused we pass 0 as deltaTime // like nothing has changed
    if (!this._running) {
        deltaTime = 0;
    }

    this._timeSinceLoopStart += deltaTime;

    // If we exceeded the loop time, we must take care of what to do next:
    // adjust the direction of the animation, call hook functions etc.
    if (this._timeSinceLoopStart >= this._duration) {

        // Just in case, we skipped more than one loop,
        // determine how many loops did we miss
        var loopsSkipped = Math.floor(this._timeSinceLoopStart/this._duration);
        this._timeSinceLoopStart %= this._duration;

        // truncate to the number of loops skipped. Even if we skipped 5 loops,
        // but there was only 3 left, we don't want to fire extra listeners.
        if (this._repeatCount != Animator.INFINITE
                && loopsSkipped > this._repeatCount - this._loopsDone) {
            loopsSkipped = this._repeatCount - this._loopsDone;
        }

        // Call the hook for each of the skipped loops
        for (var i = 1; i <= loopsSkipped; i++) {
            this._loopsDone++;
            this._reverseLoop = this._repeatBehavior ==
                Animator.RepeatBehavior.REVERSE && this._loopsDone % 2 == 1;
            this._onLoopEnd(this._loopsDone);
        }

        // Check if we reached the end of the animation
        if (this._repeatCount != Animator.INFINITE
                && this._loopsDone == this._repeatCount) {
            this._onAnimationEnd();
            this.stop();
```

```
            return;
        }
    }

    // If this is the loop that is going backwards // reverse the fraction as well
    var fraction = this._timeSinceLoopStart/this._duration;
    if (this._reverseLoop)
        fraction = 1 - fraction;

    // Give away for preprocessing
    // (acceleration/deceleration, easing functions etc)
    fraction = this._timingEventPreprocessor(fraction);

    // Call update
    this._onUpdate(fraction, this._loopsDone);
    return fraction;
};
```

The first two lines check that the animation is running. If the animator is paused, then we just recalculate the last result by setting deltaTime to zero. For the paused animator, time has stopped. It might look like a waste of resources since the last value can be cached and returned straightaway, but you rarely need to pause a single animator. If the whole game is paused, usually you will not update at all. So it is OK to waste some CPU cycles here and save a couple of cycles for a regular case.

Next, the Animator looks at the amount of time that has passed since the start of the loop. If this number exceeds the duration of the loop, the Animator goes to the next loop (or ends the animation). Note that we pay special attention to the case of skipping more than one loop. This case is not as impossible as it looks. Remember, when the browser tab is inactive, the requestAnimationFrame() doesn't execute its callbacks. Also, the Android stock browser pauses timer activities when you hide the browser window. It is quite possible to get an update after several seconds of inactivity, and skip a few dozen animator loops. If the game is not paused for the time of inactivity, it must do its best to show the consistent state.

> **NOTE:** This side effect is very useful. It allows us to identify when a long time has passed since the last update and treat it as an "auto pause." If deltaTime in our animate function is greater than 1000 milliseconds, for example, it means that the user switched to a different tab or he had to hide the browser window in his Android device. For action games where the user can lose because of inactivity, it might be a good idea to enter a pause mode instead of allowing him to taste bitter defeat.

When we know the number of loops that we've skipped, we can check if the animation has finished working, check if the current loop is going forward or backwards, and perform other housekeeping tasks. After that, we are ready to calculate and return the fraction value.

Have you noticed these four functions: _onLoopEnd(), _onAnimationEnd(), _timingEventPreprocessor(), and _onUpdate() All of them, except for _timingEventPreprocessor(), do nothing. These are *hook functions* that are inserted to allow you to extend the functionality of Animator without breaking into its code. We will speak about extending Animator in a minute.

Now here's a slightly more advanced example useful for testing motion. The code in Listing 4-32 draws a bullet (a filled and stroked circle) and animates the movement from point (50, 50) to point (300, 50). You can play with the different animator parameters here to determine what works best for you.

Listing 4-32. *Moving a Bullet with the Animator, More Custom Properties*

```
animator = new Animator(1000);
animator.setRepeatCount(Animator.INFINITE);
animator.setRepeatBehavior(Animator.RepeatBehavior.REVERSE);
animator.setAcceleration(0.8);
animator.setDeceleration(0.15);
animator.start();
var lastUpdate = new Date();

var startX = 50;
var endX = 300;

function animate(t) {
    var now = t || new Date().getTime();
    var deltaTime = now - lastUpdate;
    lastUpdate = now;

    var fraction = animator.update(deltaTime);
    var x = (1 - fraction)*startX + fraction*endX;
```

```
    ctx.fillStyle = "white";
    ctx.fillRect(0, 0, canvas.width, canvas.height);

    drawBullet(x, 50, ctx);
    requestAnimationFrame(arguments.callee);
}
animate(0);

function drawBullet(x, y, ctx) {
    ctx.fillStyle = "darkred";
    ctx.strokeStyle = "black";
    ctx.lineWidth = 4;
    ctx.beginPath();
    ctx.arc(x, y, 15, 0, 2*Math.PI, false);
    ctx.fill();
    ctx.stroke();
}
```

See how easy it is! Take some time to play more with it. Try changing the size and create a pulsating effect. Or change the size and color at the same time. Draw and try to animate a cartoon-like bomb that's anxious to explode or a spaceship that shoots missiles. Use your imagination.

Extending Animator

Let's get back to the hook functions that I mentioned. They are empty in the default implementation of `Animator`, but their main use is to give you the chance to extend it with your own cool features.

Let's utilize our sprite once more and create an extended version of `Animator` that can automatically set certain properties of an object; for example, change the height of an arbitrary object from 30 to 150 pixels, hiding the formulas inside. Wouldn't it be nice to write some code like this? We will use the hook functions to plug the custom logic into the default `Animator` implementation without changing the code for the class.

When you design the API for other developers, it is usually a good idea to think about the ways to customize your logic. Each developer has his own vision of what kind of trickery your class should perform. Instead of trying to predict every possible use case, add a few extension points as `Animator` does, and allow other developers to implement their own ideas while leaving your class consistent. Listing 4-33 shows the code from a client's perspective.

Listing 4-33. *PropertyAnimator: The Class That Can Set Any Property of the Class Within the Animation*

```
animator - new PropertyAnimator(1000, [{
            "setter": setHeight,
            "start": 30,
            "end": 100
       }, {
            "setter": setTransparency,
            "start": 50,
            "end": 255
       }]);
animator.setEasingFunction(function(fraction) {
    return fraction*fraction*fraction;
});
animator.setRepeatCount(Animator.INFINITE);
animator.setRepeatBehavior(Animator.RepeatBehavior.REVERSE);
animator.setAcceleration(0.8);
animator.setDeceleration(0.15);
animator.start();
```

For each property that animator has to change, you pass the name of the setter function, the starting value of the property, and the end value. The rest of the work is left for a framework. (What? Aren't two classes enough to call it a framework?)

Let's make the task even harder and add a support for custom functions to alter the value of the `fraction` before passing it to the setter. The usual animation rules just aren't enough for this exceptional object and I demand it to grow with a quadratic, nay, cubic increase!

> **NOTE:** The function that does preprocessing of the fraction value is often called an *easing function*. You can achieve a lot of very exciting animation effects even with the simplest easing functions. The code that applies acceleration and deceleration is a type of easing function too. Have a look at jQuery UI Effects (`http://jqueryui.com/demos/effect/easing.html`) for some inspiration on using easing functions. The pictures are interactive, so click to see different animation effects.
>
> Unfortunately, there are not enough pages in this book to cover everything I'd like to. And since easing functions are a bit of a geeky topic, I leave it to your independent exploration.

Let's try to extend our `Animator` to match these requirements. Of course, we don't want to touch the base class and add more and more code there—it will eventually become too big and slow. That's why we create a new class called PropertyAnimator.

The constructor goes first, as usual. We need just two parameters and two extra properties to support the new features (see Listing 4-34).

Listing 4-34. *The Constructor of PropertyAnimator*

```
function PropertyAnimator(duration, props) {
    Animator.call(this, duration);

    this._props = props;
    this._easingFunction = null;
}
```

Next, we need the setter for the easing function. You should check if the parameter that is passed to your setter is valid. The restrictions for the easing function are (1) it should be a function that takes one parameter as the argument, and (2) it returns a number between 0 and 1. The only restriction that we can test in the setter is that the new value is a function, as shown in Listing 4-35.

Listing 4-35. *Setter for Easing Function*

```
_p.setEasingFunction = function(easingFunction) {
    this._throwIfStarted();
    if (typeof easingFunction != "function") {
        throw "easingFunction must be a function";
    }

    this._easingFunction = easingFunction;
};
```

Don't forget to call the _throwIfStarted() from the parent class—we must be sure that we don't break things in the middle of the animation loop.

That was the easy stuff. Now we need to do two things:

- Apply the new easing function on top of the acceleration/deceleration.

- When the fraction is calculated, pass it to the setters of objects.

A piece of cake with our hook functions (see Listing 4-36). The one for preprocessing values, _timingEventPreprocessor(), is the best place to apply custom easing. And the other one, called _onUpdate(), lets us perform custom actions before finishing the update.

Listing 4-36. *Providing Custom Hook Functions to Add New Features to the Animator*

```
// Called before returning the fraction value, redefining this function we
// set the custom easing behavior instead of default one
_p._timingEventPreprocessor = function(fraction) {
    fraction = Animator.prototype._timingEventPreprocessor.call(this, fraction);
    if (this._easingFunction) {
        fraction = this._easingFunction.call(this, fraction);
        // In case if easing function returns the value more than 1 or less
        // than 0, trim it to fit the allowed interval
        if (fraction > 1)
            fraction = 1;
        if (fraction < 0)
            fraction = 0;
    }
    return fraction;
};

// Called after the fraction is calculated, at the end of update function. This
// hook allows to perform few extra actions before returning the fraction value.
// In our case, we call setters of the object
_p._onUpdate = function(fraction) {

    this._props.forEach(function(item) {
        item.setter.call(this, (1 - fraction)*item.start + fraction*item.end);
    }, this);
};
```

That was easy enough. Now it is your turn. Think of a cool animation effect and try to implement it. Play with the different easing functions. What if you use `Math.sin` or `Math.cos`, or both? It might look cool, you know! There are two examples of using Animator available together with the other source code for this chapter. The first example, 06.animator.html, shows the simple movement between two points. The second example, 07.swinging_axe.html, shows how to combine the change of position, angle, and size of the sprite to get the effect of a swinging axe.

Congratulations! Now you know not only the basics of animation, but also some advanced features too. But animation is not yet a game; the user needs a way to interact with the game world. And that's exactly what we'll do in the next chapter!

Summary

In this chapter, we learned the basics of image loading and animation. We started with loading the image. We learned two ways of getting image data to the browser—from the file and from the data URI. We learned how to handle the possible loading errors that may happen in real life, like breaks in connection or the absence of the file on the server. We learned how to organize the sprite sheet and how to render the image on canvas.

The next step was to master the animation from the very simple change of frames on the screen to the more complex subjects, such as optimizing the "consistency" of animation, dealing with the acceleration and deceleration, and custom easing functions.

We briefly overviewed the class that supports most of the techniques described in this chapter—the Animator (the full source code comes with the other materials for this chapter). We learned how to use Animator to decouple the code that updates the state of the animation (the fraction) from the code that renders the new state on the screen, which changes the frame or the position of the element.

Knowing how to handle the animation is still not quite enough to make the completed game—but we're almost there! The essential part of the game is the interaction between the player and the game world. In the next chapter, we learn how to react to user input and let the player control the characters on the screen.

Chapter 5

Event Handling and User Input

This chapter is devoted to several important topics: handling user input, implementing custom event handlers, and building comfortable game controls. The main goal is to provide you with some solid knowledge of available input mechanisms and inspire you to create a seamless and natural interface between the player and the game world.

The patterns of input are quite different between mobile devices and desktop browsers. Touchscreens provide a more intuitive way to control the interface, not only in games but also in regular applications. It is more natural to touch a button with your finger, even if the button itself is just a rectangle of glowing pixels on the screen. It is more natural to point to the place on the game map where your new building should appear, or to send your troops into battle, drawing the direction of the attack straight on the battlefield.

Touch interfaces have made huge progress towards intuitive and user-friendly controls, since they provide a direct interaction between the user and the UI. Even a two-year-old kid can deal with touchscreens, whereas the mouse and keyboard require more skill.

The browser input API is built around events, event emitters, and event listeners. The idea of passing small messages (or "events") to the listeners whenever something important happens with the object is not unique to input handling. For example, the JavaScript class responsible for communication with the server may use events to notify other classes that a new message has just been posted to a certain chatroom. The chat UI that listens to events would then update itself and show the new message to the user. In this chapter, we will look into the details of this architecture and learn how to build our own implementation suitable for most game development purposes.

The knowledge of the basics allows us to build more-advanced input models like drag-and-drop, joystick emulation, and so on. We will learn how to implement "picking," the selection of a complex shape with a mouse or touch action.

In summary, our goal is to learn the following:

- How to build the custom event emitter
- The differences between the mouse and touch interfaces
- How to build the abstraction layer to hide the details of the underlying input system (mouse or touch) and use the lowest common denominator
- How to implement drag-and-drop
- How to find a suitable solution for pixel-perfect object picking
- How to simulate a joystick on a web page

Browser Events

Touch devices give the user a completely different interaction experience than regular desktop computers, which are controlled with the mouse and keyboard. It should come as no surprise that the browser events are different too. In this section, we will learn the strengths and weaknesses of both types of controls. Afterwards, we will try to build a common input handling interface to hide the details of the underlying system from the rest of the game.

Desktop Browser vs. Android Browser Input

Whereas a desktop user is limited to the mouse and keyboard (which act like "mediators" between the person and the computer), the mobile gamer can do much more: rotate and shake the device, touch and slide the screen, move along the streets of the real world in order to complete the game objectives, take photos, and stream video.

Of course, mobile controls are not perfect either: they fail fast when it comes to activities that are common to the keyboard. A good example is the input for e-mail; typing text is easier to accomplish with a physical keyboard. Let's review the pros and cons of mobile controls to know how to use its strengths and avoid its weaknesses.

Strengths of mobile controls:

- Mobile controls feel more natural. The user points with his finger rather than a mouse cursor; he feels more like he's interacting with the objects of the game world.

- Mobile devices support multitouch. It is like having 10 mouse pointers!

- Mobile devices have accelerometer and gyroscopes that allow the device itself to be used as a controller.

Weaknesses of mobile controls:

- The user doesn't have a decent keyboard. Even typing a name is somewhat problematic.

- A mouse has several different types of interaction (hovering, clicking, right-button clicking, scrolling wheel), whereas touch has only tap and slide.

- A mouse has more buttons; some models even have 20 or so. With keyboardless touch interface, you have only one "button"—tapping. The regular way to add at least one more way to interact with the UI is long press, but that's the most that you can count on. Everything else must be compensated either by using on-screen buttons, gestures, or multitouch interactions.

- Most Android devices do not expose multitouch capabilities to the browser (except for a few Motorola devices, but not quite as you expect them to).

- Android devices do not expose the gyroscope and accelerometer data to the browser.

As you see, two points from the first list are instantly negated by the lack of browser support. Unfortunately, that's exactly how the Android stock browser works, which is why the set of games that you can actually make playable are limited to games that you can control with the mouse having a single button.

The state of things is about to change. The most recently published Android version (4.0 at the time of writing) brings some light into the world of HTML5 games. The accelerometer and gyroscope are becoming available to game developers. As for now, you can still use it, but only in web pages packed as native Android applications. (Tools like Apache Cordova, which we'll look at in Chapter 15, expose this API to JavaScript.) It is not the best choice, but it is certainly better than nothing. Right now, we will work with the stock browser and try to find the lowest common denominator for mobile and desktop input models.

Using Events to Catch User Input

Let's start with the most basic question about our motivation: why do applications implement events and event handlers? Being an experienced developer, you probably know the answer already: the reason to build the event system is to decouple components from each other. For example, instead of directly notifying a particular object about the state change, the button component can instead *fire the event*. Any subscribed party would know that the button state has changed and would react accordingly. The button doesn't have to know about its subscribers' types: the only thing it knows is that a subscriber has the function that needs to be called when something important happens.

In terms of JavaScript and DOM, an event is the browser's reaction to the change of its state or external actions. You click the button, the event is fired. You swipe your finger, another event is fired. The page is loaded, and one more event is fired. To see how many different events there are, open Google Chrome, press F12 to go to the Developer Tools window, and open the Script tab (see Figure 5-1). In the right pane, expand Event Listener Breakpoints and examine events. As you can see, browser events are categorized by type: keyboard, mouse, control, and more. There are events for almost any occasion.

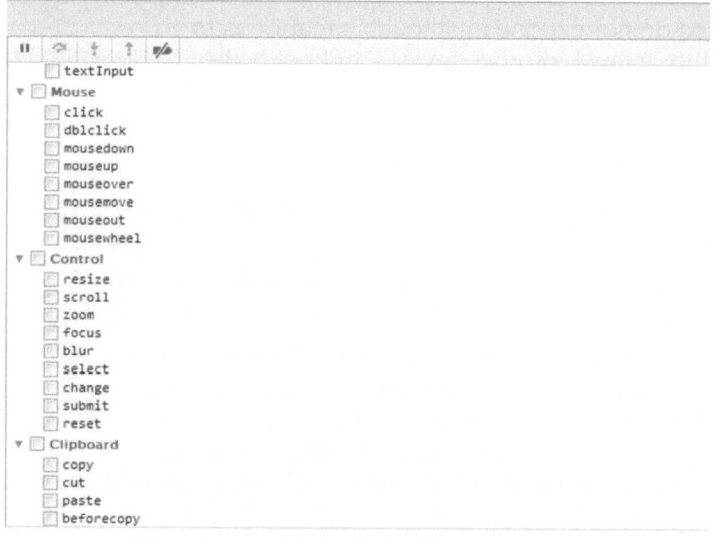

Figure 5-1. *A fragment of the long list of browser events*

Event Object

In terms of JavaScript, an event is a normal object that is passed to the registered event listener. The event object has fields and methods just like any other object that you use. The fields of the event object bring extra information about what happened. If the user taps the screen, for example, the fact that it has happened is not enough to perform a meaningful action. You also need to know the coordinates of the tap. Figure 5-2 shows the relation between the event emitter and listeners. The event object carries the details of the event— the coordinates of the tap or the state of the button—depending on the situation and the type of event.

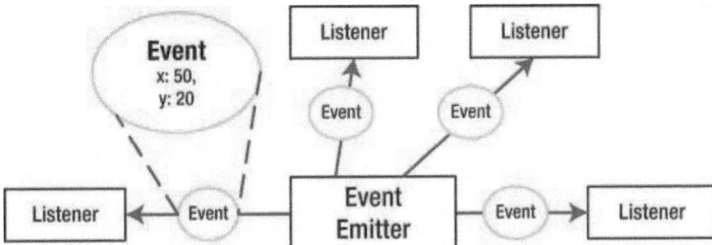

Figure 5-2. *The event mechanism explained. The emitter sends a special object called "event" to the registered listeners. That way, the listeners know that something important has happened.*

NOTE: For many years, cross-browser event handling was really painful. Browsers had completely different models for handling them. JavaScript books used to have a special chapter or two to explain how to build a road made from known hacks and workarounds to the happy cross-browser event handling. Now it looks a lot better. First of all, there are many high-quality libraries that have the enchanted event handling already implemented. In fact, every serious library that positions itself as the "essential toolset for the developer" has it.

In addition, browser vendors are finally standardizing their software.

Nevertheless, the problem is still far from being solved. Even in the simple application that we create in this chapter, we need to implement a small hack to support mobile Firefox (we will need Firefox in Chapter 9 to try out WebGL).

The event object also has several methods that are used to control the behavior of the event (more about this shortly).

Registering for Events: DOM Attributes

Now let's write some code and see how event handling works. Listing 5-1 shows one approach to event handling.

Listing 5-1. *Event Handling: The Old Way*

```
<!DOCTYPE html>
<html lang="en">
<head>
    <meta charset="utf-8" />
    <meta name="viewport"
          content="width=device-width, initial-scale=1.0, maximum-scale=1.0,
user-scalable=no, target-densitydpi=device-dpi"/>

    <style>
        html, body {
            overflow: hidden;
            width: 100%;
            height: 100%;
            margin:0;
            padding:0;
            border: 0;
        }

    </style>
    <script src="js/utils.js"></script>
    <script>
        function init() {
            console.log("document is loaded");
        }
    </script>
</head>
    <body onload="init()">
        <canvas id="mainCanvas" width="20px" height="20px"></canvas>
    </body>
</html>
```

Wait! But isn't that the code from Chapter 2 that we use all the time?!

Exactly! It is extremely hard to write a useful JavaScript program without dealing with events at all. I had to use them before introducing them. Shame on me.

Let's review the code. We added the onload parameter to the body tag of our HTML document. The value of the parameter is a fragment of JavaScript code. We could put several calls there, separated by a semicolon. However, we put just a single call to the init() function. This technique can (but really shouldn't) be used on most DOM elements. Find the event name, put "on" before it, and type the code that you need:

```
onclick="alert('bad style')";
```

Why is it considered bad style? Developers always try to structure and separate things. HTML is meant to be the language of markup. It describes the semantics and the structure of the document. HTML should not be responsible for anything else: dynamic behavior (we have JavaScript for it) or styles (we have CSS for it). By putting the event handling code straight into HTML, you violate this rule. The code will soon become messy and harder to maintain.

From a purely practical point of view, the main limitation of this approach is that you can't put multiple event handlers this way. The DOM tree can't have two attributes with the same name.

Registering for Events: Event Listeners

Now let's look at a better way of subscribing to events, shown in Listing 5-2.

Listing 5-2. *The Correct Way to Work with Events*

```
var el = document.getElementById("mainCanvas");
function onCanvasTouchStart(e) {
    console.log("touch");
}
el.addEventListener("touchstart", onCanvasTouchStart, false);
```

Each DOM element has the addEventsListener() function, which does exactly what it says. It registers the function passed as the second argument as the event listener of the DOM element. In Listing 5-2, el is the canvas element that will receive the new listener. The type of the event is touchstart, and the event listener is onCanvasTouchStart() – a function that prints a message to the console. Now onCanvasToushStart() will be called whenever there is a new touchstart event triggered on el.

Note that listener function has an argument too: it is called "e". This is one of the cases when a single-letter parameter name is just fine. Everybody knows that e means either exception or event, and 99 percent of the time, it is quite obvious what it is from the context.

After the event is processed by the listeners registered on an element, it is sent to the direct parent node. The event then triggers any listeners of the appropriate type registered on that node. Then the event goes to the parent of the parent and so on until it reaches the top of the hierarchy. This behavior is called *bubbling*—an event like air bubbles in a glass of water, which move from the bottom to the surface. But instead of water layers, the event moves through the levels of DOM hierarchy: from one level to another until it reaches the top. Then the browser performs a "default action" for that event.

The default action is what the browser normally does with the input; for example, the default action when clicking the <a> tag is navigating to a new page. The default action for the Tab key is moving focus to the next focusable element. For regular web pages, these actions are what the user wants; however, not for a web game. A tap on the canvas highlights the whole element; for example, it marks it with a border and plays a "click" sound with a rather noticeable and annoying delay. This is not what the user wants when he plays Four Balls.

A browser has two functions to control the normal event flow:

  - stopPropagation() stops the event from going to the next levels of DOM hierarchy

  - preventDefault() makes sure that browser *will not* do the default action. It is simply saying to ignore the event.

The code that calls both of these functions looks like the following snippet:

```
a.addEventListener("click", function(e) {
    e.stopPropagation();
    e.preventDefault();
}, false);
```

If a variable is an <a> DOM node, then the browser will never navigate that link because of preventDefault(). The parent of <a> will not receive the click events that happened on <a> because of stopPropagation(). We will use this technique in our API to restrict the normal flow of events that are intended solely for the main canvas element.

Getting More from Events

Many interesting things are hidden inside this little "e" that is passed as the parameter to every event listener. For the touchstart event, "e" has the array called targetTouches. In turn, every element of targetTouches has parameters called pageX and pageY, the coordinates of the touch relative to the top-left corner of the page.

Let's use this knowledge now and create a simple app that draws a bullet on a canvas when the user taps it (see Listing 5-3). This is a simple but quite useful exercise; you instantly see if event handling works and what you can expect from it: does the device in your hands support multitouch, and if so, how many touches can it process simultaneously?

Listing 5-3. *Detecting Touches on DOM Element*

```
<!DOCTYPE html>
<html lang="en">
<head>
    <meta charset="utf-8" />
    <meta name="viewport"
          content="width=device-width, initial-scale=1.0, maximum-scale=1.0,
user-scalable=no, target-densitydpi=device-dpi"/>

    <style>
        html, body {
            overflow: hidden;
            width: 100%;
            height: 100%;
            margin:0;
            padding:0;
            border: 0;
        }
    </style>
    <script>
        function init() {
            var canvas = initFullScreenCanvas("mainCanvas");
            var ctx = canvas.getContext("2d");
            canvas.addEventListener("touchstart", function(e) {
                for (var i = 0; i < e.targetTouches.length; i++) {
                    drawBullet(
                        e.targetTouches[i].pageX,
                        e.targetTouches[i].pageY, ctx);
                }
                e.stopPropagation();
                e.preventDefault();
            }, false);
        }

        function drawBullet(x, y, ctx) {
            ctx.fillStyle = "darkred";
            ctx.strokeStyle = "black";
            ctx.lineWidth = 4;
            ctx.beginPath();
            ctx.arc(x, y, 15, 0, 2*Math.PI, false);
            ctx.fill();
            ctx.stroke();
        }

        function initFullScreenCanvas(canvasId) { /* omitted */ }

        function resizeCanvas(canvas) { /* omitted */ }
```

```
      </script>
</head>
<body onload="init()">
<canvas id="mainCanvas" width="100" height="100"></canvas>
</body>
</html>
```

The most important part of the code is bolded. For each detected touch, we draw a small circle right under the user's finger. If you tap the canvas with two fingers and see only one circle, it means that this browser doesn't support multitouch. The code for this simple touch test is available with the source code for this chapter in a file 01.touch_test.html.

> **NOTE:** The targetTouches is not a real array, even though it looks like one. It doesn't have the array methods like forEach or splice. Objects like these sometimes are called *pseudo arrays*.

The code in Listing 5-3 only works for touch-enabled devices. The demo will not work on your regular desktop since desktop browsers don't fire touch events; they have click events instead. Besides, you have only one mouse pointer; that's why you will not have the targetTouches array of coordinates in an event, just one (x, y) pair.

Handling the Differences Between Touch and Mouse Interfaces

Usually we want the code to run not only on Android touch devices, but also on regular desktop systems. Aside from the obvious motivation to make your game available to more people, programmers tend to use desktop browsers for most of their development and debugging. That's why it is important to handle input correctly in both types of platforms.

Let's update the code a little and make it work in Google Chrome too. First of all, we need to detect whether we're dealing with a regular or touch-enabled device. The trick is to check whether the browser knows about touch events (see Listing 5-4). If it does, then chances are that you are on a touch device.

Listing 5-4. *Checking the Type of Device: Touch Device vs. Regular Browser*

```
/**
 * Checks if we're working with the touchscreen or with the
 * regular desktop browser. Used to determine, what kind of
 * events should we use:
 * mouse events or touch events.
```

```
*/
function isTouchDevice() {
    return ('ontouchstart' in document.documentElement);
}
```

The important line is bolded. We are checking whether the ontouchstart listener is available in the current context. If it is available, the document.document-Element will have the ontouchstart among its keys. That means that the browser is aware of touch events and supports them. Add the code for this function to the utils.js file in your project because we will often need it. The upcoming listings that rely on this function assume that it is available.

> **NOTE:** There are many other ways to test for the touchscreen support. Have a look at
> http://modernizr.github.com/Modernizr/touch.html to get an idea of
> other approaches. This page is the part of Modernizr project, a lightweight feature-
> detection library. If you need to test for more browser features (like WebSockets or
> XHR2 support), consider using this little gem: http://modernizr.com.

Now let's modify the code so that clicking the canvas in Google Chrome works too (see Listing 5-5). The full example, available with the source code for this chapter, is a file called 02.touch_and_mouse.html.

Listing 5-5. *Adding Support for a Desktop Browser*

```
function init() {
    var canvas = initFullScreenCanvas("mainCanvas");
    var ctx = canvas.getContext("2d");

    if (isTouchDevice()) {
        canvas.addEventListener("touchstart", function(e) {
            for (var i = 0; i < e.targetTouches.length; i++) {
                drawBullet(e.targetTouches[i].pageX, e.targetTouches[i].pageY,
ctx);
            }
            e.stopPropagation();
            e.preventDefault();
        }, false);
    } else {
        canvas.addEventListener("mousedown", function(e) {
            drawBullet(e.pageX, e.pageY, ctx);

            e.stopPropagation();
            e.preventDefault();
        }, false);
    }
}
```

Mouse events have only one pair of coordinates associated with each event. That's why they don't have a special object like targetTouches. The coordinates are stored straight in the event object.

pageX and pageY are the coordinates of the event relative to the page, and not the canvas. This approach works well as long as canvas is in the top-left corner of the page (which it is in most of cases). If you add other elements (debug divs, FPS counters, or a simple margin), our demo will break. We need to do a little bit of extra work to calculate the correct canvas coordinates within the page. Listing 5-6 shows the code that does that.

Listing 5-6. *Getting the Coordinates of Event When Canvas Is Not in the Top-Left Corner of a Screen*

```
if (isTouchDevice()) {
    canvas.addEventListener("touchstart", function(e) {
        for (var i = 0; i < e.targetTouches.length; i++) {
            drawBullet(e.targetTouches[i].pageX - canvas.offsetLeft,
                    e.targetTouches[i].pageY - canvas.offsetTop, ctx);
        }
        e.stopPropagation();
        e.preventDefault();
    }, false);
} else {
    canvas.addEventListener("mousedown", function(e) {
        drawBullet(e.pageX - canvas.offsetLeft, e.pageY - canvas.offsetTop, ctx);
        e.stopPropagation();
        e.preventDefault();
    }, false);
}
```

The new code takes into account the position of canvas on the page: offsetLeft and offsetTop are the parameters that hold the position of the element relative to the page. Now the demo will run fine ... on the stock browser. On mobile Firefox, it doesn't work. Why? Because Firefox doesn't have pageX and pageY properties. It has a completely useless pair of clientX and clientY coordinates that hold the position of an event relative to the current browser viewport. If a page is scrolled, the demo is broken once again. That's where browser-specific hacks come into play. The final version of our demo looks like Listing 5-7. To demonstrate that scrolling doesn't break the coordinates, I had to switch back from the game page skeleton used in Chapter 3 (see Listing 3-3) to the plain HTML5 skeleton that doesn't restrict scrolls and doesn't force the fullscreen canvas (like in Listing 3-1).

Listing 5-7. *The Final Version of the Input Demo*

```
<!DOCTYPE html>
<html lang="en">
<head>
    <meta charset="utf-8" />
    <script src="js/utils.js"></script>
    <script>
        function init() {
            var canvas = document.getElementById("mainCanvas");
            var ctx = canvas.getContext("2d");

            // Fill canvas, to see where it is
            ctx.fillStyle = "lightgray";
            ctx.fillRect(0, 0, canvas.width, canvas.height);

            if (isTouchDevice()) {
                canvas.addEventListener("touchstart", function(e) {
                    for (var i = 0; i < e.targetTouches.length; i++) {
                        var coords = getInputCoordinates(e.targetTouches[i],
                                            canvas);
                        drawBullet(coords.x, coords.y, ctx);
                    }
                    e.stopPropagation();
                    e.preventDefault();
                }, false);
            } else {
                canvas.addEventListener("mousedown", function(e) {
                    var coords = getInputCoordinates(e, canvas);
                    drawBullet(coords.x, coords.y, ctx);
                    e.stopPropagation();
                    e.preventDefault();
                }, false);
            }
        }

        function getInputCoordinates(e, element) {
          return {
             x: (e.pageX || e.clientX + document.body.scrollLeft) -
                  element.offsetLeft,
             y: (e.pageY || e.clientY + document.body.scrollTop) -
                  element.offsetTop
          }
        }

        function drawBullet(x, y, ctx) {
            ctx.fillStyle = "darkred";
            ctx.strokeStyle = "black";
            ctx.lineWidth = 4;
            ctx.beginPath();
```

```
                    ctx.arc(x, y, 15, 0, 2*Math.PI, false);
                    ctx.fill();
                    ctx.stroke();
                }

        </script>
</head>
<body onload="init()">
        <div style="height: 250px"></div>
        <canvas id="mainCanvas" width="400" height="400"></canvas>
</body>
</html>
```

As you see, we have created a special function to extract the click coordinates from the event object. In the case of the desktop browser, it uses the event itself, while for a touch interface, it uses one of the `targetTouches`. The code for this example is included in the `03.click_coordinates.html` file with the sources for this chapter.

> **NOTE:** In Chapter 3, I mentioned that the most typical HTML page structure for a game is a canvas that takes all available space. Cases when you have the scrollbars in such page are quite rare, especially on mobile devices. It is good, however, to have a more "bulletproof" code that handles these cases too, especially when it is a matter of adding only couple of lines.

The code in the last listing doesn't look all that nice: there are a lot of boilerplate lines there that should be hidden under a nice API. Besides that, touch and mouse events look very similar, but they are handled in a different manner. For example, `touchstart` works exactly like `mousedown`. Semantically they both mean the "start of interaction." Other events are related also: `mouseup` works like `touchend` since they both mean "end of interaction;" `mousemove` is like `touchmove`, they both represent "dragging." If we could get rid of differences and make the API with just three events—up, down, and move—then the event handling code would shrink to just a few lines, such as:

```
input.on("down", function(e) {
    drawBullet(e.x, e.y, ctx);
});
```

To do that, we need to introduce our own events, different from what the browser proposes by default.

Custom Events

Applications with complex internal logic usually need separate mechanisms for handling their custom events. Imagine a typical casual game: the character jumps around the level, avoiding enemies and collecting coins to gain more points. The types of events that such a system may use are coin_collected, level_completed, or level_restarted. These events are not valuable outside of the game engine; they have nothing to do with mousemove or touchstart events. They do not have to be propagated to the other DOM components or processed by the browser in any other way.

> **NOTE:** There are two different concepts that share the name Custom Events. The first concept is the CustomEvent, the interface described in the DOM Level 3 Events Specification (www.w3.org/TR/DOM-Level-3-Events/#interface-CustomEvent). It is used to add new types of events to the DOM. The other meaning of this term is "completely DOM-independent event API." In this section, we are speaking about the second type of events, even though our goal can be reached with both approaches. From a purely architectural point of view, it would be slightly better to use the CustomEvent, but for the sake of explaining the important concept, I chose the second path.

Let's look at the code in Listing 5-8, which shows how we might use custom events in the game (the functionality that supports it is implemented in the next section of this chapter). The levelManager is some object that loads the level and tracks when it is completed by the player. It has two custom events: loaded and finished. The client API makes use of these events to perform the special actions of placing the coins throughout the level and reporting level progress. An object can have many listeners for the single type of event. In Listing 5-8, there are two listeners for loaded event. One places the coins and the other prints some debug output to the console.

Listing 5-8. *An Example of Custom Events*

```javascript
// "on" is the alias for "addEventListener"
// it reads more natural
levelManager.on("loaded ",  function(e) {
    var coins = getCoins(e.levelNumber);
    placeCoins(coins);
});

levelManager.on("loaded",  function(e) {
    console.log("level " + e.levelName + " started");
```

```
});

levelManager.on("finished", function(e) {
    var numCoins = getCoins(e.coinsCollected);
    console.log("You have found " + numCoins + " coins");
});
```

Obviously, your custom events don't have to represent user input or relate somehow to the browser events. Now let's write the code to support this functionality.

Custom Event Listeners and Emitters

Building a custom event handling system is usually not a hard task. There are certain architectural decisions that you need to make before doing it, but even in the most complex cases, the task is not too challenging. In this section, we will build such a system. Let's start with `EventEmitter`, the base class for every entity that can fire events.

EventEmitter: The Base Class

Start by thinking about the architecture of the future solution. The design of the event system determines how natural it looks in your code, how easy it is to write, and the number of extra features it has. The following are few decisions to make:

- Implement event bubbling or use the "plain" subscription model?

- Should listeners have only one argument (the event object) or allow any number of arguments?

- Should memory leaks protection be implemented or not?

Let's examine this list. The first point makes sense when your game components form complex hierarchies (like the DOM tree of the browser) and events from the lower levels of hierarchy must "bubble" up to the higher levels.

The second point is more a matter of personal preference: do you want to allow event listeners like `onNewCoin(x, y, coinType)` instead of `onNewCoin(newCoinEvent)`? The multiarguments approach looks better, since it specifies the parameter names right in the declaration of the listener, but it has its own drawbacks. If the listener is only interested in the last argument, it still needs to declare all of them. Besides, you add a little extra bit of coupling; the components that emit events must know the number and the order of arguments that listeners expect. This author's personal preference is to use the single-argument approach.

The last point is inspired by Node.js (we will look at this wonderful tool in Chapter 10). The `EventEmitter` implementation of Node has a listener threshold, or the maximum number of listeners that is considered "safe." If the number is exceeded, it looks like a memory leak, and `EventEmitter` throws an exception. Sometimes this technique is useful for detecting programming errors; more than ten listeners is likely a cleanup problem that leads to memory leaks.

The code in Listing 5-9 shows how to implement the basic `EventEmitter` class without any of the extra features. If your project requires more functionality, you can always add it on top of this class. `EventEmitter` holds the array of listeners for each event type and calls them in order whenever the emit is fired. The class allows you to add listeners and remove a single listener, all listeners for a given event type, or all listeners. The code is quite straightforward and well-commented. I'm sure you'll find your way through it.

Listing 5-9. *EventEmitter, the Base Class for the Event-Firing Objects*

```
/**
 * EventEmitter is the class responsible
 * for holding the registry of listeners
 * and notifying them about the new events
 */
function EventEmitter() {
    this._listeners = {};
}

_p = EventEmitter.prototype;

/**
 * Registers the function as the listener to receive the notifications
 * about the events of the given type
 * @param type the type of the event
 * @param listener the function to add to the list of listeners
 */
_p.addListener = _p.on = function(type, listener) {
    if (typeof listener !== "function")
        throw "Listener must be a function";

    if (!this._listeners[type]) {
        this._listeners[type] = [];
    }

    this._listeners[type].push(listener)
};

/**
```

```
 * Unsubscribes the given listerer from the given event type
 * @param type the type of the event
 * @param listener the function to remove from the list of listeners
 */
_p.removeListener = function(type, listener) {
    if (typeof listener !== "function")
        throw "Listener must be a function";

    if (!this._listeners[type])
        return;

    var position = this._listeners[type].indexOf(listener);
    if (position != -1)
        this._listeners[type].splice(position, 1);
};

/**
 * Remove all listeners registered for the given type of the
 * event. If type is omitted, removes all listeners from the object.
 * @param type the type of the event (optional)
 */
_p.removeAllListeners = function(type) {
    if (type) {
        this._listeners[type] = [];
    } else {
        this._listeners = {};
    }
};

/**
 * Notifies all listeners subscribed to the given event type,
 * passing the event object as the parameter
 * @param type the type of the event
 * @param event the event object
 */
_p.emit = function(type, event) {
    if (!(this._listeners[type] && this._listeners[type].length)) {
        return;
    }

    for (var i = 0; i < this._listeners[type].length; i++) {
        this._listeners[type][i].apply(this, event);
    }
};
```

When EventEmitter is ready, look at the sample emitter built on top of it in Listing 5-10.

Listing 5-10. *Implementing the Concrete EventEmitter*

```
function LevelManager() {
    EventEmitter.call(this);
}

extend(LevelManager, EventEmitter);
_p = LevelManager.prototype;

_p.loadLevel = function(levelNumber) {
    // do the level loading
    this.emit("loaded",
        {levelNumber: levelNumber, levelName: levelNames[levelNumber]});
};
```

As you see, it is now a matter of few lines of code to fire the custom events in the application.

> **NOTE:** This is the first time in the book that we used inheritance. If you don't feel comfortable with this code, refer to the "Object-Oriented Programming" section in Chapter 1. The extend function should already be in your utils.js file. If it is not, you can find the copy of utils.js along with other sources for this chapter.

Events vs. Callbacks

In the Chapter 4, we used a slightly different approach to decoupling the components of API and sending notifications. Remember the code that loaded images with the ImageManager class?

```
this._imageManager.load({
    "house-1": "img/house-1.png",
    "house-2": "img/house-2.png",
}, function() {
    /* loading done, continue */
});
```

Instead of sending the events, ImageManager accepted a special parameter: the callback function used to notify the external API that images are loaded. Is there any difference between these two approaches? Both of them rely on a particular function (listener or callback) to notify the world about an important event, and both approaches serve the same goal: decoupling emitter from the listeners. They look quite similar.

In fact, ImageManager can be easily rewritten to also use the EventEmitter that we just created. The client code would then look like Listing 5-11.

Listing 5-11. *ImageManager, the Version That Uses Events Instead of Callback*

```
var onDone = function(event) {
    // do something when loading is done;
};

imageManager.addEventListener("done", onDone)
imageManager.addImage("star", "img/star.png");
imageManager.loadImages();
```

The differences between these approaches are the cases when they are used. The goal of callback is to deliver the result of a single asynchronous function call to the program. The callback is usually associated with the single call of the method and it is not retained after the call has finished the execution. The event listener is more permanent: it is associated with the object and not with the function call.

You can mix both approaches in a single class, of course. The ImageManager could fire events whenever a new image is added to the list, for example. At the same time, it could pass the callback along with every image. This way, the client can track the loading of a *specific* image (with the help of callback) and the *overall* loading progress (with the help of listener), as shown in Listing 5-12.

Listing 5-12. *The Example of ImageManager That Uses Both Callbacks and Events*

```
var onImageAdded = function(event) {
    console.log(event.imageName + " added to the list ");
};

imageManager.addEventListener("imageAdded", onImageAdded);

// Need to track this image, once it is loaded we will show it
imageManager.addImage("main", "img/main.png", function(ok) {
    if (ok) {
        // The main screen is loaded, display it
    }
});

// No callback here, this image is not that important
imageManager.addImage("star", "img/star.png");
imageManager.loadImages();
```

Now we have enough instruments to implement the event handling API that will hide the differences between touch and mouse-based input and allow us to focus on writing the game, rather than dealing with the specifics of the events.

Custom Events

The idea behind the custom event API is to provide the "least common denominator" interface to touch and mouse events. There are three pairs of events that work almost the same way: mousedown-touchstart, mousemove-touchmove, and mouseup-touchend. The word "almost" is what makes the developer's life harder. Let's start by analyzing events once again to discover what they have in common and what the differences are.

The first major difference is the targetTouches object. It is only available for touchscreens, but since Android browsers do not support multitouch widely yet, this difference can safely be ignored. Multitouch support is not relevant now, but later it is easy to deal with.

The following are three event groups:

- **down events**: Represented by the mousedown and touchdown events. They mark the start of an interaction: the user touched the screen or pressed the mouse button. When the user is in this state, he can perform one of two actions: start to move the controller (a mouse or a finger) or release it instantly with a "click."

- **up events:** Represented by mouseup and touchend. They work the same way, except that touchend doesn't provide the coordinates of the place where the user released her finger. There is no touch anymore; it means that there can be *no* coordinates (mice don't have this problem, since the cursor remains on the screen and the coordinates of mouseup make perfect sense). To simulate the same behavior as for the touch events, we have to track the last known coordinates of the touch, and provide them when the user releases his finger.

- **move events:** Represented by mousemove and touchmove. The most important difference is that a mouse can have two types of movement: *hovering* (moving the cursor while the button is *not* pressed) and *dragging* (moving the cursor when the button *is* pressed). We have to ignore hovering since there's no analog for touchscreens. We also have to track the state of the button in order to distinguish between hover and drag when using a mouse.

move events deserve a little bit more attention. down and up events are relatively simple: they are fully described by a pair of coordinates: x and y, where the event happened. Movement has a slightly more complex nature. For the client

API that deals with movement, it is usually not enough to know the current position of the cursor. You also need to know the *delta*, the change in position since the last movement event. That way, the client API can calculate the velocity of the movement, for example. Our goal is to build a convenient and easy-to-use API so that basic information like deltas is available out of the box. Figure 5-3 shows the delta value.

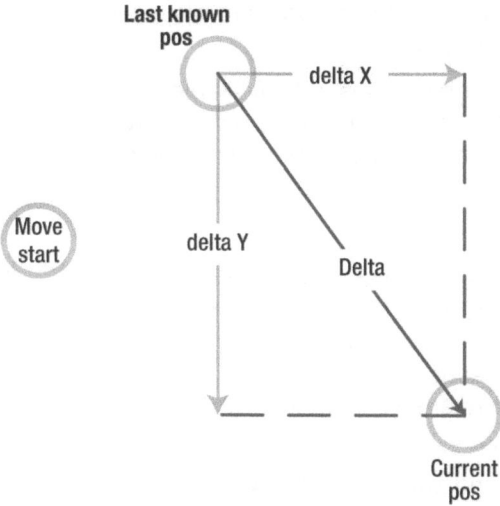

Figure 5-3. *Delta value: The actual "amount" of movement. This parameter is often used in game development.*

The other important issue is that the user can accidentally start "movement" when he doesn't really want to. Without special handling, every microscopic movement is treated as a "drag" operation, and not a "click" operation. Our anatomy works in the way that our fingers are trembling a little bit all the time, even if you can't see it, but highly sensitive touch interfaces often detect movement instead of a click. It is rather hard and annoying to use such an interface, especially when both of these actions have different meanings in the game.

In practice, the problem of micromovements is solved by assigning a special *movement threshold*, a radius around the place where you initially tapped the screen. All movements inside this area are considered to be unintentional and are ignored, as shown in Figure 5-4. The interaction starts at point A, and a couple of milliseconds later, the API detects the movement to B. Since B is within the threshold, it is considered to be an unintentional micromovement and is ignored. Next, the interaction is detected at point C. Since C is beyond the threshold, it means that the user is actually trying to move the pointer.

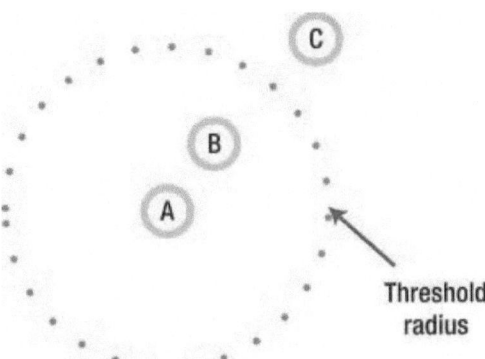

Figure 5-4. *The illustration of threshold. Since B is within the threshold, it is considered to be an unintentional micromovement.*

Now we are ready for the implementation of our API. We will make two classes: MouseInputHandler and TouchInputHandler. Both of them will act as event emitters and event listeners at the same time. They will listen to the raw DOM events of the canvas object and transform these events to our custom representation: down, up, and move events.

Figure 5-5 illustrates this concept. TouchInputHandler and MouseInputHandler act like middlemen who listen to browser events and emit platform-independent custom events. Depending on the system, these events are created either from mouse events or from touch events. The InputHandler is a convenience class: it is created at runtime, and it is either the TouchInputHandler or MouseInputHandler.

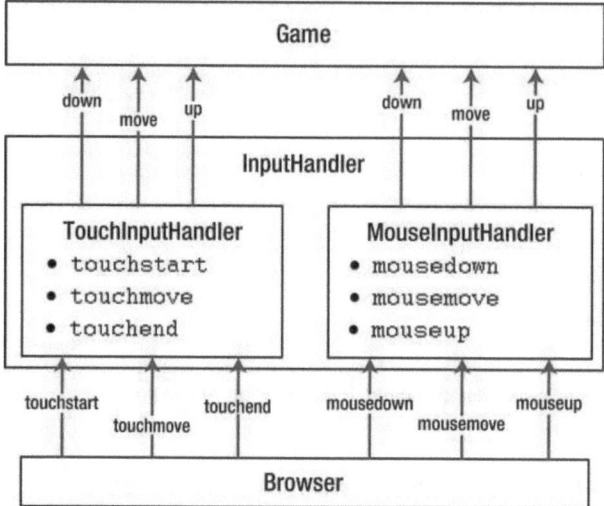

Figure 5-5. *The architecture of event handling API:*

These two classes have a lot of common code since browser event models are not that different. It makes sense to extract a common parent out of them and put the basic handling code there. MouseInputHandler and TouchInputHandler can then implement only changes. The base class is called InputHandlerBase.

Implementing InputHandlerBase

Let's write some more code now. The structure of the InputHandlerBase is relatively simple. It extends EventEmitter. It fires custom events up, down, and move—providing the lighter interface to the browser's event system.

Take a look at the code for the constructor in Listing 5-13.

Listing 5-13. *Constructor for InputHandlerBase*

```
function InputHandlerBase(element) {
    EventEmitter.call(this);

    // The DOM element
    this._element = element;

    // Last known "move" coordinates, to calculate deltas
    this._lastMoveCoordinates = null;

    // flag that indicates that we passed the "movement" threshold
    // if true, then this is the real movement, not trembling
```

```
    this._moving = false;

    // the value of the move threshold in pixels as explained on Figure 5-4
    this._moveThreshold = 10;

    // If the listener should call stopPropagation/preventDefault on
    // DOM events
    this._stopDomEvents = true;
}
extend
(InputHandlerBase, EventEmitter);
_p = InputHandlerBase.prototype;
```

As you see, there are only five fields in this class. Two of them, _moveThreshold and _stopDomEvents, are "settings" that can be changed during the lifecycle of the object by getters and setters. The code for simple getters and setters is omitted from the listing.

The next function input event. This version completely ignores multitouch; it works only with the first element of the targetTouches array (see Listing 5-14).

Listing 5-14. *The _getInputCoordinates Function Retrieves the Coordinates from the Input Event, Ignoring Multitouch*

```
_p._getInputCoordinates = function(e) {
    var element = this._element;
    var coords = e.targetTouches ? e.targetTouches[0] : e;

    return {
        x: (coords.pageX || coords.clientX + document.body.scrollLeft) -
            element.offsetLeft,
        y: (coords.pageY || coords.clientY + document.body.scrollTop) -
            element.offsetTop
    };
};
```

The core functions of InputHandlerBase are functions that transform DOM events into the more usable form: _onUpDomEvent(), _onDownDomEvent(), and _onMoveDomEvent(). TouchInputHandler and MouseInputHandler will use them as the base and add small tweaks on top.

We start with the _onDownDomEvent() function shown in Listing 5-15. It acts like a listener for the normal DOM event: touchstart or mousedown. It transforms the browser event to the custom down event and instantly fires it. It also saves the coordinates of the start of interaction. We need them later to check whether the user passed the move threshold.

Listing 5-15. _onDownDomEvent: Transforming "Start of Interaction" Events to the Custom Form

```
/**
 * Listens to the "down" DOM events: mousedown and touchstart.
 * @param e DOM Event
 */
_p._onDownDomEvent = function(e) {
    // We must save this coordinates to support the moveThreshold - this
    // may be the starting point of the movement, we can't simply
    var coords = this._lastMoveCoordinates = this._getInputCoordinates(e);

    // Emit "down" event - all coordinates together with the
    // original DOM event are passed to listeners
    this.emit("down", {x: coords.x, y: coords.y, domEvent: e});

    // Usually we want to stop original the DOM events from further browser processing.
    this._stopEventIfRequired(e);
};
```

Next comes the _onUpDomeEvent() function shown in Listing 5-16. It is slightly
more complex. As the name implies, it works with the movement events:
touchmove and mousemove. _onUpDomeEvent's main task is to keep track of deltas
and threshold. If the distance from the down event to the current point is more
than threshold, then this is not a micromovement. Once the break of threshold
occurs, we don't need to check against it anymore. The _moving flag is reset
once movement is over.

Listing 5-16. _onMoveDomEvent Keeps Track of Movement and Checks If Threshold Is Breached

```
/**
 * Listens to the "move" DOM events: mousemove and touchmove. This function
 * is slightly more complex. It keeps track of the distance travelled since the last
 * "move" action, besides it ignores the movement and swallows the event if we are
 * still within the _moveThreshold
 * @param e DOM event
 */
_p._onMoveDomEvent = function(e) {
    var coords = this._getInputCoordinates(e);

    // Calculate deltas
    var deltaX = coords.x - this._lastMoveCoordinates.x;
    var deltaY = coords.y - this._lastMoveCoordinates.y;

    // Check threshold, if the distance from the initial tap to the current position
    // is more than the threshold value - qualify it as a real movement
    if (!this._moving && Math.sqrt(deltaX*deltaX + deltaY*deltaY) >
                this._moveThreshold) {
        this._moving = true;
    }
```

```
    // If the current interaction is "moving" (we crossed the threshold already)
    // then emit the event, otherwise, just ignore the interaction.
    if (this._moving) {
        this.emit("move", {x: coords.x, y: coords.y, deltaX: deltaX, deltaY:
            deltaY, domEvent: e}));
        this._lastMoveCoordinates = coords;
    }

    this._stopEventIfRequired(e);
};
```

The next function is _onUpEvent, the listener for the touchend and mouseup events shown in Listing 5-17. Its job is very simple: transform the event into the custom form and reset the _moving flag. The movement is over, and the next one will track the threshold again.

Listing 5-17. _onUpDomEvent: Function That Takes Care of the End of Interaction and Clears _moving flag

```
/**
 * Listens to the "up" DOM events: mouseup and touchend. Touchend
 * doesn't have any coordinates associated with it so this function
 * will be overridden in TouchInputHandler
 * @param e DOM Event
 */
_p._onUpDomEvent = function(e) {
    // Works exactly the same way as _onDownDomEvent
    var coords = this._getInputCoordinates(e);
    this.emit("up", {x: coords.x, y: coords.y, moved: this._moving, domEvent: e});
    this._stopEventIfRequired(e);

    // The interaction is ended. Reset the flag
    this._moving = false;
};
```

The code for the last utility function in this class, _stopEventIfRequired(), is pretty straightforward (see Listing 5-18). It stops the propagation of the browser event and prevents the default action, as we discussed.

Listing 5-18. Stopping the Event: Usually the User Doesn't Want the Default Browser Behavior in Addition to the Game Behavior

```
_p._stopEventIfRequired = function(e) {
    if (this._stopDomEvents) {
        e.stopPropagation();
        e.preventDefault();
    }
};
```

The InputHandlerBase class defines the common flow for the API. When the user starts the interaction (doesn't matter how exactly, either clicking the mouse or touching the interface) the down event is fired. While the user is holding the controller, the class ignores all move actions that fall inside the threshold radius, since most likely these actions are not intentional. If the user reaches the threshold, the action is qualified as "movement" and InputHandler starts to fire move events. Finally, when the user ends his interaction, the up event is fired.

As you see, the custom events that we use do not expose any unnecessary platform details. Moreover, the class supports a little bit of extra functionality: _moveThreshold and tracking deltas for move events.

Given this common base, the implementation of concrete handlers is not hard at all. Let's start with the MouseInputHandler. The only way it is different from the default behavior is that you have to track whether the button is pressed before firing move events (we will ignore mouse movements without the pressed button since there is no direct analog in a touch interface).

Creating MouseInputHandler

Start with the constructor. The MouseInputHandler should use the custom listeners that we just build to keep track of browser events. The code is shown in Listing 5-19.

Listing 5-19. *Initializing MouseInputHandler: Custom Listeners Keep Track of Mouse Events*

```
/**
 * The implementation of the InputHandler for the desktop
 * browser based on the mouse events.
 */
function MouseInputHandler(element) {
    InputHandlerBase.call(this, element);
    this._attachDomListeners();
}

extend(MouseInputHandler, InputHandlerBase);
_p = MouseInputHandler.prototype;

/**
 * Attach the listeners to the mouseXXX DOM events
 */
_p._attachDomListeners = function() {
    var el = this._element;
    el.addEventListener("mousedown", this._onDownDomEvent.bind(this), false);
    el.addEventListener("mouseup", this._onUpDomEvent.bind(this), false);
    el.addEventListener("mousemove", this._onMoveDomEvent.bind(this));
};
```

Now the `MouseInputHandler` can be used; it transforms every mouse event into the custom form. But it doesn't work quite right. It fires the move event for every mouse movement, no matter if the button is pressed or not. We agreed that mouse fires move events only when the button is down, because the `touchmove` in Android is most closely represented by the drag action in a mouse interface. Start by adding the flag that tracks the button state to the constructor (see Listing 5-20).

Listing 5-20. *Adding the Flag to Track the Button State*

```
function MouseInputHandler(element) {
    InputHandlerBase.call(this, element);

    // We need additional property to track if the
    // mouse is down.
    this._mouseDown = false;
    this._attachDomListeners();
}
```

Now override all event listeners, as shown in Listing 5-21. _onDownDomEvent() sets the _mouseDown flag to true, _onUpDomEvent() sets the flag to false, and _onMoveDomEvent() checks the flag before firing event.

Listing 5-21. *Tracking the Mouse Button State and Firing the move Event Only When the Button Is Pressed*

```
/**
 * This method (and the next one) is overridden,
 * because we have to track the state of the mouse.
 * This could also be done in the separate listener.
 */
_p._onDownDomEvent = function(e) {
    this._mouseDown = true;
    InputHandlerBase.prototype._onDownDomEvent.call(this, e);
};

_p._onUpDomEvent = function(e) {
    this._mouseDown = false;
    InputHandlerBase.prototype._onUpDomEvent.call(this, e);
};

/**
 * We process the move event only if the mouse button is
 * pressed, otherwise the DOM event is ignored.
 */
_p._onMoveDomEvent = function(e) {
    if (this._mouseDown) {
        InputHandlerBase.prototype._onMoveDomEvent.call(this, e);
    }
};
```

The final touch is to get rid of the small, side effect of button-tracking. If you move the cursor away from the canvas while the button is pressed, and then release it elsewhere, the canvas will not get the mouseup event and MouseInputHandler will still think that the button is down. When you return back your cursor, the canvas reports *every* movement again. Fortunately, it is quite easy to reset the flag once the cursor leaves the canvas, as shown in Listing 5-22.

Listing 5-22. *Resetting the Button Status Once the Mouse Leaves the Canvas*

```
_p._attachDomListeners = function() {
    var el = this._element;
    el.addEventListener("mousedown", this._onDownDomEvent.bind(this), false);
    el.addEventListener("mouseup", this._onUpDomEvent.bind(this), false);
    el.addEventListener("mousemove", this._onMoveDomEvent.bind(this));
    el.addEventListener("mouseout", this._onMouseOut.bind(this));
};

_p._onMouseOut = function() {
    this._mouseDown = false;
};
```

But what if the mouse button is *not* released outside of canvas? Well, the user will have to release and press the button again. But this is the small issue: when the user leaves the canvas, he realizes that he's not interacting with it anymore. To restore the interaction, a typical user would repeat the process from the beginning: move the cursor to canvas, press the button, and drag. In practice, it is far less annoying than the "stalled" _mouseDown flag.

When you finish implementing this class, you can instantly test how the new event handling works! Of course, the demo runs only on a desktop with the mouse. The touch part is yet to be built. But look at how clean the new code in Listing 5-23 is!

Listing 5-23. *Test of Custom Input Events*

```
function init() {
        canvas = document.getElementById("mainCanvas");
        ctx = canvas.getContext("2d");

        var canvasInputHandler = new MouseInputHandler(canvas);
        canvasInputHandler.on("up", function(e) {
            drawBullet(e.x, e.y);
        });

        resizeCanvas();
}

function drawBullet(x, y) {
```

```
        ctx.fillStyle = "lightblue";
        ctx.strokeStyle = "darkgray";
        ctx.lineWidth = 5;

        ctx.beginPath();
        ctx.arc(x, y, 15, 0, Math.PI*2, false);
        ctx.fill();
        ctx.stroke();
}
```

The code that is required to handle events has been reduced from 20 lines to a mere four. Moreover, the browser-specific code is moved to the internals of API. The implementation of `MouseInputHandler` is available with the sources for this chapter in a file called `MouseInputHandler.js`.

Finally, we can implement the `TouchInputHandler`, a class responsible for touch-enabled browsers.

Creating TouchInputHandler

`TouchInputHandler` solves a different problem. The standard browser touchend event doesn't have any associated coordinates; the `targetTouches` is just empty. This is sometimes inconvenient. For example, in the previous listing we used the up event to put the token on the canvas. If we use the standard touchend instead, we'd have to track every other event! We'd have to use touchstart and touchmove to keep track of the *last known* coordinates and use them to paint the token. This is a lot of code that the core game should not care about. Let's put it into the separate class.

The idea behind it is the same as for `MouseInputHandler`, but instead of the button's state, it tracks the last known coordinate of interaction. The code in Listing 5-24 shows the class implementation. The full code can be found along with other examples distributed with this book in `TouchInputHandler.js`. This class uses the same idea as `MouseInputHandler`: take the base implementation of event listeners and modify them for their own needs. But instead of tracking the button state, this class tracks the last known coordinate of the input event.

Listing 5-24. *TouchInputHandler Has to Track the Last Known Coordinates of Input to Report Them in up Event*

```
function TouchInputHandler(element) {
    this._lastInteractionCoordinates = null;
    InputHandlerBase.call(this, element);
    this._attachDomListeners();
}
```

```
extend(TouchInputHandler, InputHandlerBase);

_p = TouchInputHandler.prototype;

_p._attachDomListeners = function() {
    var el = this._element;
    el.addEventListener("touchstart", this._onDownDomEvent.bind(this), false);
    el.addEventListener("touchend", this._onUpDomEvent.bind(this), false);
    el.addEventListener("touchmove", this._onMoveDomEvent.bind(this), false);
};

_p._onDownDomEvent = function(e) {
    this._lastInteractionCoordinates = this._getInputCoordinates(e);
    InputHandlerBase.prototype._onDownDomEvent.call(this, e);
};

_p._onUpDomEvent = function(e) {
    this.emit("up", {
            x: this._lastInteractionCoordinates.x,
            y: this._lastInteractionCoordinates.y,
            moved: this._moving,
            domEvent: e
        });
    this._stopEventIfRequired(e);
    this._lastInteractionCoordinates = null;
    this._moving = false;
};

_p._onMoveDomEvent = function(e) {
    this._lastInteractionCoordinates = this._getInputCoordinates(e);
    InputHandlerBase.prototype._onMoveDomEvent.call(this, e);
}
```

Now we have classes for both input models. The final touch is to select one, depending on the capabilities of the browser. Create the new file called InputHandler.js and add the following single line of code:

```
var InputHandler = isTouchDevice() ? TouchInputHandler : MouseInputHandler;
```

This is a small trick that is sometimes used in JavaScript. Depending on the environment, the InputHandler will be either TouchInputHandler or MouseInputHandler. This way, you can avoid picking the correct implementation in the core game files. Because input handling is the separate API, we put all four files that implement it in a separate folder called "input".

Advanced Input

Building the input layer to hide the browser API from the core logic of the game is only the first step to having good game controls. We've learned how to handle "atomic" input actions (touches, releases, and moves), so now it is time for slightly more advanced examples.

Drag-and-Drop

Drag-and-drop is a very convenient way to interact with the game designed for touchscreens. In a game that has a big world map, for example, dragging the map is the natural way to navigate the world. Besides, drag-and-drop might be used to move items between the hero stash and inventory, or to build puzzle games for kids. Moving puzzle pieces with drag-and-drop is the second most natural way to interact with them—after grabbing them with your hand. This type of input is used in our next game experiment, the isometric game in Chapter 7.

Drag-and-drop is very easy to implement. The method consists of the following three steps:

1. When the user starts the interaction, check whether he selected a draggable component. If not, abort the process since there is nothing to drag. If there are many draggable components, mark the one that is currently active. Let's call this step Picking.

2. Listen to move events and adjust the position of the component appropriately. Let's call this step Moving.

3. When the user finishes the interaction, finish the drag: execute the game logic behind drag-and-drop (move the item in the inventory, for example), and then unmark the "active" component. Let's call this step Releasing.

Let's build another demo to illustrate this concept (see Listing 5-25). We will put several rectangles onto the screen and allow the user to drag them around. All three phases are easily implementable with our API (the full code is available in the `02.drag_and_drop.html` file in this chapter's examples folder).

Listing 5-25. *Implementing Drag-and-Drop*

```
// Picking phase
input.on("down", function(e) {
    rectangles.forEach(function(rect, index) {
        if (insideRectangle(e, rect))
```

```
                selectedIndex = index;
        });
});

// Movement phase
input.on("move", function(e) {
    if (selectedIndex > -1) {
        rectangles[selectedIndex].x += e.deltaX;
        rectangles[selectedIndex].y += e.deltaY;
    }
});

// release phase
input.on("up", function(e) {
    selectedIndex = -1;
});
```

The movement phase and the release phase are simple; however, the picking phase has some pitfalls. It is fairly easy to check by the coordinates if the point falls inside a circle or square. Polygons are a little harder, but still doable. But what if the objects of the scene have shapes that are more complex? What if you want to pick an image that has transparent areas that should not be treated as "material"? Obviously, there are cases that are impossible to implement using only simple mathematical algorithms. For cases like that, there's a "pixel perfect" selection approach described in the next section of this chapter. The complete source code that implements drag and drop is available in file `04.drag_and_drop.html`.

> **NOTE:** The games that we'll create during the course of the book do not require pixel-perfect picking. This kind of input, however, is the common problem that many game developers face. So, I decided to devote a separate section for this question. Puzzle-assembling games, for example, are almost impossible to implement properly without it.

Pixel-Perfect Picking and Image Masks

The smallest thing that the user can select is a pixel. Unlike the canvas API, browser events do not deal with fractional parts of pixels: it is impossible to select the "left side of the pixel" or the "bottom corner of the pixel." The task of picking complex shapes can be formulated in a slightly different way: determine which figure of the scene the given pixel belongs to. Obviously, if we could do that, we could pick any figure with perfect accuracy. It turns out that it is possible to implement such an algorithm with relatively little effort.

Each pixel has a color. Let's imagine that we make a game where each shape has unique solid color. For example, the triangle is blue, the square is red, and the circle is green. When the user taps the screen, we can instantly tell which figure is under his finger by getting the color of the pixel and mapping it to the figure. This can be easily done with the canvas API. First, we need to get the color of a pixel; if the user tapped the screen in coordinates (51, 73), the code for the value of the pixel looks like following:

```
var imageData = ctx.getImageData(51, 73, 1, 1).data;
```

The imageData is an array that has four elements: a red value, a green value, a blue value, and an alpha value of the color. With this raw pixel data, we can tell which image is selected.

```
if (imageData[2] == 255) {
    console.log("Blue Triangle");
} else  if (imageData[0] == 255) {
    console.log("Red Square");
} else if (imageData[1] == 255) {
    console.log("Green Circle");
} else {
    console.log("Empty Space");
}
```

But most of the games we make have all kind of shapes with all kind of colors. Most sprites have multiple colors! Does it mean that this technique is useless? Not at all. Even though the images and shapes have different colors, we can paint them in the way they are "covered" with the solid color. Before going further, let's look at what this means. Figure 5-6 illustrates the idea. We have two cartoon house images, each having a palette of colors (left image). To make our technique work, we have to paint the house images, giving each a unique solid color (right image).

Figure 5-6. *Original images (left) and masks (right)*

This technique is called *masking* and the solid-colored outline of the figure is often called a *mask*. In a minute, we'll see how to create masks; for now, let's assume that it is possible.

Each pixel has a color. The color is represented by a 32-bit number, divided into four 8-bit components: red, green, blue, and alpha. We can easily translate from the color to its integer value and back. What happens if we give the unique ID to each figure in the scene and then encode this ID as the color? That's right. We get the unique color for every figure on the scene. What if we draw the mask of each figure with this unique color? The color of the pixel would then represent the ID of the figure that occupies that pixel! When the user taps the screen, we only need to translate back the red, green, and blue values of the mask color to get the integer ID of the shape.

The trick is to implement this technique now.

> **NOTE:** But won't the screen flash with every color of the rainbow once the user taps it? We need to *render* those colors afterwards! That's right, we need to render masks, but the canvas that holds them doesn't have to be the same as your "main" canvas. In a real game, the canvas for the drawing mask is never visible to the user, and masks never appear on the screen. All rendering is done in memory, behind the scenes.

Composite Operations

Let's start with a simple question: how do we draw an image mask? We need to change every opaque pixel of an image with the opaque pixel that has the color of the mask. To do it, we use a feature of 2D context called `globalCompositeOperation`. It defines the method of drawing the new pixels on top of existing ones. The default method is called *source-over*. The new nontransparent pixels are drawn on top of existing ones, like layers of paint applied one on top of the other. The pixels that are to be drawn are called the *source* and the pixels already on the scene are the *destination*. Source-over means "put the source pixels on top of the destination."

Figure 5-7 shows the components of the operation and the operation result—the one that you would expect. The house image is painted first; so, the moment the circle is painted, it is already on canvas. The house is the *destination*. The circle is painted second, so it is the *source*.

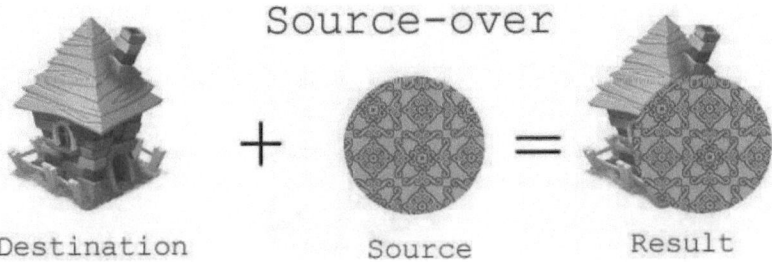

Figure 5-7. *The default composite operation: source-over*

This is the natural way of painting things. When you draw the image, you expect it to appear on top of any existing background images. This rule can easily be changed, however. If you set the `globalCompositeOperation` to "source-atop," the newly drawn pixels appear only where the background is opaque, like in Figure 5-8.

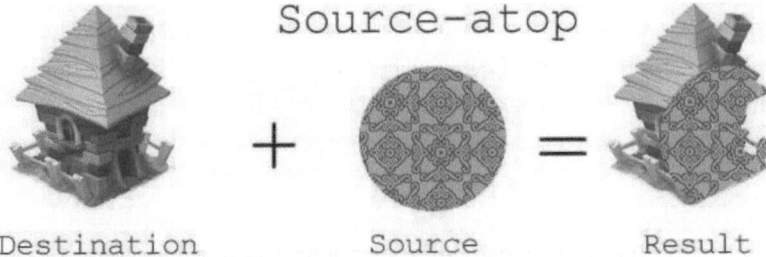

Figure 5-8. *The source-atop composite operation. Source pixels appear over the background only if it is opaque; everything else is clipped.*

That's exactly what is required to make the image mask! But instead of a circle with a fancy pattern, we will use the solid-color rectangle that covers the entire image. We first draw the image (the destination), and then cover it with the color defined by the unique object ID. This concept is pretty easy yet very powerful. Figure 5-9 shows how to make the image mask with a source-atop operation.

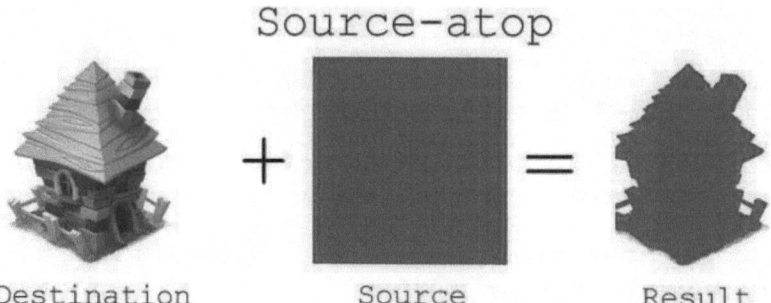

Figure 5-9. *Image mask using the source-atop operation. The solid-colored rectangle covers only nontransparent parts of the image.*

> **NOTE:** There are several other composite operations available for the canvas API. If you are interested in an in-depth exploration of this topic, have a look at the demo, called 08.composites.html, which comes with the materials for the chapter. It shows the effects of every available composite operation. For a more formal description of the math behind color compositing, refer to the paper by Thomas Porter and Tom Duff, "Compositing Digital Images." *Computer Graphics* 18, no. 3 (July 1984).

Now let's implement this technique in practice. Let's start with the two functions in Listing 5-26.

Listing 5-26. *Drawing the Image Mask with the Color Derived from Image ID*

```
function numberToColor(n) {
    var hexString = n.toString(16);
    // Add padding
    return "#" + "000000".substr(0, 6 - hexString.length) + hexString;
}

function drawImageMask(image, x, y, maskColor, ctx) {
    var w = bufferCanvas.width = image.width;
    var h = bufferCanvas.height = image.height;
    var maskCtx = bufferCanvas.getContext("2d");

    // Original image painted first. It is dest
    maskCtx.drawImage(image, 0, 0);

    // set the composite operation
    maskCtx.globalCompositeOperation = "source-atop";
    maskCtx.fillStyle = maskColor;
    maskCtx.fillRect(0, 0, w, h);
```

```
    ctx.drawImage(bufferCanvas, x, y);
}
```

The first function, numberToColor(), is a small utility that translates the numerical ID of the object to the color representation suitable for setting the fill style. The second function uses the invisible bufferCanvas to create the mask for the image. The solid-color mask is then painted from the bufferCanvas onto the context passed as a parameter. Instead of painting the image, you can insert any complex rendering code here since once the pixels are on the context, it no longer matters what the original source was, whether a PNG image or a JavaScript routine.

If you paint each image that way, it is fairly easy to grab the color of the selected pixel and to find the selected shape (see Listing 5-27). The demo that shows how to render the image mask can be found in the 05.mask.html file together with the other source code for this chapter.

Listing 5-27. *Translating from Color to Figure ID*

```
var imageData = pixelContext.getImageData(x, y, 1, 1).data;

// The black color is default, so we have to draw masks starting from
// color "1" (or take alpha values into the account). To return back
// from color to array index we have to subtract 1 back.
var index = (imageData[0] << 16 | imageData[1] << 8 | imageData[2]) - 1;
console.log("User selected index " + index.toString(16));
```

The bolded bitwise operation might require a little explanation. It restores the integer number from three-color components. The bits representation of the color is RRRRRRRRGGGGGGGGBBBBBBBB (the R block is 8 bits for red, the G block is 8 bits for green, and the B block is 8 bits for blue).

The << operation adds the given number of bits to the right of the number, filling the extra space with zeros. For example, the number 3 in binary form is 11. 3 << 1 means "add one 0 to the right," resulting in (110 which is 6) in decimal form. The whole expression means "take the 8 bits from the element 0 of the array and put it into the R block; next, take the 8 bits from the element 1 and fill the G block; and finally, fill the rest with the B block." This yields the numerical representation of the value, the operation opposite to what we've done in numberToColor().

The masking operation works only with images that do not have semitransparent pixels. If the image has translucent areas, the mask will not retain its original color; instead, it is affected by the transparency of the destination. To work with such images, they have to be preprocessed in runtime; the alpha value greater than 0 must be set to 1.

If you are going to deal with semitransparent pixels, you will have to modify the code a little and remove the alpha value from the image before applying the mask. Otherwise, the original color will not be saved and you will not be able to find the shape index that you are looking for. We can change the values of the pixels the same way as we read them (see Listing 5-28).

Listing 5-28. *Changing the Pixel Data of the Context on the Fly*

```
function drawImageMask (image, x, y, maskColor, ctx) {
    …

    maskCtx.drawImage(image, 0, 0);
    filterAlpha(maskCtx, w, h);
    maskCtx.globalCompositeOperation = "source-atop";
    maskCtx.fillStyle = maskColor;
    maskCtx.fillRect(0, 0, w, h);

    ctx.drawImage(bufferCanvas, x, y);
}

function filterAlpha(ctx, width, height) {
    var imageData = ctx.getImageData(0, 0, width, height);
    var pixels = imageData.data;
    // Pixels are stored as RGBA. Alpha values are in every
    // fourth cell of the array
    for (var i = 0; i < width*height; i++) {
        pixels[i*4 + 3] = pixels[i*4 + 3] == 0 ? 0 : 255;
    }
    ctx.putImageData(imageData, 0, 0);
}
```

The code in this section explains only the crucial points of using masks for picking the object. You can find the full demo in the 06.pixel_picking.html file with the source code supplied with the book.

> **NOTE:** The technique described here can be optimized in many ways; for example, we can check for the size and position of each image and throw away those that do not overlap the selected pixel. Besides, we keep the full-size canvas object for drawing masks while we need only a single pixel. We could instead have a one-pixel-sized canvas and save some CPU time and memory. These kinds of optimizations are pretty obvious and they are not hard to implement if you need them in your projects. Most likely, however, there will not be that many draggable objects to choose from, and the solution described here will show decent speed.

Simulating Joystick

The final part of this chapter is devoted to the simulation of real-world game controls. This is the usual practice for mobile games: trying to make a virtual version of hardware that is used for input.

Joysticks are used for all kind of games, from space simulators to third-person shooters. Whenever you need direct control over the game character, a joystick is probably the best option for a device that lacks multitouch. A virtual joystick is a circle that is sensitive to touches and moves. There's a small "stick" inside it that shows its current position. The player can alter the direction (angle) and the power (the distance from the center).

The joystick utilizes a polar coordinate system. It doesn't make much sense to use Cartesian coordinates for it. The polar coordinate system uses a different approach to specifying the position of a point in space. Instead of x and y values, it uses the azimuth and radius. The point with the Cartesian coordinates (1, 1), for example, have a radius of approximately 1.414 and an azimuth of $\pi/4$ in polar coordinates. The relation between these coordinate systems is illustrated in Figure 5-10.

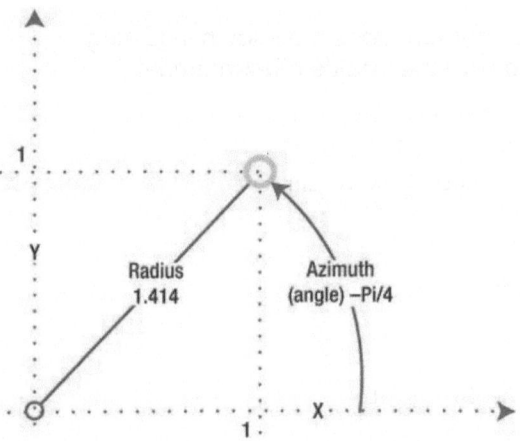

Figure 5-10. *Cartesian coordinates (x, y) and polar coordinates (azimuth, radius)*

The joystick's output is the perfect example of the case where polar coordinates are way more useful than the regular system. The "direction" is the azimuth, while the "power" (the distance from the center) is the radius. This representation suits the controller tasks much better.

The idea behind the joystick implementation is quite simple: track the touches and moves of the user and calculate the azimuth and radius of the stick position.

If the user taps outside of the "active" joystick area, the touch is ignored. Figure 5-11 shows how the simple joystick UI might look on the web page.

Figure 5-11. *The simplistic virtual joystick. The outer circle is the "active" area that the user taps to control the position of the object. The circle inside it indicates the current position of the stick).*

The code is relatively simple; the most important functions are shown in Listing 5-29. The complete implementation is found with the book's other materials.

Listing 5-29. *Implementing Virtual Joystick Control)*

```
_p._onDownOrMove = function(coords) {
    // When we receive the "down" or "move" events we save current
    // deltas and update radius and azimuth
    var deltaX = coords.x - this._x;
    var deltaY = coords.y - this._y;
    this._updateJoystickValues(deltaX, deltaY);
};

_p._onUp = function(x, y) {
    // If there's no interaction, restore the idle state
    this._updateJoystickValues(0, 0);
};

_p._updateJoystickValues = function(deltaX, deltaY) {
    var newAzimuth = 0;
    var newRadius = 0;

    // In case if the joystick is idle, we don't need to proceed with
calculations
    if (deltaX != 0 || deltaY != 0) {
        newRadius = Math.sqrt(deltaX*deltaX +
deltaY*deltaY)/this._controllerRadius;
```

```
        // User slid too far away, joystick is returned to idle state
        if (newRadius > 1) {
            deltaX = 0;
            deltaY = 0;
            newRadius = 0;
        } else {
            newAzimuth = Math.atan2(deltaY, deltaX);
        }
    }

    // If the values have actually changed, notify listeners
    if (this._azimuth != newAzimuth || this._radius != newRadius) {
        this._azimuth = newAzimuth;
        this._radius = newRadius;
        this._deltaX = deltaX;
        this._deltaY = deltaY;
        this.emit("joystickchange", {
            azimuth: newAzimuth,
            radius: newRadius });
    }
};
```

The first function is called whenever InputHandler detects an interaction— a click, touch, or movement. It calculates the deltas, or the x and y distance between the center of the controller and the touch coordinates.

Next, the values of the radius and azimuth are calculated using a few simple trigonometry formulas. Finally, if the position has changed since last time, the user is notified about it. The use of the joystick from the game code is even easier (see Listing 5-30).

Listing 5-30. *Adding Joystick to the Game*

```
function init() {
    canvas = initFullScreenCanvas("mainCanvas");
    ctx = canvas.getContext("2d");

    joystick = new Joystick(canvas);
    var r = joystick.getControllerRadius();
    joystick.setPosition(r + 50, canvas.height - r - 50);
    animateCanvas();
}

function animateCanvas() {
    var speed = 20;
    var joystickRadius = joystick.getRadius();
    if (joystickRadius > 0) {
        var joystickAzimuth = joystick.getAzimuth();
        var xSpeed = joystickRadius*Math.cos(joystickAzimuth)*speed;
```

```
        var ySpeed = joystickRadius*Math.sin(joystickAzimuth)*speed;
        controlledObject.x += xSpeed;
        controlledObject.y += ySpeed;
    }

    ... the rest of animation code goes here
}
```

A virtual joystick is a very nice tool, especially for mobile devices. It has usability issues with desktop browsers, however. The main problem is that you have to keep the mouse button pressed to move it. If your game is intended for both mobile and desktop platforms, make sure you think about usability, not only for touchscreens, but also for the good old mouse and keyboard. The final version of the joystick demo is available in a file called 07.joystick.html together with the source code for this chapter.

Summary

In this chapter, we took an in-depth look into browser event handling and user controls. We learned how the touch interfaces are different from the regular desktop browser input model. We discovered that dealing with browser events might be a cumbersome task. It is way better to create a suitable intermediate API layer that hides the details of the events and exposes the simple interface.

We learned how to build custom event handlers to use inside the game. It often doesn't make sense to utilize the heavyweight event model of the browser for simple tasks like emitting the event object to the direct subscribers.

We developed advanced ways of interaction with the game through drag-and-drop and the pixel-perfect selection model. Finally, we created the custom component that simulates the joystick—the hardware used for interacting with video games since they began.

Now that we've completed this chapter, we are ready for the next challenge: rendering virtual worlds.

Rendering Virtual Worlds

In the previous chapters, we learned how to render the animation, control the timing, and react to the user's input. The next interesting topic is rendering of the game world. This may be a trivial task if you are creating a game like chess, but what about role-playing games or strategies where the worlds are huge? Obviously, keeping the map and the game objects in your smartphone's memory is not an option—too much data, too many bytes to send over the net and too slow to render.

The next two chapters are dedicated to rendering of virtual worlds. First we will cover the basic techniques of drawing vast 2D spaces on the smartphone screen. We will explore several different approaches to optimize the rendering speed as well as volumes of data to transfer between the server and the client. We will try to focus on motivations behind each technique, discuss when and why you need to apply each of them. The material of this chapter will lay the solid ground for building the full-blown isometric engine that we will create in the next chapter.

In this chapter, we will learn the following:

- Tile maps and how to present the world as a grid of tiles

- How to render tile maps on the canvas

- How to optimize rendering performance

- How to render world objects like buildings and characters

Tile Maps

Tile maps are a very powerful technique that allows building big and complex levels using small images called *tiles*. Imagine that you're making a massive multiplayer strategy game that has a huge map of the world with rivers, plains, forests, and mountains, totaling 100,000 × 100,000 pixels. Good enough for a massive game. Obviously, we can't use an image to bring it to the user: there's simply not enough RAM to hold a super-map like that either on a mobile device or on your PC.

It turns out that the vast areas of the map are composed of very similar patterns. Snow looks almost the same everywhere—it is white and shiny. The same is also true for desert, grass, water, and similar natural areas. Perhaps we can use that to optimize our map?

The Idea Behind Tile Maps

Tiles are small images of the same size that are designed to fit each other without breaking the pattern—that's how they make up a piece of the map. Look at Figure 6-1 and you see this concept in action.

Figure 6-1. *Tile map in* Warcraft 2

This is a screenshot of the map editor from *Warcraft 2*. White lines show the borders of tiles that compose a solid picture. Note that the tiles are aligned to the grid. If you look closer, you see that tiles are not unique. In fact, they repeat pretty often. For example, there are only three or four different tiles for forest, a couple of tiles for dirt, and about a dozen tiles for the border region, where forest transforms into dirt.

Tiles are designed in a way that the user doesn't see the borders that separate one tile from another. Look at the right side of the screenshot that is not covered by a helper grid, and you'll see that the forest looks quite natural. Even though almost all the trees look the same, you don't recognize the tiled nature of this image straightaway. Neither will the player.

How does it help us with the super-map problem? Well, let's use some simple math. Let's say we have four types of terrain: snow, forest, plains, and mountains. Our designer has created four tiles for each, totaling 16 tiles. In addition, we have around 40 "border tiles" to render areas where one type of terrain transforms into the other, making the overall number of tiles 56.

If the size of each tile is 64 pixels, we can fit the entire tile set into a 512×512 image. So instead of having a monstrous $100,000 \times 100,000$ map image, we have a 512×512 tile set, which can be easily downloaded by any modern device.

The next step is to present the world as a grid of tiles. Usually, a level designer has a special tool for editing the tile maps. Break the world map into 64×64 cells and select the appropriate tile for each of them. Now the whole world can be described by a two-dimensional array. Here is an example of how such array might look:

```
var world = [
        [2, 2, 2, 8, 2, 2],
        [5, 4, 7, 3, 4, 3],
        [5, 4, 3, 3, 4, 7]
    ];
```

The real array would be much bigger, of course. The index of the array element is the coordinates of the cell in the world map (x and y), and the value is the number of the tile in the tile set. For example, in the array, the value of `world[1][2]` is 7. This means that the world map in coordinates (x=2, y=1) is rendered with the tile number 7 from the tile set. Which tile that is depends on the concrete set. It can be snow, sand, or forest. Figure 6-2 shows the same screenshot from the *Warcraft 2* map editor; the tile indexes are written over each cell. This is an example of a world fragment that can be described by our array.

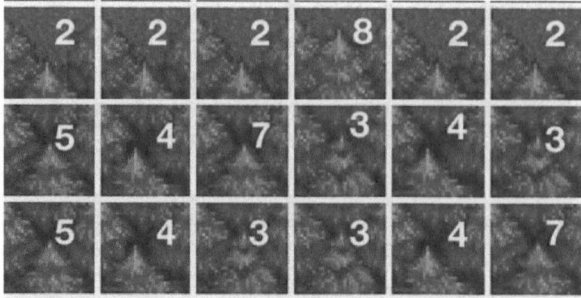

Figure 6-2. *Tile map fragment with the marked tiles*

There's one more advantage to this method: you don't need to download the array that describes the whole world map in one piece. Remember the example that we started with—a huge map for a massive online game? To describe the map we would need an array of 1500 × 1500 elements. Even though this is way better than having a monster-size image, it is still considerable traffic and memory loss. A typical player is not interested in the entire map. He usually needs to see only the area that surrounds his location; most likely, he will not move too far away from there. Even if he does start to explore, he receives portions of the map as he moves forward.

To optimize the map loading even more, we could initially load the area of 50 × 50 tiles around the player. We assume that this piece of map will most likely satisfy the immediate exploration needs. The rest can be loaded from the server when the player starts to move or scroll the map. I show how to implement this technique later in the chapter.

With proper memory management, the size of the "world map" can be virtually unlimited since it is not stored on the browser; only the piece of map that is "most important" right now is cached in the client. The rest stays on the server.

Implementing a Tile Map

In this section, we learn how to implement the tile map with JavaScript. We will start with the simplest possible implementation and then gradually make it better. In this chapter, we work with square tiles, but, of course, other shapes are also possible. For example, isometric games use diamond-shaped tiles. Turn-based tactics games might use hexagon tiles because the calculation of the distance between hex tiles is more "fair." Once we created the engine for square tiles, it is fairly easy to implement the same idea for other geometry, but the math behind it might be slightly more complex. Figure 6-3 shows the different shapes of the tiles.

Square tiles   Isometric diamond   Hexagonal tiles
                          tiles

Figure 6-3. *The tiles may have different sizes and shapes.*

In this chapter, we use a tile-set that you can find in a file called img/tiles.png that comes along with the source code for this chapter. This tile set has fourteen 40 × 40 tiles which is just fine for our needs. The tiles are taken from the free tile set from www.lostgarden.com with the kind permission of Daniel Cook. To give you an idea of how our resources look, they are presented in Figure 6-4.

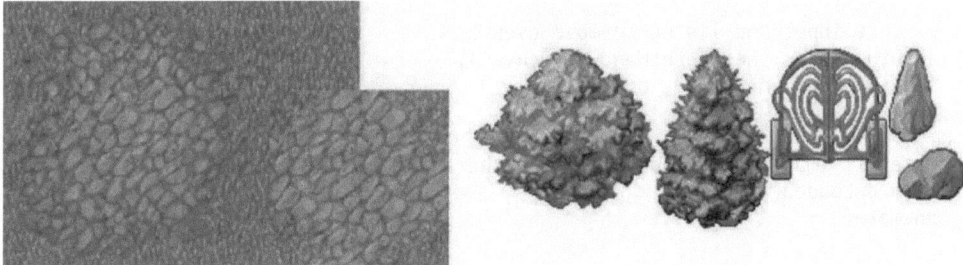

Figure 6-4. *Assets used in this chapter. On the left are tiles for rendering background. On the right are world objects.*

Setup

Let's start with drawing tiles on the screen without optimizations of any kind. Right now we are working with a rather small world that is described by the 40 × 40 array. The code is based on the skeleton from Chapter 3 (Listing 3-6), with the added support of animation from Chapter 4 (Listing 4-24) and event handling from Chapter 5 (the "Custom Events" section). Listing 6-1 shows the <script> block—a base for experiments with virtual worlds. The code sets up a typical game-dev playground: it initiates the image loading, input handling, and animation loop. For your convenience, this more advanced skeleton is saved in a folder called setup along with the other sources for this chapter.

Listing 6-1. *Setup for This Chapter*

```
<script>
    var canvas;
    var ctx;
    var imageManager;
    var inputHandler;

    var images = {
        "tiles": "img/tiles.png"
    };

    function init() {
        // Start image loading
        imageManager = new ImageManager();
        imageManager.load(images, onLoaded);

        // Init canvas
        canvas = initFullScreenCanvas("mainCanvas");
        ctx = canvas.getContext("2d");

        // Init input and listen to move events
        inputHandler = new InputHandler(canvas);
        inputHandler.on("move", onMove);
    }

    /** Once all images are loaded - starts the animation loop */
    function onLoaded() {
        animate(0);
    }

    /** Perform rendering here */
    function animate(t) {
        clear();
        requestAnimationFrame(arguments.callee);
    }

    /** Handle map move */
    function onMove(e) {

    }

    /* Clears the canvas with the solid black color */
    function clear() {
        ctx.fillStyle = "black";
        ctx.fillRect(0, 0, canvas.width, canvas.height);
    }

    function initFullScreenCanvas(canvasId) {/* not changed */}
```

```
    function resizeCanvas(canvas) {/* not changed */}
</script>
```

Now we need to get some sample map data for our virtual world—the array that describes the level. It is better to put such an array into a separate file, since it might get quite big. Create the new file js/world.js with content shown in Listing 6-2. The code in this listing is trimmed to fit the size of the book page; the full 40 × 40 version of this array can be found in the world.js file along with the other source code for this chapter.

Listing 6-2. *The world.js File That Describes the World That We Will Render*

```
var world = [
    [3,  3,  3,  3,  3,  3,  3,  3,  3,  3,  3,  3,  3],
    [3,  3,  3,  3,  3,  3,  3,  3,  3,  3,  3,  3,  3],
    [3,  3,  0,  1,  1,  1,  1,  2,  3,  3,  3,  3,  3],
    [3,  3,  5,  6, 14, 11, 13,  7,  3,  3,  3,  3,  3],
    [3,  3,  5,  6,  9,  1,  8,  7,  3,  3,  3,  3,  3],
    [3,  3,  5,  6,  6,  6,  6,  7,  3,  3,  3,  3,  3],
    [3,  3, 10, 11, 11, 11, 11, 12,  3,  3,  3,  3,  3],
];
```

Rendering Tile Maps

Now we are ready to draw the tile map. To do that, we will create the separate class called MapRenderer. The basic code for drawing a set of square tiles that form a grid is very simple. To render the world out of tile map, we need to know three things:

- the map data (the array that we just saved in world.js file)
- the image to take tiles from
- the size of a tile

We use rectangular tiles, so we don't need the width and height; it is enough to have only one parameter—tileSize. The constructor of the MapRenderer class looks quite simple (see Listing 6-3).

Listing 6-3. *The Constructor of MapRenderer*

```
function MapRenderer(mapData, image, tileSize) {
    this._mapData = mapData;
    this._image = image;
    this._tileSize = tileSize;

    // Coordinates of the map
    this._x = 0;
    this._y = 0;
```

```
    // The number of tiles in one row of the image
    this._tilesPerRow = image.width/tileSize;
}
```

Besides saving the parameters, constructor calculates the number of tiles in one row of the tile sheet. We will soon need this value to get the coordinates of the tile inside the sheet. The _x and _y variables are the coordinates of the map itself. When the user moves the viewport, we will change these to render the map in a new place (see Listing 6-4).

Listing 6-4. *Rendering a Grid of Tiles on a Screen*

```
_p = MapRenderer.prototype;

/* Draws the whole map */
_p.draw = function(ctx) {
    for (var cellY = 0; cellY < this._mapData.length; cellY++) {
        for (var cellX = 0; cellX < this._mapData[cellY].length; cellX++) {
            var tileId = this._mapData[cellY][cellX];
            this._drawTileAt(ctx, tileId, cellX, cellY);
        }
    }
};

/* Draws a single tile */
_p._drawTileAt = function(ctx, tileId, cellX, cellY) {

    // Position of the tile inside of a tile sheet
    var srcX = (tileId%this._tilesPerRow)*this._tileSize;
    var srcY = Math.floor(tileId/this._tilesPerRow)*this._tileSize;

    // size of the tile
    var size = this._tileSize;

    // position of the tile on the screen
    var destX = this._x + cellX*size;
    var destY = this._y + cellY*size;

    ctx.drawImage(this._image, srcX, srcY, size, size, destX, destY, size,
size);
};
```

As you see, drawing tiles is much easier than drawing sprites. A sprite is made of frames, and each frame has its own size and an anchor point. On the other hand, all the tiles are of the same size and they don't need anchor points. The mathematics behind tiles is not hard at all.

> **NOTE:** You should be careful when setting tile indices in arrays. If the tile index
> exceeds the overall number of tiles, canvas API will not silently ignore the attempt to
> copy pixels that fall behind image bounds. An exception will be thrown, and the tile
> map will not be rendered properly.

Let's add a function to move the map around the screen and make our
application a little more interactive. Listing 6-5 shows the code.

Listing 6-5. *Moving the Map*

```
_p.move = function(deltaX, deltaY) {
    this._x += deltaX;
    this._y += deltaY;
};
```

Now we have a class that can render a tile map on the screen. Let's plug it into
our empty skeleton! Update the functions as shown in bolded code in
Listing 6-6.

Listing 6-6. *Updating index.html File to Render the Map*

```
/** Add the variable to hold the map renderer */
var mapRenderer;

...

/**
 * Once all images are loaded - create the map renderer and
 * start the animation loop
 */
function onLoaded() {
    mapRenderer = new MapRenderer(world, imageManager.get("tiles"), 40);
    animate(0);
}

/** Perform rendering here */
function animate(t) {
    clear();

    // draw the map on the canvas
    mapRenderer.draw(ctx);
    requestAnimationFrame(arguments.callee);
}

/** Handle map move */
function onMove(e) {
```

```
    // Move the map, when user swipes the finger
    mapRenderer.move(e.deltaX, e.deltaY);
}
```

Launch this example on your Android device or desktop browser to see how it looks. Not bad, right? Figure 6-5 shows the first version of our virtual world launched in an emulator.

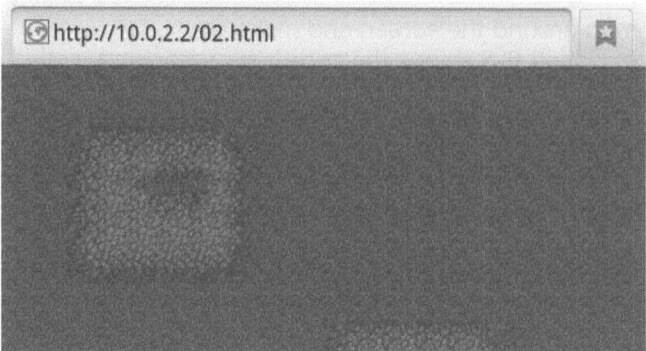

Figure 6-5. *The first version of the map*

Now think for a moment about the number of CPU loops wasted in each frame. Right now, we have two problems that make this code extremely ineffective:

- We render the whole map each time, no matter if the specific tile is visible on the screen or not.

- Even if the map is not moving, every tile is re-rendered each and every frame.

We're going to fix these issues one by one, but first let's add a small frames-per-second monitor that show us if we're really optimizing the performance or just writing lots of useless code. For the task of showing the current frames per second, I used a tiny yet very handy tool called xStats created by John-David Dalton (based on the work of Ricardo Cabello).

Measuring FPS

xStats adds a small monitor—an HTML element that displays some useful statistics about the web page:

fps (frames per second)

time spent per frame

memory usage (for desktop browsers)

Right now we are most interested in the first parameter—the frame rate. More frames means that the game runs smoother.

Let's add xStats to our project to see how many frames per second we can squeeze out of the device. Download the source from https://github.com/bestiejs/xstats.js, find the xstats.js file, and put it into the js folder along with other scripts. All you have to do to make xStats work is add three lines to the <style> block and add two lines of code to the init() function. Listing 6-6 summarizes these changes.

Listing 6-6. *Adding xStats Element to the Page*

```
<style>
    .xstats {
        position: absolute;
        top: 0;
        left: 0;
    }
</style>

...

function init() {
    imageManager = new ImageManager();
    imageManager.load(images, onLoaded);

    canvas = initFullScreenCanvas("mainCanvas");
    ctx = canvas.getContext("2d");

    inputHandler = new InputHandler(canvas);
    inputHandler.on("move", onMove);

    var stats = new xStats();
    document.body.appendChild(stats.element);
}
```

And that's it! xStats is possibly the least intrusive API for monitoring the robustness of the application. Reload the page and you'll see the running chart in the top-left corner of a page that displays the current frames-per-second value. Figure 6-6 shows how it looks (the image is zoomed 2x).

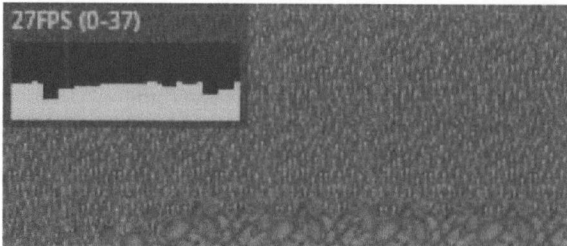

Figure 6-6. *xStats showing the frame rate*

You will likely see a constant 60 fps when you run the example in the desktop browser. It doesn't mean that it takes as much as 17 milliseconds to repaint the frame, but rather that the browser is *not requesting* the repaint more than 60 times a second.

I launched the application on my Galaxy and … wait—what? Only 27 fps, how could that happen?! Let's improve our rendering technique and maybe the game will run faster. The full example that implements the simplest map rendering and xStats monitor can be found in a v01 folder along with the other sources for this chapter.

Optimizing Rendering Performance

The current version of MapRenderer displays the tiled map properly; however, it does so in a way that is far from optimal. In this section, we try to improve the rendering performance. We will start with reducing the amount of tiles that we draw in each frame.

Draw Only What Is Required

Our first problem: we draw the entire world each time, even though the player needs only a small fragment. Instead of drawing the entire array of tiles, let's draw only the visible ones. Figure 6-7 illustrates this idea.

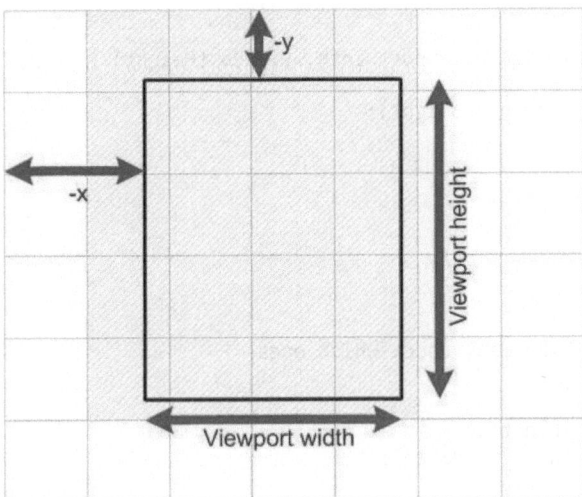

Figure 6-7. *Draw only the tiles that are currently visible in the viewport. Stroked out tiles are the ones that we will draw.*

MapRenderer needs to know the size of the viewport to find out which tiles are visible. Then, we can calculate the coordinates of the leftmost and rightmost visible tiles, using this simple formula:

```
var startX = Math.floor(-this._x / this._tileSize);
```

The expression -this._x / this._tileSize gives the number of tiles to the left of the viewport. Since this number can be decimal, we apply Math.floor() to it to get an integer index of it and receive the x coordinate of the leftmost tile that the user sees. A similar formula can be used to get the rightmost coordinate:

```
var endX = Math.floor((this._viewportWidth - this._x) / this._tileSize);
```

Both startX and endX might fall out of bounds of the world array when the user scrolls beyond the map. That's why we need to check bounds and trim values when needed.

```
startX = Math.max(startX, 0);
endX = Math.min(endX, this._mapData[0].length - 1);
```

Use the same formulas to get the topmost and bottommost y coordinates of visible tiles. Once you have all four—startX, endX, startY, and endY—you know what exactly the user sees through his current viewport, and thus you can omit any useless tiles. Let's implement this change as shown in Listing 6-7.

Listing 6-7. *Drawing Only Visible Tiles*

```
function MapRenderer(mapData, image, tileSize, viewportWidth, viewportHeight) {
    ...
    this.setViewportSize(viewportWidth, viewportHeight);
}

_p.setViewportSize = function(width, height) {
    this._viewportWidth = width;
    this._viewportHeight = height;
};

_p.draw = function(ctx) {
    // Instead of drawing every tile of the map, check which ones
    // are actually visible

    // x coordinate of the leftmost visible tile
    var startX = Math.floor(-this._x / this._tileSize);
    startX = Math.max(startX, 0);

    // x coordinate of the rightmost visible tile
    var endX = Math.floor((this._viewportWidth - this._x) / this._tileSize);
    endX = Math.min(endX, this._mapData[0].length - 1);

    // y coordinate of the topmost visible tile
    var startY = Math.floor(-this._y / this._tileSize);
    startY = Math.max(startY, 0);

    // y coordinate of the bottommost visible tile
    var endY = Math.floor((this._viewportHeight - this._y) / this._tileSize);
    endY = Math.min(endY, this._mapData.length - 1);

    // Draw only visible tiles
    for (var cellY = startY; cellY <= endY; cellY++) {
        for (var cellX = startX; cellX <= endX; cellX++) {
            var tileIndex = this._mapData[cellY][cellX];
            ...
            ...
        }
    }
};
```

You should not forget that canvas could change its size at any time. Users tend to shake and flip their smartphones and tablets causing the change of orientation, so your canvas renderer should be aware of such changes. The code that updates the size of the canvas should also update the size of the viewport so that MapRenderer has new values to calculate visible tiles. Listing 6-8 shows how to update the index.html file to keep the MapRenderer consistent with the size of the canvas.

Listing 6-8. *Updating the Size of the Viewport Each Time the Size of the Canvas Is Updated*

```
function resizeCanvas(canvas) {
    canvas.width  = document.width || document.body.clientWidth;
    canvas.height = document.height || document.body.clientHeight;
    mapRenderer && mapRenderer.setViewportSize(canvas.width, canvas.height);
}

function onLoaded() {
    mapRenderer = new MapRenderer(world, imageManager.get("tiles"),
            40, canvas.width, canvas.height);
    animate(0);
}
```

Now is a great time to see how it looks on the device! Thirty-four frames per second! Success! Well … not exactly. It still can run a lot faster; the problem that steals the most frames per second from us is when we repaint the entire map each frame, even when the visible fragment doesn't change. In other words, if the user sees the fragment of the map that is 10 × 15 tiles, we perform 150 calls to `drawImage()` on every frame, and most of the time the drawing results in exactly the same picture as the frame before. If we could cache the current state of the viewport and repaint it as a one image when we need to, we'll get a huge performance boost. That's the idea behind our next technique.

Offscreen Buffer

What if we simply create another instance of canvas that is exactly the same size as our viewport, and save the rendered map there? If the user doesn't move the map, we can use a pre-rendered snapshot instead. This technique is widespread in game development since it makes drawing complex patterns much faster. It is often referred to as the *offscreen buffer*. It's "offscreen" because you don't see the element that holds the cached fragment.

Before diving into the code, take a look at Figure 6-8, which explains the idea. Now we have two canvas instances instead of one. The second canvas is invisible, and is not even attached to the DOM. We will call it *offscreen canvas*. It holds the last frame that was drawn on the screen. If the user hasn't moved the map and hasn't changed the orientation of the device, then we can use the "cached" frame and draw it again. Otherwise, the offscreen canvas becomes invalid (this state is often called *dirty*). We need to update the offscreen canvas first, and copy the offscreen canvas back on the screen.

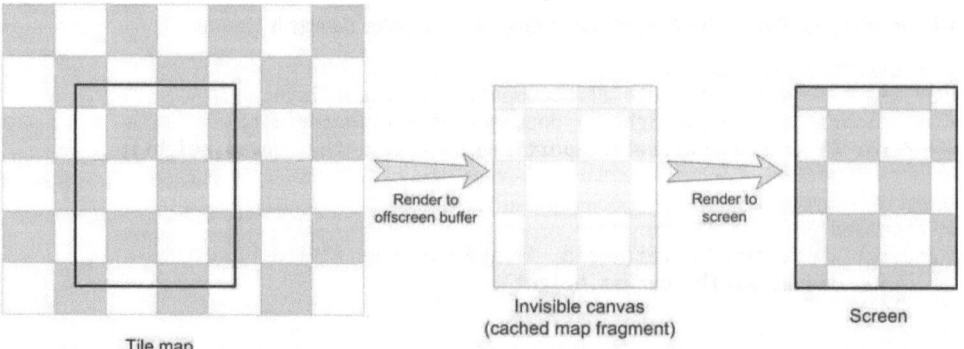

Tile map   Invisible canvas (cached map fragment)   Screen

Figure 6-8. *Instead of re-rendering the whole set of tiles every frame, we will "cache" the current frame on the invisible offscreen canvas. If the coordinates of the viewport hasn't changed, we use the pre-rendered frame, saving some cycles.*

If the user doesn't move the map, the frame is always the same and we don't need to repaint dozens of tiles. Using the offscreen buffer in this case saves many CPU cycles. Drawing big pictures is preferable in terms of performance, rather than trying to fill the same area with small tiles. That's exactly where we get the performance boost.

Now it's time for some code. Once again, MapRenderer needs a few extra fields. Let's add them (see Listing 6-9).

Listing 6-9. *Adding Support for the Offscreen Canvas to the MapRenderer*

```
function MapRenderer(mapData, image, tileSize, viewportWidth, viewportHeight) {
    …

    // offscreen canvas
    this._offCanvas = document.createElement("canvas");

    // context of the offscreen canvas
    this._offContext = this._offCanvas.getContext("2d");

    // flag that indicates, that a user has moved the viewport
    // and the offscreen canvas must be repainted
    this._offDirty = true;

    this.setViewportSize(viewportWidth, viewportHeight);
}
```

The first two fields are rather self-explanatory: offscreen canvas and its context. The third field — _offDirty—is the flag that we raise to indicate that the content of the offscreen canvas is no longer valid and needs to be repainted.

We need to keep the size of the offscreen canvas consistent with the size of the viewport. Besides, if the map has moved, we need to raise the _offDirty flag. The best way to do it is to update the move() method. Listing 6-10 shows how to implement that update.

Listing 6-10. *Keeping the Size of the Offscreen Canvas Consistent with the Viewport and Marking It Dirty Once the User Moves the Map*

```
_p.setViewportSize = function(width, height) {
    this._viewportWidth = width;
    this._viewportHeight = height;
    this._resetOffScreenCanvas();
};

/**
 * Updates the size of the offscreen canvas and marks
 * it as dirty
 */
_p._resetOffScreenCanvas = function() {
    this._offCanvas.width = this._viewportWidth;
    this._offCanvas.height = this._viewportHeight;
    this._offDirty = true;
};

_p.move = function(deltaX, deltaY) {
    Drawable.prototype.move.call(this, deltaX, deltaY);
    this._offDirty = true;
};
```

Now, the final and most important touch. Update the draw() function and make it a little smarter. Instead of drawing the tiles straight from the tile map, it checks if the offscreen buffer is "clean." A clean buffer means that the user hasn't moved the map, and the viewport has not resized; in other words, it means that the offscreen buffer holds exactly the same image that is required on this frame. So instead of drawing a piece of the world tile by tile, we can simply copy the content from the offscreen canvas to the screen.

What happens if the buffer *is* dirty? Then we need to perform exactly the same thing as we did before—render the fragment of the world tile by tile, but this time on the offscreen canvas. Once this is done, we have a clean buffer again and can draw it on the screen. Listing 6-11 summarizes these changes.

Listing 6-11. *Updating the Draw Function of the MapRenderer*

```
_p.draw = function(ctx) {
    if (this._offDirty) {
        this._redrawOffscreen();
    }
```

```
    ctx.drawImage(this._offCanvas, 0, 0);
};

_p._redrawOffscreen = function() {
    var ctx = this._offContext;
    ctx.clearRect(0, 0, this._viewportWidth, this._viewportHeight);
    var startX = Math.max(Math.floor(-this._x / this._tileSize), 0);
    var endX = Math.min(Math.floor((this._viewportWidth - this._x) /
this._tileSize), this._mapData[0].length - 1);

    var startY = Math.max(Math.floor(-this._y / this._tileSize), 0);
    var endY = Math.min(Math.floor((this._viewportHeight - this._y) /
this._tileSize), this._mapData.length - 1);

    for (var cellY = startY; cellY <= endY; cellY++) {
        for (var cellX = startX; cellX <= endX; cellX++) {
            var tileIndex = this._mapData[cellY][cellX];
            if (tileIndex > -1) {
                ctx.drawImage(this._image,
                        (tileIndex%this._tilesPerRow)*this._tileSize,
                        Math.floor(tileIndex/this._tilesPerRow)*this._tileSize,
                        this._tileSize, this._tileSize,
                        this._x + cellX*this._tileSize,
                        this._y + cellY*this._tileSize,
                        this._tileSize, this._tileSize);
            }
        }
    }
    this._offDirty = false;
};
```

As you see, most of the code from draw function migrated to the
_redrawOffscreen() function, with the only difference being that
_redrawOffscreen() works with the offscreen context.

That's it! Now our code is somewhat more complex than it was at the start of
this chapter, so let's see if it was worth the effort. A stable 45 frames! Way
closer to what we need.

Yet this code has a problem. When the user moves the map, the new version of
the draw() function performs even more work than before. Compare it yourself.
Before the last change, we repainted a few dozen tiles each frame. In the new
version, we don't do it if the map is *still*. If the map is constantly moving, we first
repaint the tiles to the offscreen buffer (the same job as before) *and then* we
paint the offscreen buffer to the screen. We optimized the case of a still, or not
moving the map a lot (45 frames is very good), but we made the case for moving
the map worse.

Some games rely on a map that is moving all the time. For example, if the viewport is tied to the character, the character's every step also moves the viewport. Let's see how we can improve the worst case.

Caching the Area Around the Viewport

So the problem that we're facing now is the following: since our offscreen canvas has the same size as the viewport, we have to redraw it on every movement. Every single pixel is causing the buffer to become "dirty." Moreover, we usually repaint the same set of tiles every time. What if we make the offscreen canvas slightly bigger than the viewport so that it can hold the small area around the viewport? This way, we could draw a set of tiles and keep them on the "buffer" until the viewport crosses the next cell of the grid. Once it happens, we need to draw a new set of tiles. We avoid repainting the same tiles over and over again. What is important here is that we don't repaint the buffer each frame while the user moves the map. We repaint it only when the user crosses the border of a tile, once per 25–30 frames. That's how we will fight the performance drop. Figure 6-9 illustrates this idea.

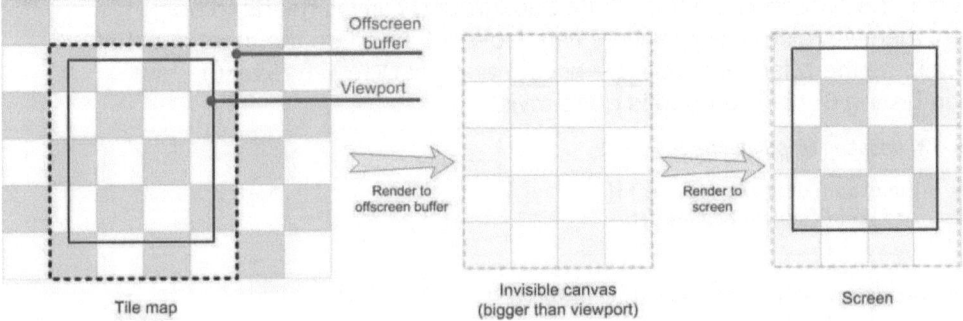

Figure 6-9. *Further optimization of map rendering. The offscreen canvas holds the area larger than the viewport; the repainting of the offscreen canvas happens only when the viewport crosses the "pre-painted" region. We chose the region to cover the integer number of the map cells.*

We have to update quite a few methods this time, but the result is worth the effort. Obviously we need to change the size of the offscreen canvas. This time we want it to be at least one cell bigger than the viewport so that we redraw it only when the visible tile set has changed.

We used to redraw the buffer on every movement. This time, before saying that the buffer is dirty, we need to check if the user has crossed the bounds of the rendered area. The _updateOffscreenBounds() function in Listing 6-12 does exactly this.

Listing 6-12. Checking If the User Has Crossed the Bounds of the Rendered Area

```
_p._updateOffscreenBounds = function() {
    var newBounds = {
        x: Math.floor(-this._x / this._tileSize),
        y: Math.floor(-this._y / this._tileSize),
        w: Math.ceil(this._viewportWidth/this._tileSize) + 1,
        h: Math.ceil(this._viewportHeight/this._tileSize) + 1
    };

    var oldBounds = this._offBounds;
    if (!(oldBounds.x == newBounds.x
            && oldBounds.y == newBounds.y
            && oldBounds.w == newBounds.w
            && oldBounds.h == newBounds.h)) {
        this._offBounds = newBounds;
        this._offDirty = true;
    }
};
```

_updateOffScreenBounds() is called for the viewport's every move in order to
check if the user has navigated to a new area of the map that hasn't yet been
rendered in the offscreen context. If the background canvas needs to be
updated, then we raise the _offDirty flag. Now, let's update the functions that
may invalidate the offscreen canvas—move() and _setViewportSize()—as
shown in Listing 6-13. The code is quite trivial.

Listing 6-13. *Updating MapRenderer*

```
_p.move = function(deltaX, deltaY) {
    this._updateOffscreenBounds();
}

_p.setViewportSize = function(width, height) {
    this._viewportWidth = width;
    this._viewportHeight = height;
    this._resetOffScreenCanvas();
};

_p._resetOffScreenCanvas = function() {
    this._updateOffscreenBounds();
    this._offCanvas.width = this._offBounds.w*this._tileSize;
    this._offCanvas.height = this._offBounds.h*this._tileSize;
    this._offDirty = true;
};
```

Once you set the new canvas size, the canvas is cleared; that's why

_resetOffScreenCanvas() explicitly sets the _offDirty. It doesn't matter if the
actual bounds have changed; there's no longer content there, so we need to

draw another. Now that we have defined the bounds of the offscreen canvas, let's see how we render it. Next, we have to update the _redrawOffscreen() function that fills the offscreen canvas with tiles. The changes are minimal: instead of using this._x and this._y to calculate the set of visible tiles, we use this._offBounds object, as shown in Listing 6-14.

Listing 6-14. *Updating the Offscreen Canvas*

```
_p._redrawOffscreen = function() {
    var ctx = this._offContext;
    ctx.clearRect(0, 0, this._offCanvas.width, this._offCanvas.height);

    var startX = Math.max(this._offBounds.x, 0);
    var endX = Math.min(startX + this._offBounds.w - 1,
                        this._mapData[0].length - 1);

    var startY = Math.max(this._offBounds.y, 0);
    var endY = Math.min(startY + this._offBounds.h - 1,
                        this._mapData.length - 1);

    for (var cellY = startY; cellY <= endY; cellY++) {
        for (var cellX = startX; cellX <= endX; cellX++) {
            var tileIndex = this._mapData[cellY][cellX];
            if (tileIndex > -1) {
                ctx.drawImage(this._image,
                        (tileIndex%this._tilesPerRow)*this._tileSize,
                        Math.floor(tileIndex/this._tilesPerRow)*this._tileSize,
                        this._tileSize, this._tileSize,

                        cellX*this._tileSize - this._offBounds.x*this._tileSize,
                        cellY*this._tileSize - this._offBounds.y*this._tileSize,
                        this._tileSize, this._tileSize);
            }
        }
    }
    this._offDirty = false;
};
```

In the previous version of the code, the offscreen canvas was exactly the same size as the viewport, so we copied the whole buffer to the screen in every draw() call. This time, the buffer is bigger than the canvas, so we need to calculate the coordinates of the area that we want to transfer. We have to do some extra calculations to make sure that we draw the correct pixels. Listing 6-15 shows how to update the draw() method.

Listing 6-15. *The New Draw Method*

```
_p.draw = function(ctx) {
    if (this._offDirty) {
        this._redrawOffscreen();
    }

    // Should draw offscreen at
    var offCanvasX = -Math.floor(this._x) - this._offBounds.x*this._tileSize;
    var offCanvasY = -Math.floor(this._y) - this._offBounds.y*this._tileSize;
    var offCanvasW = Math.min(this._offCanvas.width - offCanvasX,
                    this._viewportWidth);
    var offCanvasH = Math.min(this._offCanvas.height - offCanvasY,
                    this._viewportHeight);

    ctx.drawImage(this._offCanvas, offCanvasX, offCanvasY, offCanvasW,
                offCanvasH, 0, 0, offCanvasW, offCanvasH);
};
```

Run the test and enjoy the results! Even though we are running a little slower on a still image, we get significantly better results for the moving map! My Galaxy S now holds a steady 45 fps for this demo. The version of the code at its current state is saved into the v.04 folder along with other code for this chapter.

The same type of optimization can be applied to *loading* the blocks of the map from the server. We have divided the map into few virtual zones: *the viewport—* what the user currently sees; *the offscreen buffer—*what is pre-rendered; and the *rest of the world*. The rules are simple: when the user is reaching the end of a zone, the zone is recalculated (in our case, the offscreen buffer is re-rendered). But what if we add one zone between the *offscreen buffer* and the *rest of the world* like in Figure 6-10? We store the map data that has already transferred to the browser in that new zone, and once the user reaches the border, we load the new data from the server. This is an expansion of the idea that we already implemented.

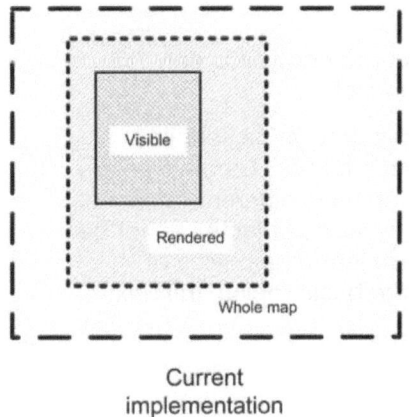

Current
implementation

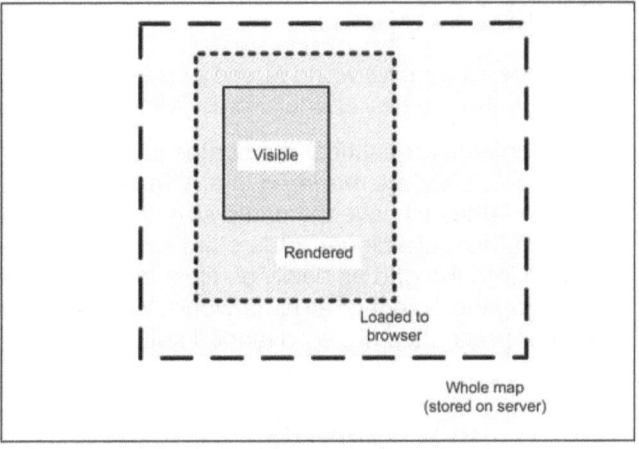

Extending the idea – the part of the map
is on the server

Figure 6-10. *Expanding the idea further. If we add the new Loaded to Browser zone, we can track when the user reaches the border, and load the new portion of the data from the server just in time.*

The map is performing reasonably well. Of course, that doesn't mean that there's no room for improvement! In fact, I think that it is quite possible to write an entire separate book describing the various algorithms of optimization, squeezing every millisecond of the processor time. But from this point on, you are ready to implement these algorithms on your own, since you already know the basic principles of optimizations and can compare the effects of each one. The optimizations that we implemented in these sections are stored in separate folders, so by simply opening each demo in your smartphone, you can compare the effects.

- v.01 has code without any optimizations (21 fps for me)

- v.02 implemented a "drawing only what is visible" strategy (34 fps)

- v.03 implemented the back buffer (about 45 fps when the map is not moving; about 30 fps when the map is constantly moving)

- v.04 implemented the caching of a small area around the viewport (about 43–45 fps, depending on whether the map is moving or not; the performance drop is too small to notice without an xStats chart).

World Objects

You have a beautiful world already created by you. But right now, it is only terrain without trees, animals, or buildings. Let's add these!

World objects (or entities) are sprites just like the sprites that we've seen in Chapter 4. They are rendered in a different way than tiled terrain. Terrain tiles are uniform—they all have the same size. World objects can have different sizes—some of them are bigger, others are smaller. That's why world objects cannot be aligned into the grid as easily as tiles. In this section, we learn the basics of rendering the object of a game world. We cover only the basic topics; the next chapter presents a more advanced solution.

Coordinate Systems

When we work with objects, it doesn't make much sense to treat them in terms of *screen* coordinates as we did for the map. It is much more convenient to speak about objects in terms of *world coordinates*. For example, it is natural to say that the object has moved when it moved inside of the world and changed its position relative to the map, rather than moved as the result of scrolling. But world coordinates are not enough to render the object. We need to pass the screen coordinates to the rendering function to display the sprite in a proper position. This way, a game object "lives" in several coordinate systems at a time. Two coordinate systems that we just described are the coordinates of the world and the coordinates of the screen. Figure 6-11 illustrates this concept.

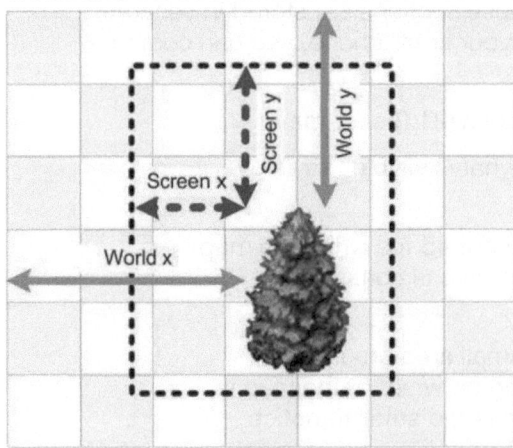

Figure 6-11. *The two coordinate systems for the game object: dashed arrows are screen coordinates; solid arrows are world coordinates.*

We need to use several different coordinate systems and be able to quickly translate the coordinates from one system to another one. If the tree is in (1270, 930) of the world coordinates, where should we draw it on the screen? Is it visible at all? This is an example of translating world coordinates to screen coordinates. The opposite example—when the user tapped the screen at (50, 120) and we need to tell if there is a tree under the tap. In this case, we need to translate from screen coordinates to the world coordinates, and check if there is a tree in a given world position.

The top-down view, like the one that we are exploring right now, is the easiest view for translating between coordinates. For example, to transform from screen coordinates to world coordinates, we can write:

```
worldX = screenX - mapX;
worldY = screenY - mapY,
```

Where mapX and mapY are the current position of the map on the screen. MapRenderer for example, stores them as this._x and this._y.

The reverse translation, from world coordinates to screen coordinates, is easy too:

```
screenX = worldX + mapX;
screenY = worldY + mapY,
```

Sometimes you also need to get the position of the tile in the world array given the click coordinates or world coordinates. For example, a user clicks a map to build a barracks and the game needs to check the type of the terrain under the click. If the user clicked a water tile, we shouldn't allow him to build something there. This third coordinate system that is often used is called *tile coordinates*. The translation formula is very simple too:

```
tileX = Math.floor((screenX - mapX) / tileSize);
tileY = Math.floor((screenY - mapY) / tileSize);
```

As you see, these calculations are not hard at all. That's because the world space is very similar to the screen space. This is not always true, however. For example, the calculations for isometric worlds, constructed from diamond or hex tiles, are somewhat more involved.

> **NOTE:** The coordinate systems are often called *spaces* in game development. For example, the rather wordy phrase "translating from the system of coordinates of the screen to the system of coordinates of the world" is often called simply "translating from the screen space to the world space." We will use these terms interchangeably.

Implementing WorldObjectRenderer

Now we are ready to implement the WorldObjectRenderer class that handles the drawing of the objects on the screen. Let's start with the helper class called WorldObject that represents the simple drawable entity like a tree or a rock. The code is shown in Listing 6-16.

Listing 6-16. *WorldObject Class*

```
function WorldObject(spriteSheet, frame) {
    this._spriteSheet = spriteSheet;
    this._frame = frame;
    this._x = 0;
    this._y = 0;
}

_p = WorldObject.prototype;

_p.getPosition = function() {
    return {
        x: this._x,
        y: this._y
    };
};

_p.setPosition = function(x, y) {
    this._x = x;
    this._y = y;
};

_p.draw = function(ctx, x, y) {
    this._spriteSheet.drawFrame(ctx, this._frame, x, y);
};
```

WorldObject is a wrapper around the SpriteSheet that associates the world coordinates with a certain frame of the sheet. The WorldObject expects the internal API to pass the correct screen coordinates during the draw() call. This class doesn't care about the viewport position or the map position.

The main work is performed in the WorldObjectRenderer class that renders the collection of objects on top of the map. The basic version of this class is quite trivial too; it passes the screen coordinates to every WorldObject and asks it to draw itself. The code is shown in Listing 6-17.

Listing 6-17. *Drawing World Objects: The First Version*

```
function WorldObjectRenderer(objects, viewportWidth, viewportHeight) {
    this._objects = objects;
```

```
        this._viewportWidth = viewportWidth;
        this._viewportHeight = viewportHeight;
        this._x = 0;
        this._y = 0;
}

_p = WorldObjectRenderer.prototype;

_p.move = function(deltaX, deltaY) {
        this._x += deltaX;
        this._y += deltaY;
};

_p.setViewportSize = function(width, height) {
        this._viewportWidth = width;
        this._viewportHeight = height;
};

_p.draw = function(ctx) {
        for (var i = 0; i < this._objects.length; i++) {
                var obj = this._objects[i];
                var pos = obj.getPosition();
                obj.draw(ctx, this._x + pos.x, this._y + pos.y);
        }
};
```

The WorldObjectRenderer has an API very similar to MapRenderer. In fact, the only difference is in the parameters of a constructor. In the next chapter, we learn how to take advantage of this feature, but for now, we will leave everything as it is.

The final step is to update the index.html file. We need to add the code that loads the new resource (the image with world objects), creates some WorldObject instances, and renders them. The code in Listing 6-18 summarizes the updates.

Listing 6-18. *Updating index.html to Render Objects on the Tiled Map*

```
var spriteSheet;
var objectRenderer;

var images = {
    "tiles": "img/tiles.png",
    "objects": "img/objects.png" // load objects image
};

// The coordinates of the frames
var frames = [
    [0, 0, 110, 96, 55, 96],
    [110, 0, 68, 108, 34, 108],
```

```
            [178, 0, 71, 79, 35, 79],
            [250, 0, 29, 56, 15, 56],
            [256, 60, 40, 31, 20, 31]
    ];

    /** Once all images are loaded - starts the animation loop */
    function onLoaded() {
        mapRenderer = new MapRenderer(world, imageManager.get("tiles"),
                         40, canvas.width, canvas.height);
        spriteSheet = new SpriteSheet(imageManager.get("objects"), frames);

        objectRenderer = new WorldObjectRenderer(getObjects(),
                                         canvas.width, canvas.height);
        animate(0);
    }

    function getObjects() {
        return [
            getTree(200, 200),
            getTree(280, 220),
            getRock(300, 270),
            getRock(150, 197)
        ];
    }

    function getTree(x, y) {
        var obj = new WorldObject(spriteSheet, 1);
        obj.setPosition(x, y);
        return obj;
    }

    function getRock(x, y) {
        var obj = new WorldObject(spriteSheet, 3);
        obj.setPosition(x, y);
        return obj;
    }

    /** Perform rendering here */
    function animate(t) {
        clear();
        mapRenderer.draw(ctx);
        objectRenderer.draw(ctx);
        requestAnimationFrame(arguments.callee);
    }

    /** Handle map move */
    function onMove(e) {
        mapRenderer.move(e.deltaX, e.deltaY);
```

```
    objectRenderer.move(e.deltaX, e.deltaY);
}

function resizeCanvas(canvas) {
    canvas.width  = document.width || document.body.clientWidth;
    canvas.height = document.height || document.body.clientHeight;
    mapRenderer && mapRenderer.setViewportSize(canvas.width, canvas.height);
    objectRenderer && objectRenderer.setViewportSize(canvas.width,
canvas.height);
}
```

Once you save the changes and update the page, you should see a screen like
the shown in Figure 6-12. Much nicer!

Figure 6-12. *Rendering of world objects*

Rendering Order

Game objects have to be rendered in order. Figure 6-13 illustrates what might
happen if you use the wrong rendering order. The rock was meant to be behind
the tree, but due to the wrong rendering order, it appears on top of it.

Figure 6-13. *Wrong rendering order*

To fix this issue, we must ensure that the objects that stand "further behind" are rendered before the objects that are closer to the player. In a 2D world, this is quite simple to implement. You sort objects by the position of their bottoms and draw them in order from furthest to closest. To do that, we add a few lines of code to the SpriteSheet class. We need to know the bounds of the frame in order to sort world objects. Listing 6-19 shows how to do it.

Listing 6-19. *Adding Code to SpriteSheet to Get the Bounds of the Frame*

```
_p.getFrameBounds = function(index, x, y) {
    var frame = this._frames[index];
    if (!frame)
        return;

    return {
        x: x - frame[SpriteSheet.FRAME_ANCHOR_X],
        y: y - frame[SpriteSheet.FRAME_ANCHOR_Y],
        w: frame[SpriteSheet.FRAME_WIDTH],
        h: frame[SpriteSheet.FRAME_HEIGHT]
    };
};
```

Next, update the WorldObject itself to report the bounds to the WorldObjectRenderer with respect to the position of an object in the world (see Listing 6-20).

Listing 6-20. *Update the WorldObject Class, Add the getBounds() Function*

```
_p.getBounds = function() {
    return this._spriteSheet.getFrameBounds(this._frame, this._x, this._y);
};
```

Finally, add the sorting code to the constructor of the WorldObjectRenderer, as in Listing 6-21.

Listing 6-21. *Sorting World Objects*

```
function WorldObjectRenderer(objects, viewportWidth, viewportHeight) {
    this._objects = objects;

    this._objects.sort(function(o1, o2) {
        var bounds1 = o1.getBounds();
        var bounds2 = o2.getBounds();
        return (bounds1.y + bounds1.h) - (bounds2.y + bounds2.h);
    });

    this._viewportWidth = viewportWidth;
    this._viewportHeight = viewportHeight;
    this._x = 0;
    this._y = 0;
}
```

Once you sort the objects this way, the rendering is correct.

This simple issue was quite easy to solve, but it has a lot of implications. When it comes to the large world where the objects can move and break the presorted order, "sort on every frame" is no longer an option. Right now, all objects are static—just rocks and trees—but once you add moving entities, things start to get much more interesting. In the next chapter, we will address this issue and build a more advanced version of the WorldObjectRenderer that can also take care of movement.

Optimizations

From an optimization perspective, objects work exactly the same way as regular tiles. The rule for them stays the same: if you don't want to lose any CPU cycles, draw only what you really need to draw. We will not go through the same exercise again by starting our implementation from the simplest case and gradually improving it—there's no point in doing the same trick twice. Let's think about a nearly optimal way of rendering objects straightaway.

We can't easily determine which objects we have to draw. Game objects do not form a grid, and we can't say "we're drawing objects from number five to number eight this pass" as we did with tiles. So we have two options. First, we can look at every object in the world and decide if we should draw it. Yes, this really *is* an option. Let's say, for example, that in your game, the main character moves between rooms; so the rooms load one by one and each room is relatively small compared to the screen size. Then chances are that you will draw at least 50 percent of the objects in the world. The same is true for social farm-like games that have a small world. In this case, it actually makes sense to save coding time by using the simplest possible scenario: check the bounding box of every object and draw those that fall inside the visible area.

However, there are other cases too, like if your world is so big that the player can only see less than 1 percent of objects on the screen at a time. Quite possible! In this case, we can't afford checking objects like that because it instantly kills the performance of the game. The only solution is to organize game objects into some sort of spatial structure that decides which objects are most likely visible "right now."

> **NOTE:** This problem is not unique for game development. There are many other types of applications that face the same issue. As an example, the question "which sprites can the user see?" is very close to "list the gas stations no more than 3 miles away from my home," which is encountered in the mapping and navigation domain. Gas stations are sprites, "3 miles away" is the size of the viewport, and "my home" is the current position of the viewport. So it's not a surprise that the problem has been seriously researched.

There are various algorithms to address this issue (most of them based on trees) by grouping entities into bounding rectangles and grouping bounding rectangles into bigger bounding rectangles on the next level (try Googling "R-Tree" for a good example on how this approach works). However, the math behind these is pretty complex, and explaining it here would take too many pages and not be interesting to most readers.

There is a much easier approach that is suitable for game development (at least on the client-side); one that doesn't require a degree in rocket science to implement. We like working with grids. Grids are simple because they have nice square cells and it is very easy to find cells that intersect the current viewport. We've used this trick with a grid of tiles, so let's use it once more! We can break the whole set of game objects into a uniform grid and check only the objects that fall into the cells that are visible.

Take a look at the image in Figure 6-14 that illustrates this idea. In the example that is shown in the picture, only four objects will be checked for the intersection with the viewport: in grid cells (2, 0), (3,0), (2, 1), and (3, 1). Only the two of them that actually intersect the viewport will be rendered. This way, we eliminate useless checks and draw only what is actually important.

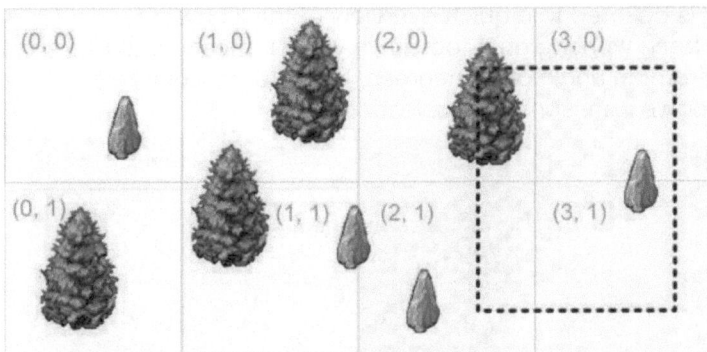

Figure 6-14. *Minimizing the amount of objects to check before drawing. The world is divided into the grid. Each object is assigned to several grid cells. Only the objects in cells from (2:0) to (3:1) are checked in each frame.*

Obviously, the game object may be placed in the border between two cells or even at the point where two such borders intersect. In this case, the object is assigned to two or four grid cells. Later, we filter such objects so that we don't draw them twice or four times.

What if the object is moving? We have to track it and make sure that it is deregistered from the grid cells when it leaves them, and registered in the new ones when it arrives. It's like traveling around the city with your cell phone: it is always looking for the best GSM transmitter to use. When you leave the range of one transmitter, you are registered in another one.

It is quite important to determine the optimal size of the grid cell. The best size depends on the specifics of your game and on the density of the game objects, if they are static (don't move, don't appear or disappear) or they are dynamic (move around, new ones appear, older ones disappear). If you make big cells, it means that you have to check more objects on each animation frame. For example, if one cell is 500 × 500 pixels and the viewport is located in the intersection of cells, it means that you have to test objects in a 1000 × 1000 pixel area, which is pretty big. If you make your cells too small, you'll soon face the problem of having a lot of empty cells. Besides, a moving object constantly has to register/unregister itself in these cells. So what is the optimal size? This questioned is best answered with some benchmarks that run on your specific setup.

In the next chapter, we build the more advanced object renderer, based on this simple idea of grids.

Isometric View

The final part of this chapter is devoted to a quick overview of the isometric projection. Until now, we've been working on a top-down view. It means that the user is looking at the scene from an angle of 90 degrees. Figure 6-15 illustrates the difference between top-down and isometric projections.

Figure 6-15. *On the left,* The Legend of Zelda, *published by Nintendo in 1986, uses an orthogonal (top-down) view. On the right,* Fallout 2, *created by Black Isle Studios and published by Interplay in 1998, uses isometric projection.*

The other interesting way of looking at things is when the camera is slightly rotated. Well, in a 2D world, we don't have the camera to rotate, of course. For a 2D game, an *isometric view* means a special way of drawing and rendering objects that creates the feeling of depth. The definition would be that isometric projection is the projection where the angles between axes are the same: 120 degrees.

Figure 6-16 shows how a cube looks in the top-down projection that we're making, and the isometric projection.

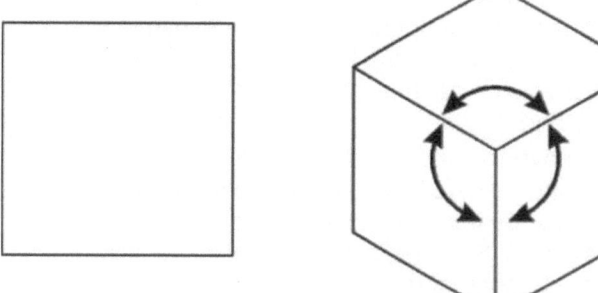

Figure 6-16. *The cube on the left is in top-down projection—either top view or side view, it looks the same. The cube on the right is in isometric projection.*

There are a lot of games that use this approach to rendering the world. The isometric view looks more natural to the user than the top-down view. When you play a board game, you don't look at the board straight from the top. When a medieval general leads his army into battle, he doesn't look at the battlefield from a hot air balloon, either.

Let's see what it takes to create an isometric-based engine on canvas. The most important point is that the optimization that we introduced in this chapter is not unique to top-down games. It works almost the same way for "iso-games" too. The only difference is the way you draw tiles and the way you translate between coordinate spaces.

In isometric games, the tiles are diamond-shaped. They are twice as wide as they are tall. Because of that, the grid that they form is not rectangular; the tiles in odd rows are half-width shifted compared to the tiles in the even rows. So the rendering code for isometric tiles needs to be adjusted. Figure 6-17 shows an example of the isometric grid.

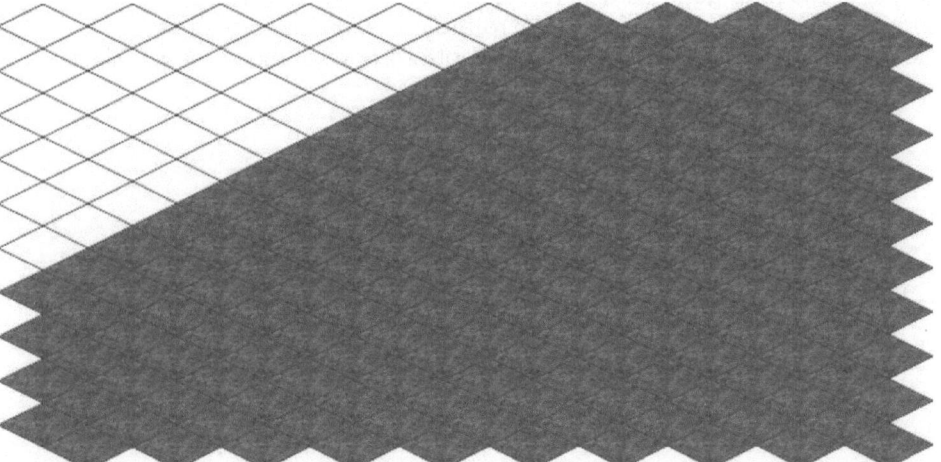

Figure 6-17. *The left part of the isometric map is filled with "empty" tiles to show how the grid looks.*

The coordinate system for isometric tiles is also different from the coordinate system of the usual "square" projection that we were working with. In isometric tile maps, there are at least two ways of setting the coordinates of tiles and rendering the tile world. Figure 6-18 shows the first way to assign coordinates to the tiles.

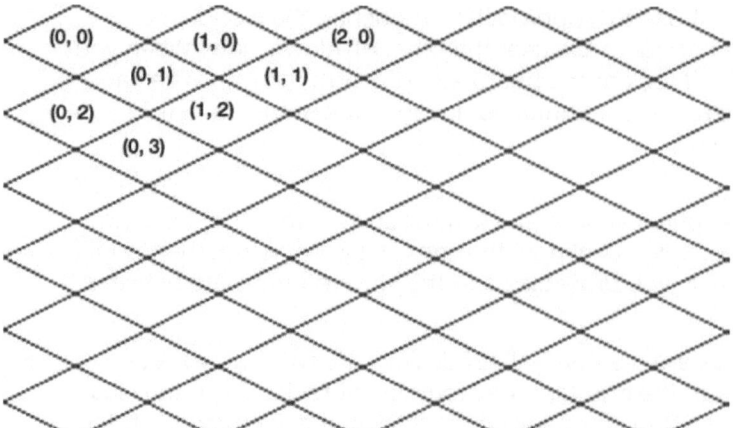

Figure 6-18. *One way to assign coordinates to the isometric grid*

Here, the axis of the map goes parallel to the axis of the canvas. The second way, shown in Figure 6-19, is the following: rotate coordinates 45 degrees counterclockwise. The x axis now goes to the bottom-right of the screen, while y goes to the bottom left.

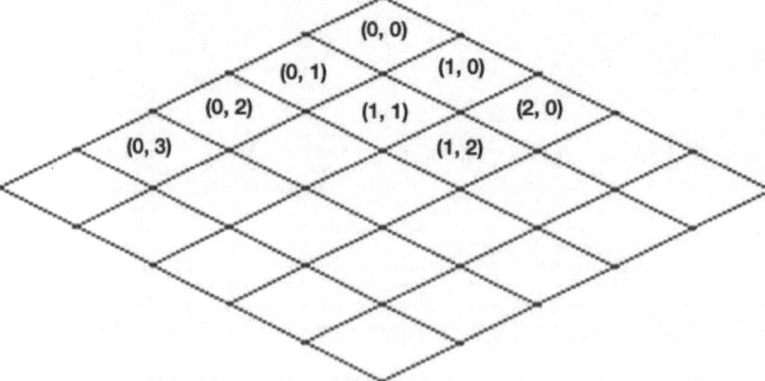

Figure 6-19. *The other way to draw the tile map*

This short introduction should give you a feeling for what isometric projection is and how isometric games look. We haven't yet looked at how to implement the isometric game, but that's why we have the entire next chapter. You have surely played at least few isometric games, if not in the age of *Fallout 2*, then recently in social networks. Isometric engines balance an appealing look with the relatively low complexity (compared to 3D engines, for example). That's why isometric games became a prime target for the developers of social applications.

Summary

In this chapter, we looked into rendering virtual worlds. We learned that implementing various approaches to the optimization of rendering is crucial for game performance, especially when it comes to mobile devices. We started from the simple implementation of the tiled engine that showed only around 20 fps, and gradually improved it to a steady 45 fps at the end. We learned how to add objects to the game world and how to render them correctly.

We looked into two different projections: top-down and isometric. The first projection is good for platform shooters and top-down is best for old-school games. Isometric projection looks more natural to the user, however, it requires more effort to implement—both in terms of math and in terms of processing power. The next chapter of the book is fully devoted to making an isometric game engine.

Making an Isometric Engine

The isometric view was once the most popular mechanic for rendering virtual worlds. It perfectly suited RPGs, strategy games, and tactical games, and it looked much better than a simple orthogonal top-down view. Many masterpieces of game development used isometric engines, such as *Fallout*, *XCOM*, *SimCity*, and many, many others. Kids of the '80s still remember how advanced and cutting-edge those games looked compared to simple "flat" engines.

Nowadays desktops use 3D for almost everything—from AAA-class games to small indie projects. Browsers, however, are still quite far from widely adopting 3D (especially mobile browsers). That's why isometric engines are still very attractive for the casual player. This type of engine can look very appealing in the browser (especially if you hire a good artist).

Social networks also factor in the popularity of isometric games. *Gardens of Time*, *The Sims Social*, and *CityVille*—the most popular Facebook games of 2011—are isometric! Indeed, numerous farms, tower defenses, and small strategies look best when implemented with an isometric view. Isometric graphics are among the most attractive engine mechanics available for mass market, and it is perfect for casual strategy projects. That's why we decided to devote an entire chapter to isometric game engines and show you how to create one from scratch.

This chapter is devoted to making a skeleton for isometric games. We will not touch the gameplay, but rather the engine that can render a big isometric world that allows the player to interact with it. This is a very solid basis for your own game project.

In this chapter, we will learn how to:

- Render the isometric terrain using a set of isometric sprites

- Optimize rendering—implement the image caching strategies described in the previous chapter for the isometric terrain

- Render game objects like buildings and characters, implementing the techniques described in Chapter 6 in practice

- Implement dirty rectangles—a strategy to minimize the redraw region and save CPU cycles

- Deal with interaction—clicking elements, dragging viewport

- Create simple UI controls

The resulting engine will look like Figure 7-1.

Figure 7-1. *The result: an isometric game engine*

As a bonus, and a boost for your own start-up, this chapter comes with a set of isometric art, created specifically for this book by a fantastic concept artist, Sergey Lesluk (http://n1tro-killer.deviantart.com). You are free to use these sprites for your own project, as long as you have purchased the electronic or paper version of this book (Choose electronic, save trees. Seriously.).

> **NOTE:** Throughout this chapter, I say "simple as farm games". In fact, popular social projects are not simple at all. They have rather complex server-side logic and infrastructure to support the gazillions of players gathering their crops every day. However, the rendering on the client side is relatively simple.

Setup

The project that we're going to accomplish is a rather big one when compared with other projects in this book, both in terms of lines of code and the number of features. We need a solid plan in order to keep track of progress and understand why we take a certain path to reach the goal. The goal is to make an isometric engine that can render terrain and objects, and interact with the user. We're omitting the gameplay details for now, but are focusing instead on architecture, rendering mechanics, optimizations, and player interaction. We will load the level, let the user scroll through it, click the ground tiles to change the terrain type (e.g. "build road"), add new objects to the map, and remove existing ones. This is the typical flow for many strategy games; the rest is just the details of gameplay (for example "do not allow building stables if wood is less than 300").

The Plan

The user will have three "modes" of interaction with the game world: movement, editing terrain, and editing objects. The user can switch between the modes at any time—we will create a small UI element for that. Look at Figure 7-1 again, the small circle with the "house" icon on the top left shows the current mode. When the user taps the circle, the mode switches.

The rendering is organized in layers (we discussed that technique in Chapter 6), and each layer is responsible for a certain type of object. We will have three types of layers in this project: one for isometric tiles, one for world objects, and one for UI elements. They are called IsometricTileLayer, ObjectLayer, and

UiLayer, respectively. They are shown in Figure 7-2. To simplify the treating of the multiple layers, we will create the LayerManager.

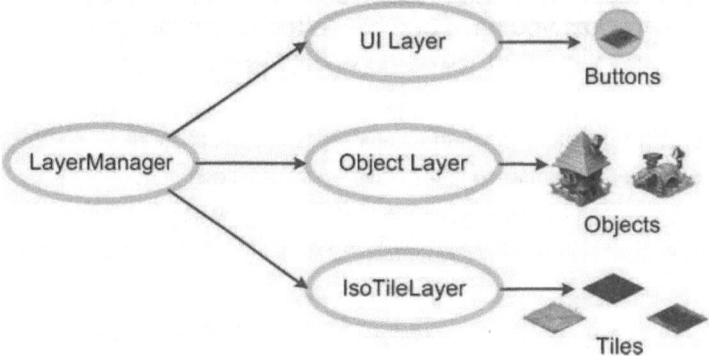

Figure 7-2. *The rendering layers of the engine*

We start by building the skeleton of the game—the HTML file and the main Game class—initiating the event handling and creating an animation loop much like we did in the previous chapter. At this point, we will have something "working" to start with. The next step is to add the isometric terrain.

The isometric terrain by itself is not a very hard task, but there are a few things to worry about, and a few optimizations to implement. The second part of this chapter is devoted to isometric terrain: rendering tiles, implementing an offscreen cache, scrolling the map, and other matters. The result is an empty, scrollable terrain with no objects.

The next obvious step is to add objects to the map. We will need the ObjectLayer, which is somewhat easier to build than IsometricTileLayer. We will introduce one more optimization briefly mentioned in the previous chapter— the *object clusters* (to limit the number of "active" objects and not to deal with the objects far away from the viewport). Finally, we will look at complex objects like arcs and portals—there is a small trick in how to implement them correctly. At this point, we will have the objects rendered on top of isometric ground. Some of them will move, to illustrate that movement is handled correctly.

The next major topic is to build the *dirty rectangles* algorithm—marking certain areas of the screen "dirty" in order to render *only these areas* in the next frame. For example, if there is a one small moving object on the screen, it doesn't make sense to repaint the whole area—just the bits covered by that object. Both isometric and object layers are affected by this change, and in the end of this section, the game will not waste any cycles on rendering the parts of the screen that are not changed anyway.

Next, we will introduce the LayerManager—the class that simplifies the handling of multiple layers—since at this point we already have two layers (terrain and objects) and we're about to add a third (UI elements). The more layers we add, the more code needs to be written to handle them (move, resize, and render them appropriately). LayerManager is the object that hides away the details like the number of layers, or their order, from the calling API. It presents a simple interface that acts like a layer itself.

With the layers and LayerManager taken care of, we will create the user interface—the round button for switching the state of the game. For now, it will stay nonfunctional since the event system is not yet ready.

The last part is to process the user input—track clicks and drag events, propagate events to the correct layer, and perform actions like changing terrain or adding objects. We will once more look at the architecture of events and build an unobtrusive system of notifications, leaving the components of the engine as independent from each other as possible. With the event system in place, we will add the final touches to the project—implementing the core game mechanics (changing terrain, adding and removing objects, changing the game state).

Preparing the Workspace

We will need a few classes that we created in previous chapters: ImageManager, utils.js, EventEmitter, and everything related to user input. Copy those from the previous chapters, or take them from the materials for this chapter. Next, copy the images into the img folder and create an empty file called Game.js—we will put the game logic there soon. After you have completed these steps, the directory structure should look like Figure 7-3.

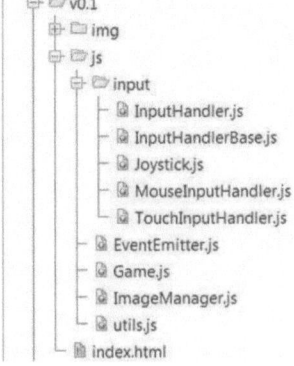

Figure 7-3. *Initial structure of the project*

Basic Code

The code for the index.html file is not very different from the initial code from previous chapters. For the sake of completeness, Listing 7-1 shows it. Once the page is loaded, the Game class gets the control (except for resize behavior that stays outside, because the Game shouldn't be aware of why and when the underlying canvas is resized).

Listing 7-1. *index.html File: The Game Entry Point*

```
<!DOCTYPE html>
<html lang="en">
<head>
    <meta charset="utf-8" />
    <meta name="viewport"
        content="width=device-width, initial-scale=1.0, maximum-scale=1.0,↩
        user-scalable=no, target-densitydpi=device-dpi"/>

    <style>
        html, body {
            overflow: hidden;
            width: 100%;
            height: 100%;
            margin:0;
            padding:0;
            border: 0;
        }
    </style>
    <script src="js/utils.js"></script>
    <script src="js/ImageManager.js"></script>

    <script src="js/EventEmitter.js"></script>
    <script src="js/input/InputHandlerBase.js"></script>
    <script src="js/input/MouseInputHandler.js"></script>
    <script src="js/input/TouchInputHandler.js"></script>
    <script src="js/input/InputHandler.js"></script>

    <script src="js/Game.js"></script>

    <script>
        var game;
        function init() {
            game = new Game(initFullScreenCanvas("mainCanvas"));
        }

        function initFullScreenCanvas(canvasId) {
            var canvas = document.getElementById(canvasId);
            resizeCanvas(canvas);
            window.addEventListener("resize", function() {
```

```
            resizeCanvas(canvas);
        });
        return canvas;
    }

    function resizeCanvas(canvas) {
        canvas.width  = document.width  || document.body.clientWidth;
        canvas.height = document.height || document.body.clientHeight;
        game && game.resize();
    }

    </script>
</head>
<body onload="init()">
<canvas id="mainCanvas" width="200" height="200"></canvas>
</body>
</html>
```

The initial version of Game.js is a set of stubs and empty functions. This class handles the core mechanics and arranges components into a working mechanism, but since there are no components yet, and there is nothing to arrange, it is still empty. Nevertheless, the Game does a couple of useful things: it loads the images and registers event listeners. During the course of this chapter, we only deal with two types of events: drag and up, so we will register listeners right away but leave them empty, until they can do the actual work. Listing 7-2 shows the initial code for this class. The code uses the bind() function, which we haven't yet looked at. I will explain it in a minute.

Listing 7-2. *Game class: The Entry Point for the Future Game*

```
function Game(canvas) {
    this._canvas = canvas;
    this._ctx = this._canvas.getContext("2d");
    this._boundAnimate = this._animate.bind(this);

    this._imageManager = new ImageManager();
    this._imageManager.load({
        "terrain": "img/terrain.png",
        "arch-left": "img/arch-left.png",
        "arch-right": "img/arch-right.png",
        "house-1": "img/house-1.png",
        "house-2": "img/house-2.png",
        "ball": "img/ball.png",
        "ui": "img/ui.png"
    }, this._onImagesLoaded.bind(this));
}

_p = Game.prototype;
```

```
/** Called once all images are loaded */
_p._onImagesLoaded = function() {
    this.resize();
    var inputHandler = new InputHandler(this._canvas);
    inputHandler.on("move", this._onMove.bind(this));
    inputHandler.on("up", this._onUp.bind(this));

    this._clearBg();
    this._animate();
};

/** Move the viewport withing the world */
_p.move = function(deltaX, deltaY) { };

/** Resize handling */
_p.resize = function() { };

/** Event handling */
_p._onMove = function(e) {};
_p._onUp = function(e) {};

/** Update objects - move, animate etc */
_p._updateWorld = function() { };

/** Render frame on context */
_p._renderFrame = function() { };

/** Called each frame, updates objects and re-renders the frame if required */
_p._animate = function() {
    requestAnimationFrame(this._boundAnimate);
    this._updateWorld();
    this._renderFrame();
};

/** Fills background with black */
_p._clearBg = function() {
    this._ctx.fillStyle = "black";
    this._ctx.fillRect(0, 0, this._canvas.width, this._canvas.height);
};
```

Once the resources are ready, the Game initializes the animation loop that contains two parts: _updateWorld() (used for logic updates, AI, etc.) and _renderFrame() (outputs the result on canvas). We already know how to handle animations and timing, so we will not implement this aspect in this project. If you want to, adding the animated character is a very straightforward task once everything else is done.

Utilities

The isometric engine is a complex project. To keep the code clean, it is worth investing a little time at the beginning and extract the common and reusable functionality in the separate classes, as well as explore some useful tricks that will make the code more readable. We will start with exploring the bind() function that fights the loss of the this keyword in event listeners.

bind(), apply(), and call() functions

As you've seen in previous chapters, the this keyword that is used within the body of a new function may refer to the different object than the this keyword used outside. The following code shows how this behaves, depending on where exactly it used; the example is taken from the ImageManager class:

```
_p._loadItem = function(queueItem, itemCounter, onDone, onProgress) {
    // this keyword points to the current instance of ImageManager
    var img = new Image();
    img.onload = function() {
        // this keyword points to the img
    };

    img.onerror = function() {
        // this keyword points to the img
    };

    // this keyword points to the ImageManager again
};
```

The value of this depends on the *execution context* of the function. The execution context (among other things) determines which variables the function "sees" and which object stands behind this. For example, consider the following code:

```
var a = {
    name: "a",
    f: function() {
        console.log(this.name);
    }
}
a.f(); // outputs "a"

var b = {
    name: "b",
    f: a.f
}
```

```
b.f(); // outputs "b"
```

The `f()` function is originally defined for the a object; it outputs the name of the object through `this` reference. But that doesn't mean that the object behind the `this` keyword will always be a. In the next line, we assign the function to the b object and then call it with `b.f()`. During the second call, the value of `this` inside the body of the function is b. Even though the function was originally defined on the other object, it outputs the name of the current "owner"—b.

The `img.onload()` callback works in a similar way. The callback function is assigned to the `Image` object, and once the image is loaded, it will be called from that object. Hence, the value of `this` will be `img`, and not the `ImageManager` instance.

But what if we *want* to make `this` always refer a certain object, no matter how the function is called? There is a way in JavaScript: the `bind()` function does exactly this. Look at the following code:

```
var a = {
    name: "a",
}

var b = {
    name: "b"
}

f = (function() {
        console.log(this.name);
}).bind(a);

a.f = b.f = f;

a.f(); // outputs "a"
b.f(); // outputs "a"! Because we used the "bound" function
f();   // Still outputs "a", even when called without the object at all!
```

`bind()` returns the new function that acts exactly as the original one, but with `this` keyword bound to the given object. In the preceding code, the function f is bound to the object so no matter how it is called—with `a.f()`, with `b.f()`, or even without the object at all, just `f()`—it always outputs the same value: `"a"`.

It is important to understand that `bind()` does not change the original function in any way; it merely creates the new version of the function and returns it to the caller. Look at the following code:

```
var f = function() {
    console.log(this.name);
};
```

```
var boundF = f.bind(a);
```

Only the function called boundF() has this keyword bound to a certain object. The original f() function behaves normally, since it did not change after the bind() call.

> **NOTE:** The mechanics behind this keyword is described in detail in the following MDN post:
> https://developer.mozilla.org/en/JavaScript/Reference/Operators
> /this.

The bind() function was introduced in ECMAScript 5th Edition, and it is not yet available for every mobile browser. To make the code cross-browser, add the following shim (see Listing 7-3) to your utils.js file.

Listing 7-3. *The bind() Function Shim That Makes Sure That the Function Is Available for Older Browsers Too*

```
if (!Function.prototype.bind) {
    Function.prototype.bind = function (oThis) {
        if (typeof this !== "function") {
            // closest thing possible to the ECMAScript 5
            // internal IsCallable function
            throw new TypeError("Function.prototype.bind - " +
                "what is trying to be bound is not callable");
        }

        var fSlice = Array.prototype.slice,
            aArgs = fSlice.call(arguments, 1),
            fToBind = this,
            fNOP = function () {},
            fBound = function () {
                return fToBind.apply(this instanceof fNOP
                    ? this
                    : oThis || window,
                    aArgs.concat(fSlice.call(arguments)));
            };

        fNOP.prototype = this.prototype;
        fBound.prototype = new fNOP();

        return fBound;
    };
}
```

> **NOTE:** The shim code is from an MDN post at
> `https://developer.mozilla.org/`
> `en/JavaScript/Reference/Global_Objects/Function/bind.`

Now it should be quite easy to understand why we used the line

```
this._boundAnimate = this._animate.bind(this);
```

in Listing 7-2. The animate() function is called as the callback of
requestAnimationFrame(). If used as is, it will lose the value of this after the first
call. Using _boundAnimate() instead of _animate() makes sure that this always
refers to the instance of the Game.

The section about the this keyword and execution contexts would not be
complete without looking at two extremely useful functions, apply() and call(),
which allow you to execute an arbitrary function with the arbitrary value of this,
without even assigning the function to the object.

```
var a = {
    name: "a",
}

var b = {
    name: "b"
}

f: function() {
        console.log(this.name);
}

f.call(a);        // Execute f, this will refer to object a
f.apply(b, []);   // Execute f, this will refer to object
```

call() and apply() let you *explicitly* provide the object for this keyword. The
only difference between the two is the way they accept the arguments for the
function—apply() accepts the array of arguments, while call()accepts them as
its own arguments one by one:

```
fun.apply(newThis, [arg1, arg2, arg3]);
fun.call(newThis, arg1, arg2, arg3);
```

Of course, if the function is bound to some object, then neither apply() nor
call() will change that behavior.

> **NOTE:** Strictly speaking, apply() and call() *will* still change the value of this keyword for the "bound" function, but not for the original one. The change will not have any effect though, because the bounded function does not rely on this.

Mathematical Functions and Rect Class

Naturally, writing a 2D engine requires some 2D math. An isometric engine is no exception. The most common math operations are the operations over rectangles— check if two rectangles are equal, test if the object is visible (object rectangle intersects with viewport rectangle), test if the user clicked the object (click is within the object rectangle), and find the minimal rectangle that should be repainted to cover all dirty areas (find rectangular convex hull).

There are too many small functions to keep them separated over the code. A far better approach is to create a class and implement all the rectangle-handling math there. Let's call this class Rect (Rectangle is too long to type). The code for the functions is really a part of the basic math course that everyone studied in school, so it doesn't make much sense to reprint it here. The whole source code is distributed with the materials for this chapter in the js/Rect.js file. Here we only list the function declarations, to know the instrument that we rely on:

```
function Rect(x, y, width, height) {
    this.x = x; this.y = y;
    this.width = width; this.height = height;
}

_p = Rect.prototype;

/* Create the new rectangle with exactly the
 * same size and position as the given one
 */
_p.copy = function() {...}

/* Return true if two rectangles are equal
 * (the size and position are the same)
 */
_p.equals = function(r2) {...};

/* Returns the string representation of the rectangle,
 * useful for debugging
 */
_p.toString = function() {...};

/* print toString() value to the console */
```

```
_p.print = function() {...};

/**
 * All functions accepting 4 args (coordinates)
 * can also accept the single arg (rectangle)
 */

/* returns true if two rectangles intersect (share some area in common) */
_p.intersects = function(x2, y2, w2, h2) { ... };

/* returns true if the rectangle completely covers the other rectangle. */
_p.covers = function(x2, y2, w2, h2) { ... };

/* Returns the rectangle that is a convex hull for
 * the this rectangle and the one passed as the parameter.
 * In other words - returnds the smallest possible rectangle
 * that covers both
 */
_p.convexHull = function(x2, y2, w2, h2) { ... };

/* Returns the intersection of two rectangles */
_p.intersection = function(x2, y2, w2, h2) { ... };

/* Returns true if this rectangle contains the point
 * with coordinates x and y
 */
_p.containsPoint = function(x, y) { ... };

/**
 * Given a grid of rectangular cels, cell size - (cellW, cellH)
 * tests which cells are overlapped by the rectangle.
 * cellsInRow and cellsInColumn are used only to limit the
 * coordinates to prevent going out of bounds in arrays for example.
 */
_p.getOverlappingGridCells = function(cellW, cellH, cellsInRow, cellsInColumn) {
... };
```

GameObject Class

The next important class that we need to create before writing the engine itself is the GameObject. This class is the root for all in-game entities: objects, layers, UI widgets, and so on. Everything that we put on the screen, render, move, or resize, is in this class. Listing 7-4 is the code for GameObject.js . The most interesting part of the listing is the setPosition(). Once GameObject makes sure that the new position is actually different from the old one, it emits the move event. Other entities, like layers, can subscribe to this event and update the world appropriately (for example, the clustering algorithm of ObjectLayer needs to track the movement of every object to keep the clusters consistent).

Listing 7-4. *The GameObject Class: The Root of Game Objects Hierarchy*

```
function GameObject() {
    EventEmitter.call(this);
    this._id = GameObject._maxId++;
    this._bounds = new Rect(0, 0, 100, 100);
}

extend(GameObject, EventEmitter);
var _p = GameObject.prototype;

GameObject._maxId = 1;

_p.draw = function(ctx) {
    // To implement
};

_p.setSize = function(width, height) {
    this._bounds.width = width;
    this._bounds.height = height;
};

_p.move = function(deltaX, deltaY) {
    this.setPosition(this._bounds.x + deltaX, this._bounds.y + deltaY);
};

_p.setPosition = function(x, y) {
    if (this._bounds.x != x || this._bounds.y != y) {
        var evendData = {
            oldX: this._bounds.x,
            oldY: this._bounds.y,
            x: x,
            y: y,
            object: this
        };

        this._bounds.x = x;
        this._bounds.y = y;
        this.emit("move", evendData);
    }
};

_p.getBounds = function() {
    return this._bounds;
};
```

```
_p.getId = function() {
    return this._id;
};
```

The GameObject extends EventEmitter, so every game object can send custom events. This is a rather handy feature. For example, the IsometricTileLayer can emit a tileClicked event with some extra parameters to notify the outer world that the user clicked a certain tile, while ObjectLayer can emit objectClicked— an event specific to its domain.

Each game object has a unique ID. This ID is useful for many things—from network synchronization (determine exactly which one of ten buildings is now destroyed) to small but important things like debugging. The code for the GameObject class uses a global counter to keep track of the maximum ID issued to the game objects, and increments it for every subsequent constructor call.

Arrays

The final utility class groups a small set of tools to make working with arrays at least a little easier. JavaScript has very poor support for array operations; even such simple functions like contains() and remove() that are typically present out of the box in other languages are absent in JavaScript. We will need only three helper methods. This class, shown in Listing 7-5, is so tiny that I put it straight into the utils.js.

Listing 7-5. *The Array Class: The Tiny Collection of Helper Methods to Make Array Operations Easier*

```
var Arrays = {
    remove: function(obj, arr) {
        var index = arr.indexOf(obj);
        if (index != -1)
            arr.splice(index, 1);
    },

    contains: function(obj, arr) {
        return arr.indexOf(obj) > -1;
    },

    addIfAbsent: function(obj, arr) {
        if (!Arrays.contains(obj, arr)) {
            arr.push(obj);
        }
    }
};
```

> **NOTE:** There is a very nice library called `Underscore.js` that has implemented most of the missing data-manipulation functions of core JavaScript. Check it out at `http://underscorejs.org`. You might find it quite convenient for your projects.

Now we have several useful utility functions at our disposal. The game skeleton is ready, and we can start adding the components of the engine—terrain, objects, UI controls, and events. We will start with terrain.

Isometric Terrain

The first step of the project is to render an isometric terrain. We've already had a fair amount of theory in Chapter 6, so now it is time to implement it in practice. Let's start with refreshing our knowledge about the coordinate systems of the game engine.

Coordinate Systems

There are at least several systems of coordinates for games like these: screen coordinates, world coordinates, and isometric grid coordinates. It is important to understand the difference between them, as well as how to translate coordinates from one system to another. Make sure that you are familiar with the material in this section before you move on; otherwise, most of the formulas in this chapter might look scary.

The game world is a vast area that has many different objects. Each object has coordinates within the world space. If you think about the world as a huge image, say 5000 × 5000 pixels, then the world coordinates are the coordinates within that image. The world coordinates are useful for in-game mechanics: AI, collision detection, and so forth. When it comes to drawing, the world coordinates have to be translated to screen coordinates.

Look at the typical world-rendering task illustrated in Figure 7-4. Let's say that we need to draw a hut that is located at (700, 500) world coordinates. `drawImage()` accepts *canvas coordinates* (or *screen coordinates*), so how do we find them? The position of the object on the screen depends on which part of the world is currently visible—or the viewport position. If the top-left corner of the viewport is located at (480, 300) world coordinates, then the screen coordinates of the object are (700 - 480, 500 - 300) = (220, 200).

The same is true for the reverse translation. When the user taps the screen, you get *screen coordinates*. For example, the EventHandler reports that the user tapped the (50, 100) point. Now you need to find which object was clicked. Objects are stored in world coordinates (in Chapter 6, we discussed why it is more convenient to store objects that way), so to find the object, you have to translate back to world coordinates. The world coordinates of the click are (480 + 50, 300 + 100) = (530, 400).

Let's continue the example and say that the user missed the object. This means that he hit one of the ground tiles. But which one exactly? To find that out, we need to translate from *world coordinates* to *isometric grid coordinates*. The formula to do that is a little more complex; we will explore it later in this chapter.

The hut in Figure 7-4 has world coordinates (700, 500), screen coordinates (220, 200), and it stands on tiles with coordinates (0, 3) and (1, 2).

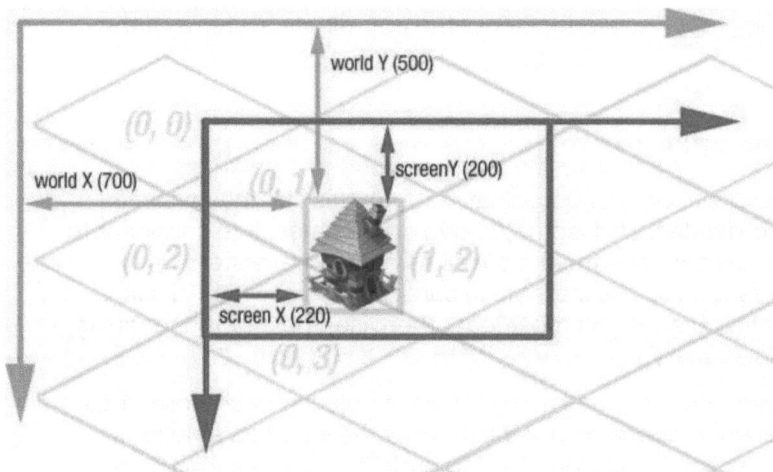

Figure 7-4. *Three different coordinate systems: world, screen, and isometric grid*

Once you understand how coordinates work and how to translate between different systems, you are ready to proceed to the next part—writing the game itself. The first step of our plan is to render the terrain.

Rendering Tiles

We start by carefully examining the resources that we have—the isometric tileset shown in Figure 7-5.

Figure 7-5. *The raw material for the rendering: a spriteset is shown on the left, a zoomed grass sprite is on the right*

What is unusual about this terrain sprite is that the edges are not entirely straight; fragments of grass fall behind the bounds of the cell. This technique is often utilized by artists to add a feeling of depth to the image, making it more realistic. If you cut a rectangular piece of your lawn and then take a picture under an "isometric" angle, you'll see that the edges are not straight at all. This is exactly how this kind of tile looks.

Tiles like these are more than common in game development. To refer to them in the text, and to differentiate them from the perfect diamond tiles in the previous chapter, we will use the word *decorated*—because of extra decorations that you have to take into account. For the perfectly straight-edged tiles, we will use the words *flat* or *simple*.

> **NOTE:** These terms are not industry standards. We need to distinguish between the different types of tiles in this section, so I decided to invent my own names to classify them.

The rendering technique for decorated tiles is slightly different compared to flat tiles. Since you might encounter both cases in your own games, we will look at the difference. Figure 7-6 illustrates a simple isometric tile case, one that has a shape of a perfect diamond. Drawing it is quite simple: the width and the height of the sprite is the same as the width of the cell in an isometric grid, and the rendering order doesn't matter. You can draw it in whatever order you like— from top to bottom, from right to left—whatever is more convenient to you. Since tiles do not overlap, the result will always be the same.

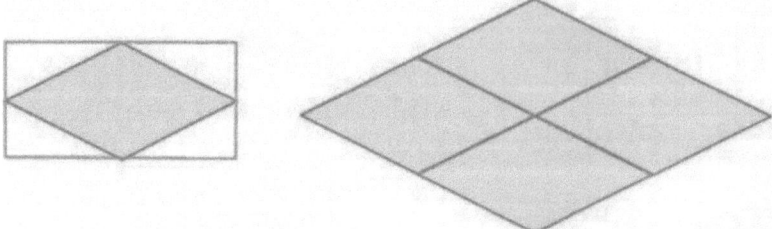

Figure 7-6. *Simple isometric tiles without overlapping elements: the drawing order doesn't matter*

Decorated tiles are different. Look at Figure 7-7. The tile is bigger than the grid cell because it has regions that overlap neighboring tiles. The left picture shows how it might be positioned inside a rectangular sprite. Note that the area that will cover the grid cell is not necessarily in the center of the sprite. The exact position of the "diamond" depends on the size of overlapping parts. The image on the right shows the individual tile, and the bottom picture is the set of tiles arranged into a grid.

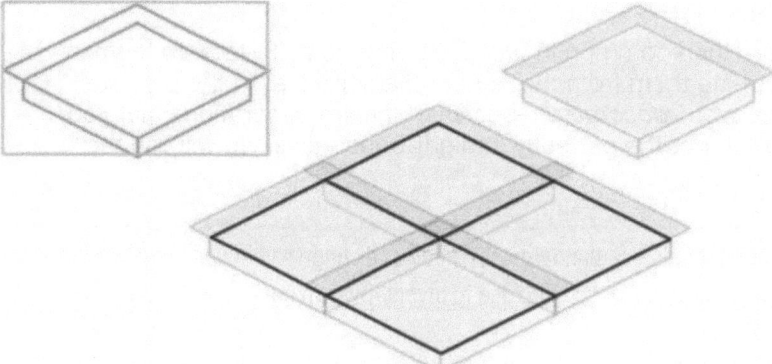

Figure 7-7. *Decorated isometric tiles: they are bigger than the grid cell and they overlap neighboring tiles*

Obviously, when you deal with decorated tiles, the order of rendering *does* matter. Figure 7-8 shows the correct order of rendering—from top to bottom.

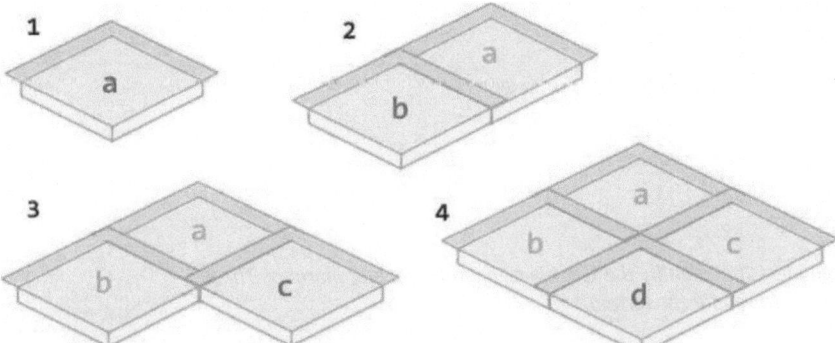

Figure 7-8. *Overlapping tiles must be drawn in order from top to bottom. If the order is broken, the result will not look like terrain because the tiles will not fit each other.*

Figure 7-9 shows the outcome of tile b being drawn first, instead of tile a. As you see, the resulting image doesn't look like the terrain.

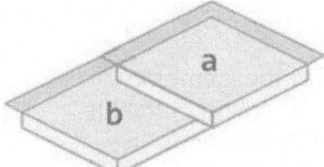

Figure 7-9. *Incorrect rendering order*

The rendering code needs to know the exact size of the "decorations" in order to arrange the tiles on the grid. Figure 7-10 shows the essential parameters of the tile. The tile width and the tile height are the size of the sprite that holds the tile—the size of the image that has both the tile and its decoration. The cell size of a single sprite in a sprite sheet is tile width × tile height in pixels. For example, our tiles are 128 pixels wide and 68 pixels high. The grid width and grid height is the size of the isometric grid cell; or in other words, the size of a perfect diamond that covers the cell. Our artist created our tiles for a cell size of 124 × 62 pixels. The final set of parameters is the *margins*, the distance from the edge of the sprite to the diamond. To render the tile, we need only the left margin and the top margin. In our case, they are 0 and 3 pixels, respectively (there is no left margin). However, this is not always the case; for example, the tile in Figure 7-10 shows the tile with both left and top margins.

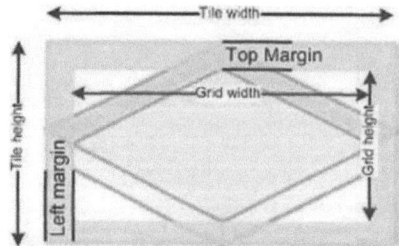

Figure 7-10. *The parameters that identify the tile: tile size, grid size, and margins. These measurements are enough to render the terrain.*

> **NOTE:** When you work with the other tile sheets, these parameters will be different. The point is that these six numbers describe the geometry of a tile, and they are enough to render the terrain. The same numbers can describe simple tiles without overlapping areas. Such tiles have no margins (0px) and "tile size" is the same as "grid size."

Now we are ready to write the rendering code. The essence of the isometric map is a two-dimensional array, where the value refers to the location of the tile within the sheet. Since the width of the tile sheet is known, it is enough to use only one number to uniquely identify the tile. Figure 7-11 shows how tile indexing works.

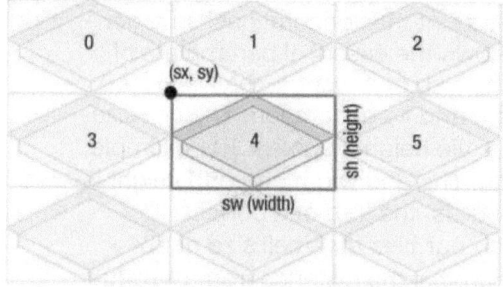
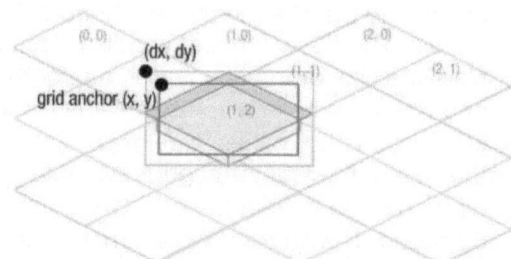

Figure 7-11. *Drawing the decorated sprite*

The sprite should then be placed on the grid, so that the diamond area of the tile fits the position of the grid cell, as shown on the right in Figure 7-11. We need to find the grid anchor—the top-left corner of the grid cell—and then render the tile over it, shifting the position by the margin values. The code in Listing 7-6 does exactly that.

Listing 7-6. *Drawing Decorated Tiles on Canvas*

```
/* We start by getting the tile position within the tilesheet */
var tileX = tileId%spritesInRow;
var tileY = Math.floor(tileId/spritesInRow);

var sx = tileX*tileWidth;
var sy = tileY*tileHeight;

/* Next, find the grid anchor - the coordinates of the cell that we render */
var gridAnchorX = cellX*cellWidth + (cellY%2)*cellWidth/2;
var gridAnchorY = cellY*cellHeight/2;

/* Finally, render the tile over the cell: */
var dx = gridAnchorX - marginLeft;
var dy = gridAnchorY - marginRight;

ctx.drawImage(tilesetImage, sx, sy, tileWidth, tileHeight, dx, dy, tileWidth,
tileHeight);
```

If you need to draw several tiles, don't forget that order matters. The following code shows how to render a bigger map area—from startCellX to endCellX, and from startCellY to endCellY, as shown in Listing 7-7:

Listing 7-7. *Drawing the Area of the Map Limited By startCellX, endCellX, startCellY, and endCellY*

```
for (var cellY = startCellY; cellY <= endCellY; cellY++) {
    for (var cellX = startCellX; cellX <= endCellX; cellX++) {
        var tileId = mapData[cellY][cellX];

        var tileX = spritesInRow;
        var tileY = Math.floor(tileId/spritesInRow);

        var sx = tileX*tileWidth;
        var sy = tileY*tileHeight;
        var dx = cellX*cellWidth + (cellY%2)*cellWidth/2 - marginLeft;
        var dy = cellY*cellHeight/2 - marginRight;

        ctx.drawImage(tilesetImage, sx, sy, tileWidth, tileHeight,
                dx, dy, tileWidth, tileHeight);
    }
}
```

Implementing IsometricTileLayer

The basic rendering should be quite clear by now. The next step is to create the IsometricTileLayer—the class responsible for rendering the map. Its task is not only to draw tiles as we just did, but also to implement a few optimization tricks.

As you remember, it is not a good idea to render each tile on every frame—it's much better to keep the pre-rendered region of the map in the invisible offscreen canvas and copy from it when required.

Create a folder called map inside your js folder, and then create a blank file in it, called IsometricTileLayer.js. We have a few more map-related classes, so it's worth keeping them separated from the other parts of the application.

We already know which parameters we need for rendering and how to draw a region of the map. Now we can write the constructor and the _drawMapRegion() method. The code is shown in Listing 7-8.

Listing 7-8. *The IsometricTileLayer and Its _drawMapRegion Method*

```
function IsometricTileLayer(mapData, tileset, tileWidth, tileHeight, cellWidth,
cellHeight, marginLeft, marginTop) {
    GameObject.call(this);
    this._mapData = mapData;
    this._tileset = tileset;
    this._tileWidth = tileWidth;
    this._tileHeight = tileHeight;
    this._cellWidth = cellWidth || tileWidth;
    this._cellHeight = cellHeight || tileHeight;
    this._marginLeft = marginLeft;
    this._marginTop = marginTop;

    this._spritesInOneRow = Math.floor(tileset.width/tileWidth);

    this._offCanvas = document.createElement("canvas");
    this._offContext = this._offCanvas.getContext("2d");
    this._offRect = new Rect(0, 0, 0, 0);
    this._offDirty = true;
}

extend(IsometricTileLayer, GameObject);
_p = IsometricTileLayer.prototype;

_p._drawMapRegion = function(ctx, rect) {
    var startCellX = Math.max(0, rect.x);
    var endCellX = Math.max(0,
            Math.min(rect.x + rect.width - 1, this._mapData[0].length - 1));

    var startCellY = Math.max(0, rect.y);
    var endCellY = Math.min(rect.y + rect.height - 1, this._mapData.length - 1);

    for (var cellY = startCellY; cellY <= endCellY; cellY++) {
        for (var cellX = startCellX; cellX <= endCellX; cellX++) {
            var tileId = this._mapData[cellY][cellX];
            var tileX = tileId%this._spritesInOneRow;
```

```
        var tileY = Math.floor(tileId/this._spritesInOneRow);

        var sx = tileX*this._tileWidth;
        var sy = tileY*this._tileHeight;
        var sw = this._tileWidth;
        var sh = this._tileHeight;

        var dx = (cellX - rect.x)*this._cellWidth +
                (cellY%2)*this._cellWidth/2 - this._marginLeft;

        var dy = (cellY - rect.y)*this._cellHeight/2 - this._marginTop;
        var dw = this._tileWidth;
        var dh = this._tileHeight;

        ctx.drawImage(this._tileset, sx, sy, sw, sh, dx, dy, dw, dh);
      }
    }
};
```

The code should already be familiar to you. The constructor saves the parameters and initializes the offscreen canvas, while _drawMapRegion() does exactly what it sounds like—it renders the fragment of the map into the given context. Here we implement the first of the tile-map optimizations that we explored in Chapter 6. We render only those tiles that are visible on the screen.

The next step is to create the offscreen buffer and write the code to manage it: handle resize, movement, and invalidation. This way we can implement the second optimization of the tile maps—re-rendering the map only when the user has moved beyond the bounds of rendered area.

Viewport and Map Bounds

The offscreen image is the image that holds the pre-rendered area slightly bigger than the area currently visible to the user. The first step is to find which part of the map the user should see now. The smaller rectangle in Figure 7-12 is the viewport, the highlighted tiles are ones that are at least partially visible, and the bigger rectangle is the size of the offscreen canvas, which is enough to hold the visible area.

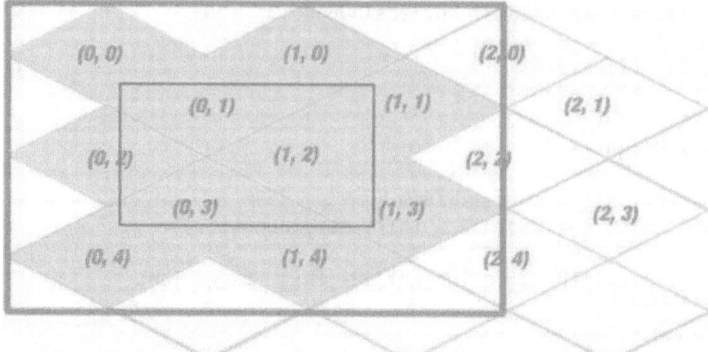

Figure 7-12. *The parameters of the offscreen canvas explained. Find out which tiles are visible, and then find the rectangle that covers them.*

In terms of grid coordinates, the smallest x and y is 0, and the biggest x and y are 1 and 4, respectively. So the bounding rectangle *in grid coordinates* is x=0, y=0, width=2, and height=5. If you pass these coordinates to the _drawMapRegion(), it will render the required fragment of map.

Of course, it is easy to find the correct tiles on the picture, but now we need to write the code that does the same thing. It might be little tricky to find the correct formula straightaway. In this section, we will start with the code and then explain why it works that way. The function in Listing 7-9 returns the bounds of the map in grid coordinates, which is what the user will see through the viewport.

Listing 7-9. *Getting the Bounds of the Map*

```
_p._getVisibleMapRect = function() {
    var x = Math.floor((this._bounds.x - this._cellWidth/2)/this._cellWidth);
    var y = Math.floor(this._bounds.y/(this._cellHeight/2)) - 1;

    var width = Math.ceil(this._bounds.width/this._cellWidth) + 1;
    var height = Math.ceil((this._bounds.height)/(this._cellHeight/2)) + 2;
    return new Rect(x, y, width, height);
};
```

Think of the *viewport* as the window through which the user sees the world. The size of the viewport is the size available for rendering. In our case, it is the size of the canvas. The x and y coordinates determine which part of the world the user sees. When the player scrolls the map, he is in fact moving the viewport to see a new region. Obviously, the IsometricTileLayer needs to know the viewport size and location to render the map.

A good place to store the viewport rectangle is this._bounds—the variable inside the layer object inherited from GameObject. The actual bounds of the game map (the size of the whole world), are almost useless for the external API: it is much better to treat layer bounds as the bounds of the viewport. This way, *moving* the layer means moving the viewport, and *resizing* means changing the size of the viewport:

```
layer.move(0, 50); // show the fragment of the map 50 px below the current
layer.setSize(300, 300); // resize the visible part of the layer to 300, 300
layer.getBounds(); // get the bounds of the viewport
```

> **NOTE:** There are two different approaches to coordinates for layers and viewports. One is to keep the layer at world coordinates (0, 0) and *move the viewport* around. The other is to "pin" the viewport in world coordinates (0, 0) and to *move the layer* instead. The result is absolutely the same: when player moves the map, he sees new regions. It is mostly a matter of one's own preferences on what to move—the layer or the viewport.

Now we need to find the map bounds covered by the viewport. Grab a sheet of paper, sketch an isometric grid, and divide it into vertical zones so that each zone has the same smallest visible x coordinate of the tile. To make it even easier, write the x coordinate on every cell of the grid. Then, do the same for y coordinates and divide the grid into horizontal zones. I sketched an example for you in Figure 7-13. In the vertical grid (on the left), zone -1 is where the tile's smallest visible x the tile (-1) is located. The horizontal grid (located on the right) for y coordinates follows the same idea: zone 2 contains the smallest y coordinate of the visible tile, which is 2.

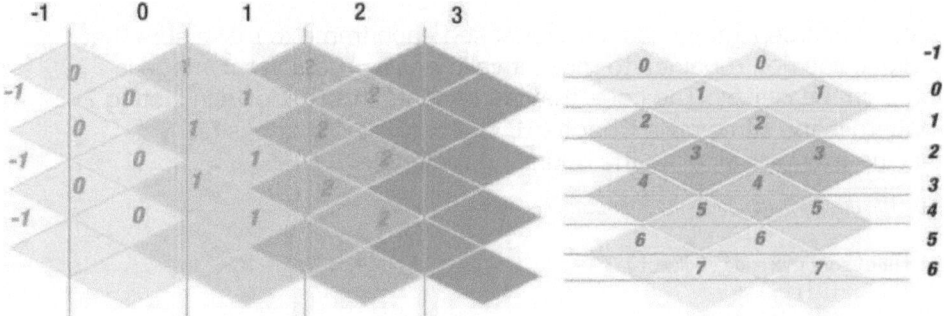

Figure 7-13. *Dividing the grid into vertical and horizontal zones*

Our goal is to write the code that finds the ID of a zone when given a world coordinate. The values that we find are the x and y values of the map bounds:

the top-left corner. Looking at the vertical zone (on the left) in Figure 7-13, you find that the zones are exactly cellWidth-sized and they start with cellWidth/2. The 0 zone has x values from 0.5*cellWidth to 1.5*cellWidth, the 1 zone has x values from 1.5*cellWidth to 2.5*cellWidth, and so on. The following code formalizes the dependency:

```
var x = Math.floor((this._bounds.x - this._cellWidth/2)/this._cellWidth);
```

Do the same for y: the zone size is cellHeight/2 and zones from -1. The next fragment of code is now clear too:

```
var y = Math.floor(this._bounds.y/(this._cellHeight/2)) - 1;
```

Now we have the coordinates of the top-left corner of the bounding rectangle. The values for width and height are even easier to get. For the width, take the minimum number of zones required to cover the viewport—that is Math.ceil(this._bounds.width/this._cellWidth). Since the rows are shifted in the isometric view, we need to add 2 to this value to cover the next and previous column:

```
var width = Math.ceil(this._bounds.width/this._cellWidth) + 2;
```

The height formula works the same way:

```
var height = Math.ceil((this._bounds.height)/(this._cellHeight/2)) + 2;
```

The hardest part is now over. Since you know what the player sees and you know how to render it on the offscreen canvas, the only thing left to do is to show the content to the user and make sure to invalidate and repaint it once the user scrolls away.

Managing Offscreen Canvas

The isometric offscreen image has to be checked each frame to make sure that it is still valid. If it is not, repaint it to make it valid again. The correct image is then painted on the canvas. The code that implements this is shown in Listing 7-10. The pattern is the same as in Chapter 6. The only thing that has really changed is the way we calculate the bounding rectangle.

Listing 7-10. *The draw() Function of the IsometricTileLayer*

```
_p.draw = function(ctx, dirtyRect) {
    if (this._offDirty) {
        this._redrawOffscreen();
    }

    var offscreenImageWorldX = this._offRect.x*this._cellWidth;
    var offscreenImageWorldY = this._offRect.y*this._cellHeight/2;
```

```
        ctx.drawImage(this._offCanvas, offscreenImageWorldX - this._bounds.x,
                     offscreenImageWorldY - this._bounds.y);
};
```

The next function: _redrawOffscreen() is also straightforward; it simply calls the _drawMapRegion() for the offscreen context. The _drawMapRegion(), in turn, knows how to paint the part of the map on a given context. The code is shown in Listing 7-11.

Listing 7-11. *Refreshing the Offscreen Buffer: The _redrawOffscreen() Function*

```
_p._redrawOffscreen = function() {
    var ctx = this._offContext;
    ctx.fillStyle = "darkgreen";
    ctx.fillRect(0, 0, this._offCanvas.width, this._offCanvas.height);
    this._drawMapRegion(ctx, this._offRect);
    this._offDirty = false;
};
```

The variable _offRect that we use in both listings holds current map bounds that are "valid." We have the offscreen image covering that map region. When the user navigates far enough and crosses the region, the _offRect changes, and the _offDirty flag becomes true. This flag notifies the rendering code that the offscreen image is not valid anymore, and has to be re-rendered. There are several functions that might change the state of the flag and toggle the reset of the offscreen canvas. For example, when the size of the canvas has changed, the content is destroyed and we need to repaint canvas. When the user moves away from the rendered part of the world, we need to render a new part, just as we did in Chapter 6. The code in Listing 7-12 summarizes the functions that you need to update to re-render the offscreen buffer once it needs to be re-rendered.

Listing 7-12. *Resetting Offscreen Canvas*

```
_p.setSize = function(width, height) {
    GameObject.prototype.setSize.call(this, width, height);
    this._resetOffScreenCanvas();
};

_p.setPosition = function(x, y) {
    GameObject.prototype.setPosition.call(this, x, y);
    this._updateOffscreenBounds();
};

_p._resetOffScreenCanvas = function() {
    this._offRect = this._getVisibleMapRect();
    this._offCanvas.height = this._offRect.height*this._cellHeight;
    this._offCanvas.width = this._offRect.width*this._cellWidth;
```

```
        this._offDirty = true;
};

_p._updateOffscreenBounds = function() {
    var newRect = this._getVisibleMapRect();
    if (!newRect.equals(this._offRect)) {
        this._offRect = newRect;
        this._offDirty = true;
    }
};
```

Add a _resetOffscreenCanvas() call to the constructor to set the initial size of the viewport and create the first offscreen image. Then implement some map-manipulation functions, which we will need later: setTileAt(), to change the terrain once the user clicks it; getTileAt(), to identify the current tile in the cell; and _getTileCoordinates(), to translate from screen coordinates to map coordinates. The reference code is shown in Listing 7-13.

Listing 7-13. *The Functions That We Will Need Later: setTileAt and getTileAt*

```
/*Updates the map setting the new tile in the given map index*/
p.setTileAt = function(x, y, tileId) {
    this._mapData[y][x] = tileId;
    if (this._offRect.containsPoint(x, y)) {
        this._dirtyRectManager.markAllDirty();
        this._offDirty = true;
    }
};

/* Returns the tile at a given map index */
_p.getTileAt = function(x, y) {
    return this._mapData[y][x];
};

_p._getTileCoordinates = function(x, y) {
    x += this._bounds.x;
    y += this._bounds.y;

    var w = this._cellWidth;
    var h = this._cellHeight;

    var x1 = Math.floor((x + 2*y - w/2)/w);
    var y1 = Math.floor((y - x/2 + h/2)/h );

    return {
        x: Math.floor((x1 - y1)/2),
        y: x1 + y1
    };
};
```

`setTile()` causes an entire offscreen repaint. Do we really need to render the whole image to change one small tile? Remember, decorated tiles need to be drawn in order: from top rows to bottom rows. When you repaint the tile, you automatically need to repaint two tiles above it and two tiles below it; those tiles, in turn, require more rows to be repainted, and so on. We assume that the terrain doesn't change a lot, so it is not worth optimizing this aspect too much. If you are interested in making this code perfect, read on to the "Dirty Rectangles" section of this chapter, which explains how to set `clip` and limit the repainting area to a single rectangle. With the help of `clip`, you only need to redraw five tiles: the changed tile itself, two adjacent tiles in the row above it, and two adjacent tiles in the row below it.

> **NOTE:** In fact, it is better to implement a much more useful optimization. When the user moves the map and we need to draw a new region, the number of new tiles is rather small (compared to the overall number of visible tiles). We have most of the image already rendered on the offscreen `canvas`, but we have to draw every single tile again. What a waste! It is much better to reuse the existing offscreen image, repaint the unchanged part to a second offscreen buffer, and then draw the few remaining new tiles. This technique is not too hard to implement, but requires one more offscreen `canvas` because you can't safely copy pixels to and from the same canvas.

Adding a Layer to Game

As a final touch, we will try out the newly created `IsometricTileLayer`. Create a simple two-dimensional array to hold the map, and save it somewhere. You can either create the map yourself or generate it randomly. For now, we just need some data to test the new layer. In my project, I used the file called `Level.js` with the content in Listing 7-14.

Listing 7-14. *The Level.js File That Describes the Level (for now, the level is only a terrain)*

```
var levelMap = [
    [1,0,0,5, .... 1,1,1,0,0],
    [1,1,0,5, .... 3,1,1,1,1],
      more here
    [1,0,1,0, .... 0,1,1,1,0]
];
```

Not the most amazing way to manage level data, but it'll do just fine for testing. Now we have created the first component of our game engine so that we can add it to the skeleton of the game and render the map on the screen. Update the code for the Game class, as shown in Listing 7-15.

Listing 7-15. *Adding the IsometricTileLayer to Game (the new code is bolded)*

```
function Game(canvas, map) {
    /* unchanged part */
    this._map = map;
    this._tileLayer = null;
}

_p = Game.prototype;

/** Called once all images are loaded */
_p._onImagesLoaded = function() {
    this._initLayers();
    /* the rest of code as before */
};

_p._initLayers = function() {
    var im = this._imageManager;
    this._tileLayer = new IsometricTileLayer(
                this._map, im.get("terrain"), 128, 68, 124, 62, 0, 3);
};

/** Move the viewport withing the world */
_p.move = function(deltaX, deltaY) {
    this._tileLayer.move(-deltaX, -deltaY);
};

/** Resize handling */
_p.resize = function() {
    this._tileLayer.setSize(this._canvas.width, this._canvas.height);
};

/** Event handling */
_p._onMove = function(e) {
    this.move(e.deltaX, e.deltaY);
};

/** Render frame on context */
_p._renderFrame = function() {
    this._tileLayer.draw(this._ctx);
};
```

Don't forget to add all the new scripts to index.html before you run the code. The code at the current state is in the v0.1 folder along with the other materials for this chapter. Feel free to use it for reference or continue your work from this point.

We have completed the first stage of the project: we have the isometric terrain that the user can scroll through. The result of our efforts is shown in Figure 7-14.

Figure 7-14. *Isometric terrain rendered on the screen of a Samsung Galaxy S*

The next step is to add objects into the game.

Rendering Objects

Good news: rendering objects is easier than rendering terrain, especially in small games without thousands of objects moving around. A game object is simply a sprite—static or animated—placed on the layer above the terrain. The "hard" part is to render *only* those objects that are required for the frame, and ignore the rest. The tiles are easier to deal with since the tile map is a grid, and it is quite easy to figure out which cells are currently visible.

For arbitrarily placed objects, it is slightly harder to find every object that intersects the viewport. The straightforward approach—to check if the viewport intersects every object—will fail fast if the size of the world is significantly bigger than the screen, and the number of objects is at least a couple of hundred. However, this approach works for many games with small worlds, like social farms.

The usual solution for this problem is to divide the world into big regions *(clusters)*, and assign objects to them. You can then check against the region— if it doesn't overlap the viewport, then none of its objects does. The region itself can have smaller subregions and so on, forming a tree-like structure. Spatial trees work that way. Alternatively, the clusters can be arranged in a grid—a simple yet very often suitable approach for client-side rendering. The goal of this section is to implement this approach in the code and wrap it into the ObjectLayer—the class for rendering objects.

Start with the bare version of the ObjectLayer, which checks the bounds of every object. The code in Listing 7-16 shows how to do it. Essentially, the code is almost the same as the code in Chapter 6, with the only difference being that it is inherited from the GameObject.

Listing 7-16. *The Basic Version of the ObjectLayer Tests Each Object*

```
function ObjectLayer(objects) {
    GameObject.call(this);
    this._objects = objects;
    this._sortObjects();
}

extend(ObjectLayer, GameObject);
_p = ObjectLayer.prototype;

_p.draw = function(ctx) {
    for (var i = 0; i < this._objects.length; i++) {
        var obj = this._objects[i];
        if (obj.getBounds().intersects(this._bounds)) {
            obj.draw(ctx, this._bounds.x, this._bounds.y);
        }
    }
};

_p.addObject = function(obj) {
    this._objects.push(obj);
    this._sortObjects();
};

_p._getScreenBounds = function(obj) {
    var worldBounds = obj.getBounds();
    return new Rect(worldBounds.x - this._bounds.x, worldBounds.y -
this._bounds.y,
        worldBounds.width, worldBounds.height);
};

_p._sortObjects = function() {
    this._objects.sort(function(a, b) {
        var aBounds = a.getBounds();
        var bBounds = b.getBounds();

        return (aBounds.y + aBounds.height) - (bBounds.y + bBounds.height);
    });
};
```

We have added two more arguments to the draw() call—the drawing offsets. Since the object might be stored in the world space, it needs a way to translate to screen space. The easiest solution is to add two parameters to draw(). We want to keep the individual objects unaware of details like the position of the viewport, but still solve the problem of rendering them on the screen.

The rendering order matters too. Objects are sorted by the y coordinate of their baseline (the place where they "touch the ground"). The objects with the lower y are rendered first. If the world has moving objects, you have to keep track of the movement and make sure that you also update the rendering order.

To test the newly created layer, let's add a few objects to the scene. I created a small class called StaticImage to represent a static unanimated sprite in the game world. In this chapter, we work only with that kind of sprite, just to keep things simple. Alternatively, you can use the version created in Chapter 6, which takes the images from the SpriteSheet, or implement your own version with the support of the animation, for example. Listing 7-17 shows the version that we use in this chapter.

Listing 7-17. *The StaticImage Class That Is Used to Render Static Objects in Our Engine*

```
function StaticImage(image, x, y, w, h) {
    GameObject.call(this);
    this._bounds = new Rect(x, y, w || image.width, h || image.height);
    this._image = image;
}

extend(StaticImage, GameObject);

var _p = StaticImage.prototype;

_p.draw = function(ctx, dirtyRect, viewportX, viewportY) {
    ctx.drawImage(this._image, this._bounds.x - viewportX, this._bounds.y -
viewportY);
};
```

Now add the new layer to the game and add a few objects to it. Use the code in Listing 7-18 as a reference, or design your own level.

Listing 7-18. *Adding ObjectLayer to the Game (update the code for Game.js as shown)*

```
_p._initLayers = function() {
    var im = this._imageManager;
    this._tileLayer = new IsometricTileLayer(this._map, im.get("terrain"),
                                   128, 68, 124, 62, 0, 3);

    // Create the new type of layer
    this._objectLayer = new ObjectLayer([]);

    // Dummy balls that we will soon use to test movement
    this._ball1 = new StaticImage(im.get("ball"), 370, 30);
    this._ball2 = new StaticImage(im.get("ball"), 370, 30);
```

```
        this._objectLayer.addObject(this._ball1);
        this._objectLayer.addObject(this._ball2);


        // Bit huts
        var img = im.get("house-1");
        this._objectLayer.addObject(new StaticImage(img, 350, 130));
        this._objectLayer.addObject(new StaticImage(img, 200, 50));
        this._objectLayer.addObject(new StaticImage(img, 150, 200));

        // Small huts
        img = im.get("house-2");
        this._objectLayer.addObject(new StaticImage(img, 550, 230));
        this._objectLayer.addObject(new StaticImage(img, 920, 250));
    };

    /* objectLayer needs to move together with the rest of the map */
    _p.move = function(deltaX, deltaY) {
        this._tileLayer.move(-deltaX, -deltaY);
        this._objectLayer.move(-deltaX, -deltaY);
    };

    /* objectLayer is resized together with the rest of the map */
    _p.resize = function() {
        this._tileLayer.setSize(this._canvas.width, this._canvas.height);
        this._objectLayer.setSize(this._canvas.width, this._canvas.height);
    };

    /* Add some movement to the static world! */
    _p._updateWorld = function() {
        // Move ball down
        this._ball1.move(0, 2);

        // Move ball right
        this._ball2.move(2, 0);
    };

    /* When the frame is rendered we need to render objects too */
    _p._renderFrame = function() {
        this._tileLayer.draw(this._ctx);
        this._objectLayer.draw(this._ctx);
    };
```

This snippet has many duplicated lines. We have to add the extra line to each of the move(), resize(), and render() functions for every new layer that we add to the game. This is not a good way to manage layers. In fact, it is quite error-prone. Forget to add a line somewhere and the rendering is broken. Later in this chapter, we will find a better way to manage multiple layers. For now, let's look at the result and proceed to the harder part of ObjectLayer. Figure 7-15 shows the current state of our game.

Figure 7-15. *Intermediate result: isometric terrain with a few huts around*

Implementing Object Clusters

The next step is to optimize the object rendering process. Right now, no matter how big or small the world is, every single object is checked against the viewport, and what's worse is that if objects are moving, the whole collection must be sorted to keep the consistent order of drawing.

It is wise to work only with a small number of objects near the viewport, and ignore other objects until they are close enough. To do that, we break the world space into several areas, or *clusters*, and assign each object to one or several such clusters. When we need to render the frame, we check only those clusters that intersect the current viewport. Figure 7-16 illustrates this idea.

The figure shows the example breakdown of the world into square clusters. Each cluster except for (2,0) holds one object. The hut between (1, 1) and (2, 1) belongs to both of these clusters since it overlaps both of them. The viewport intersects with four clusters (highlighted on the image), so only two objects participate in rendering.

Figure 7-16. *An example of cluster layout. The viewport intersects four clusters. Only two objects participate in rendering.*

To break down the world into a grid, we need to know the parameters of the grid: the size of the cell and the size of the world. Update the constructor and add these parameters to the class.

The next step is to create the data structure to store the objects within the clusters. A three-dimensional array is the obvious choice: two dimensions for the grid and a third dimension for storing objects. An array is the fast way to answer the question of which objects belong to a given cluster. For the reverse question, we need another data structure. The map from the object's ID to the rectangular set of clusters will do. After you implement these changes, your code should look like Listing 7-19.

Listing 7-19. *Break the World Space into Clusters and Assign Objects Between Them*

```
function ObjectLayer(objects, clusterSize, worldWidth, worldHeight) {
    GameObject.call(this);
    this._objects = objects;
    this._clusterSize = clusterSize;
    this._worldWidth = worldWidth;
    this._worldHeight = worldHeight;

    /* the clusters arranged into the grid*/
    this._clusters = [];

    /* object id to Rect - the cluster bounds */
    this._idToClusterBounds = {};

    /* currently visible clusters */
    this._visibleClusterBounds = {};

    /* the sorted array of objects from active clusters, no duplicates*/
    this._cache = [];
```

```
    /* true if cache needs to be fully rebuilt */
    this._cacheDirty = true;

    /* true if cache only needs to be sorted (when object moved for example) */
    this._cacheUnsorted = false;

    this._resetClusters();
}

extend(ObjectLayer, GameObject);
_p = ObjectLayer.prototype;

/**
 * Reassign each object to a cluster (or several clusters)
 */
_p._resetClusters = function() {

    // Clear clusters
    this._clusters = [];
    for (var i = 0; i < Math.ceil(this._worldHeight/this._clusterSize); i++) {
        this._clusters[i] = [];
        for (var j = 0; j < Math.ceil(this._worldWidth/this._clusterSize); j++)
{
            this._clusters[i][j] = [];
        }
    }

    // Assign every object to cluster
    for (i = 0; i < this._objects.length; i++) {
        var obj = this._objects[i];
        this._addToClusters(obj);
    }
};
```

To add the object, we first need to find the overlapping clusters (the getOverlappingGridCells() function that does exactly that is already present in the Rect class). Then we push the object to the arrays and save the bounds into the _idToClusterBounds. Listing 7-20 shows how to do it.

Listing 7-20. *Adding Objects to Clusters*

```
_p._addToClusters = function(obj, clusterBounds) {
    clusterBounds = clusterBounds || obj.getBounds().getOverlappingGridCells(
        this._clusterSize, this._clusterSize,
        this._clusters[0].length, this._clusters.length);

    var startY = clusterBounds.y;
    var endY = clusterBounds.y + clusterBounds.height;
```

```
        for (var clusterY = startY; clusterY < endY; clusterY++) {
            var startX = clusterBounds.x;
            var endX = clusterBounds.x + clusterBounds.width;
            for (var clusterX = clusterBounds.x; clusterX < endX; clusterX++) {
                this._clusters[clusterY][clusterX].push(obj);
            }
        }
        this._idToClusterBounds[obj.getId()] = clusterBounds;
        return clusterBounds;
};
```

Object Cache

Once every object is assigned to the cluster, we can start drawing them. The process would look like the following:

1. Determine which clusters are currently visible to the user.

2. Get all the objects registered in those clusters.

3. Remove duplicate objects.

4. Sort objects.

5. Draw objects.

If the user has not crossed the cluster bounds since the last frame, steps 2 to 4 will give exactly the same result. This might not be true in the case of moving objects, but we will deal with them later in this section. For now, let's assume that objects are not moving. Let's use this fact to optimize the rendering of objects even more. We will save the results after step 4 into a separate "cache" and use it for rendering.

The object cache is somewhat similar to the offscreen `canvas` of `IsometricTileLayer`, but instead of an image, it holds an array of objects. It works in a very straightforward way. Once we know the clusters that are currently visible, we add every object to the cache, checking if it is there yet. The array is then sorted and ready to use in the drawing code. Listing 7-21 shows how to initialize the object cache and prepare it for rendering. Add this code to your `ObjectLayer` class.

Listing 7-21. *Resetting the Object Cache*

```
_p._resetCache = function() {
    var cache = this._cache = [];

    var startY = this._visibleClusterBounds.y;
```

```
        var endY = this._visibleClusterBounds.y + this._visibleClusterBounds.height;
        for (var i = startY; i < endY; i++) {
            var startX = this._visibleClusterBounds.x;
            var endX = this._visibleClusterBounds.x +
this._visibleClusterBounds.width;
                for (var j = startX; j < endX; j++) {
                    var cluster = this._clusters[i][j];
                    for (var k = 0; k < cluster.length; k++) {
                        if (!Arrays.contains(cluster[k], cache)) {
                            cache.push(cluster[k]);
                        }
                    }
                }
            }
        }

    this._sortCache();
    this._cacheDirty = false;
    this._cacheUnsorted = false;
};

_p._sortCache = function() {
    this._cache.sort(function(a, b) {
        var aBounds = a.getBounds();
        var bBounds = b.getBounds();

        return (aBounds.y + aBounds.height) - (bBounds.y + bBounds.height);
    });
    this._cacheUnsorted = false;
};
```

The cache is a simple array of sorted objects without duplicates, ready for rendering. It can be in one of three states:

   ▪ *Clean.* In this case, it is used as it is.

   ▪ *Unsorted.* Meaning that some objects have moved and potentially broken the order; the cache should be simply re-sorted in this case.

   ▪ *Dirty.* The cache has to be completely discarded and then re-created.

Let's look at the following case: the user taps the screen to add an object. That object ends up in the cache because it is added to one of the visible clusters. It must be inserted into the correct place in the cache, however, and not simply appended to the end. To preserve the order, we mark the cache "unsorted". The code in Listing 7-22 shows this flow. The addObject() function should be updated to take the cache into account.

Listing 7-22. *Updating addObject() Function So That It Takes the Cache into Account*

```
_p.addObject = function(obj) {
    this._objects.push(obj);
    var clusters = this._addToClusters(obj);
    if (clusters.intersects(this._visibleClusterBounds)) {
        this._cache.push(obj);
        this._cacheUnsorted = true;
    }
};
```

The second scenario: the user removes an existing object. The order of other cached objects is preserved, and the cache stays clean. The code in Listing 7-23 shows how to remove the object from the layer; we have to update both the cache and the clusters.

Listing 7-23. *Removing Object from the Layer*

```
_p.removeObject = function(obj) {
    if (!Arrays.contains(obj, this._objects)) {
        return;
    }

    this._removeFromClusters(obj);
    Arrays.remove(obj, this._cache);
};

_p._removeFromClusters = function(obj, clusterBounds) {
    clusterBounds = clusterBounds || this._idToClusterBounds[obj.getId()];
    var startY = clusterBounds.y;
    var endY = clusterBounds.y + clusterBounds.height;
    for (var clusterY = startY; clusterY < endY; clusterY++) {
        var startX = clusterBounds.x;
        var endX = clusterBounds.x + clusterBounds.width;
        for (var clusterX = startX; clusterX < endX; clusterX++) {
            Arrays.remove(obj, this._clusters[clusterY][clusterX]);
        }
    }
    delete this._idToClusterBounds[obj.getId()];
};
```

The final use for the cache: the user scrolls away, the viewport intersects new clusters, and the cache becomes invalid (or "dirty"). Some objects must be added and some removed. The check for cache validity happens in every setPosition() and setSize() call. Listing 7-24 shows the updated setSize() and setPosition() functions; they can potentially change the clusters that the user sees, so they must trigger a re-validation of the cache when needed.

Listing 7-24. *Functions That Change the Position or the Size of the Viewport Should Check If the Cache Is Still Valid*

```
_p.setSize = function(width, height) {
    GameObject.prototype.setSize.call(this, width, height);
    this._updateVisibleClusters();
};

_p.setPosition = function(x, y) {
    GameObject.prototype.setPosition.call(this, x, y);
    this._updateVisibleClusters();
};
```

We check for cache validity in exactly the same way as we checked if the user had navigated to the dirty area in IsometricTileLayer. If the new visible clusters are different from the previously known visible clusters, then we have to rebuild the cache from scratch. Listing 7-25 shows how to do that.

Listing 7-25. *Check If the User Sees New Clusters, and If So, Invalidate the Cache*

```
/**
 * Called when the viewport has moved and checks if we are still on the same
 * set of "active" clusters
 */
_p._updateVisibleClusters = function() {
    var newRect = this._bounds.getOverlappingGridCells(
            this._clusterSize, this._clusterSize,
        this._clusters[0].length, this._clusters.length);

    if (!newRect.equals(this._visibleClusterBounds)) {
        this._visibleClusterBounds = newRect;
        this._cacheDirty = true;
    }
};
```

Finally, we need to update the rendering function and draw only the objects in the cache. If the cache is dirty or unsorted, we perform the appropriate action to bring the cache back to the clean state. Now, the rendering function draws objects on the screen, as shown in Listing 7-26.

Listing 7-26. *Updated draw() Function*

```
_p.draw = function(ctx) {
    if (this._cacheDirty) {
        this._resetCache();
    } else if (this._cacheUnsorted) {
        this._sortCache();
    }
```

```
    for (var i = 0; i < this._cache.length; i++) {
        var obj = this._cache[i];
        if (obj.getBounds().intersects(this._bounds)) {
            obj.draw(ctx, this._bounds.x, this._bounds.y);
        }
    }
};
```

This code works perfectly for static objects. But what if an object moves?

Handling Movement

Movement is simple once you think of it in terms of removing objects from clusters and adding them to other clusters. The flow for an object that has moved is shown in Figure 7-17.

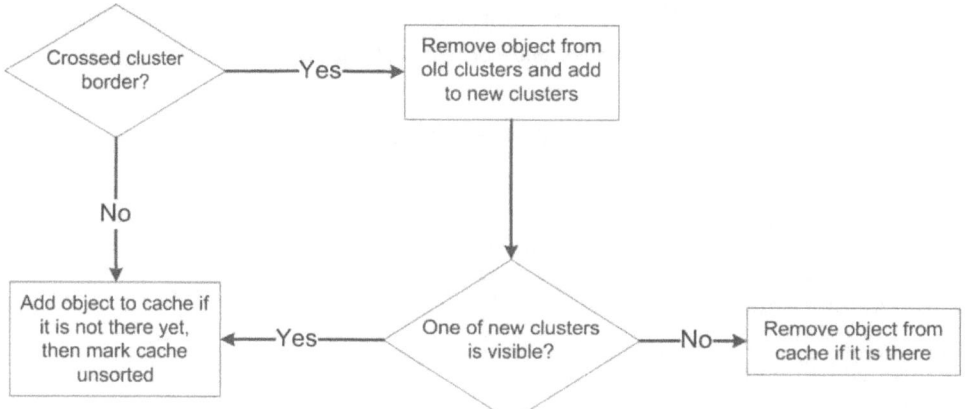

Figure 7-17. *Object movement: preserving the consistent state of clusters and the cache*

As you remember, we use custom events to track the movement of the object. The code that fires it is in the GameObject class. The first thing to do is to set up appropriate listeners for every object added to the layer, as in Listing 7-27. Once the object is removed from the layer, the listener is de-registered too.

Listing 7-27. *Tracking Moving Objects*

```
function ObjectLayer(objects, clusterSize, worldWidth, worldHeight) {
    /* unchanged code*/

    this._boundOnMove = this._onObjectMove.bind(this);
    this._addMoveListeners();
    this._resetClusters();
}
```

```
_p._addMoveListeners = function() {
    for (var i = 0; i < this._objects.length; i++) {
        this._objects[i].addListener("move", this._boundOnMove);
    }
};

_p.addObject = function(obj) {
    this._objects.push(obj);
    obj.addListener("move", this._boundOnMove);
    var clusters = this._addToClusters(obj);
    if (clusters.intersects(this._visibleClusterBounds)) {
        this._cache.push(obj);
        this._cacheUnsorted = true;
    }
};

_p.removeObject = function(obj) {
    if (!Arrays.contains(obj, this._objects)) {
        return;
    }

    obj.removeListener("move", this._boundOnMove);
    this._removeFromClusters(obj);
    Arrays.remove(obj, this._cache);
};
```

The function that handles movement is _onObjectMove() (_boundOnMove() is the version bound to the instance of ObjectLayer, but essentially is the same function). It accepts one argument—the movement event. The key point of this function is to keep layer data consistent: the clusters (both _clusters and _idToClusterBounds) and the cache. The first step is to determine if an object has moved to the new clusters. If so, we have to remove the object from the old clusters and add it to the new ones. Next, if the object is in one of the active clusters and moves vertically, we need to mark the cache as unsorted. Listing 7-28 shows how to implement this flow.

Listing 7-28. *Handling the Object Movement*

```
_p._onObjectMove = function(e) {
    var obj = e.object;
    var id = obj.getId();
    var objectBounds = obj.getBounds();

    var newClusters = objectBounds.getOverlappingGridCells(
        this._clusterSize, this._clusterSize,
        this._clusters[0].length, this._clusters.length);
```

```
        var oldClusters = this._idToClusterBounds[id];
        if (!oldClusters.equals(newClusters)) {
            this._moveObjectBetweenClusters(obj, oldClusters, newClusters);
        }

        if (newClusters.intersects(this._visibleClusterBounds) && e.y != e.oldY) {
            this._cacheUnsorted = true;
        }
    };

    _p._moveObjectBetweenClusters = function(obj, oldClusters, newClusters) {
        this._removeFromClusters(obj, oldClusters);
        this._addToClusters(obj, newClusters);
        this._idToClusterBounds[obj.getId()] = newClusters;

        // If object has left the screen, remove from cache
        if (newClusters.intersects(this._visibleClusterBounds)) {
            Arrays.addIfAbsent(obj, this._cache);
        } else {
            Arrays.remove(obj, this._cache);
        }
    };
```

The ObjectLayer can now be used with moving objects!

Composite Objects

Composite objects can't be represented as one sprite in the game world because of the way we render them. Take an arch, for example. It should allow a character to pass underneath it. But here we have an ordering problem: what do we draw first: the arch or the characters? After a bit of experimentation, you discover that it is neither. Figure 7-18 illustrates the problem.

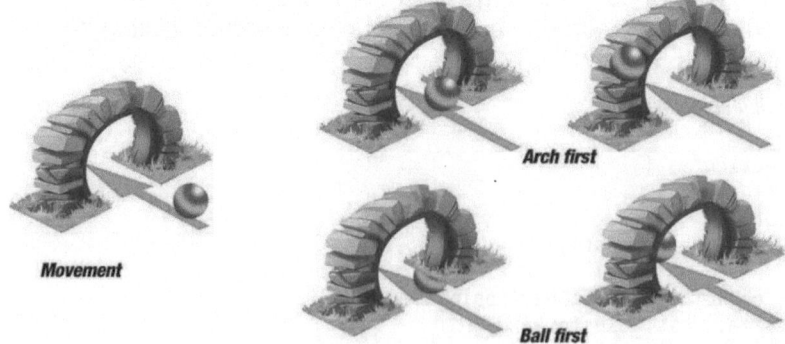

Figure 7-18. *The problem with objects like arches: no matter what the rendering sequence is, the result will be wrong at some point.*

The problem lies in our assumption that there are only two types of ordering. An object is behind another object or vice versa. With an arch like this one, we have a third state of an object—an object that is *in between* another one. Our engine can't handle this situation, and it would be rather hard to write something that handles this trick without a little help. However, I bet you've seen many games with arches and portals. So how did they solve this problem?

If you looked at the resources folder, then you already know the answer. The arch is represented by two different sprites that are ordered as usual. Then it is rendered as shown in Figure 7-19.

 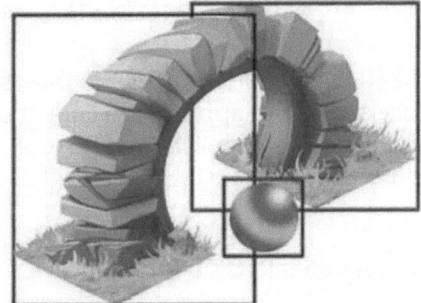

Figure 7-19. *Representing an arch as two objects*

You solve the problem this way since the engine now checks the ball position against the left and the right leg of the arch separately, and not the arch as a whole. As the ball moves, the rendering order changes, showing the correct picture all the time.

Listing 7-29 shows how this solution looks in the code. Add the following three objects to your ObjectLayer, as shown in Listing 7-29.

Listing 7-29. *Adding an Arch and a Moving Ball to the Game*

```
this._archBall = new StaticImage(im.get("ball"), 300, 600);
this._objectLayer.addObject(this._archBall);

img = im.get("arch-left");
this._objectLayer.addObject(new StaticImage(img, 120, 470));

img = im.get("arch-right");
this._objectLayer.addObject(new StaticImage(img, 234, 462));
```

Make the ball move through the arch with a simple movement rule (see Listing 7-30).

Listing 7-30. *Moving Ball Through the Arch*

```
_p._updateWorld = function() {
    // Update
    this._ball1.move(0, 2);
    this._ball2.move(2, 0);

    // Diagonal move through the arch
    this._archBall.move(2*this._archBallDirection, this._archBallDirection);
    if (this._archBall.getBounds().x > 300 || this._archBall.getBounds().x <
100)
        this._archBallDirection *= -1;
};
```

The _archBallDirection is a variable that is initialized to 1 in the constructor of the Game class (add the appropriate line). It changes depending on where the ball is moving. Launch the application and look at the movement. The ball should cross the arch correctly.

Object Layer: Next Steps

As usual, there is a lot of space for further optimization, so here are a few ideas.

- Using arrays to keep the collection of objects sorted is the simplest and most expensive approach; sorting an array is rather inefficient, as is searching for an item in it. If you have many objects, it is better to think about a specialized data structure like a binary tree that keeps objects sorted and makes it quite CPU-efficient to search for one. On the other hand, if you have only a few objects, it isn't worth the effort. There is a great article that explains how binary trees work: "Computer science in JavaScript: Binary search tree" (http://bit.ly/F4Dmc).

- The ObjectLayer can use the same offscreen canvas caching trick as IsometricTileLayer. If you have many objects on the screen at the same time (like a city with many buildings), it makes sense to save a few CPU loops by caching this layer as well.

- There are much better (although complicated to code) data structures to keep track of spatial objects. R-Tree is a good example. Consider using it; it might actually improve the performance of your game.

The state of the project at this point is saved into a folder called v0.2. Feel free to use it for reference or take the code straight from there and continue.

Dirty Rectangles

Dirty rectangles is the next major rendering-optimization that we will implement in our engine. The idea behind this technique is to "render only the areas of the screen that have changed."

Let's assume that we have a world that doesn't move by itself and the user is not moving the viewport at the moment. There might be few moving objects, but most of the screen remains static. In other words, the screen changes very little between repaints; most of the content remains the same as a frame ago, with small exceptions like an animated sprite or a moving ball. Figure 7-20 illustrates this idea. The grayed-out part of the screen is not changing between the frames; repainting it is a waste of CPU cycles. The only part that really needs to be repainted is the waving knight character.

Figure 7-20. *The area that changes between frames is much smaller than the screen; still, we repaint it all on every frame.*

Let's think about how we can optimize the repainting process once again to make it draw only the part of the screen that has really changed.

Right now, the `IsometricTileLayer` repaints its buffer every frame, even if nothing has changed at all, and that's where we lose cycles. We have to mark the changed areas on the screen and draw only those. This is exactly the idea behind the technique called *dirty rectangles*.

How It Works

This section presents an informal description of the dirty rectangles algorithm. Once we understand how it works, we will implement it in the next section and make our engine even better.

Let's say that we are in the middle of the game. We rendered the previous frame on the screen, and now it is a time to replace it with a new one. The screen, at this point, is considered "clean."

Start to update the logic of the game. If the object has moved, or the animation sequence has switched to the next frame, it means that part of the screen must be updated in order to display the changes correctly.

Figure 7-21 shows the typical game scene: a frame that has a moving character and a static background. The game engine doesn't need to re-render the whole scene to reflect the changes. It needs to repaint only two rectangles: one for the former position of the character and one for its new position. The user sees no difference between this technique and repainting the whole frame; and you will save some precious cycles.

Figure 7-21. *The idea behind dirty rectangles*

The idea behind the algorithm is to mark certain areas of the screen as "dirty" and repaint only them. The rest of the picture remains the same since canvas doesn't perform the cleanup of the content between frames. If we don't clean the old content ourselves, it remains exactly the same as before, and we can paint on top of it.

For the sake of simplicity, the areas that we mark dirty are always rectangular. There is no sense in building the finer-grained selection since rectangles are the fastest way to deal with calculating of the area to be repainted. So how do we decide if the area has to be marked dirty? The set of rules is quite simple:

- If a sprite has changed the animation frame, mark the rectangle that fully covers the old and the new frames as dirty.

- If an object has moved, mark the rectangle that wraps both the old position and new position.

- If an entity is added to the scene or removed from the scene, mark the boundaries of the entity as dirty.

- If the user moved the screen or changed the size of the canvas, mark the entire viewport as dirty.

Once you apply these rules during the world update phase, you end up with a set of dirty rectangles marking the changed areas of the game map. Now you have to decide how to use them to repaint the world.

The simplest and (usually) most efficient way is to find the smallest-size rectangle that covers all dirty areas and treat it as the repaint region. Figure 7-22 shows this technique. The left image represents a normal case: multiple dirty rectangles encompassed by one bigger rectangle. The right image shows the worst case: two moving objects will cause the entire screen to be repainted.

Regular case   Worst case

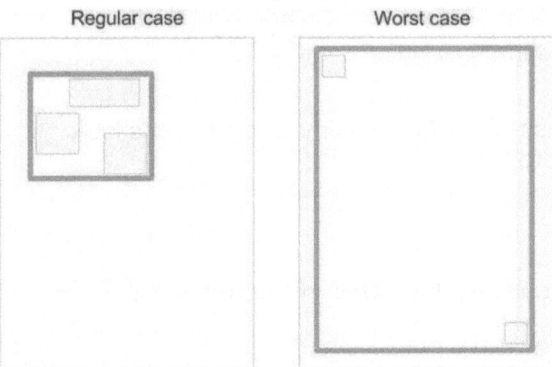

Figure 7-22. *We have a small dirty rectangle in a regular case, but the worst case results in repainting the entire area.*

This approach might look inefficient, but in most cases, it is quite enough to gain a performance boost. Now that you know how dirty rectangles work, it's time to implement this optimization in practice.

Implementation

Implementation of the dirty rectangles algorithm is not hard, but it requires careful attention: you must remember to pass the dimensions of the dirty area to every layer of our engine and let every layer update the set of dirty rectangles.

The usual practice is to introduce a special "dirty area threshold" that signals that the dirty area is too big. Once the threshold is reached, we simply mark the entire screen as dirty and do not perform any checks for dirtiness until the next frame. This little trick allows you to save a little CPU time. For example, if 75 percent of the area is already dirty, there is no big difference in terms of CPU cycles between painting a huge portion of the screen and repainting the entire frame from scratch. At this point, we can stop dirty rectangle checks and render the frame as we did in previous sections.

The central class for this optimization is called a `DirtyRectangleManager`. Its job is to keep track of dirty regions, join them into one rectangle, and keep track of the threshold. The class operates in *screen space*. Indeed, dirty rectangles is a pure rendering optimization that has nothing to do with higher-level entities such as the game world. The area that the `DirtyRectangleManager` tracks is always the same as the viewport.

> **NOTE:** The same approach is applicable not only for games, but for any GUI applications. For example, Swing—the Java toolkit for building user interfaces—has the same functionality. It renders only the part of interface that has changed from the last time—a pressed button, or moved control, and so forth.

It's time to write the code for the new class. The code is fairly small, so let's look at it in Listing 7-31, and explain it afterward.

Listing 7-31. *The DirtyRectangleManager*

```
/*
 * The constructor accepts the single parameter, the value of the threshold.
 * The value is the number between 0 and 1.
 * 0 means - every time there is the dirty rectangle,
 * repaint the whole screen, 1 means - never use the threshold,
 * repaint the whole frame only when it is really all dirty
 */
```

```
function DirtyRectangleManager(allDirtyThreshold) {
    // Save the threshold value, default is 0.5
    this._allDirtyThreshold = allDirtyThreshold == undefined ? .5 :
allDirtyThreshold;

    // The parameters of the viewport
    this._viewport = new Rect(0, 0, 100, 100);

    // Current dirty rectangle that covers all smaller dirty areas
    this._dirtyRect = null;

    // true when we have reached the trheshold
    this._allDirty = true;

    // We start from marking all screen as dirty.
    // Need to repaint it all for the first time!
    this.markAllDirty();
}

_p = DirtyRectangleManager.prototype;

/**
 * Set the size of the viewport.
 */
_p.setViewport = function(width, height) {
    if (this._viewport.width == width && this._viewport.height == height) {
        return;
    }
    this._viewport.width = width;
    this._viewport.height = height;
    this.markAllDirty();
};

/**
 * Mark the given area as dirty. This is the main function used by the
 * layers API to notify that the part of the layer has changed during the update
 * and it has to be repainted on the next frame
 */
_p.markDirty = function(rect) {
    if (!(rect.width || rect.height) || this._allDirty) {
        return;
    }

    // We are only interested in the rectangles that intersect the viewport
    // if a rectangle is far away beyond the visible part of the world, there's
no
    // sense to track it
    rect = this._viewport.intersection(rect);

    if (!rect) {
```

```
        return;
    }

    // If there is already some area marked as dirty, we find the rectangle that
covers
    // both the current dirty rectangle and the new one
    if (this._dirtyRect) {
        this._dirtyRect = this._dirtyRect.convexHull(rect);
    } else {

        // If this is the first diry rectangle, save it as the dirty area.
        this._dirtyRect = this._viewport.intersection(rect);
    }

    // Check for threshold. If it is reached, mark the whole screen dirty
    if (this._dirtyRect.width * this._dirtyRect.height >
            this._allDirtyThreshold*this._viewport.width*this._viewport.height)
{
        this.markAllDirty();
    }
};

/**
 * Clear the dirty regions. This is usually done after the repaint, when all
dirty
 * parts have the new content and they are clean again.
 */
_p.clear = function() {
    this._dirtyRect = null;
    this._allDirty = false;
};

/**
 * Mark the whole viewport as dirty.
 */
_p.markAllDirty = function() {
    this._allDirty = true;
    this._dirtyRect = this._viewport.copy();
};

/**
 * Returns true if there are no dirty rectangles registered this frame
 * (no need to repaint anything at all)
 */
_p.isAllClean = function() {
    return !(this._dirtyRect);
};

/**
 * Returns true if the whole viewport is dirty
```

```
 * (repaint everything)
 */
_p.isAllDirty = function() {
    return this._allDirty;
};

/**
 * Returns the current dirty rectangle that covers all registered dirty areas
 */
_p.getDirtyRect = function() {
    return this._dirtyRect;
};
```

The class has a variable called _dirtyRect to keep track of the area currently marked as dirty. It can be in one of two states—either "all dirty" or "normal." If _allDirty is true, then all other dirty rectangles are ignored, and getDirtyRect() returns the whole viewport. In normal mode, each new dirty rectangle is first "trimmed" by the viewport. We are not interested in the parts that are outside of the viewport (if the area is not visible, we won't redraw it anyway, dirty or not). Then the new rectangle is "joined" with the current dirty area. The convexHull() finds the smallest rectangle that covers both the new dirty region and the existing one.

As you can see, the markAllDirty() is a public method, so the client API can invoke it directly. It is useful for cases like movement—when the entire area of the screen needs to be updated and the client API knows straight away that the viewport is dirty.

Dirty rectangles is an efficient but intrusive strategy. Once you use it, then all parts of the game, even the smallest ones, must be aware of it. For example, when a sprite's animation has switched to the next frame, the sprite needs a way to mark the area as dirty. Alternatively, the entity that manages the sprite (a layer) can do that. The point is that every movement, animation, or change of map tiles—anything that makes the screen update—should go alongside with the call to the DirtyRectangleManager. That's why we add the support for the new class to the very top of our game hierarchy—the GameObject. Listing 7-32 summarizes the change.

Listing 7-32. *Making GameObject Aware of DirtyRectangleManager*

```
function GameObject() {
    EventEmitter.call(this);
    this._id = GameObject._maxId++;
    this._bounds = new Rect(0, 0, 100, 100);
    this._dirtyRectManager = null;
}
```

```
_p.draw = function(ctx, rect) {
    // To implement
};

_p.getDirtyRectManager = function() {
    return this._dirtyRectManager;
};

_p.setDirtyRectManager = function(dirtyRectManager) {
    this._dirtyRectManager = dirtyRectManager;
};

_p.markDirty = function(x, y, width, height) {
    if (this._dirtyRectManager) {
        var rect = arguments.length == 1 ? x : new Rect(x, y, width, height);
        this._dirtyRectManager.markDirty(rect);
    }
};
```

To make the use of DirtyRectangleManager optional, we assume that implementing classes will not call the this._dirtyRectManager directly, but only through the call to markDirty(). It is up to the programmer whether he uses this optimization or not. Indeed, there are games that greatly benefit from this approach, and there are games that don't. For example, in a zombie-apocalypse game where the screen is swarming with moving zombies, you don't need to bother about dirty rectangles—most of the screen is dirty all the time. On the other hand, a farm-like game with a mostly static world that eventually plays animations greatly benefits from this approach.

The draw() function now has one extra parameter, rect, which acts like a hint—the rectangle that is now repainted. The implementations use this hint to repaint only the required parts. The rect can also be null, which means "redraw everything."

> **NOTE:** The optional use of DirtyRectangleManager means a choice between using it everywhere and using it nowhere. There's no way to use it on IsometricTileLayer, for example, and ignore it in ObjectLayer.

Integrating with Layers

We created the DirtyRectangleManager and it is ready to track the updated parts of the screen. Now our task is to update the Game class and both layers: the IsometricTileLayer and the ObjectLayer so that they honor the hints from

DirtyRectangleManager and re-render only the part of the screen that has changed.

Start with updating the Game class, and then pass the DirtyRectangleManager to both layers, as shown in Listing 7-33.

Listing 7-33. *Updating Game Class to Use DirtyRectangleManager*

```
function Game(canvas, map) {
    /* unchanged */

    this._dirtyRectangleManager = new DirtyRectangleManager();

    this._imageManager = new ImageManager();
    /* unchanged */
}

_p._initLayers = function() {
    var im = this._imageManager;
    this._tileLayer = new IsometricTileLayer(this._map, im.get("terrain"),
                                    128, 68, 124, 62, 0, 3);

    this._tileLayer.setDirtyRectManager(this._dirtyRectangleManager);

    this._ball1 = new StaticImage(im.get("ball"), 370, 30);
    this._ball2 = new StaticImage(im.get("ball"), 370, 30);
    this._objectLayer = new ObjectLayer([this._ball1, this._ball2], 200, 4000,
4000);
    this._objectLayer.setDirtyRectManager(this._dirtyRectangleManager);

    /* unchanged */
};

/** Move the viewport withing the world */
_p.move = function(deltaX, deltaY) {
    this._dirtyRectangleManager.markAllDirty();
    this._tileLayer.move(-deltaX, -deltaY);
    this._objectLayer.move(-deltaX, -deltaY);
};

/** Resize handling */
_p.resize = function() {
    this._dirtyRectangleManager.setViewport(this._canvas.width,
this._canvas.height);
    this._tileLayer.setSize(this._canvas.width, this._canvas.height);
    this._objectLayer.setSize(this._canvas.width, this._canvas.height);
};
```

The code is quite self-explanatory. The _dirtyRectangleManager is updated almost like the layer. Once the player moves the map, the whole frame is dirty.

Once the player rotates the screen and changes the size of the canvas, the _dirtyRectangleManager is made aware of the new size of the viewport. Finally, both layers receive the same instance of _dirtyRectangleManager to mark the parts of screen as dirty.

Next, update the most important part—the rendering code inside the Game class, as in Listing 7-34.

Listing 7-34. *Updating the Rendering Code for the Game Class*

```
_p._renderFrame = function() {
    this._ctx.save();
    if (!this._dirtyRectangleManager.isAllClean()) {
        var rect = this._dirtyRectangleManager.getDirtyRect();
        this._ctx.beginPath();
        this._ctx.rect(rect.x, rect.y, rect.width, rect.height);
        this._ctx.clip();
        this._tiledLayer.draw(this._ctx, rect);
        this._objectLayer.draw(this._ctx, rect);
    }

    this._dirtyRectangleManager.clear();
    this._ctx.restore();
};
```

There are several important things to notice here. First, the set of calls to the Context2D API that we haven't seen yet:

```
this._ctx.beginPath();
this._ctx.rect(rect.x, rect.y, rect.width, rect.height);
this._ctx.clip();
```

As the name implies, these three calls set the clipping region on the context. Everything outside the region is ignored. The clipping region is the parameter that changes the state of the context, which is why we need to wrap the function body with calls to ctx.save() and ctx.restore().

Finally, the function checks if the rectangle is completely clean, and ignores the repaint if this is case (the biggest win of this strategy). Otherwise, each layer receives the dirty rectangle as the second parameter to the draw method.

> **NOTE:** Why pass the dirty rectangle to layers if they already have an instance of DirtyRectangleManager? Good question. The reason is that the rendering strategy is not the job of the layer. The layer should not be aware of *how exactly* the code in the game decided to render the scene. For example, a different

implementation of the DirtyRectangleManager might output an array of dirty rectangles that will require multiple calls to draw(). The job of the layer is very simple: render the content to the given rectangle. Then why do we pass the DirtyRectangleManager if all we need is a rectangle? Because layers like ObjectLayer need a way to mark areas as dirty.

Both layers should obey the new rules and render only the parts of content within the dirty rectangle. The code is quite simple: instead of checking against the viewport, check against the bounds of the dirty rectangle. So the draw() method of ObjectLayer is updated, as in Listing 7-35.

Listing 7-35. *Updating ObjectLayer to Re-Render Only the Dirty Parts of the Screen*

```
_p.draw = function(ctx, dirtyRect) {
    if (this._cacheDirty) {
        this._resetCache();
    } else if (this._cacheUnsorted) {
        this._sortCache();
    }

    // If there is no dirty rectangle - repaint all and use the _bounds
    // instead of dirty rectangle
    dirtyRect = dirtyRect || new Rect(0, 0, this._bounds.width,
this._bounds.height);

    for (var i = 0; i < this._cache.length; i++) {
        var obj = this._cache[i];

        // Draw object only if it intersects the dirty rectangle
        if (this._getScreenBounds(obj).intersects(dirtyRect)) {
            obj.draw(ctx, dirtyRect, this._bounds.x, this._bounds.y);
        }
    }
};

/*
 * Returns the screen bounds of the given object
 */
_p._getScreenBounds = function(obj) {
    var worldBounds = obj.getBounds();
    return new Rect(worldBounds.x - this._bounds.x, worldBounds.y -
this._bounds.y,
            worldBounds.width, worldBounds.height);
};
```

DirtyRectangleManager operates within screen coordinates, so we first translate the object coordinates to screen space, and then check if the object intersects the dirty area.

The next step is to update the IsometricTileLayer. It uses the offscreen image to repaint the frame. Let's change it so that only the dirty part is repainted (since most of the code is added, I will not mark the new lines bold this time). Listing 7-36 shows the updated code for the draw() function.

Listing 7-36. *Updating IsometricTileLayer to Make It Honor Dirty Rectangles*

```
_p.draw = function(ctx, dirtyRect) {
    if (this._offDirty) {
        this._redrawOffscreen();
    }

    var offscreenImageWorldX = this._offRect.x*this._cellWidth;
    var offscreenImageWorldY = this._offRect.y*this._cellHeight/2;

    // If there is a dirty rectangle,
    // calculate the intersection of the offscreen
    // image and the dirty rectangle. Then draw only the part
    // of offscreen buffer
    // that is covered by the dirtyRect
    if (dirtyRect) {
        var sx = this._bounds.x - offscreenImageWorldX + dirtyRect.x;
        var sy = this._bounds.y - offscreenImageWorldY + dirtyRect.y;
        var sw = dirtyRect.width;
        var sh = dirtyRect.height;
        var dx = dirtyRect.x;
        var dy = dirtyRect.y;
        var dw = dirtyRect.width;
        var dh = dirtyRect.height;

        ctx.drawImage(this._offCanvas, sx, sy, sw, sh, dx, dy, dw, dh);
    } else {
        // If there is no dirtyRect, redraw the whole viewport as we did before.
        ctx.drawImage(this._offCanvas, offscreenImageWorldX - this._bounds.x,
                    offscreenImageWorldY - this._bounds.y);
    }
};
```

Note that we try to keep both layer implementations independent of the dirty rectangle manager. Both of them will still operate normally if you do not pass the second parameter to draw().

Marking Dirty Rectangles

The final part is to locate places in the code that make the scene dirty and mark the rectangles. Obviously, the first part is the movement of the entire viewport— we already handled that task in the Game class. The second part is the IsometricTileLayer; the setTileAt() function changes one of the tiles in the map and the area surrounding the tile must be marked dirty. Update the setTileAt() function so that it marks part of the screen as dirty whenever someone changes the tile. Listing 7-37 shows how to do it.

Listing 7-37. *setTileAt Changes the Content of the Screen, So It Should Mark the Appropriate Rectangle As Dirty*

```
_p.setTileAt = function(x, y, tileId) {
    this._mapData[y][x] = tileId;
    if (this._offRect.containsPoint(x, y)) {
        var dirtyX = x*this._cellWidth +
            (y%2 ? this._cellWidth/2 : 0) - this._marginLeft - this._bounds.x;

        var dirtyY = y*this._cellHeight/2 - this._marginTop - this._bounds.y;
        var dirtyWidth = this._tileWidth;
        var dirtyHeight = this._tileHeight;

        this.markDirty(dirtyX, dirtyY, dirtyWidth, dirtyHeight);
        this._offDirty = true;
    }
};
```

The last place is the moving objects in ObjectLayer. Once an object has moved, two areas become dirty: the previous bounds of the objects and the new bounds. Some lines need to be added to the ObjectLayer methods; Listing 7-38 summarizes the changes. There are three places in ObjectLayer that can update the frame: _onObjectMove(), the function that is called when one of the objects changes its location; and addObject() and removeObject():, functions that either add or remove world entities. In each of these cases, the part of the screen may become dirty.

Listing 7-38. *Marking Dirty Rectangles in ObjectLayer*

```
_p._onObjectMove = function(e) {
    var obj = e.object;
    var id = obj.getId();
    var objectBounds = obj.getBounds();

    var newClusters = objectBounds.getOverlappingGridCells(
        this._clusterSize, this._clusterSize,
        this._clusters[0].length, this._clusters.length);
```

```
        var oldClusters = this._idToClusterBounds[id];

        if (!oldClusters.equals(newClusters)) {
            this._moveObjectBetweenClusters(obj, oldClusters, newClusters);
        }

        if (e.y != e.oldY) {
            this._cacheUnsorted = true;
        }

        // The object has moved, mark two rectangles dirty: the old position and the
new
        // position of the object.
        var worldBounds = obj.getBounds();
        this.markDirty(worldBounds.x - this._bounds.x, worldBounds.y -
this._bounds.y,
                worldBounds.width, worldBounds.height);

        this.markDirty(
                new Rect(e.oldX - this._bounds.x, e.oldY - this._bounds.y,
                        worldBounds.width, worldBounds.height));
    };

    /*
     * When the object is added or removed, mark its bounds as dirty to repaint the
     * area.
     */
    _p.addObject = function(obj) {
        this._objects.push(obj);
        obj.addListener("move", this._boundOnMove);
        var clusters = this._addToClusters(obj);
        if (clusters.intersects(this._visibleClusterBounds)) {
            this._cache.push(obj);
            this._cacheUnsorted = true;
            this.markDirty(this._getScreenBounds(obj));
        }
    };

    _p.removeObject = function(obj) {
        if (!Arrays.contains(obj, this._objects)) {
            return;
        }

        obj.removeListener("move", this._boundOnMove);
        this._removeFromClusters(obj);
        Arrays.remove(obj, this._cache);
        this._dirtyRectManager.markDirty(this._getScreenBounds(obj));
    };
```

We are all settled now. Every layer is responsible for reporting the dirty rectangles, and the DirtyRectangleManager is responsible for managing them and joining them into the one big rectangle that is reported back to the Game. The Game, in turn, passes this "repaint hint" downstream to layers.

Dirty rectangles is a very useful optimization. In fact, there are games where most of the frames are still, or the movements are local and rather small. In these cases, dirty rectangles saves many repaints, which is especially important on mobile devices.

UI and Layer Manager

The next phase of our project is to add the user interface (UI) elements. We have only one element—the round button that shows the current state of the game: moving, changing terrain, or building new huts. Since the UI should be placed on top of other layers, we will obviously need to add one more layer to our game. That means we have to duplicate the calls to move(), resize(), and draw(). Obviously, it wouldn't be a good idea to continue that way. We need a solution to handle a set of ordered layers at once. Let's call this new class LayerManager.

Layer Manager

LayerManager is a class that handles a set of layers in a consistent way. LayerManager delegates every call to the underlying layers, preserving the correct order. LayerManager takes care of DirtyRectangleManager too. Once the layer is added, it receives the same instance of DirtyRectangleManager that LayerManager has. The code in Listing 7-39 shows a simple yet very useful implementation of this class.

Listing 7-39. *The LayerManager*

```
function LayerManager() {
    GameObject.call(this);

    // The collection of layers to manage
    this._layers = [];
}

extend(LayerManager, GameObject);

var _p = LayerManager.prototype;

/**
```

```
 * Proagate setSize call to every layer
 */
_p.setSize = function(width, height) {
    GameObject.prototype.setSize.call(this, width, height);
    for (var i = 0; i < this._layers.length; i++) {
        this._layers[i].setSize(width, height);
    }
};

/**
 * Proagate setPosition call to every layer
 */
_p.setPosition = function(x, y) {
    GameObject.prototype.setPosition.call(this, x, y);
    for (var i = 0; i < this._layers.length; i++) {
        this._layers[i].setPosition(x, y);
    }
};

/**
 * Proagate setDirtyRectManager call to every layer
 */
_p.setDirtyRectManager = function(dirtyRectManager) {
    GameObject.prototype.setDirtyRectManager.call(this, dirtyRectManager);
    for (var i = 0; i < this._layers.length; i++) {
        this._layers[i].setDirtyRectManager(dirtyRectManager);
    }
};

/**
 * Draw layers in order, passing the dirtyRect
 */
_p.draw = function(ctx, dirtyRect) {
    for (var i = 0; i < this._layers.length; i++) {
        this._layers[i].draw(ctx, dirtyRect);
    }
};

/**
 * add the new layer to the collection
 */
_p.addLayer = function(layer) {
    if (this._dirtyRectManager) {
        layer.setDirtyRectManager(this._dirtyRectManager);
    }
    this._layers.push(layer);
};

/**
 * Return i-th layer from the collection
```

```
    */
_p.getLayerAt = function(i) {
    return this._layers[i];
};
```

The idea behind LayerManager is to hide the collection of layers and make them behave as the single layer. Every action that is performed on the LayerManager is propagated to layers of the collection.

Once the LayerManager is in place, the code for the Game becomes much easier to read and maintain. And what's more important, we got rid of duplication! Now there's no need to keep a list of places in the code that need to be changed whenever you add a new layer. Take a look at the updated Game class in Listing 7-40 to see the difference.

Listing 7-40. *The Updated Game Class That Uses LayerManager Can Get Rid of Code Duplication and Handle Multiple Layers As One*

```
_p._initLayers = function() {
    var im = this._imageManager;

    // Tiled layer
    this._tiledLayer = new IsometricTileLayer(this._map, im.get("terrain"),
                                     128, 68, 124, 62, 0, 3);

    // Object layer
    this._ball1 = new StaticImage(im.get("ball"), 370, 30);
    this._ball2 = new StaticImage(im.get("ball"), 370, 30);
    this._objectLayer = new ObjectLayer([this._ball1, this._ball2], 200, 10000,
10000);

    var img = im.get("house-1");
    this._objectLayer.addObject(new StaticImage(img, 350, 130));
    this._objectLayer.addObject(new StaticImage(img, 200, 50));
    this._objectLayer.addObject(new StaticImage(img, 150, 200));

    img = im.get("house-2");
    this._objectLayer.addObject(new StaticImage(img, 550, 230));
    this._objectLayer.addObject(new StaticImage(img, 920, 250));

    // Layer manager
    this._layerManager.addLayer(this._tiledLayer);
    this._layerManager.addLayer(this._objectLayer);
};

_p.move = function(deltaX, deltaY) {
    // Had to duplicate call for every layer here
    this._dirtyRectangleManager.markAllDirty();
    this._layerManager.move(-deltaX, -deltaY);
```

```
};

_p.resize = function() {
    // Had to duplicate call for every layer here
    this._dirtyRectangleManager.setViewport(this._canvas.width,
this._canvas.height);
    this._layerManager.setSize(this._canvas.width, this._canvas.height);
};
```

For those of you who like design patterns, the LayerManager is an example of composite—the class that allows handling a collection of objects as if it is a single object. In fact, LayerManager can be treated as a layer itself—there is nothing wrong with adding an instance of LayerManager to another LayerManager.

UI

The only UI element that we have is the round button that shows the current "mode" of the game: moving, building, or terrain. Figure 7-23 shows, how the UI will look at the end of this section. The circle in the top-left corner acts as a "mode indicator" and a button at the same time. Right now, it shows that the user is in construction mode, and clicking the screen adds or removes new buildings. If the user taps the button, the mode switches to "terrain," and after another click, to "movement."

Figure 7-23. *The simple UI of the game: the round button in the top-left corner*

For now, the button is pretty useless, since we haven't implemented the interaction yet, but let's try to place it on the screen anyway to prepare everything for the next phase of our project. The RoundStateButton class renders the button on the screen and returns the current state of the button. Listing 7-41 shows the simple implementation of this class.

Listing 7-41. *Implementation of the RoundStateButton*

```
/*
 * The RoundStateButton constructor accepts the image with three frames:
 * one frame for each state. frameWidth and frameHeight are the dimensions
 * of the single frame
 */
function RoundStateButton(image, frameWidth, frameHeight) {
    GameObject.call(this);
    this._bounds = new Rect(0, 0, frameWidth, frameHeight || image.height);
    this._image = image;
    this._frame = 2;
}

extend(RoundStateButton, GameObject);

// Constants to reference states
RoundStateButton.TERRAIN = "terrain";
RoundStateButton.OBJECTS = "objects";
RoundStateButton.MOVE = "move";

var _p = RoundStateButton.prototype;

/**
 * Render the current frame on the canvas.
 */
_p.draw = function(ctx, dirtyRect, viewportX, viewportY) {
    ctx.drawImage(
        this._image,
        this._bounds.width*this._frame,
        0,
        this._bounds.width,
        this._bounds.height,
        this._bounds.x - viewportX || 0,
        this._bounds.y - viewportY || 0,
        this._bounds.width,
        this._bounds.height);
};

/**
 * Set the current button state to the given value
 */
_p.setFrame = function(frame) {
    this._frame = frame;
};
```

```
/**
 * Switch to the next state. This function is executed when user
 * taps the button. Emits the event to notify the outer
 * world about the change
 */
_p.nextFrame = function() {
    this._frame = (this._frame + 1) % 3;
    this.emit("change", {object: this});
};

/**
 * Get the string representation of the current state
 */
_p.getState = function() {
    return [RoundStateButton.TERRAIN, RoundStateButton.OBJECTS,
              RoundStateButton.MOVE][this._frame];
};
```

Now that we have a RoundStateButton, we need to decide how to place it on the screen. The difference between the button and the other entities that we worked with so far is that the button is not bound to world coordinates, but rather screen coordinates. When the user scrolls the map, the button stays in place. One option is to treat it as a special entity and manage it separately from the other objects. A much better choice would be to add it to one of the layers and let LayerManager do the rest. None of the existing layers will handle the task correctly because the ObjectLayer and the IsometricTileLayer are both designed to work in world coordinates; the layer that we need for a button should not move once the map is moved. Let's create a new layer class and call it UiLayer. Listing 7-42 shows this simple class.

Listing 7-42. *The UiLayer Class*

```
/**
 * UiLayer - the layer that operates in screen coordinates and doesn't move
 * when the user scrolls the map. This layer is "bound" to the screen, so it can
 * safely ignore the calls to move() and setPosition().
 */
function UiLayer(objects) {
    GameObject.call(this);
    // The array of the objects to render
    this._objects = objects;

    // For every object of this layer, bind the listener for "change" event
    // to mark the area dirty
    this._addChangeListeners();
}
```

```
extend(UiLayer, GameObject);
_p = UiLayer.prototype;
_p.setPosition = function(x, y) {
    // Ignore
};

_p.move = function(deltaX, deltaY) {
    // Ignore
};

/**
 * Draw every object on the screen with the respect to dirtyRect
 */
_p.draw = function(ctx, dirtyRect) {
    // If no dirtyRect is provided - draw every visible object
    dirtyRect = dirtyRect || this._bounds;

    for (var i = 0; i < this._objects.length; i++) {
        var obj = this._objects[i];
        var bounds = obj.getBounds();
        // Draw only those objects that intersect the dirty rect
        if (bounds.intersects(dirtyRect)) {
            obj.draw(ctx, dirtyRect, this._bounds.x, this._bounds.y);
        }
    }
};


/**
 * Add new UI element on the screen
 */
_p.addObject = function(obj) {
    this._objects.push(obj);
};

/**
 * Remove the existing object from the screen
 */
_p.removeObject = function(obj) {
    if (Arrays.contains(obj, this._objects)) {
        Arrays.remove(obj, this._objects);
    }
};

/**
 * If one of the objects says that it has changed - mark the area as dirty.
 * Objects of this layer are stored in screen coordinates so there's no need
 * to translate from world coordinates in this function.
 */
_p._onObjectChange = function(e) {
```

```
    var obj = e.object;
    this.markDirty(obj.getBounds());
};

/**
 * Track change events on every object
 */
_p._addChangeListeners = function() {
    var boundOnChange = this._onObjectChange.bind(this);
    for (var i = 0; i < this._objects.length; i++) {
        this._objects[i].addListener("change", boundOnChange);
    }
};
```

Note how the layer "connects" to the button via the custom event mechanism, just like the GameObject that reports the movement to the interested layer. Once the external API calls nextFrame() on the button, it emits the event and notifies all registered listeners about the change. The layer listens to the event and marks the bounding rectangle of the button as dirty. Another option is for the button to mark the dirty area itself, but I prefer to keep the game objects as simple as possible. You are free to implement your own architecture, of course. I will omit the code that adds another layer to the Game; after many exercises, you should already be comfortable with most of the code. If you need a hint, just look at the final version of the project in the v1.0 folder.

Interaction

Welcome to the final section of this chapter and to the final phase of the project. We already have the terrain, the objects, and the UI. To make it all "live," we need to think about the interaction between the user and the game. Let me remind you about the goal for this section:

- The game can be in one of three states: moving, terrain, and objects. In every state, the drag event moves the map.

- If the game is in a *moving* state, the up event does nothing.

- If the game is in a *terrain* state, the up event changes the underlying tile.

- If the game is in an *object* state, and the player clicked the existing object, it is removed; otherwise, a new ball is added to the game world.

There are some subtle requirements that we should remember in order to design a flexible and reusable API:

- We should not hard-code any particular reaction to an event into the layer code. Another game might reuse the isometric terrain, for example, but have its own rules for handling clicks.

- The layers should not know about the other layers, for the same reason. The ObjectLayer should not assume that there is any layer on top of it or underneath it, for example. The layers should not assume that they are managed by the LayerManager.

Now, before you read on, I challenge you to take paper and pencil and try to design the interaction flow yourself. This is a great exercise, and it gives you a very good level of understanding on how event-based architectures should work. Now go draw a couple of diagrams. When you're done, read on—it's time to make our game come alive.

Event Propagation and Handling

Look at the model of the game that we've built, shown in Figure 7-24. We have the hierarchy of entities. The top level is LayerManager, which internally consists of one or many layers. Each layer, in turn, consists of either objects or tiles. Each of these entities might be interested in events.

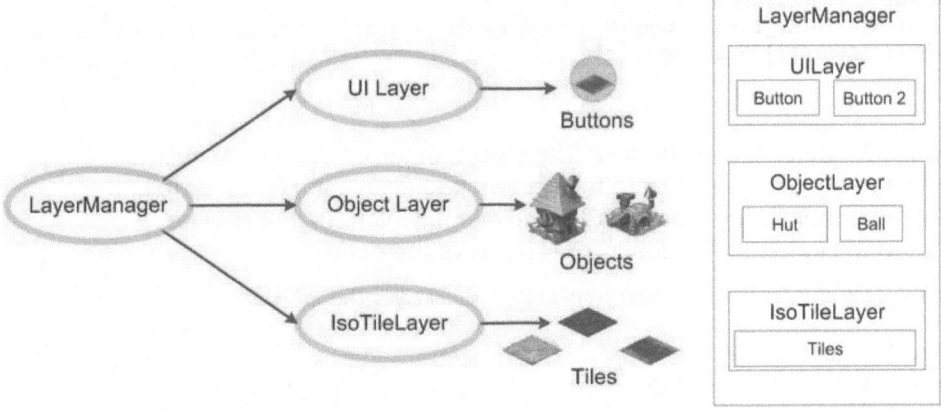

Figure 7-24. *The components and layers of the game*

The model looks very much like a traditional model of the HTML document, a hierarchy—or like a DOM tree. It would be natural to implement a similar event model, since it is well thought-out and programmers are already very familiar with it.

The first step is to build the event propagation model. In this example, we will work only with the up event. You can do the same for other events too.

Find the _onUp() function in the code for the game and modify it so that it sends every incoming event to the LayerManager (see Listing 7-43).

Listing 7-43. *Passing the Event to the LayerManager*

```
_p._onUp = function(e) {
    this._layerManager.emit("up", e);
};
```

This function was bound to the up event earlier in this chapter, but now it does something useful—it sends the same event to _layerManager. Next, in LayerManager, send the same event to every layer in sequence (see Listing 7-44).

Listing 7-44. *LayerManager Sends the Event to Every Layer It Controls*

```
function LayerManager() {
    GameObject.call(this);
    this._layers = [];
    this.addListener("up", this._onUpEvent.bind(this));
}

_p._onUpEvent = function(e) {
    for (var i = this._layers.length - 1; i >= 0; i--) {
        this._layers[i].emit("up", e);
    }
};
```

Every layer will receive the event now. The layers, in turn, transfer the event to the elements or transform them into the game-specific events. For example, the ObjectLayer can transmit the objectClicked event, which might be more convenient to the external API. Listing 7-45 shows the code.

Listing 7-45. *ObjectLayer Transforms the up Event to the Custom objectClicked Event*

```
_p._onUpEvent = function(e) {
    // Ignore the end of dragging
    if (e.moved)
        return;

    var x = e.x + this._bounds.x;
    var y = e.y + this._bounds.y;
    var obj = this.getObjectAt(x, y);
```

```
        if (obj) {
            obj.emit("up", e);
            this.emit("objectClicked", {object: obj, layer: this, cause: e});
        }
};
```

The UiLayer works exactly the same way, as shown in Listing 7-46.

Listing 7-46. *UiLayer Transforms the Up Event to the obectClicked Event*

```
_p._onUpEvent = function(e) {
    if (e.moved)
        return;

    var obj = this.getObjectAt(e.x, e.y);
    if (obj) {
        obj.emit("up", e);
        this.emit("objectClicked", {object: obj, layer: this, cause: e});
    }
};

/**
 * Returns the object at a given x, y coordinates,
 * if no object there - return null
 */
_p.getObjectAt = function(x, y) {
    for (var i = 0; i < this._objects.length; i++) {
        if (this._objects[i].getBounds().containsPoint(x, y)) {
            return this._objects[i];
        }
    }
    return null;
};
```

The IsometricTileLayer is slightly different since individual tiles are not represented as objects. This layer simply emits a custom tileClicked event. Listing 7-47 shows how to update the code for the IsometricTileLayer to react on events. The layer now emits tileClicked events whenever a user taps the tile.

Listing 7-47. *Updating IsometricTileLayer*

```
_p._onUpEvent = function(e) {
    if (e.moved)
        return;

    var coords = this._getTileCoordinates(e.x, e.y);
    if (coords.x >= 0 && coords.x < this._mapData[0].length &&
        coords.y >= 0 && coords.y < this._mapData.length) {
```

```
        this.emit("tileClicked", {x: coords.x, y: coords.y, layer: this, cause:
e}));
    }
};
```

Now, when the user taps the canvas, the event is propagated through the layers much like DOM events do. Next comes the most interesting part. Let's add the event listeners to the Game class that implement our logic. Add the following two lines to _initLayers():

```
this._tiledLayer.addListener("tileClicked", this._onTileClicked.bind(this));
this._objectLayer.addListener("objectClicked",
this._onObjectClicked.bind(this));
```

After you have added these lines, the Game class listens to the new events that our layers emit: tileClicked and objectClicked. This is exactly what we need for our game logic! Clicking the tile means that the tile has to be changed if the state of the button is TERRAIN. Clicking the object should remove it, if the state is OBJECTS. Finally, clicking the terrain if the state is OBJECTS means that the user clicked an empty space, so a new object must be added. Implementing this in code is simple. Listing 7-48 shows how to do it.

Listing 7-48. *Implementing the Core Logic*

```
_p._onTileClicked = function(e) {
    if (this._ui.getState() == RoundStateButton.TERRAIN) {
        var newTileId = (this._tiledLayer.getTileAt(e.x, e.y) + 1)%9;
        this._tiledLayer.setTileAt(e.x, e.y, newTileId);
    } else if (this._ui.getState() == RoundStateButton.OBJECTS) {
        this._addDummyObjectAt(e.cause.x, e.cause.y);
    }
};

_p._onObjectClicked = function(e) {
    if (this._ui.getState() == RoundStateButton.OBJECTS) {
        this._objectLayer.removeObject(e.object);
    }
};

_p._addDummyObjectAt = function(x, y) {
    var layerPosition = this._objectLayer.getBounds();
    var obj = new StaticImage(this._imageManager.get("ball"),
            x + layerPosition.x, y + layerPosition.y);
    var bounds = obj.getBounds();
    obj.move(-bounds.width/2, -bounds.height/2);
    this._objectLayer.addObject(obj);
};
```

The last part of adding event handling is to react to the clicks on the round button and update its state. It is just fine to add the handler straight to the RoundStateButton class. I can hardly think of a scenario when clicking the button like that can mean anything but "change the state" (don't forget to register this listener in the constructor):

```
_p._onUpEvent = function(e) {
    this.nextFrame();
};
```

Add this code and try out the application. You'll soon find out that the code does a little bit *too much*. Clicking the button not only changes the button state, but also goes to the next layers and changes the terrain or alters objects. The object deletion also looks wrong: once the object is deleted, the event goes to the IsometricTileLayer, where the object is created once again!

Stopping the Propagation

In some cases, we don't want the event to continue moving through the layers any further. There are a few examples in the previous section. Once the button is clicked, you don't want any underlying layers to receive the same event. The event should end with the UiLayer. For exactly the same reason, the DOM API has event-manipulation methods: stopPropagation() and preventDefault(). We need to implement a similar mechanism ourselves. The question is how to save the state of the event and track whether it was stopped or whether it should continue to move through the layers.

There are two options. The first is to make events into constructed objects, create a separate class hierarchy for them, and add two methods there, similar to the DOM API methods: stopPropagation() and isPropagationStopped(). The other way is to choose the easy path and agree upon setting a certain flag on an event to mark that it should not go any further. For a project like this one, it makes sense to use the simpler approach; we want to keep events small, easy, and lightweight.

Let's call the flag "stopped." So, whenever you write

```
e.stopped = true;
```

you are saying, "I am finished with this event. Do not let any other components of the game react on it."

There are two places in the code that should stop events. First is the objectClicked event handler in the Game class. If you click an object to remove it, you must stop the event from further propagation. Otherwise, the event hits the IsometricTileLayer and the Game creates a new dummy ball again! This is the behavior that we've just seen. Change the listener code in the Game class, as shown in Listing 7-49.

Listing 7-49. *The Game Class Should Stop the Event Once It Has Reacted Upon It*

```
_p._onObjectClicked = function(e) {
    if (this._ui.getState() == "objects") {
        this._objectLayer.removeObject(e.object);
        e.cause.stopped = true;
    }
};
```

Note that the game receives the onObjectClicked event, and not the up event that it needs to stop. To access the original event, we use the e.cause property—the small hack that we used just for this purpose.

The second obvious place is the button's event handler. If the user hit the button, he only wants to change the state and nothing else. Such an event should not be propagated. Modify the code for RoundStateButton, as in Listing 7-50.

Listing 7-50. *Stopping the Event Once the User Clicks the Button*

```
_p._onUpEvent = function(e) {
    this.nextFrame();
    e.stopped = true;
};
```

The final part of the solution is to update LayerManager—the class that decides if the event should move to the next layer. The code modifications are quite simple. They are shown in Listing 7-51.

Listing 7-51. Stopping the Events in LayerManager

```
_p._onUpEvent = function(e) {
    for (var i = this._layers.length - 1; i >= 0; i--) {
        this._layers[i].emit("up", e);
        if (e.stopped)
            return;
    }
};
```

> **NOTE:** There is one more way to mark an event as stopped: the return value from the event handler. Usually, the returned value is false. If one of the handlers returns false, the next layer will not receive the events.

Run the game once again—and enjoy your fully controllable world! Figure 7-25 shows a screenshot of the game engine running on a smartphone. You can navigate through the world, change the terrain, and add and remove objects. These simple actions form the basics for the wide variety of games that you can now build by yourself.

Figure 7-25. *The finished engine running on a smartphone*

The code is available in the v1.0 folder. Take it, and make a real game out of it! The best thing that you can do now is think about making your own isometric game. For example, add "resources" to the game that replenish over time. Make controls to select the type of structure to build and to allow construction only when there are enough resources. Add animated units using what you learned in Chapter 4, build a gameplay out of it, and assemble a game that you will enjoy.

Summary

Congratulations! You've done a great job learning how isometric engines work! This was one of the longest chapters in the entire book, and we learned many things during the course:

- A more in-depth insight into building isometric engines

- Using decorated tiles—working with resources from actual game artist Sergey Lesiuk

- Implementing a layer for an isometric terrain

- Using offscreen buffers to speed up the rendering

- Using object layers—arranging game objects into manageable data structures

- Implementing clusters—a way to limit the set of objects that rendering code has to deal with

- Implementing dirty rectangles—the strategy that allows us to mark certain areas of the screen as "dirty" to repaint only those parts (this is an invaluable optimization for games with only a few moving entities)

- Building the user interface—a simple control over the game state

- Implementing LayerManager—a way to work with multiple layers as a single object

- Reacting to user input—propagation events and stopping propagation

Now that you have an isometric engine at your disposal, the next step is to make an actual game with it! Don't hesitate to try something out. Build a single-player prototype of a social strategy game, add some resources and challenges, and play around with the user interface, dialogs, and controls. Try to do "upgrades" on buildings if there are enough resources. Add animation, make a loading screen, or add several different levels.

There are lots of ideas that you can try now! Once you reach Chapters 10 and 12, you learn how to add networking capabilities to a game.

But right now, you *already* have enough knowledge to make commercial-looking games. With canvas graphics, animations, events, and world-rendering tricks to top it all off, you have all the required tools to build a playable game. Don't hesitate—grab the code and try out some of your own ideas!

3D in a Browser

In the first part of the book, we learned how to make 2D games. For many, many years of browser game development, 2D games were the most advanced cutting-edge technology that one could use. 3D games are the result of a natural evolution process that aims to make the game look as realistic as possible. The only limiting factor that doesn't allow us to run *Skyrim* on a smartphone is, of course, the processing capabilities of portable hardware.

3D engines require much more processing time compared to regular 2D engines. In a 2D engine, the rendering job is relatively simple: take pixels from image, copy them to canvas; if there is transparency involved, calculate the composite color. For a 3D engine, on the other hand, it is a lot harder, and the underlying math is much more complex. That's one of the reasons why browsers (neither desktop nor mobile) didn't have native support for 3D until recently.

This chapter is devoted to the development of 3D applications in a browser. There is an API that was created to be the "standard" implementation of 3D in a browser called WebGL. Right now, WebGL is only making its first baby steps in the mobile market. The only browser available for Android smartphones and tablets that supports it is Firefox Mobile (at least at the time of writing). Sony Xperia PLAY supports WebGL in the stock browser. Due to the massive expansion of WebGL in desktop browsers, it is obvious that soon we will have this wonderful API in many mobile devices.

When more devices are capable of handling 3D at a good level, without doubt we will have 3D games in our browsers. That's why it is important for a game developer to know how 3D rendering works and what it takes to implement it in your own project. This chapter is devoted to the general concepts behind 3D and acts as a gentle preparation for Chapter 9, where we learn the basics of WebGL.

In this chapter, we will cover the following topics:

- The essentials of 3D rendering: how to present a volumetric figure on a flat screen

- Basics of matrix algebra: the main mechanism behind 3D

- Perspective and projections: making a scene look more natural

The goal of this chapter is to build a simple demo that can render the wireframes of a 3D model. We will start with the simplest shape—a cube.

Introducing 3D Rendering

So what is 3D essentially? How does it differ from the regular 2D graphics that we've seen in previous chapters? 3D graphics is an illusion, just like animations. When you're rendering an animation, you are switching frames fast enough to create the feeling that an object moves. But in reality, there's no physical movement involved in this process. Pixels stay in their positions, they just change color, and nevertheless it looks like the figure on the screen is moving.

Rendering a 3D scene works in a similar way. The display itself is flat, but we render the scene in a way that makes the user feel like he is looking at a 3D world through a window. Now, you must be asking the usual question: If 3D is basically a special case of 2D, and we already know how to work with 2D scenes, why don't we just use the canvas 2D context and draw a 3D scene there? That's a fair question. In fact, we can build a very simple 3D engine using only canvas, but we will face two major problems. First is the amount of work and math involved in such a project. The math and optimizations behind 3D engines and 2D engines is different by an order of magnitude. But even if you have a couple spare years to learn everything you need to know about 3D and implementing it as a 3D engine, you'll come up against the second crucial problem: the processing power that you will need to implement custom 3D rendering.

Ever since gamers, game developers, and hardware manufacturers understood that 3D is cool, they also understood that the CPU is not that great in rendering 3D. So they decided to add video card chips that are solely responsible for 3D calculations. Often more expensive than CPUs, these pieces of hardware are laser-focused on 3D graphics. In JavaScript in browsers, you can't directly access the GPU (graphics processing unit) and send rendering instructions there. You are limited to the JavaScript engine that executes every instruction in a CPU. Since a CPU isn't optimized for this type of operation, rendering takes far more time compared to rendering with a GPU.

In fact, before WebGL appeared, building fully custom 3D renderers was the only way of creating 3D in a browser without Flash or Java. People were inventing their own 3D engines, and some of these experiments were really impressive. But sadly, the bottom line is that you will not be able to write a decent-quality 3D game inside a 2D context. WebGL works very differently—it allows you to send all of the heaviest 3D calculations to the GPU.

Most cell phones in the market do not have a separate GPU yet, but that's really a question of time. What happens if you launch WebGL in such a phone? Will it work at all? Quick answer: yes, it will. But it still uses the CPU to render a scene and you won't get many frames per second on such a setup. When a 3D scene is rendered by the GPU, it is called *hardware rendering*, which means that the math and heavyweight calculations are done with a GPU that is optimized specifically for this kind of task. The opposite is called *software rendering*. It is when you render your scene with a CPU, for example, from JavaScript without WebGL, or on a device that doesn't have hardware that is supported by it.

> **NOTE:** Even on your desktop PC, you might have problems with WebGL acceleration. There is a special "blacklist" of hardware-driver-OS combinations that are known to cause issues with WebGL. If your PC falls into the blacklisted category, your WebGL context will not be accelerated, or WebGL will be disabled completely. If you still want to enable it at your own risk, there's a launch parameter on every browser that forces it to ignore blacklists. On Chrome, launch the browser with the option to ignore-gpu-blacklist. On Firefox, go to about:config and set webgl.force-enabled=true.

How 3D Rendering Works

This was one of the hardest sections to write in the entire book. 3D rendering is really a complex topic and it is quite possible to write a separate book or two with the title "How 3D Rendering Works." I try to explain just the important essentials of 3D rendering and later give you a good basis to understand the more advanced algorithms behind it. I will also try to make the math as lightweight as I can, but I still need to write some formulas here and there.

The Math

Let's start with the good news about 3D. The math that you are using in flat, two-coordinate 2D space works just fine in 3D. Everything in 3D is just 2D with one extra dimension, called "z". In 2D, the middle of the segment is calculated as

x = (x1 + x2) ÷ 2, y = (y1 + y2) ÷ 2

Add one more dimension, and you've got your 3D-version:

x = (x1 + x2) ÷ 2, y = (y1 + y2) ÷ 2, z = (z1 + z2) ÷ 2

The same is true for the distance between two points. In two dimensions, the formula is

d = sqrt((x1 − x2)^2 + (y1 − y2)^2)

Add the third dimension, and your formula will become

d = sqrt((x1 − x2)^2 + (y1 − y2)^2 + (z1 − z2)^2)

Why is that important right now? Because sometimes it is way easier to understand how things work in 2D than in 3D. It is easier to understand 2D drawings and formulas, but once you get the hang of them, switching to 3D is not hard at all. If you find it hard to understand something about 3D, either in this chapter or anywhere else, try to think about the same concept in a 2D space. If you can find a similar case, you'll get the 3D in no time.

Of course, every rule has its exceptions. In 2D, for example, lines are either parallel or they cross somewhere. In 3D, it is quite possible that lines are neither parallel nor do they cross.

A 3D Example

Let's start with a very basic real-life example. What is the most common case of 3D rendering on a 2D surface? That's right—taking a picture or video with your cell phone camera. The camera makes a "shot" of a 3D scene and captures it on a 2D surface. A decade ago, the surface was analog film, and nowadays it is a digital matrix. Look at the picture in Figure 8-1 to see how it works.

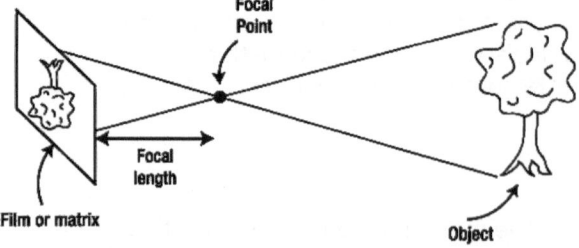

Figure 8-1. *A photo camera is a good example of 2D projection that is used to represent a certain fragment of a 3D scene.*

The light reflected by the objects is captured by the lens and transferred to the matrix. The image appears rotated top-down because the lens transforms it that way.

Digital cameras often have a zoom feature. You press a button and the picture magically becomes closer to you. What really happens is you change the distance between the focal point and the lens, thus increasing or decreasing the field of view (see Figure 8-2). A larger field of view means more objects are visible, with each object occupying less space—that's the rough equivalent of "zoom out" on a camera. A smaller field works in the opposite: objects take more space in the viewport and you see them in greater detail, like when you press "zoom in."

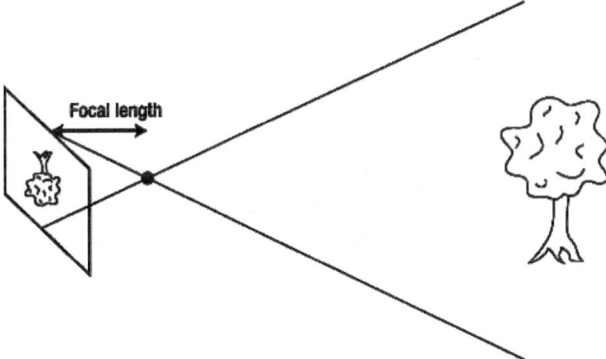

Figure 8-2. *Changing the focal length works like zooming in or out: the bigger the field of view, the smaller the image appears on the screen.*

Rendering a 3D scene works almost the same way, but since we don't have any lens or such, we don't need to put the "target" 2D surface behind the focal point. It is treated as if it is standing right in front of the camera (see Figure 8-3).

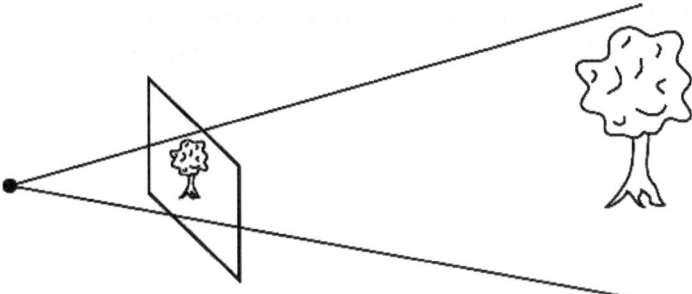

Figure 8-3. *In computer graphics, there are no lenses. That's why the plain that "captures" the scene projection is placed in front of the focal point. Still the rules for the field of view remain the same: the more you see, the smaller individual objects become.*

Now let's see how taking a picture is different from rendering a 3D scene. Unlike the real world, a 3D scene is made of triangles (so far that is the best way to represent a 3D model). Triangles do not have any physical properties, unlike the objects that you see and touch every day. They don't have weight, color, material, and so forth. These properties have to be simulated with other, more complex mathematical models.

When you click the button on a camera to take a picture, the tricky part is already done for you by natural laws: the light is properly reflected from surfaces—distorted by the fog or the flows of hot air, filtered by translucent objects—and then it is simply delivered to your camera or to the retina in your eye. In 3D, it is your task to implement these natural laws and calculate what is actually visible to the user. That's where the complexity of 3D engines comes from.

The good news is that you don't have to build a super-realistic simulation of every single optics law to build a 3D engine. If we throw away the lighting and materials, the engine is pretty simple—it just shows the wireframe of the polygons on the scene. The "Hello World" that everybody does when learning 3D programming is displaying a spinning 3D cube. That's what we'll do now, without touching WebGL yet. Why? Because it is probably the best example to kick-start our understanding of 3D.

The Hello World 3D Engine

In this section, we create the simplest possible 3D engine using the plain canvas API that we already know. We will start by looking at how to represent a 3D model in JavaScript. Then we briefly cover matrices—the mathematical abstraction that helps to render the model on the screen. With the help of matrices and transformation, we will make cube rotate on the screen. Finally, we explore perspectives and projections to make the model look more natural. The practical goal is to display a nice, rotating cube like the one shown in Figure 8-4.

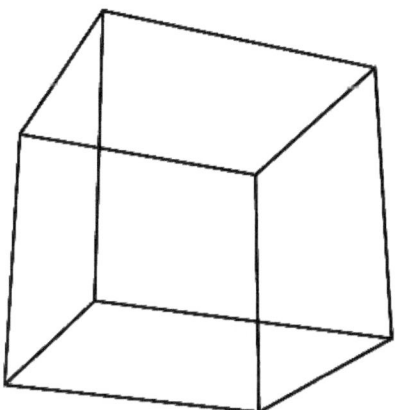

Figure 8-4. *The final version of the application that we make in the course of this chapter illustrates how to render a rotating 3D cube.*

Model and Scene

What do we need to know about the scene to render it? First of all, we need the list of vertices that make up a cube or any other model that we render. Next, we need to know which points are connected by an edge and which is not. Let's define the cube for our JavaScript experiment.

The Model

In 3D space, the model is represented with vertices, edges, and faces. A *vertex* is simply a point in space; an *edge* is a line that connects two vertices; and a *face* is a flat surface limited by the edges.

A cube has eight vertices, twelve edges, and six faces: each edge connects a pair of vertices and each face is the square limited by four edges. Each point in 3D space is represented by three coordinates (x, y, z). Let's first look at Figure 8-5, which shows the scheme of the cube, the coordinate directions, and the coordinates of the cube's vertices.

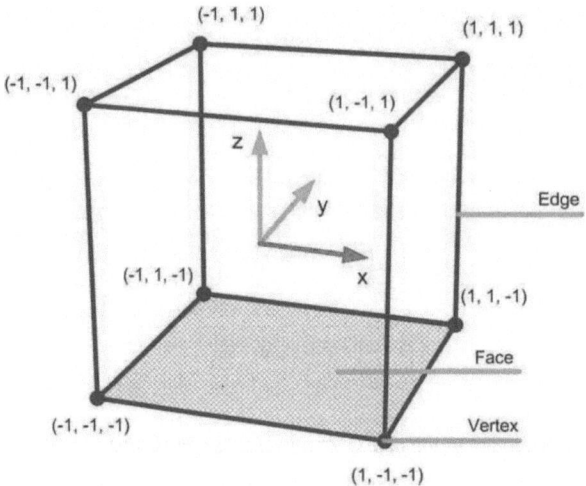

Figure 8-5. *Representation of the cube in space*

> **NOTE:** 3D space doesn't have up, down, left, or right directions—only three axes, each one pointing in its own direction. The one of that is "up" is for you to decide; however, the typical convention is that z axis represents height.

The origin of coordinates is in the middle of the cube—the (0, 0, 0) point. For simplicity, the length of the edge is 2, so each coordinate element is 1 or -1. Now, let's save the information about vertices in the array. It has eight elements because there are eight vertices. Each element is a point in 3D space presented by another array that holds three coordinates. Listing 8-1 shows how this looks in the code.

Listing 8-1. *The Vertices of the Cube*

```
var vertices = [
    [-1, -1, -1],  [-1, -1,  1],  [-1,  1, -1],  [-1,  1,  1],
    [1, -1, -1], [1, -1,  1], [1,  1, -1], [1,  1,  1]
];
```

The second part of the model are edges. An edge is the line that connects two vertices. We do not need to store the coordinates of edges because we already have them in vertex array. Instead, the edge saves to indices from the first array. For example, the first edge in Listing 8-2 is saved as [0, 1]. It means that it connects the vertex with index 0 to the vertex with index 1. Take a look at the first array for the coordinates of these points and you see that they are (-1, -1, -1) and (-1, -1, 1). The code for an edges array is shown in the Listing 8-2.

Listing 8-2. *The Edges of the Cube, Each Element Refers the Index in Vertices Array*

```
var edges = [
    [0, 1], [0, 2], [0, 4], [1, 3],
    [1, 5], [2, 3], [2, 6], [3, 7],
    [4, 5], [4, 6], [5, 7], [6, 7]
];
```

The Scene

Now that we have a cube, we definitely want to observe it under different angles. In the real world, we usually can't move the world itself, so we move the camera. In 3D graphics, the camera often stays fixed in a space, looking in a particular direction. In WebGL, for example, the camera looks down the z axis so that objects with smaller z values appear further away. To show the user the part of the scene that he needs to see, we need either to adjust the angle and position of the camera, or to change the angle and position of the world. This works exactly the same way as in the previous chapter: to create a feeling that the user is navigating to a new area of the map, we leave the viewport looking at point (0, 0) and move around the map itself.

Rotation is only one transformation that you can apply to your model. The other simple types include moving the object around the scene or scaling the object on every axis. It is not hard to write a couple of nice functions that handle these cases, but it turns out that the task becomes harder and harder once you start to stack these transformations one on top of the other. For example: first move the object five units to the left, then rotate it 3.14 radians around the z axis, and then scale it three times on the x axis. It would be a nice math exercise to implement this kind of logic, but let's not get ahead of ourselves, and instead take a look at the mechanism that proved its efficiency.

Rendering

Now that we have defined the coordinates of the model and stored them in the array, it is time to render the cube on the screen. But how do we transform those points into the wireframe? In this section, we learn how 3D rendering works on a very basic level. To render a 3D figure, we must find the projection of its vertices on the screen. Once the projections are found, we can draw the line between each two points connected by the edge—and this is enough to render the wireframe!

The mathematical apparatus for finding projections and 3D rendering is called a *matrix theory*. Let's start with a very basic element—the matrix. Once we know how matrices work, we will apply this knowledge to our task. We will render the cube, rotate it, and then apply the perspective projection so that the cube looks more natural.

Matrices

So, what is the matrix? No, it's not only the parallel reality where Neo fights Agent Smith. The matrix is also a fundamental data structure that is essential for every 3D program. Figure 8-6 shows how a matrix looks.

$$A = \begin{bmatrix} 1 & 3 & 5 & 7 \\ 2 & 8 & 3 & 1 \\ 4 & 5 & 3 & 2 \\ 1 & 0 & 0 & 2 \end{bmatrix}$$

Figure 8-6. *An example of the matrix*

Essentially, the matrix is a grid that has rows and columns. A matrix can have different sizes, of course. Figure 8-6 is a 4 × 4 matrix. The natural way to represent matrices in JavaScript is by using the two-dimensional arrays. What is really exciting about them is that a 4 × 4 matrix can hold any number of transformations in any order that you apply to your scene. How? Each matrix represents a certain transformation: a rotation, scaling, translation, or any combination of these. Figure 8-7 shows some examples.

$$\begin{bmatrix} 0.5 & 0 & 0 & 0 \\ 0 & 1 & 0 & 0 \\ 0 & 0 & 1 & 0 \\ 0 & 0 & 0 & 1 \end{bmatrix} \begin{bmatrix} 1 & 0 & 0 & 0 \\ 0 & 1 & 0 & 0 \\ 0 & 0 & 1 & 0 \\ 5 & 2 & 0 & 1 \end{bmatrix} \begin{bmatrix} 0.7 & -0.7 & 0 & 0 \\ 0.7 & 0.7 & 0 & 0 \\ 0 & 0 & 1 & 0 \\ 0 & 0 & 0 & 1 \end{bmatrix}$$

Figure 8-7. *Matrices representing different transformations. From left to right: shrinking for 50% on x axis, moving to five units by x axis and two units by y axis, rotation around z axis approximately 45 degrees.*

If you have never worked with matrices, Figure 8-7 probably looks like three grids of meaningless numbers. Things become much clearer when you know how to multiply matrices, however. The rules are somewhat unintuitive and it is way easier to show them on 2 × 2 matrices. Let's say, we want to multiply matrix A by matrix B.

The general rule of matrix multiplication is as follows: to get the cell that stands in mth row and nth column of the result matrix, you must take the mth row of the left matrix and the nth column of the right matrix, multiply their elements, and add them. To get the number in the first cell (row 1, column 1), you must take the first row of the left matrix and the first column of the right matrix, multiply them element-by-element, and add the results. This operation is illustrated in Figure 8-8.

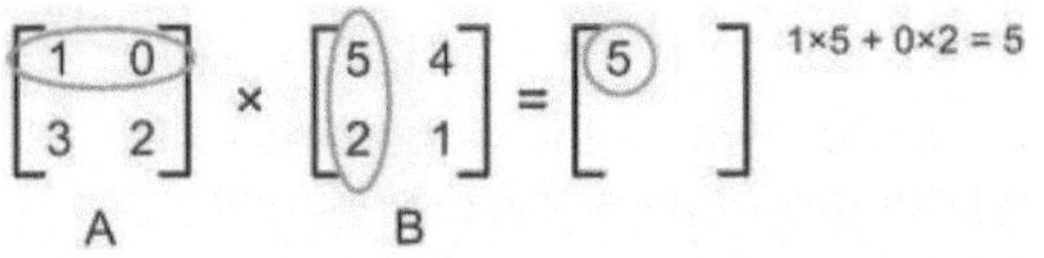

Figure 8-8. *Multiplying matrices to get the first element*

For the cell in the first row and the second column, you must take the first row of the left matrix and the second column of the right matrix, and do the same: multiply them element-by-element, and add the results. Figure 8-9 shows how to do it.

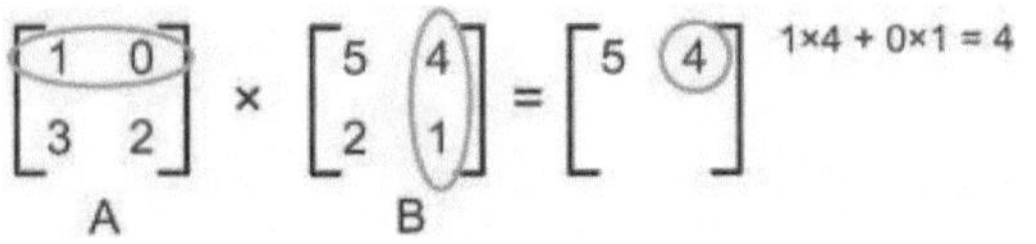

Figure 8-9. *The next step of multiplication: second element in first row*

Figure 8-10 shows how to calculate the last two cells of the resulting matrix.

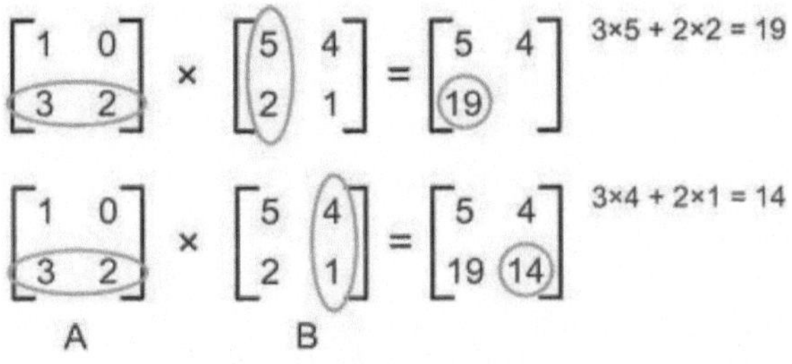

Figure 8-10. *The final result of multiplying matrices*

Now for the long-awaited feature. To apply the transformation that is represented by the matrix, you must multiply the coordinates of the point by the matrix. You get the new coordinates—the coordinates *after* the transformation. If you apply the same transformation to each vertex of the cube, the cube itself is transformed: rotated, scaled, or moved to a certain location on the scene. Here's how it works. First, you need to write the coordinates of the point in a form of matrix: [x, y, z, 1]. You must add the "1" coordinate to multiply the matrix and then apply the regular rules of matrix multiplication. Let's see what happens when we take the first vertex of a cube and apply the second matrix from the example to it. Figure 8-11 shows the result of multiplication.

$$\begin{bmatrix} -1 & -1 & -1 & 1 \end{bmatrix} \times \begin{bmatrix} 1 & 0 & 0 & 0 \\ 0 & 1 & 0 & 0 \\ 0 & 0 & 1 & 0 \\ 5 & 2 & 0 & 1 \end{bmatrix} = \begin{bmatrix} 4 & 1 & -1 & 1 \end{bmatrix}$$

Figure 8-11. *Applying transformation to the vertex coordinates*

The point is moved by five on the x coordinate and by two on the y coordinate. That's exactly what we wanted to get! If we repeat this process for every point of the cube, then every point is moved, and the cube itself ends up in a new position. Figure 8-12 shows schematically how it looks. Dotted edges mark the position of the cube when the transformation is applied to every vertex. The highlighted point is the point that we just transformed.

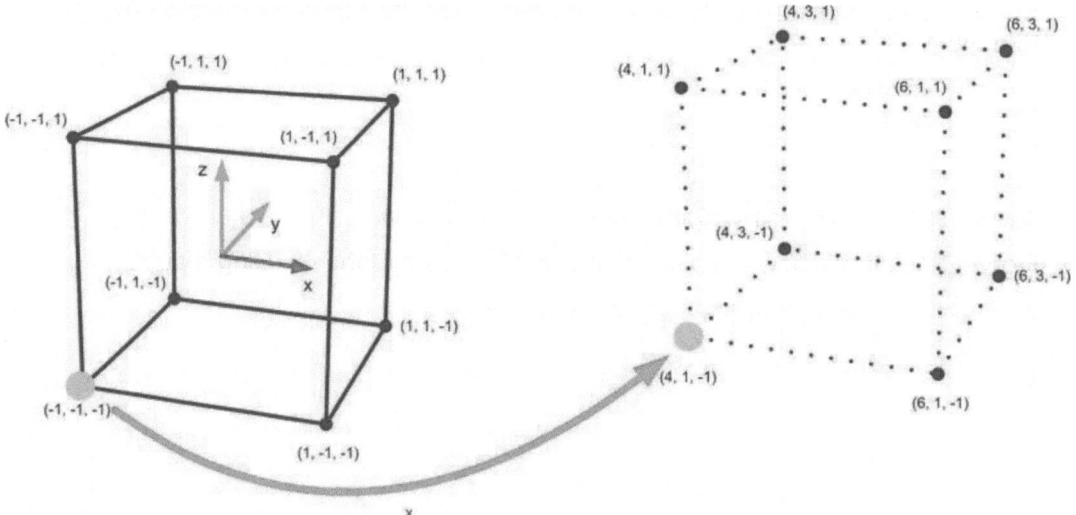

Figure 8-12. *The "translate" transformation of cube. If every vertex is moved, then the cube itself is moved too.*

Well, that's not really an amazing result, since we could simply add five and two to the appropriate coordinates without dealing with matrices at all. The real use of matrices comes when you need to apply a bunch of transformations to the set of points. For example, if you have ten different transformations, one on top of the other, and a model with a lot of vertices, you either have to apply these transformations to the points of the model one-by-one, or create a single matrix that implements all the transformations and use it instead. Guess which is better.

> **NOTE:** That humble "1" that we added as the fourth component of the point's coordinates is not there just to make the multiplication valid. 3D engines strictly represent points in a slightly different coordinate system, called homogeneous coordinates. Why is it used in computer graphics? Because this type of coordinate is much easier to deal with when it comes to projections. If you want, you can easily find an in-depth explanation of this idea on the Internet and in mathematical literature, but you will not really need anything beyond this in your own 3D masterpieces. However, I do encourage you to learn how things work under the hood once you're comfortable with the basic concepts.

Creating a matrix that combines several transformations is as simple as multiplying the matrices that represent individual transformations. If you multiply the matrix that moves the vertex to the right by one that moves the vertex to the top, and then with one that rotates it around the x axis, you get a matrix that does all three in one pass: moves to the top-right and also rotates the model.

There are two important points to know about matrices. First, the order of multiplication makes a difference. When you operate with numbers, the result is the same for (5 × 3) and (3 × 5), whereas with matrices it is not. To illustrate this, have a look at Figure 8-13, which shows how the order of transformations changes the result.

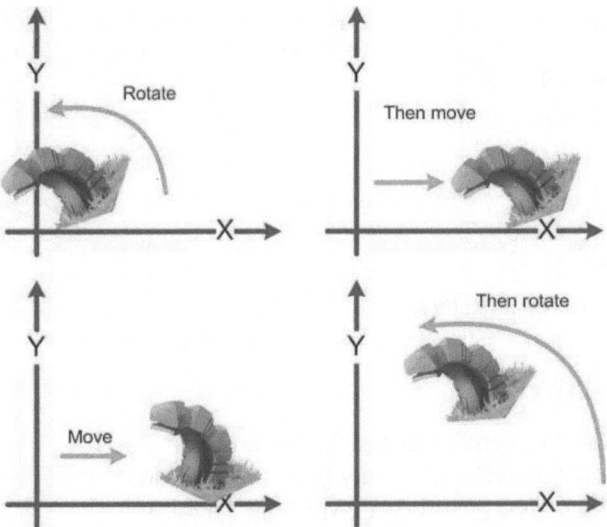

Figure 8-13. *Changing the order of transformations makes a difference*

The trick is that when you use the described matrix model, transformations are applied in reverse order: the last transformation is applied first. It is somewhat confusing at first, but you get used to it eventually.

The second point is, just as "1" in regular algebra doesn't change another number when multiplied by it, there's a matrix called *identity matrix* that doesn't change the matrix to the left or to the right during multiplication. This matrix represents the "no transformations" state. Figure 8-14 shows how it looks.

$$\begin{bmatrix} 1 & 0 & 0 & 0 \\ 0 & 1 & 0 & 0 \\ 0 & 0 & 1 & 0 \\ 0 & 0 & 0 & 1 \end{bmatrix}$$

Figure 8-14. *Identity matrix stands for "no transformations"*

Finally, Figure 8-15 presents the short list of the most-used transformation matrices. Don't be scared by the sines and the cosines in the rotation matrices—you don't have to dive into the details of exactly how points are transformed, or exactly why that sine or cosine stands there.

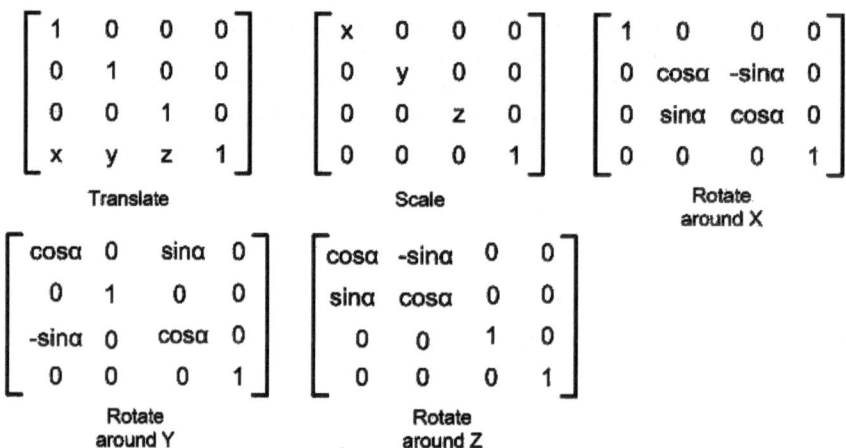

Figure 8-15. *Different types of transformations written as matrices*

Implementing Transformations

Now we are fully prepared to draw the first version of our "cube-engine." Let's start with the good news. There's a nice JavaScript library that does all the hard work of matrix manipulation for us; it's called gl-matrix (https://github.com/toji/gl-matrix). Thanks to Brandon Jones, we have a wonderful and very fast tool at our disposal. Get a copy of the file called gl-matrix.js or gl-matrix-

`min.js` and add it to your project. As the name suggests, the library is supposed to be used with WebGL, but since it implements the general matrix math that is the same all over the planet, we will use it for our project.

The idea behind rendering the wireframe of the cube is to implement two simple steps:

1. Transform each vertex the way we want (we want to rotate it).

2. Draw a line between each of the two vertices that have an edge that joins them.

The steps of this process are illustrated in Figure 8-16.

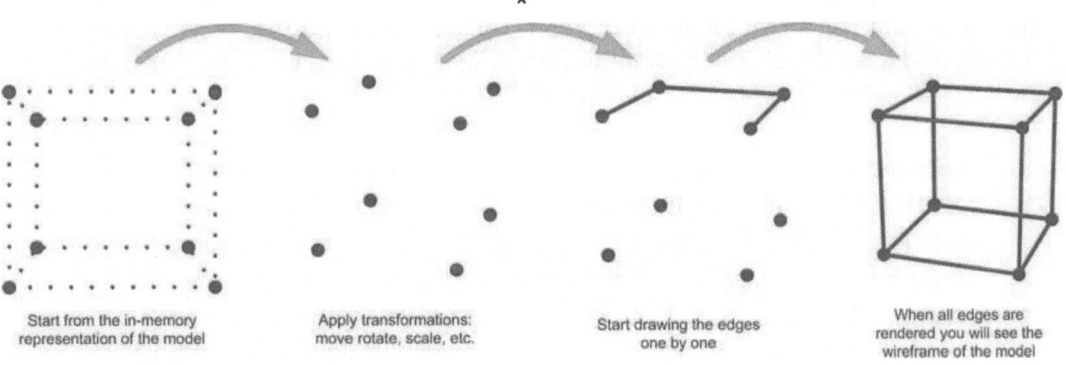

| Start from the in-memory representation of the model | Apply transformations: move rotate, scale, etc. | Start drawing the edges one by one | When all edges are rendered you will see the wireframe of the model |

Figure 8-16. *Steps to render the cube wireframe*

Let's start with the first part. We need to apply two transformations to our cube: rotation over the x axis and rotation over the y axis (feel free to apply any others if you want). gl-matrix has several convenient methods that hide the details of the matrices inside the library. The code that creates the transformation matrix is shown in Listing 8-3.

Listing 8-3. *Creating the Transformation Matrix*

```
var modelView = mat4.create();
mat4.identity(modelView);
mat4.rotateX(modelView, xRot);
mat4.rotateY(modelView, yRot);
```

In the first line, we create an empty matrix. The created matrix is filled with zeros, so we have to initialize it to the identity matrix before we can use it (otherwise it will transform any point to coordinates (0, 0, 0)). The third line adds the x axis rotation to our matrix. It is equivalent to first creating the rotation matrix, and then multiplying our identity matrix by it. The last line finishes the preparation, and we are now ready to spin the cube.

> **NOTE:** Why do we call the matrix variable a `modelView`? That's the name that is
> used by OpenGL, and it means that the matrix represents… uh, the view of the
> model: all the transformations that are applied to the vertices to represent the model
> exactly as we want it. Why not just "matrix"? Because there are other matrices that
> are too involved in the process. For example, we will deal with the projection matrix
> that calculates the perspective later in this chapter.

The process of "spinning" is very simple: we apply the matrix to every vertex
one-by-one. We receive the transformed coordinates and project them to the
camera surface by simply dropping the z coordinate. We also have to scale up
the cube a little bit so that it fits the screen. The size of the cube is only 2 (from -
1 to 1), and if we translate it straight to pixels, it will look tiny. Listing 8-4 shows
how to calculate the coordinates of a projection.

> **NOTE:** The size of two? Two what? Pixels, inches, meters, melons? In 3D graphics, it
> doesn't matter. It is up to you to make some sort of convention in your project to
> define these numbers. The only rule is to keep your metric consistent over the
> project. If you decide that "two" means "two meters," don't forget it afterwards;
> otherwise, you may accidentally create a model of a rabbit that is the size of a small
> car. But that's not a problem either: you can always scale it with the magic matrix to
> fit your scene. In this chapter, I use the word "units" when I need to refer to the sizes
> of a 3D scene.

Listing 8-4. *Calculating the Coordinates for Projections of Each Point*

```
// It is convenient to create such indices to match the indices of array
var X = 0;
var Y = 1;
var Z = 2;

// Screen coordinates
var points = [];

// Scale factor, for now pick one that you like best
var scaleFactor = canvas.width/8;

for (var i = 0; i < vertices.length; i++) {
    // Transform point to the homogenous coordinates, prepare to
    // multiply
    var point = [vertices[i][X], vertices[i][Y], vertices[i][Z], 1];
```

```
    // Apply the transformation
    mat4.multiplyVec4(modelView, point);

    // Add the calculated coordinates to the array
    points[i] = [
        Math.round(canvas.width/2 + scaleFactor*point[X]),
        Math.round(canvas.height/2 - scaleFactor*point[Y])];
}
```

As you can see, there's nothing too scary once you know the secret of matrices.

The last part is to draw edges. We have an array of edges and an array of the points' projections. Combine the two—and voilà—the cube is spinning (don't forget to update the rotation values). Listing 8-5 shows the full code for the project. Try to launch it on your cell phone and your desktop browser.

Listing 8-5. *The Full Source Code for the Spinning Cube Demo*

```
<script src="js/utils.js"></script>
<script src="js/gl-matrix-min.js"></script>

<script>
    var canvas = null;
    var ctx = null;

    var X = 0;
    var Y = 1;
    var Z = 2;

    var vertices = [
        [-1, -1, -1],  [-1, -1,  1],  [-1,  1, -1],  [-1,  1,  1],
        [1, -1, -1], [1, -1,  1], [1,  1, -1], [1,  1,  1]
    ];

    var edges = [
        [0, 1],  [0, 2], [0, 4], [1, 3],
        [1, 5], [2, 3], [2, 6], [3, 7],
        [4, 5], [4, 6], [5, 7], [6, 7]
    ];

    var xRot = 0;
    var yRot = 0;

    function init() {
        canvas = initFullScreenCanvas("mainCanvas");
        ctx = canvas.getContext("2d");
        animate(0);
    }
```

```
function animate(t) {
    ctx.clearRect(0, 0, canvas.width, canvas.height);
    renderCube();
    requestAnimationFrame(arguments.callee);
}

function renderCube() {

    var modelView = mat4.create();
    mat4.identity(modelView); // Set to identity
    mat4.rotateX(modelView, xRot);
    mat4.rotateY(modelView, yRot);

    var points = [];
    var scaleFactor = canvas.width/8;

    for (var i = 0; i < vertices.length; i++) {
        var point = [vertices[i][X], vertices[i][Y], vertices[i][Z], 1];
        mat4.multiplyVec4(modelView, point);

        points[i] = [
            Math.round(canvas.width/2 + scaleFactor*point[X]),
            Math.round(canvas.height/2 + scaleFactor*point[Y])];
    }

    ctx.strokeStyle = "black";

    // draw the wireframe
    ctx.beginPath();
    for (i = 0; i < edges.length; i++ ) {
        ctx.moveTo(points[ edges[i][0] ][X], points[ edges[i][0] ][Y]);
        ctx.lineTo(points[ edges[i][1] ][X], points[ edges[i][1] ][Y]);
    }

    ctx.stroke();
    ctx.closePath();
    xRot += 0.01;
    yRot += 0.01;
}

function initFullScreenCanvas(canvasId) {
    var canvas = document.getElementById(canvasId);
    resizeCanvas(canvas);
    window.addEventListener("resize", function() {
        resizeCanvas(canvas);
    });
    return canvas;
}

function resizeCanvas(canvas) {
```

```
        canvas.width  = document.width || document.body.clientWidth;
        canvas.height = document.height || document.body.clientHeight;
    }
</script>
```

If you launch the demo, you'll see that the cube looks somewhat unnatural; for some reason, it doesn't look like a real cube at all. The problem is that we used orthographic projection, and the real world works in a different way. The full source code of this demo is available in a file called `01.spinning_cube.html` with the other resources for this chapter.

Projections

In the real world, things that are far away look smaller than things that are close to the camera. Our demo doesn't take this into account—that's why the cube looks wrong. As you've seen in the code, we simply drop the z value, and it doesn't participate in the calculation of the projection at all.

Our demo uses the *orthographic projection*, which is rendering 3D figures without any perspective. In orthographic projection, a car that is 5 meters away from the camera is rendered the same size as a car that is 20 meters away. This projection looks somewhat unnatural, but it is often used for blueprints. The *perspective projection*, in turn, works more naturally: objects further away are smaller than objects close to the camera. Figure 8-17 illustrates the difference between the two projections.

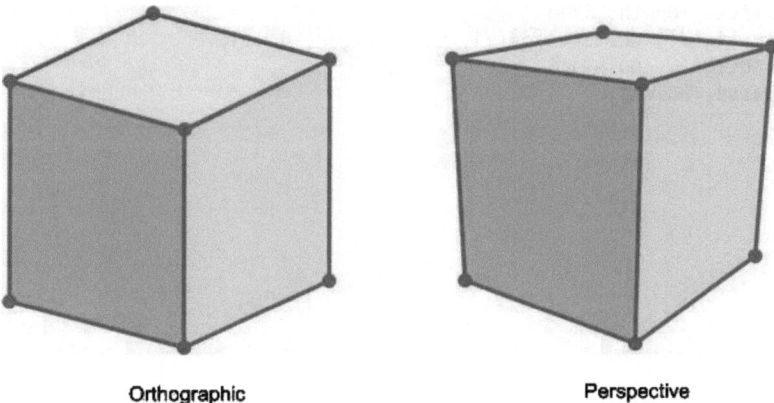

Orthographic   Perspective

Figure 8-17. *The image on the left shows orthographic projection. The image on the right shows perspective projection.*

As you see, the picture on the right that shows the same cube with perspective projection looks far more realistic than what we have now on the left. How do we fix our engine so that it takes perspective into account? That's right. We add another matrix.

I will not go into any more mathematical detail on how the projection matrix is actually implemented. You only need to know two things to make cool 3D games. First, if you multiply the result of the modelView transformation by this matrix, you get the projection transformation—which takes perspective into account. Second, Brandon is a nice guy who included a convenient method in his library that creates a perspective matrix when given a set of human-readable parameters.

Listing 8-6 shows how we create the matrix.

Listing 8-6. *Creating the Projection Matrix*

```
var persp = mat4.create();
mat4.perspective(45, canvas.width/canvas.height, 0.1, 100, persp);
```

The parameters are vertical angle of view, aspect ratio, distance to the "near plane," and distance to the "far plane," respectively. The near plane and far plane are the bounds of the scene. It is saying, "I don't want to see anything closer than 0.1 and anything that is beyond 100." The last parameter is the matrix that is initiated with these values (see Listing 8-7). Figure 8-18 illustrates how the perspective parameters affect the resulting frame.

Listing 8-7. *Using the Projection Matrix*

```
for (var i = 0; i < vertices.length; i++) {
    var point = [vertices[i][X], vertices[i][Y], vertices[i][Z], 1];
    mat4.multiplyVec4(modelView, point);
    mat4.multiplyVec4(persp, point);

    ...
}
```

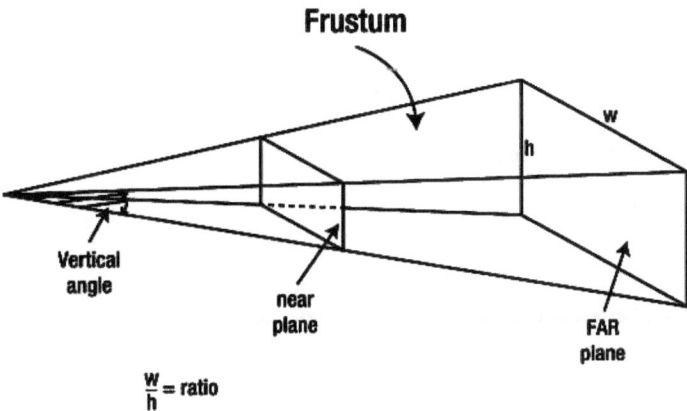

Figure 8-18. *Defining scene bounds with perspective*

The coordinates that we receive after applying the perspective matrix have to be normalized before we can draw vertices onto the screen. Without overcomplicating matters, we translate the homogeneous coordinates (those with one extra component) to the usual screen coordinates that have only two axes: x and y (see Listing 8-8).

Listing 8-8. *Normalizing the Coordinates*

```
var ndcPoint = [
    point[X]/point[W],
    point[Y]/point[W]
];
```

The resulting x and y fall between -1 and 1. The NDC in `ndcPoint` stands for normalized device coordinates. Now the only thing we have to do is "stretch" them to fill the whole canvas, as shown in Listing 8-9. The full complete demo of perspective projection is available in a file called `02.perspective.html` included with the source code for this chapter.

Listing 8-9. *Translating to Window Coordinates*

```
points[i] = [
Math.round(canvas.width/2*(1 + ndcPoint[0])),
    Math.round(canvas.height/2*(1 - ndcPoint[1]))];
```

Listing 8-10 shows the full code for the `renderCube()` function, which is aware of perspective (the new code is in bold).

Listing 8-10. *Final Version of renderCube*

```
function renderCube() {

    var modelView = mat4.create();
    mat4.identity(modelView); // Set to identity
    mat4.translate(modelView, [0, 0, -10]);
    mat4.rotateX(modelView, xRot);
    mat4.rotateY(modelView, yRot);

    var persp = mat4.create();
    mat4.perspective(45, canvas.width/canvas.height, 0.1, 100, persp);

    var points = [];

    for (var i = 0; i < vertices.length; i++) {
        var point = [vertices[i][X], vertices[i][Y], vertices[i][Z], 1];
        mat4.multiplyVec4(modelView, point);
        mat4.multiplyVec4(persp, point);

        var ndcPoint = [
            point[X]/point[W], // W = 3, the position of fourth coordinate
            point[Y]/point[W]  // in an array
        ];

        points[i] = [
            Math.round(canvas.width/2*(1 + ndcPoint[0])),
            Math.round(canvas.height/2*(1 - ndcPoint[1]))];
    }

    ctx.strokeStyle = "black";

    // draw the wireframe
    ctx.beginPath();
    for (i = 0; i < edges.length; i++ ) {
        ctx.moveTo(points[ edges[i][0] ][X], points[ edges[i][0] ][Y]);
        ctx.lineTo(points[ edges[i][1] ][X], points[ edges[i][1] ][Y]);
    }

    ctx.stroke();
    ctx.closePath();
    xRot += 0.01;
    yRot += 0.01;
}
```

Hey! You just created a very simple 3D engine—but it's yours! That's a really big accomplishment! And you know what? You just repeated a fragment of the OpenGL rendering pipeline—the heart of this API. Let's review what we've done.

1. We used vertex coordinates and edges as the input.

2. We applied a transformation on vertices, rotating our model around two axes.

3. We applied the perspective matrix to the result of the previous transformation.

4. We normalized the coordinates.

5. We translated the coordinates of the source vertices to the coordinates of the 2D canvas.

6. We drew the edges to show the rotating cube.

Of course, WebGL's process is way more involved, but the main parts—the transformations of the vertices, the usage of matrices, perspective, and other concepts that we've highlighted in this chapter—stay the same. Now you have a solid basis for understanding the math behind basic WebGL operations.

The final question is can we actually draw something beyond these stupid cubes, rectangles, and circles? Of course we can. There's a very good model that I found somewhere on the Internet. I won't paste a few hundred vertices in the next pages, but you can find them in the sources that come with this book. Enjoy the teapot in Figure 8-19!

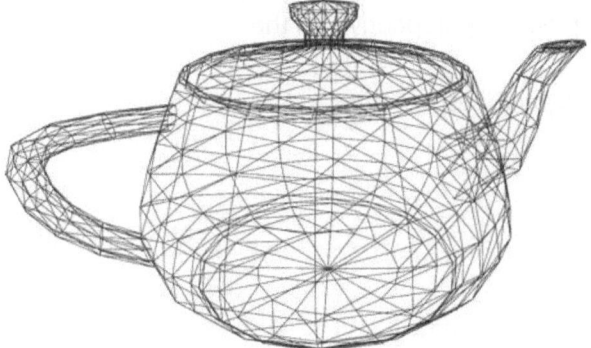

Figure 8-19. *The teapot rendered using the same technique as the cube*

The complete demo of spinning teapot is available with the other resources for this chapter, file name 03.teapot.html.

Summary

This chapter was devoted to understanding the basics behind 3D engines. Calculating the position of vertices and applying perspective is just a first step that a real engine does for every frame in a game. The other steps might be more complex—for example, dropping polygons that are not visible to save resources, applying texture to the faces of the model, calculating the effects of lighting, and many others. 3D engines usually have more involved mathematics than 2D engines, and they constantly evolve. Developers and mathematicians work to bring better algorithms and make the rendered picture even more realistic.

Even the most complex 3D math starts with the position of vertices in the world, and calculating the transformations of the model. If you had never worked with 3D graphics before, then now you are one of very few 3D developers who actually understands what he is doing.

In this chapter, we built the simplest possible 3D demo—a rotating cube. During the course, we learned several important aspects:

- The in-memory representation of the model
- How to use matrices to move, rotate, or scale models
- How to render a wireframe
- The projections and how to implement perspective on the scene

Now we are ready to explore a more advanced topic: WebGL API.

Using WebGL

WebGL is a very promising initiative that has already conquered most of the desktop browser world. WebGL is an API that exposes the resources of the graphics card to your JavaScript application. With WebGL, you can create a 3D game and run it in the browser without having to implement all the 3D math yourself, as we did in Chapter 8. WebGL is based on OpenGL ES 2.0 (OpenGL for Embedded Systems, a subset of the OpenGL API suitable for mobile devices).

WebGL is only making its first steps in mobile web. It is not yet widely supported by Android devices. In fact, only Firefox Mobile supports this important API for game developers. The other early birds are Sony Ericsson Xperia phones—they also support WebGL in the native browser. At the time of writing, every major desktop browser except for IE supports WebGL.

This chapter is devoted to WebGL. This technology is not yet ready for the mass market of Android web games, but it is getting more and more popular among game developers. The goal of this chapter is to introduce you to this bleeding-edge API and to prepare you for creating games once there are more devices that support it. This chapter is a light introduction to 3D programming. We build several demos that show how to use aspects of WebGL. We will do the following:

- Initialize WebGL context in a mobile browser
- Learn the WebGL rendering pipeline
- Use the OpenGL Shading Language (GLSL), which is a language for shaders
- Display basic primitives
- Load textures and learn how to render them

■   Load a 3D model from the binary source

The goal of this chapter is to give you a solid, basic understanding of WebGL. You will learn the structure of a 3D program and will have enough knowledge to continue exploring on your own. There are many resources to explore on your own once you've read this chapter.

Basics of WebGL

Making a sample WebGL web page that shows that 3D rendering works is a somewhat more complex task than rendering a triangle or a circle in a 2D context. The reason for the complexity is because the rendering is performed on a graphics card, not in JavaScript code, and the API that you have to use in order to pass the rendering parameters to the GPU is rather low-level. WebGL has a steep learning curve—it involves a decent amount of mathematics, but after reading the previous chapter, you quickly master it.

In this chapter, we will use Firefox for running and debugging our demos on both a desktop and a smartphone. Download and install the most recent version for your desktop from `www.mozilla.org/en-US/firefox/new/`. Then install Firebug (`http://getfirebug.com`), the plug-in that adds the development tools to Firefox similar to what we used in Chrome. Install the recent version of Firefox Mobile (`www.mozilla.org/en-US/mobile/`) or find it in the market from your device.

> **NOTE:** Using a compatible browser on the desktop doesn't guarantee that WebGL will work for you. It is important to have a supported video card and a fresh driver. WebGL has blacklists and whitelists that determine the level of support for each individual case. More about this in the official WebGL wiki at `www.khronos.org/webgl/wiki/BlacklistsAndWhitelists`. If your video card or driver is blacklisted, there is a way to enable WebGL at your own risk. In Firefox, go to the about:config page, find the webgl.force-enabled flag, and set it to true. It will make Firefox bypass the blacklist.

Initializing WebGL

WebGL is exposed to JavaScript as the context of the canvas, so most of the code remains unchanged. There are several WebGL specific settings, however. The skeleton that we use in this chapter is shown in Listing 9-1.

Listing 9-1. *The Basic Setup for WebGL*

```
<!DOCTYPE html>
<html lang="en">
<head>
    <-- regular meta and style omtitted -->

    <-- gl-matrix - we will need it in every example -->
    <script src="js/gl-matrix.js"></script>
    <script>
        var canvas;

        /* The WebGL context*/
        var gl;

        function init() {
            canvas = initFullScreenCanvas("mainCanvas");

            gl = getWebGLContext(canvas);
            gl.clearColor(0.0, 0.0, 0.0, 1.0);
            gl.enable(gl.DEPTH_TEST);

            drawScene();
        }

        /**
         * Returns WebGL context.
         */
        function getWebGLContext(canvas) {
            var ctx;
            try {
                ctx = canvas.getContext("webgl") ||
                        canvas.getContext("experimental-webgl");
            } catch (e) {}

            if (ctx)
                return ctx;

            throw "Could not initialize WebGL";
        }

        /**
         * Renders the scene
         */
        function drawScene() {
            gl.viewport(0, 0, canvas.width, canvas.height);
            gl.clear(gl.COLOR_BUFFER_BIT | gl.DEPTH_BUFFER_BIT);

            // We will add rendering code here.
        }
```

```
            function initFullScreenCanvas(canvasId) {
                var canvas = document.getElementById(canvasId);
                resizeCanvas(canvas);
                window.addEventListener("resize", function() {
                    resizeCanvas(canvas);
                });
                return canvas;
            }

            function resizeCanvas(canvas) {
                canvas.width  = document.width || document.body.clientWidth;
                canvas.height = document.height || document.body.clientHeight;
                gl && drawScene();
            }
        </script>
    </head>
    <body onload="init()">
    <canvas id="mainCanvas" width="20px" height="20px"></canvas>
    </body>
</html>
```

This is a little bit more when compared to the 2D example. First, we acquire the WebGL context that is called either webgl or experimental-webgl. Next, we set general "environment" settings—the gl.clearColor is the background color of the scene. The last parameter, gl.enable(gl.DEPTH_TEST), tells WebGL to take into account the distance to the object, so that objects that are far away are covered by objects that are closer to the spectator.

The "main" drawing function is drawScene(). For now, it simply initializes the scene: it sets the parameters of the viewport according to the size of canvas, and clears the entire area. When you open the page in a browser, you should see a black screen. If you did everything right, you are ready to draw on the newly created context. The code from Listing 9-1 is available in a file called 01.init.html.

Geometry

The most basic primitive in the 3D space is the triangle. 3D scenes are usually made of triangles, and graphics cards are optimized to render them because it is the simplest primitive to work with. WebGL has other types of primitives too: lines, triangle strips, and triangle fans—but they are less common. In this chapter, we only work with triangles.

Do you remember how we represented a 3D model of a cube in Chapter 8? We used two arrays to describe the spatial geometry: one was an array of vertices and the other was an array of edges. The edge is the line connecting two vertices, so the second array was holding the references to the elements of the first.

In WebGL, we use the same strategy except that we need faces (triangles) instead of edges. Have a look at the data structure in Listing 9-2. Each commented block of the vertices array define the face of the cube: front, back, top, bottom, left, and right. Each face of the cube is a square that is made of four points. The cube face is then broken down into two triangles that are listed in a faces array.

Listing 9-2. *The Cube Geometry in WebGL*

```
var cube = {
    vertices: [
        // Front
        -1.0, -1.0,  1.0,
         1.0, -1.0,  1.0,
         1.0,  1.0,  1.0,
        -1.0,  1.0,  1.0,

        // Back
        -1.0, -1.0, -1.0,
        -1.0,  1.0, -1.0,
         1.0,  1.0, -1.0,
         1.0, -1.0, -1.0,

        // Top
        -1.0,  1.0, -1.0,
        -1.0,  1.0,  1.0,
         1.0,  1.0,  1.0,
         1.0,  1.0, -1.0,

        // Bottom
        ...

        // Right
        ...

        // Left
        ...
    ],

    // Two triangles for each face
    faces: [
        0, 1, 2,    0, 2, 3,    // Front
        4, 5, 6,    4, 6, 7,    // Back
        8, 9, 10,   8, 10, 11,  // Top
        12, 13, 14, 12, 14, 15, // Bottom
```

```
        16, 17, 18,   16, 18, 19, // Right
        20, 21, 22,   20, 22, 23  // Left
    ]

    x: 0,
    y: 0,
    z: -10,

    rx: 0,
    ry: 1.2,
    rz: 0
};
```

This object also stores the position of the cube (x, y, and z properties) and its orientation in space (rx, ry, and rz, which are the rotation along each axis). This is everything required to draw it on the scene. Generally, it is not a good idea to mix geometry data with position and orientation; if you needed to draw several similar cubes in different places in the scene, you have to duplicate the same geometry for each one, thus wasting precious mobile memory. It is best to separate geometry from instance properties like rotation, color, texture, size, and so forth, because while the geometry is the same for each cube, other properties can change. For the sake of simplicity, however, we still use this approach for the next few examples.

The other very similar thing between our self-made engine and WebGL is the matrix geometry. WebGL also relies on two main matrices to render the scene: the `modelView` matrix that holds the transformations of the model (rotation, position, and scale), and the `projection` matrix that describes the viewport. Listing 9-3 shows how we initialize these matrices.

Listing 9-3. *Initializing modelView and Projection Matrices*

```
/* Projection and modelview matrices */
var modelViewMatrix = mat4.create();
var projectionMatrix = mat4.create();
```

mat4 is the object provided by the gl-matrix.js—the library that we first tried in Chapter 8 and continue to use for this chapter.

Now we have everything in place to render the cube on the screen. In a canvas-based 3D engine, we could use this data directly to render the wireframe of the model, calling `lineTo()` for every pair of vertices connected with the edge. WebGL works in a completely different way: it sends the data to the graphics card, and asks it to render the geometry afterward. The whole process of transforming vertices, faces, lights, and textures into pixels on a display is known as the *pipeline*.

OpenGL ES 2.0 Rendering Pipeline

The OpenGL rendering pipeline (just "pipeline" for short) is the process of transforming input data into a rendered 2D picture that you can see on the display. Each time you need to render the model, you go through the same set of steps—some are "fixed" and some are "programmable."

The understanding of this process is extremely important, not only for WebGL, but also for overall 3D graphics programming since it is one of the most basic concepts. First, look at Figure 9-1, which illustrates the stages of the pipeline. It is a somewhat simplified representation of what is really happening behind the scenes, but this figure should give you a bird's-eye view of the process.

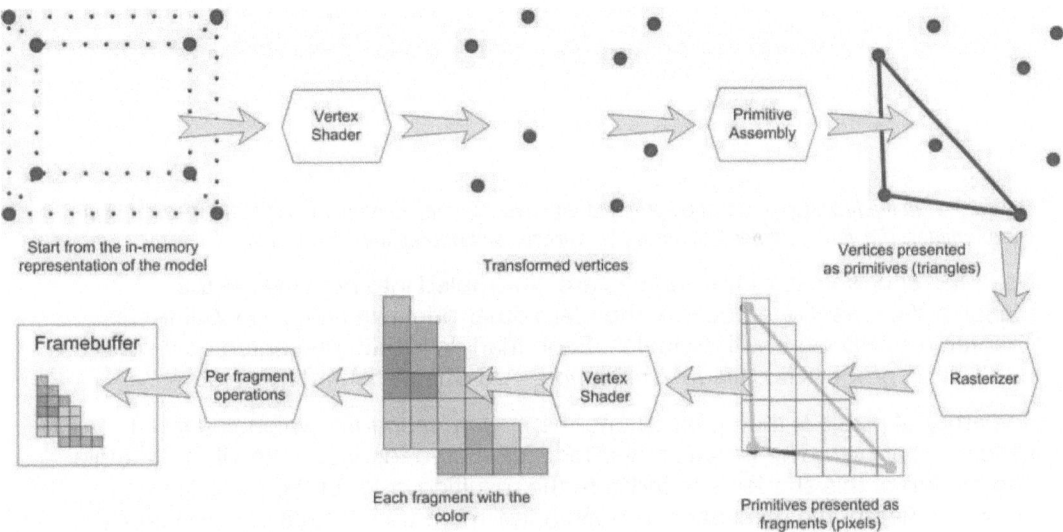

Figure 9-1. *The OpenGL ES 2.0 pipeline*

The input to the pipeline is everything required to render a model—the vertex positions of the original model, colors, location and properties of light sources, textures, orientation, scale, viewport properties, and so on. This data inputs into a program called the *vertex shader*.

A vertex shader runs for every vertex. Its task is to determine the projection of the vertex to the screen (remember, in Chapter 8 we did it manually by multiplying matrices). In other words, its main task is to return the coordinates for every vertex it receives. Besides this simple task, it can do all kinds of other useful calculations—for example, determine the resulting light color and intensity when given several light sources of different types. A vertex shader can also transform the geometry itself, doing things such as creating a waving banner out of a plain wireframe, or implementing a simulation of liquid physics. The possibilities are endless, and what is very important about shaders is that they are executed on the GPU (where available) that is optimized for that kind of math. In other words, shaders work much faster than JavaScript transformations. We learn how to write simple shaders in the next section of this chapter. Figure 9-2 shows the first step of the WebGL rendering process—passing the data to the shader.

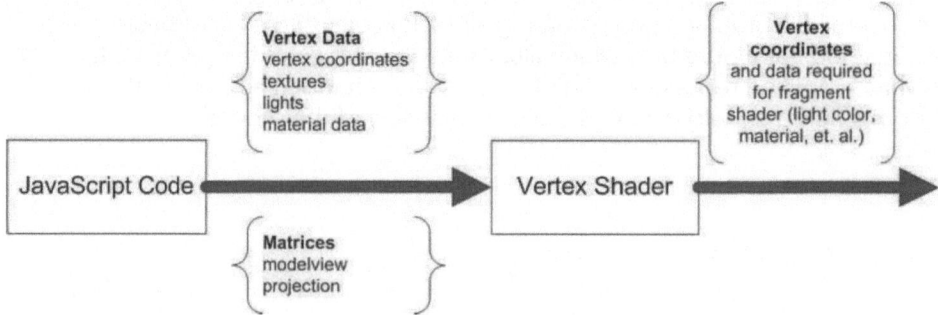

Figure 9-2. *In the first step of a WebGL program, the data required to render the model is passed to the vertex shader. The vertex shader transforms the vertices and returns the coordinates.*

Next, the coordinates of the vertices are assembled into primitives—the triangles. As I mentioned before, there are other primitive types too, but in this chapter, we only work with triangles. Each triangle is then presented as a set of pixels. This process is called *rasterization*. You do not control these steps.

The array of pixels is then passed into the *fragment shader*, which you must write on your own. The fragment shader is executed for each pixel of the triangle and the job of this shader is to indicate the resulting color of the pixel. With the color and depth, the pixel goes through a few more transformations and finally ends up on the screen. The second part of the process is shown in Figure 9-3.

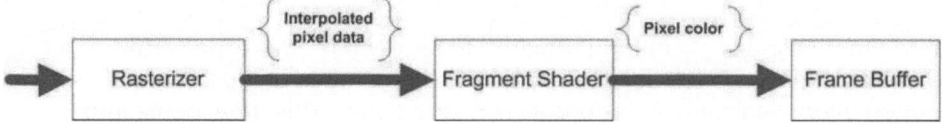

Figure 9-3. *In the second part of rendering process, data received from the vertex shader is interpolated and passed to the fragment shader. The fragment shader outputs the pixel color.*

The overall process might look somewhat complex—indeed, this is more than just ctx.drawRect()—but it gives you significantly more control over the details of rendering. In fact, there are only three components needed to create a WebGL program: model and environment data, the vertex shader, and the fragment shader.

Let's start with the first step: getting the geometry data and sending it to the pipeline.

Using Buffers

Video cards don't know anything about JavaScript or browsers, which is why you can't send JavaScript objects directly into the rendering pipeline. The data must be converted into the internal format suitable for graphical hardware. In terms of WebGL, we must *create the buffer*.

Buffers work like arrays in JavaScript, except they are stored outside of the JavaScript engine and you don't have direct control over them. You load the data required for rendering into separate buffers: the coordinates of vertices, the lists of faces, the colors of vertexes, or the coordinates of textures. What exactly you load depends on your program, of course. Once the data is loaded, you can tell WebGL what to do with it. Buffers are the primary way to send the information between your script and pipeline, so it is important to understand how they work.

The first thing you need to do is declare the new buffer:

```
var vertexBuffer = gl.createBuffer();
```

The vertexBuffer acts like a pointer to the actual buffer created elsewhere; for example, in the memory of the graphics card. In WebGL, every buffer-related operation is performed over the currently active buffer. To upload the geometry data, for example, we first have to activate a buffer:

```
gl.bindBuffer(gl.ARRAY_BUFFER, vertexBuffer);
```

The first argument is the buffer type. There are two types of buffers in WebGL:

- gl.ARRAY_BUFFER: The buffer that holds the data itself (for example, vertex coordinates or vertex colors).

- gl.ELEMENT_ARRAY_BUFFER: The array that holds the references to the elements of the other array—usually the ARRAY_BUFFER, which stores the vertex data. For example, we need to specify three vertices to describe the face of 3D model. Since vertices are already stored, there's no need to duplicate their coordinates and create another buffer with the same data. It is enough to know the indices of vertices inside the other buffer, not their real coordinates in space. That's what ELEMENT_ARRAY_BUFFER stands for.

Now the buffer is ready to receive data:

```
gl.bufferData(gl.ARRAY_BUFFER, new Float32Array(model.vertices),
gl.STATIC_DRAW);
```

The first parameter is the type of the buffer. The second wraps the `model.vertices` array into the JavaScript object called `Float32Array`. The third `gl.STATIC_DRAW` acts like a hint on how the data is used. `STATIC_DRAW` means that the data will not change.

> **NOTE:** `Float32Array` is the part of Typed Array API—the step toward the better processing of binary and typed data with JavaScript. You can find more about this API on the MDN page at `https://developer.mozilla.org/en/JavaScript _typed_arrays`.

Let's prepare both of the cube's buffers (the vertex buffer and the index buffer), as shown in Listing 9-4.

Listing 9-4. *Preparing Buffers for WebGL*

```
function initModel(model) {
    // Vertex buffer
    model.vertexBuffer = gl.createBuffer();
    gl.bindBuffer(gl.ARRAY_BUFFER, model.vertexBuffer);
    gl.bufferData(gl.ARRAY_BUFFER, new Float32Array(model.vertices),
gl.STATIC_DRAW);

    // Face buffer
    model.faceBuffer = gl.createBuffer();
    gl.bindBuffer(gl.ELEMENT_ARRAY_BUFFER, model.faceBuffer);
    gl.bufferData(gl.ELEMENT_ARRAY_BUFFER, new Uint16Array(model.faces),
gl.STATIC_DRAW);
}
```

This kind of initialization is performed only once—at the start of the program or before the first use of the geometry. Once they are created this way, buffers are ready to be used with shaders to show the cube on the screen.

Shaders and GLSL

Shaders are the most complex part of the WebGL learning curve. There are two reasons for that: (1) shaders are written in their own language, which looks more like C than JavaScript, and (2) it is rather hard to debug them. Let's start by looking at the code for the simplest possible vertex shader, which calculates the projection of a point to the screen (see Listing 9-5).

Listing 9-5. *The Simplest Vertex Shader*

```
attribute vec3 aPos;
uniform mat4 uMVMatrix;
uniform mat4 uPMatrix;

void main(void) {
    gl_Position = uPMatrix * uMVMatrix * vec4(aPos, 1.0);
}
```

Intuitively, it is clear how this program works.

- The shader somehow receives three parameters from the outer world: aPos, uMVMatrix, and uPMatrix.

- The type of matrix is a 4×4 matrix and the type of aPos is a three-element vector.

- We create a four-element vector out of a three-element vector by adding 1.0.

- Shader multiplies two matrices, and then multiplies the result by the vector. It looks much like the projection of a point to the screen. From a mathematical point of view, this is exactly the same code as in Chapter 8.

- The result is then assigned to the gl_Position.

If you previously worked in C, this code should look more familiar to you. Of course, you can't write your own shaders based solely on intuition. In this chapter, however, we will describe only the basic concepts of the language. If you are interested in more in-depth details, refer to the GLSL specification or more advanced shader examples.

> **NOTE:** The complete specification of the GLSL language used in WebGL is available on the Khronos Group web site at www.khronos.org/registry/gles/specs /2.0/GLSL_ES_Specification_1.0.17.pdf.

GLSL is a programming language, just like JavaScript, PHP, or C, but unlike most languages that you've seen, it is not intended for general-purpose tasks like writing a web server or database. GLSL is intended solely for manipulations with 3D graphics. We need its basics to write WebGL programs, so let's start with the smallest building block of every language: variables and data types.

Data Types

Unlike JavaScript, GLSL is a strongly-typed static language. This means that every variable has its own type, which doesn't change during the execution of the program. The following line, for example:

```
int x = 1;
```

declares that the integer variable x has an initial value of 1. It is impossible to assign a floating-point value to x in the next line or in any other place of the program. Once declared, the type of variable cannot change. The concept of strict types should be familiar to those of you who worked with languages like C or Java. Table 9-1 shows the most common GLSL types.

Table 9-1. *Types in GLSL*

Type	Example Values	Description
void	--	Usually a return value of the function. Means "nothing is returned."
int	2, -1, 0	Integer number, no floating-point values.
float	1.2, 0.3, .4, -5.2	Floating point values.
bool	true, false	Boolean values—true or false.
vec2, vec3, vec4	`vec2 v = vec2(0.0, 0.0)` `vec3 v3 = vec3(v, -1.0)`	2, 3, 4 components vector. Can be constructed from numbers or from other vectors.

mat2, mat3, mat 4	`mat2 m;`
	`m [0] = vec2(1.0, 1.0);`
	`m [1] = vec2(1.0, 1.0);`
		Usually passed from JavaScript, the example shows the matrix filled with 1.0. Matrices always contain floating-point values.

sampler2D, samplerCube		For use with textures.

Now you can reread part of the shader program in Listing 9-5 to determine the types of variables. You'll also notice that GLSL supports common matrix operations. You can multiply matrix-by-matrix, or matrix-by-vector, and receive a valid result. There's no need to manually implement matrix math in your shader.

There is another component in the variable definition: modifiers like `attribute` and `uniform`. This property of the variable is called a *storage qualifier*. It can be any one of the qualifiers shown in Table 9-2.

Table 9-2. *Storage Qualifiers in GLSL*

Qualifier	Example	Description
No qualifier	`int a`	Regular variable or function parameter.
const	`const int a = 1;`	Constants, the value will not change.
uniform	`uniform mat4 uMVMatrix;` `uniform uLightColor;`	Passed to the shader from JavaScript. The uniform value doesn't change between different vertices; for example, since the projection matrix is the same for every vertex, it is uniform. Another example of uniform is the color of the light. Uniforms are not initialized inside the shader, since their values come from JavaScript.
attribute	`attribute vec3 aPos;` `attribute vec3 aNormal;` `attribute vec3 aColor;`	Per-vertex data that can change from vertex to vertex; for example, the vertex coordinates or color might be different for each vertex. Attribute is the way to pass data from JavaScript to the vertex shader.
varying	`varying vec2 vTexCoord;` `varying vec3 vColor;`	A varying variable provides a way to pass data from the vertex shader to the fragment shader. The values passed via varying are interpolated before they appear in the fragment shader (more about this later in the chapter).

To better understand how storage qualifiers affect the behavior of the variable, Figure 9-4 shows how the data is injected into the shaders, and how they can exchange the data afterward. As you see, JavaScript can set only *attributes* (when the per-vertex data is required) and *uniforms* (when the data is the same for the whole set of vertices). The vertex shader can use both attributes and uniforms to pass the data to the fragment shader. The fragment shader can have its own uniforms, but no attributes, since it doesn't need the information about the specific vertex.

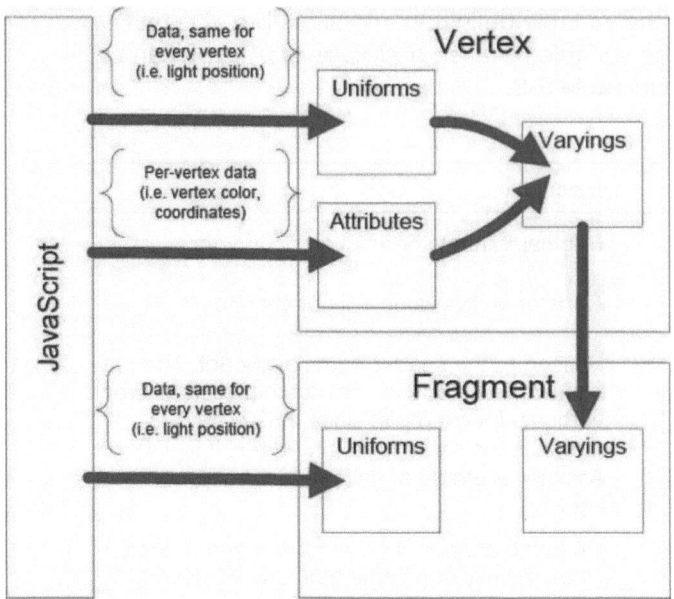

Figure 9-4. *The storage qualifiers of GLSL variables and how they are transferred between the WebGL layers: JavaScript, vertex shader, and fragment shader.*

Now you can read the whole vertex shader. Let's look at the code once more.

```
attribute vec3 aPos;
uniform mat4 uMVMatrix;
uniform mat4 uPMatrix;

void main(void) {
    gl_Position = uPMatrix * uMVMatrix * vec4(aPos, 1.0);
}
```

The shader defines one attribute, aPos, which stores the position of the current vertex. It also has two matrix uniforms—for the modelView matrix and for the projection matrix. The shader doesn't have any "varying," so it will not pass any data to the fragment shader.

Operations and Functions

In terms of operations, GLSL works like most programming languages. The following are a few examples of typical constructs.

if-else:

```
if (shininess != 0.0) {
    // Do calculation for shiny surface
```

```
} else {
    // otherwise
}
```

for loop:

```
for(int i=0; i < limit; i++) {
    // Do something in the loop
}
```

while and do-while loops:

```
while (value < limit) {
    // Loop body
}
```

```
do {
    // Loop body
} while (value > 0)
```

The entry point of the shader is a function called main(). It accepts no arguments and returns no value. Every shader must have a main() function declared like in the example code. The result of the function is written into the magic variable. It is called gl_Position in the fragment shader.

For simple examples like the ones in this chapter, we put all the code in the main function. However, you can define your own functions for convenience. For an in-depth explanation of function syntax, refer to section 6.1.1 of the GLSL specification referenced earlier in this chapter. Here is an example of a simple function:

```
float transform(float t) {
    return sin(t*t);
}
```

GLSL has numerous built-in functions for geometrical and matrix calculations. Table 9-3 shows the most commonly used GLSL functions.

Table 9-3. *Functions Most Commonly Used in GLSL Programs*

Function name	Description
sin, cos, tan, asin, acos, atan, radians, degrees	General-purpose trigonometry functions.
abs, sign, floor, ceil, fract, mod, min, max, clamp, pow, exp, log, exp2, log2, sqrt, mix	General math functions.

length, distance, dot, cross, normalize, faceforward, reflect, refract	Geometry functions, mostly used with vectors.
equal, notEqual, lessThan, lessThanEqual, greaterThan, greaterThanEqual, any, all, not	Vector per-component functions (applied for each component of two vectors).
texture2D, texture2DProj, texture2DLod, texture2DProjLod	Texture lookup functions.

The function names are self-explanatory, except for the texture-related ones. We'll discuss them a little later in the chapter.

As you can see, GLSL is a relatively small and math-focused language. If you take a little more time to explore it, you will see that it is a very powerful tool for 3D rendering. Don't worry if you don't feel very comfortable with it yet. This section is intended to give you just a general feeling of the language. You will understand it better by following the examples in this chapter and experimenting with shaders.

Throughout this section, we've been working with the vertex shader. Let's take a look at an example of the Hello World fragment shader (see Listing 9-6).

Listing 9-6. *The Simplest Fragment Shader That Makes Every Pixel White*

```
precision mediump float;
void main(void) {
    gl_FragColor = vec4(1.0, 1.0, 1.0, 1.0);
}
```

For every given pixel, it returns the same color—white. The first line looks new. It defines the default precision of the floating-point values in the shader. It doesn't make much sense to dive deeply into what this means exactly, but medium precision is quite enough for the shader's tasks.

> **NOTE:** More information about precision is available in the GLSL specification at www.khronos.org/registry/gles/specs/2.0/GLSL_ES_Specification_1 .0.17.pdf, section 4.5, "Precision and Precision Qualifiers."

Basic Example: Render a 3D Cube

Now we have all the required knowledge to assemble a working WebGL program that outputs something. Just like in Chapter 8, we will render a cube on the screen. The goal of this section is to understand how the different parts of WebGL script work together. We will learn how to compile and link shaders, configure the pipeline, how to load the data into the pipeline, and draw a cube.

Using Shaders in a Web Page

To use shaders in your program, you have to perform several steps: compile the shaders, combine one vertex shader and one fragment shader into the program, link it, and tell WebGL to use it in the pipeline. Inside the JavaScript code, the shaders' source code is stored as simple strings, as shown in Listing 9-7.

Listing 9-7. *Saving the Code for Shaders into JavaScript Strings*

```
var vertexShaderSource =
    "attribute vec3 aPos;" +
    "uniform mat4 uMVMatrix;" +
    "uniform mat4 uPMatrix;" +

    "void main(void) {" +
        "gl_Position = uPMatrix * uMVMatrix * vec4(aPos, 1.0);" +
    "}";

var fragmentShaderSource =
    "precision mediump float;" +

    "void main(void) {" +
        "gl_FragColor = vec4(1.0, 1.0, 1.0, 1.0);" +
    "}";
```

This is not the best way to manage them. In fact, this method is far from perfect: the code in one language that is saved as a string in another language is hard to manage, read, and understand. Of course, you don't have to do the same in your production game. For example, you can save the code in a plain text file, load it with an XHR call, and read the contents afterward. You can also make a library of shaders and save it as an XML file with some extra descriptions and meta-info. It is completely up to you how to manage them. Just remember that at the end of the day, you need the JavaScript string with the source code in order to compile the shader.

When the source is written and ready, execute the code in Listing 9-8.

Listing 9-8. *Compiling Vertex Shader*

```
var vertexShader = gl.createShader(gl.VERTEX_SHADER);
gl.shaderSource(vertexShader, source);
gl.compileShader(vertexShader);
if (!gl.getShaderParameter(vertexShader, gl.COMPILE_STATUS)) {
    // Something went wrong
    alert(gl.getShaderInfoLog(vertexShader));
}
```

The code creates the shader object, loads the source code, and tries to compile it. Then, it checks the compilation status and if there is an error, shows it to the user (don't forget to turn off the alert for the production build). The process of creating a fragment shader is the same, except that the shader type is gl.FRAGMENT_SHADER instead of gl.VERTEX_SHADER.

Now you have two shaders that you have to assemble into the *shader program*, the solid unit that is ready to be used in the pipeline (see Listing 9-9).

Listing 9-9. *Creating a Shader Program out of Two Compiled Shaders*

```
var shaderProgram = gl.createProgram();
gl.attachShader(shaderProgram, vertexShader);
gl.attachShader(shaderProgram, fragmentShader);
gl.linkProgram(shaderProgram);

if (!gl.getProgramParameter(shaderProgram, gl.LINK_STATUS)) {
    alert("Error initializing shaders");
}

gl.useProgram(shaderProgram);
```

WebGL uses the two shaders that we've created to render the geometry. The first shader calculates the projections of the vertices on the screen, and the second fills every pixel of the cube with a solid white color. The next step is to get the location of parameters inside the program to insert them later from the JavaScript code:

```
var pMatrixUniform = gl.getUniformLocation(shaderProgram, "uPMatrix");
var mvMatrixUniform = gl.getUniformLocation(shaderProgram, "uMVMatrix");
```

Finally, tell WebGL that the shader program has the attribute for vertex data (see Listing 9-10). The variable is used later to set the value for the attribute.

Listing 9-10. *Working with Attributes of Shaders*

```
var vertexPositionAttribute = gl.getAttribLocation(shaderProgram, "aPos");
gl.enableVertexAttribArray(vertexPositionAttribute);
```

Before moving forward, let's review the components of the WebGL program. They are shown in Figure 9-5.

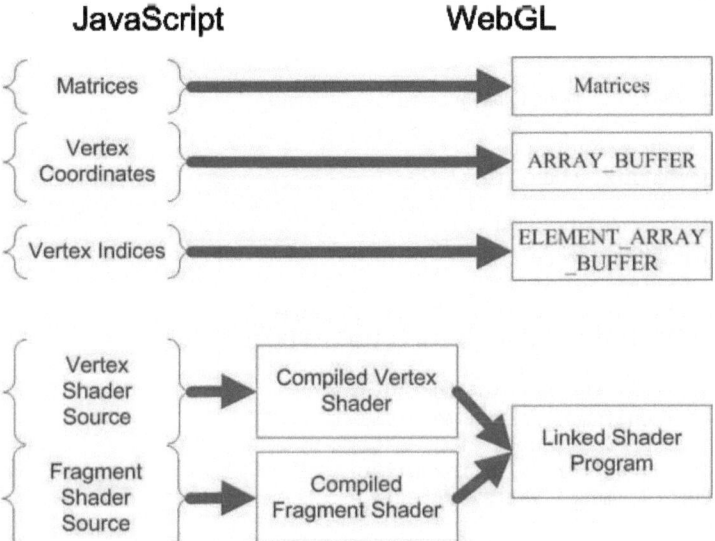

Figure 9-5. *The transformations of data from JavaScript to WebGL*

Now, both WebGL and the program are ready to receive geometry and render it on the screen.

Rendering Hello World

Now every component is in place and we are ready to start the rendering. The function that renders the screen is called drawScene() (see Listing 9-11). Its job is to use the prepared components and pass it to WebGL. This function doesn't perform the actual rendering; it only passes the data into the pipeline. The rendering is performed by the WebGL implementation—either by the graphics card or by the software emulator when a graphics card is not present.

Listing 9-11. *Drawing the Cube: drawScene is the Main Function That Does the Rendering*

```
function drawScene() {
    gl.viewport(0, 0, width, height);
    gl.clear(gl.COLOR_BUFFER_BIT | gl.DEPTH_BUFFER_BIT);

    mat4.perspective(45, width / height, 0.1, 100.0, projectionMatrix);

    // Reset the modelView matrix
    mat4.identity(modelViewMatrix);
```

```
    // Update the modelView matrix, "move" the model to the correct position
    mat4.translate(modelViewMatrix, [model.x, model.y, model.z]);

    // Update rotation
    if (model.rx)
        mat4.rotateX(modelViewMatrix, model.rx);

    if (model.ry)
        mat4.rotateY(modelViewMatrix, model.ry);

    if (model.rz)
        mat4.rotateZ(modelViewMatrix, model.rz);

    // Pass the projection matrix as the uniform to the program
    gl.uniformMatrix4fv(pMatrixUniform, false, projectionMatrix);

    // Pass the modelView matrix as the uniform to the program
    gl.uniformMatrix4fv(mvMatrixUniform, false, modelViewMatrix);

    // Tell WebGL that the active buffer is vertexBuffer
    gl.bindBuffer(gl.ARRAY_BUFFER, model.vertexBuffer);

    // Pass the elements of the active buffer as the values of "aPos" attribute
    gl.vertexAttribPointer(vertexPositionAttribute, 3, gl.FLOAT, false, 0, 0);

    // "Activate" faceBuffer
    gl.bindBuffer(gl.ELEMENT_ARRAY_BUFFER, model.faceBuffer);

    // Use the faceBuffer to draw total of model.faces.length triangles
    // each element of the buffer pointing to the vertex in the vertexBuffer
    gl.drawElements(gl.TRIANGLES, model.faces.length, gl.UNSIGNED_SHORT, 0);

    // The pipeline has started, it will render the cube now.
}
```

Now you have everything to launch Hello World. Let's review the steps that you have to take in a typical WebGL application:

1. Load the geometry and related data like vertex color, normals, and so forth.

2. Pass the geometry data to WebGL and receive buffer objects.

3. Load the source of the fragment shader and the vertex shader.

4. Compile both shaders and make sure there are no errors.

5. Create a shader program and link it. Make sure that there are still no errors.

6. Receive the locations of the program's input parameters by their names.

7. Update modelViewMatrix: set the size, position, and rotation of the model.

8. Associate matrices and buffers with the program parameters.

9. Execute gl.drawElements() to start the pipeline and to render the figure.

10. Repeat the last four steps for every model on the scene. Change the shader program if required.

Yes, it looks like the checklist you'd go through before flying a passenger jet. Luckily, most of the steps are easy to isolate into separate functions, and then forget about them for a while. Listing 9-12 shows the source code for the Hello World application that renders a white 3D cube on the screen without textures or lights. The comments are stripped where possible to save space, and some pieces of the code are isolated into the functions. The whole source code can be found with the materials for this chapter in a file called 02.basic.html.

Listing 9-12. *The Hello World Example in WebGL*

```
<!DOCTYPE html>
<html lang="en">
<head>
<!–regular meta and styles -->
<script src="js/gl-matrix.js"></script>

<!-- The geometry data of the cube -->
<script src="js/geometry.js"></script>

<script>

// Canvas object
var canvas;

// The WebGL context
var gl;

// The only shader program that we'll use
var shaderProgram;

// Projection and modelview matrices
var modelViewMatrix = mat4.create();
var projectionMatrix = mat4.create();
```

```
// Location of parameters in shader program
var pMatrixUniform;
var mvMatrixUniform;
var vertexPositionAttribute;

var vertexShaderSource = /* vertex source stripped, see Listing 9-7 */

var fragmentShaderSource = /* fragment source stripped, see Listing 9-7 */


function getWebGLContext(canvas) {
    /* Return the WebGL context as in Listing 9-1 */
}

function initShaders() {
    var fragmentShader = createShader(gl.FRAGMENT_SHADER, fragmentShaderSource);
    var vertexShader = createShader(gl.VERTEX_SHADER, vertexShaderSource);

    shaderProgram = gl.createProgram();
    gl.attachShader(shaderProgram, vertexShader);
    gl.attachShader(shaderProgram, fragmentShader);
    gl.linkProgram(shaderProgram);

    if (!gl.getProgramParameter(shaderProgram, gl.LINK_STATUS)) {
        alert("Error initializing shaders");
    }

    gl.useProgram(shaderProgram);

    vertexPositionAttribute = gl.getAttribLocation(shaderProgram, "aPos");
    gl.enableVertexAttribArray(vertexPositionAttribute);

    pMatrixUniform = gl.getUniformLocation(shaderProgram, "uPMatrix");
    mvMatrixUniform = gl.getUniformLocation(shaderProgram, "uMVMatrix");
}

function createShader(shaderType, source) {
    var shader = gl.createShader(shaderType);
    gl.shaderSource(shader, source);
    gl.compileShader(shader);
    if (!gl.getShaderParameter(shader, gl.COMPILE_STATUS)) {
        alert(gl.getShaderInfoLog(shader));
        return null;
    }

    return shader;
}

function initModel(model) {
    model.vertexBuffer = gl.createBuffer();
```

```
    gl.bindBuffer(gl.ARRAY_BUFFER, model.vertexBuffer);
    gl.bufferData(gl.ARRAY_BUFFER, new Float32Array(model.vertices),
gl.STATIC_DRAW);

    model.faceBuffer = gl.createBuffer();
    gl.bindBuffer(gl.ELEMENT_ARRAY_BUFFER, model.faceBuffer);
    gl.bufferData(gl.ELEMENT_ARRAY_BUFFER,
                    new Uint16Array(model.faces), gl.STATIC_DRAW);
}

function drawScene() {
    gl.viewport(0, 0, canvas.width, canvas.height);
    gl.clear(gl.COLOR_BUFFER_BIT | gl.DEPTH_BUFFER_BIT);

    mat4.perspective(45, canvas.width / canvas.height, 0.1, 100.0,
projectionMatrix);
    mat4.identity(modelViewMatrix);
    drawModel(cube);
}

function drawModel(model) {
    mat4.translate(modelViewMatrix, [model.x, model.y, model.z]);

    if (model.rx)
        mat4.rotateX(modelViewMatrix, model.rx);

    if (model.ry)
        mat4.rotateY(modelViewMatrix, model.ry);

    if (model.rz)
        mat4.rotateZ(modelViewMatrix, model.rz);

    gl.uniformMatrix4fv(pMatrixUniform, false, projectionMatrix);
    gl.uniformMatrix4fv(mvMatrixUniform, false, modelViewMatrix);

    gl.bindBuffer(gl.ARRAY_BUFFER, model.vertexBuffer);
    gl.vertexAttribPointer(vertexPositionAttribute, 3, gl.FLOAT, false, 0, 0);

    gl.bindBuffer(gl.ELEMENT_ARRAY_BUFFER, model.faceBuffer);
    gl.drawElements(gl.TRIANGLES, model.faces.length, gl.UNSIGNED_SHORT, 0);
}

function init() {
    canvas = initFullScreenCanvas("mainCanvas");

    gl = getWebGLContext(canvas);
    gl.clearColor(0.0, 0.0, 0.0, 1.0);
    gl.enable(gl.DEPTH_TEST);
```

```
        initShaders();
        initModel(cube);
        drawScene();
}

/* Rest of the code is the same as in Listing 9-1*/
</script>
</head>
<body onload="init()">
<canvas id="mainCanvas" width="20px" height="20px"></canvas>
</body>
</html>
```

When you load the page in the browser, you should see a result that looks like what's shown in Figure 9-6: a white silhouette of a cube on a black background.

Figure 9-6. *The WebGL Hello World result*

Exploring WebGL

Congratulations, you've made it to the most exciting part of the chapter. We will now take the basic cube example and gradually improve it, explaining the possibilities of WebGL on the go. The first obvious improvement is to render each face with its own color, not just white. Since alone color is too simple to impress someone, we will add textures. Finally, we will look at using 3D models with WebGL and techniques for working with binary data.

Color

Let's start with the color. As you already know, the color of the pixel is determined in the fragment shader. In this section, we change the fragment shader so that it paints every face of the cube with its own color.

There are many ways to encode the color: you can save color as the single integer, as the hex-string, as a CSS string, or as the four floating-point values. The last way is the most convenient for our case because of the way the fragment shader returns the result:

```
gl_FragColor = vec4(1.0, 1.0, 1.0, 1.0);
```

The four parameters of the vector are red, green, blue, and the alpha components of the color.

Let's add another array to our cube describing the color of each vertex (see Listing 9-13). Since the entire cube face has the same color, each vertex has exactly the same value.

Listing 9-13. *Associating Color with Each Vertex of the Cube*

```
var cube = {
    vertices: [
        // Front
        -1.0, -1.0,  1.0,
         1.0, -1.0,  1.0,
         1.0,  1.0,  1.0,
        -1.0,  1.0,  1.0,

        // Back
        -1.0, -1.0, -1.0,
        -1.0,  1.0, -1.0,
         1.0,  1.0, -1.0,
         1.0, -1.0, -1.0,

        // Rest of the vertices go here
    ],

    // Two triangles for each face
    faces: [
        // Definitions of faces as in Listing 9-2
    ],

    colors: [
        // Front
        0.5, 0.0, 0.0, 1.0,
        0.5, 0.0, 0.0, 1.0,
        0.5, 0.0, 0.0, 1.0,
```

```
        0.5, 0.0, 0.0, 1.0,

        // Back
        0.0, 0.5, 0.0, 1.0,
        0.0, 0.5, 0.0, 1.0,
        0.0, 0.5, 0.0, 1.0,
        0.0, 0.5, 0.0, 1.0,

        // The color is assigned to every vertex in a similar way
    ],

    vertexBuffer: null,
    faceBuffer: null,
    colorBuffer: null,

    x: 0,
    y: 0,
    z: -10,

    rx: 0.4,
    ry: 1.2,
    rz: 0
};
```

Take another a look at the checklist of the typical WebGL program from the previous section, and stop and think. Which steps should we update to include the extra information, and how will the vertex shader change?

1. The fragment shader needs to accept the parameter with the encoded color of the vertex. The parameter is `varying` because the color changes from vertex to vertex, and this is the only variable type of parameter that the fragment shader accepts from the outside (see Figure 9-4, which shows how script and shaders exchange the information).

2. The only source of `varying` parameters for the fragment shader is the vertex shader. We need to add the extra `attribute` parameter to the vertex shader so that it can be saved as `varying` and passed to the fragment shader.

3. The data for the new parameter is supplied as the buffer—alongside with the other vertex information like coordinates. We need to create the new buffer and use it to send the color data to the shader.

Let's start with updating the fragment shader.

Updating Shaders

Let's add another input parameter. The type is vec4, since a color has four components, and the storage qualifier is varying since the color changes from vertex to vertex. The updated GLSL code for the shader is in Listing 9-14.

Listing 9-14. *The Fragment Shader That Supports Colors*

```
precision mediump float;

varying vec4 vColor;
void main(void) {
    gl_FragColor = vColor;
};
```

As you see, the fragment shader does not do any kind of processing. It simply assigns the received color to gl_FragColor; however, this is enough to paint our rectangle.

The vertex shader in this case acts like the entry point for the parameter: it cannot do anything with the information about the vertex color since it is not its job to set the color of the pixel. It silently passes the value to the fragment shader. To do this, create a new attribute to receive the per-vertex values from the buffers. Then create a varying to pass the data to the fragment shader. Finally, assign the value of the attribute to varying. The color information ends up in the fragment shader. The code for the vertex shader is shown in Listing 9-15.

Listing 9-15. *The Vertex Shader That Passes the Color Data to the Fragment Shader*

```
attribute vec3 aPos;
attribute vec4 aCol;

uniform mat4 uMVMatrix;
uniform mat4 uPMatrix;

varying vec4 vColor;

void main(void) {
    gl_Position = uPMatrix * uMVMatrix * vec4(aPos, 1.0);
    vColor = aCol;
}
```

This way, the color is available to the fragment shader too. Think of varying variables as the output from the vertex shader and, at the same time, the input of the fragment shader. Look at Figure 9-4 once again if you are not quite comfortable with this principle.

How Varyings Work

Why make useless assignments to simply pass values within the same program? Good question. The reason for this sort of complexity is that the fragment shader doesn't have access to the vertex data.

The fragment shader works with pixels, and a pixel belongs to the whole face—not a single vertex. If all three vertices of the face are the same color, every resulting pixel should be of that color too. But what if vertices hold different colors? The resulting color of the pixel depends on how close is it to each of the vertices. Hence the name "varying"—the exact value that the fragment shader receives depends on the position of the pixel within the face. Everything that you save in the varying variable in the vertex shader is used as the value for interpolation. This concept works not only with colors, but with other per-vertex values too: normals, texture coordinates, and so forth.

To better understand this concept, look at Figure 9-7, which shows how WebGL treats the values of varying variables. Each vertex is assigned a color: pure red, pure green, and pure blue.

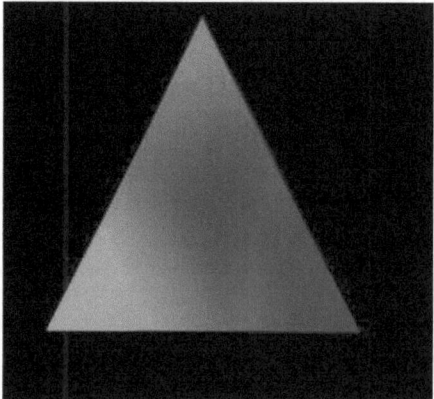

Figure 9-7. *The result of linear interpolation between three colors*

The color of each pixel is the result of linear interpolation of per-vertex values. The color in the middle is gray because it is a mix of all three colors: red, green, and blue in the same proportion.

Passing Color Data to the Vertex Shader

The final part is to update the main script. We need to create an extra buffer, fill it with data, register a new variable location in the shader program, and associate the new buffer with it. The code that does this doesn't need any further explanation. Use Listing 9-16 for reference, or use the full version that comes with the source code for this chapter, the file named 03.color.html. The code in Listing 9-16 is trimmed to show only the changed lines.

Listing 9-16. *The Updated Version of the Demo That Uses Textures*

```
function initShaders() {
    // The shaders are initialized as usual, see Listing 9-12 for reference

    vertexPositionAttribute = gl.getAttribLocation(shaderProgram, "aPos");
    gl.enableVertexAttribArray(vertexPositionAttribute);

    vertexColorAttribute = gl.getAttribLocation(shaderProgram, "aCol");
    gl.enableVertexAttribArray(vertexColorAttribute);

    pMatrixUniform = gl.getUniformLocation(shaderProgram, "uPMatrix");
    mvMatrixUniform = gl.getUniformLocation(shaderProgram, "uMVMatrix");
}

function initModel(model) {

    model.vertexBuffer = gl.createBuffer();
    gl.bindBuffer(gl.ARRAY_BUFFER, model.vertexBuffer);
    gl.bufferData(gl.ARRAY_BUFFER, new Float32Array(model.vertices),
gl.STATIC_DRAW);

    model.faceBuffer = gl.createBuffer();
    gl.bindBuffer(gl.ELEMENT_ARRAY_BUFFER, model.faceBuffer);
    gl.bufferData(gl.ELEMENT_ARRAY_BUFFER,
                    new Uint16Array(model.faces), gl.STATIC_DRAW);

    model.colorBuffer = gl.createBuffer();
    gl.bindBuffer(gl.ARRAY_BUFFER, model.colorBuffer);
    gl.bufferData(gl.ARRAY_BUFFER, new Float32Array(model.colors),
gl.STATIC_DRAW);
}

function drawModel(model) {
    // Rotate and position model as in Listing 9-12

    gl.bindBuffer(gl.ARRAY_BUFFER, model.vertexBuffer);
    gl.vertexAttribPointer(vertexPositionAttribute, 3, gl.FLOAT, false, 0, 0);

    gl.bindBuffer(gl.ARRAY_BUFFER, model.colorBuffer);
    gl.vertexAttribPointer(vertexColorAttribute, 4, gl.FLOAT, false, 0, 0);

    gl.bindBuffer(gl.ELEMENT_ARRAY_BUFFER, model.faceBuffer);
    gl.drawElements(gl.TRIANGLES, model.faces.length, gl.UNSIGNED_SHORT, 0);
}
```

Update your application or grab the code that comes with this book. Your WebGL demo should look much better now (see Figure 9-8).

Figure 9-8. *The result of adding color data to each vertex of the cube*

Textures

Now, what about textures? From the perspective of the fragment shader, a texture is not too different from a plain color. The only difference is that instead of a color value, the shader receives the image coordinates and extracts the color data from it.

Before diving into the code, let's look at how the textures work. A texture is a regular image: anything that a browser can load and display on a page. Each vertex of the model is associated with a certain point of the image, called the *texture coordinate*. The job of the fragment shader is to find the color for the pixel when given the interpolated texture coordinates and the image itself. Take a look at Figure 9-9, which illustrates how texturing works.

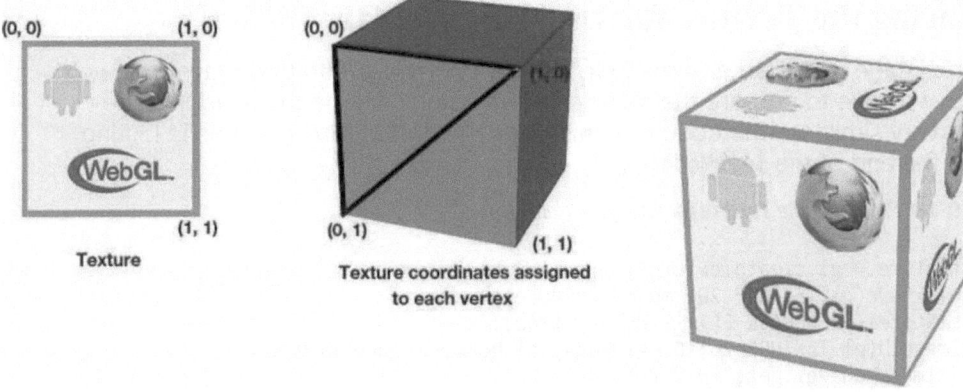

Figure 9-9. *Texturing: The color of the pixel is determined by the texture image and the texture coordinate.*

Just like with the color value, the texture coordinate is a varying variable: it is interpolated based on the values of vertices. Let's add textures to our demo.

Loading the Texture

You are already familiar with the process of loading images; we even have a convenient class that manages the loading. Let's rewrite the init() function a little. It waits for the textures to load and renders the scene afterward (see Listing 9-17).

Listing 9-17. *Load the Texture Before Rendering the Scene*

```
function init() {
    canvas = initFullScreenCanvas("mainCanvas");
    imageManager = new ImageManager();
    imageManager.load({"texture": "img/texture.png"}, initWebGL);
}

// The rest of the initialization goes to the
// separate function
function initWebGL() {
    gl = getWebGLContext(canvas);
    gl.clearColor(1.0, 1.0, 1.0, 1.0);
    gl.enable(gl.DEPTH_TEST);

    initShaders();
    initModel(cube);
    drawScene();
}
```

Preparing the Texture for Use with WebGL

Now the image is loaded and ready to be used. Just like with the arrays and buffers, we have to prepare the texture before using it inside the shaders. The code is very similar to the code that initializes the buffer. Add the lines in Listing 9-18 to the end of the `initModel()`.

Listing 9-18. *Preparing the Texture for Use with WebGL*

```
model.texture = gl.createTexture();
gl.bindTexture(gl.TEXTURE_2D, model.texture);
gl.pixelStorei(gl.UNPACK_FLIP_Y_WEBGL, true);
gl.texImage2D(gl.TEXTURE_2D, 0, gl.RGBA, gl.RGBA, gl.UNSIGNED_BYTE,
        imageManager.get("texture"));
gl.texParameteri(gl.TEXTURE_2D, gl.TEXTURE_MAG_FILTER, gl.LINEAR);
gl.texParameteri(gl.TEXTURE_2D, gl.TEXTURE_MIN_FILTER, gl.LINEAR);
```

The texture is created, then it is marked as "currently active" and all the texture-related operations that follow are performed against this specific resource. The third line normalizes the coordinates by flipping the y axis. This is required because of the differences in coordinate systems in WebGL and the image. The third line feeds the data from the image to the texture. Finally, the last two lines set the strategy of rendering the texture when there are either multiple texture pixels matching a single fragment, or vice versa. In other words, the last two lines tell what to do when the texture is too big or too small. `gl.LINEAR` tells it to use the weighted average of the four closest texture elements.

Texture Coordinates

We need to assign the texture coordinate to each vertex of the model, and create and initialize the appropriate buffer to transfer this data to the shader. You already know how to do that (see Listing 9-19).

Listing 9-19. *Adding Texture Coordinates to the Model*

```
var cube = {
    // Definitions for vertices and faces stay the same

    textureCoords: [
        // Front face
        0.0, 0.0,
        1.0, 0.0,
        1.0, 1.0,
        0.0, 1.0,
```

```
    // Back face
    1.0, 0.0,
    1.0, 1.0,
    0.0, 1.0,
    0.0, 0.0,

    // Texture coordinate is set for each vertex
    ],
    vertexBuffer: null,
    faceBuffer: null,
    colorBuffer: null,

    textureCoordsBuffer: null,
    texture: null,

    // Position, rotation and other parameters as before
};

function initModel(model) {
    // code not changed

    // Initialize one more buffer for texture coordinates
    model.textureCoordsBuffer = gl.createBuffer();
    gl.bindBuffer(gl.ARRAY_BUFFER, model.textureCoordsBuffer);
    gl.bufferData(gl.ARRAY_BUFFER, new Float32Array(model.textureCoords),
        gl.STATIC_DRAW);
}
```

The texture coordinates are a value between 0 and 1; they are not the exact pixel coordinates. This is a rather convenient approach—the coordinates don't depend on the size of the texture. You can use a texture of any size (256×256, 512×512, 1024×1024, or whatever) without changing the code. It is WebGL's job to find the exact matching pixel of the texture.

Updating Shaders

Now it's time to update the shaders. Just like with the color, the texture coordinates are the value associated with the vertex. You have to create one extra varying variable and pass the coordinates to the fragment shader (see Listing 9-20).

Listing 9-20. *The Vertex Shader That Passes the Texture Coordinates to the Fragment Shader*

```
attribute vec3 pos;
attribute vec2 aTex;
```

```
uniform mat4 uMVMatrix;
uniform mat4 uPMatrix;

varying vec2 vTex;

void main(void) {
    gl_Position = uPMatrix * uMVMatrix * vec4(pos, 1.0);
    vTex = aTex;
}
```

The fragment shader receives the coordinates, but it also needs the image data to get the color. In GLSL there are several special objects called "samplers" that act like a store of pixel information. You can think of samplers as images inside GLSL. The texture doesn't change from vertex to vertex, so the sampler is uniform (see Listing 9-21).

Listing 9-21. *Assigning the Color from the Texture to the Pixel*

```
precision mediump float;

varying vec2 vTex;
uniform sampler2D uSampler;

void main(void) {
    gl_FragColor = texture2D(uSampler, vTex);
}
```

As you can see, assigning the color from the texture is very simple. There's a built-in function—texture2D()—that takes the sampler and texture coordinates, and returns the matching color.

Passing Texture Data to the Fragment Shader

The final step is to register the new attribute aTex and new uniform uSampler, and pass the texture data to the shader program (see Listing 9-22).

Listing 9-22. *Passing the Texture Data to the Vertex Shader*

```
gl.activeTexture(gl.TEXTURE0);
gl.bindTexture(gl.TEXTURE_2D, model.texture);
gl.uniform1i(samplerUniform, 0);
```

The result is a nice textured cube, as shown in Figure 9-10.

Figure 9-10. *The textured cube*

File 04.texture.html, the final version of the code that shows the textured cube, is found with the source code for this chapter.

Loading Models

The cube is a basic 3D shape that has been used like the Hello World example for ages. In a real 3D demo or game, however, the cube has somewhat limited use. Let's learn how to use other 3D models within the WebGL application. We will start with looking at different types of 3D models and the tools to work with them. Then we'll learn how to load the model to your application.

3D Models Overview

There are two types of 3D models: high-polygon (hi-poly) models and low-polygon (low-poly) models. Generally, high-poly models are used for static rendering. For example, a model of an ancient vase that has 10,000 triangles looks gorgeous, but a mobile processor will never render it fast enough to use in a game. Low-poly models are the models for games. They have significantly fewer polygons, and they are created specifically for real-time 3D applications. So what you need, obviously, is a low-poly model.

To display an arbitrary 3D model in WebGL, you need at least the coordinates of vertices and an array of faces. If the model is textured, you also need the coordinates of the texture for each vertex. The best option is to convert the existing model into the JSON format and use it in your script, just as we used the model of the cube. Since WebGL is gaining popularity, there are several tools to do this. Most of them convert models from the Wavefront (.obj) or Collada (.dae) format to JSON because these formats are among the simplest for parsing. OBJ files store data as plain text with a minimum amount of meta information. DAE files are XMLs, so it is not hard to convert them to another text format, such as JSON. Some game engines load DAE models straightaway, without the intermediate step of converting them.

What if your model is not in OBJ or DAE format? You can use a 3D editing tool to convert between formats. Blender (www.blender.org) is a free 3D editor that has many custom plug-ins to work with 3D models. Figure 9-11 shows a screenshot of one of the free models loaded in Blender.

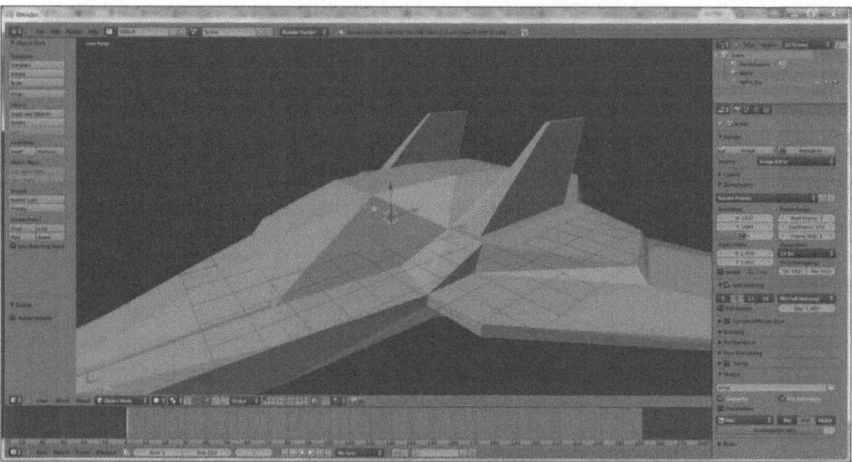

Figure 9-11. *A space frigate loaded in Blender*

On Blender's official tutorial page at www.blender.org/education-help/, you can find more information about Blender and how to use it to load and convert a 3D model.

Sometimes, instead of creating a JSON representation, it is much more convenient to load the model in the original format. One of the reasons is the size of the resulting file. A model of a character saved in the binary format (MD2) is only around 218 KB, while the same model converted to JSON is 6 MB. Even zipping the model doesn't help a lot; a zipped JSON is still ten times bigger than the original binary model.

On the other hand, parsing binary data on the client side is a rather heavyweight operation, both in terms of processing and in terms of coding. The task is considered "advanced" since the data that is fed to WebGL must still be in the form of JavaScript arrays; so to load the 3D model in a custom format, you must write your own parser.

Working with Binary Data

In this section, I show you some very basic techniques on dealing with binary data. Binary files can store all kinds of information: music, pictures, databases, and so forth. Sometimes it is quite useful to be able to parse them in JavaScript. We will look at the example of the MD2 file parser—an old format for animated characters that was used in *Quake II* (http://en.wikipedia.org/wiki/MD2_ (file_format)). The goal is not to dive deep into the specifics of the format, but to learn the general principles of parsing such files. If you are curious about the whole implementation, the source code for the MD2 parser is included with the source code for this chapter.

The main problem with working with binary data is that our target devices' in-browser JavaScript engines can't deal with it out-of-the-box. There's no regular way to load something like an MD2 model from the server and parse it on the client-side. XHR (XMLHttpRequest) is expecting to receive text, not a stream of bytes.

> **NOTE:** There is support for binary data in XHR Level 2 calls; however, it is not yet widely supported by mobile browsers. Read more about it in Chapter 11. If you are unfamiliar with XHR, you might want to read Chapter 11, and then return to this section afterward.

There is an ugly hack that developers often use to overcome this limitation. Take a look at the code in Listing 9-23.

Listing 9-23. *Receiving the Unchanged Binary Data with Ajax Call*

```
var req = new XMLHttpRequest();
req.open('GET', "models/marine.md2", false);

// Override Mime, such charset will prevent browser from messing with bytes
req.overrideMimeType('text/plain; charset=x-user-defined');
req.send(null);
var data = req.responseText;
```

This charset prevents the browser from treating the response as plain text and converting it to a regular JavaScript string. Next, it is not hard to get the byte data out of such a string:

```
var byteValue = data.charCodeAt(offset) & 0xff;
```

The last part of this line strips garbage out of the character code to leave only the original number as received from the server. Some numbers might have more than one byte; for example, the two-byte integer (usually called a "short") or four-byte float. To read such numbers, you simply combine bytes with binary shift operations, as shown in Listing 9-24.

Listing 9-24. *Reading Numbers That Have More Than One Byte*

```
var b0 = buf.charCodeAt(off) & 0xff;
var b1 = buf.charCodeAt(off+1) & 0xff;
var short = b0 + (b1 << 8);
```

There are several small libraries that can handle all the dirty byte-swapping work for you. The one that I used for my MD2 converter is BinaryFile.js by Brandon Jones. BinaryFile takes the Ajax response as the input and hides the details of the calculations. Your client code looks like the code in Listing 9-25.

Listing 9-25. *Reading Binary Data with BinaryFile.js*

```
for (var i = 0; i < model.header.num_tris; i++) {
    vert.push([bf.readShort(), bf.readShort(), bf.readShort()]);
    tex.push([bf.readFloat(), bf.readFloat(), bf.readFloat()]);
}
```

Using this technique, you can request the model from the server, take the specification of the format, and read the model information byte-by-byte.

The result: you can use custom binary models in your WebGL applications and save some network traffic at the expense of a slightly longer loading time. The time to load several megabytes over mobile internet is, however, usually more than the time required to process the model.

Summary

In this chapter, we learned how to create WebGL applications. WebGL is a very powerful tool that allows you to bring real accelerated (where possible) 3D on web pages.

WebGL is a rather low-level and complex API. It requires a good understanding of 3D mechanics and the mathematical principles of 3D visualization. Another point of complexity is that to create a WebGL page, you need to write two programs in GLSL language called shaders. The language of shaders has a C-like syntax and is math-oriented (there are no functions to work with strings or user input, but there are many functions to work with vectors and matrices).

WebGL is still not widespread on mobile devices, so this chapter gives only a very brief introduction to the subject. There are still a lot of topics to master to make full-blown WebGL applications with animation, lights, materials, physics simulations, environmental effects like fog or rain, and the many other possibilities available with this rich API.

In this chapter, we learned how to initialize WebGL, load the basic geometry, write shaders, use color and textures, and work with models and binary data.

Since WebGL has a steep learning curve, the most important advice is to get started and make your first demo work. After you are comfortable with the basic principles, the other topics become much easier to understand.

There are several higher-level 3D engines that simplify typical tasks like loading models, adding lights, adding textures, and so forth.

WebGL is a vast topic to explore. If you would like to learn more about this API, you will find the following websites useful:

- `http://learningwebgl.com`: Collections of WebGL lessons and tutorials, along with WebGL news and links to cool experiments.

- `www.khronos.org`: The official website of Khronos Group.

- `http://mrdoob.github.com/three.js`: The home page of Three.js, the WebGL-based 3D engine with many advanced features.

Chapter 10

Going Server-Side

Do you want to know if your friend is a lucky game developer? Ask him what his favorite programming language or platform is. Java fans are lucky: they can create their masterpieces using only the tool and language that they know—Java. They don't need to learn something beyond it to start working over the game. PHP developers have a little bit less luck—their favorite language is intended only for server scripting, so they need to learn something else in order to make a shiny game client. They also have an option to pair with an ActionScript developer who has the opposite problem: they can't write efficient server code with their favorite tool.

Until recently, JavaScript developers were completely out of luck—not only did they have to learn the server-side languages in order to build even the simplest network game, but they also had to deal with the different implementations of DOM engines in browsers. The learning curve and the amount of workarounds that one had to implement in a production-quality product were daunting.

That was the dark age of JavaScript game development. Now it is gone and JavaScript developers are the luckiest guys in town. First, when canvas appeared, we got rid of most of the problems that were caused by the DOM bugs in browsers. It turns out that a line drawn in canvas inside IE looks the same in Chrome and Firefox. Moreover, we can now write the server code in our favorite language thanks to Ryan Dahl, the creator of Node.js—the tool that has completely changed the way of thinking about JavaScript.

In this chapter, we will learn how to efficiently use Node.js to create full-blown server-side support for our applications. There are a lot of cases when you need networking. Even the smallest game feature that involves sharing data with the world requires networking: a high score board or a simple in-game chat is a good example of a JavaScript application that requires something beyond canvas.

We will write a minimum amount of client-side JavaScript in this chapter; it is fully devoted to server development. Also, the material in it is obviously not limited to smartphones or tablets. You can use this knowledge for regular desktop web sites and applications too.

In this chapter, we will learn the following:

- How to install Node.js, and write and debug simple scripts that can be executed in server environment

- How the Node.js program is organized

- How to use NPM to discover and install Node.js modules

- How to build a simple server for the Four Balls game with the Express framework

> **NOTE:** In this chapter, I use the word "Node" for Node.js, and for convenience, I sometimes refer to the JavaScript files written specifically for Node.js as "node scripts." Also, sometimes I use such phrasing as "reading the file with Node.js," meaning "reading the file with JavaScript that runs on Node.js."
>
> A word of caution before we start. Node.js is a fast-evolving software and so are the open-source libraries that are built for it. They improve every day to bring a better, more friendly and more efficient software to developers. APIs change very fast. In the time that passed between the initial draft of this chapter and its final version, several parts of the frameworks described here have changed. The e-mail-sending framework was deprecated in favor of a more powerful one, and the installation procedure of Node itself became way simpler.
>
> Most of the code in this chapter should work just fine; however, if something is not working straightaway for you, visit the online documentation of the library that doesn't work in the way you want it to. Also, you might want to visit the author's page from time to time (http://juriy.com) to look for updates there, as well as the source code hosted on the Apress site. I will try to keep the code as up-to-date as possible and list all the changes that you need to implement to make your code work with the latest versions of libraries.

Node.js Basics

The Idea behInd Node.js (http://nodejs.org) is to bring the awesomeness of JavaScript to the server. As I mentioned already, Node.js is a tool that allows you, as a web developer, to write the code in a language that is familiar to you. But of course, that's not the only reason that makes Node.js a good choice for online gaming needs. In this section, we cover the basics of Node.js. We start with looking at the Hello World program, and then install Node and get ready to write our own scripts.

Introducing Node.js

Before diving into the internals of Node.js, let's look at what it really is and how you work with it. Essentially, Node.js is a small command-line tool that can run code written in JavaScript. To do so, it uses an extremely efficient JavaScript engine—V8 (http://code.google.com/p/v8/), but instead of working in the browser, it works directly with the operating system, exposing its resources to the programmer. No more moving divs and changing the backgrounds of buttons. With Node.js, you can do everything that you can do with a regular desktop programming language: open and read files, use sockets, build HTTP servers, download images, parse XML, stream sound—whatever you want.

Node.js is definitely not a web server. It works more like a JavaScript-driven virtual machine that has HTTP as the first-class protocol—meaning that it comes out of the box and is fully supported by Node.js. You *can* write a web server in Node.js if you want, but it doesn't mean that you have to. You could also write a tool that finds duplicated photos in your media library and doesn't have a single networking-related instruction. Still, in the vast majority of cases, you use Node for processing network requests (either HTTP or TCP/IP) since this is where it shows its full potential.

If you're like me, you're eager to see how the code looks, so here it is. The famous Hello World written for Node.js:

```
console.log("Hello World");
```

Hey, what did you expect? It's supposed to be simple! I know that you're not excited about this example, but I didn't want to break the old-school Hello World traditions. We will learn how to run this script in a minute.

In Listing 10-1, let's look at something more complex: writing a web server that returns the data to the user.

Listing 10-1. *Slightly More Advanced Example of Node.js Script*

```
var http = require('http');
http.createServer(function (req, res) {
    res.writeHead(200, {'Content-Type': 'text/plain'});
    res.end('Hello World\n');
}).listen(1337, "127.0.0.1");
```

Don't worry if you don't fully understand this code, we have the rest of the chapter to make it familiar. The main point that you should notice is that this is regular JavaScript code, and if you think about it for a second, you can understand how it works. In the first line, we receive the object `http`, and then we call the `createServer()` on it, passing the function as an argument. The function acts like an event listener in a regular browser: it is invoked when a certain event happens. In this case, the event that triggers a call is the HTTP connection initiated by the user.

Programming Model

The philosophy of Node.js is to use asynchronous operations for IO whenever it is possible. That's what allows Node to be so fast: it saves every microsecond where regular servers tend to think about it as an unavoidable loss. Node scripts are entirely made of callbacks that might look slightly strange if you already have experience with other server-side languages.

It is better to explain with a code example. Listing 10-2 shows the code for a Node script that reads the file from the file system and prints the output to the console:

Listing 10-2. *Reading the Content of the File with Node.js*

```
var fs = require('fs');
fs.readFile('some/file/here', function (err, data) {
    if (err)
        throw err;
    console.log(data);
});
```

The idea is just the same as in Listing 10-1. You are asking Node.js to retrieve the content of the file for you, and let your callback know when this is done. Now compare this code to the fragment of PHP in Listing 10-3 that performs exactly the same task.

Listing 10-3. *Example Code in PHP That Performs the Same Task of Reading the File and Outputting Its Content*

```php
<?php
    $content = file_get_contents('some/file/here');
    echo $content;
?>
```

Listing 10-3 looks somewhat simpler, of course. But this kind of simplicity has a very high cost. PHP code blocks the execution of the script while it reads the file: it waits until the file is fully read before moving to the second line. What happens to the other users who want to access the server at the same time? They wait until the execution of the file-read operation is done. In practice, of course, a web server spawns a lot of threads so that users don't have to wait until a single available thread is ready. But this model has its limits: spawning and supporting a thread is not a cheap operation. When more users request the page from the server, it spawns more threads until it hits the thread limit or the server runs out of memory and CPU resources.

Node.js works in a different way. Once you have requested the file data, you're letting the script go. You provide the callback that is executed when the IO operation is done, and free the server to work with the next user. In other words, a server thread is not blocked during the reading operation. While the file is being read by some external process, a server also serves the request of another user or two. Once the file is fully read, it finishes the current job and calls the callback that you've provided.

Figure 10-1 illustrates the typical flow for a blocking server. In this example, the first request causes the execution of a long-running operation on the server, like reading the big file or querying database for the complex data. The operation takes considerable time to finish. The other requests—2 and 3—are very fast to process. Their results are returned to the browser almost immediately.

In the case of the blocking server shown in Figure 10-1, requests 2 and 3 have to wait while the server is busy performing a long-running operation, even if the actual job is done elsewhere (for example, in the database software). The server can respond only when the long-running operation is finished, even if during that time it sits idly, performing no useful job.

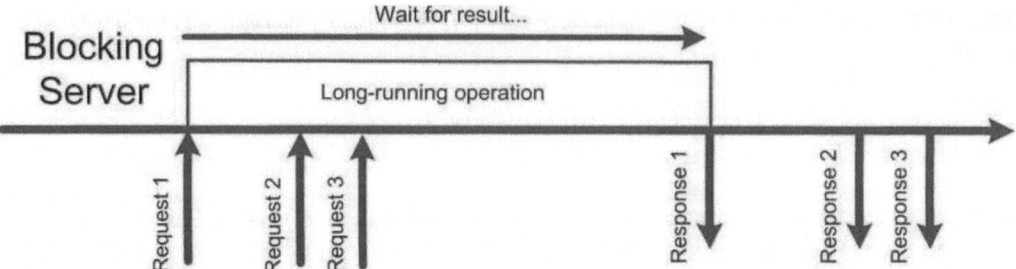

Figure 10-1. *Blocking server flow*

Node.js uses a different approach, as shown in Figure 10-2. While the long-running operation is in progress, Node.js can serve other requests. For example, it can return the responses for requests 2 and 3. When the long-running task is finished, Node.js calls the registered callback and the script can serve the result for request 1.

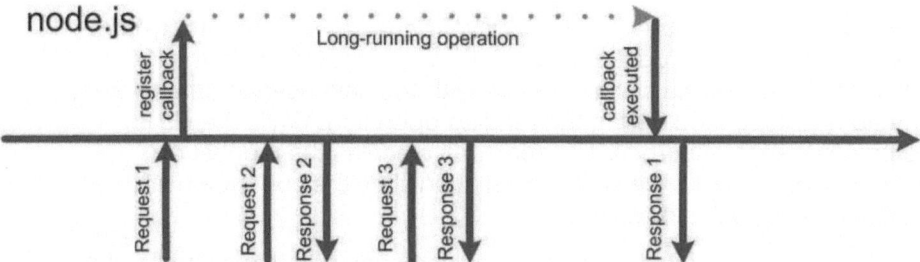

Figure 10-2. *Node.js flow. While the long-running request is processed in the background, Node.js serves the other requests.*

Dan York found a good metaphor to describe the difference between the traditional and asynchronous IO (http://tinyurl.com/49wl5lk). He compares the *traditional* IO with a fast-food restaurant line. When it is your turn, you give your order, and you wait until your order is done. Even though the cashier is doing nothing useful at the moment, he's just waiting for the order to arrive from the kitchen, he is blocked. While you and the cashier are waiting for the order to come, the other customers have to wait until you are done. Spawning a lot of threads is like adding more cashiers: it definitely makes things happen faster, but this solution is not scalable since you are limited by space and budget. Besides, the problem itself is not actually solved—the cashiers are standing there, wasting their time while they wait for the kitchen people to do their job.

In an *asynchronous* model, the cashier asks you to step aside once you made your order, and he serves another customer in the meantime. It may well happen that the next customer wants something very simple, like a muffin, which is already baked so the cashier serves that customer instantly. Eventually, the cashier is notified by the kitchen that your order is ready. He finishes serving his current customer and returns to you. Now he's got what you need and he gives it to you.

See the difference? In the second example, the cashier is utilizing his time to the maximum: he doesn't waste time standing and staring at you while the kitchen staff is making a burger—every second is used to satisfy the needs of the clients. Obviously, in this metaphor, the client is the request from the browser, the cashier is the web server thread, and the kitchen is the IO operation that might be quick, but may take some time to finish.

If you already have experience working with the server-side stack, it might be hard for you to change your way of thinking about the structure of the code— you got used to the synchronous model, where operations are executed one by one. Hopefully this small explanation has clarified things for you a little. Now let's move on to installing Node.js. It's time to try this amazing stuff.

Installing Node.js

Before writing any real Node.js code, we have to install it. There are two pieces of software that are important for development, the first being Node.js itself. This is an executable that does the hard job of running scripts and doing all the complicated low-level OS stuff. The second part is NPM, the package manager for Node.js. It is the de facto standard for downloading and installing additional packages for Node, such as the frameworks, tools, and utilities that you require during the development.

> **NOTE:** Node.js has a very active community and there are a lot of *modules*— extensions that you can use to simplify development so that you don't have to reinvent the wheel every time. There are hundreds of them, from FTP servers and command-line parsers, to PDF generation and image processing. In this chapter, we use a few of them too.

Installation of Node.js is fairly simple: select the installer package from `http://nodejs.org/#download` (choosing the Windows or Mac version, depending on your OS) and follow the installation instructions. Update the PATH environment variable to point to the destination directory (if you don't remember how to set environment variables, refer to Chapter 1's "Installing Java Development Kit"). I prefer to create an extra variable called NODE_HOME and to refer to it in PATH afterward.

> **NOTE:** On my own system, I use the path `c:\apps` for all development-related
> applications, tools, and utilities. For example, Node.js resides in `c:\apps\node`. I
> like it better than standard Program Files... because it is short and there are no
> spaces in it. It also doesn't have any special treatment in Windows, meaning fewer
> issues with security restrictions. And finally, it starts with "a" and is the first folder
> that appears in the command prompt when you click Tab to autocomplete the name.

When this is done, open the command prompt and type:

```
> node --version
```

If everything is fine, you should see the version number of your Node.js build.
For me, it is v0.8.3—the latest stable version at the time of writing.

NPM, the package manager for Node.js, is installed in the same directory. Type
the following command to check whether NPM is available:

```
> npm --version
```

Once you hit Enter, you should see the version of NPM. For me, at the time of
writing, it is 1.1.43.

To try out the real script, copy the Hello World example code to the file named
`hello.js` then type the following command line:

```
> node hello.js
```

If everything is set up correctly, Node will output the greeting in the console.
This first but important example is available in the folder named `01.hello_world`.
It can be found along with the other materials for this chapter.

Debugging Node Scripts

Sometimes we all make mistakes, so it is great to have the tools to quickly
discover and fix them. IntelliJ Idea and WebStorm both have the same excellent
plug-in by Maxim Mossienko that allows you to debug JavaScript straight from
the IDE.

The plug-in adds an extra type of run configurations: Node JS, Node JS Remote
Debug, and Nodeunit for running unit tests. Create your own run configuration
and provide the path to the Node executable and to the "main" application file.
The rest of the parameters are optional. Figure 10-3 shows the configuration
screen of the Node JS plug-in in the WebStorm IDE.

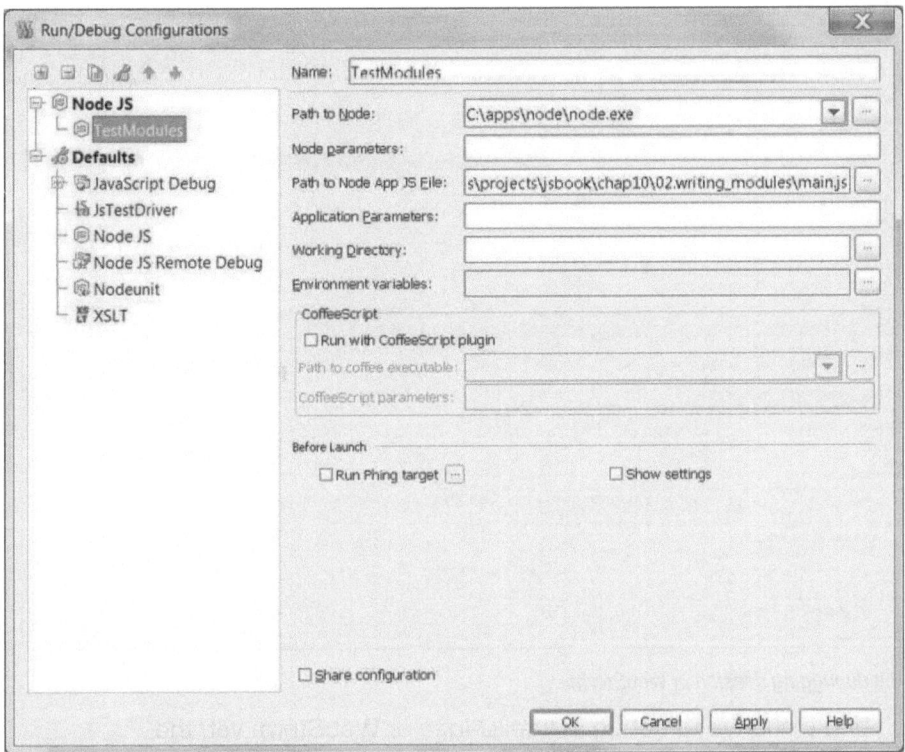

Figure 10-3. *The IntelliJ module for debugging Node.js scripts*

Now you can set a few breakpoints in your code and click the Debug button.
The execution pauses once it reaches one of your breakpoints. You'll have a
chance to explore the values of variables, place watches, and do whatever you
usually do to make your code work. Figure 10-4 shows the open debug session
for a sample Node.js application.

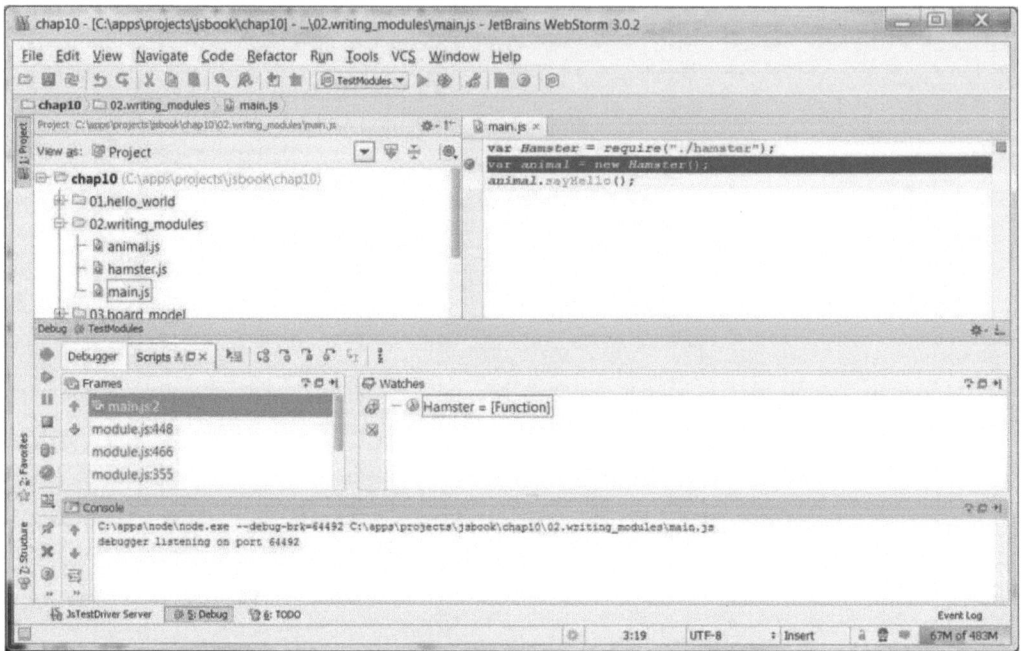

Figure 10-4. *The debugging session in WebStorm*

If you haven't had a chance to debug in IntelliJ Idea or WebStorm yet, the process is almost the same as in Web Developer Tools of the WebKit browser. If you want to read more on debugging in Idea, a nice document for you to start with is at http://wiki.jetbrains.net/intellij/Debugging_JavaScript_with _IntelliJ_IDEA. It tells you about usual browser scripts, but Node.js works in exactly the same way.

Eclipse doesn't yet have a dedicated Node plug-in, but since Node uses V8, it is possible to use the V8 debugger in order to work with Node from Eclipse. The details on how to set it up are described at https://github.com/joyent/node /wiki/Using-Eclipse-as-Node-Applications-Debugger.

There's one more thing to say about Node before we move to the next section. It is evolving at the speed of light. If you want to make a multiplayer game with this tool, get into the habit of checking out what's new on the horizon every week or two. The whole Node ecosystem lives in an extremely dynamic rhythm. While you're thinking about how to deal with a problem, someone else is already publishing a tool that solves it.

Now that you know how to set things up and debug Node, you are ready to run your first real script.

Writing Scripts for Node.js

In this section, we learn how to write Node.js scripts beyond Hello World. Most Node.js programs consist of *modules*—reusable components that are written and distributed in a special way. To write a server application, we have to use other developers' modules, as well as write a couple of our own modules.

First, navigate away from the folder where you installed Node. You will not need it anymore. Create a separate folder for your new server project and create a file called `hello-server.js` with the content in Listing 10-4.

Listing 10-4. *Running the HTTP-Enabled Hello World*

```
var http = require('http');
http.createServer(function (req, res) {
    res.writeHead(200, {'Content-Type': 'text/plain'});
    res.end('Hello World\n');
}).listen(80);
```

Run it from the command line with the following command:

```
> node hello-server.js
```

Then open `http://localhost` in your desktop web browser. You should see the Hello World page.

Exceptions and Stack Traces

Before running this script, you need to make sure that your nginx instance is down, otherwise you get a message like:

```
node.js:201
        throw e; // process.nextTick error, or 'error' event on first tick
        ^
Error: listen EADDRINUSE
    at errnoException (net.js:614:11)
    at Array.0 (net.js:704:26)
    at EventEmitter._tickCallback (node.js:192:40)
```

Ouch. That wasn't all that friendly. Don't worry, if you make a mistake in your own script, you can count on a better explanation. Try adding an erroneous line like the following to your script:

```
var http = require('http');
http.createServer(function (req, res) {
    foo.bar = 123;
    res.writeHead(200, {'Content-Type': 'text/plain'});
    res.end('Hello World\n');
}).listen(80);
```

Then execute it once again. You should see something like this:

```
node.js:201
        throw e; // process.nextTick error, or 'error' event on first tick
             ^
ReferenceError: bar is not defined
    at Object.<anonymous>
(c:\apps\projects\jsbook\chap10\01.hello_world\main.js:3:7)
    at Module._compile (module.js:432:26)
    at Object..js (module.js:450:10)
    at Module.load (module.js:351:31)
    at Function._load (module.js:310:12)
    at Array.0 (module.js:470:10)
    at EventEmitter._tickCallback (node.js:192:40)
```

The bolded lines are pointing to the exact place in your code that caused the problem, and the error message is rather friendly too.

Let's write some real code now! We have an interesting task for the next two chapters: build the basis for the multiplayer implementation of the Four Balls game from the beginning of the book. We will make a multiplayer game out of it: players invite each other to play a game and exchange turns via network.

Global Namespace and Node Modules

Node.js has a very active community of developers who create extensions and tools for it. Such an ecosystem can't exist without good support for structuring and sandboxing contributors' API. Just imagine a case when two programmers (let's call them John and Frank) are making their frameworks. John defines a global variable called count that he uses to hold the number of image files loaded from the server. Frank doesn't know anything about John's code, and creates his own variable with the same name; but he uses it to keep track of the number of mousedown events. Let's say that you want to use both frameworks together. What if these variables clash? Obviously, if we don't take special care, we will have a big mess to clean up. Most likely, one of the frameworks will break, or maybe both of them will.

Before looking at how Node solves this issue, let's try to think about the solution. In the previous parts of the book, we broke down the functionality of our program into classes, and put each class into a separate file. This approach works fine for applications, but fails when it comes to distributable APIs. The root cause of all problems is JavaScript's global scope, which is the same for all files. Any careless use of global scope brings in errors.

But what if we promise to be very careful and we do not rely on the global scope at all? We will not create or read global variables, only define them in classes and methods. Will it help? It will certainly make matters a little better, but it will not solve the general problem because the constructor of a class is a global variable itself, and classes with the same name clash.

Take a look at the code in Listing 10-5. It simulates the loading of two big and useful frameworks: one dealing with math and the other dealing with strings. Both frameworks have a class called Utils. Guess what happens?

Listing 10-5. *Perfectly Valid JavaScript Code That Leads to Rather Unexpected Behavior*

```
<script>
    // The class defined in Mathematics API
    function Utils() {
    }

    Utils.prototype.add = function(x, y) {
        return x + y;
    };
</script>
<script>
    // The class defined in Strings API
    function Utils() {
    }

    Utils.prototype.add = function(x, y) {
        return x + "" + y;
    };
</script>
<script>
    // Now we want to add two numbers... easy, right?
    console.log(new Utils().add(2, 3));
</script>
```

The result is obviously 23 since the Strings API has overwritten the global variable Utils, holding the constructor of the class. Now add only works correctly for strings. The usual approach to address this problem is to use *packages*—special namespaces that are unique to the API. For example, if every developer used the name of his web page to identify his works, it would be much easier to avoid clashes. Listing 10-6 shows an example of how it usually looks.

Listing 10-6. *Addressing Naming Problems by Creating Namespaces*

```
<script>
    // The class defined in Mathematics API
    if (typeof com == "undefined") {com = {};}
    if (!com.juriy) {com.juriy = {};}
    if (!com.juriy.math) {com.juriy.math = {};}
```

```
          com.juriy.math.Utils = function () {
          };

          com.juriy.math.Utils.prototype.add = function(x, y) {
              return x + y;
          };
</script>
<script>
          // The class defined in Strings API
          if (typeof com == "undefined") {com = {};}
          if (!com.juriy) {com.juriy = {};}
          if (!com.juriy.strings) {com.juriy.strings = {};}
          com.juriy.strings.Utils = function() {
          };

          com.juriy.strings.Utils.prototype.add = function(x, y) {
              return x + "" + y;
          };
</script>
<script>
          // Now we want to add two numbers... easy, right?
          console.log(new com.juriy.math.Utils().add(2, 3));
</script>
```

My web site is at http://juriy.com. If everything's fine, I'm going to keep it for the next 60 years—long enough to use it as the unique identifier of my APIs. The last example doesn't have the problems of the first version of the code—it shows the correct result. Of course, the code is less clean, but we can always clean it up with some convenience functions. Still, even this approach has a problem.

What if I support several versions of my API and I decide to make a new major version that's not backward compatible? I have introduced a real problem, since there are frameworks that rely on my old API and there are frameworks that rely on the new one—and you can't have both in your application because they use the same namespace: com.juriy.math!

> **NOTE:** This might sound like an artificial problem, but in the real world, it is not, especially when it comes to the software and components in a high-enterprise environment. The components there might not be updated for ages, because old libraries are well tested, bugs are known, and workarounds already found. There's very little motivation to update anything. "If it ain't broke, don't fix it," as the saying goes.

A lot of platforms simply ignore the last issue. For example, Java doesn't have a good way to support multiple versions of the same library out of the box. The library in Java is distributed as a jar file, and Java programmers have a special term to describe what happens when they face this issue: Jar Hell. As you might have guessed, this is one of the worst problems to deal with. Don't worry. Node.js is very smart when it comes to modules: it will not let you down.

The root cause of the problem is the same: the global namespace. Namespaces that we just introduced are plain objects that are saved in the global scope. The solution to this serious problem is surprisingly simple: don't use the global scope for defining APIs at all. With JavaScript closures, it is a matter of a few lines of code. Listing 10-7 shows how to isolate two APIs from each other.

Listing 10-7. *Isolating API from the Global Scope*

```
<script>
    // The class defined in old String API
    var oldApi = (function () {
        function Utils() {
        }

        Utils.prototype.add = function(x, y) {
            return x + "" + y;
        };
        return Utils;
    })();

    // The class defined in new String API
    var newApi = (function () {
        function Utils() {
        }

        Utils.prototype.add = function(x, y) {
            return x + "!THIS IS COOL TO JOIN STRINGS!" + y;
        };
        return Utils;
    })();

    console.log(new oldApi().add("foo", "bar"));
    console.log(new newApi().add("foo", "bar"));
</script>
```

As you can see, both the old API and the new one define the object with the same name—Utils—but they don't clash because they are isolated from the global scope by the wrapper. In JavaScript, a new function creates a new scope—you can define any new variables inside it without being afraid of overwriting something that was already defined.

This approach is very similar to what Node does. When you call

```
var foobarApi = require('foobar');
```

Node looks for a file called `foobar.js`, executes the content of the file in the separate scope, and returns whatever the code in that file decided to share with the outer world.

The foobar in the example is called a module. Module is a reusable API that you can use in your application. As I mentioned earlier, every major platform has a similar concept of reusable components—some call them *libraries*, other call them *extensions*, and yet others call them *plug-ins*. Node calls them *modules*. Every platform uses its own rules for packaging and distribution of such components, as well as the rules of discovery—where to look for them when one needs them. Node.js has its own rules, of course, that we will explore right after writing our first Node.js module!

Writing the First Module

Writing a module for Node is not hard at all. In fact, it is not too different from writing plain script for the browser, with two major differences: you don't have to worry about the global scope and you have to explicitly state which variables or constructors you want to share with the rest of the world.

Create a new file called `animal.js` and copy the code from Listing 10-8 into the new file.

Listing 10-8. *Creating Own Module*

```
function Animal() {
    console.log("New animal is born");
}

var _p = Animal.prototype;

_p.sayHello = function() {
    console.log("Hello, I'm a humble animal");
};

function makeNewAnimal() {
    return new Animal();
}

exports.Animal = Animal;
```

You don't need to explicitly wrap the module into the function call because Node does the scope isolation for you. exports is the "pseudo-global" variable that is available to every module. By assigning properties to exports, you share them with the rest of the system. As you see, we've exported only the constructor. The function makeNewAnimal is not exported, so it stays private for this module.

We can access the newly created module, as shown in Listing 10-9.

Listing 10-9. *Accessing the Module*

```
var animalApi = require("./animal");

var animal = new animalApi.Animal(); // Creates the new instance of animal
console.log(typeof animalApi.makeNewAnimal); // Undefined, method is not visible
animal.sayHello(); // Prints greeting
```

The require function loads the animal.js file from the current folder, executes the code there, and returns the object that has all the "exported" fields. After this is done, you can access whatever you exported—call functions, create objects from constructors, and so forth. The third line shows that the function that is defined inside the module—but not exported—stays inaccessible.

The syntax is a little unusual. Some people would prefer to export the function itself and not an object that has the function as one of the values. The syntax would be a tad clearer then:

```
var Animal = require("./animal");
var hamster = new Animal();
```

To do that, you have to use module.exports, which refers to the object that is actually available outside of the module. Listing 10-10 shows the common pattern, when your module needs to export only one variable (usually it is the constructor).

Listing 10-10. *Exporting the Single Variable*

```
// Export constructor only
exports = module.exports = Animal;

function Animal() {
    console.log("New animal is born");
}

// The rest of the code goes here
```

One module can have as many classes, functions, and variables in it as you want, but you can have only one module in a file. The other important point is inheritance. It works exactly the same way as the inheritance in a browser. To make a "clean" experiment, make another file named `hamster.js` and save it near `animal.js`. Copy the code from Listing 10-11 into the new file.

Listing 10-11. *Inheritance in Node Modules*

```
var Animal = require("./animal");
var util = require("util");

function Hamster() {
    Animal.call(this);
    console.log("It's the hamster");
}
util.inherits(Hamster, Animal);

var _p = Hamster.prototype;

_p.sayHello = function() {
    console.log("(chewing carrot)");
};

exports = module.exports = Hamster;
```

In the second line, we load one of Node's core modules—util. Even though there's no `util.js` file around, it is still loaded correctly. This module is compiled straight into the Node's binary and doesn't require any extra files.

Now let's get back to the inheritance problem. The first part looks exactly the same as in our browser code. We call the super constructor as usual. The second part, the call to the `inherits()` function of the `util` module, is very similar to our own implementation (called `extend()`).

Update the main script to use `Hamster` instead of `Animal` and check the output. The sample code is shown in Listing 10-12. Note that we import only the module that we actually use, not its dependencies.

Listing 10-12. *Updated Main Script*

```
var Hamster = require("./hamster");

var animal = new Hamster();
animal.sayHello();
```

Here's the output:

```
C:\apps\node\node.exe C:/apps/projects/jsbook/chap10/02.writing_modules/main.js
New animal is born
It's the hamster
(chewing carrot)
```

That's it. Now the hamster is a happy descendant of the animal. Note that the main script doesn't need to load the animal module anymore. It is enough to call it from `hamster`. When you create a Node.js script, you require only those modules that you actually need. All dependant modules are loaded automagically.

The complete code example for this section that shows how to organize your own modules can be found in the `02.writing_modules` folder.

> **NOTE:** The architecture behind the Node.js modules is the implementation of the CommonJS (`www.commonjs.org`) specification. The goal of CommonJS is to create a common set of rules on how to write modules for JavaScript. Theoretically, modules following the predefined pattern should run fine on different environments: Rhino, Node, Browser, and so forth. In practice, however, the server-side JavaScript is very different from the browser JavaScript, and this makes the implementation of the CommonJS less usable for the browser environment.
>
> The tradeoffs are described in detail in a nice post by James Burke—the creator of RequireJS (CommonJS-style modules for the browser) at `http://tagneto.blogspot.com/2010/03/commonjs-module-trade-offs.html`. Basically, CommonJS doesn't play well with the browser environment, which is why we don't use it straight from the start of the book.

Discovering Modules

There are two main ways to refer a module in Node.js, and we've seen both already. The first is by specifying the path to the module file, either absolute or relative. For example, `require("./hamster")` loads the module by specifying a relative path (the absolute path starts with / and refers to the root of the filesystem). The second way is where the magic happens—when you refer the module only by its name, like `require("http")`.

In the latter case, Node.js looks into the directory with the name `node_modules` inside the directory of the current module (or the main file). Node looks for one of three files that describe the module, in the following order:

1. the `node_modules/<module-name>.js` file

2. the `node_modules/<module-name>/package.json` file

3. the `node_modules/<module-name>/index.js` file

package.json is the json file that must have at least one attribute called name that points to the main file of the module. Listing 10-13 shows the example of the simplest possible package.json file.

Listing 10-13. *Simplest Module Descriptor*

```
{
    "main": "hamster"
}
```

The main file may, in turn, require other modules and provide an interface to the complex functionality. In big modules, the main files usually don't implement any specific functionality, but rather do housekeeping tasks: loading dependant files, adding keys to exports, and so forth. This form of discovery allows it to distribute complex modules as a folder that can be checked out from the version control system, for example.

If none of the three is found in the folder, Node goes to the parent folder and repeats the whole process there. If the requested module is still not found, it goes up one more level until it reaches the root of the filesystem. This approach allows you to set up the default versions of the modules somewhere at the top of the filesystem, which is available to all your Node projects. However, if the specific project needs a version of the library that is different from the default, you can easily override it in the project's own node_modules folder. You can also add an arbitrary folder to the search process by defining the NODE_PATH environment variable.

Sometimes you need to know where exactly the module was loaded from (typically when something doesn't work as you expected). There's a way to do it in Node.js:

```
> node
> require.resolve("hamster");
'c:\\apps\\projects\\jsbook\\chap10\\node_modules\\hamster\\hamster.js'
```

This last listing shows the so-called REPL mode (read-eval-print loop). If you start Node without specifying the js file, you can type commands right into the terminal. This is a quick way to check something if you are too lazy to create and save a text file.

The scope of this book doesn't cover the building and distribution of the complex Node modules, but if you're interested in this topic and want to explore more, the official documentation on modules (http://nodejs.org/api/modules.html) is the good place to start.

Using NPM

NPM is the standard package management In Node.Js. It Is not a simple download-and-extract type of software but a complete toolset that allows you to install and manage modules, create your own, search for them in the online registry by keyword, and do a lot more. NPM itself is a Node application, even though you call it from the command line like a regular Windows program. NPM is developed and maintained by Isaac Z. Schlueter.

Instead of writing more about what NPM can do, let's issue a couple of commands and see how the real action looks. We've learned enough theory about Node.js; now we need to pick a nice framework to build our multiplayer application. We want a web framework that follows the REST style (https://www.ibm.com/developerworks/webservices/library/ws-restful/). Let's ask NPM if he knows such a framework:

```
> npm search web rest framework
```

The output is a nice list of search results that highlight the keywords with different colors. Figure 10-5 shows how the output looks on my machine.

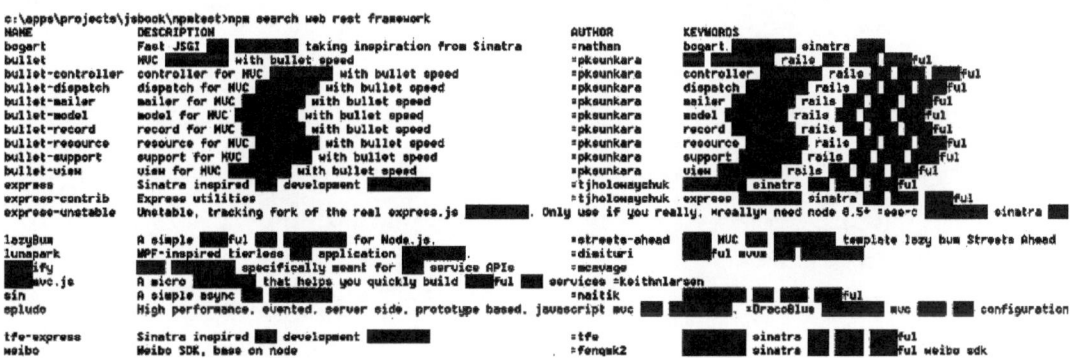

Figure 10-5. *The results of NPM search*

Now you can read through the results and choose the framework that you like. Of course, you usually first search online about the framework, read forums and mailing lists, and only then choose the tool to work with. For this book, I've chosen Express (http://expressjs.com)—one of the most popular frameworks on the market.

Let's install it now.

```
> npm install express
```

After few dozen progress-reporting lines, you see that NPM reports that the model is installed along with the required dependencies:

```
express@3.0.0beta7 node_modules\express
├──── methods@0.0.1
├──── fresh@0.1.0
├──── range-parser@0.0.4
├──── cookie@0.0.3
├──── commander@0.6.1
├──── debug@0.7.0
├──── mkdirp@0.3.3
├──── response-send@0.0.1 (crc@0.2.0)
├──── send@0.0.3 (mime@1.2.6)
└──── connect@2.3.9 (bytes@0.1.0, cookie@0.0.4, crc@0.2.0, qs@0.4.2,
formidable@1.0.11)
```

The installation process takes a little time—NPM needs to download the package and its dependencies before installing it onto the system. Open the project's folder and take a look at the structure of the files that appeared after we issued these two commands. You should see something similar to the structure shown in Figure 10-6.

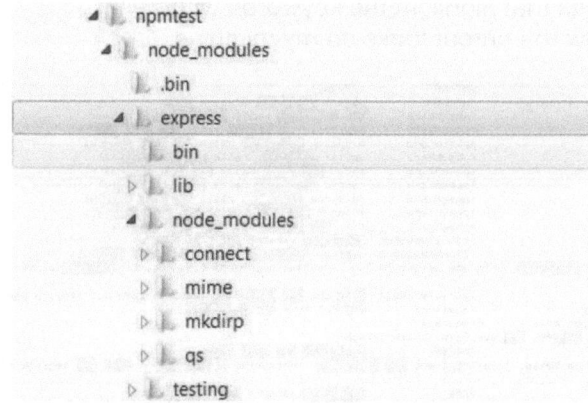

Figure 10-6. *The structure of the folders created after the installation of Express*

As you can see, NPM created the `node_modules` folder that now has the `express` folder in it. Since Express as a module relies on several other modules, its dependencies are also available in its own `node_modules`.

Let's verify that the module is installed, and output some slightly more verbose info about each module. The output looks like Figure 10-7 (on my Windows machine).

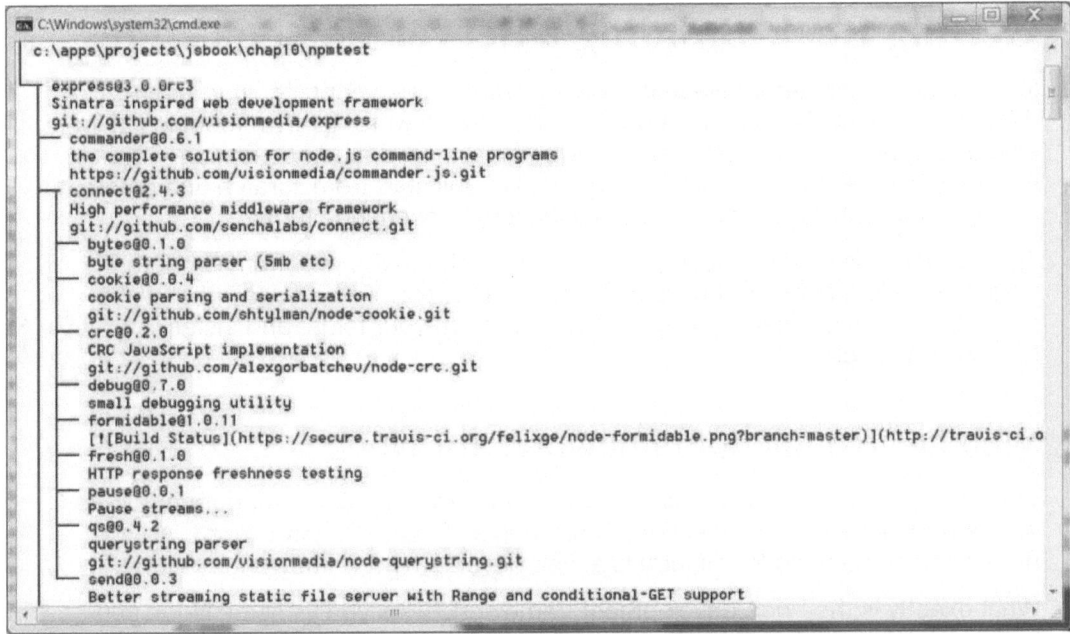

Figure 10-7. *The detailed information about each installed module*

Now you can see not only the names and versions of the available packages, but also a short description, the path to the module folder, and the source of the module—links to Git repositories. Now we know that Express is a "Sinatra-inspired web development framework" and that the source of the module can be checked out at `git://github.com/visionmedia/express.git`. That's a lot of info! You can also use synonyms for the `list` command: `ll`, `ls`, and `la` (`ll` and `la` showing the "long" version, `ls` the short version).

If you have forgotten the details of the command for some reason, use

```
npm <command> help
```

It brings up the browser window and opens the documentation section from the local filesystem.

This is pretty much everything that you need to know about NPM to get started with Node. We've just completed the learning curve of Node.js—we are ready to write our server now.

Getting Real: Building a Server for the Game

Now we know a lot about Node.js: how to write simple scripts, how to debug them, how to install additional modules, and how to write our own modules. It is a time to apply our knowledge and build the more advanced application—the multiplayer version of the Four Balls game. We will start from scratch and create a simple text-only page that allows two players to exchange turns.

This section tells how to accomplish this task with the Express framework that we just installed. Let's start by learning about Express. To be certain that we're starting from a clean setup, delete all the files from your folder and install Express once again.

Web Development Frameworks for Node

What is Express (http://expressjs.com) and why will we use it for our game? As we learned in the previous section, Express is a "Sinatra-inspired web development framework." Sinatra is a web development framework for Ruby.

What exactly is the "web development framework"? As you've seen, Node can handle HTTP traffic out of the box, so why do we need to install something beyond it? Let's take a step back and think of common activities that you usually need to perform when you want to build a web site. At the very least, you need to parse the URL, extract GET or POST parameters from it, then route the call to the script that does something useful. Next you'll need to serve static data—images, CSS, client-side JavaScript, and so forth. Sometimes you also need to handle user sessions, error pages (404s and 500s), and logging. Well, you could do that yourself, of course, if you want to, but you'd just be reinventing yet another wheel.

But do we *really* need all these facilities just to make a simple Four Balls game? Okay, you got me. In fact, we don't. We could probably get by with a smaller framework like Connect (http://senchalabs.github.com/connect/) that just does basic things like cookies and request routing; but once you start adding features to your project, you end up doing one of two things: installing Express or reinventing the wheel. The good news is that Express is built on top of Connect, and once you learn how to work with the big brother, you can handle Connect in no time.

> **NOTE:** This chapter is devoted to server-side programming, which means that we
> will not touch smartphones at all. Once you start thinking about Android, things get
> slightly more complex—you need to implement a lot of client-side features that don't
> have anything to do with the server. I want to avoid the mess of making both client
> and server in one go, so I've divided this material into three chapters. This means
> that, sorry guys, there are no bells and whistles in this chapter; the interface is just
> enough to test that the server is working—and no more. But fear not. In the next
> chapters, we'll get back to our usual environment and make a cool-looking game
> client too.

Basic Output

The starting point is the Hello World application as usual (see Listing 10-14). It is
good to have something working before diving deep into the details.

Listing 10-14. *Hello World with Express*

```
var app = require('express').createServer();

app.get('/', function(req, res){
    res.send('hello world');
});

app.listen(80);
```

After installing Express (if it is not yet installed), save the script into the `main.js`
file and run it with the following:

```
> node main
```

Go to `http://localhost`. You should see our favorite line there. The first line of
the code loads a module called `express`(we've already installed it) and then calls
the `createServer()` function of the exported object. The `app` variable now holds
the `Server` object that we use to set up the application itself. This demo adds
only one routing rule: all `GET` requests to the root of the web site output the line
Hello World. The last line attaches the server to port 80. Make sure that you
don't have nginx around—in this chapter, we only use Node to serve files.

Let's add some real action by creating a simple game screen—just for the sake
of verifying that the server works fine. We'll load the empty `BoardModel` from
Chapter 3 and then display it via HTML page.

> **NOTE:** The code for the original BoardModel can be found with the materials for
> Chapter 3 in the js/BoardModel.js file.

To do so, we first need to translate BoardModel into the Node module. Luckily,
there's not much to change. We have updated the inheritance code from it
(since it is not valid in Node) and assigned the constructor to the exports
variable. Listing 10-15 shows the result. I'm stripping the old function's code
(when I pasted the entire source, it was three pages long; and if you're like me,
then you're not patient enough to read three pages of code). If you want to look
at the full source code for this class, you can either download the code for this
chapter or refer to Chapter 3. I'm leaving the function names to remind you
about the interface of the BoardModel. We have added one extra method, called
toString(), which returns the human-readable string representation of the
board state.

Listing 10-15. *BoardModel as the Module of Node.js*

```
function BoardModel(cols, rows) {
    this._cols = cols || 7;
    this._rows = rows || 6;
    this._data = [];
    this._currentPlayer = BoardModel.RED;
    this._totalTokens = 0;

    this.reset();
}

BoardModel.EMPTY = 0;
BoardModel.RED = 1;
BoardModel.GREEN = 2;

BoardModel.NONE = 0;
BoardModel.WIN = 1;
BoardModel.DRAW = 2;
BoardModel.ILLEGAL_TURN = 3;

_p = BoardModel.prototype;

_p.reset = function() { … };

_p.getCols = function() { … };

_p.getRows = function() { … };

_p.makeTurn = function(column) { … };
```

```
_p.getPiece = function(col, row) { … };

/**
Few more private methods go here
*/

/**
 * This method is added in the most recent version to build the
 * simple string representation of the BoardModel.
 */
_p.toString = function() {
    var value = "";
    for (var row = 0; row < this._rows; row++) {
        for (var col = 0; col < this._cols; col++) {
            value += "[" + this._cellToString(this._data[row][col]) + "]";
        }
        value += "\n";
    }
    return value;
};

_p._cellToString = function(value) {
    switch (value) {
        case 0:
            return " ";
        case BoardModel.GREEN:
            return "X";
        case BoardModel.RED:
            return "O";

    }
};

exports = module.exports = BoardModel;
```

Now let's update our main script to show the board instead of Hello World. Listing 10-16 shows how this can be done.

Listing 10-16. *Displaying the Board at the Main Page of the Site*

```
var app = require('express').createServer();
var BoardModel = require("./BoardModel");

var board = new BoardModel();
board.makeTurn(2);
board.makeTurn(3);

app.get('/', function(req, res){
    res.setHeader('Content-Type', 'text/plain');
    res.send(board.toString());
});
```

```
app.listen(80);
```

It should now be pretty obvious what the code is doing. The only thing that is different is that we send an additional Content-Type header with the response. In Listing 10-14 the text that we passed was sent to the browser with the `Content-Type text/html` (this is the default value that Express uses when there is no explicit `Content-Type` specified). If we did the same here, the browser would display the board as one line of square braces. HTML doesn't treat the `\n` symbol as a new line; that's why we need to set `Content-Type` explicitly to `text/plain`. We have also dropped a couple of pieces to make sure that the page renders something meaningful. Figure 10-8 shows how Chrome renders the web page that we just created.

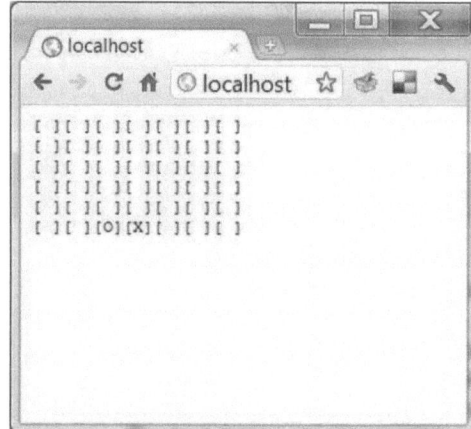

Figure 10-8. *The rendered board*

That's obviously correct, but… it doesn't look nice at all. Besides, you can't click anything because it is not HTML, it is plain text. Even though we decided that we don't care about what looks nice while we are on the server, we still need the ability to interact with the board somehow.

Don't rush updating your code to make it HTML-like. If you're writing the page markup inside the JavaScript code, it means that something is fundamentally wrong with the approach. The UI should be saved in nice HTML files that you can give to your designer for styling. Imagine what he'll say if you send him a couple hundred lines of JavaScript.

> **NOTE:** The complete code as it looks on the current stage of the project can be found in the 03.board_model folder.

Rendering Web Pages

The goal of this section is to output HTML to the browser instead of plain text. While it is quite easy to adjust the code for toString() function, we don't want to do that. The BoardModel is the class that represents the state of the game and the game logic; rendering HTML is clearly out of its responsibilities.

We will start with learning how to send static files—HTML, CSS, and JavaScript files—to the client browser. Afterward, we will explore templates—the mechanism that separates the application logic from rendering logic. At the end, we will be able to change the look of the page without touching the other parts.

Serving Static Files

It is fairly easy to send the plain HTML or CSS to the user. You need to tell Express that you want to use "static middleware"—a module for serving static files—and then just put the files into the folder that you pointed out as the root for your static files. Listing 10-17 shows how to do it. Once you update the code as shown in the listing, Express will serve any files from the public folder upon the request of the browser.

Listing 10-17. *Serving Static Files*

```
var express = require('express');
var BoardModel = require("./BoardModel");

var app = express.createServer();
app.use(express.static(__dirname + '/public'));

var board = new BoardModel();
board.makeTurn(2);
board.makeTurn(3);

app.get('/', function(req, res){
    res.setHeader('Content-Type', 'text/plain');
    res.send(board.toString());
});

app.listen(80);
```

The __dirname is one of the global variables of Node. It holds the path to the directory where the script resides (be careful, it depends on the script; if it is used from the module, then it refers the directory of the module, and not the initial file). Now if you put the file called about.html into the public folder inside your project, it is accessible via http://localhost/about.html. Create this file and try it out. Make a small page and make sure that Node serves it correctly.

> **NOTE:** Why do we use a special folder here and not the root of the project? There's a good security reason for that. Since your server is written in JavaScript, and JavaScript files are just another type of static content, Node happily serves the sources of the server and all its modules if you do so. Besides, it is always better to separate client scripts from the server scripts.

Now we know how to serve static files, but it still doesn't solve the problem of rendering the board. We need to pass the current board data to HTML somehow. That's where templates come in handy.

What Are Templates

A template is a special file that defines the generic structure of the document and puts in placeholders instead of actual dynamic data. Listing 10-18 shows how the template might look.

Listing 10-18. *An Example of a Template*

```
<!DOCTYPE html>
<html lang="en">
<head>
    <meta charset="utf-8" />
</head>
<body>
    <% if (user) { %>
        <h1><%= user.name %></h1>
    <% } %>
</body>
</html>
```

This is the code for EJS (https://github.com/visionmedia/ejs), one of the available template engines. Notice that the template is mostly an HTML file, so the designer will feel quite comfortable with it. Besides, the template has an embedded language that can be used for rendering purposes. In Listing 10-18, a template checks if there is a variable called user; and if so, it outputs the name of that user in <h1> tags. With EJS this language is JavaScript. As you'll see in a minute, JavaScript is not a must.

The template by itself is not enough to render an HTML page. As you see, the template is referencing the data—the variable called user that is not present in the template itself. That gives you the clear separation between the rendering logic and the rest of the application.

The component that combines the template code and the data, and outputs the HTML page is called the *template engine*. Figure 10-9 shows a high-level overview of the process.

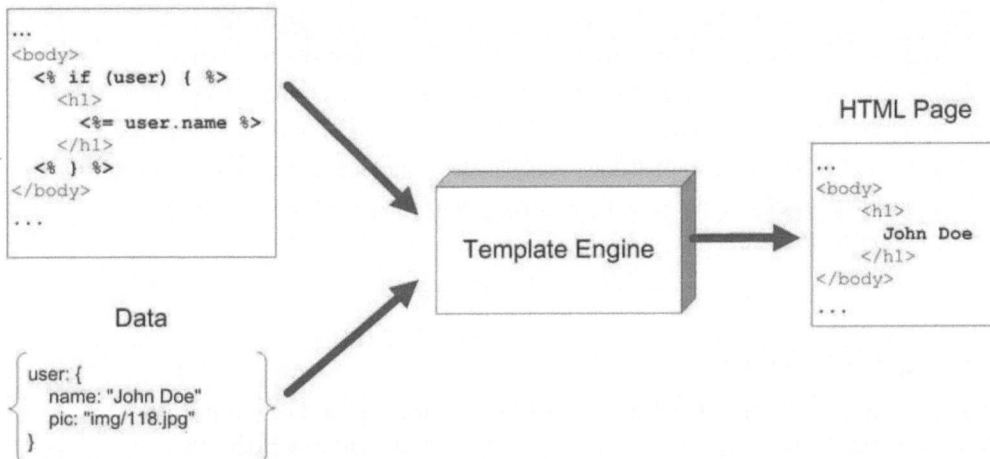

Figure 10-9. *The idea behind the templates. To produce an HTML page, a template engine needs two components: the template and the data model.*

Basically, it doesn't matter how the template code looks, as long as the engine knows how to enrich it with data and translate it into a usable form. This feature allows you to build pretty interesting template dialects that aim to make the markup look better. Listing 10-19 shows the example of a template for one of the most popular engines—jade (http://jade-lang.com).

Listing 10-19. *An Example of a Jade Template*

```
!!! 5
html(lang="en")
  head
    title= pageTitle
    script(type='text/javascript')
      if (foo) {
        bar()
```

```
      }
    body
      h1 Jade - node template engine
      #container
        - if (youAreUsingJade)
          p You are amazing
        - else
          p Get on it!
```

Node supports several template engines—Haml, Jade, EJS, CoffeeCup, and jQuery Templates. If you have a couple of spare hours, look through them and find the one that you like best.

> **NOTE:** The author of this book prefers templates that don't create a whole new language just to make a good old HTML file. There are two reasons for that: HTML is plain, simple, and here to stay: if you give an exotic template to a designer, nine out of ten will ask, "Hey, what's this?" It is important that people other than programmers be able to easily read and modify the file. The second reason is that we know JavaScript already and we like it; we can use it for templates and there is no good reason not to use it.

Creating a Template

Let's apply the knowledge about the template to our project. Let's create a template that renders the game board. First, you need to install EJS, the templating engine.

```
>npm install ejs
ejs@0.4.3 ./node_modules/ejs
```

Now create a folder called views and put a file called board.ejs there. The file itself is the EJS template. Listing 10-20 shows the complete code for the template. The most important parts are highlighted in bold.

Listing 10-20. *Rendering the Game Board with EJS Templates*

```
<!DOCTYPE html>
<html lang="en">
<head>
    <meta charset="utf-8" />
    <meta name="viewport"
        content="width=device-width, initial-scale=1.0, maximum-scale=1.0,
user-scalable=no, target-densitydpi=device-dpi"/>
    <style>
        .cell {
```

```
            display: inline;
            font-family: monospace;
            font-size: 2cm;
            cursor: pointer;
        }

        h1 {
            font-family: monospace;
        }
    </style>
</head>
<body>
    <h1>Welcome to the Four Balls!</h1>
    <div class="board">
        <% for (var i = 0; i < board.getRows(); i++) {
            for (var j = 0; j < board.getCols(); j++) {
                %><div class="cell"><%
                switch(board.getPiece(j, i)) {
                    case BoardModel.GREEN: %>X<% break;
                    case BoardModel.RED: %>O<% break;
                    default: %>-<% break;
                }
                %></div><%
            }
            %><br /><%
        } %>
    </div>
    <a href="about.html">About</a>
</body>
</html>
```

The bolded JavaScript does not appear on the page that goes to the browser. This script is used by the EJS engine to generate HTML content only. The resulting document is in plain old HTML. To distinguish between the normal HTML markup and the script, EJS uses <% %> symbols. Everything between them is interpreted; everything outside these symbols stays on the page as is.

The final part is to update our main script: we use our newly created template instead of plain text representation. We need to pass the correct data to the template to make it work, of course. Listing 10-21 shows the updated main.js file.

Listing 10-21. *The Updated Server Code That Takes Templates into Account*

```
var express = require('express');
var BoardModel = require("./BoardModel");

var app = express.createServer();

app.set('views', __dirname + '/views');
```

```
app.set('view engine', 'ejs');

app.use(app.router);
app.use(express.static(__dirname + '/public'));

var board = new BoardModel();
board.makeTurn(2);
board.makeTurn(3);

app.get('/', function(req, res){
    res.render('board', {
        BoardModel: BoardModel,
        board: board,
        layout: false
    });
});

app.listen(80);
```

A lot of changes here! First of all, there are two new lines that set two values. The method set() assigns the value to the application-level setting. This setting can be then used by various modules in order to adjust their behavior. The first bolded line sets the directory to look for templates. The second line tells Express that we are using the ejs engine to render templates. The next two lines add middleware to the server. We explicitly tell the server that we will first try to serve the request with the app.get(…) function. Only if nothing appropriate is found there do we move to static files.

The last block executes render() instead of send(). As you have guessed, render() instructs Express to take the first argument, check the current view engine, find the board.ejs file, and pass it along with the template data to the engine. The final parameter layout: false turns off the default behavior of Express, as it tries to look for the layout.ejs file and embed the actual template into it. This feature is good for a multipage site where there's actually a common structure of HTML documents. But since we have only one file, we don't need it.

Save the file and restart Node. You should see a somewhat nerdy-looking board that I've designed using my own skills and inspiration (shown in Figure 10-10). Since the template is now separated from the rest of the server, I can give it to my web designer. Even though the template has a few lines of JavaScript code, it isn't too scary.

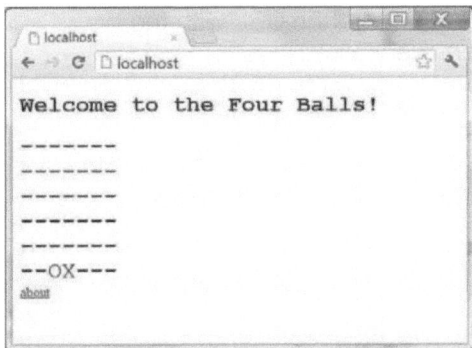

Figure 10-10. *The board rendered with template. Better give it to designer before showing to your friends.*

The code for the current state of the project can be found in the 04.templates folder along with the other code for this chapter.

Parsing User Input

Let's make this small demo playable and give the user the ability to click the column and make his move. To do that, we need to extract GET parameters from the request string and update the board afterward. Clicking the cell navigates the user to a URL like http://localhost/?turn=3. Our server checks if the parameter exists, and updates the board.

To access a parameter passed via a query string, you can use the query array of request object. The code is fairly simple, as shown in Listing 10-22.

Listing 10-22. *Accessing Query Parameters*

```
app.get('/', function(req, res) {
    var turn = req.query["turn"];
    if (!isNaN(turn)) {
        board.makeTurn(turn);
    }
    res.render('board', {
        BoardModel: BoardModel,
        board: board,
        layout: false
    });
});
```

Now, we'll have to add a minor tweak to the template (views/board.ejs file), so that clicking the cell takes the user to the correct URL. Listing 10-23 summarizes the changes. Clicking a cell brings the user to the URL with the turn parameter. The server updates the board on every click.

Listing 10-23. *Adding onclick Events*

```
<!DOCTYPE html>
<html lang="en">
<head>
    …
    <script>
        function turn(col) {
            location.href = "/?turn=" + col;
        }
    </script>
</head>
<body>
    <h1>Welcome to the Connect Four!</h1>
    <div class="board">
        <% for (var i = 0; i < board.getRows(); i++) {
            for (var j = 0; j < board.getCols(); j++) {
                %><div class="cell" onclick="turn(<%= j %>)"><%
                switch(board.getPiece(j, i)) {
                    case BoardModel.GREEN: %>X<% break;
                    case BoardModel.RED: %>O<% break;
                    default: %>-<% break;
                }
                %></div><%
            }
            %><br /><%
        } %>
    </div>
</body>
</html>
```

Now you can launch the game once again and try clicking different cells of the board. It works!

CAUTION: Those of you who know the principles of REST must be thinking, "This guy is doing it all wrong—somebody stop him." I just violated the semantics of a GET request that should not alter the state of the system. When you are designing the API or the server, your GET requests should only retrieve the data, not modify it. For modifying, we have POST. This time, I used GET to update the board only for the sake of simplicity. But what is the danger of using GET? Well, click any cell to make a turn, then refresh the browser a couple of times. That's the side effect of this poor design decision. Don't do that in real life.

There are two more ways to pass the parameter to the server: via POST (in this case it is encoded in the body of the request) and via the path itself: for example, our URL could look like `http://localhost/turn/5`; then 5 would be the parameter (`turn` could be the parameter too, by the way). If you want to read more about this trick, check out the documentation for Express (`http://expressjs.com/guide.html#route-param pre-conditions`) or read on to the next chapter—we use it there.

Working with Sessions

Right now, any user can join the game and start clicking the board because there is a single shared board for the whole server. Once you start making the real game, you need to separate the users from the games. In other words, for each playing user, you need to store the reference to the board that he's playing on. This is an easy task once you know how to work with sessions.

Sessions are a way to identify users and keep track of their actions. If you haven't worked with them before, then you should think about the session as an object that is associated with the user's browser. This object resides on the server, so the user can't change it. For example, we can keep track of how many pages the user has visited by adding a counter to the user session, and increasing it each time we serve a page for that user.

To add session support to our server, we need to use another piece of middleware: I think you're starting to see a pattern. Listing 10-24 shows the required configuration.

Listing 10-24. *Adding Session Support to the Server*

```
app.use(express.cookieParser());
app.use(express.session({ secret: "gameserversession" }));
app.use(app.router);
app.use(express.static(__dirname + '/public'));
```

That's all you need to track your users. After you add these lines, your request object that is passed to the handler function is enriched with a new field called `session`. You can add new properties and read properties that you have set before, and pass them to the templates. The example in Listing 10-25 shows how to create a new session parameter, `totalTurns`, which is increased each time the user makes a turn.

Listing 10-25. *Working with Session Parameters*

```
app.get('/', function(req, res) {
    if (!req.session.totalTurns) {
        req.session.totalTurns = 0;
    }

    var turn = req.query["turn"];
    if (!isNaN(turn)) {
        board.makeTurn(turn);
        req.session.totalTurns++;

    }
    res.render('test', {
        BoardModel: boardApi.BoardModel,
        board: board,
        totalTurns: req.session.totalTurns,
        layout: false
    });
});
```

The typical use of sessions is to distinguish between users: to support authentication and authorization when needed. The most popular use case is to check if the session has the userID property, and if it does, it means that the user is logged in and can see the restricted area of your web site. If there's no such property, it means that the user is anonymous and he should proceed to the sign-in form. When the user enters a correct login and password, his session is updated and the userID is set.

We use session to associate the user with the progress. Obviously, a real multiplayer solution must support multiple simultaneous games, and not just one as we did. So we'll use sessions to keep track of which game instance out of the many running on the server is the correct one for him. We add this feature to our game in Chapter 12.

The last important notice about the sessions: by default, session data is stored in memory, so sessions will not survive a server restart. If you want to have a more reliable solution, you should consult the Express documentation at http://expressjs.com/guide.html#session-support.

The source code for the project on its current state is available in the 05.sessions folder.

Understanding Middleware

We've used this term a lot through this chapter, so I think it's a good time to explain what it really is. Middleware is a special term that Express picked to indicate a module that can be used to filter the HTTP request somehow, and enrich req and resp variables for the next middleware. Almost everything you do in Express happens in one of these nice little modules. To better understand them, it is useful to think about them as layers (see Figure 10-11).

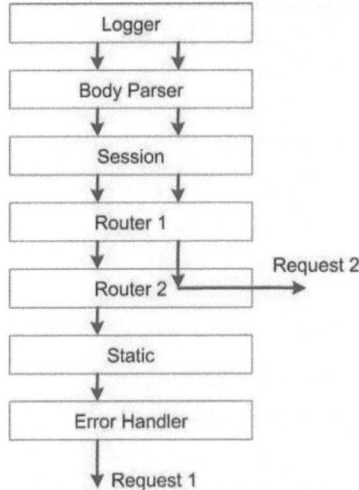

Figure 10-11. *Layers of middleware. Requests go through each "layer" that does a specific task. Request processing can stop on a certain layer or go through all of them.*

Each new request is passed to the first level. It can stop and return there, or pass to the next level, and so forth. As you have seen, middleware sometimes relies on the result of the previous layers. For example, our get handler needed a session to work correctly. If we put it *above* the sessions—we will not have session data available at the time when it is called. The same is true for sessions themselves. Sessions need cookies to be parsed. Cookies store the session ID of the current user, and without it, we can't load the user's session data. Sessions can't work without cookies being parsed by one of the previous layers. This means that the cookieParser middleware *must* be placed before the session middleware.

The typical middleware stack looks like Listing 10-26.

Listing 10-26. *A Typical Middleware Stack of a node.js Server*

```
app.use(express.logger(...));      // Similar to access log of Apache HTTP server.
app.use(express.bodyParser(...));  // Extracts whatever useful is stored in the request
                                   //body (usually POST requests)

app.use(express.cookieParser(...)); // Parses cookies and populate req.cookies
app.use(express.session(...));      // Enables session support and
                                    //populates session and sessionStore
```

```
app.use(app.router);                 // Executes router functions
app.use(express.static(...));        // Serves static files
app.use(express.errorHandler(...));  // Reports exceptions if any
```

You have a certain amount of control over the execution of other layers of middleware. This control is given to you via the next() function, which is usually passed as the third parameter to your callbacks. Before this point, we were ignoring the third parameter:

```
app.get('/', function(req, res) {
...
});
```

To receive the callback, simply add a parameter like this:

```
app.get('/', function(req, res, next) {
...
});
```

The execution of the request stops on the middleware that decided *not to call* next. Ignoring next means that the middleware decided to return the result, and it doesn't want to pass the execution to lower levels.

Take a look at Listing 10-27, which demonstrates how this trick can be used to implement some crazy content filtering. Let's say that there's a very special static page that we will show only to the user who has taken at least ten turns. We could add a route to match that page address and check the security restriction in it.

Listing 10-27. *Passing Control Through Layers*

```
app.get('/prize.html', function(req, res, next) {
    if (req.session.totalTurns && req.session.totalTurns > 10) {
        next();
    } else {
        res.send("Not enough clicks yet!");
    }
});
```

When the router receives a request to /prize.html, it checks for the number of turns that the user made. This value is stored in the session. If the value is more than ten, we simply call next(). By doing so, we allow other middleware to do its work. Otherwise, if the number of clicks is not enough, we simply handle the request ourselves. Since we don't call next(), the request processing stops here and static middleware will not even know that the user was trying to get the page. This trick is only possible when your router stands above static in the stack. Otherwise, you will not be able to filter requests, since static serves the content before you do it.

If you encounter an error in your layer of middleware and decide to let it go, you should pass the error as an argument to the next function. The error is then caught and processed by one of the registered error handlers. Read on to learn how it works.

Housekeeping

The final part of this chapter is devoted to the small but useful housekeeping tasks that every web server should do: logging, error reporting, and support for different environments. You probably noticed a couple of new bits of middleware in the previous section: `logger` and `errorHandler`. Let's look at them to finalize our acquaintance with the Express framework.

Reporting Errors

Both logging and reporting are pretty important tasks—it is impossible to imagine a serious web server that is running in a production environment and ignores at least one of the two. We start with the error reporting system and write some code that will do something wrong and produce the error (see Listing 10-28). That's the easy part—introducing bugs are so much easier than solving them!

Listing 10-28. *Creating Artificial Error to Show How It Is Handled by the Server*

```
var express = require('express');
var app = express.createServer();

app.set('views', __dirname + '/views');
app.set('view engine', 'ejs');

app.use(express.cookieParser());
app.use(express.session({ secret: "gameserversession" }));
app.use(app.router);
app.use(express.static(__dirname + '/public'));

app.get('/', function(req, res) {
    var foo = {};
    var bar = foo["bar"].baz;
    res.send("This shouldn't be visible");
});

app.listen(80);
```

Obviously, trying to access the property of undefined must break something. Run the server and run the request. The error message is passed to the console as well as rendered on the web page. For my environment, the stack trace looks like the following:

```
TypeError: Cannot read property 'baz' of undefined
    at C:\apps\projects\jsbook\chap10\err.js:18:25
    at callbacks
(C:\apps\projects\jsbook\chap10\node_modules\express\lib\router\index.js:272:11)
    at param
(C:\apps\projects\jsbook\chap10\node_modules\express\lib\router\index.js:246:11)
    at pass
(C:\apps\projects\jsbook\chap10\node_modules\express\lib\router\index.js:253:5)
    at Router._dispatch
(C:\apps\projects\jsbook\chap10\node_modules\express\lib\router\index.js:280:4)
    at Object.handle
(C:\apps\projects\jsbook\chap10\node_modules\express\lib\router\index.js:45:10)
    at next
```

Errors like that might look fine for a developer, but they certainly won't do for production, for two reasons. First off, the error report is obviously not user-friendly. Your end user doesn't need to know what exactly went wrong and which lines of code were involved in breaking the server. The only thing that user really needs to know is that something has happened and your application can't process the request. He should probably try once again—the error might be temporary, after all.

It is also good to tell the user, "While you are reading this, the error report is already being investigated by our support team, and we're doing our best to fix it." The attention to such small details is the key to making your project look solid. The stack trace in the browser window makes your system look completely broken, as if its internal wires and gearwheels are staring at the user through a hole in the hull. At the same time, a nice custom page makes you feel like the error is nothing really serious. Hey, we're game developers—we must make fun error pages! For some inspiration on error page design, look at github's 404 page (see Figure 10-12) at `https://github.com/404`.

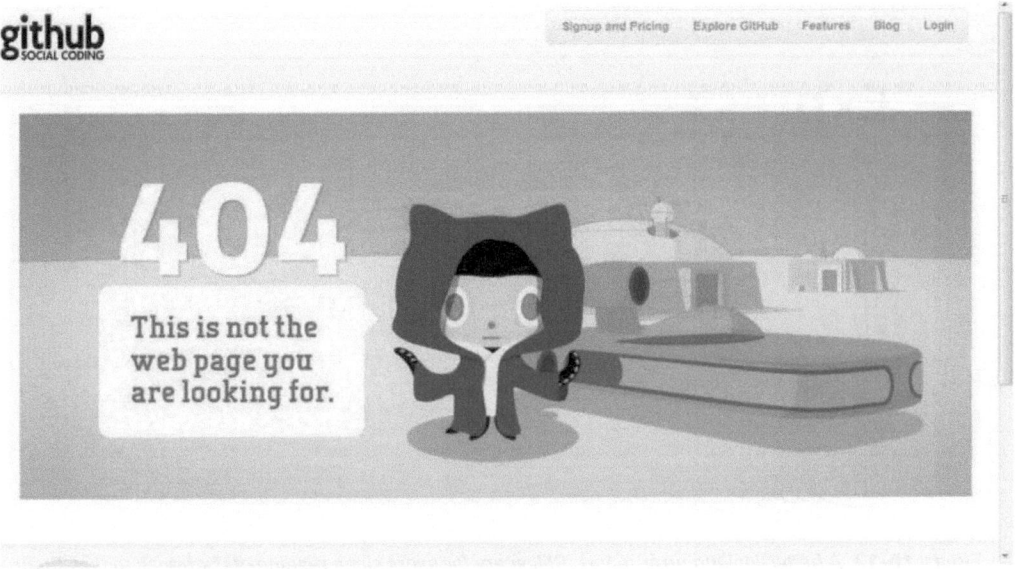

Figure 10-12. *An example of a great error page that has some dynamic features. When you move the mouse around it, it feels "alive" thanks to a simple parallax effect.*

The second problem with the default error handling is that the error is not reported anywhere but in the log. Imagine that your friend is calling you and he says, "Hey, I've just tried to play your great new online game, but it shows a fancy error screen when I enter the fey forest." If you leave the default error handling, you will not even know what has happened—the error only goes to the console. This is not considered to be a reliable way to report such important information. Sure, you can save the console output to a log file, but you'll have to read through it regularly in order to check if everything is still fine. Trust me, you'll be too lazy to do it sooner or later. Programmers are lazy—this is one of our virtues. What if you can say to your friend, "Thanks for reporting. I'm already looking into it. I got the report on my e-mail." This all is doable with Express.

The first step is to add the `errorHandler` middleware that can be configured to show a better-looking (but still geek-friendly) error page in the browser. Add the following line to the end of your middleware list:

```
app.use(express.errorHandler());
```

This middleware is only intended for the development phase. Figure 10-13 shows how the exception screen will look.

Express

500 TypeError: Cannot read property 'baz' of undefined

at C:\apps\projects\jsbook\chap8\err.js:19:25

at callbacks (C:\apps\projects\jsbook\chap8\node_modules\express\lib\router\index.js:272:11)

at param (C:\apps\projects\jsbook\chap8\node_modules\express\lib\router\index.js:246:11)

at pass (C:\apps\projects\jsbook\chap8\node_modules\express\lib\router\index.js:253:5)

at Router._dispatch (C:\apps\projects\jsbook\chap8\node_modules\express\lib\router\index.js:280:4)

at Object.handle (C:\apps\projects\jsbook\chap8\node_modules\express\lib\router\index.js:45:10)

at next (C:\apps\projects\jsbook\chap8\node_modules\express\node_modules\connect\lib\http.js:203:15)

at C:\apps\projects\jsbook\chap8\node_modules\express\node_modules\connect\lib\middleware\session.js:323:9

at C:\apps\projects\jsbook\chap8\node_modules\express\node_modules\connect\lib\middleware\session.js:338:9

at Array.0
(C:\apps\projects\jsbook\chap8\node_modules\express\node_modules\connect\lib\middleware\session\memory.js:57:7)

Figure 10-13. *A better-looking error report. Still scary for users since reading stack traces makes them think their computer will explode.*

For the production environment, we should provide a better error page. If you register an arbitrary four-argument function to the use() method, it is treated as the error handler and works as middleware. It is fully integrated into the life cycle and can decide if it wants to handle a certain error itself or pass it to the next layer. Listing 10-29 illustrates how multiple error-handling middleware might work together.

Listing 10-29. *Adding Custom Error-Handling Middleware*

```
app.use(express.cookieParser());
app.use(express.session({ secret: "gameserversession" }));
app.use(app.router);
app.use(express.static(__dirname + '/public'));
app.use(function(err, req, res, next) {
    if (canHandleMyself()) {
        res.render("error", {layout: false});
    } else {
        // Pass to the standard errorHandler middleware defined below
        next(err);
    }
});
app.use(express.errorHandler());
```

The code in the example is very simple, but it implements a useful functionality: it hides the scary details of the error from the user and shows a fancy error page. With the current setup, it looks for the error.ejs file in the views folder and renders it instead of the default errors. I leave it up to you to design the error page that you like. The canHandleMyself() is the function that you implement yourself. If you don't need several layers of error-handlers, feel free to rewrite the code so that it returns the custom error page all the time.

```
app.use(function(err, req, res, next) {
    res.render("error", {layout: false});
});
```

Now we're coming to the final task of saving the error somewhere and notifying the support team about the error. I show you how to write an exception to the log file in the next section of this chapter, along with other logger-related issues. Let's move to notifications for the support team. The most obvious choice is to send an e-mail. As usual for such a typical task, there's a module that does it already. It is called nodemailer (https://github.com/andris9/Nodemailer). You install it by running

```
npm install nodemailer
```

and then use it like in Listing 10-30.

Listing 10-30. *Using Mailer to Notify Support Team About the Error*

```
var express = require("express");
var email = require("nodemailer");

var app = express.createServer();

app.set('views', __dirname + '/views');
app.set('view engine', 'ejs');

app.use(express.cookieParser());
app.use(express.session({ secret: "gameserversession" }));
app.use(app.router);
app.use(express.static(__dirname + '/public'));

// Send the email to the team
app.use(function(err, req, res, next) {
    res.render("error", {layout: false});
    var transport = nodemailer.createTransport("SMTP", {
        service: "Gmail",
        auth: {
            user: "juriy.bura@gmail.com",
            pass: "mysecretpass"          // No, this is not my real password
        }
    });
    transport.sendMail({
        from : "node@juriy.com",        // from
        to : "juriy.bura@gmail.com",    // to
        subject : "Error report",       // subject
```

```
        body: "We got error here!\n" + err.stack // error description
    }, function(error, responseStatus){
        if(error){
            console.log("ERROR " + error);
        } else {
            console.log(responseStatus.message); // response from the server
        }
    });
});

// Render a nice page to the user
app.use(function(err, req, res, next) {
    res.render("error", {layout: false});
});

app.get('/', function(req, res) {
    res.send("Here's the page");
});

app.listen(80);
```

That's it! Now the error reporting of your application is (almost) commercial grade! If you want more fun, search NPM for other modules, post to Twitter, send Jabber messages, connect to SMS services, and send bugs directly to your phone—it is all up to you now.

The last but most important pitfall of error processing: never, ever, allow any exception to fall from your error reporting code. Express swallows the original error and reports the new error to the underlying middleware instead.

Logging

The other important aspect of the application is logging - writing the usage information to the console or a file. The default logging facilities of Express are rather poor, but are enough for us. The simplest setup is to add the logging middleware on top of your stack:

```
app.use(express.logger());
```

Once this is done, you'll see much more output from your application in the console. Every request is logged now.

```
127.0.0.1 - - [Mon, 14 Nov 2011 22:35:11 GMT] "GET / HTTP/1.1" 500 - "-"
"Mozilla/5.0 (Windows NT 6.1; WOW64) AppleWebKit/535.7 (KHTML, like Gecko)
Chrome/16.0.912.36 Safari/535.7"
127.0.0.1 - - [Mon, 14 Nov 2011 22:35:11 GMT] "GET /favicon.ico HTTP/1.1" 404 -
"-" "Mozilla/5.0 (Windows NT 6.1; WOW64) AppleWebKit/535.7 (KHTML, like Gecko)
Chrome/16.0.912.36 Safari/535.7"
```

```
127.0.0.1 - - [Mon, 14 Nov 2011 22:35:12 GMT] "GET / HTTP/1.1" 500 - "-"
"Mozilla/5.0 (Windows NT 6.1; WOW64) AppleWebKit/535.7 (KHTML, like Gecko)
Chrome/16.0.912.36 Safari/535.7"
```

There's a lot of information in these lines: host, time, request, status, user agent, and so forth. If you don't need such verbose information, change the "format" of logger. Format is the string made of several tokens, each representing a bit of information. The following is an example of a format line that prints only the HTTP method, the URL of the page, and the amount of time spent for processing it:

```
app.use(express.logger({
    format: ":method :url - :response-time ms"
}));
```

If you pass that line to the logger, you'll get a much nicer (but of course, less informative) output.

```
GET / - 5 ms
GET /favicon.ico - 3 ms
GET / - 4 ms
GET /favicon.ico - 3 ms
```

The list of possible tokens can be found at the page with the Connect documentation—http://extjs.github.com/Connect/logger.html (remember, Express uses Connect's middleware).

Writing to the console is not the best decision when it comes to production. It is much better to write to a file. Doing so is a little tricky. Connect's logger doesn't have a way to pass the name of the file directly, but it rather accepts something called stream. In terms of Node.js, it is the writable stream—anything that you can write to—TCP/IP socket, file, Unix socket, console, whatever (see http://nodejs.org/docs/api/streams.html). In order to send the logger's output to a file, you need to open a stream on it and pass it to the logger. Listing 10-31 shows how this is done.

Listing 10-31. *Writing Logs to a File*

```
var express = require("express");
var email = require("mailer");
var fs = require("fs");

var fileStream = fs.createWriteStream(__dirname + "/node.log",
    { flags: 'a',
      encoding: "UTF-8" });

var app = express.createServer();

app.set('views', __dirname + '/views');
app.set('view engine', 'ejs');
```

```
app.use(express.logger({
    format: ":method :url - :response-time ms",
    stream: fileStream
}));
```

In the third line, we load the `fs` module that allows us to work with the filesystem. Then we create the `WriteStream`, giving the file name and a set of parameters that indicate how exactly we want the file to be opened.

The "flags" indicate that the file is open for writing and the cursor is placed at the end of the file. This way, your log survives server restarts. Finally, we pass the created stream to the logger middleware and enjoy the result.

Of course, you can write to the same file yourself. Listing 10-32 is an example of an error-handler that saves the stack in the file, as I promised.

Listing 10-32. *Writing the Error Information to the Same Log File*

```
// Write logs
app.use(function(err, req, res, next) {
        fileStream.write(err.stack);
        next(err);
    }
);
```

We're almost done with the housekeeping, but we have only one small task left: supporting different server configurations. Usually enterprise-grade servers have quite a few configuration files that describe a dozen different environments: development, testing, preproduction, production, and so forth. The motivation is quite simple: you want different server features to be enabled in different configurations.

Server Configurations

We decided to hide the error messages from the user, but we don't want to hide them from ourselves. When you write a lot of code and test changes every minute, you want to see error traces immediately, without having to look at the console. In other words, you want this "nice page" feature on production but not in the development environment. Most likely, you don't want to spam yourself with letters, and you don't need logs either.

Obviously, you want to switch server modes without having to write even a line of code (we're all lazy, remember). This task is usually solved by adding support for configuration files, but Express has a more lightweight mechanism for that. Node has reserved a special environmental variable called NODE_ENV to hold the identifier of the environment. There are two "magic" values for it: development (the value that is used by default) and production (that enables the "production mode").

Express has a function called configure that allows you to define the parts of the configuration that are executed only in specific environments. Listing 10-33 shows the code fragment for the "production" configuration.

Listing 10-33. *An Example of Environment-Specific Configuration*

```
// For production we want logs to be written to the file and have the verbose format
app.configure("production", function() {
    loggerStream = fs.createWriteStream(__dirname + "/node.log", { flags: 'a'});
    app.use(express.logger({
        format: "default",
        stream: loggerStream
    }));
});
```

This way, the code that initializes logging is executed only in the "production" environment—when you explicitly set the NODE_ENV to production. By default, Express simply ignores this part. If the configure function is used without arguments, it is called for any available environment.

Now you have the tool to define the different behaviors of your server for different modes of operation. Take a look at the following complete code, which illustrates this idea (I've stripped the code of long functions to save some space):

```
var express = require("express");
var BoardModel = require("./BoardModel");
var nodemailer = require("nodemailer");
var fs = require("fs");

var loggerStream;
var app = express.createServer();

// Every environment has the same settings for views
app.configure(function() {
    app.set('views', __dirname + '/views');
    app.set('view engine', 'ejs');
});

// For production we want logs to be written to the file and have the verbose format
app.configure("production", function() {
    loggerStream = fs.createWriteStream(__dirname + "/node.log", { flags: 'a'});
    app.use(express.logger({
        format: "default",
        stream: loggerStream
    }));
});
```

```
// For development, we don't use logger at all

// Main stack is the same for both environments
app.configure(function() {
    app.use(express.cookieParser());
    app.use(express.session({ secret: "gameserversession" }));
    app.use(app.router);
    app.use(express.static(__dirname + '/public'));
});

// Write logs and hide pages - only for production
app.configure("production", function() {
    app.use(function(err, req, res, next) {
            loggerStream.write(err.stack);
            next(err);
        }
    );

    // Send the email to the team
    app.use(function(err, req, res, next) {
        /* Email code */
        next(err);
    });

    // Render a nice page to the user
    app.use(function(err, req, res, next) {
        res.render("error", {layout: false});
    });
});

// Development is fine with the standard error handling
app.configure("development", function() {
    app.use(express.errorHandler({stack: true, dump: true}));
});

app.get('/', function(req, res) {
    // Generate the error to see the flow.
    // On production you should see the nice error page designed
    // for users. On development you'll see the stack trace on the web page
    // and on the console
    var foo = req["bar"].baz;
    res.send("Here's the page");
});

app.listen(80);
```

Sometimes you want to use a different source for an "environment" setting—a configuration file or your special command-line option, for example. In this case, you can always override this value by calling

```
app.set("env", "production");
```

The environment switch feature is rather nice, but the truth is you need it only when you are really going into the production phase, meaning that you're going to show the application to someone besides your friends. Before that, you should just remember that you have this feature at your disposal and use a single development environment, as we did for most of the chapter.

The result of this chapter is available in the directory called 06.housekeeping. Don't forget to replace the e-mail settings to your own if you want to test mail notifications.

Summary

In this chapter, we moved from client-side development to server-side without switching languages. We learned a great and fast-evolving tool called Node.js that allows us to run JavaScript code as if it is the native code of the operating system. Node.js allowed us to create a web server and implement very basic user interaction. What is more important: we've learned the basic building blocks of server-side programming that we'll use in the next chapters to build a full-blown multiplayer application—a game of Four Balls with some pretty advanced features.

We also learned one of the most popular and powerful web development frameworks for Node.js called Express. We started with a simple Hello World application and gradually increased the set of features. We learned how to handle query parameters (user input), how to keep track of the user's activity with sessions, and how to separate the logic of the server from the HTML views with template engines.

We took a small tour into the architecture of Express, and learned about the different middleware that encapsulates small sets of functionality: cookies, query parsing, logging, sessions, and so forth. We learned about the middleware stack and how the request is processed by it.

Finally, we did some housekeeping tasks: we studied the error handling, logging, and configurations of Express. Now we are ready to continue. With the knowledge that we've acquired, we can start building a multiplayer client that uses Ajax to fetch data from the server and send information about the user's actions—like clicks, chat messages, or match game proposals.

Talking to the Server

After reading the previous chapter, you are ready to create a game server and provide a decent infrastructure around it with templates, error handling, and logging. To build a real multiplayer application, however, a server is not enough. The second essential part of the networking architecture is the client. The goal of this chapter is to provide a good level of knowledge of networking from the client's perspective. In order to do that, we will learn the following:

  ▪ How to load the data from the server without having to reload a web page

  ▪ A newer version of the XMLHttpRequest object called XHR Level 2

  ▪ How to load binary data from the server and parse it on the client side

  ▪ The limitations of mobile devices

  ▪ A few things about *reverse Ajax* and the options available to implement real-time client-server communication

  ▪ The definition of a *transport* and the types of trade-offs involved when a developer chooses a transport for his game

We will start this chapter by taking a brief look into the evolution of networking: from historical APIs to cutting-edge technologies that will be available in the near future. Afterward, we will be ready for tasks that are more sophisticated: exploring different ways of communication between the client and the server, and building real-time solutions that support sending messages in both directions.

The Evolution of Networking in Browsers

Let's take a (very) short history course to see how networking has helped web applications become what they are now, the kind of problems developers faced, and how most of these problems were solved.

In the early years, web browsers were programs that could only render plain HTML pages, follow links, download and display images, and provide a few utility functions like searching and bookmarking. Nobody thought about a browser as an environment for building rich applications or games. The regular pattern of using the web was to

- Load a page
- Read through its content
- Click a link, type an address in the address bar, or reload the page if new content is desired

Clearly, this model gave total control over the web page to the user; without his explicit action, the content remains the same. This model is perfect for passive surfing and exploring static data. For example, a web site that allows the user to read the chapters of a book can work without any dynamic features like JavaScript and Ajax; it remains readable and user-friendly.

There are many examples when this model is not sufficient for comfortable surfing, however. Reloading the web page means reloading every bit of it; in some cases, this may be redundant and wasteful. Imagine a page that has a hierarchical menu on the left-hand side. If all pages were static, clicking the menu item to expand it would cause the whole page to reload. Even if traffic is not an issue, the process of rendering the page from scratch is distracting to the user—at the very least, the page blinks.

This model had to "expire" eventually. Indeed, its practical use involved a lot of overhead, and even basic interactive applications like chat or web games were impossible to implement when there was no way to load new data from the server without reloading the page. Then Ajax appeared on the scene.

Ajax is a technology that allows loading server data without reloading the web page. It was first implemented by Microsoft as a small component called XMLHTTP. Later, XMLHttpRequest made it possible to query the server, receive the response, and update only the part of the page that needs to be updated.

Ajax felt like the natural evolution of the web—allowing a web page to execute HTTP requests without reloading allowed developers to create a whole new world of web applications; far more sophisticated web pages where the interaction between the user and the browser isn't just a by-product of the surfing process. Of course, it was possible to make a dynamic web page even before Ajax appeared—for example, by loading the never-ending stream of content into the IFRAME—but these techniques were only hacks: they lacked reliability and good cross-browser support.

> **NOTE:** Strictly speaking, AJAX is an acronym for Asynchronous JavaScript and XML. Acronyms are typically spelled in uppercase. However, this word has become a common noun and most online media spell it as Ajax. In this book, I will use the second naming approach.
>
> Ajax is not a standard, an implementation, or the name of an API. It is a buzzword that developers use for any approach that involves loading data from the server without reloading the page. We look at an example of an Ajax call later in this chapter.

Ajax has its own limitations, and the main one is HTTP itself. HTTP is the request-response protocol where the communication between the client and the server follow a predefined order:

1. The client sends a request describing exactly what it wants to read or update.

2. The server analyzes the request, forms a response, and sends it back to the client.

3. The connection is closed.

4. To send another fragment of data, the client has to initiate a new connection.

The server cannot send the message to the client by itself: this model of communication assumes that the server only *responds* to the *requests* from the page. The weaknesses of plain old Ajax is easy to understand when you use an example. Imagine that you are writing a multiplayer game that has an internal mail system. At some point, the server receives a new mail message that it needs to deliver to the user: we want to show a blinking "new mail" icon in the corner of the screen. Even though the server now has the new data for the user, it cannot do anything with it because the server cannot initiate the new connection with the page. Instead, the server has to wait patiently for the new Ajax request, and only then respond with the new update. The obvious drawback of this model is that clients have to constantly poll the server to check whether there is a new message for them (more about this model and its problems in the next section of the chapter).

Rich applications, especially games, often require better networking. They need a connection that works like TCP/IP: once the page opens it, it stays open, and either party (client and server) can send their messages at any time and in any order. Using a connection like that, the server could instantly send the mail notification to the client and not have to wait for a new request from the page.

The next logical step of evolution was WebSocket, a technology to fill the gap of real-time, two-way communication between the web page and the server. WebSocket allows you to open a real TCP connection and send data without any HTTP overhead. Technologies like this one are pushing the whole area of HTML5 game development forward, opening possibilities that were unthinkable just a few years ago.

> **NOTE:** On the Android platform, WebSocket is only available in Chrome for Android. The absence of WebSocket in the standard browser is the reason for thousands of complaints coming from Android web developers. To make matters worse, iOS, Android's main competitor, already supports it. There is no doubt that the Android stock browser *will* support it eventually, but for now, we just have to wait.

WebSocket is exactly what web application developers wanted from the very start: a persistent two-way connection that is capable of sending messages with minimal overhead and latency. Games need it more than any other application since gaming is where latency is critical. If you have a chat application and the chat message arrives with a 200-millisecond delay, you are running a perfect chat, and your users will love it! If you're about to make a real-time 3D shooter, that kind of latency is far too long—the game will appear inaccurate or choppy since 200 milliseconds is the difference between hitting your target and hitting the wall behind him.

Web developers and browser vendors have invented many different techniques to build a reliable solution for client-server communication. These techniques are called *transports*. WebSocket and Ajax polling are two different transports, both of them serving the same goal: to get the updates from the server back to the client as soon as possible. Many libraries hide the details of transports under an abstraction layer, so that developers don't have to worry about implementation details like error handling or restoring broken connections.

Server Setup

Most examples from this chapter and the next require a server to run. Feel free to take the server code from the previous chapter as your starting point for the examples, or write a ten-line express application from scratch. We will omit the code from the housekeeping section of the previous chapter. Instead, we will concentrate on the actual functionality, and keep listings small. Remember that this is not an option for a production environment: you should return to Chapter 10 before bringing your project to the public and reviewing it once again. Listing 11-1 is the starting point for the server.

Listing 11-1. *Basic Server Code Used in This Chapter*

```
var express = require("express");
var app = express.createServer();

app.set('views', __dirname + '/views');
app.set('view engine', 'ejs');

app.use(express.bodyParser());
app.use(express.cookieParser());
app.use(express.session({ secret: "gameserversession" }));
app.use(app.router);
app.use(express.static(__dirname + '/public'));
app.use(express.errorHandler());

app.get('/', function(req, res) {
    res.sendfile(__dirname + "/public/index.html");
});

app.listen(80);
```

Using XMLHttpRequest API for Basic HTTP Requests

All major browsers provide the XMLHttpRequest object as the supposed and standard way of making HTTP requests from the web page to the server. You have most likely used it already: either directly creating a new instance yourself, or indirectly via the abstraction layers provided by JavaScript libraries like jQuery or Prototype.js.

> **NOTE:** As W3C admits, the name of this object is rather misleading: *"First, the object supports any text-based format, including XML. Second, it can be used to make requests over both HTTP and HTTPS (...) Finally, it supports "requests" in a broad sense of the term as it pertains to HTTP; namely all activity involved with HTTP requests or responses for the defined HTTP methods."*
> —www.w3.org/TR/XMLHttpRequest/

The `XMLHttpRequest` API comes in two versions: the regular older version that most browsers provide, and the new `XMLHttpRequest` Level 2 version that adds plenty of new and very useful features to the original API.

> **NOTE:** `XMLHttpRequest` is often shortened to XHR. I use both names in this book interchangeably. `XMLHttpRequest` Level 2 is another, very long name for the API, which is why it is often shortened to Level 2, XHR Level 2, or even XHR2. The last name is somewhat misleading since it looks like we're speaking about a different object, so I use the other two versions.

The Level 2 specification (www.w3.org/TR/XMLHttpRequest2) doesn't define a completely different interface, but rather extends the existing one by adding support for transferring files to the server, sending and receiving binary data, tracking the upload progress, and adding better life-cycle notifications. This means that all code written for the "original" `XMLHttpRequest` also works in the Level 2 version.

Even though the specification has been in a "working draft" state since 2008 (the earliest and least-mature state of the document according to the W3C process), most browsers have already implemented the new features (http://caniuse.com/xhr2). The Android stock browser is among them, starting with Android 3.0. At the time of writing, the market share of devices that have Android 3.0 or higher is not enough to safely drop the old API and move to Level 2, but it is only a matter of time. I highlight both old and new API in this section so that you can shift to a new implementation once the market is ready for it.

HTTP Request with Plain Old XHR

`XMLHttpRequest` object is the basis of most methods to add networking to a web page. Nowadays, it is hard to find a web page that doesn't use it for dynamically checking forms, loading pieces of UI on demand, or implementing other kinds of logic. XMLHttpRequest was standardized in 2006, but since then, web applications have become much more sophisticated and demanding. Based on previous experience, W3C is working on the new standard (XMLHttpRequest Level 2) that aims to resolve the problems of the original implementation.

Let's start with a very basic Hello World example. We will send the GET request to the server and print the response to the console. In this section, we will use the old approach (before Level 2). Take a look at the web page code in Listing 11-2, and the server-side code that supplies the data in Listing 11-3.

Listing 11-2. *Sending XHR Request To Retrieve Textual Data from the Server*

```
function init() {
    var xhr = new XMLHttpRequest();
    xhr.onreadystatechange = function (e) {
        if (xhr.readyState == 4) {
            console.log("Got " + xhr.status +
                " saying [" + xhr.responseText + "]");
        }
    };
    xhr.open("GET", "data.json");
    xhr.send();
}
```

Listing 11-3. *Server Code That Supplies the Data to the Request from Listing 11-2*

```
app.get("/data.json", function(req, res) {
    res.contentType("application/json");
    res.send(JSON.stringify({hello: "World"}));
});
```

Launch the example, and look at the output. It should print this single line to the console:

```
Got 200 saying [{"hello":"World"}]
```

The client-side function looks quite similar to the code that we used to download the images from the server (Chapter 4). The major difference is that we receive a textual response instead of an image. Additionally, onreadystatechange has some extra code that checks the current state of the request: the function does the actual data processing only if the readyState of the XHR object is 4; otherwise, it simply returns, ignoring the call.

XMLHttpRequest (even the old version) supports a more fine-grained control over the life cycle of the HTTP request, compared to the Image object, which only indicates if the image has loaded successfully or if there has been an error. The browser calls onreadystatechange for every change in the state of

XMLHttpRequest. The state itself is stored in the property called `readyState`, which we check inside the body of a function.

The state "4" means `DONE`. When the object's state is `DONE`, it means that XHR has reached the last phase of its life cycle and the text of the response is fully available (in the case of a successful call). The states are as follows:

- UNSENT (0): The object has been constructed, but the `open()` method hasn't yet been called. At this point, there has been no network activity.

- OPENED (1): After the call to open method but before the call to send. Network communication has not started yet.

- HEADERS_RECEIVED (2): After the send has been called, the redirects resolved, and the server has sent its headers. The network communication is in progress, but the response is not yet available.

- LOADING (3): The response body is downloading from the server.

- DONE (4): The response body is downloaded and available.

In the most cases, the only state that you check against is state 4. Use the code from Listings 11-2 and 11-3 to update the client (`public/index.html file`) and the server (`main.js file`), and then run the example. The full source for this example is available under the `01.XHR` folder along with the other materials for this chapter.

Handling Errors with XHR

If there was an error during the execution of the request, the object still ends up in the `DONE` state, but the response data (the HTTP response code, headers, and response body) may not be available. A slightly better version of the code that explicitly checks for an error looks like what's in Listing 11-4.

Listing 11-4. *An Updated Version of Listing 11-2 That Checks for the Errors*

```
function init() {
    var xhr = new XMLHttpRequest();
    xhr.onreadystatechange = function (e) {
        if (xhr.readyState == 4) {
            if (xhr.status == 200) {
                console.log("Got " + xhr.status +
                " saying [" + xhr.responseText + "]");
            } else {
```

```
                    console.log("Got error " + xhr.status + "
                    saying [" + xhr.statusText + "]");
                }
            }
        };
        xhr.open("GET", "no.json");
        xhr.send();
    }
```

This version of the code is somewhat better. Before reporting that the request was successful, it checks the HTTP status code returned by server. 200 is the code for OK— the normal successful response. This way, the XHR call treats all server-side problems as errors, so they won't go completely unnoticed. When the code from Listing 11-4 is launched with the default server that doesn't know how to treat the request for /no.json, for example, it prints the following message to the console:

```
http://localhost/:27 Got error 404 saying [Not Found]
```

This message has enough detail to describe and diagnose the problem: the server sent the response code 404, which indicates that the given resource could not be found. Sometimes, however, this check is not enough. If there's a networking problem or if the user aborted the request by calling xhr.abort(), the status line is less informative:

```
Got error 0 saying []
```

If the server had no chance to process the request, or even see it, both the HTTP status code and the status text are undefined, making it impossible to tell what exactly went wrong. There is no way to diagnose the root cause of a problem programmatically from JavaScript. XHR API allows you to distinguish between two types of errors: *server error* and *any other error*. Obviously, "any other error" is too broad a description to rely on— loss of network connection, failed DNS lookup, too many redirects or programmatic aborts—any of these and many other problems fall into the same category.

The chance of seeing one of these problems is significantly lower than the usual 404 or 503 status codes; if the browser could load the web page itself, it means that the web server was available at that time and the bandwidth was strong enough for initial content. Usually it means that Ajax requests will complete fine too. The chance is slightly higher for mobile games though, mainly because of the quality of mobile internet that highly depends on the environment (if the user runs down to his concrete cellar, he'll probably lose the signal).

Hint: there are several ways to check how your application will work in low connectivity. The simplest way to test the networking problems is to abort your requests randomly. The second technique is to abort the connection from the server-side without writing back any data, as follows:

```
app.get("/no.json", function(req, res) {
    req.socket.end();
    req.socket.destroy();
});
```

In more sophisticated cases (for example, when you want to test low-bandwidth connections, packet loss, etc.), you should use special network emulation software.

XMLHttpRequest Level 2

The new Level 2 specification has added some missing features to XHR objects, including better event handlers, support for sending and receiving binary data, support for file uploads, and tracking upload progress, among others. In this section, we compare the old API with Level 2 by using two examples: a regular HTTP request and a binary request. Both of these tasks are extremely important for game development. Even though both tasks are doable with the old API, Level 2 looks more convenient and doesn't require any hacks.

Let's look at the code, shown in Listing 11-5, of the same Hello World application—but updated to use some features of the new version of XHR.

Listing 11-5. *The Level 2 Version of the Hello World Request*

```
function init() {
    var xhr = new XMLHttpRequest();

    xhr.onload = function(e) {
        if (xhr.status == 200) {
            console.log("Got response saying [" + xhr.responseText + "]");
        } else {
            console.log("Got server error " + xhr.status +
                " saying [" + xhr.statusText + "]");
        }
    };

    xhr.onerror = function(e) {
        console.log("Got network error");
    };

    xhr.onabort = function(e) {
        console.log("Request is explicitly aborted");
    };
```

```
    xhr.open("GET", "data.json");
    xhr.send();
}
```

This solution is certainly better than the original version. There are three different callbacks for handling the outcomes of the HTTP request:

- onload, for the regular outcome when the HTTP call is completed normally (the response code is not taken into the account, so both 200 and 503 codes are treated as normal);

- onabort, when the user aborts the request; and

- onerror, when a network error occurs.

The main advantage of this code is that it is easier to read and it's the first step toward better-quality error reporting. In XMLHttpRequest Level 2, abort is treated as a separate event.

Level 2 has a lot more to give than fine-grained callbacks, and one of the most important new features is the ability to handle binary data.

Working with Binary Data

Being able to handle binary data is extremely useful for game development. Game resources such as 3D models are often saved in binary formats either for historical reasons or to save traffic and keep the size of the assets small. Before XHR Level 2, there was no standard way to do it. The only possible solution relied on the custom function overrideMimeType(). This approach is illustrated in Listing 11-6.

Listing 11-6. *Loading Binary Data with the Original XMLHttpRequest (Custom charset Hack)*

```
function init() {
    var xhr = new XMLHttpRequest();
    xhr.open('GET', 'bin/marine.md2');

    xhr.overrideMimeType('text/plain; charset=x-user-defined');

    xhr.onreadystatechange = function(e) {
        if (this.readyState == 4 && this.status == 200) {
            for (var i = 0; i < this.responseText.length; i++) {
                var byte = this.responseText.charCodeAt(i) & 0xff;
                // process byte here
            }
        }
    };
```

```
        xhr.send();
    }
```

The code in the Listing 11-6 overrides the MIME type returned by the server, and forces the browser to interpret the binary response as if it is text with an unknown charset: x-user-defined. This is a way to ensure that the browser does not process the response, and bytes that were sent by the server remain intact.

The XHR Level 2 specification added explicit support for binary communications. A browser that supports new features can send and receive arbitrary binary data without the need to implement workarounds, like in Listing 11-6. Take a look at the code in Listing 11-7 to see how it works.

Listing 11-7. *The Support for Binary Data Exchange in XHR Level 2*

```
function init() {
    var xhr = new XMLHttpRequest();
    xhr.open('GET', 'bin/marine.md2');
    xhr.responseType = 'arraybuffer';

    xhr.onload = function(e) {
        var byteArray = new Uint8Array(xhr.response);
        for (var i = 0; i < byteArray.length; i++) {
            var byte = byteArray[i];
            // process byte here
        }
    };
    xhr.send();
}
```

The code in Listing 11-7 doesn't use any hacks, thus it is far easier to read and work with. To enable it, you have to set the responseType property of the XHR object to ArrayBuffer or Blob. In this case, the browser treats the response from the server as binary data, and you have access to the bytes without applying any hacks. The other possible values of responseType are document for DOM object and text for plain text responses. The default is text. Note that in Listing 11-7, we use a different property of XHR to access the response data: response instead of responseText as before.

The binary data support in XHR Level 2 relies on the other specifications: typed arrays (www.khronos.org/registry/typedarray/specs/latest/) and File API (www.w3.org/TR/FileAPI/). Typed arrays added the standard way of manipulation with the binary data. Before typed arrays, developers had to handle data types themselves: create bytes, floats, integers, and other atomic types out of byte sequences. In Listing 11-7, the response from the server is treated as an array of "unsigned 8-bit integers" or, in other words, bytes.

There are other types too, for example: `Int32Array` for 32-bit signed integers (equivalent of `int` in C) or `Float64Array` for double-precision floating-point type (equivalent to `double` in C). The second binary type of response is `Blob` (`http://dev.w3.org/2006/webapi/FileAPI/#blob`), a data structure from the File API specification that is very similar to the `ArrayBuffer`, with the only difference being that `Blob` keeps the information about the type of data that it holds—if it is a PNG image, zip array, or MD2 model.

> **NOTE:** All three specifications—`XMLHttpRequest` Level 2, File API, and typed arrays—are in a working draft state at the time of writing this chapter. This means that they could change in a few months. Browser vendors, however, are already building their implementations upon these specs. Right now, you still have to consider the devices and browsers that do not support new features; there are still too many of them. As usual, the best source of information concerning browser support is at `http://caniuse.com/fileapi` and `http://caniuse.com/typedarrays`, as well as extensive testing with emulators and real devices.

If you want to know more about the other exciting features of the new API, take a look at a wonderful HTML5 Rocks post by Eric Bidelman titled "New Tricks in XMLHttpRequest2" (`www.html5rocks.com/en/tutorials/file/xhr2/`). Another good source of inspiration is the W3C specifications—documents that are referred to throughout this book—since they are developer-friendly and well written. You should read them to get the big picture of how the new features are supposed to work, and where the web is moving.

Reverse Ajax

This section is devoted to the low-latency communication between the client and the server, where both parties can send messages to each other. The typical use of XHR assumes that the client is the only source of new events; for example, when the user fills out a form, he might require a response from a validation service, and at that moment, he *requests* the server to perform certain actions and to return the *response*. What if we have an application where the server should be capable of sending requests to the client? For example, in a chat application, the server may want to send the new chat messages to the client; or, in other words, to send the request to the client.

The set of techniques that allow server to speak to the client is often referred to as *reverse Ajax*. Technically, it is impossible for the server to connect to the web page and send the message directly, since the only party that can establish a connection is the web page. However, with a certain level of collaboration between the server and the client, it is possible to achieve this result.

The idea behind every such technique is to establish some sort of persistent connection between a page and a web server so that the server can use it to push the message back to the client once there is an update. When there is no activity, the connection sits idle, but once the server has a new event to publish, it can use the open connection to deliver it to the client straightaway. This model is different from regular Ajax since it allows the server (and not the client) to be the initiator of communication.

> **NOTE:** There are several names for this architecture, and neither is standardized. The most popular names are reverse Ajax, server push, and comet. All these names, except comet, suggest that the initiative for communication is now on the server side: the server can now *push* the messages to the client and this model is the *reverse* of how regular Ajax works.

The Problem

The lobby of any online game service is the perfect example of a situation when server-push architecture is essential. Imagine that the user has connected to the game and he needs to find out who else is playing. The list of other players must be interactive; the user wants to know the status of the other players (ready to play, playing, away from keyboard). He also wants the list to be updated in real time.

In this case, the server works as the dispatcher of events: when two players decide to start a match, the server should notify all other subscribed users that the status of the ones who are playing has changed and they are not available for new game requests until they finish their game (the usual practice for match-based online games).

The Solutions

Now we should find a way to show the lobby updates to every user who is viewing the page. Every available approach for solving this task falls into one of three categories:

- *Best solutions*: APIs designed specifically to solve a task like this.

- *Acceptable solutions:* Solutions that are merely "good enough," taking into account available APIs and limitations.

- *Obsolete solutions:* Approaches that are generally no longer used, but may still be available in some libraries..

In this section, I pay most attention to the second group, acceptable solutions. Best solutions are described only briefly because they cannot be used in the Android browser. Obsolete solutions are not illustrated in the code: they are present in this chapter only for the sake of "completeness" of the review of transports.

> **NOTE:** As mentioned earlier in the chapter. different approaches to the implementation of server push are commonly called *transports*.

The Best Solutions

There are two APIs specifically designed to handle real-time communications and sending events from the client to the server:

- **WebSocket**: spec (www.w3.org/TR/websockets/) support (http://caniuse.com/websockets)

- **Server-Sent Events (SSE)**: spec (www.w3.org/TR/eventsource/) support (http://caniuse.com/eventsource)

Unfortunately, neither of these is available to the stock Android browser. However, since both APIs are making their way to the desktop browsers, chances are that the Android platform will eventually support them too (for example, WebSocket is supported by Chrome for Android). This small section gives a very brief overview of the client-side code for both. It is highly possible that either WebSocket or SSE is available for the new Android release at the time you read this chapter.

WebSocket

WebSocket provides the API and a lightweight protocol over TCP to keep the connection between the client and the server. If Android supported it, the task would be relatively simple. Each client would initialize the connection to the server, which stays open for the lifetime of the application. When the player changes his state, the server would send the message to all open WebSocket connections. The hypothetical WebSocket client code would look like this:

```
var webSocket = new WebSocket('ws://example.com/lobby');
webSocket.onmessage = function (e) {
    // e.data holds the response from the server,
    // update the UI or log it to the console
    console.log('Server: ' + e.data);
};
```

The difference between the WebSocket and XHR is that both client and server can send messages to each other, and the connection stays open after the message is sent.

Server-Sent Events

Server-Sent Events (SSE) is the API that defines the new DOM element called EventSource. When this object is constructed, it connects to the server and starts listening for new events. The following shows how the client code would look if supported by Android:

```
var es = new EventSource('lobby');
source.addEventListener('message', function(e) {
    // now you can manipulate the event data
    console.log(e.data);
}, false);
```

SSE and WebSocket look quite similar from the client's perspective; however, they have major technical differences. Eric Bidelman did a really good job explaining the nuances of using APIs in his post on HTML 5 Rocks, "Stream Updates with Server-Sent Events" (www.html5rocks.com/en/tutorials/eventsource/basics/):

> "... APIs, like WebSockets, provide a richer protocol to perform bi-directional, full-duplex commu nication. Having a two-way channel is more attractive for things like games, messaging apps, and for cases where you need near real -time updates in both directions. However, in some scenarios data doesn't need to be sent from the client. You simply need updates from some server action.
>
> ... SSEs are sent over traditional HTTP. That means they do not require a special prot ocol or server implementation to get working. WebSockets on the other hand, require full-duplex connections and new Web So cket servers to handle the

protocol. In addition, Server-Sent Events ha ve a variety of features that WebSockets lack by design such as automatic reconnection, event IDs, and th e ability to send arbitrary events."

(This fragment is published with the kind permission of Eric Bidelman.)

The solutions described in this section can be used in projects that target mobile devices and desktops. There should be a reliable fallback, however, to achieve the same result on Android smartphones. The next section is dedicated to such fallback transports. They are not as beautiful as the "best" solutions from this section, but they are proven to work.

> **NOTE:** Don't be misguided by the name of this section: *best* doesn't mean *flawless*. Both WebSocket API and SSEs have their own drawbacks and pitfalls. The word "best" means that the semantics of these APIs suit this task better than other APIs, like XHR.

The Acceptable Solutions

"Acceptable" solutions are the trade-off between beautiful code that relies on cutting-edge technology and stable hacks that have been field-tested by millions of users over the last few years.

First, let's look at the simplest way to simulate the server-to-client communication with XHR. The client polls the server every few seconds by asking, "Any new events for me?" If there are new events, they are transferred to the client; otherwise, the server just returns the empty response. The communication between the client and the server in this case is illustrated in Figure 11-1. The "useless" requests that did not bring any information to the client or to the server are shown in gray. As you can see, to receive only one event, both the client and the server need to process many connections just to give the server a chance to respond.

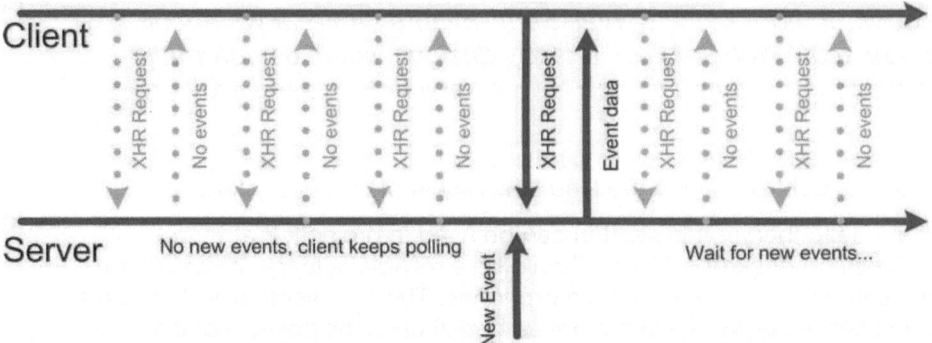

Figure 11-1. *The simplest polling technique requires the server and client to perform a lot of unnecessary work.*

With the simple polling approach, the response is written and the connection is closed even if there are no new events. Then the client waits for a certain amount of time (called a "polling interval") and reconnects again. The drawback to this approach is that the latency is equal to the polling interval in the worst case. Decreasing the interval value is also not an option: a lot of bandwidth will be wasted just to send headers. The server will starve under the enormous load (processing an HTTP request has its own small CPU and memory overhead). More clients means more wasted CPU time.

HTTP protocol has one interesting feature: it doesn't require the server to respond immediately to the client's request. In fact, the server can keep the HTTP connection open for as long as needed. The first technique in this section relies on this fact to reduce the number of useless calls.

XHR Long Polling

XHR long polling works almost like the traditional polling. The only difference is that the server keeps the connection open when it doesn't have any new events. Once there is a new event for the client, the server responds and closes the connection afterward. This way, the client connection may stay open for several seconds, waiting for new data. Figure 11-2 illustrates this idea.

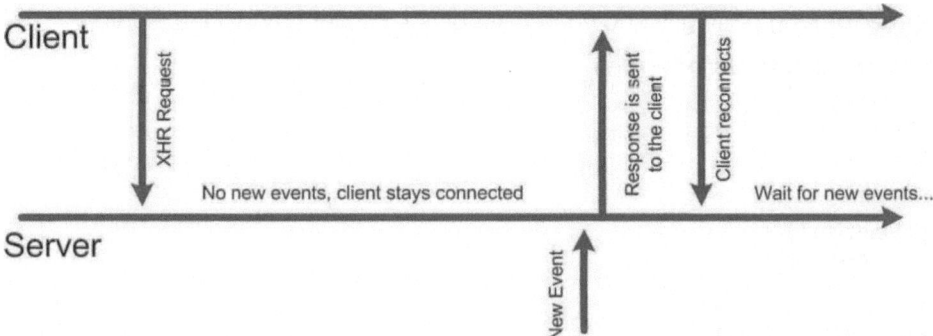

Figure 11-2. *With XHR long polling, the server holds the connection open until it has some data to send to the client.*

As you can see, XHR long polling uses considerably fewer requests to keep the connection with the server. The maximum latency overhead is the time that the web page needs to reconnect to the server.

Long polling has its own drawbacks, however: the long-running XHR requests may be terminated by middleware proxy servers or even by the browser itself. For example, Android 2.2 running on Samsung Galaxy kills the XHR connection if it is idle for about 20 seconds. To make matters worse, the rules for breaking "stalled" connections may vary from browser to browser and from proxy to proxy. The safe timeout is around 15 seconds. If this time has passed and the server doesn't have anything to respond, it should send the empty response and close the connection.

The second drawback is that in message-intensive environments, long polling loses its advantage and it is reduced to regular polling. This is one of the reasons why this technique is not suitable for fast-action, real-time games like racing, online RPGs, or strategy games. The client would spend a lot of time reconnecting to the server (see Figure 11-3).

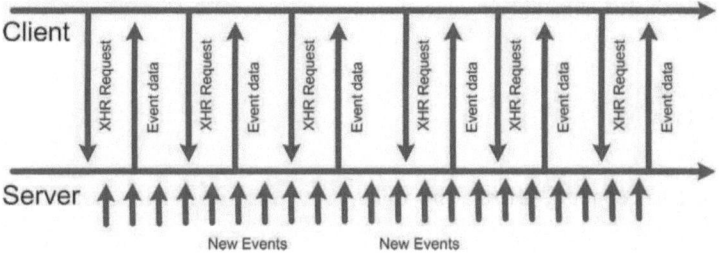

Figure 11-3. *The problem with long polling in a message-intensive environment. The long polling is reduced to simple polling: requests are sent each second.*

Example code for long polling is shown in Listings 11-8 (client) and 11-9 (server).

Listing 11-8. *The Example XHR Long Poll Client*

```
function init() {
    pollServer();
}

function pollServer() {
    var xhr = new XMLHttpRequest();

    console.log("Requesting");
    xhr.open('GET', 'lobby');

    xhr.onload = function(e) {
        console.log("RESPONSE:" + xhr.responseText);
        setTimeout(pollServer, 4); // Poll server again after the response
    };

    xhr.onerror = function(e) {
        console.log("Error, retrying");
        setTimeout(pollServer, 4); // Poll server again in case of error
    };
    xhr.send();
}
```

Listing 11-9. *The Simplest Long-Poll Server*

```
var clients = [];

// send notification with random intervals
(function() {
    notifyClients();
    setTimeout(arguments.callee, Math.floor((Math.random()*10000)));
})();

/**
 * Sends the new event data to every connected client
 */
function notifyClients() {
    clients.forEach(function(res) {
        res.send("new event data");
    });

    clients = []; // They will reconnect, empty the array
}

app.get("/lobby", function(req, res) {
    clients.push(res);
```

```
    console.log("Added client, now " + clients.length + " connected");
});
```

This implementation should not be used for production, of course; it only illustrates the basics of the technique behind long-poll transports. As you can see, the server does not return the response immediately. Instead, the response object is saved in the `clients` array for later use. Once the data is available, the server broadcasts it to clients and clears the array. The clients are now disconnected and they will connect once again in a few milliseconds.

The real-world implementation would be much more sophisticated. It should gracefully handle disconnects and errors, save the messages for the clients in queues so that they are not lost while the client is reconnecting, and so on. In the next chapter, we will use Socket.IO—the library that has already implemented the hard part of transport handling.

The complete source code for this simplistic long-poll implementation is available in the `02.longpoll` folder along with the other sources for this chapter.

XHR Streaming

There is a method to getting rid of one major long-poll problem: reconnecting after each received message. The approach is called *XHR streaming*. Technically, it is not an entirely new transport, but a slight modification of the long poll.

Here's how it works: if you set the content type of the response to a custom value (like `"application/x-custom-event-stream"`), the browser will not wait to receive the whole response body. Instead, it will append everything that the server writes to the `responseText` of the XHR object and trigger the `onreadystatechange` (and `onprogress` in Level 2) to give you a chance to extract the new messages from the stream. Have a look at the updated client and the server code in Listings 11-10 and 11-11.

Listing 11-10. *XHR Streaming Transport: Example Client*

```
function init() {
    pollServer();
}

function pollServer() {
    var responseMarker = 0;
    var xhr = new XMLHttpRequest();

    console.log("Requesting");
    xhr.open('GET', 'lobby');
```

```
    xhr.onload = function(e) {
        console.log("Server closed the stream, reconnect");
        setTimeout(pollServer, 4);
    };

    xhr.onprogress = function(e) {
        if (this.readyState == 3 && this.status == 200) {
            var response = xhr.responseText.substr(responseMarker);
            responseMarker = xhr.responseText.length;
            console.log(response);
        }
    };

    xhr.onerror = function(e) {
        console.log("Error, retrying");
        setTimeout(pollServer, 4);
    };
    xhr.send();
}
```

The code for the client has significantly changed. This version of the code relies on the onprogress() function to fetch new events, instead of the usual onload(). Also, the new messages are appended to the end of responseText, so to use the described approach, the latest message has to be manually extracted from the whole response string.

Listing 11-11. *XHR Streaming: Example Server*

```
var clients = [];

// send notification with random intervals
(function() {
    notifyClients();
    setTimeout(arguments.callee, Math.floor((Math.random()*10000)));
})();

/**
 * Sends the new event data to every connected client
 */
function notifyClients() {
    clients.forEach(function(res) {
        res.write("new event data");
    });

    // clients = []; // Do not clean the array, clients stay connected
}

app.get("/lobby", function(req, res) {
    res.contentType("application/x-custom-event-stream");
```

```
    clients.push(res);
    console.log("Added client, now " + clients.length + " connected");
});
```

The server remained almost the same. The changed parts are bolded. First, the server sends the custom contentType to the browser. Then it writes the new messages to the clients' streams as they arrive. The write() function does not close the underlying connection, so there is no need to clear the array of clients at this point (it has to be cleared anyway when the client disconnects, otherwise, the array holds junk; but for the sake of this simple demo, it works just fine). The main advantage of streaming is that in a message-heavy environment, the client doesn't have to re-establish the connection after each message.

The complete sample application that demonstrates the XHR streaming transport is found in the 03.streaming folder along with the other code for this chapter.

The Obsolete Solutions

This section covers the transports that were used some time ago, but were substituted by the other API that solved the problem in a better way. These transports are

- JSONP polling

- Flash Socket

- Forever IFRAME

JSONP Polling

JSONP polling was meant to solve the problem of loading the data from the server that is located on a different domain from the client's. For example, if the server is at http://server.example.com and the client HTML page was loaded from http://client.example.com, they could not communicate via XHR because of the limits of the *same origin policy*, a security restriction that prevented XHR from sending requests to other domains.

The technique behind JSONP was to create the new <script> element and append it to the body of the document. Since the script element can load scripts from any domain, there are no security restrictions that could prevent the request from retrieving the data.

The JSONP transport is obsolete because there is a new API that regulates the sharing of resources between domains in a standard way: cross-origin resource sharing or CORS (www.w3.org/TR/cors/). The specification describes special headers that the server must send to the client in order to allow access to its resources. Using CORS is preferable since JSONP provides significantly less control over the life cycle of the request (for example, you can't cancel it once started) and error handling. The last important reason to use CORS is because it is a supported standard and not a hack like JSONP.

Flash Socket

Flash Socket is the transport that relies on the Flash plug-in to handle the communication with the server. The Flash component notifies JavaScript of new events. Flash handles notification, while JavaScript handles the processing logic. Many people would disagree that this transport is obsolete; indeed, Flash does a really good job handling persistent low-latency connections, much like WebSocket does. However, Adobe dropped support of Flash Player for mobile devices—and that is the reason why this transport cannot be relied on anymore (at least not on smartphones).

This transport is obsolete not because the communication technology was substituted by a better API, but because the core component that the transport relies on is now at the end of its life.

Forever IFRAME

Forever IFRAME is the oldest of transports: it relies on a feature of HTTP 1.1 and its chunked encoding that was introduced to handle very large documents. The IFRAME opens a connection to the server that is never closed. The task of the server is to feed new chunks of data—script elements with commands to handle new events. Each time the server needs to send an event, it appends another <script> block into the endless page. The script is immediately evaluated by the client, and that is how the transport provides low-latency communication.

This transport is obsolete because it was substituted by several better solutions described earlier in this section. Two major drawbacks of Forever IFRAME were inconsistent behavior across browsers and poor error handling.

Testing Transports in the Field

One of the main requirements of a good transport is reliability. We live in an imperfect world where mobile data connections can break from time to time. As a developer, you cannot do anything about it. Your goal here is to make sure that a temporary loss of connection does not kick the player out of the game, and when the connection is restored, he can continue to play. Moreover, the messages that the game tried to send during the period of low connectivity should not be lost. They should be saved somewhere for sending and delivering to the server once the device is back online.

The best way to test your game is to start a server and try to play on your way from home to office. Start with the Wi-Fi connection in your home, and then switch to 3G once you are on the street. Take a bus and ride couple of stops, then move to the subway and continue your experiment from there. Finally, grab a coffee and go to the park. Don't forget to answer incoming calls or to send a few text messages when you have a spare minute.

Now, honestly answer the following questions:

- How was your online gaming experience?
- Were there any freezes or crashes?
- Did you lose any data, turns, or server updates?
- Was the game engine able to restore synchronization once the server became available?
- Did your game show some sort of message to warn you that you're not connected?
- How did it look from your opponent's side? Did he know that you're losing your connection? Should he? Did he have a chance to end the match when he saw that you're not responding for several minutes?

If you are satisfied with every answer after conducting this kind of experiment for the first time, send me a postcard. I want to live in a city that has perfect mobile data coverage.

Running around the city is not the best way to debug networking, but how do you debug it if your office Wi-Fi works perfectly? There are a few tools that simulate a bad network; they are designed specifically for these cases.

DDMS (Dalvik Debug Monitor Server)

The simplest tool for simulating a bad network is an Android emulator along with a standard utility called the Dalvik Debug Monitor Server, or DDMS. It is located in the Tools folder of your emulator installation. Run the application and find the Emulator Control tab on the right (see Figure 11-4). It has a few options to control the behavior of the data, the bandwidth, and the delay.

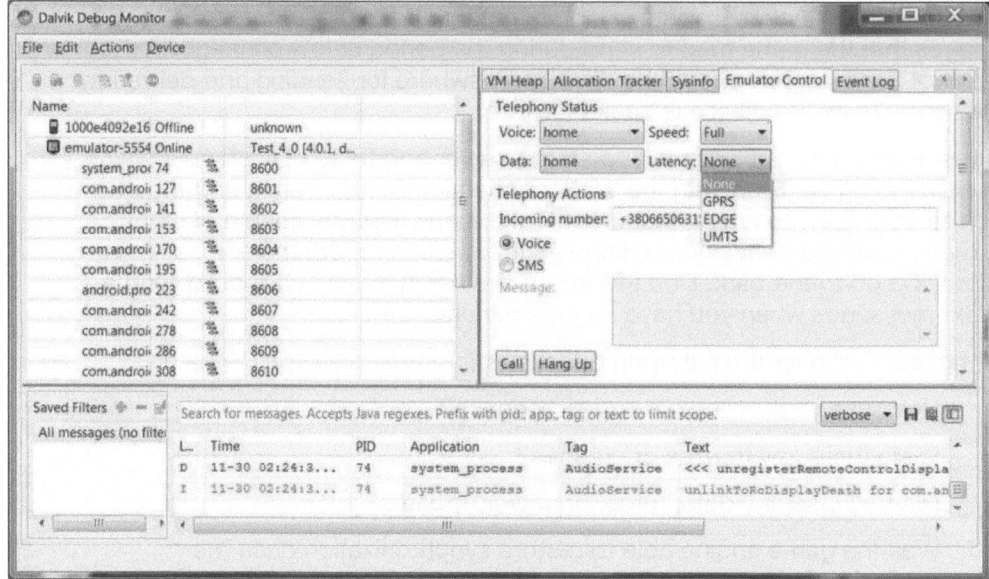

Figure 11-4. *The DDMS window shows several options to simulate a realistic network*

There's also an option to completely kill the emulator's connectivity, but it's not a good idea to select it: DDMS and ADB (Android Debug Bridge) communicate with the emulator via the network. If you turn networking off, you will not be able to turn it on again the same way since the emulator will not respond anymore. The Telephony Actions section allows you to simulate an incoming voice call or SMS.

Specialized Software That Simulates a Bad Network

DDMS is somewhat limited since it can only simulate low bandwidth and network delays. It can't simulate loss of packets and temporary disconnects. Fortunately, there are several solutions available to simulate a poor network, although most of them require some knowledge of networking.

Unfortunately, an in-depth discussion of network configurations and setting up a system that will help you to simulate realistic mobile traffic are outside the scope of this book. However, I will give you information on DummyNet and WANem, which are good software to start with.

DummyNet (http://info.iet.unipi.it/~luigi/dummynet/) is a tool for traffic shaping and low-connectivity simulation. It was originally developed for FreeBSD, but later ported to all major platforms, including Windows and Linux.

You can find a tutorial on setting rules for DummyNet at `http://cs.baylor.edu/~donahoo/tools/dummy/tutorial.htm`.

The WANem project (`http://wanem.sourceforge.net`) is a tool based on a custom Knoppix distribution. Basically, WANem is a separate OS that should be loaded either from a live CD or inside a virtual box so that it can run on every modern OS. WANem has an intuitive web interface that allows people who just want to test web game connectivity to set up the environment for testing without having to dive deep into the networking details. There are other tools out there, but DummyNet and WANem seem to be the most popular.

Summary

In this chapter, we reviewed the broad range of techniques available for loading data from the server. There are two major types of communication:

- Ajax: The "classical" model in which the client is the only party that can initiate the communication.

- Reverse Ajax: The "inverted" model, also known as server push and comet, in which the server can push the messages to the client.

We learned that there are multiple available APIs for both techniques, but most of the devices in the market do not support newer APIs at a good level. For Ajax, we learned how to request data from the server via plain XMLHttpRequest, as well as a better version of the same API—XMLHttpRequest Level 2. We also studied the problem of loading binary data and parsing it on the side of the client.

Reverse Ajax allows us to build a relatively reliable and low-latency communication channel between the server and the web page for communication that is close to real time.

In order to do that, the client and server have to establish a connection and keep it open as long as possible. The server can then use this connection to send updates. There are several ways to establish this kind of communication and support the connection, and these approaches are called *transports*.

At the time of writing, there is no transport that works like a silver bullet for game development purposes. Each available transport is a trade-off between browser support, latency, reliability, CPU cycles, and traffic.

In the next chapter, we will apply our knowledge to a practical task: building the client-server implementation for our Four Balls game.

Making Multiplayer Games

This chapter is devoted to the practical application of the skills that we have learned in the previous two chapters. The goal is to make a fully functional multiplayer Four Balls game out of the single-player version that we developed in the Chapter 3. After reading this chapter, you will know how to:

▪ Implement the basic multiplayer architecture

▪ Distribute the game logic between the client and the server

▪ Share the JavaScript components between the browser and Node.js

▪ Use Socket.IO for handling the real-time communications

We will start by looking at the anatomy of the networking game, from the challenges of a typical casual online game to the more advanced fast-action, real-time games that are likely to show up on the mobile web in the near future. The next section is devoted to the essential components of the multiplayer game that support the online experience.

We then discuss Socket.IO—the module for Node.js that takes the burden of providing the best available transport for real-time networking. The last section is devoted to the implementation of the game: we will take the code for the single-player version and add support for lobby and multiplayer matches. The code will show the common patterns of Socket.IO; once you learn them, you can add more advanced features to the project yourself.

The Anatomy of a Network Game

Network applications always consist of two components: the client and the server. In the PC game development industry, server-side logic is often embedded into the game. For example, when two users want to play *Diablo 2*, they don't have to set up the separate dedicated server software; instead, they launch the game and select the LAN Game mode. Then one of the launched applications takes the role of server and allows other people to connect and play together, handling transmission of data packets, voice communication, in-game chats, and other usual multiplayer functions. In such cases, there might be no separate server application, like a server.exe file somewhere in the game folder. Nevertheless, these two components—client and server—are present in every game that supports networking.

Web games work in a different manner: a game client is usually a web page with some amount of logic embedded as JavaScript. The page is prepared and served by the web server, and then it is loaded and rendered by the browser. From this point, it can work as a standalone application (like ones described in detail in previous chapters), or as a "client" that can "speak" to the same or different server and allow the user to play with other people like himself.

The task for this chapter is to make a more advanced version of the Four Balls game. We will add very basic support for networking—a lobby and a multiplayer version of the game. The materials in this chapter allow you to build a working skeleton of a network-enabled web application that you can extend further to suit real-world requirements.

For someone who has never developed a simple online multiplayer game, this might sound like a very easy task. Indeed, we have already implemented the hardest parts of the game—the graphical engine and the logic—so we can reuse the pieces of the code and assemble a server in no time. In practice, however, this is not true. As a rule of thumb, take the effort that you've spent to make a good single-player game, multiply it by ten, and you'll get the effort that you need to make a good multiplayer version of the same game. Figure 12-1 shows the amount of work required to complete the network version of the simple game. The core game itself is a small part of the whole infrastructure.

Figure 12-1. *The relative proportions of effort in developing a good multiplayer game*

Why so much time? The reason why multiplayer games are more involved is that they require a certain infrastructure to support the seamless online experience: lobbies, ratings, high scores, friend lists, avatars, chat rooms—these are only a few examples to begin with. Look through the advanced online gaming communities and you will find even more components. When users play online, they not only want to leverage their offline experience and waste some network traffic, but they want to meet new people, find the right opponents, see their achievements, progress, and prove that they are better than others—that's what makes online games fun to play. The development of such infrastructural tools is often more challenging than implementing the core of the game: the logic and UI.

> **NOTE:** This chapter assumes basic knowledge of HTTP protocol. At the very least, it assumes that you know about request headers and how they are different from the request body; that you know about GET and POST, and the differences between them; that you know how a developer should serialize parameters when he wants to send them to the server; that you know what a server response code is, and other basic HTTP matters.

Game Architecture: Moving from Single Player to Multiplayer

Let's find out the optimal way to upgrade the single-player game that we created in Chapter 3 to a multiplayer version. First, a client-server solution involves two components that share responsibilities and logic: the client and the server. We need to analyze the best way to split the tasks between the two. Since we already have implemented some components, we want to re-use them where possible. There are two points to consider: first, the components designed for the single-player game often cannot be used without at least minor changes; and second, how to share the code for the component between the client and the server.

When these two issues are addressed, we are ready to design the architecture of the game and implement it in code. The general process is as follows:

1. Find out the responsibilities of client and server.

2. Review the game components that we already have and think about how to re-use them.

3. Design the architecture of the game.

4. Implement it.

The Job of Client and the Job of Server

Splitting the set of responsibilities between the client and the server is not always a trivial task, but most of the time architects make their decision based on the game type, security requirements, requirements for responsiveness, and so forth. The major decision is where to put the logic of the game—for example, the verification of the turns. In this section, we look into the different types of games, not only Four Balls.

The old rule of the web said, "Never trust the input of the client." It means that everything that the client can send to the server can also be sent by a malicious user who wants to hack your system and access functionality that he is not supposed to. A simple example of the possible problem is the game that supports sending the resulting score to the worldwide record board. If the user has enough technical skills, he can easily hijack the process of transmitting the result to the server, and send any number that he wants. Usually, it is easier to do this with text-based protocols like HTTP and slightly harder for binary protocols, but in any case, it is doable if the hacker has enough time and patience. So any user can become the top in your leader board. In the best case, the cheater is recognized and banned.

Taking security considerations into account, the solution seems obvious: put every possible bit of logic to the server, and do not allow the client to make any unchecked input. Such a paranoid approach works very well when you deal with a turn-based game where the whole verification logic is done on the server. The server is the arbiter that does not allow the client to cheat, no matter what. However, this is not always possible.

The legitimacy of single-player game clients that contact the server only to send the high score are impossible to verify, because the client is not sending any evidence that he took the valid actions to achieve that score. The server acts like the university professor who tells his students, "If you did the assignment, raise your hand." If he does not check if the students who claim it actually did it, they soon start to cheat to get bonuses or good marks.

Another broad category of games that are very hard to restrict from cheats are fast-action multiplayer games like online shooters. They often have to sacrifice the verification for better playability and lower complexity of the server. There are at least two reasons why perfect verification of the users' actions is impossible: volumes of data, and lags that make verification inaccurate.

If the volume of data to send for verification is too big, then verification becomes too expensive, both in terms of traffic and in terms of required processing power. The rate of fire for the Heckler & Koch MP5K series is about 900 rounds per minute (15 rounds per second). How much traffic and CPU cycles would it take to verify every fired bullet? Not to mention when there are ten people firing simultaneously on a multiplayer map. This problem is solvable of course: you can send the direction for every tenth bullet in a burst, and interpolate the rest, for example.

The second issue that makes server-side verification less attractive for real-time action games is network delays, or *lag*. Figure 12-2 illustrates the problem. This is the top-down view of a virtual game battlefield where the player tries to fire at a fast-moving target with a projectile weapon. The client sees that the player hit the target, but due to the lag, the server version of the game is different from the client version, and the server thinks that player missed. Needless to say, the player will be very unhappy as he watches the enemy that he just shot happily running away.

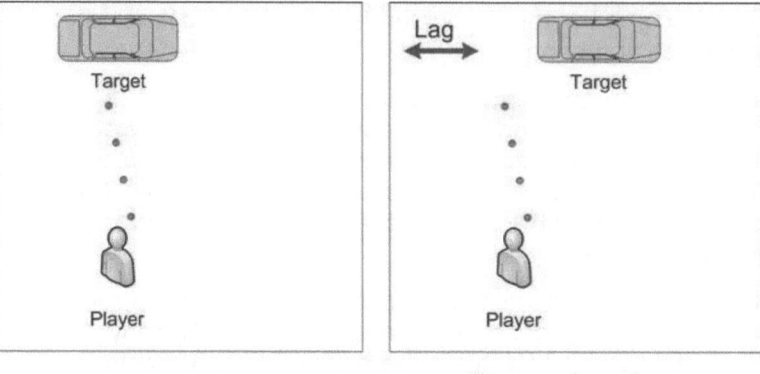

Figure 12-2. *Due to the lag, the server receives a different result of a shot than the client.*

There are a lot of sophisticated algorithms to solve the problems of lag, which are often called *lag compensation techniques*. For example, if the networking delay for the particular client is 300 milliseconds, then when the server receives the event, it tries to step 300 milliseconds back and look at the game world as the player saw it at the moment of shooting. Unfortunately, these techniques open possibilities for a whole different kind of network protocol exploits that allow a malicious player to get an unfair advantage in the game.

> **NOTE:** As I mentioned, Android games are not yet ready for problems of this kind, since fast-action online games are impossible without good support from the networking layer. Until WebSockets or any other similar API is available to the default Android browser, the games where milliseconds matter are not possible to implement with acceptable quality.

Getting back to the Four Balls game, the task of bringing logic to the server is not too hard: there are no lags to compensate for as in 3D shooters, there is no physics or such to replicate on the server, and the rules are quite easy. We will make our server validate every turn that players make—and this is the strategy for our verification solution. If the turn is valid, the server broadcasts it to both players; otherwise, it sends an error to the player who tried to send the wrong move.

Game Components

At the very least, the multiplayer game should have a lobby, the list of players that look for opponents and are ready to play. It means that besides the components that we already have, we need to create at least two more: the lobby UI to render it on the client and the server-side support for notification about new users.

The very important change in the game architecture is that the client now has multiple screens (or states): the lobby and the game. Before this point, our games were rendered on a big canvas and the only state of the game was "playing." When you create a commercial game, however, it has several different screens that render in a completely different manner and support a completely different set of user actions. For example, the following are a few screens for an online strategy game:

- Main menu
- World map
- City screen
- Building & Trading screen
- Battlefield screen
- In-game Help screen
- Settings screen

These screens act like a sub-modules of the game: they provide access to the different aspects of the game and you should treat them as independent software components. If you decide to update the Battlefield screen, it means that only this module is updated, not the whole project. The game that we are going to implement is very simple: it has only two screens (lobby and game board), but we still need to think of a good way to show the correct one to the user and process the input according to the current state of the application. This last task is very easy in HTML touch interfaces: the touch is always dispatched to the component that you touched, so invisible components will not receive any events.

The only important piece that we are missing is the choice of the transport. For this chapter, we will use the Socket.IO library. We'll start learning it right after we discuss the project structure.

Project Structure

The folder structure of the project is usual for the typical Node project. Let's review it to make sure that the structure of folders is clear. Figure 12-3 shows how the project looks when it is finished.

Figure 12-3. *The structure of the project*

The main.js file is the entry point of the Node.js application. Files intended for browser HTML files and client-side JavaScript files reside in the public folder.

Create the structure of the folders described, and put the code for the offline game that we created in Chapter 3 into the public folder. I renamed the old index.html file offline.html to keep the single-player version accessible. The new index.html file is the entry point to the multiplayer version.

Game Lobby with Socket.IO

Socket.IO is the project created by Guillermo Rauch (http://devthought.com) and available at github (https://github.com/LearnBoost/socket.io) or as an NPM module. The goal of this project is to "blur the differences between the different transport mechanisms" as the official project page says (http://socket.io/). More formally, Socket.IO is the convenient client-server library that allows you to implement in-page networking without thinking about the transport details. Allow Socket.IO to answer low-level questions like "What is the best transport to use on this device?" or "How can I deal with the messages that might come while the client is reconnecting?" or "How can I keep track of all clients and broadcast them a message when needed?" The saved time is better spent building a better game.

NOTE: It would be unfair to say that the Socket.IO is the only available browser-networking library. There is another nice project called Faye (https://github.com/faye/faye) by James Coglan (http://jcoglan.com). It provides a similar solution and has some good feedback from the developers. There are two reasons why I picked Socket.IO and not Faye for this chapter, and neither reason is technical or quality-based. First, Faye implements a higher-level communication protocol called Bayeux (http://svn.cometd.org/trunk/bayeux/bayeux.html), and trying to keep things simple, I did not want to spend a couple more pages explaining the protocol itself. The second reason is purely social: Socket.IO has a larger community around it, and it is growing continuously. In the time that I have spent writing this chapter, about 50 more members have joined the mailing list.

Nevertheless, I encourage you to go and check Faye yourself to form your own opinion about this little gem.

Socket.IO is based on the idea of sockets. Socket.IO sockets have nothing to do with the real TCP Sockets or Unix Sockets. It is no more than the abstraction layer on top of the transport that a particular client uses. Take a look at Figure 12-4 to see how this works. The server can hold the connection with multiple clients, and each client would use the suitable transport. Neither client nor server performs any transport-specific actions, like creating XHR objects and sending requests. The single interface of communication is Socket—the rest is handled by the library. I'm sure that you are anxious to see a live example.

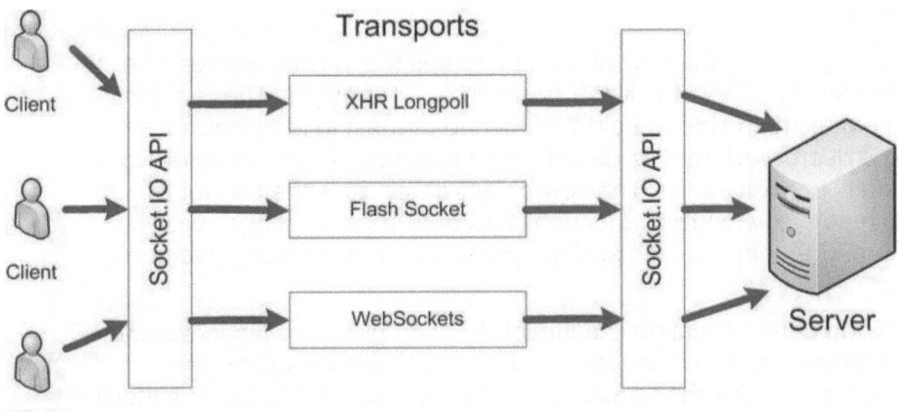

Figure 12-4. *Socket.IO hides the details of underlying transports and provides the simple, reliable API for client-server communications.*

Client-Server Communications

Let's start by taking a first step toward the lobby implementation. When the initial client connects to the server, he should receive the "you are connected" message; the following clients should receive the "new user joined" message.

First, you need to install Socket.IO (don't worry if Socket.IO reported that it can't compile native extensions, the project still works):

```
> npm install socket.io
```

Next, initialize the Socket.IO server. It can work standalone but it is more useful as the wrapper around Express' server (see Listing 12-1). The requests that are intended for Socket.IO are intercepted and processed independently from the main web site flow. The integration between the functionality of Express and Socket.IO is rather seamless and simple.

Listing 12-1. *Adding Socket.IO Support to the Express Server*

```
var express = require("express");
var http = require("http");

var app = express();
var server = http.createServer(app);

var io = require("socket.io").listen(server, {
    "polling duration": 10
});
…
// next goes the regular Express setup

server.listen(80);
```

As you probably guessed, the new object, io ,wraps the existing server. The second parameter, listen, is the list of possible server options. The "polling duration", the maximum time to hold the opened request in long-polling approaches, is decreased from its default value because some mobile devices tend to forcefully break it earlier. The new object called io is the Socket.IO server that is ready to listen to connections and exchange messages with clients. Without further delay, let's add the user-tracking functionality to our server.

From now on, the communication is a straightforward process. Whenever the new client connects, the server creates a new object called socket—the abstraction layer that hides the transport details. You can then listen to various socket events that clients might emit(), or emit() messages yourself. If you want to notify multiple clients about a certain event, you call broadcast(). The code in Listing 12-2 implements the basic lobby functionality and is a good demonstration of the basics of Socket.IO.

Listing 12-2. *Adding the Basic Lobby Functionality to the Server*

```
var maxUserId = 0;
io.sockets.on("connection", function (socket) {
    var userId = maxUserId++;
    var userName = "User " + userId;
    var user = {id: userId, name: userName};

    socket.emit("info", { text: "You have connected" });
    socket.broadcast.emit("user-joined", user);

    socket.on("disconnect", function () {
        socket.broadcast.emit("user-left", user);
    });
});
```

The second line listens to the "connection" event that is triggered for every newly established connection. Note that the Socket.IO connection has nothing to do with Express sessions. For example, if you open two tabs in Google Chrome and access the same page, they share the same Express session (since they share a session ID stored in cookies) but Socket.IO recognizes them as two different sockets. The API passes the socket object as the parameter to the function.

The next two lines make a new object with some user information to have a human-readable way of identifying users. Each user has an ID and a unique default name. If your game has the authentication and authorization algorithms, you would probably get the user name from the database, or from the social networking API, but in this simple example, all users are called User 1, User 2, and so on.

The most interesting parts of the code are two calls to emit() and broadcast(). In the first line, we send the message to the user who just connected (or, in terms of Socket.IO, we emit the event) with the "info" type and some object with the greeting text. The second line "broadcasts" the event—or sends the message to all *other* users, except the connected one. The final part listens to the "disconnect" event and once again, broadcasts the message to notify the other players about the change in the lobby.

Let's build the client now. Look at Listing 12-3 for the client-side code. As usual, this is a simple web page; however, it has a little bit of Socket.IO magic.

Listing 12-3. *The Client for Socket.IO Server*

```html
<!DOCTYPE html>
<html lang="en">
<head>
    <meta charset="utf-8" />
    <meta name="viewport"
        content="width=device-width, initial-scale=1.0, maximum-scale=1.0,
        user-scalable=no, target-densitydpi=device-dpi"/>

    <style>
        html, body {
            overflow: hidden;
            width: 100%;
            height: 100%;
            margin:0;
            padding:0;
            border: 0;
        }
    </style>

    <script src="js/utils.js"></script>
    <script src="/socket.io/socket.io.js"></script>

    <script>
        var socket;

        function init() {
            socket = io.connect();

            socket.on("user-joined", function (user) {
                console.log (user.name + " joined");
            });

            socket.on("user-left", function (user) {
                console.log (user.name + " left");
            });

            socket.on("info", function (info) {
                console.log (info.text);
            });
        }
    </script>
</head>
<body onload="init()">
</body>
</html>
```

The code in Listing 12-3 uses exactly the same approach as the server. It retrieves the socket object and uses it as the single entry point of communication with the server. The `socket` is then used to listen to messages, or to emit new ones (more about this later). Note that there's no file called "`/socket.io/socket.io.js`" on the server. Socket.IO server handles the requests to this script and returns the file itself, so you don't have to worry about it. That code looks incredibly simple and clean!

> **NOTE:** A few years ago, I had to implement a custom browser-networking library that relied only on two transport implementations: XHR long-polling and XHR streaming. It took me about three weeks to build the server and the reliable client that did exactly the same trick as we just built in three minutes.

Now you can try this code out. It doesn't have any UI elements so far, but the expected console output proves that you've done everything right, and you have a very basic Hello World application working.

The code for the application at the current state is available along with the other materials for this chapter is a folder called `01.basic_io`.

Adding the Lobby Screen to the Game

We have established the basic communication, now we should make a lobby screen. Writing messages to the console is not a particularly good way to notify users about game events.

The lobby is a list of clickable buttons—each button stands for the user. When a player clicks the button, the game should start. The rule of thumb that you should never forget is: do not try to reproduce a rich user interface by the means of raster graphics of `canvas`. The regular mistake that people make at this point is to start reinventing the wheel and rendering the buttons in the 2D context. Sometimes this approach makes sense, but 99 percent of the time, it is a huge waste of your efforts and browser resources. Modern browsers have spent years gradually improving the rendering algorithms for typical UI elements. I cannot believe that somebody can do the same on `canvas` in a rather limited time frame that you usually have for a game development. Don't try to do a slider, or button, or drop-down list on the `canvas` yourself. Use HTML facilities until you have a really good reason not to use them.

We implement the user list for the lobby as a separate class called `LobbyUsersList`. It wraps the UI element and uses it as the placeholder for the list of users. The code for this class is rather simple: it does nothing but DOM manipulation. The small trick that I used here—the class of the list item is same as the name of the user's state in lobby: playing or ready. This way, we can easily change the visual style of the button depending on the readiness of the person to play. Listing 12-4 shows the code for this class.

Listing 12-4. *LobbyUsersList Class: The Client-Side Component for Displaying Currently Available Users*

```
function LobbyUsersList(listElement, clickCallback) {
    this._users = {};
    this._listElement = listElement;
    this._clickCallback = clickCallback;
}

var _p = LobbyUsersList.prototype;

_p.add = function(userId, username, status) {
    // If the user is already present for some reason,
    // just update the information about him
    if (this._users[userId]) {
        this.setStatus(userId, status);
        this.setName(userId, username);
    } else {
        // Otherwise, create new element and append it to DOM tree
        var el = this._getUserListElement(userId, username, status);
                        this._users[userId] = el;
        this._listElement.appendChild(el);

        // When the list item is clicked, it extracts the current
        // data about the user, and executes the callback
        el.addEventListener("click", (function(e) {
            var userId = el.getAttribute("data-userid");
            var userName = el.innerHTML;
            var state = el.className;
            this._clickCallback.call(this, userId, userName, status);
        }).bind(this));
    }
};

_p.setStatus = function(userId, status) {
    // Setting "status" means just updating the class name
    if (this._users[userId]) {
        this._users[userId].className = status;
    }
};

_p.setName = function(userId, name) {
    // Name is innerHTML
    if (this._users[userId]) {
        this._users[userId].innerHTML = name;
    }
};
```

```
_p.remove = function(userId) {
    if (this._users[userId]) {
        this._listElement.removeChild(this._users[userId]);
        delete this._users[userId];
    }
};

_p._getUserListElement = function(userId, userName, status) {
    // Create the new element (list item)
    // and set values
    var el = document.createElement("li");
    el.className = status;

    // We save the custom data, associated with this element,
    // using HTML5 data attributes
    // http://dev.w3.org/html5/spec/Overview.html#embedding-custom-non-visible-
data-with-the-data-attributes
    el.setAttribute("data-userid", userId);
    el.innerHTML = userName;
    return el;
};
```

This class is cheating a little bit: it joins the model (the list of users, user names, ids, and states) with the view (HTML elements that represent individual items). The code is rather self-explanatory. If we add the user list element to the page and hook the Socket.IO events, we receive a fully functional lobby (see Listing 12-5).

Listing 12-5. *The Code That Creates a Lobby*

```
<html>
<head>
    // usual head lines are stripped
    // ...
    <script>
        var socket;
        var userList;
        function init() {
            socket = io.connect();

            socket.on("user-joined", function (user) {
                userList.add(user.id, user.name, user.status);
            });

            socket.on("user-left", function (user) {
                userList.remove(user.id);
            });

            socket.on("user-playing", function (user) {
                userList.setStatus(user.id, "playing");
```

```
                });

                socket.on("user-ready", function (user) {
                    userList.setStatus(user.id, "ready");
                });

                socket.on("user-list", function (data) {
                    for (var userId in data.users) {
                        var user = data.users[userId];
                        userList.add(user.id, user.name, user.status);
                    }
                });

                socket.on("info", function (info) {
                    console.log (info.text);
                });

                var listElement = document.getElementById("online_users");
                userList = new LobbyUsersList(listElement, onChallenge);
            }

            function onChallenge(userId, userName, status) {
                alert("you challenge user " + userName + " who is " + status);
            }
        </script>
    </head>
    <body onload="init()">
        <div id="lobby">
            <ul id="online_users"></ul>
        </div>
    </body>
</html>
```

The client code knows how to react to six types of server events:

- "user-joined": sent when a new user has joined the lobby

- "user-left": sent when a user has left the game

- "user-playing": sent when a user has started a new game (he is not available for other games and cannot be invited)

- "user-ready": sent when a user has finished the game and is ready for the new invitations

- "user-list": the list of all users in the room (useful to initialize the lobby list)

- "info": generic message to display in console for debugging

Right now, the server knows how to send only "user-joined", "user-left", and "info" messages. Let's add one more message type—"user-list" to fill the list of users with those already online. To do that, we need to track every connected and disconnected user. Luckily, it is not hard to do at all. Listing 12-6 shows how to do it.

Listing 12-6. *Tracking Connected and Disconnected Users*

```
var maxUserId = 0;
var users = {};

io.sockets.on("connection", function (socket) {
    var userId = addUser(socket);

    socket.on("disconnect", function () {
        socket.broadcast.emit("user-left", users[userId]);
        delete users[userId];
    });
});

/**
 * Registers the user on the server. Notifies everybody that
 * he joined the lobby, sends the list of the online users
 * to the newly connected one.
 * @param socket the socket object of the connected client
 * @returns the ID of the newly created user
 */
function addUser(socket) {
    var userId = maxUserId++;
    var userName = "User " + userId;

    var user = {id: userId, name: userName, status: "ready"};
    users[userId] = user;
    Object.defineProperty(user, "socket", {
            value : socket,
            enumerable : false}
    );

    socket.emit("info", "You have connected");
    socket.emit("user-list", { users: users });
    socket.broadcast.emit("user-joined", user);
    return userId;
}
```

We moved the code for adding the user into the separate function—addUser(). It is way easier to manage it that way. Each new user receives the unique id, a userName, a status, and a socket. We assigned a socket property in a quite unusual way—via the Object.defineProperty(). If we assign the socket in a usual way, like

```
user.socket = socket;
```

then every time the user object is sent to the client, the `socket` object is sent too. Obviously, we don't need that data in our application. The easiest way to fix this behavior is to declare the property as non-enumerable. Such a property is accessible only if you know its name, it will not appear in `for..in` loops, and is omitted by the code that serializes JSON into the string. That's exactly what `Object.defineProperty()` does in our code.

Now you can test the code. Try connecting to the server with your device, open a few browser windows, and see how new list items appear on the screen. Then close the window and see how one of the items disappears. The look of our lobby is rather poor. It is not suitable for the game. Indeed, the basic styling of an HTML list doesn't look attractive, either on the desktop browser or on the phone. Figure 12-5 shows the result of our work.

Figure 12-5. *Lobby rendered without any extra CSS*

The result doesn't look particularly fascinating, but if we add some CSS magic, the list becomes a lot better. Add the CSS code in Listing 12-7 to the page.

Listing 12-7. *The CSS Styling for Lobby*

```
<style>
    html, body {
        overflow: hidden;
        width: 100%;
        height: 100%;
        margin:0;
        padding:0;
        border: 0;
    }


    #online_users {
        font-size: 2.5em;
        cursor: pointer;
        list-style: none;
        padding-left: 0;
    }

    #online_users li {
        margin: 0.2em;
```

```
        padding: 0.2em 0.2em 0.2em 0.2em;

        font-weight:bold;
        text-align:center;
        border: 3px solid #456f9a;
        background-image: -webkit-gradient(linear, 0% 0%, 0% 100%, ➥
    from(#7FA6CD), to(#5F88B0));
        box-shadow:3px 3px 3px #000000;
        border-radius: 6px;
    }

    #online_users li.ready {
        color: white;
    }

    #online_users li.playing {
        color: #006400;
    }
</style>
```

After styling, the usual list becomes a rather attractive list of buttons (see Figure 12-6). Okay, maybe it is not *that* attractive—but if you hire a real designer, you can be sure that it will be nice.

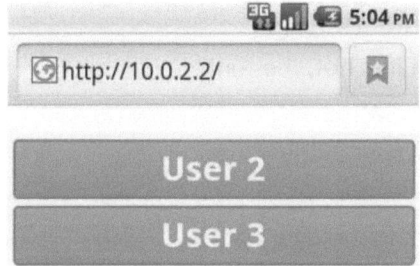

Figure 12-6. *The Same Lobby with CSS Styles*

The project at the current state is saved in the 02.lobby folder along with the other sources for this chapter. Feel free to play around with it and improve the look and feel of the lobby.

Adding the Gameplay

The goal of this section is to finish the implementation of the multiplayer version of Four Balls. We now have a working lobby, so that players can challenge each other to a game. Let's add the game-handling itself.

Before diving into the code, let's look at the shared components that are required on both the client and the server. This class is BoardModel—it holds the logic of making turns, and it can check if the turn is legal.

Sharing Logic Between the Client and the Server

Right now, the game board works well in single-player mode. When the user tries to make a move, a BoardModel puts the new token on the field if the move was correct, or ignores the action otherwise. In a multiplayer game, tapping the screen is not enough to place the token on the board. The turn first goes to the server, and then the server checks that the valid player is making a valid turn, and only then will the server send back the turn result to the client.

A well-designed game should perform the turn validation on the client too. Doing so improves usability: the wrong turns are reported straightaway without sending the response to the server. The algorithm for making the turn looks like the following:

1. User taps the game board.

2. The client detects the tap and calculates the number of the column under the tap.

3. The game client checks if the turn was valid (if it is not, the turn is simply ignored and algorithm terminates).

4. The turn is sent to the server and the server performs the same type of validation.

5. The turn result is sent to both players, and the next player can now take his turn (if the game is not over, of course).

As you see, we have to reuse the validation logic in the client and the server—steps 3 and 4 are doing the same action: step 3 validates the turn on the client-side and step 4—on the server side. Since both parts of the game are written in JavaScript, it is natural to try to reuse the same code and possibly the same file without useless code duplication.

There is only one problem with this approach. The modules of Node.js are defined in a different way than regular browser-based classes. Node.js uses several "magic" variables that do not exist in browser environment. For example, in Node.js you have to use exports in order to make parts of your module visible to the outer world, while in a browser, you simply declare new functions and they are appended to the global window object. In other words, what is different is the method of publication of the class for Node.js and the browser environment.

Luckily, it is not too hard to adjust the code for the component so that it works in both cases. Let's first look at the code in Listing 12-8.

Listing 12-8. *Wrapping the Code for the Class to Use in Browser and in Node.js*

```
(function(exports) {
    function BoardModel(cols, rows) {
        /* regular constructor here */
    }

    /* the rest of the code from BoardModel.js */

    // Publish the API to the outter world
    exports.BoardModel = BoardModel;

})(typeof global == "object" ? exports : window);
```

Start reading the code from the last line. The last line tries to detect the current execution environment. If there is a `global` object defined in the current scope, then the code is executed by Node.js, otherwise by the browser.

> **NOTE:** This kind of check is far from perfect of course. For example, if someone defines the `window.global` variable in the browser, this code fails. At the time of writing, however, there is no better way to detect the execution environment for the JavaScript module.

The last line of the listing passes either an `exports` or `window` object as the parameter to the anonymous function. The next fragment of the code is rather simple: the constructor and other functions and variables are defined as usual, except they now belong to the inner scope of the function (and not to the global scope as before). Finally, we have to make the constructor available to the outer world: `exports.BoardModel = BoardModel` does exactly this. With Node.js, the constructor is later available via a call to `require()` as usual; whereas in a browser, this code is equivalent to `window.BoardModel = BoardModel`, which simply appends the constructor to the global scope of the browser.

This technique is far from perfect, but it is much better than code duplication. To finish the task, add the updated `Board.js` file to the `public/js` folder. From this location, it is available to both the client and Node.js.

Take the old version of the `BoardModel.js` file from Chapter 10. Update it as shown in Listing 12-8 and save into `public/js/BoardModel.js`. This file is required on both the client and the server. That's why we put it in the location that is accessible to both. The client can read anything from `public` folder, while the server can read anything at all, including the `public` folder.

Server-Side

Given that we adopted the main logic-handling class for Node.js, the server is now ready to handle real game sessions! The player starts in a lobby where he can challenge other players or wait to be challenged (we implemented this functionality already). Once challenged, the player enters a new "mode of communication" with the server. He now can send and receive the game turns. Once the game is finished, the player is returned to the lobby.

Let's look at the protocol of communication between a client and a server, which we need to implement to support all these features. When a player selects an opponent from the list, he sends the challenge. In a real-world game, the player should have an option to accept or decline the challenge, but in this simple example, the challenge is always accepted. The server handles a few error cases at this point. For example, the player cannot challenge himself or another player who is in the middle of another match. If there were no errors, both players receive a message that indicates the start of the game. At this point, both clients should change the active screen and display the board instead of the lobby, allowing the players to take turns. Once the match is over, both players return to the lobby and can challenge new opponents.

Figure 12-7 illustrates the main game flow.

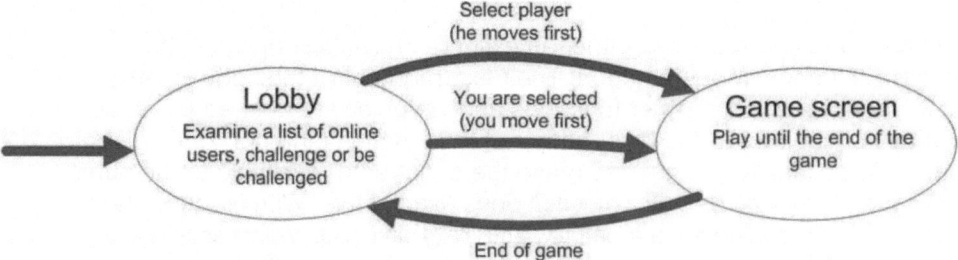

Figure 12-7. *The multiplayer game flow*

Now, let's start with the main server class. It has to handle a new type of message called *challenge*. Look at the code in Listing 12-9, which implements the connection-handling part of the server-side flow. The code for `onConnection()` function is mostly known to you already, the new part is the handling of challenges—the invitations to start the game. We first check if the challenge is valid; and if it is, we initiate the game between the users. The game is initiated inside the startGame() function, which we will look at in a minute.

Listing 12-9. *The Main Server File*

```
/* set up express and socket.io as usual */

io.sockets.on("connection", onConnection);

/**
 * Global counters and user registry
 */
var maxUserId = 0;
var maxGameId = 0;
var users = {};

/**
 * The connection handler, the "main" function of the multiplayer
 * server
 * @param socket
 */
function onConnection(socket) {
    var userId = addUser(socket);

    // Handling challenges, check the validity of challenge, and
    // if valid, set two users (the challenger and his opponent) into
    // the "playing" mode with the help of startGame()
    socket.on('challenge', function (challengedUserId, respond) {
        if (userId == challengedUserId) {
            respond({ error: "Cannot challenge self" });
        } else if (!users[challengedUserId]) {
            respond({ error: "Cannot find user " + challengedUserId });
        } else if (users[challengedUserId].status != "ready") {
            respond({ error: "User is not ready to play" });
        } else {
            startGame(users[userId], users[challengedUserId], respond)
        }
    });

    socket.on('disconnect', function () {
        console.log(users[userId].name + " disconnected");
        socket.broadcast.emit('user-left', users[userId]);
        delete users[userId];
    });
}


/**
 * Registers the user on the server. Notifies everybody that
 * he joined the lobby, sends the list of the online users
```

```
 * to the newly connected one.
 * @param socket the socket object of the connected client
 * @returns the ID of the newly created user
 */
function addUser(socket) {
    var userId = maxUserId++;
    var userName = "User " + userId;

    var user = {id: userId, name: userName, status: "ready"};
    Object.defineProperty(user, "socket", {
            value : socket,
            enumerable : false}
    );
    users[userId] = user;

    socket.emit('info', {text: "You have connected"});
    socket.emit('user-list', { users: users });
    socket.broadcast.emit('user-joined', user);
    return userId;
}
```

The second part of the server is the startGame() function. The game is initiated between the two players: "the initiator" (the one who selected the opponent from his lobby) and his opponent, "the target." The function creates the special initGame message that is sent to both parties. The message contains the data about the players so that the client application can draw the players' names somewhere on the screen. Next, we notify all online users that the initiator and the target are now "playing." Their names are now highlighted differently in the user list and everybody sees that they are busy.

Finally, the function creates the new GameSession—the object that handles the in-game interaction between the players. GameSession constructor accepts four parameters:

- gameId: the number that uniquely identifies this session

- player1: the player who takes the first turn (the target in our case)

- player2: the player who takes the second turn (the initiator in our case)

- onEndGame: a callback function that is called when the game is over

The code for the startGame() function shown in Listing 12-10 should now be quite easy to read.

Listing 12-10. *The startGame Function: Initiating the Game Between Two Players*

```
function startGame(initiator, target, initiatorRespond) {
    initiator.status = target.status = "playing";

    var initGame = {
        player1: initiator,
        player2: target
    };

    initiatorRespond(initGame);
    target.socket.emit('challenged', initGame);

    io.sockets.emit("user-playing", initiator);
    io.sockets.emit("user-playing", target);

    var gameId = maxGameId++;
    new GameSession(gameId, target, initiator, function() {
        initiator.status = target.status = "ready";
        io.sockets.emit("user-ready", initiator);
        io.sockets.emit("user-ready", target);
    });
}
```

The respond object that is passed as the second argument to the listener function allows the server to send the *response* to the *specific* message from the client. Here's how the corresponding client-side code looks:

```
// Client-side code. data is the
socket.emit('challenge', userId, function (data) {
    if (data.error) {
        // Something bad has happened, maybe the other party has left
    } else {
        // The game has started
    }
}
```

As you can see, Socket.IO passes the response to the callback method. This is rather convenient, especially when the client sends multiple messages of the same type: otherwise, it is impossible to match the particular request message with the particular received response without extra coding effort.

Finally, we need to create a GameSession class that is responsible for running a game between two players. Let's start with the constructor in Listing 12-11. Everything is quite simple: the game session is initiated with the default values: the current player is 0 and empty BoardModel. Then we add the game-specific listeners to the socket, the listeners that would listen to "turn" events.

Listing 12-11. *The GameSession Class*

```
exports = module.exports = GameSession;

var board = require("public/js/BoardModel");
var BoardModel = board.BoardModel;

function GameSession(id, player1, player2, onEndGame) {
    this._roomName = "game" + id;
    this._players = [player1, player2];
    this._currentPlayer = 0;

    this._boardModel = new BoardModel();
    this._onEndGame = onEndGame;

    for (var i = 0; i < this._players.length; i++) {
        this._setupGameListeners(i);
    }
}
```

The only fragment of code that is not completely clear at this point is the _roomName variable. Why do we need it in this code? Socket.IO has quite a useful concept called a *room*. A room is a convenience API that allows you to group sockets when you need it and quickly send a particular message to the members of the room. This is somewhat similar to the rooms in a chat application or "topic subscription" in the more advanced messaging APIs. Once you send something to the room, every subscribed socket receives the message.

Listing 12-12 shows the final part of the GameSession code, the _setupGameListeners() function that implements the main game flow. In this simplistic model, the only thing that a player can do during the match is to take a turn. Eventually, one of the players wins or the game enters the draw state. When this happens, the listeners are de-registered.

Listing 12-12. *Reacting on Players Turns and Ending the Game*

```
var _p = GameSession.prototype;

_p._setupGameListeners = function(playerIndex) {
    var socket = this._players[playerIndex].socket;
    socket.join(this._roomName);

    socket.on("turn", (function(column) {
        if (playerIndex != this._currentPlayer) {
            // For some reason, the wrong player is trying to make a turn
            socket.emit("error", {
                cause: "It is not your turn now"
```

```
        });
        return;
    }

    // Let's try to make a turn and see what happens
    var turn = this._boardModel.makeTurn(column);

    // Check if that was illegal turn
    if (turn.status == BoardModel.ILLEGAL_TURN) {
        socket.emit("error", {
            cause: "This turn is illegal"
        });
        return;
    }

    // The turn is legal, we can broadcast it to both parties
    socket.manager.sockets.to(this._roomName).emit("turn", turn);

    // Next player is the "current" now
    this._currentPlayer = (this._currentPlayer + 1)%2;

    // If there's a win condition or it is a draw,
    // then players are already in lobby. Clean up listeners.
    if (turn.status == BoardModel.WIN || turn.status == BoardModel.DRAW) {
        // End game, leave room and de-register listeners
        for (var i = 0; i < this._players.length; i++) {
            this._players[i].socket.removeAllListeners("turn");
            this._players[i].socket.leave(this._roomName);
        }
    }

    // Call the callback
    this._onEndGame();
}).bind(this));
};
```

The server is ready. It does everything that we planned to do: lobby, game handling, and the transition between the two. The final part of the game is the client-side HTML. We've already started to make it; we have the working lobby and components from the single-player version.

> **NOTE:** The current implementation doesn't cover situations such as one of the players being disconnected from the game or not making a move for a long time. We leave it as an exercise for the reader. It is quite easy to implement with a `"disconnect"` listener and a `setTimeout()` to track the stalled player.

Client-Side

The client needs some adjustments too. Right now, the client code can only handle the lobby, not the game itself. Copy the scripts from Chapter 3: the Game.js and BoardRenderer.js to the public/js folder of your project. BoardRenderer.js doesn't need to change at all, but the Game.js becomes slightly different.

Let's quickly review the single-player architecture of Four Balls.

- The BoardModel class is responsible for keeping the game state and validating the turns. In a multiplayer version, it is slightly changed to use it in both the browser environment and Node.js (see Listing 12-8).

- The BoardRenderer class is responsible for rendering the board on canvas. It will not change at all, because it is a pure client-side class. You may leave it as it is.

- The Game class is responsible for running the game and in particular for reacting on clicks. This class has the most changes in the multiplayer version because the game flow is now completely different. Instead of putting the token on board right after the click, we now have to wait for the server-side approval of the turn.

The most important change is in the Game class, the way the client reacts to the player tapping the screen. In the single-player version of the game, the client could decide if the turn is valid by itself, without asking the server. In the multiplayer game, the server is the mastermind, responsible for the flow of the game. Therefore, instead of placing the new token straight on the board, the Game class should now send the turn message to the server, and show the token only when the server confirms that the turn was valid.

The new implementation is quite different from the original one, so rename your file and constructor to OnlineGame.js. Look at the code in Listing 12-13, which illustrates the changes (set in bold) to this class. If the code doesn't look familiar to you, feel free to refer to "Wiring Components Together: The Game Class" in Chapter 3 to see the original version of the Game class.

Listing 12-13. *The Changes to the Game Class*

```
function OnlineGame(canvas, socket, endGameFn) {
    this._boardRect = null;
    this._canvas = canvas;
    this._ctx = canvas.getContext("2d");
    this._boardModel = BoardModel.newDefaultBoard();
```

```
        this._boardRenderer = new BoardRenderer(this._ctx, this._boardModel);
        this.handleResize();

        this._socket = socket;
        this._endGameFn = endGameFn;
        socket.on("turn", (function(turn) {
            this._makeTurn(turn.x);
        }).bind(this));

        socket.on("error", function(error) {
            alert(error.cause);
        });
}

_p = OnlineGame.prototype;

/**
 * Handles the click (or tap) on the Canvas. Translates the canvas coordinates
 * into the column of the game board and makes the next turn in that column
 * @param x the x coordinate of the click or tap
 * @param y the y coordinate of the click or tap
 */
_p.handleClick = function(x, y) {
    // get the column index
    var column = Math.floor((x - this._boardRect.x)/this._boardRect.cellSize);

    if (this._boardModel.isTurnValid(column)) {
    // Do not place token yet, just send the turn to the server
        this._requestTurn(column);
    } else {
        alert("Invalid turn");
        // Ignore this turn
    }
};

/**
 * Tell server that we are making turn. Do not place any tokens at this point
 * @param column the column to drop the piece to
 */
_p._requestTurn = function(column) {
    this._socket.emit("turn", column);
};

/**
 * Called when the server has responded, place the token and check
 * the result. If the game has ended - return to the lobby.
 * @param column the column where new piece was dropped
 */
_p._makeTurn = function(column) {
    // Make the turn and check for the result
```

```
        var turn = this._boardModel.makeTurn(column);

        // If the turn was legal, update the board, draw
        // the new piece
        if (turn.status == BoardModel.ILLEGAL_TURN) {
            alert("Ouch, we're out of sync with server");
            return;
        }

        this._boardRenderer.drawToken(turn.x, turn.y);

        // Do we have a winner after the last turn?
        if (turn.status != BoardModel.NONE) {
            _p._notifyAboutGameEnd(turn);
            this._reset();
            this._endGameFn();
        }
    }
};

/* rest of the functions not changed */
```

As you see, the player action is treated differently than in the single-player version. The online version of the class waits until the server confirms that the turn was recorded in the server-side board. That's why we had to split the code that makes the turn in three steps. First, we check the validity of the turn against the local version of the board with _boardModel.isTurnValid(), then we send the turn to the server with _requestTurn(column), and finally we receive the response from the server and place the token to the board in the _makeTurn() function. Only after that does it render the new token on the canvas. The code for the class is trimmed. The full version is available as usual with the source code for the book in a 03.game directory.

The BoardModel class needs to be updated too. We need to extract the turn validation logic into the separate function. For this game, the validation code is a one-line bounds check. Update BoardModel.js with the isTurnValid() function from Listing 12-14.

Listing 12-14. *Update BoardModel: Extract the Validation Logic into the Separate Function*

```
_p.isTurnValid = function(column) {
    // Check if the column is valid and if there's the empty row in the
    // given column. If there's no empty row, then the turn is illegal
    return (column >= 0 && column < this._cols &&
                            this._getEmptyRow(column) != -1);
};
```

To finish the application, we need to update the index.html file, the entry point for the client. This file is a merge between the lobby-handling code and the single-player Four Balls implementation. Now our game has two screens: the lobby screen and the game screen. We implement the change of screens with two div tags, only one of which is visible at any given moment. The code that does the switching is shown in Listing 12-15.

Listing 12-15. *Switching Game Screens*

```
function switchScreen(screenId) {
    document.getElementById(currentScreen).style.display = "none";
    document.getElementById(screenId).style.display = "block";
    currentScreen = screenId;
}
...

...
<body onload="init()">
    <div id="lobby">
        <ul id="online_users"></ul>
    </div>
    <div id="game" style="display: none">
        <canvas id="mainCanvas" width="30px" height="30px"></canvas>
    </div>
</body>
```

By default, the lobby screen is visible, and the game screen is hidden. Once you call switchScreen("game") the canvas with the game board appears on the screen, while the lobby div disappears (with the help of style.display = "none". The important thing to note here is that the lobby continues to function as usual. It still receives the events from the server and keeps the user list up-to-date. Once the game is over and the lobby screen is back, it is in a perfectly valid state.

Look at the source code for index.html file in Listing 12-16. Some parts, such as meta and CSS styles, are omitted in the listing to keep it shorter and focus on the main points. The full code can be found along with the other source code for this chapter in a 03.game folder (the file name is index.html).

Listing 12-16. *The Main HTML File*

```
<!DOCTYPE html>
<html lang="en">
<head>

    <!-- meta and css as usual, omitted here -->

    <script src="js/LobbyUserList.js"></script>
    <script src="js/BoardModel.js"></script>
    <script src="js/BoardRenderer.js"></script>
    <script src="js/OnlineGame.js"></script>
    <script src="/socket.io/socket.io.js"></script>
```

```
<script>
    var socket;
    var userList;
    var game;
    var currentScreen = "lobby";

    function init() {
        var canvas = initFullScreenCanvas("mainCanvas");

        // Copied from Chapter 3, you can implement a better way of handling
        // of user input with the help of classes from Chapter 5
        if (isTouchDevice()) {
            canvas.addEventListener("touchstart", function(e) {
                var touch = event.targetTouches[0];
                game.handleClick(touch.pageX, touch.pageY);
                e.stopPropagation();
                e.preventDefault();
            }, false);
        } else {
            canvas.addEventListener("mouseup", function(e) {
                game.handleClick(e.pageX, e.pageY);
                e.stopPropagation();
                e.preventDefault();
            }, false);
        }

        socket = io.connect();
        game = new OnlineGame(canvas, socket, onGameEnd);

        socket.on("user-joined", function (user) {
            userList.add(user.id, user.name, user.status);
        });

        socket.on("user-left", function (user) {
            userList.remove(user.id);
        });

        socket.on("user-playing", function (user) {
            userList.setStatus(user.id, "playing");
        });

        socket.on('user-ready', function (user) {
            userList.setStatus(user.id, "ready");
        });

        socket.on('user-list', function (data) {
            for (var userId in data.users) {
                var user = data.users[userId];
                userList.add(user.id, user.name, user.status);
            }
```

```
    });

    socket.on('challenged', function (data) {
        switchScreen("game");
        alert("Challanged by " + data.player1.name);
    });

    socket.on("info", function (info) {
        console.log (info.text);
    });

    var listElement = document.getElementById("online_users");
    userList = new LobbyUsersList(listElement, onChallenge);
    switchScreen("lobby");
}

function switchScreen(screenId) {
    document.getElementById(currentScreen).style.display = "none";
    document.getElementById(screenId).style.display = "block";
    currentScreen = screenId;
}

function onChallenge(userId, userName, status) {
    socket.emit('challenge', userId, function (data) {
        if (data.error) {
            // Something is wrong, maybe the other party has left
            alert(data.error);
        } else {
            // The game has started
            switchScreen("game");
            alert("Playing with " + data.player2.name);
        }
    });
}

function switchScreen(screenId) {
    document.getElementById(currentScreen).style.display = "none";
    document.getElementById(screenId).style.display = "block";
    currentScreen = screenId;
}

function onGameEnd() {
    switchScreen("lobby");
}

function initFullScreenCanvas(canvasId) { /* code not changed */ }

function resizeCanvas(canvas) { /* code not changed */ }

function isTouchDevice() { /* code not changed */ }
```

```
    </script>
  </head>
  <body onload="init()">
  <div id="lobby">
      <ul id="online_users"></ul>
  </div>
  <div id="game" style="display: none">
      <canvas id="mainCanvas" width="30px" height="30px"></canvas>
  </div>
  </body>
  </html>
```

As you see, the code in Listing 12-16 is based on the index.html code from Chapter 3. From that time, we've learned how to handle user input in a much better way. Feel free to update the code and use InputHandler.js to detect clicks.

The code is now ready. You can launch the game, join the lobby, challenge other players, and play a game online.

This project is just the starting point (though a very important one) toward the real multiplayer games. Its main task is to get you started with the multiplayer concepts and the corresponding code. Once you feel comfortable with these concepts, move on and make a more advanced version of the game, probably with chat, leader boards, funny user avatars, and tournaments.

Take a look at the result of your work in Figure 12-8. There are several clients playing on the same server; some of them in game, others are in lobby.

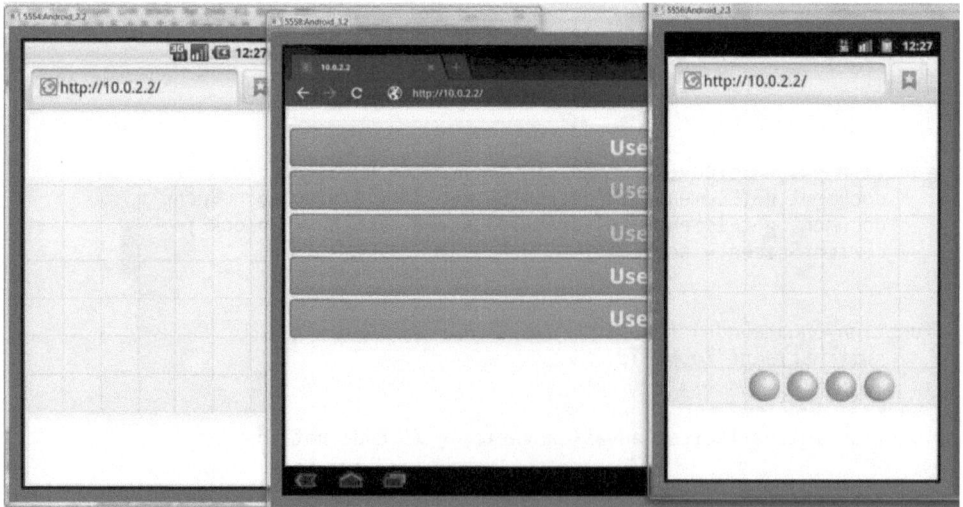

Figure 12-8. *Several opened sessions of the game*

Summary

In this chapter, we learned how to make a multiplayer game out of the single-player version. It takes a lot of effort to build a commercial-grade online game, even when the single-player version is up and running. The online experience involves not only the game itself, but also the large infrastructure around it: chats, tournaments, ratings, and so forth. It is important to keep the user interested in the game, even when he has mastered it already.

We learned how to use Socket.IO to simplify the communications between the client and the server. We analyzed the game architecture and determined the classes that need to be shared between the client and the server. We found a method to represent the JavaScript class in a way that both Node.js and browser can use. The logic of the game is now distributed between the client and the server. The client performs the "quick and dirty" checks of the turn validity to give users an early warning, while the server acts like a final arbiter that is responsible for updating the state of the game. We created a lobby, and implemented the opponent selection and the game process.

The result of this chapter is the prototype of the network application that demonstrates the typical flows of the online games: lobby and the game. The final version of the source code for this chapter can be found in a folder called `03.game`.

AI in Games

Artificial intelligence (or AI for short) is what makes the computer-controlled characters behave like real creatures: chase prey, find their way through the level, plan assaults, expose emotions, or even learn from the player. In other words, AI is a term that refers to a set of algorithms that make the game agents, look intelligent.

This chapter is a gentle introduction to several of the most commonly used AI algorithms and the approaches behind them. The topic itself is rather broad and it is impossible to fit an extensive overview of AI into the bounds of a single chapter, but I will try to give you a good starting point for further exploration of this wonderful subject. Once you master the basics, feel free to explore more-advanced AI algorithms.

In this chapter, we will learn about the following:

- AI and the type of AI needed for your game
- Types of graphs, their uses in real life, and how to implement a graph in JavaScript
- Building a waypoint graph
- Pathfinding
- A popular pathfinding algorithm called A*
- Decision making with a decision tree

I find AI to be one of the most interesting parts of game development. You can build an exciting game world without sound, 3D effects, networking, and even without traditional graphics. Look at *NetHack*, *ADOM*, and *Dwarf Fortress*. I know these examples are somewhat geeky, but these games are extremely addictive once you've learned how to play them. They all are built around an AI that creates a random virtual world, inhabits it with creatures, and makes up the gameplay.

> **NOTE:** The term AI is used in a much broader sense than game development. Artificial Intelligence presents a huge scientific interest in solving practical tasks— like natural language recognition and synthesis, financial analysis and prediction, image processing, and face recognition—and exploring the mechanisms behind the human thinking, such as memory, learning, decision making, and so on. In this book, the word "AI" is used solely in the context of game development. For more information, refer to the wonderful article "What is Artificial Intelligence" (`www-formal.stanford.edu/jmc/whatisai/whatisai.html`) by John McCarthy, a prominent scientist and the inventor of the term "AI".

Do I Need AI in My Game?

"Do I need AI in my game, and if so, how smart should it be"? This is the first question that you have to ask yourself before you spend too much time implementing algorithms. The real need for AI highly depends on the type of game that you are making, and the gameplay that you try to build. For example, solitaire-type games do not need an AI, and neither do online F1 simulators where players compete only with each other and not with computer-controlled bots.

The second part of the question is harder to answer. So how smart should your AI be? The truth is—a "smarter" AI doesn't always mean better gameplay. In some cases, simple and straightforward algorithms do a much better job than complex approaches. The zombie-invasion game, for instance, can be quite interesting with only a few rules that describe the behavior of zombies: if no player around—wander; otherwise—chase player. Zombies do not need to be the tactical geniuses to be fun, right?

Of course, there are games where AI plays a quite important role. Here are few examples: a 3D shooter that presents the player with intelligent opponents, a rally game where AI has to predict the effects of physics on a car, and a tactical simulator where computer-controlled guards realistically react on an intrusion. For these games, AI is a major part of the gameplay.

The rule of thumb is that the AI should be smart enough to look natural in the given game and under given circumstances. What exactly is "natural" depends on two factors. One is the game genre. A zombie standing with its face to the wall looks much more natural than the human guard doing the same thing. The second factor is the amount of time that the player observes the computer-controlled character. If the typical character appears on the screen only to vanish under a blast of bullets in the next second, he would not even have a chance to show how smart he is. On the other hand, if the player observes the character for a long time (like in *The Sims*), the unrealistic nonhuman behavior becomes much more obvious.

In this chapter, I decided to present two types of algorithms that are most commonly implemented in games: one is pathfinding and the other is decision making. Decision-making answers the question "what to do," while pathfinding tackles "how to reach the point in a world." These algorithms are quite easy to master and they allow building a broad range of games.

> **NOTE:** The examples in this chapter are built with the small, open-source framework that I created for the AI experiments. You can grab your copy from `https://github.com/Juriy/gameai`. It is a set of tools to render a tiny, 2D world and perform common geometric calculations that are often required in AI. This chapter describes the algorithmic part of the AI, so the code doesn't depend on a framework too much. The framework is only used to visualize the results: render walls, animate agents, and so forth.

Introducing Pathfinding

Pathfinding is the set of techniques that help a character to move from one point in the world to another. For example, when you order a unit to go to the tower, it must first find the path to the tower. Figure 13-1 illustrates a sample game world with a couple of buildings and obstacles. The goal of the pathfinding is to help agents navigate through the world.

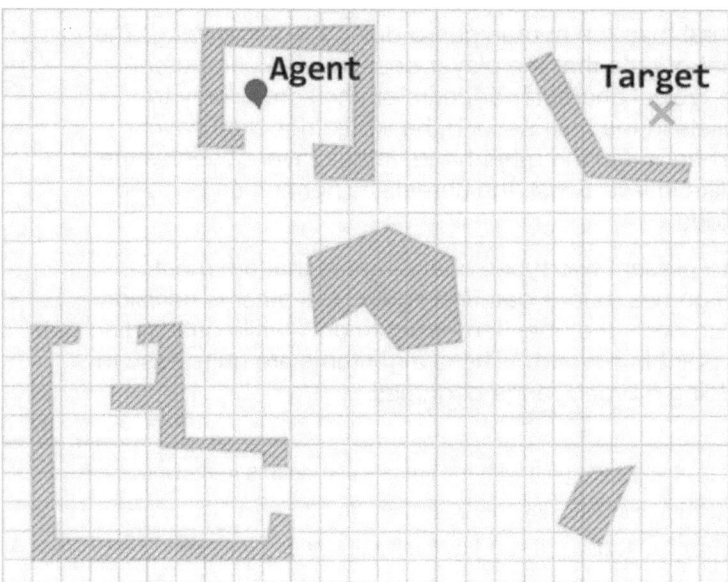

Figure 13-1. *The task of pathfinding: find the path between two points in the game world.*

The path should also be as short as possible. If a unit decides to take the long way when there is a short one, his behavior looks unnatural. So we should try to find the best path and not just any path.

> **NOTE:** Distance is not the only way to measure how good the path is. There are other options for path optimizations. For example, the fastest way for me to get out to the street to buy a bottle of soda is to jump out of the window from the third floor. Usually, however, I decide not to take this route. This is an extreme example, but in the game world, these kinds of cases are a lot more common. The character might decide to jump off a platform, losing some health but getting the ammo faster than his/her opponent. If health is low, however, it is more important to stay alive and take the slower way. These cases are more complex and they involve both pathfinding and decision making. In this chapter, we examine a case in which distance is the only criteria.

Analyzing the complete world geometry to find the path between two points might be a very complex task. The much simpler solution is to place waypoints throughout the level, so that they are connected by the line of sight and a character can navigate between them. The task of pathfinding is much easier then. Instead of navigating through the world, which can be incredibly complex, the character navigates through the set of predefined waypoints. Figure 13-2 illustrates this idea. As you **see**, once the waypoints are set, you only need to move between them.

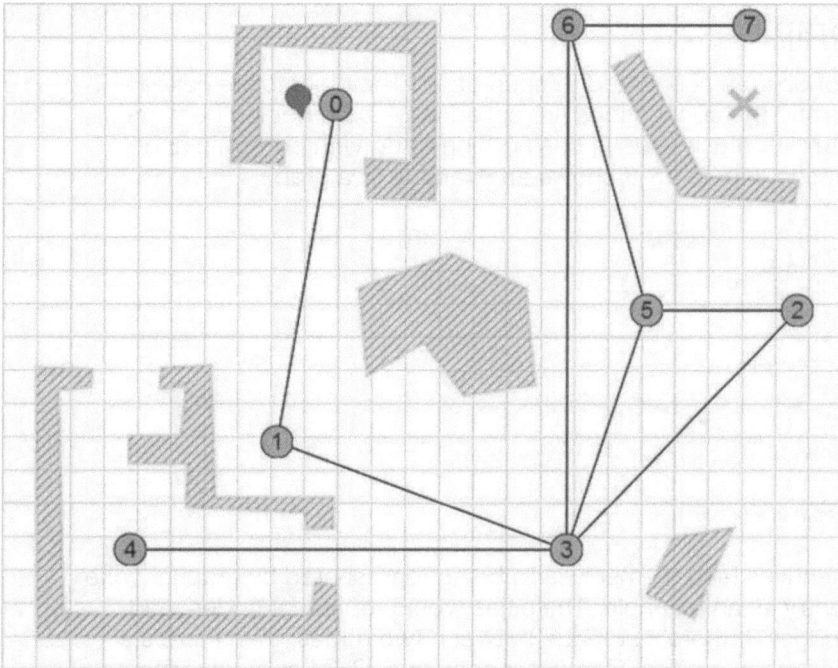

Figure 13-2. *The task of pathfinding simplified with the help of waypoints*

As you see in Figure 13-2, the agent now has to move from his current location to point 0, then to points 1, 3, 6, and 7, and finally moves straight toward the destination point. The only remaining question is how to make our AI find the correct sequence of waypoints: 0-1-3-6-7? There are multiple ways to get from 1 to 7. For example, an agent could go through point 5, or through point 2 and point 5, but these paths are longer than the correct one. To answer this question, we will take a step back and learn few basic facts from the mathematical apparatus called *the graph theory*.

Graphs

Many AI algorithms (not just pathfinding) take advantage of the graph theory. This section is a quick and informal introduction to graphs, mostly to get you familiar with the terms that we use in the following sections. If you are already familiar with graph theory and know straightaway what an "acyclic weighted graph" is, feel free to skip this section and move straight to the algorithms.

What Is a Graph?

A graph is a set of objects connected to each other. The objects are called *nodes* or *vertices* and the connections are called *edges*. Do not let the names "edge" and "vertex" confuse you—it has nothing to do with polygons and WebGL programming. Figure 13-3 shows an example of a graph.

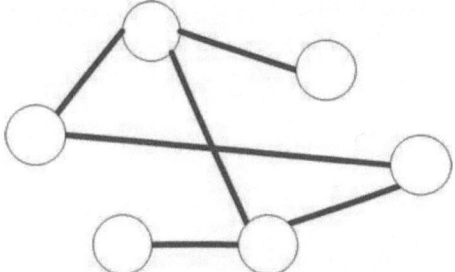

Figure 13-3. *An example of a graph*

Many real-world entities lend themselves to being represented by graphs. Take the map of a country as an example. The cities would represent nodes, and roads would be edges. If there's an edge between two nodes, then there's a direct road connecting two cities. Computer networks, GSM cells covering a certain area, and social connections between you, your friends, and friends of your friends are also examples of graphs.

Graphs prove themselves a good abstraction for many tasks: finding the shortest route between two cities; building an efficient network topology that handles high loads; and finding people in the social network that are likely to be the friends of the user. In games that involve movement and combat, it is common to represent a level as a graph of waypoints. This structure is much easier to analyze and to make decisions fast.

The way the graph is drawn on the surface can be arbitrary: the only thing that is important about the graph is the nodes and the connections between them. The layout is merely the representation of the structure in a surface. The graphs in Figure 13-4 are equivalent: in fact, this is exactly the same graph but drawn slightly differently. To make it even clearer, the nodes are marked with numbers.

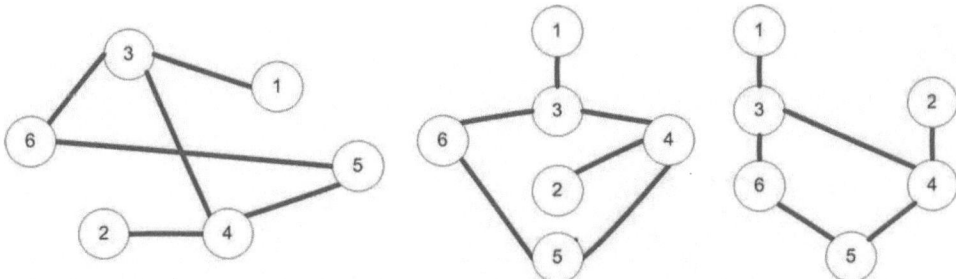

Figure 13-4. *The same graph drawn with the different layouts*

A graphical representation is not convenient for development, of course. The usual way to represent a graph in script is to use a matrix—each row and each column stands for a node. If two nodes are connected, then the matrix element on the intersection of the corresponding row and column is 1, otherwise it's 0. The matrix in Figure 13-5 represents the graph from Figure 13-4, without drawing it on the screen.

$$\begin{bmatrix} 0 & 0 & 1 & 0 & 0 & 0 \\ 0 & 0 & 0 & 1 & 0 & 0 \\ 1 & 0 & 0 & 1 & 0 & 1 \\ 0 & 1 & 1 & 0 & 1 & 0 \\ 0 & 0 & 0 & 1 & 0 & 1 \\ 0 & 0 & 1 & 0 & 1 & 0 \end{bmatrix}$$

Figure 13-5. *The matrix representation of the graph. If, for example, there is "1" on the intersection of the column i and row j, it means that vertexes i and j are connected with an edge.*

The edges of the graph may have directions. In this case, the graph is called a directed graph. An example of a directed graph is shown in Figure 13-6.

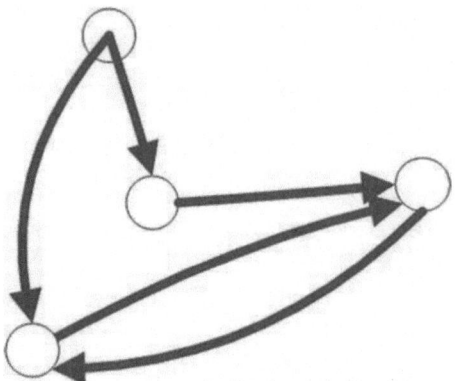

Figure 13-6. *A directed graph*

Finally, the edges of the graph might have *weights*. Weight is simply a number that shows how much it costs to move between the nodes. For example, if the vertices are cities and the edges are roads, think of the weight of the edge as the length of the road. Figure 13-7 shows the graph with added weights.

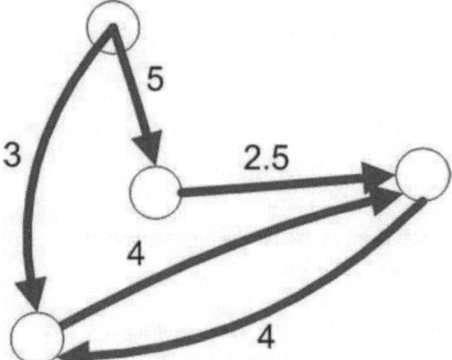

Figure 13-7. *A weighted graph*

A graph is a perfect way to represent waypoints. The edge between the nodes means that an agent can get from one waypoint to another by following the straight line, or performing other trivial action. If we work with the plain level, like in Figure 13-1, we can use an undirected graph. If you can get from point 1 to point 2, it automatically means that you can get back. In more complex cases, you might need to use the directed graph. For example, if there is a one-way portal or a crate that a character can jump into but can't scramble back. The weight of the edge is the distance between the waypoints.

Implementing Graphs in JavaScript

Graph implementation is fairly straightforward. The exact code might vary, of course, but the code in Listings 13-1 and 13-2 give you a general impression of how simple the graph really is. The code implements the generic graph structure suitable for pathfinding. First, let's look at the class that represents the graph node.

Listing 13-1. *The Graph Node Implementation*

```
function Node(id, x, y) {
    this.id = id;
    this.x = x;
    this.y = y;
    this._connections = [];
}

var _p = Node.prototype;

_p.addConnection = function(node, weight) {
    this._connections.push({
        node: node,
        weight: weight
    });
};

_p.getConnections = function() {
    return this._connections;
};
```

Even thought the generic graph doesn't need the information about the node position, pathfinding requires it. The algorithm that we will discuss in a moment takes into account the distance between the nodes, and that's why we will need to save the coordinates of every node. The **id** parameter is there only for convenience. It is much easier to debug graph algorithms when nodes have a name or unique number.

Each node has an array of connections. The array is a list of the other graph nodes connected to the current one (with respect to direction, if the graph is directed).

The graph itself is simply a set of nodes (see Listing 13-2).

Listing 13-2. *The Graph Is a Set of Nodes*

```
function Graph(nodes) {
    this._nodes = nodes;
}
```

It is often convenient to present the graph in the form of a two-dimensional array or matrix. If there is an edge between nodes i and j, then the [i][j] is 1, otherwise 0. For example, the 3×3 array in Listing 13-3 presents a graph that has three nodes.

Listing 13-3. *Array That Stores the Connections Between the Nodes*

```
var nodes = [
    [0, 1, 0],
    [1, 0, 1],
    [0, 1, 0]
];
```

The graph that is described by this array is shown in Figure 13-8. It has connections between nodes 0 and 1, and nodes 1 and 2.

Figure 13-8. *The graph described by the array in Listing 13-3*

This method of specifying connections is widely used in mathematics. As for the JavaScript development, for small graphs it is cleaner to put the matrix in your code rather than many calls to **node.addConnection()**. Let's update the graph's constructor. It accepts the optional array of connections and updates the nodes with the data from the array. Because we are making the graph for the pathfinding, the code also calculates the distance between the nodes and sets the connection weight to that value. Listing 13-4 shows the updated constructor.

Listing 13-4. *The Updated Graph Constructor That Accepts the Array of Connections*

```
function Graph(nodes, connections) {
    this._nodes = nodes;

    if (!connections)
        return;

    for (var i = 0; i < connections.length; i++) {
        for (var j = 0; j < connections[i].length; j++) {
            if (matrix[i][j]) {
                nodes[i].addConnection(nodes[j],
                    Graph.distance(nodes[i], nodes[j]));
            }
        }
    }
}
```

```
Graph.distance = function(node1, node2) {
    return Math.sqrt(
        (node1.x - node2.x)*(node1.x - node2.x) +
        (node1.y - node2.y)*(node1.y - node2.y));
};
```

With **Node** and **Graph** classes in place, we can transform waypoints into a graph
suitable for the pathfinding algorithms. For example, the graph used in the game
world we saw in Figure 13-2 is created with the code in Listing 13-5.

Listing 13-5. *Creating the New Graph from Node Coordinates and Connection Matrix*

```
function createGraph() {
    var coords = [[248,76],[205,329],[592,230],[420,410],
                  [95,410],[479,230],[420,16],[555,16]];
    var matrix =
            [[1, 1, 0, 0, 0, 0, 0, 0],
             [1, 1, 0, 1, 0, 0, 0, 0],
             [0, 0, 1, 1, 0, 1, 0, 0],
             [0, 1, 1, 1, 1, 1, 1, 0],
             [0, 0, 0, 1, 1, 0, 0, 0],
             [0, 0, 1, 1, 0, 1, 1, 0],
             [0, 0, 0, 1, 0, 1, 1, 1],
             [0, 0, 0, 0, 0, 0, 1, 1]];

    var nodes = [];
    for (var i = 0; i < coords.length; i++) {
        nodes.push(new Node(i, coords[i][0], coords[i][1]));
    }
    graph = new Graph(nodes, matrix);
}
```

It is worth adding a couple more functions to draw the graph on the **canvas**.
These functions have nothing to do with the AI algorithms, so they are not
included in this chapter. You can find them in the **Graph.js** file that comes along
with the source code for this chapter. The final example code will look like
Listing 13-6. The code includes few calls to the utility functions, like rendering
grid and obstacles from the AI playground framework that I mentioned at the
start of the chapter. They are quite trivial; you can implement them yourself or
grab the fresh version straight from GitHub.

Listing 13-6. *The Graph-Rendering Example*

```
<!DOCTYPE html>
<html>
<head>
<title>Graph Rendering Demo</title>
```

```
<-- add required script tags -->

<script>

var map = new Map(mapData);
var canvas;
var ctx;

var agent;
var graph;

function init() {
    agent = new Agent();
    createGraph();
    agent.setPosition(220, 70);
    agent.setOrientation(Math.PI/2 - 0.2);

    canvas = document.getElementById("mainCanvas");
    ctx = canvas.getContext("2d");
    drawFrame();
}

function createGraph() {
    var coords = [[248,76],[205,329],[592,230],[420,410],
                  [95,410],[479,230],[420,16],[555,16]];
    var matrix =
            [[1, 1, 0, 0, 0, 0, 0, 0],
             [1, 1, 0, 1, 0, 0, 0, 0],
             [0, 0, 1, 1, 0, 1, 0, 0],
             [0, 1, 1, 1, 1, 1, 1, 0],
             [0, 0, 0, 1, 1, 0, 0, 0],
             [0, 0, 1, 1, 0, 1, 1, 0],
             [0, 0, 0, 1, 0, 1, 1, 1],
             [0, 0, 0, 0, 0, 0, 1, 1]];

    var nodes = [];
    for (var i = 0; i < coords.length; i++) {
        nodes.push(new Node(i, coords[i][0], coords[i][1]));
    }

    graph = new Graph(nodes, matrix);
}

function drawFrame() {
    ctx.fillStyle = "white";
    ctx.fillRect(0, 0, canvas.width, canvas.height);

    Grid.draw(ctx, canvas.width, canvas.height);
    graph.draw(ctx);
    agent.draw(ctx);
```

```
      map.draw(ctx);
    }
  </script>
</head>

<body onload="init()" >
<canvas id="mainCanvas" width="625" height="500"></canvas>
</body>
</html>
```

This code gives you a good start to test your AI algorithms.

Building Pathfinding AI

There are two steps to building simple pathfinding AI: find a method to build the pathfinding graph for the level, and implement the algorithm to find the routes on the graph. Let's start with the algorithm.

A* Algorithm

A* (pronounced "A star") is the de-facto standard for pathfinding in modern games. A* solves the task of finding the best path between the two nodes of the graph. In terms of pathfinding, the "best" path is the cheapest path—the one that has the smallest possible sum of connection weights. The path from node A to node B that goes through connections with weights 3-3-2 (total 8) is obviously better than the path that goes through the route 5-3-4 (total 12). For our simple example, the weight of the connection is the distance between the nodes; however, other metrics are also possible: for example, when the game involves different terrain types like dirt or rocks, or the level has teleports that can instantly move the player to another part of the world. We will start with a very informal explanation of the algorithm.

Informal Description

The idea behind A* is to move through the nodes of the graph so that the most promising routes are explored first. A route is a list of connections from the starting node to some other node in the graph. The cost of the route is the sum of the connections' weights that form the route. Figure 13-9 shows the route between the nodes 0 and 3 that has a cost of 485 (256 to go from 0 to 1, and 229 to go from 1 to 3). This figure shows exactly the same graph as Figure 13-2, but without the surrounding obstacles. Once the pathfinding graph is built, we don't care about the geometry of the level anymore, we work only with the node positions and connection weights.

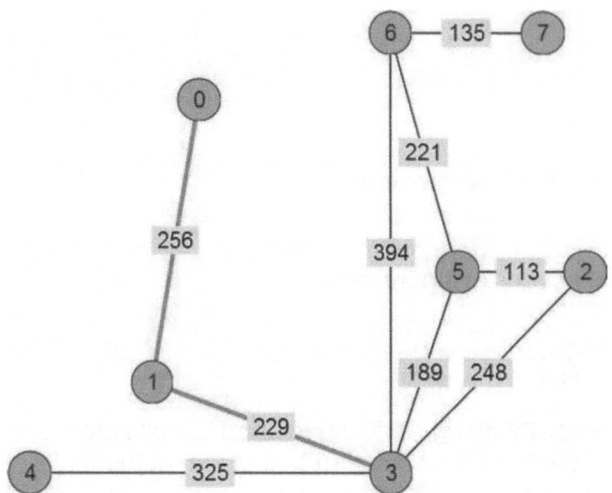

Figure 13-9. *The route between nodes 0 and 3; the cost of this route is 485.*

If we need to find the path between nodes 0 and 7, the first two steps are obvious. We move to node 1, and then to node 3, because we don't have any choice here—there is only one possible path. But at node 3, we have an option to explore four other nodes: 2, 4, 5, and 6. The question is which one to choose first.

A* chooses the path that is likely to be the shortest. To find which one that is, we need to calculate the *estimated cost* of the route. To estimate the cost of the route without knowing the number of additional nodes we need to visit, we divide the route into two parts. The first part is the "known" part—the nodes that we have already visited before the current one. The cost of this part is easy to calculate—just add the weights of the connections that led to the current point. The second part of the route, from the current point to the destination, is unknown, but we still need to estimate it. To do that, we pretend that there is a direct connection from the current node to the destination. The weight of such connection would be the distance between these two points. Add it to the first part and you get a rough estimate of what the route might cost.

This is an optimistic estimate of the route length—you know that the route will be at least that long, maybe more, but never less. It turns out that this heuristic gives rather good results.

Now let's try to pick the best route from node 3. Table 13-1 summarizes the calculations that we need to perform for each of the four possible routes.

Table 13-1. *Calculating the Estimated Cost for the Routes*

Route	Cost	Distance to Goal	Estimated Cost
0-1-3-**2**	485 + 248 = **706**	217	923
0-1-3-**4**	485 + 325 = **810**	605	1415
0-1-3-**5**	485 + 189 = **674**	227	**901**
0-1-3-**6**	485 + 394 = **879**	135	1014

The most promising route is the route that has the smallest estimated cost, which is route 0-1-3-5. As you see, this route is not the correct one, but the next step of the algorithm fixes that.

On the next step, A* goes to node 5 and calculates the cost of the route 0-1-3-5-6. This route is longer than 0-1-3-6, which we tried on the previous step. Even though the route 0-1-3-6 was not selected that time, it is chosen as the most promising route now.

The process is repeated: pick the best node, mark it as "current," find adjacent nodes, check which is the best, mark it as current, and so on until we reach the destination node. The algorithm guarantees that if the path exists, it will be found.

When a node is visited, we keep track of the connection that led to the node: we will use this information once we have found the target and need to build the whole route. Each node tracks the total cost of the route and the estimated total cost of the route. So each visited node has three numbers associated with it:

- The previously visited node that led to this one
- The cost of the route (so far)
- The estimated cost of the route to the destination

Node Lists

A* keeps track of all nodes that have been visited or processed. There are two lists called *open list* and *closed list*. When the node has been processed and all its connections have been evaluated (in other words, the node was "current" at some step of algorithm), it is considered to be a *closed node* and it is moved to the closed list. The node that has been visited through one of the connections and has an associated route length and cost estimate is called an *open node* and is moved to the open list. Look at Figure 13-10, which illustrates how nodes are moved between the lists.

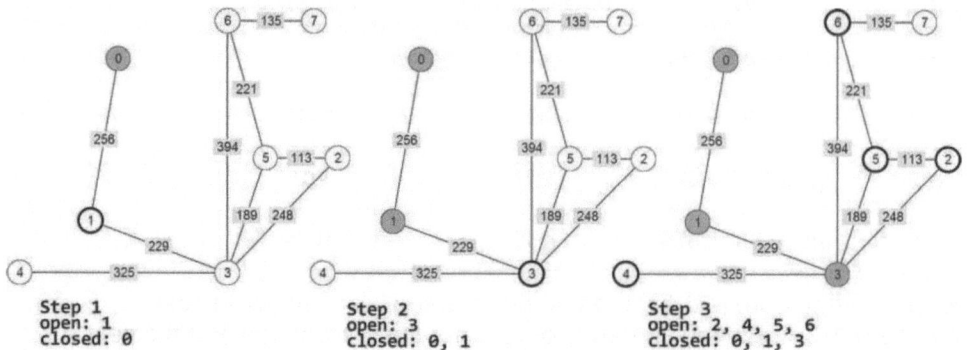

Figure 13-10. *The lists of A*: the filled nodes are in the closed list, bolded nodes are in the open list, the rest of the nodes are unprocessed.*

The first step starts at node 0. At the end of the first step, node 0 is closed (since every connection has been processed), and its neighboring nodes are open (since we have cost estimations for them, but we haven't yet processed their connections). The second step starts with choosing the best node from an open list. Since there is only one node, node 1, we chose it. All nodes connected to node 1 are now processed, and then node 1 is moved to the closed list too. Next, we add nodes 2, 4, 5, and 6 to the open list, and find which one of them is the most promising. When all four nodes are inspected, node 3 is moved to the closed list.

During the run of the algorithm, we may eventually try to evaluate the node that is already in one of the lists. If the new route to the node is better than the previous one, then we simply treat the node as unprocessed: update the associated values and move the node to the open list, if it is not there already.

Formal Description

Now we are ready for the formal description of the algorithm. A* starts with putting the first node into the list of the open nodes. Next, the following steps are performed while the list of open nodes is not empty:

1. Find the most promising open node (minimal estimated cost). This node is now "current."

2. For every node connected to the current node:

    a.   Calculate the route cost and estimated route cost.

b.   If the node is in the closed list and the new route cost is less than the one associated with the node, remove it from the closed list, update the values as if it is the new node, and then put it in the open list.

c.   If the node is in the open list and the new route cost is less than the one associated with the node, update the values and leave it in the list.

d.   Otherwise, update the values and put the node into the open list.

3. Move the current node from the open list to the closed list.

Once the end node is found, the route can be constructed by tracing back the node connections that formed the route.

Implementation

The implementation of A* is quite simple (see Listing 13-4). Given the earlier explanation, you should be comfortable with the code for the **findPath** function.

Listing 13-7. *The JavaScript implementation of A**

```
_p.findPath = function(startNode, endNode) {

    function updateNodeValues(node, prevNode, routeCost) {
        node.routeCost = routeCost;
        node.estimatedCost = routeCost + Graph.distance(node, endNode);
        node.prevNode = prevNode;
    }

    var openList = [];
    var closedList = [];

    startNode.routeCost = 0;
    openList.push(startNode);
    var routeFound = false;

    while (openList.length > 0) {
        // The smallest element (consider a better way
        // of getting smallest element).
        var currentNode = openList.sort(function(a, b) {
                                        return a.estimatedCost
                                        - b.estimatedCost})[0];

        if (currentNode == endNode) {
            routeFound = true;
```

```
                break;
        }

    currentNode.getConnections().forEach(function(connection) {
        var node = connection.node;
        var newRouteCost = currentNode.routeCost + connection.weight;

        if (closedList.indexOf(node) > -1) {
            // The node is in closed list
            if (newRouteCost < node.routeCost) {
                // Remove from closed list
                closedList.splice(closedList.indexOf(node), 1);

                updateNodeValues(node, currentNode, newRouteCost);
                openList.push(node);
            }
        } else if (openList.indexOf(node) > -1) {
            // The node is in open list
            if (newRouteCost < node.routeCost) {
                updateNodeValues(node, currentNode, newRouteCost);
            }
        } else {
            // The node is not processed
            updateNodeValues(node, currentNode, newRouteCost);
            openList.push(node);
        }
    });

    // Remove from open list
    openList.splice(openList.indexOf(currentNode), 1);
    // Add to closed list
    closedList.push(currentNode);
}

var route = [];
if (routeFound) {
    var routeNode = endNode;
    while (routeNode) {
        route.push(routeNode);
        routeNode= routeNode.prevNode;
    }
    route.reverse();
}

// Cleanup, so that old values don't mess around
this._nodes.forEach(function(node) {
    delete node.routeCost;
    delete node.estimatedCost;
    delete node.prevNode;
});
```

```
    return route;
};
```

With some extra drawing effort, you can highlight the route to see the result shown in Figure 13-11.

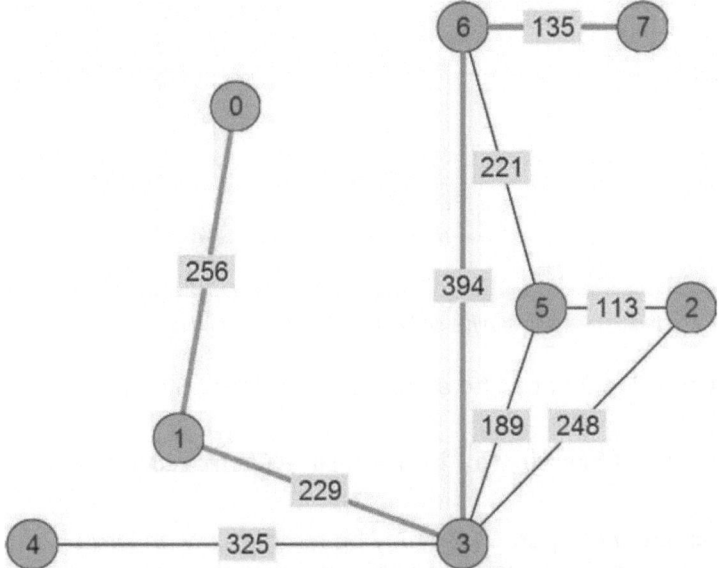

Figure 13-11. *The highlighted path between the nodes*

Notes on Implementation

The exact implementation of the algorithm might vary a lot, depending on the game that you are building. For example, in tactic games, where units move within a square grid, you do not really need a waypoint graph. The grid itself plays the role of the graph. Every tile has exactly four connections: east, west, north, and south (or eight if you allow moving diagonally), and it is easy to predict which tile is next to the current one. If the tile is marked as a "wall," there is no connection in that direction. Figure 13-12 shows an example of such a game world.

The weight of the move is usually constant too. The distance is calculated differently: Euclidian distance doesn't work because you do not allow the character to move straight through the tiles. The distance that is used in this case is called a *Manhattan distance*. It represents the world where you can only move along an axis—like in the city of Manhattan, where you drive through a grid of streets and avenues but not through the skyscrapers. Manhattan distance is calculated by the formula |x2 − x1| + |y2 − y1|. For that kind of pathfinding, you can stick with the much easier implementation of the A* algorithm.

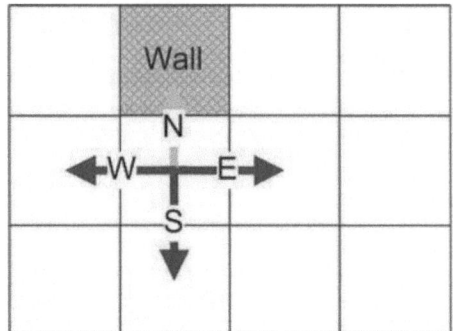 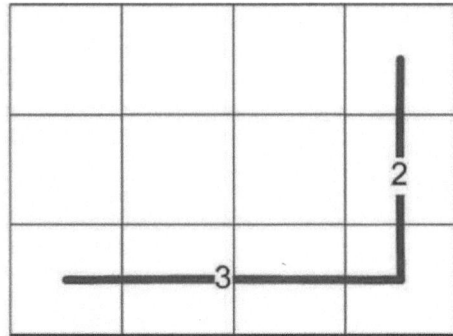

Figure 13-12. *A game world based on square tiles can survive without graphs for pathfinding.*

Lastly, the implementation has a line that can be a performance killer on large graphs:

```
var currentNode = openList.sort(function(a, b) {return a.estimatedCost - b.estimatedCost})[0];
```

The problem is that sorting an array of open nodes may be terribly slow on large graphs with thousands of nodes (on small maps you will not notice the difference). If you need an efficient algorithm, you should look for the data structure that holds the elements presorted. For example, the priority queue implementation based on the binary tree. The discussion of these algorithms is out of the scope of this chapter, but you can easily find several nice implementations on the Internet. The small library at `https://github.com/vadimg/js_bintrees` is a good place to start.

Methods of Building the Pathfinding Graph

The correctly built pathfinding graph is the key to intelligent AI movement. There are many approaches to building a graph, and this section is a brief overview of some of them.

- *Full manual graph.* You set the coordinates of the nodes and connections yourself.

- *The line-of-sight approach.* Allows you to set only node positions and calculate the connections based on the level geometry.

■ *The navmesh.* The nodes of the graph are polygons rather than points.

Full Manual Graph

The first way of creating a graph manually is to define every node and connection by hand and then let the character pick the node that is closest to him. For a game with large levels, this approach can be rather inefficient, since the game designer must be very careful while placing nodes. Figure 13-13 shows a possible problem: the character picks the closest node, but there is a wall in the way.

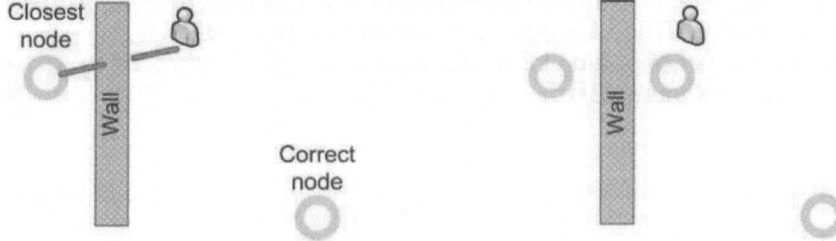

Figure 13-13. *On the left, the problem with a naïve pathfinding graph: due to the mistake of the level designer, the character attempts to move through the wall to reach the node. The corrected version is on the right.*

This problem can be fixed by checking if the closest node is visible before selecting it. While it is usually not hard to code it, the algorithm might be rather expensive to execute at runtime.

Manual placing of the nodes is quite a cumbersome task too. There are a few ways to make the life of level designer easier.

Raycasting (Line of Sight)

In many 2D games, if the node is visible from the other node, then it is reachable. Using this simple rule, we can generate the edges of the waypoint graph automatically: it's much easier to place vertices. Take a look at Figure 13-14, which shows this idea. The nodes are placed by the level designer. Then we cast a virtual ray between every pair of nodes and check if there are any obstacles in between. If the line of sight is clear, the edge is added to the graph:

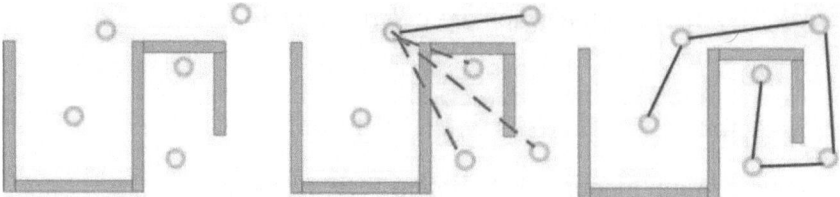

Figure 13-14. *Line of sight is used to generate edges of the waypoint graph automatically.*

Navigation Meshes

The most popular technique in modern game development is navigation meshes, or simply *navmeshes*. The idea behind it is to let the level designer prepare the graph, but instead of putting individual nodes, he draws polygons to mark a "movable" area (see Figure 13-15).

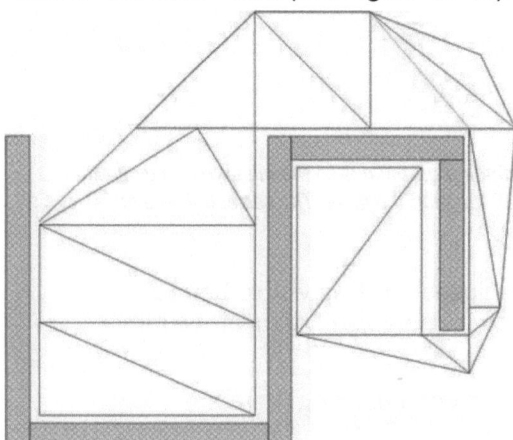

Figure 13-15. *An example of the navmesh and a navigation graph built with it*

There are many advantages of using this approach. The character doesn't need to pick the closest waypoint anymore, so he will not try to step through the wall to get there. A level designer is comfortable with moving polygons around and he will be comfortable with navmeshes too. The last important property of a navmesh is that the character should be able to move from any point on his polygon to any point on any adjacent polygon. In other words, the character does not need to follow paths that might look like rails. With navmeshes, the character can implement smarter and more natural movement algorithms.

Once you build the pathfinding graph and implement the pathfinding algorithm, you can build the actual movement of the character through the level. Use the techniques described in Chapter 4 to build the animation of the character that moves from one waypoint to the other.

Decision Making

Now the agent can move through the level, but the behavior is not quite intelligent yet. What should the character do next? Run, chase the enemy, find food, or take some rest? This is the usual question for the decision-making AI. In everyday life, every human being needs information of some sort in order to make a decision. For example, if I am a little hungry, and there is a sandwich on my desk, I will eat it. If I am really hungry, and there is no sandwich on the table, but there is a sandwich in a kitchen, I will go and grab that one. To make a decision, I had to observe my internal state (am I hungry or not?) and the world around me (where is the sandwich?).

In the simplest case, a decision-making AI acts almost the same way. However, the internal and external conditions are presented in a more formal way:

```
makeDecision() {
    if (!isHungry()) {
        workMore();
    } else if (isLittleHungry()) {
        if (isSandwichOnTheDesk()) {
            eat();
        } else {
            workMore();
        }
    } else if (isVeryHungry()) {
        if (isSandwichOnTheDesk() || isSandwichInTheKitchen()) {
            eat();
        } else {
            workMore();
        }
    }
}
```

This type of the presentation is called a *decision tree*, because it is easy to represent and configure in the form of a tree (see Figure 13-16).

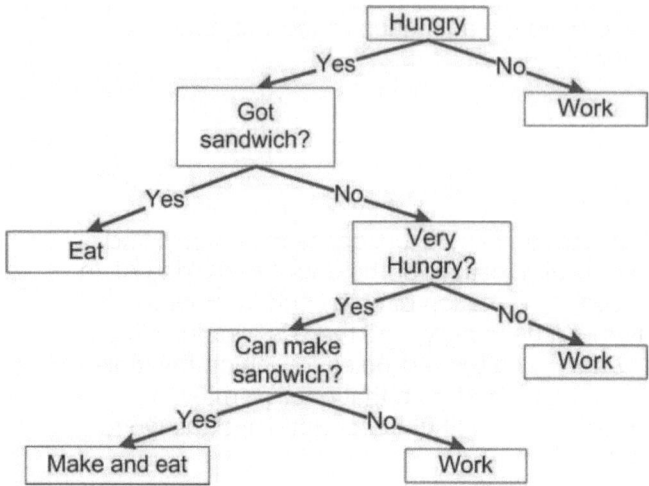

Figure 13-16. *An example of a decision tree*

When each node is a separate JavaScript object that can check the condition and return either a decision or another node, the resulting system can be configured to implement rather interesting AI behaviors.

There are many different types of decision trees. For example, the tree doesn't have to contain only yes/no branches. It can have multiple branches, or probabilistic conditions, as shown in Figure 13-17.

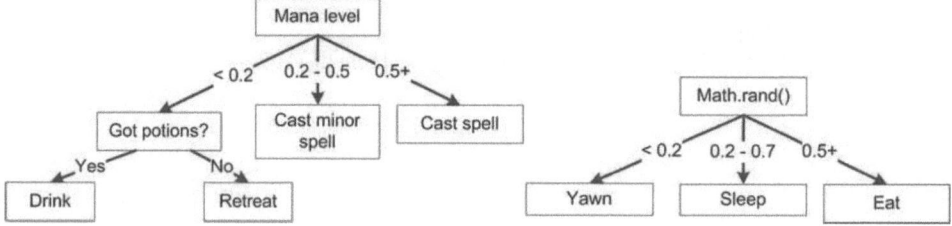

Figure 13-17. *Multiple branches and probabilistic conditions on a decision tree*

The code in Listings 13-6 to 13-8 shows the JavaScript implementation of such a decision-making agent. It has just two "needs"—to eat and to sleep. It sleeps whenever it wants to, but the chance of it eating is only 30 percent. The listings are rather self-explanatory. The code is based on two types of decision nodes. The **NumericDecision** checks the parameter of the object; it then delegates to the **leNode** if it is "lesser or equals" than the threshold, or to the **gNode** if it is greater than the threshold. The numeric decision is used to trigger the hunger behavior. If the hunger level is above 50, the agent will think about finding food (with 30 percent chance). The second type of node that we need is **ProbabilisticNode**—it chooses the action depending on the value of the random number.

Listing 13-6. *The Decision Tree Nodes*

```
/**
 * Numeric decision is based on the value of the certain agent parameter.
 * If value is lesser or equal than the threshold, the leNode is executed
 * otherwise - gNode.
 */
function NumericDecision(name, threshold, leNode, gNode) {
    this._name = name;
    this._threshold = threshold;
    this._leNode = leNode;
    this._gNode = gNode;
}

NumericDecision.prototype.execute = function(agent) {
    var node = agent[this._name] > this._threshold ? this._gNode : this._leNode;
    node.execute(agent);
};

/**
 * Probabilistic decision is executed depending on the chance value
 * 0 - never
 * 1 - always
 * between 0-1 with the
 */
function ProbabilisticDecision(chance, trueNode, falseNode) {
    this._chance = chance;
    this._trueNode = trueNode;
    this._falseNode = falseNode;
}

ProbabilisticDecision.prototype.execute = function(agent) {
    var node = Math.random() < this._chance ? this._trueNode : this._falseNode;
    node.execute(agent);
};
```

Now that we have the nodes, we can add some actions too. The **EatAction** makes the agent go to a predefined point where the food source is located, and start eating. The **SleepAction** makes the agent sleep wherever he is, and finally, the **WanderAroundAction** makes the agent select a random point on the map and navigate there.

Listing 13-7. *Actions: The Leafs of Decision Tree*

```
/**
 * Eat - reduce hunger
 */
function EatAction() { }
EatAction.prototype.execute = function(agent) {
    console.log("Decided to eat");
    navigateTo(220, 70);
    eat();
};

/**
 * Sleep - increase energy
 */
function SleepAction() {}
SleepAction.prototype.execute = function(agent) {
    console.log("Decided to sleep");
    sleep();
};

/**
 * Do nothing
 */
function WanderAroundAction() {}
WanderAroundAction.prototype.execute = function(agent) {
    console.log("Wandering around...")
    goToRandomPoint();
};
```

Finally, we need to create the tree and let it make the decision. Listing 13-8 shows how to do it.

Listing 13-8. *Initializing the Decision Tree*

```
/**
 * Initialize the tree
 */
function buildDecisionTree() {
    var wander = new WanderAroundAction();
    var sleep = new SleepAction();
    var eat = new EatAction();

    return new NumericDecision("hunger", 50,
        new NumericDecision("energy", 30,
            sleep,
            wander),
        new ProbabilisticDecision(0.3,
                eat,
                new NumericDecision("energy", 30,
```

```
                    sleep,
                    wander)));
}
```

Once the decision tree is initialized, you can call **tree.execute()** whenever an agent needs to make a decision. It is worth mentioning that decision making should not happen on every frame of the game. The decision-making logic happens only when the character needs to reconsider what he is doing. In the simple example that comes along with the source code for this chapter, the character makes the decision when he finishes the action sequence and needs to do something new.

The decision itself might require a complex action. For example, the decision to recharge a weapon might involve finding the ammo location, moving there (with the help of a pathfinding algorithm), taking the ammo and recharging, and finally returning to the front line. Such a set of complex actions is usually referred to as *behavior*.

There are many other approaches to building AI: fuzzy logic, goal-oriented designs, state machines, rule systems, and their combinations. There's a lot of material to cover, but for many casual games, it is quite enough to have only pathfinding and a decision-tree-based AI engine. If you are interested in further research, read the wonderful book by Ian Millington and John Funge, *Artificial Intelligence for Games*, Second Edition (Morgan Kaufmann, 2009). It has a set of well-explained AI algorithms, which if used wisely can make your game bots act very smart.

The code that combines both pathfinding and decision-making techniques can be found in a file called **04.decisions.html** along with the other sources for this chapter. Don't forget to visit the JavaScript AI playground project on GitHub (**https://github.com/Juriy/gameai**) from time to time. You might find something useful for your own game there.

Summary

This chapter is the starting point for an in-depth exploration of AI topics. Artificial intelligence plays an important role in game development, but you should carefully evaluate the level of AI required in your particular game. Sometimes the most interesting game uses the simplest AI techniques. The most basic and usual task that AI performs is pathfinding—finding a path between two points in the level. The A* pathfinding algorithm works with the waypoint graph—a mathematical representation of the reachable area of the game world.

We learned about the different ways to construct the graph and highlighted the common pitfalls of each technique. We also peeked at the different ways to represent the navigation data for a level, called the navmesh.

We also looked at a decision tree—the simple algorithm that helps an agent pick the next action. This is probably the simplest algorithm out of the family, yet it allows us to implement very interesting and natural-looking behaviors.

JavaScript Game Engines

This chapter is devoted to the review of the third-party tools: game engines and graphic libraries made for web browsers. Game engines make the life of developers easier since they provide higher-level facilities for making games. For example, if you are making a game from scratch, you have to deal with every detail yourself: loading images, breaking them up into frames and sprites, rendering world, detecting clicks, and so forth. We have done it already in Chapter 7, and you probably remember that there are quite a lot of aspects to take care of. A good 2D game engine would give you all these facilities right out of the box.

The usual question at this point is "why have we wasted so much time learning the basic stuff if we could just pick the game engine and start making games?" The reason is quite simple: game engines are not a silver bullet, and they can't be used at maximum efficiency without understanding the basic principles behind them. Besides, when you find an engine that suits your needs, you might still want to extend it with a few features that are required specifically for your game. Now that you have that knowledge under your belt, let's take a look at some leading open-source tools that aim to make your life as a game developer easier.

This chapter is devoted to game engines and graphic libraries. We will explore the following subjects:

- A game engine and how it is different from a graphical API

- The Entity Component System

▣   How to write a game with the 2D game engine Crafty.js

> **NOTE:** There are quite a few products for both 2D and 3D graphics, so if you are wondering why I have chosen to cover Crafty and not Engine X, I'll explain how I made the decision. First, the tool must be free and open source. It is useful to read through the engine's code to see how it works under the hood. Examining a mature engine's code is a good way to learn new tricks. Second, the project should have at least moderately recent activity. If it hasn't been updated for three or four months, the engine's authors have probably lost interest in it. Third, the size of the community is important: an active and helpful community is always a plus.

Graphical APIs, Libraries, and Game Engines

We already started to speak about the game engines, graphical libraries, and APIs, but we haven't yet highlighted the differences between these classes of tools. This section aims to give you a basic understanding of how they are different, their purpose, and limitations.

Let's say that you are holding a smartphone to test the game that you have just created. The JavaScript code is rendering frames as the character fights its way through hordes of enemies. To be 100 percent precise, it is not JavaScript that renders the frame. The rendering commands that you send to a canvas travel a long way before they end up being executed on the hardware that does the actual job.

One of the best things about JavaScript game development is that you don't care about low-level details like the architecture of a graphical system or the hardware specifics. This is possible because the browser provides the *graphical API*—the set of functions that we use for rendering.

Graphical APIs

A graphical API is a layer of abstraction that stands between your code and the underlying system. Its main goal is to make rendering platform-agnostic. Figure 14-1 shows a bird's-eye view of graphical APIs.

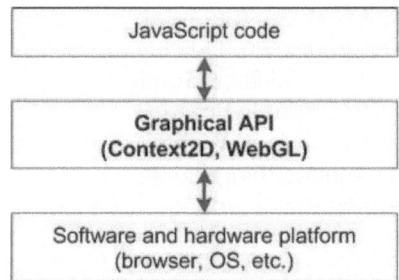

Figure 14-1. *A high-level view of graphical APIs. The role of a graphical API is to provide a layer of abstraction between JavaScript code and the underlying system.*

So far, we have worked only with graphical APIs: Context2D and WebGL. From the perspective of an HTML5 game, these APIs are low-level: they have a small set of functions that act like tiny building blocks—small bricks that you use to create your application. Working on the level of the graphical API gives you full control over the rendering, at least as "full" as allowed by the underlying context.

The downside of such APIs is that you usually have to write many lines of code to implement your ideas. For example, to draw a line with Context2D, one must set the stroke style and then call beginPath(), moveTo(), lineTo(), and finally stroke(). At least five calls to display the very simplest thing!

You can polish your code to perfection with graphical APIs. Considering the example from the previous paragraph, if you know that your game needs to render many lines, you fine-tune the function that does it. You can group the lines by color, and reduce the number fillStyle() and stroke() calls to a minimum—squeezing every bit of performance out of the CPU. The higher-level APIs usually do not allow this level of control, and sometimes you have to sacrifice the performance of the game to gain the speed of development.

Graphical Libraries

Graphical libraries are the "Swiss Army knife" type of tools built on top of raw APIs that provide standard solutions to typical tasks that arise when you deal with graphical content. Usually, they are more specialized than graphical APIs. For example, a library can be focused on general geometry and deal with shapes, or on photo processing and change brightness and saturation, or apply sophisticated artistic effects and filters. A third tool might specialize in charts and simplify graph-rendering tasks.

Graphical libraries have their advantages: they implement features that might otherwise take a considerable amount of time to make on your own. Quickly, think of a way to apply the "sharpen edges" filter on the canvas! Most people can't answer this question straightaway; they would spend valuable time Googling, writing code, testing it, and finally adding it to the project. WebGL is another good example of a low-level API that sometimes makes things look much harder than they should be. Several graphical libraries make writing WebGL applications a real pleasure.

Some graphical libraries are game-oriented, meaning that their focus is to solve typical game-development tasks. In Chapter 7, we created a set of classes to load the levels, draw isometric terrain, render objects, mark dirty rectangles, and so forth. In fact, we wrote a game-oriented library, ready for building games on top of it. Figure 14-2 shows the relation between graphical libraries and other components of the rendering system.

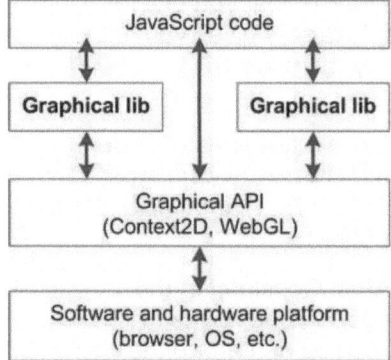

Figure 14-2. *Graphical libraries are a set of tools that work on top of graphical APIs and provide typical solutions to typical graphics-related tasks.*

The world is moving very fast, and it will not wait for you to make every tool by yourself. It is almost impossible to write a project without the help of the right tools. We've already used some of them throughout the pages of this book: Node.js and Express framework, Socket.IO and Cordova. Graphics are not different—if you know that there is a library that solves your problem, give it a shot before you invent your own wheel.

Game Engines

Game engines' primary targets are games. Game engines solve a broad spectrum of problems specific to game development. They are much more complex than typical libraries and they are not limited to handling graphics.

Game engines usually provide the complete solution for building games, including components for physics, AI, sound, video playback, networking, social features, and level editors. Game engines can provide infrastructural solutions like chat rooms, high score tables, or social network integrations.

A game engine is not only an API and not only a set of helper classes that a programmer uses to speed up development. It is a framework with its own architecture that *helps* the programmer build a well-thought-out application. If you want to get a feeling on how a big commercial game engine looks, try Unreal Engine (www.unrealengine.com) or Unity3D (http://unity3d.com).

The relation between the game engine and the other layers of the system is shown in Figure 14-3.

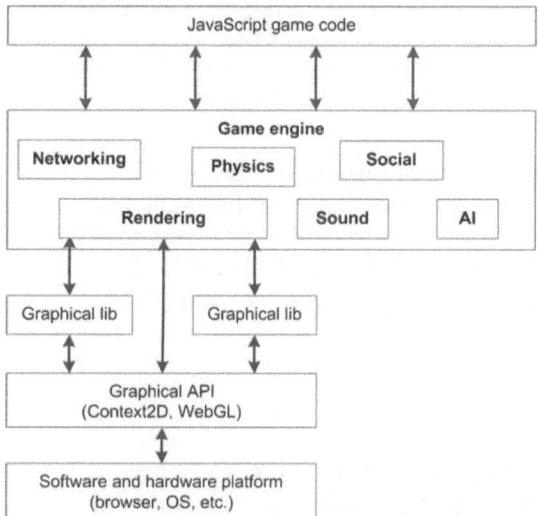

Figure 14-3. *Game engines provide complex solutions for game development; rendering is only a part of it.*

NOTE: In this section, I am not advocating that you use (or not use) any sort of tools for your project. There are no silver bullets and no APIs that suit every case. Be pragmatic: think of what you will actually gain from the tool and what its tradeoffs are. Perhaps the API is designed for a version of Android more recent than the one you initially planned to support. Perhaps the tool is not free but requires some investment. Or perhaps it will save you half the development time and push your game to the market faster than the competition!

Crafty

Crafty (http://craftyjs.com) is a well-thought-out and lightweight 2D game engine. The core file is only 81K minified, yet it still supports many great features out of the box:

- Custom event system

- Sprite sheets, animations, and tile maps—including isometric maps

- Collision detection and "gravity"

- Input handling and audio playback

This is a short list. The full set of features is described in the official documentation at http://craftyjs.com/api/. Crafty also supports modules, so if you are missing anything, you can look at the "components" page at http://craftycomponents.com.

Crafty is built upon the idea of the "Entity Component Paradigm" (or Entity Component System)—a special way of treating game entities that perfectly fits game development. As the first step in our introduction to Crafty, let's see how the entity component system is different from the traditional object-oriented approach, and what types of game-development problems you can solve with its help.

Entity Component System

Let's think about a typical game with many different objects that have different qualities. A strategy game is a good example. There are two main categories of game entities: buildings that are constructed by engineers and that stand still on the ground, and units that can move, shoot, fly, heal other units, carry passengers, and do other useful things. Now think about the hierarchy of classes for such a game. The generic "game entity" should be on the top of the hierarchy. Then we have two types of entities: buildings and units. Each unit, in turn, can fly or walk, damage or heal, transport or be transported, or even both. If you continue building the class tree like that, you soon end up with a rather complex architecture that is hard to manage. An example of such a heavyweight hierarchy is shown in Figure 14-4.

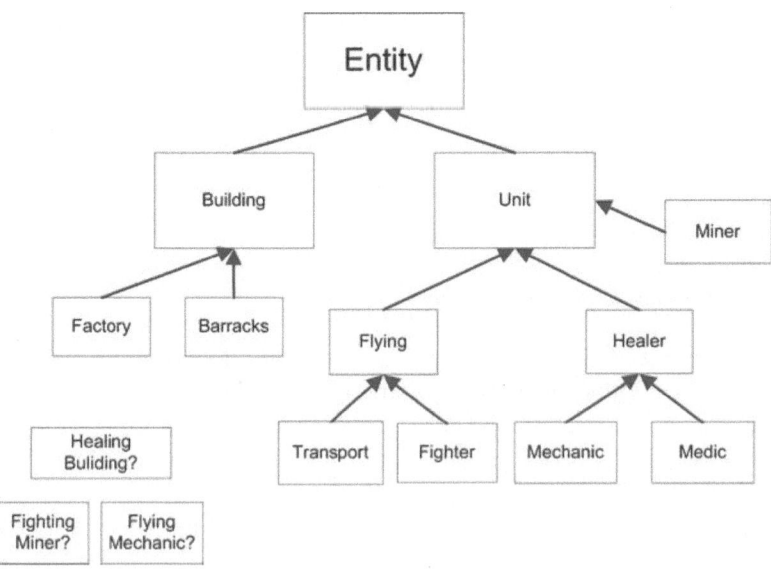

Figure 14-4. *A typical problem with inheritance of game entities*

Even if you manage to break entities into branches of a tree, you soon face the problem of adding new entities that must belong to two branches at once. What if there is a building that can heal nearby units? On the one hand, it belongs to the "building" hierarchy, but on the other hand, it must be inherited from "Healer." Healer belongs to "units," however. This means that it has many methods that are useless for a building. The same happens if you try to add the "Fighting Miner" or the "Flying Mechanic." In fact, this issue is a typical problem with inheritance. Multiple interchangeable qualities that do not depend on each other is the worst-case scenario for inheritance.

The alternative is to use the "composition" approach. Extract specific qualities like "Fighter," "Healer," "Builder," or "Flyer" into separate objects, as shown in Figure 14-5. Crafty uses the term *components* to describe such qualities. Each component has methods and properties that are specific to the quality that it describes. For example, a Flyer can have properties like pitch, yaw, and flightSpeed, and have methods like doBarrelRoll() or land(). Whereas a Mechanic would have sparePartsLeft and startFixing().

Figure 14-5. *The "qualities" or "components" of the game entities*

The components are then "injected" into the objects, so that they describe the exact game unit that you want. Figure 14-6 shows some possible sets of qualities for units.

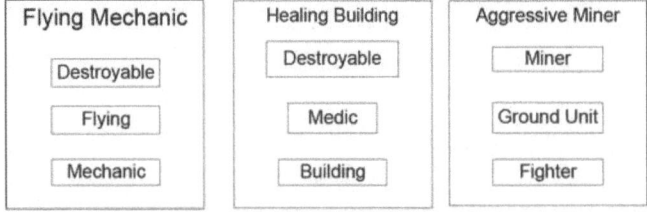

Figure 14-6. *Combining components to describe the qualities of the unit*

By using this approach, the Flying Mechanic is composed of three components: destroyable (since someone can shoot it), flying (because it can fly and has parameters like flight speed and flight distance), and mechanic (meaning that it can fix broken units). Similarly, the Healing Building and the Aggressive Miner are also composed of three components.

In JavaScript, the implementation of such a system is very straightforward. Essentially, the component is a collection of functions and variables that you have to add to the object in order to describe certain qualities. For example, Flyer and Mechanic components could look as follows :

```
var Flyer = {
    pitch: 0,
    yaw: 0.31,
    doBarrelRoll: function() {
        // code goes here
    }
}
var Mechanic = {
    sparePartsLeft: 10.
    startFixing: function() {
        // code goes here
```

```
    }
}
```

If we need to create a Flying Mechanic unit, we have to combine the code from both components into a single object so that result looks as follows:

```
var FlyingMechanic = {
    pitch: 0,
    yaw: 0.31,
    sparePartsLeft: 10,

    startFixing: function() {
        // code goes here
    },

    doBarrelRoll: function() {
        // code goes here
    }
}
```

Combining components programmatically is quite easy too. A sample implementation is presented in Listing 14-1. Note that this is not a Crafty implementation, but rather a simplified model that shows how this system works.

Listing 14-1. *Combining Components Programmatically*

```
var flyingMechanic = {};
[Flying, Mechanic].forEach(function(component) {
    for (var prop in component) {
        flyingMechanic[prop] = component[prop];
    }
});
```

This code simply copies the components' properties and functions to the flyingMechanic object. The result will be exactly what we expect: an object that combines the qualities of a flying unit and a mechanic.

The old OOP principle expresses this way of organizing objects: "favor composition over inheritance." The practical implementation of this rule in game development is often called the *Entity Component System*. A game entity is initially empty. Then it is enriched with components, each one describing certain qualities of that entity. Each component adds new parameters and methods to the object. This is the main idea of Crafty, and in a minute, we will see how the code looks.

> **NOTE:** There is another name for Entity Component System that is used more widely: mixins. The name comes from a type of ice cream that can be customized with tasty add-ons like raisins, nuts, or candies. You can find a more in-depth review of mixins (in programming, not ice cream) in a great blog post called "A Fresh Look at JavaScript Mixins," available at `http://bit.ly/1ZVgQs`.

Now that we know Crafty's core ideology, it is time to write a real game with it!

Crafty Hello World

Start by downloading the latest version of Crafty (it is version 0.4.9. at the time of writing) from the official site (`http://craftyjs.com`). A game made with Crafty typically starts with some small initialization code, such as that in Listing 14-2.

Listing 14-2. *Crafty Initialization*

```
<!DOCTYPE html>
<html lang="en">
<head>
<meta charset="utf-8" />
<meta name="viewport"
      content="width=device-width, initial-scale=1.0, maximum-scale=1.0, user-
scalable=no, target-densitydpi=device-dpi"/>

    <style>
        html, body {
            overflow: hidden;
            width: 100%;
            height: 100%;
            margin:0;
            padding:0;
            border: 0;
        }

    </style>
    <script src="js/crafty.js"></script>
    <script>
        window.onload = function() {
            // Init crafty in full screen
            Crafty.init();

            // Init canvas
            Crafty.canvas.init();
```

```
        // Rest of the game code goes here
    };
    </script>
</head>
<body>
</body>
</html>
```

Crafty does not need any HTML elements to get started: it creates the required DOM elements itself. Moreover, Crafty tries to do its best to determine whether the user is running a desktop or mobile browser. If the browser is mobile, Crafty makes the canvas element take up the whole screen, listens to touch events for input, and adds an appropriate meta attribute to set the properties of the viewport.

The next step is to define one or more *scenes*. A scene is the game screen, like the loading screen, the game board, the high score screen, and so forth. The Four Balls game from Chapter 12 had two main states: "lobby" and "game". Scenes in Crafty are a similar concept, despite having a different name. The code in Listing 14-3 shows how to create four scenes for a typical game workflow.

Listing 14-3. *Setting the Scenes of the Game: Loading, Game, Win, and GameOver*

```
window.onload = function() {
    Crafty.init();
    Crafty.canvas.init();

    Crafty.scene("loading", function() {
        // Loading scene, show loading screen for example
    });

    Crafty.scene("game", function() {
        // Start of the scene
    }, function() {
        // End of the scene
    } );

    Crafty.scene("win", function() {
        // Win scene
    });

    Crafty.scene("gameover", function() {
        // Gameover scene
    });

    // Start the "loading" scene
    Crafty.scene("loading");
}
```

The game that we create in this chapter follows a simple flow, shown in Figure 14-7.

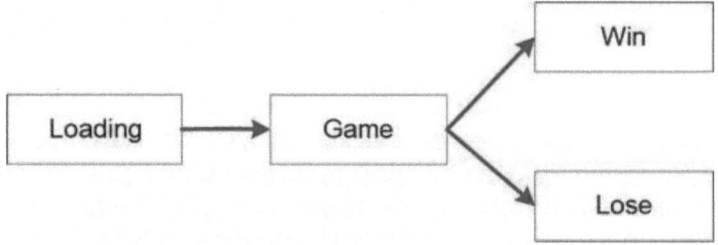

Figure 14-7. *The flow of our example game*

The `Crafty.scene()` function either defines or runs the scene. The two functions passed as parameters are `intro` (the code that runs when the scene starts) and `outro` (the code that runs before the next scene takes control). The first function is the "meat" of the game—it is the place to show the visuals and run the logic. Let's add a simple loading screen to the game. Create a nice logo for the game and put it into the `img/logo.png` file. Alternatively, just use the logo file provided with this chapter. The first step is to create the sprite out of the file:

```
Crafty.sprite(420, 75, "img/logo.png", { logo: [0,0] });
```

This line tells Crafty that we want to load a sprite from the image `"img/logo.png"`. Our sprite has one frame, its size is 420 × 75 pixels, the frame's name is `logo`, and its position within the sprite sheet is (0, 0). Crafty will create a new component, called `logo`. Now let's create the entity that uses our new component:

```
var logoEntity = Crafty.e("2D, Canvas, logo");
```

With the help of the `Crafty.e()` function, we create the new game entity. This entity is a combination of three components: 2D, canvas, and `logo`. The first two components are built into Crafty; they determine how exactly the entity is drawn. The third component— the `logo`—is the one that we just created. Let's place our new entity at the center of the screen. The following lines do exactly this.

```
logoEntity.attr({
    x: (Crafty.DOM.window.width - 420)/2,
    y: (Crafty.DOM.window.height - 75)/2
});
```

Listing 14-4 shows the brushed-up version of the code. The bold lines indicate the new code for the logo.

Listing 14-4. *Showing the Logo at the Start of the Game*

```
var logo = { sprite: "img/logo.png", width: 420, height: 75 };

window.onload = function() {
    Crafty.init();
    Crafty.canvas.init();

    Crafty.scene("loading", function() {
        showLogo();
    });

    Crafty.scene("game",
        function() { /* Start of the scene */ },
        function() { /* End of the scene */ } );

    Crafty.scene("win", function() {});

    Crafty.scene("gameover", function() {});

    // Start the "loading" scene
    Crafty.scene("loading");
};

function showLogo() {
    Crafty.background("#000");
    Crafty.sprite(logo.width, logo.height, logo.sprite, { logo: [0,0] });
    Crafty.e("2D, Canvas, logo").attr({
        x: (Crafty.DOM.window.width - logo.width)/2,
        y: (Crafty.DOM.window.height - logo.height)/2
    });
}
```

If you run the application, you will see the splash screen of the future game, shown in
Figure 14-8.

Figure 14-8. *The future game's logo*

Crafty Game

Now let's build a simple game using Crafty. I call this game "Escaping Knight". The goal of the game is to catch a knight that tries to escape from his guard route and go to a tavern. The player tries to catch the knight by tapping on the sprite. The game is not particularly challenging, but it demonstrates a whole host of useful techniques:

- Game life cycle (from loading to game screen, to win or lose screens)
- Loading and rendering sprites
- Creating animation
- Reacting on user input
- Interacting with sprites

The finished game will look like Figure 14-9.

Figure 14-9. *The finished Escaping Knight game*

Loading sprites

There's nothing easier than preloading a set of images in Crafty. For the Escaping Knight game, we will need only a few of them: a tile set for rendering the terrain, four tiles for various objects (houses and an arch), one sprite sheet for the running knight character, and two banners for the "Game Over" and "You Win" screens. Listing 14-5 shows the code that loads them. We will preload only the sprites that we need for the game level, the banners for "Win" and "End Game" will be loaded lazily—just before the player needs to see them.

Listing 14-5. *Preloading a Set of Sprites for the Level*

```
var images = ["img/terrain.png", "img/house-1.png", "img/house-2.png",
    "img/arch-left.png", "img/arch-right.png", "img/knight.png"];

Crafty.load(images,
    function() {
        // Called when images are loaded
    });
```

We want to add this code to the "loading" screen, since images must be loaded before the start of the gameplay process. Once every image is in place, we are ready to move to the next scene. The final version of the "loading" scene will look like Listing 14-6.

Listing 14-6. *The "Loading" Scene That Preloads the Resources Required for the Game*

```
var images = ["img/terrain.png", "img/house-1.png", "img/house-2.png",
    "img/arch-left.png", "img/arch-right.png", "img/knight.png"];

var logo = { sprite: "img/logo.png", width: 420, height: 75 };

Crafty.scene("loading", function() {
    Crafty.background("#000");
    showLogo();
    Crafty.load(images,
        function() {
            Crafty.scene("game");
        });
});

function showLogo() {
    Crafty.sprite(logo.width, logo.height, logo.sprite, { logo: [0,0] });
    Crafty.e("2D, Canvas, logo").attr({
        x: (Crafty.DOM.window.width - logo.width)/2,
        y: (Crafty.DOM.window.height - logo.height)/2
    });
}
```

In a local environment, images are loaded almost instantly, so chances are you will not see the loading screen at all. For development purposes, you might want to add an artificial delay and show the loading screen for at least two seconds (see Listing 14-7). Once your game goes live, simply remove this code.

Listing 14-7. *Delaying the Loading Scene So That You Have a Chance to See the First Image*

```
Crafty.scene("loading", function() {
    Crafty.background("#000");
    showLogo();
```

```
var startTime = new Date().getTime();
Crafty.load(images,
    function() {
        var timeLoading = new Date().getTime() - startTime;

        setTimeout(function() {
            Crafty.scene("game");
        }, Math.max(2000 - timeLoading, 0));
    });
});
```

At this point, the images are loaded and ready for rendering on the screen. The next task is to render the level.

Rendering Terrain and Objects

You have already seen the code that creates a sprite out of an image. In fact, the `Crafty.sprite()` method was designed to work with sprite sheets. The following code illustrates how this works:

```
Crafty.sprite(128, 68, "img/terrain.png", {
    grass: [0,0], grass2: [1,0], roadNW: [2,0],
    bricks: [0,1], roadSW: [1,1], roadNS: [2,1],
    roadWE: [0,2], roadNE: [1,2], roadSE: [2,2]
});
```

The sprite sheet consists of 128 × 68 pixel images. Each image occupies one "cell" of the sprite sheet. The `Crafty.sprite()` function simply associates the cell coordinates with a particular name, like `grass`, `bricks`, or `roadWE`.

The sprite can then be used just like any other component:

```
Crafty.e("2D, Canvas, grass").attr({x: 30, y: 20});
```

The code for rendering the level should now be a piece of cake for you (see Listing 14-8). We will render the isometric map using exactly the same technique as in Chapter 7. If you need to refresh your knowledge of isometric math, feel free to peek back at Chapter 7.

Listing 14-8. *Rendering the Background*

```
var ground = [
    ["grass", "grass", "grass", "grass", "grass", "grass", "grass", "grass"],
    ["grass", "roadSE", "grass", "roadNS", "grass", "grass", "grass", "grass"],
    ... more here
    ["grass", "grass", "grass", "grass", "grass", "grass", "grass", "grass"]
];
```

```javascript
var objects = [
    { sprite: "house2", x: 290, y: 198 },
    { sprite: "house1", x: 476, y: 282 },
    { sprite: "archRight", x: 553, y: 95 },
    { sprite: "archLeft", x: 440, y: 102 }
];

/**
 * Create the sprite component for every tile and every building that we are
 * going to render
 */
function createSprites() {
    Crafty.sprite(128, 68, "img/terrain.png", {
        grass: [0,0], grass2: [1,0], roadNW: [2,0],
        bricks: [0,1], roadSW: [1,1], roadNS: [2,1],
        roadWE: [0,2], roadNE: [1,2], roadSE: [2,2]
    });

    Crafty.sprite(32, 64, "img/knight.png", { princess: [0,0] });
    Crafty.sprite(128, 106, "img/house-1.png", { house1: [0,0] });
    Crafty.sprite(128, 159, "img/house-2.png", { house2: [0,0] });
    Crafty.sprite(151, 183, "img/arch-left.png", { archLeft: [0,0] });
    Crafty.sprite(142, 130, "img/arch-right.png", { archRight: [0,0] });
}

/**
 * Add isometric tiles to the scene
 */
function drawTerrain() {
    for (var j = 0; j < ground.length; j++) {
        for (var i = 0; i < ground[j].length; i++) {
            Crafty.e("2D, Canvas, " + ground[j][i]).attr(
                    {x: offsetX + i*124 + (j%2)*62, y: offsetY + j*31}
            );
        }
    }
}

/**
 * Add huts and arch
 */
function drawObjects() {
    objects.forEach(function(object) {
        Crafty.e("2D, Canvas, " + object.sprite).attr(
                {x: offsetX + object.x, y: offsetY + object.y}
        );
    });
}
```

The first function creates the sprite objects for every loaded image. drawTerrain() and drawObjects() are rather self-explanatory: they use the same sprite-drawing technique as in the previous examples, the only difference is that the sprites are now arranged in an order suitable for isometric view.

> **NOTE:** Crafty has built-in support for an isometric view (http://craftyjs.com/api/ Crafty-isometric.html). However, this chapter draws the terrain "by hand" just to keep things simple and straightforward.

If you launch the application, you should see a rendered landscape with a couple of houses and an arch that appears right after the loading screen, as shown in Figure 14-10.

Figure 14-10. *Isometric terrain and objects rendered with Crafty*

Animation

Animation in Crafty is a matter of a few lines of code. Not more than you just wrote to load the sprites. To define the animation, you need to assign the SpriteAnimation component to the entity and specify the frames of animation sequence. The following code shows how to define the animation for the knight:

```
Crafty.e("2D, Canvas, knight, SpriteAnimation")
    .attr({x: 100, y: 280})
    .animate("move ", 0, 0, 15)
```

This code says, "grab the sprite sheet of the knight component and create an animation sequence called move." The sequence starts at cell (0, 0)—the top-left corner of the image—and loops 15 frames to the right. If this concept sounds a little vague, Figure 14-11 should make it clear (the image is showing only 5 out of 15 frames).

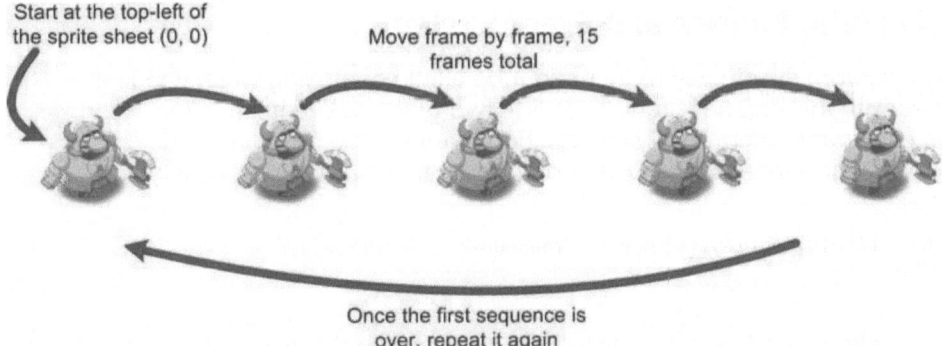

Start at the top-left of
the sprite sheet (0, 0)

Move frame by frame, 15
frames total

Once the first sequence is
over, repeat it again

Figure 14-11. *The way Crafty treats animation sequences: the first parameter is the coordinates of the "anchor" frame, the last one is the number of frames in the sequence.*

When the animation sequence is created, you can execute it straightaway, as shown in Listing 14-9.

Listing 14-9. *Starting an Animation Sequence*

```
Crafty.e("2D, Canvas, knight, SpriteAnimation, Mouse")
    .attr({x: 100, y: 280})
    .animate("move ", 0, 0, 15)
    .animate("move", 15, -1)
```

The last line launches the sequence that we just defined. The first parameter is the name of the sequence ("move"), the second parameter is the duration of the animation, and the final one is the repeat count, where -1 stands for infinity.

Reload the page and enjoy the knight running in the same place. If you want him to move somewhere, add the highlighted code in Listing 14-10.

Listing 14-10. *Moving the Knight*

```
Crafty.e("2D, Canvas, knight, SpriteAnimation, Mouse")
    .attr({x: 100, y: 280})
    .animate("move", 0, 0, 15)
    .animate("move_right", 15, -1)
    .bind("EnterFrame", function() {
        this.x += 0.8;
        this.y += 0.4;
    });
```

The bind() function registers a listener to the EnterFrame event. EnterFrame is fired for every animation frame, giving you the chance to update the position of the sprite. Refresh the code, and see the knight running away! Time to catch him!

Interaction with Entities and Event System

Crafty has a custom event system that might be a little confusing when you first start to work with this engine. Crafty supports two types of events: native browser events and custom Crafty events. For example, the following code adds a DOM event listener to the DOM component that backs up the entity (if there is one):

```
Crafty.addEvent(this, entity._element, "mousedown", function() {
    alert("hi");
});
```

The code in Listing 14-11 creates a listener to the custom Crafty event.

Listing 14-11. *Adding a Custom Crafty Event Listener to the Entity*

```
Crafty.e("2D, Canvas, SpriteAnimation, Mouse")
    .attr({x: 100, y: 280})
    .bind("MouseDown", function() {
        alert("hi");
    });
```

As we discussed in Chapter 5, browser events are often not enough for building complex games, which is why Crafty distinguishes between the two. Browser events are considered to be "low-level"—use them when you need to specify nonstandard behavior or to deal with nasty corner cases. Otherwise, Crafty events are the best way to deal with most cases in a consistent way.

To fire your own event, call the `trigger` method. Let's update the code that renders the character and makes it notify the outer world about win and lose conditions. When the user taps the knight, the user wins the game; if the knight reaches the safe zone, the user loses. Listing 14-12 shows how to implement this idea in code.

Listing 14-12. *Triggering Win and GameOver Events*

```
function drawPrincess() {
    Crafty.e("2D, Canvas, knight, SpriteAnimation, Mouse")
        .attr({x: 100, y: 280})
        .animate("move ", 0, 0, 15)
        .animate("move ", 15, -1)
        .bind("EnterFrame", function() {
            this.x += 0.8;
            this.y += 0.4;
            if (this.x > 500) {
                Crafty.trigger("GameOver");
            }
        }).bind("MouseDown", function() {
            Crafty.trigger("Win");
```

```
        });
}
```

Once you call the `trigger` somewhere in the code, you can react to the event, adding a listener for a certain event type:

```
Crafty.bind("Win", function() {
    Crafty.scene("win");
});
```

Note that the event is called `MouseDown`. Even though there's no mouse on Android devices, Crafty mimics `MouseDown` events, wrapping `touchstart` browser events much like we did in previous chapters.

> **NOTE:** Don't forget to specify the right components for every bit of functionality that you are adding to each game entity. Without the `SpriteAnimation` component, the knight entity will not "know" about animation-related methods. Similarly, to use the mouse, we had to add the `Mouse` component to the entity to make it aware of input events.

Final Version

The game is now almost ready, but we just need to add two banners for "Game Over" and "You Win" messages. Showing them is no different from drawing a logo, as we did in Listing 14-4.

The source code for our simple, Crafty-written game is shown in Listing 14-13. (Some code has been trimmed to make it shorter. You can find the full version in the supplied materials for this chapter. The file is called `01.crafty.html`.

Listing 14-13. *A Bird's-Eye View of a Completed Crafty Game*

```
var images = ["img/terrain.png", "img/house-1.png", "img/house-2.png",
    "img/arch-left.png", "img/arch-right.png", "img/knight.png"];

// The level
var ground = [
    ["grass", "grass", "roadNW", "grass", "roadNS", "grass", "grass", "grass"],
    /* ... more tiles here */
];

/* Location of sprites */
var objects = [
{ sprite: "house2", x: 290, y: 198 }, { sprite: "house1", x: 476, y: 282 },
{ sprite: "archRight", x: 553, y: 85}, { sprite: "archLeft", x: 440, y: 92} ];
```

```javascript
/* Banners - images and sizes */
var logo = { sprite: "img/logo.png", width: 420, height: 75 };
var winBanner = { sprite: "img/win.png", width: 420, height: 90 };
var gameOverBanner = { sprite: "img/gameover.png", width: 420, height: 90 };

window.onload = function() {
    Crafty.init();
    Crafty.canvas.init();

    Crafty.scene("loading", function() {
        Crafty.background("#000");
        showLogo();
        Crafty.load(images,  function() { Crafty.scene("game"); });
        });
    });

    Crafty.scene("game", function() {
        createSprites();
        drawTerrain();
        drawObjects();
        drawKnight();

        // Once we get events - go to the appropriate scene
        Crafty.bind("Win", function() { Crafty.scene("win"); });
        Crafty.bind("GameOver", function() { Crafty.scene("gameover"); });
    });

    // These scenes only show banners
    Crafty.scene("gameover", showGameOverBanner);
    Crafty.scene("win", showWinBanner);

    // Start the "loading" scene
    Crafty.scene("loading");
};

/* Create sprite entities */
function createSprites() {
    Crafty.sprite(128, 68, "img/terrain.png", {
        grass: [0,0], grass2: [1,0], roadNW: [2,0],
        /* Other terrain tiles are described in a same way*/
 });

    Crafty.sprite(159, 148, "img/knight.png", { knight: [0,0] });
    Crafty.sprite(128, 106, "img/house-1.png", { house1: [0,0] });
    Crafty.sprite(128, 159, "img/house-2.png", { house2: [0,0] });
    Crafty.sprite(151, 183, "img/arch-left.png", { archLeft: [0,0] });
    Crafty.sprite(142, 130, "img/arch-right.png", { archRight: [0,0] });
}
```

```
/* Render isometric terrain */
function drawTerrain() {
    for (var j = 0; j < ground.length; j++) {
        for (var i = 0; i < ground[j].length; i++) {
            Crafty.e("2D, Canvas, " + ground[j][i]).attr(
                    {x: i*124 + (j%2)*62, y: j*31}
            );
        }
    }
}

/* Render huts and arch */
function drawObjects() {
    objects.forEach(function(object) {
        Crafty.e("2D, Canvas, " + object.sprite).attr(
                {x: object.x, y: object.y}
        );
    });
}

/* Animate a knight and make it run */
function drawKnight() {
    Crafty.e("2D, Canvas, knight, SpriteAnimation, Mouse")
        .attr({x: 20, y: 170})
        .animate("move_right", 0, 0, 15)
        .animate("move_right", 15, -1)
        .bind("EnterFrame", function() {
            this.x += 0.8;
            this.y += 0.4;
            if (this.x > 450) {
                Crafty.trigger("GameOver");
            }
        }).bind("MouseDown", function() {
            Crafty.trigger("Win");
        });
}

function showLogo() {/* Show banner as in Listing 14-4*/}
function showWinBanner() { /* Show banner as in Listing 14-4*/ }
function showGameOverBanner() { /* Show banner as in Listing 14-4*/ }
```

As you see, Crafty is a very nice and convenient game engine that easily handles rather complex tasks. With its good start and active community, it will soon become a mature game development engine—without a doubt.

Summary

In this chapter, we explored the topic of game engines. We started by describing three layers of interaction with the graphical system: the graphical APIs, libraries, and game engines. We learned the differences between them, and their purposes and limitations.

We built the game with the help of Crafty—a 2D game engine that focuses on bringing together typical tools for game developers, including sprite sheets, animation, event handling, game states and transitions, and many other features. We created a rather complete game (omitting the gameplay, of course) that has the majority of the features of a completed product—and the total size of the source code was only about 140 lines of JavaScript.

Even though game engines might look like a silver bullet, they are not. They save you a lot of time and effort, but the efficient use of every game engine requires knowledge of the mechanics underneath. Even if you choose to use one of these, the skills that you gain throughout the chapters of this book will bring you a better understanding of the engine's black art.

Chapter **15**

Building Native Applications

Most applications that people use on their Android devices are *native*—programs written in Java and tightly integrated with the OS. Games are no exception. Most games for Android are native games. Applications created throughout this book are of a different type—they are web applications. They already work pretty well, and there's no doubt that with some extra polishing, it would be simple to bring the web app to the commercial level. However, there are a few reasons why you might want to build a native Android version of your game.

Why build a native application out of a working web version? That is a good question. Indeed, web applications have many advantages. They are easier to deploy, you don't have to install them, they support more platforms, they are much easier to update… so why spend extra time for native apps? The following is a summary of the most important features that make native apps very attractive:

- Distribution via markets

- Access to the native API

- Fullscreen mode

- Using HTML5 APIs that are not yet available to the browser

- Native apps don't necessarily need to have an internet connection, and the user may be able play the game offline.

In this chapter, we will discuss the advantages and disadvantages of native applications. In addition, we will learn how to:

- Install and configure Apache Cordova (formerly PhoneGap and Apache Callback)
- Wrap the existing web game as a native application
- Access the phone resources (such as the phonebook or GPS)
- Sign the application and prepare it for market publishing
- Register on Google Play
- Publish the game and download it via a Google Play application
- Update the application, and release a new version

Creating an Android app from scratch is a rather complex task: it requires certain knowledge of Java and Android architecture. If you are not familiar with these technologies, it may take considerable time and effort to master them to a level when you can write a commercial-grade game. Fortunately, there is a way to gain the benefits of a native application without losing the familiar web environment, and this chapter is fully devoted to that subject.

> **NOTE:** This chapter is written in the form of a step-by-step guide. Certain steps are far from the usual web development tasks; they require some experience in other areas to understand them completely. I will try to give you a good general understanding of the process and provide the first step toward understanding how native applications work; however, Java programming falls outside of the scope of this book. If you want to learn more, feel free to read other sources. For an introduction to Java, try *Java 7 for Absolute Beginners* by Jay Bryant (Apress, 2012). If you already have some Java under your belt, a good resource is *Beginning Android Games*, 2nd Edition, by Mario Zechner and Robert Green (Apress, 2012). Android development has become a very popular topic recently, so you will find it easy to locate good materials online.

Native Applications

Let's start with very generic questions. What is a native application? What does it look like and what is it made of? Native Android apps are written in Java. A typical Android project consists of Java files, Java libraries, and resources and assets like images, XML configuration files, and media files. There's one special file called AndroidManifest.xml that holds the information about the app. The application itself is distributed in the form of an APK file: a zip archive that has a certain internal structure.

The process of building an APK is rather long; when the coding part is done, the developer has to complete the following steps to make a file that is ready for deployment on a device:

- Run the tool to autogenerate several Java files

- Compile Java sources

- Transform compiled sources to Android byte code

- Package everything into the APK file

- Sign the APK with the key

- Perform the alignment—the optimization of the APK archive

As you can see, the process is rather complex, and it would be a huge waste of time to do everything manually every time you needed to test a tiny change to your application. Android developers use a tool called Ant (http://ant.apache.org) to simplify the process. Ant is an automated build system; it can execute build scripts written in XML that describe every action required to build the app. It works like .bat files on Windows or make on Linux, but Ant is cross-platform and has many Java-specific extensions. With its help, an Android application can be created with a single command from the command line.

> **NOTE:** Most IDEs have plug-ins to support Android development and hide the details of the application-building process away from the developer. Both Eclipse and IntelliJ Idea have a great support for Android development. If you think about diving deeper into the native Android development, start with setting up an IDE that you like, just as we did in Chapter 1. As for this chapter, command-line tools along with a text editor are quite enough to reach our goals.

From a logical point of view, Android applications are made of various components and UI elements—buttons, progress bars, combo boxes, and so on. There are dozens of such components, both default and custom. One of them is the "browser," or WebView as it is called in Android. WebView is a regular component like a button or a progress bar; any application can use it to render HTML pages like a normal browser does.

It is not hard to make a one-screen application that has `WebView` occupying the entire available space and use it to render an HTML file with the game. Even though the page is rendered as usual, it is not a "simple" page anymore. It is a real native application, and it has access to system resources otherwise forbidden for a web page. An application like this combines the best of both worlds: the simplicity of a web page and the behavior of a native app.

Let's look closer at the advantages of this approach:

- The markets. Application markets like Google Play are an extremely important channel of distribution. A web page by itself is harder to promote compared to a native application published on the market. When you work with the markets, it is easy to gather community feedback and notify the users about the features in new versions. Finally, yet importantly, if you decide to ask users to pay for the application, markets are the optimal way to handle billing.

- Access to the native API. Everything available to a regular application is available for your web page too. For example, you can access the filesystem, SQLite databases, connectivity facilities, sensors, and everything else that a regular Android application can. Sometimes you have to do some Java coding in order to do that or use existing third-party components. However, this kind of unrestricted resource access gives you a way to build completely different, more sophisticated solutions.

> **NOTE:** Of course, when I say "unrestricted access," I do not mean that you can hack into the user's device and do whatever you like. Android native applications use a different permission scheme than web pages. When a user installs an application, he is prompted to confirm that he "allows" certain types of actions: access network, send SMS, read the phonebook, and so forth. Afterward, the application can use the device's resources. The main difference is that a web page doesn't have an option to request such permissions.

- Fullscreen mode. This feature is extremely important for game development. On handheld devices, every inch of screen counts. The address bar and taskbar take away lots of useful space! A game could use it to show a bigger part of the map, or to display its own status bar or HUD (heads-up display). Besides, the fullscreen game feels different to the user. It feels more like the usual Java games that they used to play.

- Using APIs that are not yet available to the browser. The Android browser (especially on older Android versions) lacks the implementation of some very nice HTML5 specifications. Some of these APIs could be implemented with the help of native resources. WebSockets and FileSystem API cannot be shimmed in a regular web page—they lack the permissions to work with the OS on the required level. With a native page, one can implement a standards-compliant shim and use it instead of a real API.

You can see that there are many reasons to use such an approach. So let's use this technique to prepare our Four Balls game for the Android Market—and publish it!

Setting up Apache Cordova (PhoneGap)

No surprise that there's already a tool that simplifies the wrapping of a web page. This tool is Apache Cordova (`http://phonegap.com`).

NOTE: Cordova was originally known as PhoneGap. Later it moved to Apache Incubator and became Apache Callback. A few months later, it was renamed once again and now it is known as Apache Cordova. When searching for blog posts, examples, and tutorials, it is better to use the oldest name in search terms, since PhoneGap is how the project was known for most of its lifetime. In this chapter we use the most current name—Cordova.

Cordova is a tool that solves several tasks.

- It simplifies the "web to native" wrapping process.

- It gives access to native resources: phonebook, camera, and so forth.

- It provides a platform for third-party plug-ins, which is a standard way to extend the core functionality with custom features.

Cordova is not an Android-specific project; it has a similar set of tools for iOS, Symbian, Blackberry, and several other platforms. The ultimate goal of this project is to provide a way for developers to port existing HTML5 applications to different mobile platforms as native apps, distribute them via markets, and access the device-specific APIs. This is exactly what we need.

Let's start by installing Cordova and its dependencies.

Setting up Cordova

There's no special setup for Cordova—download the archive from the official site (http://phonegap.com) and extract the folder called lib/android from the archive. There's no need to set any environment variables and such; simply remember where you extracted it.

Setting up Apache Ant

Apache Ant (http://ant.apache.org) is the automated build system, and an XML-based language for complex build scripts. In order to use Apache Cordova and create native application, we first need to install Ant.

> **NOTE:** If you are using a Mac, you may already have Ant installed. Open the command line and type ant -version. If you see the version number (like 1.8.2), then Ant is ready for work; otherwise, install it as described next.

Download the latest version of the Ant distribution from the official web site at http://ant.apache.org/bindownload.cgi and extract the contents of the archive into the folder of your choice. Create the environment variable ANT_HOME and point it to the folder that you just extracted. Modify the PATH variable and add ANT_HOME\bin to the path so that the executables are available from the command line.

Type

```
>ant -version
```

You should see the output with the information about the build—the version and the date:

```
Apache Ant(TM) version 1.8.2 compiled on December 20 2010
```

If you see something similar, Ant is successfully installed on the system.

Building Native Application

At this point we need to create a real native Android project. We will not do a lot of Java programming, even though we have to edit a couple of Java files. As mentioned earlier, the details of Android development are outside the scope of this book. If you trust me a little, however, and follow along, you'll have a good idea of what you can do. If you prefer to dig a little deeper, feel free to check out the official Hello World tutorial for native Android development (http://developer.android.com/resources/tutorials/hello-world.html).

Creating an Empty Android Project

The first step is to create an empty Android project and try to launch it on a device. Navigate to the folder where you want to set the project, and execute the following command that shows the list of possible *targets*. A target is simply a platform on which you build your application.

```
>android list targets
Available Android targets:
----------
id: 1 or "android-8"
    Name: Android 2.2
    Type: Platform
    API level: 8
    Revision: 3
    Skins: HVGA, QVGA, WQVGA400, WQVGA432, WVGA800 (default), WVGA854
    ABIs : armeabi
----------
id: 2 or "android-10"
    Name: Android 2.3.3
    Type: Platform
    API level: 10
    Revision: 2
    Skins: HVGA, QVGA, WQVGA400, WQVGA432, WVGA800 (default), WVGA854
    ABIs : armeabi
----------
...
```

Decide on the minimum version of Android that you plan to support. We will make an application for Android 2.2 and above. On my computer, the corresponding id of the target is 1. Look at the preceding output: the bolded lines show where to look for the Android version and its id. When you have the version id, execute one more command in the console:

```
> android create project --package com.juriy.fourballs --activity FourBalls --
target 1  --path fourballsnative
```

This command creates a new, empty Android project, ready for compilation, packaging, and testing on the device. Let's take a closer look at the parameters; they become important once you start to prepare for production.

- --package is the "namespace" of your application. Java developers have a convention of deploying their libraries so that classes with the same name don't clash with each other. If you have a class called Sprite and so does the other library in the project, both classes work fine as long as their packages are different. A package is any dot-separated list of words; however, the usual practice is to take the domain name that you own and write it in reverse order. For example, I have the domain juriy.com; I can use package com.juriy, com.juriy.whatever, or even a longer com.juriy.game.client.utilites. You have to choose the name of the package to make a project.

- --activity is the name of the main class. Choose whatever sounds best to you. FourBalls, Main, or anything else will do.

- --target is the version id of the platform, as described earlier.

- --path is the folder where you put your files. Since there is no folder called fourballsnative, mine was created for me.

Once the project is created, you see that there are quite a lot of new files and folders. Look at Figure 15-1. You see a similar structure. If you don't have experience in Android development, don't try to understand what these files are for. It is enough to know that this is the typical structure of an Android project.

Figure 15-1. *The typical structure of Android project*

Now you have built the empty project. It doesn't yet have Cordova, but it can be compiled and tested on a device or emulator.

Testing the Empty Android Project

Before we start to add Cordova libraries, let's make sure that the project we created actually works. Start the emulator or connect the device with a USB cable. Make sure that the debug mode is on (if you don't know how to enable the debug mode, refer to Appendix A). Make sure that you are in the project folder's root. Execute the following command:

```
> ant clean debug install
```

Ant uses a build script called `build.xml` to create a debug version of the app. It signs the app with a debug key (every Android application must be signed with a key—more about that later) and installs it on the currently running emulator or connected device. If it finds neither an emulator nor a device, the build will fail. If you did everything right, you should see the newly created application in the list of installed apps and be able to run it. The application looks rather dull—a black screen with gray "Hello World, FourBalls" text, as shown in Figure 15-2.

Figure 15-2. *The empty Hello World Android project*

> **NOTE:** You need to have either the device or the emulator running when you execute
> the "install." If neither is running, the build script will fail. If your script is failing even
> though the emulator is open, execute the following two commands in sequence:
>
> ```
> > adb kill-server
> ```
>
> ```
> > adb start-server
> ```

Basic Cordova Project

Now we have to do the main work toward building the "wrapped native app."
That is add the Cordova libraries to the empty project, modify Java files, and put
the web resources (HTML, scripts, CSS, etc.) into the correct places. This part
of the chapter contains many "dark magic" steps. I encourage you to dive
deeper into native Android app development to gain a better understanding of
this process.

Preparing the Project for Cordova Development

First, we need to copy several files and provide a certain folder structure to add
Cordova support to our application. Follow these steps:

1. Find the `cordova-2.0.0.jar` (the version number might differ, of
    course) in the folder where you extracted Cordova under
    `/lib/android`.

2. Copy it to the `libs` folder of your project.

3. Create a new folder, `assets`, and another folder, `www`, inside it to
    use as the root for web application files: HTMLs, JavaScript
    files, and so forth.

4. Find the `cordova-2.0.0.js` file in the same location as the `jar`
    from the first step and copy it into the newly created `www` folder.

5. Create an `index.html` file—a plain HTML with some text in it.
    We will use it in a minute to test that everything is working. I
    used the dummy in Listing 15-1.

6. Copy the `xml` folder from the Cordova distribution into the `res`
    folder of your project.

Listing 15-1. *Dummy HTML to Test That the Cordova Project Is Working*

```html
<!DOCTYPE html>
<html lang="en">
<head>
    <meta charset="utf-8" />
    <meta name="viewport"
          content="width=device-width, initial-scale=1.0, maximum-scale=1.0,
user-scalable=no, target-densitydpi=device-dpi"/>

    <style>
        html, body {
            overflow: hidden;
            width: 100%;
            height: 100%;
            margin:0;
            padding:0;
            border: 0;
        }

        #main {
            font-size: 20px;
        }
    </style>
</head>
<body>
    <div id="main">
        Cordova is working!
    </div>
</body>
</html>
```

After you finish these steps, the structure of the project should look like what you see in Figure 15-3. Take a close look to check that you did everything right.

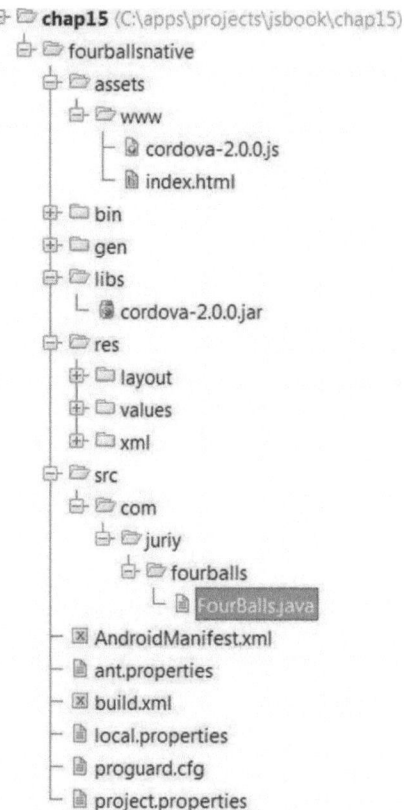

Figure 15-3. *The updated project structure*

Updating the Java Files and Android Manifest

Now we have to change the Java files a little bit. Find the only `.java` file, called `FourBalls.java`, in the `src` subfolder. This file is highlighted in Figure 15-3. Change the text as shown in Listing 15-2.

Listing 15-2. *The Main Java Class*

```
package com.juriy.fourballs;

import android.app.Activity;
import android.os.Bundle;
import org.apache.cordova.*;

public class FourBalls extends DroidGap {
    @Override
```

```
    public void onCreate(Bundle savedInstanceState) {
        super.onCreate(savedInstanceState);
        super.loadUrl("file:///android_asset/www/index.html");
    }
}
```

Make sure that you set *your* package in the first line of the file. Leave the rest intact—Cordova takes care of everything else. The last thing that you must do is edit the AndroidManifest.xml file that is located in the root of your project. The bolded lines in Listing 15-3 are the lines that you need to add.

Listing 15-3. *AndroidManifest.xml File Modifications*

```
<?xml version="1.0" encoding="utf-8"?>
<manifest xmlns:android="http://schemas.android.com/apk/res/android"
      package="com.juriy.fourballs"
      android:versionCode="1"
      android:versionName="1.0">

  <supports-screens
    android:largeScreens="true"
    android:normalScreens="true"
    android:smallScreens="true"
    android:resizeable="true"
    android:anyDensity="true"
  />

    <!-- Uncomment this line if your page will interact with the server -->
    <!-- <uses-permission android:name="android.permission.INTERNET" /> -->

    <application android:label="@string/app_name" >
        <activity android:name="FourBalls"
                  android:label="@string/app_name"
                  android:configChanges="orientation|keyboardHidden" >
            <intent-filter>
                <action android:name="android.intent.action.MAIN" />
                <category android:name="android.intent.category.LAUNCHER" />
            </intent-filter>
        </activity>
        <activity android:name="org.apache.cordova.DroidGap"
                  android:label="@string/app_name"
                  android:configChanges="orientation|keyboardHidden">
            <intent-filter>
            </intent-filter>
        </activity>
    </application>

    <uses-sdk android:minSdkVersion="8" />
</manifest>
```

> **NOTE:** The final bolded line sets the `minSdkVersion` parameter—the minimum version of Android that the application runs on. Well, not the Android OS itself, but rather the corresponding "internal" version of the Android SDK. In this example, we target Android 2.2, which has SDK version 8. For other version numbers, refer this to this web page: `http://developer.android.com/guide/appendix/api-levels.html`.

Testing the Project

Now the project is ready for testing. Launch the emulator if you have closed it, and execute once again.

```
> ant debug install
```

The application should now look like the screenshot shown in Figure 15-4.

Figure 15-4. *Basic Cordova-enabled project*

Congratulations! The project is working! Porting the Four Balls game is now a piece of cake. Just copy the files from Chapter 3 to the www folder and rebuild the app. The resulting application doesn't look like a web page anymore; it doesn't have the address bar or browser menus, and the user will not guess that you created this game (almost) without writing Java code. Once you're finished, your game should look like Figure 15-5.

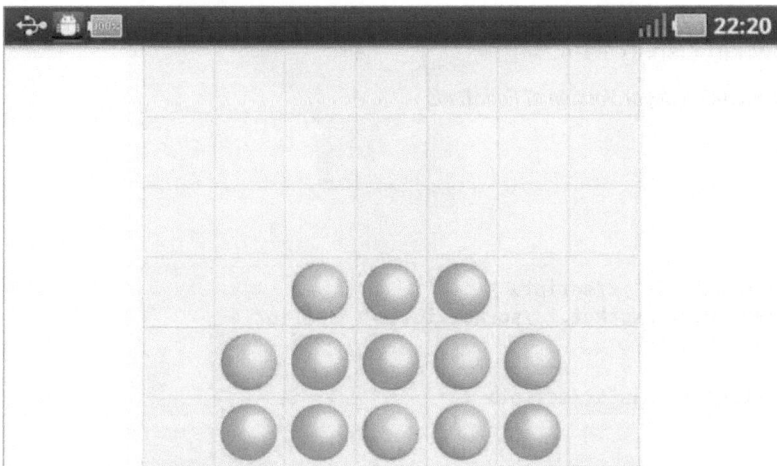

Figure 15-5. *The finished Cordova application. The Four Balls game now looks quite native.*

Networking

Let's continue our experiments with Cordova and create a native version of the multiplayer game. In this case, it is not enough to copy the app's code to assets/www.

First, you have to rewrite the lines that use relative URLs to access server-side resources. When you launch a Cordova application, it loads the page directly from the filesystem. This means that every relative URL refers to the filesystem too, and not the server as is usual. For example, consider the typical XHR call:

```
var xhr = new XMLHttpRequest();
xhr.open("GET", "user/182.json", true);
xhr.send(null);
```

Usually, the request ends up on the server, which loads the required info from the database and forms the dynamical response. With the Cordova application, the request tries to load the data from the /assets/www/user/182.json file, and obviously fails. Fixing this problem is a straightforward task; use absolute URLs instead of relative ones:

```
xhr.open("GET", "http://myserver.com/user/182.json", true);
```

But what about the same-origin policy of the browser? Usually, you can't access anything but your own server! Good news: there's no such policy restriction for Cordova-loaded pages. You just enter any URL you like, and receive the response.

Copy the code from Chapter 12's multiplayer game application and adjust the absolute URLs, as shown in Listing 15-4.

Listing 15-4. *Fixing URLs for the Multiplayer Version of Four Balls*

```
<!DOCTYPE html>
<html lang="en">
<head>
    ...

    <script src="js/OnlineGame.js"></script>
    <script src="http://10.0.2.2/socket.io/socket.io.js"></script>

    <!-- Events -->
    <script src="js/EventEmitter.js"></script>

    ...

        function init() {
            socket = io.connect("http://10.0.2.2");

    ...
```

After this change, the resources load correctly. Of course, you have to adjust the URL to fit your own system setup. The code in Listing 15-4 was used for testing on the emulator.

Second, we need to adjust the set of permissions for the application. By default, an Android native app is *not* allowed to use internet connections. To gain this privilege, an application has to explicitly state that connectivity is required. Then the user has to approve the list of permissions when he first installs the app. The security model of Android is much better than the restrictive security model of the browser. If the user trusts your app, he may allow almost unlimited access to the device: filesystem, sensors, phonebook, and so forth (but it is always better to ask for only the permissions you need and nothing else).

To add the permission, modify the AndroidManifest.xml once again, as shown in Listing 15-5.

Listing 15-5. *Requesting Permissions to Connect to the Internet from the Native Android App*

```
<?xml version="1.0" encoding="utf-8"?>
<manifest xmlns:android="http://schemas.android.com/apk/res/android"
      package="com.juriy.connectfour"
      android:versionCode="1"
      android:versionName="1.0">
...
    <!-- Uncomment this line if your page will interact with the server -->
    <uses-permission android:name="android.permission.INTERNET" />
```

Uncomment the commented line, rebuild the application, and run it. Don't forget to start the Node server before you start the app! The multiplayer version of *Four Balls* is now a native application too.

Final Touches: Name, Icon, and Fullscreen Mode

The native application is almost ready for distribution. Let's add a couple final touches to make it look even better. First, the name of the game that shows in the application list doesn't look nice—it is the name of the main activity—FourBalls—camel case and no spaces (it was automatically generated for us).

To change the name, find the `res/values/strings.xml` file and add a space in the `"app_name"` (see Listing 15-6).

Listing 15-6. *Adding a Human-Readable Name for the Application*

```
<?xml version="1.0" encoding="utf-8"?>
<resources>
    <string name="app_name">Four Balls</string>
</resources>
```

If you rebuild and install the app, the name looks much better.

Now let's deal with the icon. The default Android app icon is a humble placeholder that should be used only during early development. In production, the app must have its own attractive icon. Android has its own guidelines on how to style it at `http://developer.android.com/guide/practices/ui_guidelines/icon_design_launcher.html`. It is a good idea to give this link to your designer before asking him to make a set of icons.

The icon must be a 32-bit PNG with an alpha channel. Android runs on a large variety of different devices that have different screens in terms of size and density. That's why an icon for a production-level game should be created in several resolutions: 36×36, 48×48, 72×72, and 96×96 for extra-high-density screens (only if your target is Android 2.3 or higher). Create a simple image on a transparent background and save it for each resolution, or use the one that comes along with the chapter materials. Now create four new subfolders in res and put the corresponding icon file in each one:

- res/drawable: 48×48 (the default; you can leave only this folder, but in this case, the icon is resized to match a particular density and may not look good for all resolutions)

- res/drawable-hdpi: 72×72 (high)

- res/drawable-mdpi: 48×48 (middle)

- res/drawable-ldpi: 36 × 36 (low)

Also, if you are going to publish your application on Google Play, create a high-res 512 × 512 icon and save it in a project folder for now. We will use it in the next section. The res folder should now look like Figure 15-6.

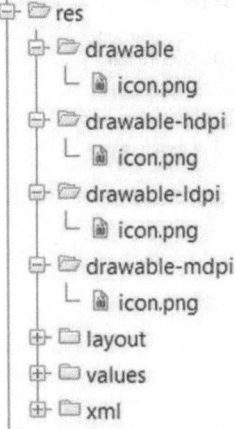

Figure 15-6. *Icons of different sizes are placed into the appropriate folders*

Modify the following line in the AndroidManifest.xml:

```
<application android:label="@string/app_name" android:icon="@drawable/icon">
```

Android automatically uses the correct icon depending on the screen density. Rebuild the application and enjoy the new look, shown in Figure 15-7!

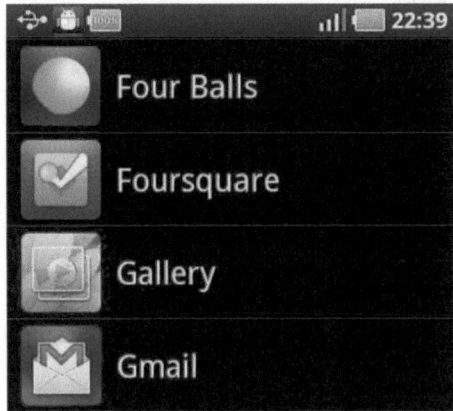

Figure 15-7. *A custom icon makes the application look better*

The final improvement is to hide the standard Android status bar. Game applications usually work in fullscreen mode. We already got rid of the browser address bar, and the next step is to gain a few more pixels by hiding the status bar too. Open FourBalls.java and add the lines shown in bold in Listing 15-7.

Listing 15-7. *Enabling Fullscreen Mode for the Application*

```
package com.juriy.fourballs;

import android.app.Activity;
import android.os.Bundle;
import org.apache.cordova.*;
import android.view.WindowManager;

public class FourBalls extends DroidGap {
    @Override
    public void onCreate(Bundle savedInstanceState) {
        super.onCreate(savedInstanceState);
        super.loadUrl("file:///android_asset/www/index.html");
        getWindow().setFlags(WindowManager.LayoutParams.FLAG_FULLSCREEN,
                        WindowManager.LayoutParams.FLAG_FULLSCREEN |

WindowManager.LayoutParams.FLAG_FORCE_NOT_FULLSCREEN);

    }
}
```

Rebuild and run the application once again. You should now see that the status bar is gone and Four Balls uses every available screen pixel. Figure 15-8 shows the difference between the previous version of application and the new one—without the status bar.

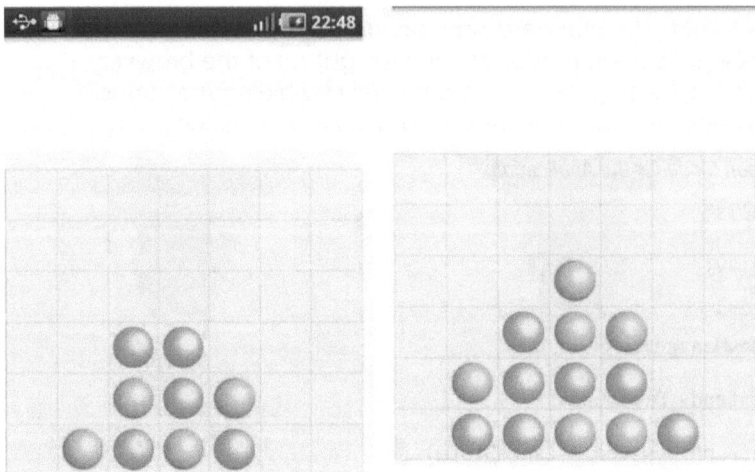

Figure 15-8. *The game with a status bar (left) vs. the game without a status bar (right)*

Using Native APIs

To complete our introduction to Cordova, let's try one more very important feature—using native device resources that are not available to the browser. Regular Java applications can access them directly via the Java API. JavaScript doesn't have direct access to such API, so Cordova's job is to provide a layer between the two. From a high level, the architecture looks like Figure 15-9.

Figure 15-9. *Communication between native resources and the HTML page*

In other words, for every piece of Java API that you want to use, Cordova must provide a "Java to JavaScript adapter" and explicitly expose the API to the web page. That's why Cordova supports a system of plug-ins. If you miss a "native" feature, you can always write a plug-in yourself without waiting for developers to implement it in the core framework.

The basic template that we'll use in this section is somewhat different (see Listing 15-8).

Listing 15-8. *Basic Template for Working with Native Resources*

```html
<!DOCTYPE html>
<html lang="en">
<head>
    <meta charset="utf-8" />
    <meta name="viewport"
          content="width=device-width, initial-scale=1.0, maximum-scale=1.0,
user-scalable=no, target-densitydpi=device-dpi"/>

    <style>
        html, body {
            overflow: hidden;
            width: 100%;
            height: 100%;
            margin:0;
            padding:0;
            border: 0;
        }

        #main {
            font-size: 20px;
        }
    </style>
    <script src="cordova-2.0.0.js"></script>
    <script>
        document.addEventListener("deviceready", onDeviceReady, false);

        function onDeviceReady() {
            /* code here */
        }
    </script>
</head>
<body>
    <div id="main">
        Cordova is working!
    </div>
</body>
</html>
```

First, we need to load the cordova-2.0.0.js file that provides the native access facilities. Next, the "main" entry point has changed. Usually, we use the body onload event to insert the JavaScript starting code. With the Cordova app, the page can load faster than Cordova is ready to provide its facilities, and as a result, you can't call "native" functions reliably from body onload. Cordova provides its own event that indicates that the native functions can be used, and Listing 15-8 illustrates how it works. When you receive the deviceready event, you can safely call any Cordova code. Note that you don't have to change anything in your app if you don't use native calls.

To test how it works, we will read the entire device phonebook and display every contact in the list. To do it, we first need to specify in AndroidManifest.xml that the application now needs one extra permission—the permission to read from the contact database. Add the following lines to the manifest, right after the INTERNET permission (see Listing 15-9). The second permission, ACCESS_NETWORK_STATE, is required by Cordova itself.

Listing 15-9. *Requesting Permission to Read Contacts*

```
<supports-screens
        android:largeScreens="true"
        android:normalScreens="true"
        android:smallScreens="true"
        android:resizeable="true"
        android:anyDensity="true"
        />

<!-- Uncomment this line if your page will interact with the server -->
<uses-permission android:name="android.permission.INTERNET" />

<!-- Used to read from the contacts database -->
<uses-permission android:name="android.permission.READ_CONTACTS" />

<!-- Required by Cordova -->
<uses-permission android:name="android.permission.ACCESS_NETWORK_STATE" />

<application android:label="@string/app_name"
            android:icon="@drawable/icon">
    <activity android:name="FourBalls"

    ...
```

Now, update the index.html file with the code in Listing 15-10.

Listing 15-10. *Reading Phonebook Contacts from JavaScript*

```
<script>
    document.addEventListener("deviceready", onDeviceReady, false);

    function onDeviceReady() {
        var options = new ContactFindOptions();
        options.filter = "";
        options.multiple = true;
        var fields = ["displayName"];
        navigator.contacts.find(fields, onSuccess, onError, options);
    }
```

```
        function onSuccess(contacts) {
            var list = document.getElementById("contacts");
            alert("Got contacts " + contacts.length);
            for (var i = 0; i < contacts.length; i++) {
                list.innerHTML += "<li>" + contacts[i].displayName + "</li>";
                }
        }

        function onError() {
            alert("Could not get contacts");
        }
    </script>
</head>
<body>
<div id="main">
    Contacts:
    <ul id="contacts"></ul>
</div>
</body>
</html>
```

Notice that there are a few new objects and new listings: `ContactFindOptions`, `contacts.find`, and so forth. These elements are Cordova-specific, so obviously this code will not run in a regular browser, even on the mobile device.

The result is the list of contacts shown in Figure 15-10.

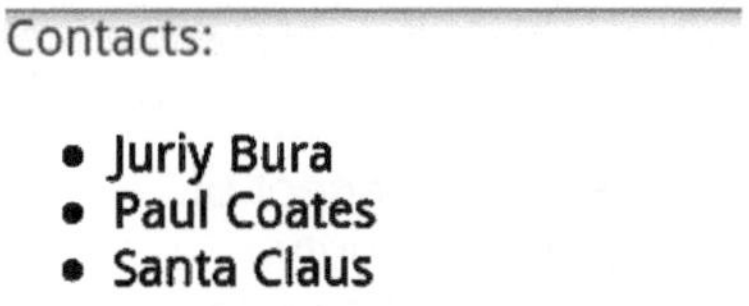

Contacts:

- Juriy Bura
- Paul Coates
- Santa Claus

Figure 15-10. *List of contacts, running on an emulator*

You can read more about available APIs on the official documentation page at `http://docs.phonegap.com`. There are many useful examples to start with. This section highlights only the generic concepts of API usage. It is up to you now to explore the whole list of possibilities.

There's one final but very important point I'd like to mention. Remember the basic rule of using permissions: ask for only what you really need. The more permissions you ask, the smaller the chance that the user will believe that your application is a harmless game and not some malware that wants to steal their private data. For example, it is fine to ask for `INTERNET` permission, or to ask for `READ_CONTACTS` permission. However, if an application is asking for both, it has everything required to upload your whole address book to the arbitrary site. This is definitely not what the user wants. For the next section of the chapter, we'll revert the permission to read the address book, and make our game a harmless, innocent application again.

Preparing for Markets

Now that the native application is ready, it is time to publish it on the market. This is typically the main motivation for "going native." The process has several steps:

- Create a key and sign the application.
- Register on the Android Market (requires $25 at the time of writing).
- Publish the application.
- Update the application as changes are made and when a new version comes out.
- The goal of this section is to bring our great Four Balls game to public and bring it to Google Play store. The first step, according to our list, is to sign the application.

Signing Applications

If you haven't worked with Java, .NET, or similar platforms, then the concept of signing might be somewhat unfamiliar to you. Signing is a powerful security instrument that allows the user to verify the integrity and authenticity of certain data. In Android development, the "data" is the application that you distribute.

Every application must be signed: not only the applications to be distributed via market but any application at all. Every example that that we created in this chapter was implicitly signed—the Ant build script signs it with the debug key. However, Google Play store doesn't accept debug keys, so you need to create a real key in order to share your work with other people.

> **NOTE:** There is a very good explanation of the signing process in the official Android documentation (`http://developer.android.com/guide/publishing/app-signing.html`). In this section, I do not go into a detailed explanation of digital signature concepts and replicate the online information, but instead I give a quick guide on how to prepare the application for Android Market publishing.

Creating a Digital Key

To sign an application, you need to create a digital key. The command-line tool for managing keys comes along with JDK; it is called a *keytool*. The key is stored in a *keystore*—the file that contains the information about multiple keys. Execute the following command to generate the keystore with one 2048-bit RSA key:

```
> keytool -genkey -v -keystore juriy-android.keystore -alias android-release -
keyalg RSA -keysize 2048 -validity 10000
```

The keytool prompts you to answer several questions, as shown in the following output from my example key creation. Answering the questions is not obligatory, so answer whatever suits you.

```
Enter keystore password:
Re-enter new password:
What is your first and last name?
  [Unknown]:  Juriy Bura
What is the name of your organizational unit?
  [Unknown]:
What is the name of your organization?
  [Unknown]:
What is the name of your City or Locality?
  [Unknown]:  Kiev
What is the name of your State or Province?
  [Unknown]:
What is the two-letter country code for this unit?
  [Unknown]:  UA
Is CN=Juriy Bura, OU=Unknown, O=Unknown, L=Kiev, ST=Unknown, C=UA correct?
  [no]:  yes

Generating 2.048 bit RSA key pair and self-signed certificate (SHA1withRSA) with
a validity of 10.000 days
        for: CN=Juriy Bura, OU=Unknown, O=Unknown, L=Kiev, ST=Unknown, C=UA
Enter key password for <android-release>
        (RETURN if same as keystore password):
[Storing juriy-android.keystore]
```

The keystore is a simple file that has one or many keys and certificates. Each key in the keystore is protected by its own password and has an alias—the name that you use to refer the key. Once the file is created, which should look like the following, check that it is a valid keystore and that it has a key with the android-release alias:

```
> keytool -list -v -keystore juriy-android.keystore
Enter keystore password:

Keystore type: JKS
Keystore provider: SUN
```

```
Your keystore contains 1 entry

Alias name: android-release
Creation date: 10 Jul 2012
Entry type: PrivateKeyEntry
Certificate chain length: 1
Certificate[1]:
Owner: CN=Juriy Bura, OU=Unknown, O=Unknown, L=Kiev, ST=Unknown, C=UA
Issuer: CN=Juriy Bura, OU=Unknown, O=Unknown, L=Kiev, ST=Unknown, C=UA
Serial number: 4f357fb2
Valid from: Fri Feb 10 22:36:02 EET 2012 until: Tue Jun 28 23:36:02 EEST 2039
Certificate fingerprints:
        MD5:  EA:48:BE:09:AA:8A:05:20:AC:04:D6:13:B2:7A:09:05
        SHA1: 74:ED:15:74:98:D0:A2:1F:89:76:46:E2:B6:2A:48:37:D9:66:AD:5D
        Signature algorithm name: SHA1withRSA
        Version: 3


*****************************************
*****************************************
```

If you see something like the preceding, then the keystore is ready.

Signing the Application

The next step is to build the "release" version of your application, and sign it with the key. To do that, you need to tell the Ant script where to find the keystore and which key (alias) to use. Execute the following command:

```
> ant -Dkey.store=<path-to-keystore>.keystore -Dkey.alias=<key-alias> clean release
```

At some point of the build script, Ant prompts you to enter two passwords: one for the keystore and another for the key. The password appears on the screen as you type, so make sure that nobody's looking over your shoulder. Alternatively, you can put two extra lines into the ant.properties file in the project root:

```
key.store=../<path-to-keystore>
key.alias=<key-alias>
```

If you do so, you can omit the extra parameters in the command line and just type

```
> ant clean release
```

> **NOTE:** If you are as paranoid about your passwords as I am, you can sign the package manually. The process is somewhat more complex, since it requires you to sign and then "align" the application. Refer to the official Android tutorial for details (`http://developer.android.com/guide/publishing/app-signing.html#signapp`).

The final step is to check that the signed application is really signed. Execute the following line in a console, and check that the output says `jar verified`, as in the following.

```
> jarsigner -verify bin/FourBalls-release-unsigned.apk
jar verified.
```

If you did everything right and see this output, then you are ready for the market!

After you have signed your application with the "production" key, you will not be able to install it on top of the "debug" version. If you see a message like the following during your build process:

```
[exec] Failure [INSTALL_PARSE_FAILED_INCONSISTENT_CERTIFICATES]
```

then uninstall the older version application:

```
> adb uninstall <package>
```

In my case, I type

```
> adb uninstall com.juriy.fourballs
```

The reason is that Android will not reinstall the application silently if the certificates don't match.

Publishing on Google Play

This step requires a small financial outlay. To create an account, you need to pay a registration fee, which is $25 at the time of writing.

> **NOTE:** If you are not yet ready to publish your app, I suggest you either skip this section, or just read over it quickly to get an idea of how to work with the market. You already know enough to create the application, publish it on your own site, and show it to your friends and business partners. The next few pages of the chapter are solely devoted to Google Play store.

Go to `https://play.google.com/apps/publish/`, login with your Google account, and follow the registration procedure. The first step of registration is shown in Figure 15-11.

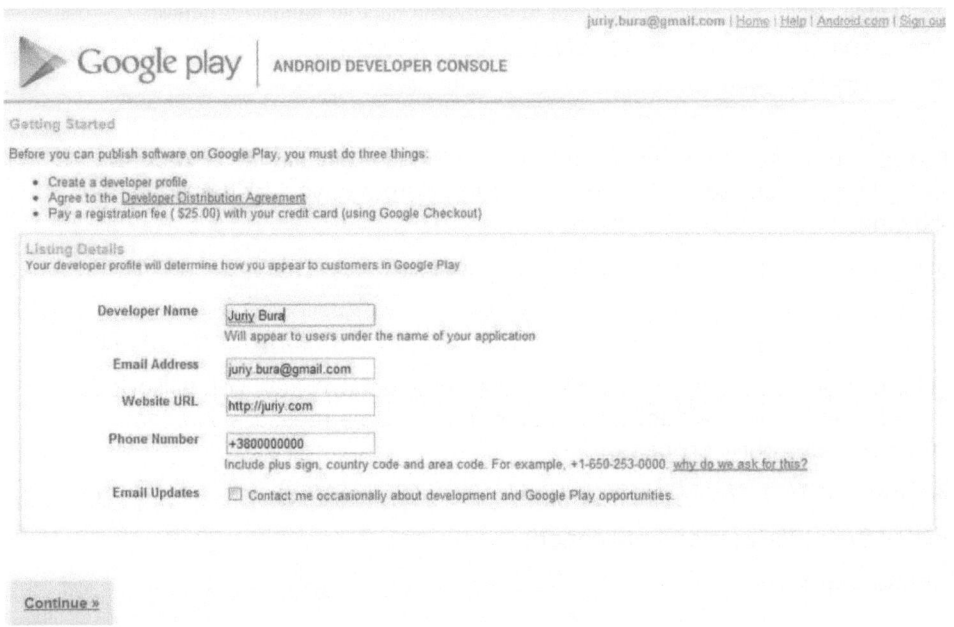

Figure 15-11. *The first step in registration on the Android Market*

After you agree with the license agreement and pay the registration fee, you are ready for publishing. The initial web page will look like Figure 15-12. Click the Upload Application button and select the signed version of the file. It will not be immediately published, so don't worry if you don't feel 100 percent ready to go public.

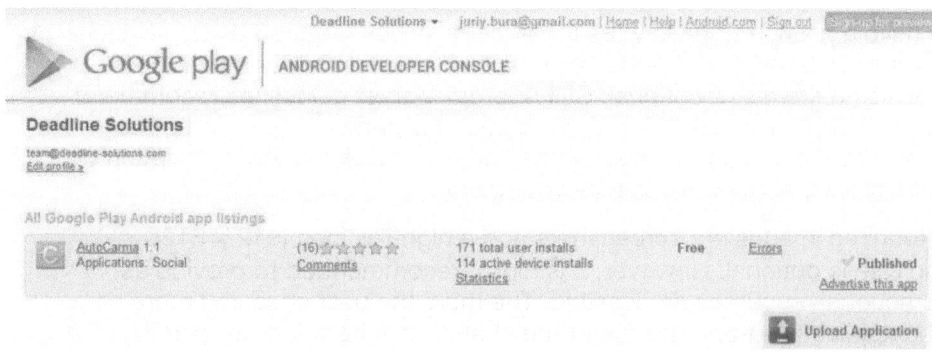

Figure 15-12. *The developer console when you first enter it. No published applications so far.*

The screenshot in Figure 15-10 shows a page that already has one published application. If you have just started, you have an empty list of apps.

When the file is uploaded, you see a quick summary of the APK, as shown in Figure 15-13.

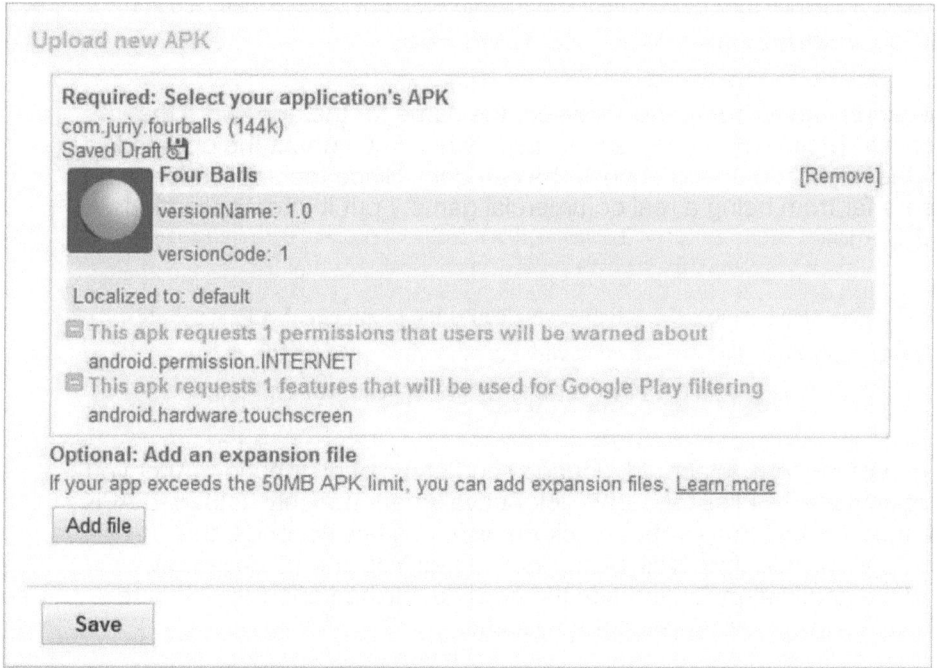

Figure 15-13. *A new APK summary screen*

Here you have a chance to review the list of permissions required by application. Click Save and proceed to the publication form. The form itself is rather long; most of the listed items are optional. Still Android Market guidelines recommend treating every field as required. For a new game, it is particularly important to show a few bright and colorful screenshots and to provide a good description of the product. Make people want to play your game!

The only required images are screenshots and a high-res icon (512 × 512). Everything else is optional. However, it is highly recommended to provide as many promotional resources as possible. The more the user sees, the more he will like the application—and the better the chance that he will download it.

> **NOTE:** There are several ways to create screenshots for your application. The simplest way is to load the page in an emulator and create the screenshot with the usual screen-capturing tools. The other alternative is to connect to your device via a small utility called DDMS (Dalvik Debug Monitor Server), which is found in the Tools folder of your Android SDK. Connect the device with USB Debugging enabled, run the tool, select the device from the list, then select Device Screen Capture. Here you go! You have a screenshot exactly like on a real device screen.

Follow the guide and fill out the form: select the name for the app, write the description and promo text, list changes (used when you submit the updated version of the application), and choose the category. Since the application that I will release is far from being a real commercial game, I put it into Applications, Libraries & Demo.

> **NOTE:** For your convenience, the screenshots, icons, and promotional graphics that I used with Google Play store are provided with the other resources for this chapter. You can use them as a reference point or placeholders for your own applications.

The final part of the form is about languages and areas of distribution. After you fill it out, open the APK Files tab, and click Activate near the only uploaded APK file. When the APK becomes active, click Publish. In a few seconds, the application is published and available for download! You should have now returned to the application list and see the newly published app there. Figure 15-14 shows how your developer console looks.

Figure 15-14. *The developer console after the app is published*

> **NOTE:** The publishing process might take some time, so don't worry if your application is not immediately available. Taking a coffee break usually helps the application publish faster.

Visit the application page, using the URL in the form (`https://play.google.com/store/apps/details?id =<package_name>`), where the `<package name>` is the name of the package that you set at the start of this chapter. My newly published game is available at `https://play.google.com/store/apps/details?id=com.juriy.fourballs`. If you click the link to this page from your Android device, you are prompted to open the market application and install Four Balls. This is the "home page" of the app in the Android Market. Figure 15-15 shows how the page looks in a desktop browser, and Figure 15-16 shows how the page looks on the market application on the device.

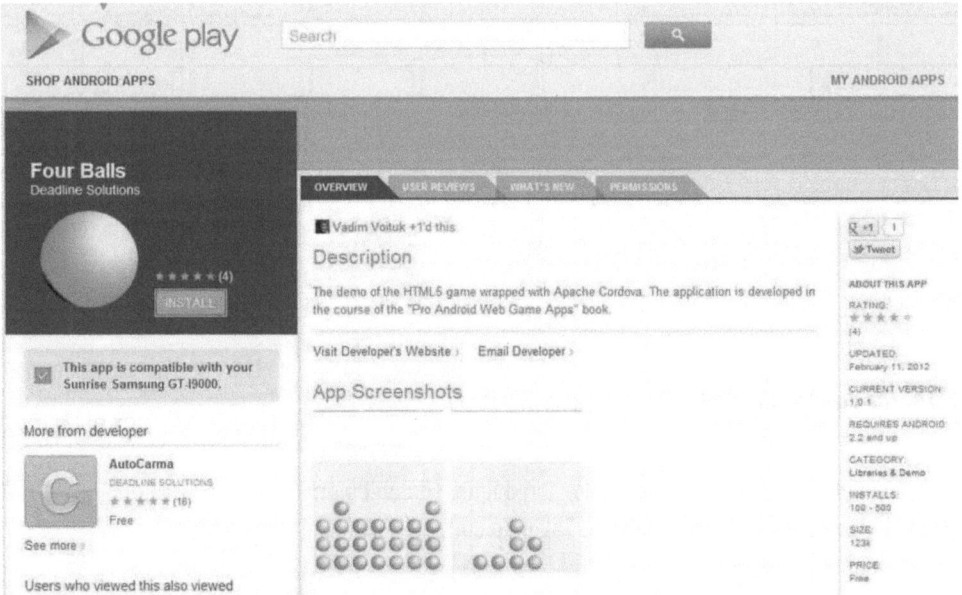

Figure 15-15. *The application page on Google Play store in a desktop browser*

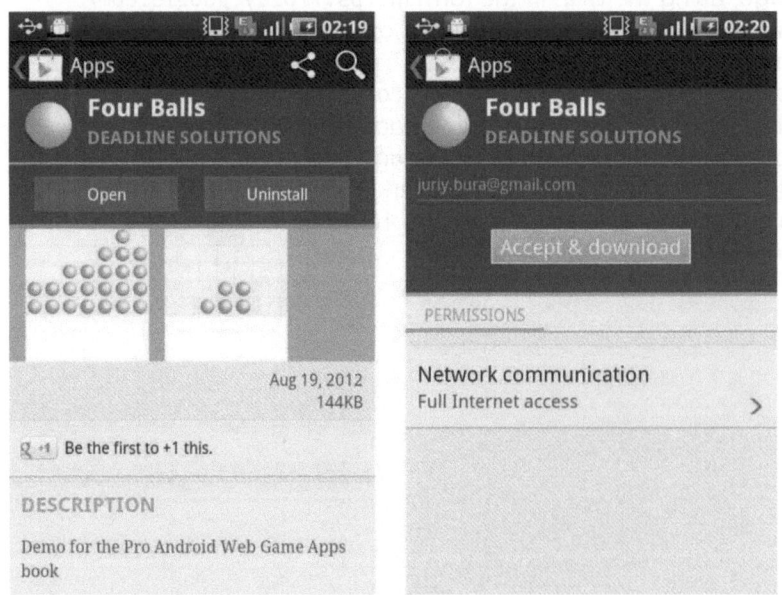

Figure 15-16. *On the left, the application page is open on the device. On the right, the installation prompt shows a list of the required permissions.*

If you want to learn more about the publishing process, visit the official Android documentation page at `http://developer.android.com/guide/publishing/publishing.html`.

Updating Your Application

Once your application gets popular, you probably want to update it with some new features to attract even more users. The final section of this chapter is devoted to pushing the updates to Google Play store. Let's look at a simple scenario: you decided that a white background doesn't look good on a device and you want to change it to black. You fixed a line of JavaScript code in a minute, and now you are eager to publish a new version. Before you create a new signed build, open the `AndroidManifest.xml` file once again and update the bolded lines in Listing 15-11.

Listing 15-11. *Updating the Application Version in Android Manifest*

```
<?xml version="1.0" encoding="utf-8"?>
<manifest xmlns:android="http://schemas.android.com/apk/res/android"
     package="com.juriy.fourballs"
     android:versionCode="2"
     android:versionName="1.0.1">
...
```

The `versionCode` parameter must be an integer and is required for the market to compare between the version that is installed on the user's device and the newest available version on the market. The second parameter, `versionName`, is what the user the sees. Save the file and rebuild the application.

Once it is packed and signed, open the Google Play store developer's console, select the Four Balls application, and upload the new APK. Since it is the new version of the app and it has changed compared to the last one, complete the Recent Changes field to let your users know why they should update. The application has changed its appearance, so you should also update the screenshots and promo graphics. Paying attention to such small details is essential for the success of the app.

Upload the new APK. Click the Deactivate button near the first version of the APK, and then Activate near the new version—1.0.1. Click Save and wait several minutes. The update appears on the market, and every user who already has the application is prompted to get the new version.

Working with the market is not hard at all. Once you publish your first application, you become comfortable with the whole process. The market is a very powerful distribution channel, and once your game is working in the browser, you should think about putting it onto the market.

Summary

In this chapter, we learned how to wrap existing web pages with Apache Cordova and create a native Android application. We learned how to deal with the specifics of such a setup: server URLs, application permissions, and access to the native application resources.

We learned how to make a "production" version of the application: create a key, sign the app, and prepare it for Google Play store publishing.

In the last part of the chapter, we looked at how to use Google Play store—from creating the account to publishing your application, sharing it with other people, and updating it with newer and better versions.

Native applications have many advantages. It doesn't matter how you create such an app, with Java or with an HTML5 technology stack. If the user can load the app to his device and play your game, then you achieved your goal.

Chapter 16

Adding Sound

Sound is one of the final touches that you need to add in order to make a complete, market-ready game. In mobile gaming, sound often plays a secondary role. There are several reasons for that.

- Mobile games are mostly casual. People play mobile games while traveling, in long lines, at airports, and in dull meetings— places where sound might actually disturb others.

- If the player has headphones, most likely he's listening to the music he likes—songs from his huge MP3 collection.

- Sound consumes battery life, so even though the amount of actual power loss is very small, some users would rather save it for something else.

- The lack of sound doesn't hurt the playing experience for most casual games. In desktop games like *Counter Strike*, players know the location of the enemies just by listening to their steps. In games like *Fallout 3*, sound is a way of diving deeper into the game world. In contrast, casual games are perfectly playable in "muted" mode.

Nevertheless, sound is a pretty important aspect of mobile games, and you should not ignore it in your own project. A game without it feels more like an uncompleted garage project rather than a commercial product. Look at *Angry Birds*—the canonical example of a crazy-popular casual game: the quiet grunting of pigs awaiting their destiny and the vigorous battle cries of birds really make this game even more fun to play.

Your job as a developer is to make users *want* to turn the sound on. Even if only 15 percent of them actually play with the sound, they will certainly give you an extra star in their market rating.

This chapter is devoted to sound. We will learn about the following topics:

- Sound support in Android browsers
- Workarounds for common problems
- SoundManager2—the ultimate web sound library
- Sound in native applications (Cordova API)
- Common sound usability patterns

Audio on Web Pages

Let's start by looking at the APIs available to the "big brothers"—the desktop browsers that tend to follow the latest HTML5 tendencies. There are two audio APIs available for working with sound: the simple HTML5 audio tag (www.whatwg.org/specs/web-apps/current-work/#the-audio-element) and the sophisticated full-blown Web Audio API (https://dvcs.w3.org/hg/audio/raw-file/tip/webaudio/specification.html).

The Audio Tag

The audio tag is the simplest possible way to play sound within a web page. The API is straightforward and unsophisticated, as shown on Listing 16-1.

Listing 16-1. *Using the Audio Element on a Web Page*

```
<head>
    <script>
        var audio;
        function init() {
            audio = new Audio("sound/theme.mp3");
        }

        function play() {
            audio.play();
            setInterval(function() {
                audio.volume -= 0.1;
            }, 200);
        }
```

```
        function pause() {
            audio.pause();
        }

        function changeVolume(deltaVolume) {
            audio.volume += deltaVolume;
        }
    </script>
</head>
<body onload="init()">
    <div>
        <button onclick="play()">Play</button>
        <button onclick="pause()">Pause</button>
        <button onclick="changeVolume(0.2)">Vol. Up</button>
        <button onclick="changeVolume(-0.2)">Vol. Down</button>
    </div>
</body>
```

The new Audio("sound/theme.mp3") line is a convenience constructor that creates the tag on the fly.

The code in Listing 16-2 gives the same result.

Listing 16-2. *The Alternate Way to Initialize Sound by Adding the audio Tag to the Page*

```
<script>
    var audio;
    function init() {
        audio = document.getElementById("player");
    }

    /* rest of the code is unchanged*/
</script>
</head>
<body onload="init()">
<div>
    <audio id="player" src="sound/theme.mp3"></audio>
    <button onclick="play()">Play</button>
    <button onclick="pause()">Pause</button>
    <button onclick="changeVolume(0.2)">Vol. Up</button>
    <button onclick="changeVolume(-0.2)">Vol. Down</button>
</div>
</body>
```

The audio tag implements the bare minimum of audio functionality: load the file, play/pause the track, change playback volume. It can also show simple player controls on the web page (rarely required for games). Even though it is hard to imagine a simpler API, this functionality is often enough for casual games: load the background music, set the volume, start the playback in a loop, and occasionally play other sounds for various game events.

The Web Audio API

The Web Audio API is the next-generation audio processing API for the web. It allows you not only to *play* audio, but also to *process* it in real time, playing with the raw audio data—the waveform. To better understand the function of the API, think about the real-time image processing that we can do with the canvas API. Given thousands of raw pixels, we can do truly amazing things— dynamically render worlds; create 3D figures; provide effects like lightning and fire; cover parts of the map with a "fog of war," and more. It is possible because we can manipulate the raw pixel data, not just static pre-rendered images.

Sound is no simpler than images, and sometimes it is even more complicated. Imagine a 3D adventure game where the player enters a room and sees two NPCs (non-player characters), who talk to each other and the player. The resulting sound wave depends on many different parameters:

- The position of each NPC relative to the player (the closer to the player, the louder the sound)

- The direction the player is facing (the left and right channels should each receive different sounds in order to make it realistic)

- The size of and the material in the room: a voice in a cave sounds totally different from a voice in a concert hall or on the street

As you can see, it is nearly impossible to pre-render the sound for such complex situations. The Web Audio API allows you to take the "source" of the sound and process it right before playback: mix several tracks together; apply effects like cave echo or radio static; add filters; and finally, send the result to the audio device.

Unfortunately, this API is only available for a few desktop browsers and is still far from coming to mass-market Android devices. For the sake of completeness of the material, however, Listing 16-3 provides sample code that shows how this API works.

Listing 16-3. *Playing Sound with Web Audio API*

```
var context;
var buffer;
function init() {
    try {
        context = new webkitAudioContext();
    } catch(e) {
        alert('Web Audio API not supported');
```

```
        return;
    }

    // Load the binary data from music file
    var request = new XMLHttpRequest();
    request.open('GET', "sound/theme.mp3", true);
    request.responseType = 'arraybuffer';

    request.onload = function() {
        // Decode data and play sound
        context.decodeAudioData(request.response, function(buff) {
            buffer = buff;
            var source = context.createBufferSource();
            source.buffer = buffer;
            source.connect(context.destination);
            source.noteOn(0);
        });
    };
    request.send(null);
}
```

> **NOTE:** An audio API doesn't need a source file. Just as you can draw a line on a blank canvas, you can generate sound data on the fly and play it. You can create applications such as a "virtual piano" without having a separate sound file for each key, or make something even more sophisticated, like "realistic" alien speech syntheses based on certain pronunciation parameters.

The difference between the Web Audio API and HTML5 audio tag is roughly the same as the difference between the canvas API and the IMG tag. The latter gives you a simple way to render static media, while the Web Audio API gives you full control over the process (at the cost of more complex code, of course).

Sound in Android Browser

Sadly, the Android browser has rather poor support for sound APIs. The Web Audio API is still cutting-edge technology, and it has yet to make its way onto mobile platforms. However, even basic support for the audio tag is somewhat buggy and limited in Android. The situation with native applications is much better, but the standard browser still has a lot of space for improvement.

The first version of Android to support the Audio element was Android 2.2, and that "support" was rather... specific. Even though the element itself was recognized by the browser, it couldn't play *any* audio files. It looked more like a dummy for future expansion. So, real support for audio wasn't released until Android 2.3 Gingerbread. It was still very far from perfect, however.

Speaking of audio files, the "support" for playing audio doesn't automatically mean that every possible audio format is recognized by the browser. Just as the IMG tag can display only a few file formats—PNG, JPEG, GIF, and a couple more—the audio tag is limited to specific file formats. To make matters slightly worse, there is no single opinion on which formats browsers should support. Some vendors insist on using open-source and free formats such as OGG, while others push closed, proprietary formats like MP3 and h.264. In other words, there is no single file format supported by every browser. That's why the audio tag allows you to set several alternative files as the audio source. The browser chooses the one that it "knows."

Pre-Gingerbread devices form a massive 23 percent of the market at the time of writing. Simply dropping the support for sound for every fourth customer is not an option, of course. Luckily, there is a library that solves most of Android's sound problems. SoundManager2 (www.schillmania.com/projects/soundmanager2/) utilizes a simple approach: if the browser is too silly to play audio, we let Flash do the heavy part. Rich out-of-the-box media support was one of the reasons why Flash became so popular—Flash Player knows how to deal with playback.

> **NOTE:** SoundManager2 is not an Android-specific solution. Its mission is to bring seamless sound capabilities to a broad range of browsers, starting with the oldest ones. The idea of using Flash is not entirely new, either. Socket.IO, the networking API that we used in Chapter 12, also has an option of falling to *Flash Sockets*—the Flash-based implementation of the persistent connection between the web page and the server. As you can see, small Flash components often work like a "Plan B" for browsers that are still catching up.

The best feature of SoundManager2 is its ease of use. Just a couple lines of code—and your game has music!

In this chapter, we add sound to an existing game—Escaping Knight—the one that we created in Chapter 14 while testing the Crafty game engine. Copy the code from the Chapter 14 game, or use your own project.

Using SoundManager2

Now it is a time to add some sound to the tale about the escaping knight. But first, we need to set up the project.

Initial Setup

The first step is to download the latest version of SoundManager (2.97a at the time of writing) from the official site at www.schillmania.com/projects/soundmanager2/doc/download/.

Then, unpack the archive somewhere on your hard drive. The distribution contains many demos and tools, but we need only a few of them in our project. Perform the following steps:

1. Copy the /script/soundmanager2.js file from the distribution to your js folder.

2. Copy the entire swf folder to the root of your project.

3. Create a new folder called sound in a root of the project. We will put our sound files there.

4. Take the theme.mp3 file, distributed with this book, and copy to the folder created in the previous step.

Your directory structure should look like Figure 16-1.

Figure 16-1. *The starting directory structure*

> **NOTE:** The script folder of the SoundManager2 distribution contains several files.
> They all have exactly the same production functionality. Files with the *nodebug* suffix
> have different defaults (all debugging is turned off); they have no comments and no
> debugging methods. Files that have *jsmin* in their name are preprocessed with JSMin
> (www.crockford.com/javascript/jsmin.html), the JavaScript "code minifier"
> that removes all extra spaces in the source code, making the file much smaller and
> faster to download. During development, we always use the original unprocessed file
> with debugging enabled. Once you go to production, consider replacing it with a
> nodebug-minified version.

Now we are ready to add some nice sound to the game. Add the code in Listing
16-4 to the page.

Listing 16-4. *Initializing SoundManager2*

```
<script src="js/soundmanager2.js"></script>
<script>
    soundManager.url = 'swf/';
    soundManager.flashVersion = 9;
    soundManager.onready(function() {
        soundManager.createSound({
            id:'theme',
            url:'sound/theme.mp3',
            autoLoad:true,
            onload:function() {
                this.play();
            }
        });
    });
</script>
```

The soundManager is the "magic" object that appears on the global namespace
once you load the soundmanager2.js file. The first two lines initialize the basic
settings—the path to the swf folder and the version of swf that SoundManager
will use. There are two options—8 and 9—and the default is 8. Version 9
unlocks some fancy new features, and your players will most likely have the
appropriate version of Flash Player on their devices.

> **NOTE:** If you are pragmatic and you want to know the percentage of customers (not
> only mobile) that have older versions of Flash Player, refer to the official version
> usage statistics from Adobe at

www.adobe.com/products/flashplatformruntimes/statistics.
displayTab3.html.

The next line adds the onready event listener that fires once the soundManager is
operational and ready to perform actual sound-related tasks. Finally, we load the
sound from the MP3 file, and instruct soundManager to start playback once the
sound is ready.

Run the page in the browser, and enjoy the background music. Note that if you
are using the emulator, you probably hear no sound at this point. This is
because the emulator doesn't have the Flash plug-in. If you are going to debug
sound with the emulator, you need to install the player manually on the
emulator.

The music theme plays only once. Usually the background theme should repeat
and play continuously. Let's make the music loop.

Looping

Looping by itself is quite easy to implement—all you need is to set the number
of loops (see Listing 16-5).

Listing 16-5. *Looping the Background Theme*

```
soundManager.url = 'swf/';
soundManager.flashVersion = 9;
soundManager.onready(function() {
    soundManager.createSound({
        id: 'loopTest',
        url: 'sound/theme.mp3',
        loops: 10000,
        autoLoad: true,
        onload:function() {
            this.play();
        }
    });
});
```

SoundManager doesn't support infinite loops, so when you need infinite
playback, just use a big number like 10000—it will give you around 13 hours of
continuous playback for a five-second sound sample—more than enough for a
casual game.

However, music looping is much trickier than this. Just as tiles must match their
neighbors to create the illusion of solid terrain, the end of the loop must match

the beginning. Otherwise, a gamer will clearly hear that the composition has ended and started again milliseconds later. It will not be continuous ambient background music, but a set of irritating loops.

If you save your files in MP3 or a similar lossy format, you may find another surprise. Even though the sound loops perfectly in the sound editor, you hear a "clank" after each iteration once the sound is played in the game. This is a well-known problem caused by the peculiarities of lossy compression algorithms. Take a look at Figure 16-2, which shows a simple waveform—a generated tone (like the one that television companies use to censor harsh language). The top part of the image shows the original waveform, and the bottom part shows the same waveform saved as an MP3.

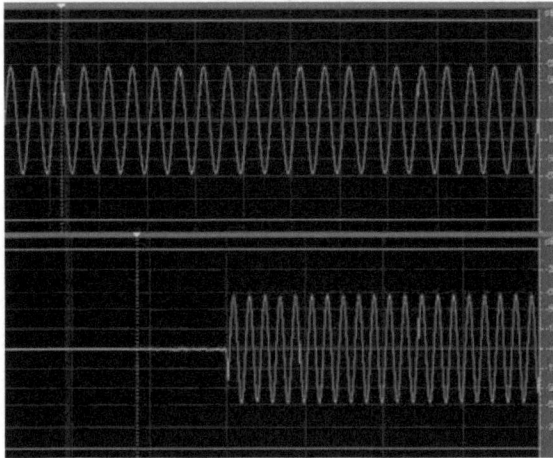

Figure 16-2. *The original waveform (top) and the compressed MP3 file. The first 50 milliseconds are almost silent because of the compression algorithm.*

Notice that the compressed one starts with 50 (or so) milliseconds of silence. That's how MP3 works: it simply can't save every bit of the sound as we would like it to, and it results in an irritating "clank" sound. However, this is not an excuse for game development, of course. We want smooth playback for our background theme.

There are two ways to address this issue. If the sample starts and ends with a relatively quiet fragment, or even silence, the "clank" is not audible. It is still there, but the player thinks that this is a quiet part of the musical composition and it will not irritate him.

The other way is to use specialized encoding software that can re-encode MP3 and make the clank slightly "lighter." The exact mechanism behind this is beyond the scope of this chapter. If you are interested in a more in-depth explanation, follow these useful links:

- `www.schillmania.com/projects/soundmanager2/demo/api/#loo ping`: The SoundManager documentation on looping.

- `www.flickr.com/photos/schill/4499319436/`: A quick "how to" on making smooth sound loops for SoundManager.

- `www.compuphase.com/mp3/mp3loops.htm`: The home page of a utility called MP3Loop. As the name implies, this utility is used to create "looping" MP3 files. The page has a pretty good explanation of why the MP3 encoder behaves that way and how to fix it.

From now on, we will assume that your MP3 files are already prepared for your game.

Adding Sound to the Game

Now we are ready to add the sound to the game itself. Our game will have three sounds: the main theme, a click sound, and a "game over" sound. The main theme sound should loop once it is loaded, while other two sounds play on certain game events. Load all three sound files as shown in the following code listings. First, load the sounds and set the theme sound to play on load (see Listing 16-6).

Listing 16-6. *Loading Sounds and Playing the Theme Once It Is Loaded*

```
soundManager.url = 'swf/';
soundManager.flashVersion = 9;
soundManager.onready(function() {
    soundManager.createSound({
        id: 'theme',
        url: 'sound/theme.mp3',
        loops: 10000,
        autoLoad: true,
        onload:function() {
            this.play();
        }
    });

    soundManager.createSound({
        id: 'click',
        url: 'sound/click.mp3',
        autoLoad: true
    });
```

```
    soundManager.createSound({
        id: 'gameover',
        url: 'sound/gameover.mp3',
        autoLoad: true
    });
});
```

Now you have the main theme playing in a loop. The sound that I used is too loud for a casual game, though. You can set the volume straight in the code (value between 0 and 100), as shown in Listing 16-7.

Listing 16-7. *Setting Sound Volume*

```
soundManager.createSound({
    id: 'gameover',
    url: 'sound/gameover.mp3',
    volume: 40,
    autoLoad: true
});
```

Now let's add the click sound. When a player taps the screen, this sound plays. Note that Android has its own tap sound that plays along with our custom sound unless you call "prevent default" on the tap event. The code for playing the tap sound looks like Listing 16-8.

Listing 16-8. *Playing the Click Sound Whenever the User Taps the Screen or Presses the Mouse Button*

```
Crafty.addEvent(this, window, "touchstart", function (e) {
    e.preventDefault();
    soundManager.getSoundById("click").play();
});
Crafty.addEvent(this, window, "mousedown", function (e) {
    e.preventDefault();
    soundManager.getSoundById("click").play();
});
```

Unfortunately, the call to preventDefault()also causes Crafty to ignore tap events on the Knight sprite. We have to make the sprite render on a separate DOM element and then add the event listeners manually, as shown in Listing 16-9.

Listing 16-9. *Drawing the Character*

```
function drawCharacter() {
    var knight = Crafty.e("2D, DOM, knight, SpriteAnimation, Mouse")
        .attr({x: 100, y: 280})
        .animate("move_left", 1, 0, 3)
        .animate("move_right", 0, 1, 2)
        .animate("move_right", 15, -1)
```

```
        .bind("EnterFrame", function() {
            this.x += 0.3;
            if (this.x > 500) {
                Crafty.trigger("GameOver");
            }
        });

    Crafty.addEvent(this, knight._element, "touchstart", function() {
        Crafty.trigger("Win");
    });

    Crafty.addEvent(this, knight._element, "mousedown", function() {
        Crafty.trigger("Win");
    });
}
```

When the game is over, we need to stop the main theme and play the "game over" theme once. Let's create a function for that (see Listing 16-10).

Listing 16-10. *Playing the gameover Sound*

```
function playGameoverSound() {
    soundManager.getSoundById("theme").stop();
    soundManager.getSoundById("gameover").play();
}
```

The final touch is to call this function from both "win" and "game over" scenes (see Listing 16-11).

Listing 16-11. *Play the gameover Sound for Both Win and Lose States*

```
Crafty.scene("gameover", function() {
    playGameoverSound();
    showGameOverBanner();
});

Crafty.scene("win", function() {
    playGameoverSound();
    showWinBanner();
});
```

That's it! With just 40 lines of code, most of which is configuration, we added some nice sound effects to the game!

Playing Sound in Cordova Applications

If you are making a native application, you have many more tools at your disposal—in fact, the whole Android API is yours. Using it to play sounds in a

Cordova app is wasteful—Android can play sound on its own. Cordova has a simplistic API for media playback at `http://docs.phonegap.com/en/1.0.0/phonegap_media_media.md.html`.

The code for playing audio from within a native-wrapped app looks like the following:

```
var media = new Media("/android_asset/www/sound/sound.mp3");
media.play();
```

That's it. Don't forget to load the core phonegap API. As for looping, things are quite complicated once again. The Cordova API doesn't know how to loop media. Cordova developers are ignoring community requests on this subject, simply saying, "Looping is not implemented on Android." The hacky way to get around this limitation is shown in Listing 16-12.

Listing 16-12. *Looping Track with Cordova*

```
var media = new Media("/android_asset/www/sound/sound.mp3",
        null, null,
        function(status) {
            if (status == 4) {
                media.stop();
                media.play();
            }
        }
);
media.play();
```

The code listens to the "status" of the media, and once the playback is finished, it starts it again. The results are far from perfect—the delays between the loops are more than noticeable, but it is better than nothing. Besides, there are a few plug-ins that bring better sound support to Cordova. An article at `www.scirra.com/tutorials/283/phonegap-low-latency-audio/page-1` describes one of them.

User Experience

Sound is a powerful feature that should be used wisely. Sound, by its nature, is much more evocative than other types of feedback that you might use in your game. That's why you should make sure that your splendid audio actually brings fun and not annoyance.

Follow common sense when you design the sound capabilities of your app. Remember, your user might be sitting in a boring lecture in the middle of the auditorium, surfing the web and looking for something more exciting. Now he finds your page. If your application plays all its bells and whistles, the user will be none too pleased.

As a rule of thumb in the web, sound is *disabled* by default. Alternatively, you can ask the user if he wants to enable it on the first launch—but never create pages with the sound turned on. The worst thing you can do is create an intro sound that plays with a significant delay: if the user has switched to a different tab, he will have a tough time finding the page that plays the tune.

If you are making a native application, you may leave the sound turned on by default, although I would suggest that you be nice and still ask the user if he wants sound or not.

A casual game should be playable without any sound. The following are more tips on good sound design:

- Design sound with a Mute button. Make it easily accessible from within the game screen (two clicks at most).

- Add volume controls. Allow the player to set the volume of the background music and effects independently.

- Use consistent sounds. Just as icons from the same collection have the same size and suit each other, sounds should have the same "style" and volume.

- Don't use sounds that are too loud or too disturbing, or sounds that bring negative emotions. A realistic baby cry for the game over event, for example, will not motivate your player to try again.

Follow this simple advice, and your game audio will fit smoothly and naturally into the game process.

Summary

In this chapter, we learned how to work with sound in the browser. Sound APIs are still far from perfect, especially when it comes to mobile devices. Libraries like SoundManager2 are designed to make sound easily accessible from JavaScript. When the browser is not capable of playing certain sound formats, SoundManager uses the Flash plug-in and allows you to play media anywhere, even on rather outdated browsers.

We learned how to play individual sounds and sound loops, how to deal with lossy sound format problems, and how to play seamless loops. We also looked at the sound capabilities of Apache Cordova to add sound to native applications.

We added sound capabilities to Escaping Knight—the game created with the Crafty engine in Chapter 14. We used three sounds—a background loop, a "click" effect, and a "game over" tune.

Going Further

In this book, we learned the fundamental techniques of Android web game development. Now you have a clear understanding how to make your own Android web game from scratch: 2D or 3D, single-player or multiplayer, with sound, animations and AI. But game development doesn't end here.

The world of mobile entertainment is a world that moves extremely fast. Things that sounded fantastic even few years ago are now a reality: GPS, 3D graphics, rich media, networking, voice recognition, augmented reality – all brewed together under a shiny screen of the brand new smartphone. The endless possibilities for fundamentally different games are now open to you and ready to be explored.

The future is exciting and ready for your craziest ideas.

Debugging Client-side JavaScript

One of my friends once told me that "debugging JavaScript code in Android is like chopping wood with a spoon." The Android browser doesn't have any sort of debugger by default. There's no way to follow the typical debugging scenario: place a breakpoint, add some watches, and then proceed in "step-by-step" mode until you find the problem in the code. So the only thing that you have is `console.log`—writing some values to the device's log and reading it afterwards. Still, there are several tools and tips that will hopefully make your debugging experience, if not enjoyable, then at least somewhat easier.

This appendix is devoted to those debugging tools. Debugging is the most important part of the development process. Errors in the code are unavoidable and the best that we can do is to try to fix them fast and without much effort.

The good news is that you usually perform 90 percent of the work in your regular browser, and only the final 10 percent of polishing on the device. Usually if you have a bug that shows up on your smartphone, you have exactly the same bug in the desktop browser, and desktop browsers have a lot of very nice tools to locate the problem and fix it.

Android's default browser is based on WebKit. Obviously, your primary desktop equivalent that you'll use for early testing and debugging should be from the same family. The most popular WebKit-based browsers are Safari and Google Chrome. Both have a powerful set of "developer's tools." If you find yourself comfortable with debugging in one of these browsers, you will surely be able to do the same with another.

In this appendix, we will learn how to do the following:

- Use the desktop browser to debug common problems

- Use default instruments available in Android

- Work with weinre to simplify some of the debugging tasks

Debug Example

In this appendix, we use an approach based on a hands-on example. Let's try to do the simplest possible debugging session for our web page. We will need some JavaScript code to work with (see Listing A-1).

Listing A-1. *Buggy JavaScript Code Sample*

```
<!DOCTYPE html>
<html lang="en">
<head>
    <meta charset="utf-8" />
    <script>
        function getMax(a, b) {
            if (a > b)
                return a;
            if (b > a)
                return b;
        }

        function init() {
            writeToDiv(getMax(1, 2));
            writeToDiv(getMax(4, 1));
            writeToDiv(getMax(1, 1));
        }

        function writeToDiv(value) {
            document.getElementById("result").innerHTML += value + "<br/>";
        }
    </script>
</head>
<body onload="init()">
    <div id="result"></div>
</body>
</html>
```

The main function—getMax() from Listing A-1—is meant to return the larger of two numbers. Given numerical input, it should always return a number. Copy the listing into a new HTML file and load it into the browser: use either nginx (described in Chapter 1) or Node.js (described in Chapter 10) to serve the page to the browser. The following output is not quite as we expected:

```
2
4
undefined
```

Instead of three numbers, the page is showing two, and then the ugly undefined. Obviously, the function has a bug! Time to fight it.

Debugging in a Desktop Browser

The first thing to do when you encounter a bug is to check if it can be reproduced in the desktop browser. If it does, then you can use the full set of development instruments to find and fix the problematic line.

Open Google Chrome and load the page. Then press F12 to open the Developer Tools window. Welcome to your ultimate debugging tool. Click the Scripts button in the top row. Now you should see the code for the buggy page that we just created. If the code doesn't show up immediately, you might need to select the correct file with the script from the drop-down list, as shown on Figure A-1.

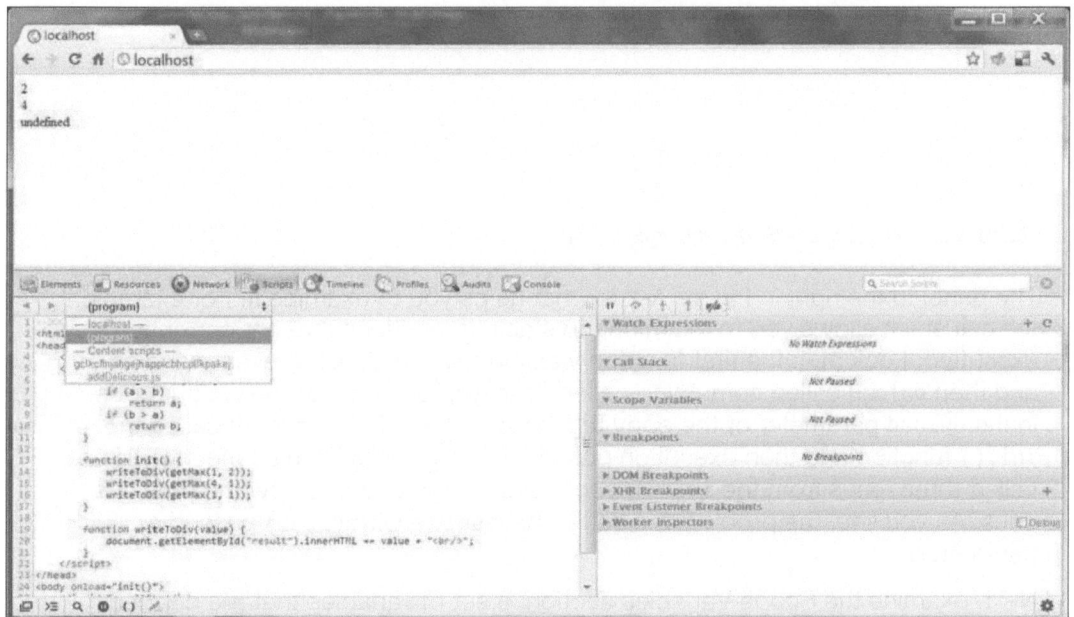

Figure A-1. *The Scripts tab with the page code and a drop-down with a list of the loaded files*

The idea behind debugging JavaScript is the same as for every other language: to locate the code that looks suspicious, to put the breakpoint at the start of the code fragment, and then execute the script line-by-line, making sure that variables have the correct values in each step.

There's the panel with the line numbers to the left from the window with the code. Find the first instruction in getMax() function: if (a > b) and click the corresponding line on the left panel (line number 7 in Figure A-1). You should now see the small blue arrow that indicates the breakpoint. Now reload the page. The line that you just marked is highlighted with a blue background (see Figure A-2). The execution is stopped and you can examine the state of the script.

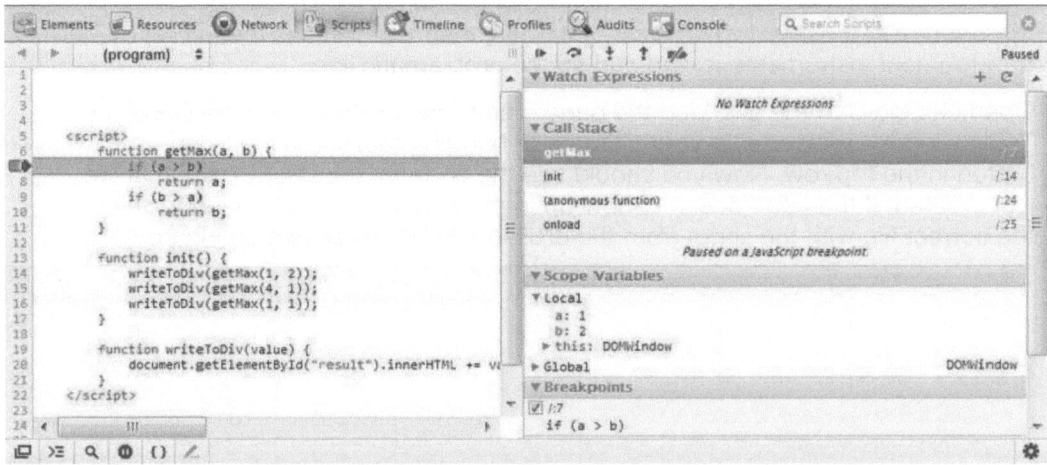

Figure A-2. *Debugging JavaScript in Google Chrome*

The panel to the right in Figure A-2 is what helps you to examine it. For example, the call stack allows you to examine the stack of functions that are currently executing. Look at it: the first function was onload, which is the event handler, and then onload called something called "anonymous function"—it is our code in the onload parameter of the body tag: onload="init()". In turn, it called the init() function and then execution passed to the getMax(). This function will be called three times from the init(), each result is appended below the previous ones. As you see, the problematic call is the last one with (1, 1) passed as parameters.

Next, examine the Scope Variables section: a set of variables that are currently reachable from the current line of code. When you need to trace the result of an expression, you open the Watch Expressions block, click the small plus sign, and type the expression to evaluate. For example, if you type Math.max(a, b), you will see what we expect from our custom function (see Figure A-3). If variables are not accessible in the current scope, you will see ReferenceError instead of the expression result.

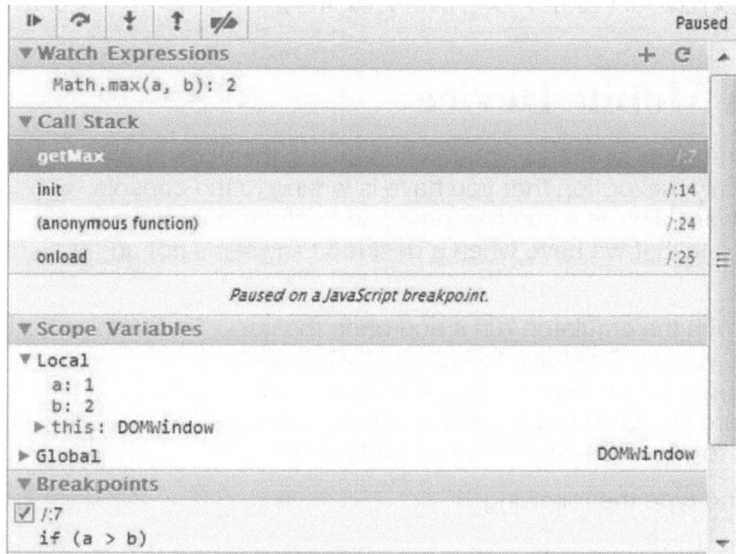

Figure A-3. *A closer look at the Scripts tab right panel, which allows you to inspect the current execution state and manage breakpoints*

Press F10 to go to the next instruction and press F11 to "step into" the function. Walk through the code step-by-step until you reach the broken code—in this case, the third call: writeToDiv(getMax(1, 1)). Looks like everything is breaking up when the parameters are equal. That's right, the if checks do not pass, and the return statement is not called at all: that's why we have the undefined value. Well, now that you know where the problem is—you can easily fix it!

> **NOTE:** This is another example of a typical dynamic language problem. In JavaScript, the same function can return values of different types: strings, numbers, objects, or undefined. A static language would check for the return type of the function at the time of compilation, and an error like this would never make it to production. In JavaScript, this code is perfectly valid.

That's easy, right? Maybe even too easy. This bug can be traced by reading four lines of the code without a debugger. But that's not always the case. Sometimes you need much more to debug the function that just doesn't want to work the way it should. Chrome's debugger can do much more. The detailed debugging tutorial is outside the scope of this book, but you can find more information about Chrome Developer Tools at http://code.google.com/chrome/devtools/docs/overview.html.

Debugging on a Mobile Device

Now let's consider the worst-case scenario: you have to debug the code on the device (or emulator). The only real option that you have is writing to the console and reading the logs afterward. This is a cumbersome and ineffective technique, but unfortunately the only one that we have when a desktop browser is not an option.

If you are going to debug with the emulator, run it and open the page. If you're working with a real device, you will first have to enable USB debugging; otherwise, you will not access device logs. Go to Settings ➤ Applications ➤ Development and make sure that USB Debugging is active. Afterward, connect your smartphone or tablet to your PC with the cable, and proceed.

Open the command line and type the following:

```
> adb logcat -v raw browser:I *:S
```

This shows the logs of the device (or the emulator) in real time, filtering them to display only the messages that you're actually interested in; in this case, the console output from the browser.

> **NOTE:** You don't believe in magic and want a better explanation of how this all works? Okay, adb (Android Device Bridge) is the tool that you use to communicate with your Android device or emulator from your PC. With this tool, you can issue commands directly to the device or use the device's services. Besides examining logs, you can install or uninstall programs, reboot devices, or even access the shell of your Android device.
>
> The command that we just issued (logcat) is used to view logs. The second parameter, -v raw, tells logcat to omit the extra logging information like the id of the process that is writing to the log, or the log level. The last parameter is the filter. By default, logcat is extremely verbose: each and every Android component tends to write logs about anything interesting that is happening around. Without a filter, logcat is almost useless. Try to run it without the last parameter to see it yourself.

> Each log entry in Android has a log level and a tag. The log level indicates the severity of the message: Verbose, Debug, Info, Warn, Error. The tag usually indicates the component that is writing to the log. The last parameter that we pass to logcat contains two filters:
>
> browser:I
>
> It means: write every output for the tag browser with a log level of Info and higher (do not show Verbose).
>
> The second filter
>
> *:S
>
> tells it to not show anything else *but* what we told it to show us in the other filters. The asterisk (*) stands for "every other tag". S means Silent – no logging.
>
> Running logcat with these options will show only the output we're looking for.

Now let's add some debugging output to our application to see how it works. Listing A-2 is the updated version of the code that prints out the arguments and the return value of the function that we're trying to debug.

Listing A-2. *The Updated Example with Logging Statements to Debug with logcat*

```
function getMax(a, b) {
    console.log ("getMax a=" + a + " b=" + b);
    if (a > b)
        return a;
    if (b > a)
        return b;
}

function init() {
    var result;
    writeToDiv(result = getMax(1, 2));
    console.log(result);
    writeToDiv(result = getMax(4, 1));
    console.log(result);
    writeToDiv(result = getMax(1, 1));
    console.log(result);
}
```

Now reload the page in your device's browser and look at the `logcat` output. After each message, `console.log` prints the address of the page and the line number.

```
> adb -d logcat -v raw browser:I *:S
--------- beginning of /dev/log/main
--------- beginning of /dev/log/system
Console: getMax a=1 b=2 http://192.168.1.142/:19
Console: 2 http://192.168.1.142/:29
Console: getMax a=4 b=1 http://192.168.1.142/:19
Console: 4 http://192.168.1.142/:31
Console: getMax a=1 b=1 http://192.168.1.142/:19
Console: undefined http://192.168.1.142/:33
```

As you might have guessed, that's what "chopping wood with a spoon" is all about. This method is extremely slow and inefficient, but hey, it's better than nothing. Besides, you have to change the code for the application to add logging, which can introduce more bugs. The bottom line is: whenever it's possible to debug with a desktop browser, do it.

Logging (Almost) Without Code Changes

One bad thing about logging is that you have to change the code to make it work. You have to put the logging statements here and there just to debug the problematic fragment. Sometimes all you need to log is the function name, input parameters, and result. So here in Listing A-3 is a trick that adds the moderate logging capabilities to any given function without significantly affecting its code.

Listing A-3. *Convenience Logging Wrapper*

```
function getMax(a, b) {
    if (a > b)
        return a;
    if (b > a)
        return b;
}

/**
 * Creates the "logging" wrapper that logs every function call:
 * passed arguments and result.
 * @param tag logging tag (usually the name of the function)
 * @param fun function. Make sure to pass function itself, not the function
result!
 */
function wrapWithLogging(tag, fun) {
    return function() {
        var result = fun.apply(this, arguments);
```

```
        var argumentsString = Array.prototype.join.call(arguments, "|");
        console.error(tag + "(" + argumentsString + ") = " + result);
        return result;
    };
}

function init() {
    getMax = wrapWithLogging("getMax", getMax);

    writeToDiv(getMax(1, 2));
    writeToDiv(getMax(4, 1));
    writeToDiv(getMax(1, 1));
}
```

As you can see, the `wrapWithLogging` takes the target function as an argument and wraps it in the anonymous function that executes the target, and then writes the parameters and a return value to the console. Let's have a closer look at the code.

```
return function() {
        var result = fun.apply(this, arguments);
        var argumentsString = Array.prototype.join.call(arguments, "|");
        console.error(tag + "(" + argumentsString + ") = " + result);
        return result;
    };
```

In the first line, we execute the original function with whatever arguments were passed to it. Then we form a simple string representation of the function's arguments, write the message to the console, and return the result of the original call.

Then, in the following code, we substitute the original function with the wrapped one and leave the rest of the code intact:

```
getMax = wrapWithLogging("getMax", getMax);

writeToDiv(getMax(1, 2));
writeToDiv(getMax(4, 1));
writeToDiv(getMax(1, 1));
```

> **NOTE:** This trick with the function might look like black magic. The good news is that it really isn't. There are just a few things that you should know about JavaScript to make it all clear. In JavaScript, everything is an object. Even a function is an object. So if you have code like this:

```
function foo() {
    return 1;
}
```

then foo() (with parentheses) will execute the function and return the result, while foo (without parentheses) will refer to the function itself and not its result. Following the same logic, the return type of the function can be another function—just like in our case.

The second part that may not be so obvious is the arguments variable. It is the variable that is available from within any JavaScript function. It behaves like an array: you can access individual arguments with the bracket syntax arguments[0] or get the arguments.length, but you can't use the array methods on it since it is *not* an array. Hence, the following trick with join:

```
Array.prototype.join.call(arguments, "|");
```

We have to use the function from Array since the arguments object doesn't have own join() function.

The console output is just what we need, as follows:

```
Console: getMax(1|2) = 2 http://192.168.1.142/:25
Console: getMax(4|1) = 4 http://192.168.1.142/:25
Console: getMax(1|1) = undefined http://192.168.1.142/:25
```

This helper is somewhat limited. For example, it will not be that useful for the functions that take objects as arguments: my simple wrapper doesn't know how to fetch an object's properties and print them neatly. It will not save you from having to put the log statements inside the function body, when needed, if the function arguments are objects.

weinre

weinre (http://people.apache.org/~pmuellr/weinre/ is a great tool that aims to fill the gap of remote debugging between the PC and Android stock browser. It doesn't have the whole set of capabilities that a desktop debugger does, but it is still very useful. Even though it doesn't allow you to place breakpoints and analyze the variables, it has a rich set of tools for DOM manipulations, tracking the timeline of the script, and executing JavaScript on the fly, straight on the device.

Download the latest version of weinre-jar zip from
`http://people.apache.org/~pmuellr/weinre/builds/`. Unpack the zip file and
run the following from the command line:

```
java -jar weinre.jar --httpPort 8000 --boundHost -all-
```

The `weinre.jar` file is an executable Java program that starts the debug server,
which acts like a mediator between the device and PC. It provides a debug
interface to the WebKit browser that connects to it and exchanges commands
with the debug target—the web page running on the device or the emulator. The
preceding command starts the server on port 8000.

To finish the setup, add the following line to the web page that you're going to
debug:

```
<script src="http://10.0.2.2:8000/target/target-script-
min.js#anonymous"></script>
```

It instructs the HTML page to load the special script served by debug server,
and then start the communication. Change the IP address and the port
according to what you have in your environment. For example, the preceding
line is used to launch the page from the emulator that refers to the host OS via
10.0.2.2. Port 8000 is configured via weinre.jar startup options.

Load the page on the device. Now go to `http://localhost:8000/client` in
desktop Chrome (the interface is usable in Safari too, but looks slightly better on
Chrome). Figure A-4 shows the opened debugging session. The browser
window in the background shows the debug interface. As you see, it looks
exactly like the Chrome dev tools that we tried in the first section of this
appendix.

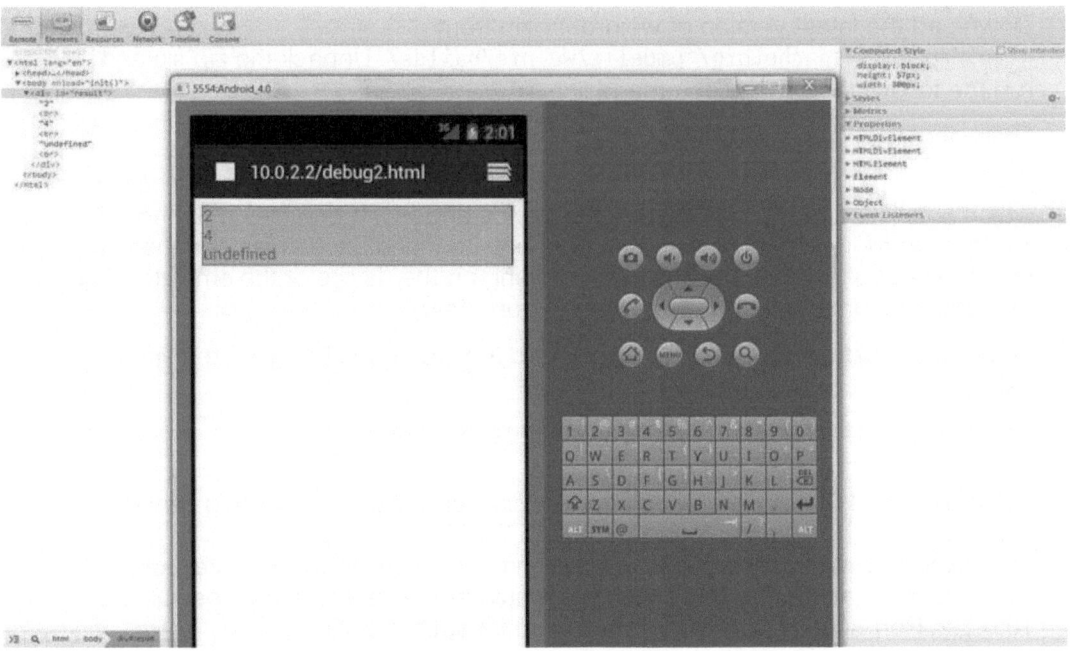

Figure A-4. *The weinre debugging session. The opened Elements tab allows you to explore and modify the content of a device's DOM tree.*

For more information on weinre, refer to its home page at http://people.apache.org/~pmuellr/weinre/. The Chrome Dev tools documentation page is at http://code.google.com/chrome/devtools/docs/overview.html.

Summary

Android lacks support for full-scale debugging in browsers, and that can make debugging an extremely hard task. Luckily, most of the problems that you will face are not device-specific and can be debugged on a desktop browser. WebKit-based browsers (Chrome and Safari) provide an excellent set of "development tools" that are laser-focused on solving all kinds of problems: layout, logic, or timing.

In this appendix, we learned how to do the following:

■   Debug a web page in a WebKit-based browser

- Use standard Android facilities: `console.log` and `logcat` to trace the problem

- Set up weinre to debug the possible layout or timing issues of the web page

Index